1001 FOODS
YOU MUST TASTE BEFORE YOU DIE

1001 FOODS
YOU MUST TASTE BEFORE YOU DIE

GENERAL EDITOR FRANCES CASE

PREFACE BY GREGG WALLACE

UNIVERSE

A Quint**essence** Book

First published in the United States of America in 2008 by
Universe Publishing
A division of Rizzoli International Publications, Inc.
300 Park Avenue South
New York, NY 10010
www.rizzoliusa.com

ISBN: 978-0-7893-1592-2

Library of Congress Control Number: 2008922855

2008 2009 2010 2011 / 10 9 8 7 6 5 4 3 2 1

This book was designed and produced by
Quint**essence** Publishing Limited
226 City Road
London EC1V 2TT
United Kingdom

Project Editor	Victoria Wiggins
Copy Editor	Beverly LeBlanc
Editor	Fiona Plowman
Assistant Editors	Rebecca Gee, Frank Ritter
Editorial Assistant	Helena Baser
Art Editor	Dean Martin
Commissioned Photography	Rob Lawson
Designer	Gaspard de Beauvais
Picture Researcher	Sunita Sharma-Gibson
Editorial Director	Jane Laing
Publisher	Tristan de Lancey

Color reproduction by Pica Digital Pte Ltd., Singapore.
Printed in China by SNP Leefung Printers Ltd.

Contents

Preface
By Gregg Wallace

For someone like me, who has spent nearly all his working life handling fresh produce, this book is delightful. Listed in these pages are quite simply the best food products from around the globe. Nobody, no matter how clever or well traveled, could claim to know all the culinary wonders of the world—even a television "ingredients expert" like myself!

Of course, a book of this scale and magnitude could not possibly work without illustrations. My time as a judge on the BBC TV show *MasterChef* taught me just how difficult it is to explain taste and smell. No writer finds it easy to describe perfectly the appearance of a particular French goat cheese, or an incredible-looking fruit like the mangosteen. The photographs in this book are beautiful, and I admire the book's attempt to bring flavor and aroma to the page.

I have a personal love of food history. It is not something I suppose many people consider, but every food originates somewhere. The golden age of European exploration brought to Old World dining tables a treasure trove of new flavors, textures, and sights. *1001 Foods* is packed full of wonderful anecdotes and the history behind many familiar and not so familiar ingredients. I am always boring my children and dinner guests with food histories, and this book has more than doubled my knowledge.

As a seller of fresh produce, I found the sections on fruits and vegetables especially fascinating. I would like to boast that I recognized each and every fruit and each and every vegetable, but I didn't. I loved the descriptions of produce that I know very well, and found it nearly impossible to disagree with the writers. But this book also does a terrific job of filling in the gaps in my knowledge, particularly in the complex world of aromatics. As I write this, I'm scratching my head and trying to think of a comparable work. I am lucky to have a kitchen full of cookbooks from around the world, and I will be putting this book alongside my *Larousse gastronomique* and Alan Davidson's *Oxford Companion to Food*. Like those two works, I expect *1001 Foods* to age beyond its years through frequent thumbing.

I have had this book with me now for just over a week and I can't help turning through the pages to see what has been written about the foods I am preparing for each mealtime. Reading it, I've found myself pondering the possibility of a Herculean but divine journey of exploration across the world, sampling each of the 1001 ingredients as I go. This is surely a wild dream, but a hugely pleasant one nonetheless. And even if I never manage this journey of gastronomic discovery, what I will undoubtedly do the next time I travel is make a list of the favored products of my destination. In fact, as I look through the book, I realize just how many gems I have missed on previous travels. There is only one thing for it—I am going to have to revisit those countries with *1001 Foods* tucked into my suitcase. Owning this book is a must for anyone who enjoys cooking or eating well. Wherever you go in the world, or however you cook, the cornerstones are good ingredients. Nothing can be achieved without them and any attempt made at good cooking will be a struggle.

Allow me a little indulgence here. Because there is so much included in the book's pages, everyone is going to have their favorite chapters. Of course, my major interest is fruit, vegetables, and herbs—all of which are brilliantly described—but the coverage of preserved meats has filled me with special admiration. Food preservation is a subject dear to my heart. In order to survive, every race of people had to learn ways of preserving slaughtered beasts. As well as providing tremendous detail of the dried and salted meats that are familiar to me, this book whetted my appetite for meats I never even knew existed.

Anyone who has watched *MasterChef* will know what a sweet tooth I have. I fell in love with *1001 Foods* as soon as I realized it had devoted a whole chapter to confectionery and sweetmeats. Candy plays a huge part in our childhoods and some people, like me, never lose their passion for them. I cannot believe I went skiing in Scandinavia last winter and had no idea I could have bought myself a big bag of salted, fish-shaped licorice drops. I am now also on a mission to get my hands on the Iranian honey-and-nut combo known as Qum sohan. And I am horrified that honeycomb toffee has been available in Britain for years, and I've never tried it. As soon as I've finished writing this, I am going to put "honeycomb toffee" into a search engine and order myself a packet.

This is a truly beautiful book—full of information and filled with treats you will not have tried. I'm now on a mission to try as many as I can.

Surrey, England, 2008

Introduction
By Frances Case, General Editor

Food is not only an essential part of our lives, but also a source of great joy. In the words of the eighteenth-century gastronome Jean-Anthelme Brillat-Savarin (who himself has a cheese named after him), "The discovery of a new dish confers more happiness on humanity than the discovery of a new star." Today, there is a growing passion for food around the world, and for food from all over the world.

With the food in supermarkets becoming less recognizable as food and containing all sorts of odd chemicals we would not expect to find on the kitchen shelf—from nitrites and stabilizers to trans fats and glutamates—we want to get closer to the land, closer to our heritage. This explains the surge in popularity of growing our own fruit and vegetables, buying organic, traceable foods, and the belief that "less is more": the fewer ingredients a supermarket-bought meal contains, the better.

Responsible eating is hip. We are concerned about the risk to the environment of food production and the air miles required to transport foods from overseas. Farmers' markets are springing up in every major city from San Francisco to London, with urban markets priding themselves on offering things grown within a few miles of where they are sold. Restaurants such as London's Konstam go further, promoting the fact that they source all their ingredients within the city's limits.

Another concern is sustainability, especially as more people have access to gourmet and unusual ingredients than in previous generations. The sustainability of seafood is a hot topic, and this book warns of foods that we should not eat from the wild—at least until their stocks recover. Some are already almost impossible to find. Overfishing of certain sea creatures has decimated stocks, and climate change is already having an impact on marine ecosystems.

Take toheroa, the iconic, fast-burrowing New Zealand shellfish, or elvers, the Anglo-Spanish delicacy of baby eels, collected from the Sargasso Sea. Even tuna and cod are under threat, and one of the saddest things about researching this book was reading about delicacies that no longer exist because they have been made extinct in the wild over the last decade: like the giant catfish of the Mekong, famed for its delicacy and exterminated because of it. Of the world's fish stocks, seventy-six percent are overexploited, and many are severely depleted: scientists now agree that we must find a radical new approach to farming the seas to ensure the health of our oceans for future generations.

Regionality provokes strong passions, especially when it comes to foods. Many European cheeses are made on or around the mountains where herds of cows, goats, or sheep are bred, and which also form national boundaries. European Union (E.U.) product laws exist to protect such traditional foods and ensure that substandard products do not enter the market and damage their reputation. *Appellation d'origine contrôlée* (AOC) guidelines governing traditional production methods were drawn up as far back as the fifteenth century, and are strictly enforced. For example, a patriotic debate rages over whether Vacherin, a mountain cheese matured in spruce, is French or Swiss, with both sides laying claim to the name and insisting that their Vacherin is the authentic one; a similar dispute occurs over Emmentaler and Emmenthal. More than forty French cheeses have been granted the AOC label, and even lentils from Le Puy-en-Velay carry it.

For any country, shared heritage means shared food, and national delicacies that might seem unpalatable to some are often based on a plentiful supply of a particular animal or vegetable. The Scandinavians, for example, have a passion for moose, and it is no coincidence that Sweden has the largest moose population in the world. Many Polish dishes are based around cabbage and potatoes, both of which grow in abundance in the region. There is a natural balance between supply and demand.

Cooking shows on television are now hugely popular. The chefs who present them are bona fide celebrities who can increase sales of a particular ingredient by 300 percent by using it in a recipe. Martha Stewart, Delia Smith, Nigella Lawson, Wolfgang Puck, and Anthony Bourdain are household names in many countries. Their programs attract huge audiences. Nigella Lawson's most recent series, *Nigella Express*, peaked with 3.3 million viewers per episode in the United Kingdom. The Food Network cable channel is distributed to 90 million U.S. households. We now spend more time watching cooking on television than we do actually preparing food in our kitchens: and probably more time reading about it, too.

For this book we have assembled an international team to reflect the cuisines and delicacies specific to each continent and country. Despite this, we are bound to have trodden on some national toes. Pavlova, for example, is the national dish of both Australia and New Zealand, a matter not necessarily known to both nations. So, to any Ukrainians finding their national dish described as Polish, any Lithuanians whose Sunday special has been attributed to Estonia, and any Norwegians feeling that their cuisine has been hijacked by the Swedes, I offer my sincere apologies.

Selecting the 1001 foods featured in this book has not been easy. We have tried to include a mix of affordable and unusual ingredients, alongside luxury items—a difficult balancing act. Each foodstuff we chose to include had to justify its place in the list of greats: there are hundreds of types of mushroom, so which ones deserve to be included, and why? Some of the tastes in here will provoke strong personal reactions—sulfurous truffle will not necessarily be to everyone's taste, any more than stinky-sweet surströmming (fermented Baltic herring), but one is considered a delicacy by more people than the other. Luxurious, indulgent foods, such as single-estate chocolate, oysters, and lobster, sit alongside less celebrated ones, such as the delicacy of hop shoots—without question the most expensive green food on earth.

We have included a fantastic range of fruits and vegetables, from "superfoods" such as pomegranate and edamame to everyday heroes such as fennel, peppers, and shallots. (Our terms, as Jeffrey Steingarten magnificently remarked in *The Man Who Ate Everything*, are culinary, not botanical, so you will find tomatoes in the vegetable chapter, along with their companions in the vegetable drawer.)

1001 Foods encourages you to branch out and explore—broadening your palate—with tasting notes that should give you an idea of what you are getting into. Some of the foods may not be easy to track down, and some are extraordinary: miracle berries, so sweet that lemons taste like candy for minutes after you have eaten them; turu, the Amazonian tree worm that tastes of oysters; and yellow oil crabs, the Shanghai specialty of female crabs so sunburned that their roe has melted and turned into buttery oil. Other foods are simply marvelous examples of the familiar, the best of their kind, such as Azores pineapples, lovingly grown under glass as they once were for the grand houses of Europe; heritage Blenheim apricots; and Cox's Orange Pippin apples. The focus of this book is on taste, not texture, although we do include some iconic, texture-led Chinese delicacies—jellyfish, sea cucumber, and bird's nest.

Food myths and lore are intrinsically tied to the appeal of certain delicacies, from the aphrodisiac properties of oysters and asparagus to fact-based claims made about certain foods. Popeye munched on spinach to maintain his bulging muscles, and most of us will benefit—perhaps not to the same extent—from eating more of this iron-rich vegetable. We wanted to make this a global guide, with offerings from all seven continents, but Antarctica proved stubbornly resistant (any readers on a research station, please write in).

1001 Foods is about foods and their tastes, rather than the dishes you can make from the ingredients. There is a book of "1001 Dishes" to be made, but this is not it: so, while curried goat or lobster thermidor are dishes everyone should taste before they die, you will not find them here. Neither is this book a simple dictionary of ingredients. Every food in here has been selected because it is special in some way—whether iconic to a nation (or the world), simply delicious, part of a fascinating story, unique, or unusual. We love seasonal foods: the Christmas breads and cakes were hard to choose between, and I wish we had discovered the Finnish pastries *joulutorttu* before we finalized the list.

I would like to thank our wonderful team of contributors, who produced fantastic copy, often to ludicrously tight deadlines. Special thanks to Michael Raffael, whose passion for cheese and patient exploration of the finer points of E.U.-cheese law went well beyond the call of duty, and to C. J. Jackson and her team at the Seafood Training School, a charitable company promoting awareness of fish in both the public and the industry. Tony Hill imparted an incredible knowledge of spices, and was willing to find, buy, and taste absolutely anything. Special thanks also to Beverly LeBlanc, for her Americanizing, practicality, and ability to perform miracles; Shirley Booth, for her unswerving enthusiasm for and knowledge of all things Japanese; Anne-Marie Sutcliffe, for covering both Mani and Greece; Rob Lawson, for his fantastic photography; Suzanne Hall, for her enthusiasm for all things that grow; and Victoria Wiggins and Fiona Plowman, for keeping the whole project on the road against considerable odds. Personally, I would also like to thank Victor Sutcliffe, Howard Case, Frances Voss, Michelle Jeffares, and Zachary Sutcliffe, for putting up with me during the book's production, for parts of which we oh-so-ironically subsisted largely on takeouts.

The main goal of this book is to encourage you to try new foods, broaden your palate, and discover new favorites. You may not enjoy everything you taste—the Sardinian cheese casu marzu immediately springs to mind—but you will certainly have fun experimenting.

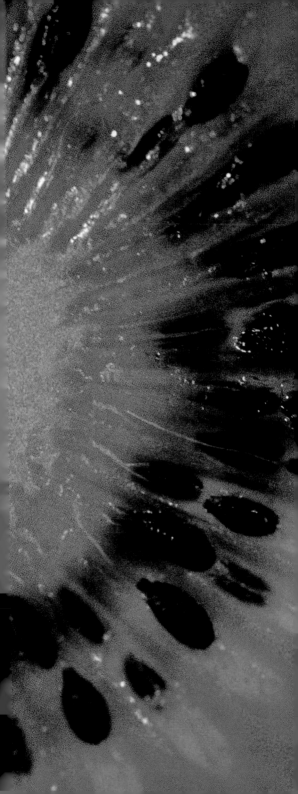

Elderberry Flower

Rose Petal

Found all over North America, Europe, and Asia, the elder—*Sambucus canadensis* in northern North America, *Sambucus nigra* in Europe—is a neglected plant. Yet, provided they are cooked, both flowers and berries are a boon.

The flowers in their characteristic wide, flat clusters have a distinctive fragrance, and can be added to sorbets and desserts or used to flavor gooseberry jelly, popular in Britain. The Austrian preference for making fritters from the sprays and serving them with confectioners' sugar is said to have caught on after World War II, when starving families gleaned what food they could from the fields, although elderberry-flower fritters have a heritage that stretches back to medieval times.

The berries make a fine jam popular in Hungary and other parts of central Europe; they are also used as an ingredient in an Austrian compote called *hollerröster*, and in Scandinavian mixed fruit soups. In England, elderberry flowers are used to make a cordial or a mildly vinous Champagne; elsewhere they are infused in boiling water as a cold remedy. **GM**

In Iran, the scent of rose petals provides a mysterious background to dishes both sweet and savory. According to Margaret Shaida's *The Legendary Cuisine of Persia* (2002): "Just as the rose is as much a part of Persian literature as the nightingale, so its delectable fragrance is as much a part of Persian cuisine as the lemon and saffron."

The Mohammadi roses grown around the city of Kashan, south of Tehran, are prized because the hot desert air enhances their scent. Dried or powdered petals can be mixed with rice *polows*, included in the spice blends known as *advieh*, added to sweet preserves, or made into jams. It takes 90 pounds (40 kg) of their pink or red petals—a day's work for professional pickers—to extract one-third of an ounce (10 ml), or about 2 teaspoons, essential oils.

Rose water spread with the influence of Persian cuisine west to Turkey and east to India. It brings exoticism to Turkish Delight (*lokum*), and is also utilized in ice creams, rice puddings, sherbets, cakes, and confectionery throughout South Asia and the Middle East. **MR**

Taste: *Elderberry flowers have a sickly, gooseberrylike scent and flavor. Elderberries taste somewhere between a blackberry and a ripe plum, but with a strong bitterness.*

Taste: *Rose petals have little taste, but their perfume infuses a dish so fast that they call for subtle dosing. Used in rose water, they add a note of the exotic to many dishes.*

Roses are traditionally picked at dawn to preserve the freshness of their petals. ❯❯

Black Currant

It is odd that a flavor that is now summoned to describe the taste of the finest Bordeaux *crus* could have spent so much of its existence as a poor relation of red currants and white currants. But *Ribes nigrum* suffered this until the last century and remains, despite a vitamin C content far higher than lemons, relatively rare, except in liqueurs such as the Burgundian *crème de cassis*, and Ribena, the British branded fruit syrup, which guzzles almost three-quarters of the United Kingdom's commercial crop.

Yet, gardeners know the small berries have more to offer than just juice. While some varieties are plumper and sweeter, others sharper and more intensely flavored, all come into their own as a culinary fruit. Harvested in early summer, they are bottled, jammed, or mixed with other fruits in a compote, where they deliver a distinctive aroma. In professional kitchens, the black currants are often used to add punch to sauces such as those served with roasted duck fillets. Black currants are suited to mixing with blander ingredients: in ice cream, in sorbets, or as a topping for cheesecakes. **MR**

Taste: *The aroma of fresh black currant is powerful and fragrant. The berries contain a sharp juice and seeds that benefit from poaching in syrup to unwrap their berry tang.*

Mountain Huckleberry

Like a supercharged blueberry, rich in aroma, flavor, sugar, and antioxidants, yet with a deep purple color that continues even under its skin, the mountain huckleberry is the most frequently harvested and highly coveted of the dozens of varieties of wild huckleberries that grow in North America. A member of the same genus as the blueberry and cranberry, *Vaccinium membranaceum* is typically found in the northwest United States, where it goes by a whole range of names. The huckleberry remains culturally important to Native Americans who have relied on it as a food source.

Low elevation picking begins in early July and can continue into late September. Pickers regard huckleberry patches a closely guarded secret, and will move to elevations as high as 10,000 feet (3,000 m) to continue harvesting as the season progresses. It is believed millions of pounds of huckleberries are harvested each season. Because of concerns that demand is outstripping supply, there are current attempts to domesticate the plant, which has proven difficult to grow in cultivation. **CLH**

Taste: *The taste is similar to blueberries, but juicier with both sweet and tart notes. Huckleberries are used in desserts, preserves, and candies, and as a sauce for meats.*

Berry-picking is one of the pleasures of a northwestern American childhood. ❯❯

Cranberry

An essential part of Thanksgiving Day feasts, these sour little scarlet berries are native to both the Old World and the New World: local varieties are prized every bit as much in Scandinavia as they are in the United States.

It is the North American cranberry, *Vaccinium macrocarpon*, however, that has made its mark on the world. High in bezoic acid, a natural preservative that enables the berries to be stored for months without deteriorating, the berries were a staple in the diets of Native Americans, who used them fresh and dried, or pounded with meat into the trail mix known as pemmican. They became, in turn, a basic of the early settlers and of colonial sailors, who carried them on voyages stored in barrels of water. When, in 1677, the colonists sent a gift of their choicest products to placate Charles II, king of England, cranberries went along with the cod and corn; by 1689 they were being eaten at Thanksgiving.

Gathering in the commercial cranberry crop takes the form either of dry harvesting, when the berries are combed off the vines with rakes, or, more spectacularly, wet harvesting. In the latter case, the cranberry fields are flooded and special machinery is employed to beat the berries off the vines. The floating red berries are then gathered together and collected for worldwide distribution.

Old World cranberries are mostly used in sauces, jams, preserves, and liqueurs: the sauces pair particularly well with game. North American berries are also used for sauces, but appear in salads, relishes, garnishes, breads, candies, cakes, and side dishes. Cranberries are high in vitamin C and their juice is also popular. **SH**

Taste: *Very firm with crunchy flesh, cranberries have a pungent, tart, acidic taste that requires sweetening. Some varieties have a distinctive taste of pine.*

To wet-harvest cranberries,
Ⓚ *farmers flood the bog they grow in.*

Cloudberry

Found in the far northern regions of Europe and North America, cloudberries are circumpolar in distribution. For centuries, these bright berries, which resemble yellow raspberries, have played a major role in the diet of Scandinavians, the northern Sami tribes of Lapland, and the Inuits of Alaska and Canada, where the berry is known as the baked-apple berry or bakeberry.

The natural habitat of the cloudberry, *Rubus chamaemorus*, is peaty bogs and marshes. The low, creeping plant sprouts small white flowers, then forms red berries that turn a deep yellow color as they ripen in late summer. Cloudberries are as yet largely uncultivated, and so must be laboriously harvested from the wild, which makes them both exclusive and expensive. Once gathered, however, they can be frozen and stored for long periods.

Cloudberries are highly valued in Scandinavia, where a rich heritage of gathering and using wild berries still thrives today. The Swedish botanist Carl Linnaeus praised the berry in his masterpiece *Flora Lapponica* (1737) and reported how copious amounts of preserved cloudberries were transported every year to the tables of the Swedish capital. The Finns, who call them *lakka*, use them to make a liqueur and eat them with a Lappish farm cheese. In Sweden, cloudberries are often made into a jam and eaten with pancakes or ice cream. The Inuits traditionally mixed them with fat and snow to make *akutaq*, known as Eskimo ice cream. Aside from their delicious taste, cloudberries are appreciated for health reasons. High in vitamins, including vitamin C, they were historically eaten by Nordic seafarers to prevent scurvy. **CC**

Taste: *Cloudberries have an intense freshness, unique tangy flavor, and juicy texture that is best enjoyed freshly picked and carefully warmed, with a pinch of sugar.*

Wild Raspberry

Stretching across Europe and Asia and into North America, the raspberry (*Rubus idaeus*) thrives in thickets, open woods, and hedgerows, and has been harvested wild for thousands of years. The ancient Greeks were most likely the first to cultivate the fruit, and according to Pliny named it after Mount Ida, because the plants grew so thickly on its slopes.

Wild raspberries can be red, yellow, white, or shades in between: like their cultivated relatives, they are slightly hairy and are plucked easily from the thorny bush. Like blackberries, they are not botanically berries, but clusters of tiny individual seed fruit, or drupelets, set around a central core. This "receptacle" stays on the branch when the raspberry is picked, leaving a small, cuplike fruit.

Raspberry's fruit, leaves, and bark have long been used to treat ailments or minor wounds: the leaves, in particular, have a long history of usage during pregnancy and childbirth. Once harvested, the berries can deteriorate quickly, making them difficult to transport: those that do not survive the journey can be used in jams, pastries, pies, or teas. **CLH**

Taste: *Wild raspberries are sweet, tart, and highly aromatic. The berry is fragile and juicy, and the flavor of some varieties found in the wild can be spectacular.*

Black Mulberry

"And the gods touched their parents. Ever after / Mulberries, as they ripen, darken purple." This, according to Ovid, explains how the suicide of the star-crossed lovers Pyramus and Thisbe led to the white mulberry becoming the black mulberry (*Morus nigra*). Myth attaches itself to this most luscious, but fragile, of fruits, the best tasting of the many varieties of mulberry found all over the world.

The mulberry is native to southwest Asia, but has been grown in Europe since classical times, and was probably introduced into Britain, France, and Spain by the Romans. It has also been successfully introduced into the Americas and Australia. It is not a true berry, but a cluster of berries, and harvest is challenging. The fruit tend to collapse when picked, and can stain a virulent purple: some prefer to wait until the fruit ripen sufficiently to fall from the tree.

Mulberries rot very quickly and should only be washed immediately before eating, but any surplus can be made into a delicious jelly. In Afghanistan, they are dried, powdered, and mixed with flour to make bread. **AMS**

Taste: *The black mulberry is very sweet, but has sufficient acidity to give a burst of flavor that is comparable to a blackberry, but less seedy in both taste and texture.*

Black mulberries are white when young, but turn black; the white mulberry is a separate species. »

Boysenberry

Softer and larger than blackberries, with a sweeter flavor, smaller seeds, and a color closer to maroon or indigo than black, boysenberries have a complicated heritage. They are named after Rudolph Boysen, a California farmer who developed the fruit in 1923, but failed to sustain a crop, and are a cross between blackberries, raspberries, and loganberries—which are, in turn, believed to be a hybrid of a blackberry and a raspberry.

Similar to the blackberries found growing wild around the globe, although some varieties do not have any thorns, boysenberries are grown commercially in parts of the United States, where they are a popular ice-cream flavor, as well as Chile, New Zealand, and Australia. Boysenberries do well in jams, jellies, pies, tarts, and cobblers, or simply served with cream and, perhaps, a hint of sugar.

Good raw, where they top breakfast cereals and can adorn green salads, their flavor is enhanced by being lightly cooked. Chefs use them to create sauces and purees to accompany meats and poultry, sometimes paired with ingredients such as ceps. **SH**

Marionberry

While in Britain and northern Europe blackberries are still often left to be picked wild from the hedgerows, in North America their cultivation is a serious business. Marionberries are a succulent type, a cross between two modern breeds of blackberries with some raspberry heritage: shiny black in color, they are moderately firm and relatively large in size, with a very fruity fragrance. Marionberries were developed and grown in Oregon during the 1950s, as part of a selective breeding program, and take their name from Marion County in that state.

Marionberries are available fresh for only about a month, typically between 10 July and 10 August, although they can also be found frozen at other times. They make richly flavored jellies, jams, pies, ice creams, and sorbets, and work well as an addition to pancakes and waffles. The puree makes a very flavorful marinade and appears in sweet-and-sour sauces. Regional chefs offer dishes such as a granola made of toasted oats and nuts over honey yogurt with Marionberry puree, rattlesnake glazed with Marionberries, and other imaginative mixes. **SH**

Taste: *Boysenberries have a rich, sweet flavor with tart undertones. They have hints of blackberry, strawberry, and raspberry in their flavor.*

Taste: *Marionberries have an intense blackberry flavor that is sweet and a little musky. At their best they strike a perfect balance between sweet and tart.*

Fresh boysenberries should be eaten within three
❰ *days of picking because they deteriorate quickly.*

Alpine Strawberry

The French name *fraises des bois*, like the Italian *fragole di bosco*, suggests that these tiny, delectable strawberries are a wild fruit. But while they are, indeed, found wild, they are more often cultivated by gardeners, as they have been since the fourteenth century. Charles V of France had his gardener plant 12,000 sets as early as 1386.

Unlike their larger cousins, alpine strawberry plants (*Fragaria vesca*) fruit right through the summer. In size they can be smaller than a currant or the size of a manicured little fingernail. Some are drier or juicier or sweeter than others, but they are always strongly fragrant and distinctive.

Alpines are extremely perishable, so rarely make a commercial crop. Sensitive fingers are required when picking, for they easily bruise and discolor. During the seventeenth century, plants were dug up in the wild for replanting in gardens; during the British Regency fruiting plants were placed on tables for diners to eat at will. Although alpines shine in a *tarte aux fraises des bois* and make a luxurious sorbet, the taste of the fresh fruit cannot be bettered. **MR**

Taste: *Alpines are best enjoyed as a handful of perfectly ripe fruit. Individual fruit might be a little sour, but a mouthful gives a complete, intense strawberry flavor.*

Alpine strawberries are at their best picked
Ⓚ *fully ripe from the garden or the wild.*

Mara des Bois Strawberry

For many millennia, tiny alpine strawberries were beloved in Europe. They were picked 8,000 years ago and the Romans valued them highly. Yet, the discovery of America revealed sturdier, larger species that were introduced to Europe and hybridized with existing fruit. Faced with this competition, the soft, low-yielding alpines began to fall from favor.

In 1991, a French laboratory created the Mara des Bois strawberry, a hybrid of four different strains of berry, with the aim of capturing the fragrance and flavor of an alpine strawberry and packaging it in a berry with the firm texture of contemporary varieties. Available on the market for an extended growing season, from springtime until the first frosts, this fantastically fragrant fruit fetches a premium price and accounts for about a tenth of France's strawberry harvest. The color ranges from brick red to pinkish purple, while the berries can be as small as a pea or as large as a plum. Cultivation is expanding from its heartland in southwest France to California, the United Kingdom, and beyond. **HFL**

Taste: *Combining the musky fragrance of wild strawberries with the firm-fleshed attributes of its genitors, a balance of sweetness and acidity marks this melt-in-the-mouth berry.*

Casseille

Hybridizing fruit is hardly a new science. Pears can be crossed with apples. Tangelos are part mandarin orange, part grapefruit. Known botanically as *Ribes x culverwellii*, the casseille, or jostaberry, is a relatively recent example: a happy marriage between a black currant and a gooseberry, developed by Erwin Bauer in Munchenberg, Germany, in 1975.

The berries look like oversized black currants, but the pulp has the texture of gooseberries. They are easy to pick from bushes, with none of the awkward hanging bunches associated with currants or the thorns common to gooseberries. Their size, similar to small Muscat grapes, is ideal for the kitchen.

Even in Britain, where the gooseberry is relatively widely grown, casseille has not yet made an impact; the French, however, have been quick to seize the opportunities presented by a fruit that is much more than a novelty. Although it can be eaten raw, the main attraction is as a very versatile ingredient that lends itself well to jams, preserves, compotes, *bavarois*, sorbets, and ice creams, as well as the liqueur known as crème de casseille. **MR**

Taste: *A casseille conserve has a less assertive taste than black currant, but similar. It is fresher, lighter on the palate, and less cloying than black currant's syrupy intensity.*

Gooseberry

What is sauce for the goose is sauce for the mackerel. The English name "gooseberry" and the French name—literally "mackerel currant"—both point to the early use of the European gooseberry as a base for sauces where its tartness offset the oiliness of meat or fish. The berries are not always sour. In fact, when picked mature they are sweet and juicy. The fresh berries come in four colors: yellow, green, red, and "white." The more common canned are usually green. Some are furry, others prickly, others smooth; some are as pale as pearls, others almost black.

Ribes grossularia has attracted little interest on mainland Europe, but in northern England, and especially in the county of Cheshire, it has been highly prized. Annual competitions to judge the largest gooseberry of the year date back to 1786, and by the mid-nineteenth century there were 250 amateur gooseberry societies in Britain.

In Britain, gooseberry pies and jams are popular, but in the most typical of British dishes, gooseberry fool, gooseberry is mixed with whipped cream, sometimes flavored with elderberry flowers. **MR**

Taste: *Underripe gooseberries picked for cooking are hard and sharp. In ripe fruit, the plentiful seeds are coated in a slippery pulp with a sweet and refreshing taste.*

Hairy gooseberry fruit with their many seeds have a unique texture when baked whole in desserts. »

Miracle Berry

Native to West Africa, where it grows on small, azalealike shrubs, the intensely sweet miracle berry gets its name from the miraculin it contains, although any weight watcher with a sweet tooth will assert that it is a genuine miracle worker, too. Used for hundreds of years in its homeland, the fruit was brought to the attention of the West by U.S. explorer David Fairchild in the 1930s.

Miraculin is a type of protein that persuades the taste buds that sour foods are actually sweet. This attribute was exploited to the full in 1995 by a Tokyo café that claimed the unique selling point of having no dish on the menu containing more than 100 calories. The Japanese dieters who packed the tables happily tucked into cakes and desserts made from mouth-puckering quantities of lemons and limes after having eaten just one berry beforehand. Miraculin works by binding its active glycoprotein molecule with some trailing carbohydrate chains to receptors of the taste buds; the molecule changes their function for a short time. The fruit does not make sweet food taste sweeter, because it is not a sweetener in itself; its effects depend on what is eaten afterward, and it has been used to make bitter medicines more palatable.

The scarlet berries, also known as miracle fruits and serendipity berries, are grape-sized and develop from small, white flowers. Although they have been used by West Africans as a sweetener for centuries, they long remained unknown elsewhere because the bushes do not flourish in cooler climes and the berries were impossible to export since they rotted quickly. Freeze-drying has changed all that, and the berries can now be enjoyed around the world. **WS**

Taste: *Discard the pit and chew the vaguely sweet, but bland, flesh of a miracle berry and everything you eat in the next few hours, however sour, will taste sweet.*

Sea Buckthorn

This spiky plant (*Hippophae rhamnoides*), with its bright orange berries, is native to northern Asia and Europe and was one of the first to establish itself in Scandinavia after the Ice Age. Hardy and vigorous, it is a pioneer species, tolerant of exposure, that grows in sandy mountains and coastal areas. The fruit of this plant has long been praised for its health-giving properties, mentioned in ancient Tibetan medical texts and also in Chinese traditional herbal medicine and in Indian Ayurvedic medicine. Today the fruit of sea buckthorn, phenomenally rich in vitamins C and E, is being newly marketed as a "super berry," with research being carried out into it as a source of cholesterol-lowering compounds.

The hardy bush is covered by long thorns, a fact reflected in its common names of sea buckthorn, Alpine sandthorn, and Siberian pineapple. This natural defense makes the berry difficult to pick and harvest, although thornless varieties are cultivated in Russia. In Scandinavia, a special tool is used to press the juice out of the berry while it is still on the spiky bush; in other places, the bushes are shaken—mechanically or by hand—to loosen the berries.

In Scandinavia, the sour-sweet berries are a particularly special delicacy. They have appeared at the prestigious Nobel Prize dinner, as a main ingredient in the traditional ice cream. The juice is used as an ingredient in desserts, jams, sauces, and alcoholic drinks, such as schnapps. Health-food shops sell dried sea buckthorn berries in powdered form, to add to smoothies or sprinkle over yogurt and porridge, and it is also available as a juice, often mixed with other fruit juices. The plant is also used in herbal medicine and skin-care products. **CC**

Taste: *Sea buckthorn has a unique, citric taste and a fresh aroma that has been likened to passion fruit. Many prefer it as a juice blended with sugar rather than as a raw fruit.*

The fruit-covered branches of sea buckthorn fan out to form a pleasing ornamental plant. »

Açaí

Riberry

Known as the "purple pearl of the Amazon," the açaí is deep violet, almost black in color, with firm flesh surrounding a sturdy seed. Yet, its culinary potential would have gone unnoticed if indigenous tribes had not realized centuries ago the pulp required processing. The resulting thick puree forms a wonderful base for juices, mousses, and ice creams, and lasts far longer than the fresh fruit.

Açaí grows in bunches from a tall, leafy palm, *Euterpe oleracea*, which can reach a height of 65 feet (20 m) or more deep in the rain forest around the Amazon River and its tributaries. Locals pick the fruit daily and send it down-river for sale at markets such as *Ver-o-Peso* (See-the-Price), the colonial covered market in the regional capital of Belém.

Açaí makes a great, energy-charging breakfast; however, sophisticated chefs in Rio and São Paulo, who are keen to encapsulate different facets of their country in their cuisine, use it as a base for sauces to accompany roast meats and desserts such as crème caramel and ice cream. Outside Brazil, it is gaining increasing renown as a nutritional superfood. **AL**

Botanically related to the common spice clove, the riberry (*Syzygium leumannii*) is a small rain forest tree originally found in northern New South Wales, where it was a forage food of the Bundjalung people and other local clans. It is now commonly used as a decorative urban planting all along the east coast. Ten-year-old plants and even potted specimens can bear impressive bunches of rose to scarlet heart-shaped fruits in the few months around Christmas. The fruits are hand-picked and stemmed, then washed and cleaned. They are then stored frozen or made into preserves such as spreads and vinegars.

Delicious in desserts, particularly in combination with chocolate—commercial riberry confit pairs wonderfully with a rich chocolate mousse—they are equally at home In a riberry vodkatini or tossed through stir-fry dishes. A classic Australian combination is kangaroo cooked medium rare with a port wine *jus* and riberry confit. The sweetness of the sugar-cured fruits can be offset with red wine vinegar; drained of their syrup, preserved riberries are ideal with cheese. **VC**

Taste: *The acidity of açaí fruit and the discreetly bitter notes, which some compare to chocolate, come into their own when balanced with sugar or honey.*

Taste: *The seedless fruits have a refreshing watermelon texture and aromatics of cinnamon and clove; clove is more dominant in seeded varieties.*

Extravagant claims are made for the health benefits of this rain forest fruit, used by indigenous tribes.

Marula

Traditional wisdom has it that wild animals become intoxicated from eating the slightly fermented fallen fruits of the marula tree: certainly elephants are partial to the fruit and in South Africa the marula is known as the "elephant tree." Be that as it may, however, marula (*Scelerocarya birrea*) has fed a diversity of users in southern Africa, possibly from as early as 10,000 BCE. Thriving in dry, sandy soils and drought-resistant, the tree is a familiar sight in the savanna and the veldt today.

The marula is considered a sacred tree in many parts of Africa and is attributed with many powers, including those of fertility and virility. Among the Venda people, the bark was used to select the sex of an unborn child: an infusion of bark from a male tree was believed to produce a son, while an infusion from a female tree would summon a daughter. Given the tree's sacred status, the harvesting of marula fruits from the wild is the cause for celebration and harvest festivals.

The marula is a prolific tree, bearing many fruit, and historically a valued food source in many parts of Africa. The fruits are about the size of a golf ball, ripening from green to pale yellow, and contain several times more vitamin C than an orange. The smooth, shiny, yellowish skin surrounds white flesh. When completely ripe, marula fruit are used in various jams and jellies. The fruit is also used to make wine, beer, the South African moonshine brandy known as *mampoer*, and as an ingredient in the cream liqueur, Amarula. The hard, brown nut inside the fruit contains edible kernels also prized as a foodstuff, used in porridge or as a flavoring. Oil extracted from the kernels is used in cosmetics. **HFi**

Mazhanje

Highly valued in Africa as a cash crop, mazhanje is the tropical fruit of *Uapaca kirkiana*, an indigenous tree that grows at medium altitudes in areas that receive good rainfall and are free of frost. Antelopes and elephants are also partial to fruit that has fallen to the ground and is fermenting. Popular in Zimbabwe, the fruit owes its name to the Shona language; it is known as wild loquat in English and by a host of different names across Africa.

The fruit tree grows in the Miombo ecological zone of woodland in southern Africa that takes in countries such as Zimbabwe, Angola, Namibia, Botswana, South Africa, Zambia, Tanzania, and Mozambique. The berrylike fruit can be up to 1.5 inches (4 cm) across and has a bitter, reddish-brown skin and a yellow-brown pulp embedded with several hard, white seeds. The flesh can be eaten raw, but the tough skin, which contains bitter tasting tannins and seeds, is discarded. A ripe fruit can weigh up to 1.75 ounces (50 g). Mazhanje is low in fat and high in potassium, and is highly regarded as an important famine food.

The fruit is usually collected in the wild by women and children, either from low-lying branches or from the ground, and is then sold at roadsides. The ripe fruit pulp is used to sweeten maize-meal porridge and is also made into a variety of local beers, cakes, and a jam that is eaten with bread. It is common for the jam to be sold a spoonful at a time. The tropical fruit also may be broken up, placed in water, and left to ferment to make a sweet, heady wine. In Malawi, the fruit is used to produce an opaque beer called *napolo ukana* and a gin called *kachasu*. **CK**

Taste: *Marula has an earthy, fruity scent. Remove the skin, then pop the central seed and the pulp around it into your mouth. The flesh has a refreshing, sweet-and-sour taste.*

Taste: *The ripe flesh of the mazhanje fruit has a honey sweet flavor that tastes like a cross between an orange and a pear; it has a fleshy, squashlike texture.*

Fermenting marula berries are known to intoxicate wild animals, and are also used to make beer.

Barhi Date

Mamoncillo

The fruit of a palm tree, *Phoenix dactylifera*, which grows in clusters in hot climates from California to North Africa, the date has been cultivated since prehistoric times. By the beginnings of the ancient civilizations in Egypt and Mesopotamia it was already a staple, and in the Middle East and North Africa it is still a vital fruit.

The maturation cycle is known around the world by its Arabic names. *Khalal* denotes a date that has reached full size but is still hard and pale; *bisr* is when the fruit begins to color; during *rutab* the date begins to soften at the tip; at *tamr* the dates are ready to be packed. Barhi dates are one of few cultivars that are enjoyable to eat at the khalal stage.

Barhis, which probably originated in Basra, Iraq, are popular across the Arab world, and have been grown in California since the early twentieth century. Firm, round, pale yellow, and as crunchy as an apple at the khalal stage, they are naturally high in sugar. During the rutab stage they become known as "honey balls" for the sweet liquid that pools inside their fragile surface. **FC**

Mamoncillo fruit begs to be plucked and eaten on the spot from the roadsides of Central and South America and all across the Caribbean. Clusters of these emerald green, round fruits ripen during the tropical summers on the native trees, which also conveniently offer a shady place to snack. On scorching hot afternoons the juice and flesh of the fruit can be slurped out of hand. The fruit also finds its way into the desserts, salsas, and cocktails that are served on the sun-drenched beaches.

Known by many other names, including genip, honeyberry, and Spanish lime, *Melicoccus bijugatus* belongs to the same family as rambutan and longan. Physically similar to these relatives, its orange-pink, opaque flesh surrounds a large oval seed. Wrapped in an inedible leathery shell that almost cracks when bitten or pierced, the inner fruit is slippery and releases easily with a gentle squeeze.

Mamoncillo is available preserved in syrup, but the fresh fruit offers the best flavor. Enterprising chefs toast the inner seeds and use them in much the same way as nuts or pumpkin seeds. **TH**

Taste: *Barhi dates are crisp, firm, and slightly fibrous, with a mild astringency until the flavors open up. Expect notes of sugarcane, cinnamon, cooked fruit, and candied nuts.*

Taste: *Mamoncillo is slightly tarter than either lychee or longan, but maintains a fruity sweetness that is an unusual, yet refreshing, cross between mango and grape.*

In many regions, dates are still hand harvested
Ⓧ *by pickers who hazardously shin up the palms.*

Davidson's Plum

Jamun

Native to the rain forests of southeast Queensland, the fruit known by Aborigines as *ooray* hangs in clusters amid the dark green, leathery leaves of *Davidsonia pruriens*. It starts off green, deepens to a dark purple or brilliant burgundy upon ripening, and varies when mature from 1 to 2½ inches (2.5–6 cm) in diameter. Like the European plum, to which it is not related, the Davidson's plum is soft and juicy, although its firm skin—but for the few sparse hairs that scatter it—is more similar to a date's. The twin pits, which form a teardrop shape, are densely coated with short fibers.

The rich color and brilliant pink juices make Davidson's plum a desirable ingredient in otherwise less colorful preparations, while its tang provides balance to chutneys, jams, and sauces. It is one of Australia's most versatile native foods with a pleasantly acid character that, like lemon, works equally well in sweet and savory dishes. Limited wild harvest supplies are being replaced by cultivated sources from the coasts of Queensland and northern New South Wales. **SC-S**

As much a part of an Indian summer as strawberries are of Western summers, the scorching afternoon siestas of a blazing June are often punctuated by itinerant fruitsellers singing out, *"Jamun kah-ley, kah-ley!"* (black, black jamuns). Hordes of children come scampering out to wolf them down with a sprinkling of coarse salt.

Jamuns are about the size and shape of large black olives and grow on tall, shady trees, which are a popular summer refuge from the heat and sun. Ripe jamuns hang down in bunches and annual contracts are given out to harvest them from trees in public areas, as from June the ripe fruit fall with every gust of wind to be crushed underfoot, staining the streets a livid purple.

Also known as jambul, jambolan, and java plum, *Syzygium cumini* grows over much of the Indian subcontinent and all the way into Southeast Asia, and is found as far afield as Hawaii and Zanzibar.

Besides being a summer snack, the dried and powdered fruit is also used as a digestive or in the kitchen to flavor gravies. **RD**

Taste: *Davidson's plums are sour on their own. Simply stew them in their own weight of sugar to tame the acidity and soften the grass, resin, and green bell pepper notes.*

Taste: *Varying from sweet to tart, jamuns are mouth-puckeringly astringent when even slightly unripe. Either way, they stain the mouth a deep shade of violet.*

An Indian laborer with his harvest of jamuns. The berries turn from green to nearly black as they ripen.  »

Illawarra Plum

The Illawarra plum, or brown pine (*Podocarpus elatus*), belongs to an ancient species. A southern hemisphere conifer, it stands tall and proud in dense subtropical, riverine, and seashore rain forests along Australia's east coast. Its family name, *Podocarpus*, comes from the Greek for "foot" and "fruit," a reference to the fleshy dark edibles that are botanically the stem of the fruit, yet in culinary terms the fruit itself.

Aborigines and the early settlers of southern New South Wales valued Illawarra plums highly, but in Queensland, where there was a greater variety of bush fruit, they were usually left to the possums. The tree produces its plums prolifically: they are a grapelike swelling of juicy flesh that can be up to 1¼ inches (3 cm) long, with a hard, inedible, smaller pit attached to their outside edge.

Most supplies of this classic wilderness food come from wild harvest. The plums are used in both sweet and savory foods, but are most often enjoyed in preserves, fruit compotes, baking, and sauces. Chile and sugar make happy accompaniments. **SC-S**

Taste: *The fleshy part of the fruit is subtly sweet with a mild, pleasantly resinous quality. The core is resinous and the flesh closest to it tastes so piney it should be avoided.*

Cashew Apple

The cashew apple (or cashew fruit) is one of Brazil's most enticing fruits. With the cashew nut sprouting from one end of its fleshy, almost pear-shaped growth, this pseudo-fruit conceals a lot of juice below its fibrous peel. The fruit's intense aroma spreads easily and can perfume a kitchen within seconds.

Widely cultivated along the coast of Brazil's stunning northeast region, to which it is probably native, the cashew apple has long been a favorite of the indigenous population. Ancient tribes used it to make a thick, creamy wine called *mocororó*, which was served at festivals; today the cashew apple makes one of Brazil's most popular fruit juices.

Anacardium occidentale is also the base ingredient in an unusual juice drink called *cajuína*, made by filtering the juice and cooking it in a water bath. It is enjoyed in ice creams, mousses, trifles, jams, and chutneys; reduced on a low heat for many hours it produces the dark, very sweet syrup known as cashew honey. In Goa, the cashew apple is used to produce a liqueur called Fenny. **AL**

Taste: *Cashew apples range in color from pale yellow to vermilion, and have a tangy astringent bite. If underripe, the tannins will cause an unpleasant aftertaste.*

The cashew nut is removed from the cashew apple and processed as soon as the fruit is harvested. »

Lucuma

This fruit (pronounced loo-ku-mah) is known as the "gold of the Incas;" its Latin name is *Pouteria lucuma*. Although mainly found in Peru, lucuma is also grown in Chile, Brazil, and Ecuador, and it is next to impossible to find it fresh away from these countries. Lucuma is referred to as one of the lost crops of the Incas; these are indigenous foods that are now being introduced in the West for the first time.

Similar to a small mango in appearance, lucuma is green-skinned when young, ripening to a warm red. Round or oval in shape, the fruit has golden flesh and a distinct, fragrant flavor, said to be similar to that of maple syrup. The unripe fruit contains a bitter white latex. In South America, lucuma is revered as an ancient and well-loved food, commonly included in celebratory feasts and banquets. One tree can produce as many as 500 fruits in the course of a year, helping to sustain people when field crops are out of season or damaged by drought. At such times the species literally becomes the tree of life.

The fruit can be eaten fresh when ripe and is also consumed in the form of a refreshing drink. Most lucuma is dried and powdered and used in ice creams and other sweets. In Peru, lucuma is one of the most popular flavorings for ice cream. Lucuma pulp is also frozen for export.

Like most golden fruits, lucuma is an excellent source of beta-carotene, as well as being rich in iron and niacin. Powdered lucuma has been gaining popularity among health-conscious Westerners as a low-glycemic sweetener for cakes and cookies. Its syrupy, shortbread flavor makes it an ideal substitute for wheat when making gluten-free versions of traditional treats. **KMW**

Taste: *Usually eaten fresh, out of hand, the highly juicy flesh is slightly fibrous, with an exquisite aroma and a delicate, caramel-like flavor.*

Red Mombin

In conditions as varied as the torrential downpours of the Amazon forest and the dry heat of the savanna, the red mombin flourishes across Latin America under a bewildering range of names—most notably jocote in parts of Mexico (from the Aztec *xocotl*), ciruela, and Spanish plum. Many varieties grow throughout the region—more than twenty in Mexico's Yucatan region alone. The Spanish introduced the fruit to the Philippines, where it grows well and is known as siniguelas. In the Philippines, the fruit is eaten raw or features as an ingredient in the traditional sour stew, sinigang.

With its delicate, thin skin, the red mombin has a simplicity typical of wild fruits: a pleasant, sweet flavor, with contrasting sour nuances, balanced by a citric fragrance. The fruit is small, only 1 to 2 inches (2.5–5 cm) in length, and ranges in shape from rounded to oval, like an olive. It grows on the tree singly or in clusters of two or three and comes in many varying colors, from yellow and orange to deep red or violet. Red mombin fruit is generally harvested in the wild, but research is being undertaken into its potential for cultivation because the tree is easy to propagate and fast-growing.

Naturally juicy and refreshing, *Spondias purpurea* yields a juice perfect for energizing the body on hot days. In Brazil, the juice forms a base for ice creams; in Costa Rica, it is the star of a preserve called "jocote honey." In Nicaragua, where the Pacific Coast was famous for its red mombins back in colonial times, the fruits are also enjoyed "green," before they ripen. To make the most of their intense acidity, they are seasoned with salt and sold by the bagful on the streets of cities such as the capital, Managua. **AL**

Taste: *With the concentrated sweetness of yellow plums and a light acidity reminiscent of a sour orange, the red mombin is fantastic raw, in ice creams, and in cocktails.*

Latin America is seeing greater consumption of red mombin, mainly supplied by local markets. »

Ambarella

Originally native to the Society Islands of the South Pacific, the ambarella fruit (*Spondias dulcis*) is now widely grown in tropical and subtropical areas including Southeast Asia, India, Sri Lanka, Australia, Jamaica, Trinidad, and Venezuela. It is consequently known by a bewildering host of names, including golden apple, pomme cythere, Otaheite apple (which derives from Otaheite, the old name for Tahiti), Tahitian quince, hog plum, Brazil plum, Polynesian plum, and Jew plum.

The oval, egg-sized ambarella fruit grows on a handsome, tall, glossy-leafed tree, borne in hanging clusters of between two to ten fruits. The fruit, which is sometimes likened to an inferior mango, has a thin but tough skin with a rough, knobbly surface that ripens from green to a yellowy orange, and contains a few small pale seeds embedded in the center.

In many countries the fruit is often eaten when unripe, enjoyed for its tangy sourness and crisp texture. Its juice is extracted for cold drinks (often mixed with the juice of other tropical fruits). The flesh can be stewed, sweetened, and then sieved to make a sauce to accompany meat. The ripe flesh is also used to make a cinnamon-flavored preserve similar to apple butter. The unripe fruit is made into pickles, chutneys, and relishes, used to flavor stews and soups, and added to curries in Sri Lanka. High in pectin, it is often used in jams. In Indonesia, where it is called *kedongdong*, the crisp, sour flesh of the green, unripe fruit is used in *rujak*, a traditional salad dish of raw vegetables tossed with a salty-sweet dressing; the young leaves are steamed and served with salted fish and rice. Sliced and dipped in salt and cayenne, it is a popular street snack. **CK**

Wampee

A distant relative of the orange, wampee (*Clausena lansium*) looks like a large grape and grows in bunches of up to eighty fruit, each fruit having five segments of soft, highly aromatic flesh. The dense wampee trees with their dark green leaves are native to southern China but provide much-needed shade throughout Southeast Asia. The tree also grows well in greenhouses in England.

The fruit has many local names, including *wang-pei* in Malaysia, *galumpi* in the Philippines, *hong bi* in Vietnam, and *som-ma-fai* in Thailand, where the wampee has been recognized as the country's finest fruit. In Vietnam and China, the halved, sun-dried, immature fruit is used as a remedy for coughs and bronchitis. Dried wampee fruit is very popular in Thailand where it is eaten as a sweet preserve.

Wampee fruits turn yellow when ripe. Although the skin is thin, papery, and easily peeled, it is also minutely hairy, resinous, and quite tough, and therefore should be peeled away before eating. Each fruit contains one or more large seeds, but a seedless variety has been developed in recent years.

In China, wampee is served to accompany meat dishes, and the fruits are also made into pies, jams, and drinks, including a champagnelike aperitif made by fermenting the fruit with sugar and then straining off the juice. A fully ripe, peeled wampee can be eaten fresh, after discarding the large seed or seeds. Jelly can be made only from the acidic underripe fruit. The fruit is reputed to have a cooling effect, and the Chinese also prize the fruit as a digestive aid—contending that "When too many lychees have been eaten, wampee will counteract any adverse effects." **WS**

Taste: *Crisp and firm in texture, ambarella fruit has a pleasant, juicy, slightly sour taste. Its flavor and musky aroma are similar to an underripe pineapple.*

Taste: *The jellylike flesh varies from sweet and tangy to sharp and almost sour. Freshly picked, wampees are thirst quenching, refreshing, and a delightful palate cleanser.*

Islands in the South Pacific offer fruit and vegetable ✪ *species yet to make an impact in the wider world.*

Mirabelle

Greengage

These golden, honey-sweet, walnut-size plums were first recognized as a separate variety in the seventeenth-century French tract, Lectier's *Catalogue of Cultivated Garden Trees*. Although the fruit is widely grown, Mirabelles have been most closely identified with Lorraine, in France, where there are two specific varieties. Both the smaller Mirabelle de Nancy and its sister the Mirabelle de Metz fall under an EU Protected Geographical Indication that guarantees their provenance. They are grown in orchards and ripen in midsummer, and their smooth skins are often speckled with reddish dots.

When baked, Mirabelles have a sticky, lip-smacking taste at its best in *tarte aux mirabelles*. The halved plums are packed on top of a crust prepared with a yeasted dough, then baked in a hot oven until the fruits are lightly caramelized, when the tart is sprinkled with a little sugar and cinnamon and given a final glaze. Mirabelle sits alongside kirsch and Poire William as one of the eaux-de-vie for which Alsace and Lorraine are most celebrated: the fruit is also popular in jams, jellies, and preserves. **MR**

The story goes that the carrier who was delivering the first greengage trees from France to England thought the label on his consignment of green plums, which read Gage, was the name of the fruit. So while many Europeans know the fruit as a variation of Reine Claude, the wife of Francis I of France (1494–1547), Anglo-Saxons memorialize William Gage, who imported them to Suffolk in 1724.

Not botanically distinct from other plums, most greengages have green skins with very sweet green or yellow flesh. Round rather than oval, they tend to be smaller than other European plums. (Some, however, such as the Oullins gage, can be red or green, and larger than the average plum.) They were developed in France and Italy from the domestic plum, possibly crossed with a wild green plum from Asia Minor; France still grows more greengages than anywhere else. The season in western Europe extends from early July until late September, but fruit produced in volume for transport can be tasteless compared to those found in a home garden or picked fresh from the orchard. **AMS**

Taste: *At the peak of maturity, Mirabelles have a syrupy, almost cloying sweetness that is unlike any other plum. Their flavor in an open tart is incomparable.*

Taste: *Greengages are best eaten raw and very fresh. Their rich and honeyed sweetness comes as a surprise, in contrast to the acidity their skin color suggests.*

Blenheim Apricot

Nectarine

Cultivated in China for more than four millennia, over the centuries the apricot has traversed the globe. By the first century CE cuttings had reached Europe by way of the Middle East. Later, Spanish colonists took the fruit to Mexico and from there to California. By the turn of the twentieth century, a burgeoning apricot industry was in place in the state, and groves of California's trademark variety, the Blenheim, flourished all around San Jose. But acreage was lost to development, as communities grew, and the farmers moved out to poorer land. Although prized for its flavor and scent, the Blenheim is particularly delicate, and does not hold up well to transport or storage, so during the second half of the century it gave way to sturdier varieties.

Approaching the close of the twentieth century, the Blenheim was in danger of extinction, but the current interest in heirloom fruit varieties is helping rescue it from the brink. Small, often organic, farms are creating a new generation of enthusiasts to support this delicate fruit, seeking it out at farmers' markets or orchard stands in early summer. **CN**

This succulent fruit, produced in orchards around the world, has suffered from its popularity. Few varieties are grown commercially and those are too often picked and marketed underripe. But rare varieties, such as the yellow-fleshed Vaga Loggia Duracina, which grew in Jefferson's Monticello garden, enjoy a special reputation for their flavor.

Peaches were probably first domesticated in China 3,000 years ago. Nectarines evolved from them as a kind of sport or genetic anomaly. With their smooth skins, they look a little like large plums, but are not at all related: their English (and French) name probably comes from German or Dutch and points to the nectarlike sweetness and juiciness of their flesh. Their popularity grew, in Europe, during the seventeenth century. Louis XIV was especially partial to those growing in his *potager* at Versailles.

As with peaches, there are cultivars with white fruits and yellow, with freestones and clingstones. They are best eaten as a table fruit, although many recipes exist, notably the luxurious nectarines macerated in Champagne. **MR**

Taste: *Not as juicy-sweet as a peach, apricots tend to have a lovely flavor between sweet and tart. The Blenheim has a rich, full flavor that is remarkably potent for an apricot.*

Taste: *Ripe nectarines have a smooth skin and buttery-textured pulp that is juicy, but denser than most peaches. The flavor is perfumed and sweet, with a hint of acidity.*

Pêche de Vigne

Pêche de vigne appears for a fleeting few weeks during late summer, most often in the orchards around the Rhône valley. Its grayish, fuzzy exterior conceals fragrant red or pink flesh connoisseurs consider the very best peach on the planet.

The name means "peach of the grapevine" and some say it derives from French *vignerons*, who plant young peach trees at the end of their rows so the plants contract diseases or pests before the grapevines do—somewhat like a canary in a coal mine. Others say it comes from the color of the flesh, which can be as bright as red wine lees.

The peach originated in China more than 3,000 years ago; there the peach tree symbolizes immortality and springtime. The fruit found its way to the West via the silk roads to Persia—hence its botanical name, *Prunus persica*—which is most likely where Greeks, under the leadership of Alexander the Great, discovered it and took it to Europe.

Best simply peeled and eaten *au naturel*, pêches de vigne are also wonderful sliced and submerged in red dessert wine or a rich rosé. **LF**

Taste: *The sweet-smelling flesh of pêche de vigne combines the light, but slightly musky, flavor of a juicy white peach with the spirit of sun-kissed raspberries.*

Prunus persica *peach trees blossom in spring.* »

Green Mango

Alphonso Mango

Any mango (*Mangifera indica*) is called a green mango in its unripe state. The deliciously sour flavor makes this a popular fruit throughout South and Southeast Asia, where the mango has been cultivated for millennia, although it is now grown and enjoyed in tropical and subtropical climates around the world.

In India, where green mangoes are a symbol of imminent richness, they play an important role in harvest and New Year feasts across the nation, which coincide with the fruit's annual debut around March or April. The tangy, tender fruit are sliced or diced and added to lentils, vegetables, or fish dishes in summer; pickled in mustard oil and spices to last throughout the year; or sun-dried and powdered to become the sour spice *amchur*. In Thailand, they are used in salads and as a souring agent; in the Philippines, green mango juice is sought after; in Central America, they are served with salt and spices.

Green mangoes are best plucked fresh from the tree, peeled, and eaten with a sprinkling of cayenne pepper or coarse salt. The sour tang is addictive. **RD**

Mangoes have been a part of India's mystique for millennia, referenced in ancient Hindu scriptures, Chinese Buddhist chronicles, and by countless visiting Europeans down the centuries. This varietal of *Mangifera indica* is known as *Haphoos* locally, a corruption of its name Alphonso, supposedly after the Portuguese nobleman-adventurer Afonso de Albuquerque, who arrived in Goa in 1504.

The Alphonso is western India's pride and joy, dubbed "the king of mangoes" in a nation that grows nearly seventy percent of the world's mangoes in more than 135 varieties. It appears in Indian fruit stores early on in the mango season, reaching its peak from mid-May to mid-June, and, because it travels well, is increasingly found elsewhere.

No Indian summer can start without biting into a luscious Alphonso then chasing the juice that runs down the forearm with the tongue. Simply cut off the two "cheeks" of the fruit by slicing vertically from stem to tip on each side of the seed, score the flesh in a grid pattern (without piercing the skin), push the skin up to turn out the flesh—and tuck in! **RD**

Taste: *Green skin encloses white or pale yellow flesh. The texture varies from hard to spongy, whereas the flavor can be mouth-puckeringly astringent or delightfully sour.*

Taste: *The Alphonso's deep orangy-saffron flesh covers a large, flat seed. The vanilla aroma provides sweet citrus hints; the buttery-sweet flavor offers a dash of tartness.*

Firmer than their ripe siblings, green mangoes
🛇 *have a sour tang that is valued in many cultures.*

Salak

Longan

Known as snakeskin fruit because of their leathery, scaly skin, salak, or zalak, are native to Indonesia, but also grow in Thailand and Malaysia. The fruit grows in bunches at the base of a short-stemmed palm and is similar in size and shape to a fig or small pear, with a plump, rounded base and pointed tip. The easiest way to peel salak is to pinch the tip to loosen the thin, reddish-brown skin so it can be pulled away to reveal three segments of creamy, ivory flesh that closely resemble fat cloves of peeled garlic. Each segment contains a hard, inedible seed.

The texture of the different varieties of salak range from moist and juicy to very dry. General consensus holds that the best salak grow on the island of Bali, where they are refreshingly crunchy. Salak from the Yogyakarta region of Java, known as *pondoh,* is thought to have the sweetest flesh, but its pungent aroma is offputting to some. Sweet and acidic, salak are usually eaten fresh, but they are also pickled or canned in syrup. Their texture makes them good in cooked desserts and they are often added to pies and puddings. **WS**

As the spring comes to a close in southern China, country farmers seem to defy gravity as they travel into the cities with overloaded baskets strapped to all sides of their bicycles. Branches bejeweled with the treat of fresh longan fruit are taken straight from the tree at higher altitudes to hungry city dwellers by makeshift couriers in what has become a seasonal culinary tradition.

Handfuls of the fruit (*Dimocarpus longan*) are the perfect snack and can be bought for only a few yuan. The size of large grapes, longans have hard shells that must be pierced to allow the slippery flesh to escape. The art is part skill and part comedy, but streets become littered with remnants of the game.

Sometimes called "dragon's eyes," longans are best fresh from the tree or the nearest farm vendor, but can also be found dried, jellied, canned in syrup, and even distilled into a mildly alcoholic cordial. While exported to and increasingly grown in Western markets, the sweetness of the fruit diminishes in transport compared to when eaten in China, where numerous cultivars are grown. **TH**

Taste: *Salak tastes like pineapple crossed with the sharp crunchiness of a Granny Smith apple. Its tangy character becomes more pronounced the dryer the flesh becomes.*

Taste: *The fruit is sweet and musky, sometimes, although not always, sharp, but reminiscent of lychees and kiwis. The soft, juicy flesh is completely sealed within the shell.*

The dense clusters of longan fruits are simply cut from the tree during harvesting. ❯❯

Lychee

The fruit of a tall evergreen, *Litchi chinensis*, and native to the subtropical parts of Asia, the lychee's mesmerizing qualities are clear from early Chinese lore. The tenth-century writer Ts'ai Hsiang devoted a treatise to the subject; the emperor Hsuan Tsung was reportedly brought down by his concubine's fondness for the fruit; from the first century CE, fast horses used to carry lychees to the imperial court.

Scarlet when ripe on the tree, and—more or less—heart-shaped, this aromatic little fruit has long been associated with romance and credited with aphrodisiac powers, too. The skin has a rough, leathery texture, which is easily broken by slight pressure, revealing the translucent whitish flesh around the smooth brown seed at its core.

Like most fruits, lychees are best eaten fresh. Unlike many fruits, however, they keep much of their natural flavor even when canned or made into juice. The refreshing quality of lychees is savored in the humid conditions of their subtropical homeland, and has led to their being cultivated in similar climates around the world. **JN**

Taste: *Lychees are sweet and have delicate floral notes with hints of melon. The texture is similar to firm grapes that are plump with juice, although a little more glutinous.*

Thailand's floating markets have become a big
◉ tourist attraction as well as an outlet for local produce.

Rambutan

If the lychee is the blowsy diva of the tropical fruit world, the rambutan is the elegant, honey-voiced recitalist. That said, the appearance of *Nephelium lappaceum* is pure music hall, with a flashy scarlet or yellow coat covered in thin, green-tipped hairs. Native to Malaysia, but now grown more widely across Asia, in Australia, and in parts of the Americas, rambutans are valued for their pearly, succulent flesh and their sheer sweetness, accented with a lightly citric tang in some varieties. Like peaches, they come in clingstone and freestone varieties.

They are best bought fresh and ripe and eaten by hand the same day: cooking and canning both attenuate their flavor, and adding sugar overwhelms their natural taste. Despite their appearance, they are easy to peel, making them a perfect fruit for snacking. A close cousin of the rambutan called *pulasan (Nephelium mutabile)* has thicker, juicier flesh that when perfectly ripe can be even better than rambutans. Neither rambutans nor *pulasans* travel well, and are hard to find outside their growing regions. **CTa**

Taste: *A pure burst of sweetness distinguishes the first bite of a ripe rambutan; successive bites reveal a faint, almost lilylike perfume. Sweet-sour cultivars add a lemony note.*

Passion Fruit

Pomegranate

The passion fruit is the fruit of a tropical vine, *Passiflora edulis*, which is native to Brazil, although members of the same family are found in tropical regions around the globe. The name, which suits its extraordinary flavor, originates with Christian missionaries who named the flower the "passionflower" in the belief that the shapes of its various parts were symbolic of the crucifixion of Christ: its five stamens supposedly represent the five wounds of Christ, and its three styles the nails that pinned him to the cross.

On plantations, a single vine will easily produce about 100 fruits each year. The darker, purple-brown passion fruits, which wrinkle when ripe, are better for eating than the prettier, smoother, yellow varieties. Cut open, the fruit reveals a golden-orange pulp, which clusters in teardrop-shaped arils around edible black seeds.

The flavor and aroma carry well, making passion fruit a popular flavoring for desserts, drinks, and fragrances. It is probably best enjoyed scooped raw from the half-shell with a spoon. **FC**

The fruit whose seeds, in ancient Greek mythology, led to Persephone's captivity by Hades, the god of the underworld, has been cultivated in its Asian homeland for several millennia, and has acquired iconic and religious status in many cultures: it is cited in the Koran as an example of the good things God provides, and prescribed as adornment for priestly robes in the book of Exodus. It is a national symbol of Armenia, where folklore says it contains 365 seeds, one for each day of the year.

The pomegranate is the fruit of a small tree, *Punica granatum*, and varies widely in shape and color. Those for eating have a hard rind colored anywhere between a mild yellow and a bright crimson, while the interior is laced with clusters of glassy-looking, crystalline arils colored on a spectrum between white and scarlet and separated by yellowish, pithy membranes. Used in cooking throughout the Caucasus and Middle East, the flavor is often harnessed as a juice or syrup: many commercial versions in the United States and Europe gain their taste from other red berries. **FC**

Taste: *The intensely sharp flavor has notes of mandarin, orange, and pineapple. Most enjoy the contrast of the succulent pulp and the crunch of the mild-flavored seeds.*

Taste: *Pomegranate pulp is tart, reminiscent of a sweeter cranberry. The skin encasing each aril is firm, delivering a satisfying burst; the seeds have a distinct bitterness.*

All varieties of **Passiflora** *produce spectacular flowers, but the fruits are not equally appealing.*

Mangosteen

Known in parts of Asia as "the queen of fruits" (with the durian as its king), the mangosteen is the fruit of *Garcinia mangostana*, a tall, ultratropical tree that can take fifteen years to reach maturity. Airfreighted fruit can occasionally be found in gourmet food stores in many countries, although these are smaller and less flavorsome than those picked fresh.

The mangosteen inspires lyricism wherever it is encountered: Queen Victoria allegedly offered a knighthood to anyone who could bring her a mangosteen ripened to perfection and ready to eat. The hard, maroon rind, whose juice can easily stain, contains between four and eight elegant segments of soft, snow-white flesh; some contain a gelatinous, edible seed.

Mangosteens are best eaten raw, cut neatly in half so the white fruit rests within the cup of the crimson half-shell and can be carefully extracted with the fingers. Unripe mangosteens, however, are preserved in Malaysia, and mangosteen juice has been used as a common folk remedy in parts of Asia and marketed with medicinal claims in the West. **FC**

Taste: *On the palate, the flavors are considerably subtle: a light sweetness is balanced by a delicately sharp tang reminiscent of mandarin orange, mixed with floral notes.*

In transit, the delicate flesh of the mangosteen is protected from bruising by its thick, fibrous shell.

Pequi

There are perhaps few fruits with a scent or flavor as intense as that of the pequi (*Caryocar coriaceum*), which is native to the central savanna region of Brazil. The fruit, which ranges in color from white to egg-yolk yellow, is a highlight of Goiás state's most typical landscape—scrubland dominated by small and twisted trees—and of its home cooking. It stars in two signature dishes, pequi rice (a type of country risotto) and chicken pequi (a traditional chicken stew). Many chefs enjoy the challenge of creating new dishes that combine this aromatic fruit with other ingredients without letting it dominate.

When using the pequi whole in dishes, caution is required beyond the strictly culinary. The pit must be carefully chewed, as it conceals a stone bristling with thorns that can damage the mouth and tongue. (Most chefs opt to use the flesh with the pit removed.) In addition to savory dishes, pequi is also used to make an aromatic liqueur for rounding off meals: this can linger on the palate for many hours. Cultivated pequi fruit are preferable to the wild sort, which are endangered. **AL**

Taste: *Pequi's musky aroma is almost untamable and its balsamic oiliness unmistakable. Using it requires care to stop other ingredients next to it from becoming bit players.*

Feijoa

Golden Kiwifruit

The feijoa, *Acca sellowiana*, is native to Uruguay and parts of Brazil, Paraguay, and Argentina, where, although common in the wild, it is cultivated relatively rarely. Most exported fruit comes from its adoptive home, New Zealand, where the big bush is as much appreciated for its vibrant red flowers as for its frosty green fruit.

Also known as the pineapple guava, each fruit is a smooth or knobbly barrel measuring 3 to 4 inches (7–10 cm), not dissimilar to a small avocado, but with a sensual, intensely perfumed aroma and flavor. The slippery, coated seeds in the translucent central core, the granular texture of the creamy white flesh, and the distinct aroma of guava demonstrate its relationship to the fruit whose name it bears. As with the quince, just a few can scent a room.

Traditionally the feijoa was made into a savory jelly or bottled to eat during winter. Today, its unique flavor is appreciated when cooked with apples in deep pies or under a cobbler or crumble topping, although many prefer to halve the chilled fruit and scoop the flesh out raw. **GC**

The kiwifruit is indigenous to the Yangtze River basin, China, where its local names include monkey peach, macaque peach, and sun peach. It reached its adoptive home, New Zealand, with missionaries at the turn of the last century. *Actinidia deliciosa* originally produced a small, cigar-shaped fruit that New Zealanders tended to cook, producing a gooseberrylike flavor—hence the name, Chinese gooseberry. The fruit's modern success began in the 1960s when the locally bred Hayward variety, with bigger fruit like a flattened barrel, was renamed the kiwifruit. Today it is grown in many countries.

Golden kiwifruit, a variety developed in New Zealand, has a yellow flesh speckled with tiny black seeds at the white core. It has a sweeter, more intense tropical flavor than those with the bright green flesh. The kiwifruit is unique, although sliced or segmented it can become a garnishing cliché. Halved and spooned out, sliced onto cakes, pavlova, or fruit salad, it remains popular. Avoid misuse in ice cream and sorbet; if the seeds are broken by a blender they become particularly bitter. **GC**

Taste: *On the palate, feijoa mixes pineapple and guava. The initial sweetness mellows to leave a slightly citric herbal flavor, which declines when the fruit is cooked.*

Taste: *The rich, full, honeyed flavor of ripe golden kiwifruit is initially reminiscent of apples but develops unique sweet aromas and a deliciously long, acidic finish.*

The flowers make the feijoa a most attractive evergreen
◎ *shrub; its fruits should not be eaten if overripe.*

Strawberry Guava

With its intense aroma and surprising sharpness on the palate, this cousin of the guava is considered by many gastronomes the best and tastiest fruit in the guava family. Native to Brazil, where it grows wild in some states and is a great countryside delicacy, *Psidium cattleianum* is a spectacularly fertile plant. An evergreen tree, it bears two crops a year in some locations, and fruits virtually year-round in others: a habit that would make it a true plant of the future, but for its tendency to colonize new habitats, wiping out competing native vegetation, which means many countries now class it as an invasive weed.

The round fruit looks like an egg with skin that varies from green to red, although yellow types are the best, with juicy, "seedy," white pulp. Delicious eaten unaccompanied and particularly appetizing when fresh, it is also excellent used in jams and sweets: *araçazada* is a popular Brazilian treat, prepared using puree and cut simply into tablets. The strawberry guava features in ice creams, liqueurs, juices, jellies, jams, pastes, and sherbets, and also works well in cocktails involving punch. **AL**

Carambola

Pastry chefs love this fruit for the pretty five-pointed stars it slices into, but *Averrhoa carambola* deserves its nickname of "star fruit" for more than its physical charms. To Southeast Asian palates, carambola has the same ineffably cooling aura as watermelon or papaya. Sweltering tropical humidity or an overheated constitution are agreeably countered by star fruit juice or slices, seasoned with a pinch of salt.

Carambola's juicy bite makes it a good appetite stimulant and palate cleanser: in countries including Singapore, Malaysia, and Taiwan, it is even considered a cure for sore throats. Today, the star fruit is extensively cultivated outside its homeland, from Australia to China via Latin America and Israel: in the United States, some winemakers have produced crisp white wines from its juice.

Carambolas are often confused in literature with a close relative, *Averrhoa bilimbi*. Bilimbis taste very similar to carambolas, except much more acidic and astringent; they are used to sour curries, pickles, and chutneys in India and Southeast Asia. Both fruits are also often candied in sugar syrup. **CTa**

Taste: *The juicy pulp has a sourness not usually found in this type of fruit, and the taste is sharp and refreshing, a little like melon mixed with touches of lime.*

Taste: *Barely ripe carambola has a verjuicelike sharpness. As it ripens, it acquires notes of pear, melon, and gooseberry, with a balance of flavors that is lightly sweet and sour.*

Averrhoa carambola *deserves its nickname of "star fruit" for more than its physical shape.* ❯

Date Plum

Reputed to be the fabled food eaten by the lotus-eaters in Homer's *Odyssey*, the date plum (*Diospyros lotus*) is sometimes confused with the American persimmon, a close cousin. The potential confusion is farther increased by the fact another persimmon variety, the kaki (*Diospyros kaki*), is also sometimes called a date plum.

The date plum's precise origins are not clear, but it grows today, both in the wild and in cultivation, in southeastern Europe and as far east as Japan, China, and Korea. The size of a large cherry, the fruit varies in color—from yellow to brown-blue-black, depending on ripeness—and has a flavor that is sweet and astringent at the same time. Most fruits contain flat, brown seeds.

Date plums can be eaten raw or cooked. Raw, they can be eaten out of hand, but, unless they are fully ripe, they will be overly harsh and astringent. The fruit can also be used to make jams, puddings, and other fruit desserts. In Asia, the date plum is often dried, when it assumes a more recognizable datelike flavor. **SH**

Taste: *Neither a plum nor a date, a ripe date plum has a very soft flesh and a rich, sweet, slightly spicy taste, similar to that of a persimmon, but less astringent.*

Loquat

Native to China, the *Eryobotrya japonica* is known as the *pipa*, after the ancient Chinese four-string "lute." In the United States and Europe, the loquat is also known as a Japanese medlar—*nèfle du Japon* in France, *nespola giapponese* in Italy—or even, sometimes, just plain medlar.

Oval shaped, the loquat has a beautiful color, similar to a ripe apricot or mango, depending on the variety. They have been cultivated in China for more than 1,000 years and have been popular in Japan for centuries, but, although they are grown in other parts of the world—notably in the Americas, Turkey, and Australia—they are not an easy fruit to find. When ripe, the loquat bruises very easily and visibly, making it difficult to transport: the skin, which is peeled rather than eaten, is very thin. The tree is sometimes grown as an ornamental plant.

Delicious raw, the loquat is also dried or cooked, as all the fruit on a tree ripens within a very short time. It can be made into preserves, jellies, syrups, and liqueurs, while in China both the leaves and the dried fruit are used in treatments for coughs. **KKC**

Taste: *The flesh of the loquat has a sweetness, texture, and fragrance that brings apricots to mind. The taste, however, is different—both juicier and sharper.*

Loquat fruit trees thrive in the fertile valleys of southern Spain. »

Cape Gooseberry

Agbalumo

British cookbook author Jane Grigson memorialized "the orange-red berry glimmering through its dried out, gauzy calyx." Long before Europeans arrived in the New World, Native Americans were extracting these pretty round fruit from their papery, parchmentlike husks and eating them out of hand or drying them. It was Australian settlers in the early nineteenth century who christened the Cape gooseberry, however, after the Cape of Good Hope, in South Africa, from where it had traveled to them.

Cape gooseberries belong—like other physalis fruits—to the Solanaceae (nightshades) family, and should not be confused with *Physalis ixocarpa*, the tomatillo. Today, Cape gooseberries are highly popular and widely cultivated in Hawaii, where they are known as poha berries and used for both sweet and savory dishes: combined with couscous and cilantro, they form an accompaniment to scallops. In Colombia and Andean countries, they are used in yogurts, ice creams, and savory sauces; in Brazil and parts of Europe, they are dipped in dark chocolate and served as petits fours. **SH**

One of the foods Nigerians are most likely to miss when they live far from home is agbalumo, a fruit highly prized for its sweet-and-sour qualities. The fruit of a tropical canopy tree, *Chrysophyllum albidum,* that is found in lowland mixed rain forest areas in such African countries as Sudan, Kenya, Ghana, Sierra Leone, Uganda, Cameroon, Côte d'Ivoire, and of course Nigeria where the tree is cultivated. The fruit is also known as the "white star apple," after its five-pointed-star-patterned flesh.

Round in shape with a slight point, the fruit measures about 1¼ inches (3 cm) in diameter. The green-gray fruit turns to orange-red, yellow-brown, or yellow, sometimes with speckles, when it is ripe. Agbalumo has a red fleshy interior and creamy white core. It is very popular with children, who as well as eating the flesh, play games with the flat, beanlike, inedible brown seeds. The fruit also takes on the texture of chewing gum when continually chewed. Agbalumo is eaten raw and the pulp is also used to make jams and jellies. Locals also ferment and distill the fruit to produce wine and spirits. **CK**

Taste: *Bittersweet, slightly tart, and very juicy, Cape gooseberries have some of the acidity of a cherry tomato and notes of citrus fruits, pineapple, peaches, and cherries.*

Taste: *The soft luscious flesh of the ripe agbalumo fruit has a mouthwatering, creamy texture and a sweet-and-sour flavor that is distinctly moreish.*

Each Cape gooseberry develops inside a calyx that is brightly colored when young.

Bael

Cherimoya

When British botanists visited India in the early nineteenth century they encountered a bewildering array of unfamiliar exotic fruits and they renamed many of them, such as the pineapple and custard apple, as variations of the English apple. The bael, which is also known as bilva, Buddha fruit, holy fruit, and Bengal quince, was dubbed "wood apple."

The thorny bael tree is native to India, but grows all over Southeast Asia. The tree is sacred in the Hindu religion; the god Shiva is said to live under a bael tree and its oval, pointed leaves are used in religious rituals. The tree is prized for its medicinal properties and is used to treat a range of maladies from dysentery to the common cold.

Related to the citrus family, the bael makes a popular breakfast in Indonesia where it is sweetened with palm sugar. In Bangkok, a family-run cottage industry turns dried bael into a tangy syrup with a subtly, smoky flavor. In India, the seeded fruit pulp is mixed with sugar and sometimes tamarind for a refreshing drink. The fruit can also be made into teas, jams, pickles, and even taffy. **WS**

The lumpy exterior of this pear-shaped fruit belies the creamy, elegant interior, one that has led it to be called "the jewel of the Incas." Mark Twain described it as "the most delicious fruit known to men."

Native to Ecuador and Peru, the cherimoya (*Annona cherimola*) is now cultivated not only in Hawaii, where Twain encountered it, but in many subtropical areas around the world, as well as the California coast and New Zealand. Its name is from the language the Incas spoke—Quechua—and means "cold seeds." The cherimoya is one of several fruits also called "custard apple," because of the custardy texture of its flesh.

When ripe, cherimoyas yield to slight pressure. They can then be halved or sliced, and the flesh scooped out with a spoon. (The seeds and the skin are not edible.) They make a valuable addition to a fruit salad of apples, berries, and bananas, or give an interesting flavor contrast when served with red or white wine. Delicious served with ice cream or yogurt, or mixed with cream into a fool, cherimoya also makes a good ice cream or sorbet. **SH**

Taste: *The pale orange pulp smells sweet, but has a citric, refreshing taste that has a cooling effect on the body. Wild fruits are very tannic compared with cultivated varieties.*

Taste: *The cherimoya's delicious, creamy white flesh tastes like a gentle blend of banana, papaya, and pineapple with subtle hints of coconut, mango, and vanilla.*

Bael fruit is used in Ayurvedic medicine as an
Ⓚ *ingredient of remedies for numerous ailments.*

Smyrna Fig

Medlar

Like the figs that were first cultivated more than four millennia ago, these sensuous fruit are the product of a peculiar synergy between a small wasp, a semiwild fig tree known as a caprifig, and a cultivated tree. The wasp hatches in the caprifig, which is not edible, and fertilizes the Smyrna tree that is planted nearby.

Smyrna figs take their name from the Greek form of the Turkish port of Izmir, on the Aegean, and in the Mediterranean can produce two crops a year. The fruit from the second of these crops is generally smaller and sweeter, and best enjoyed straight from the tree. Figs bred for transport and distribution through the modern food chain are tougher and less succulent. The skin color varies from green to deep violet, but the pulp is always red and full of "seeds" (botanically, tiny individual fruit).

When the fruit is dried, the seeds add a nuttiness or crunchiness not found in other kinds of fig. The boxes in which they are packed sometimes contain a bay leaf to repel weevils, which might otherwise burrow into the dried fruit. **MR**

When ripe, the medlar, or *Mespilus germanicus,* is the wizened brown fruit of the eponymous tree. The seed boxes are exposed at the rear end, hence its historic English name of openarse. A similar insult is leveled at it in France, where it is called *cul de chien* (dog's bottom). Its official title, however, derives from the Greek *mespilon,* although the Greeks themselves acquired the fruit from the ancient Persians: it is still highly valued in Iran.

The medlar is famous for the fact that it must be eaten in late autumn when the fruit is in a state of putrescence. French writer Jean-Anthelme Brillat-Savarin recognized as much when he classified it among foods eaten in a state of decomposition in *The Physiology of Taste* (1825). Not to everyone's taste, D. H. Lawrence called medlars "wineskins of brown morbidity, autumnal excrementa." However, pigs are fond of medlars, and in the Edwardian writer Saki's story "The Boar-Pig," the malevolent animal is disarmed by a "handful of overripe medlars." The Victorians used them to make medlar cheese and jelly, but they are much less common today. **GM**

Taste: *Smyrna figs have a surface texture that is plump, but slightly yielding. The pulp, which contains the small seeds, is juicy and melting, and the taste is honeyed.*

Taste: *Medlars come into their own when picked after the frosts. The flesh is opaque, gelatinous, and very sweet, reminiscent of very sugared reinette apples in a tart.*

Figs were among the fruits that the
⊗ ancient Egyptians offered to their gods.

Tamarillo

Taste a tamarillo and you will remember it always. Smooth scarlet or golden eggs, the fruits hang by threads from a bush that emits the musky scent common to many other Solanaceae. *Cyphomandra betacea* was once called the tree-tomato, and is known as *tomate de arbol* in parts of South America: when cut, it looks very much like a tomato.

A native to the Peruvian Andes, the tamarillo was cultivated in the United States in 1913 and reached New Zealand shortly afterward. As the intense acid-sweet flavor is too much for many to eat raw, the tamarillo is generally found cooked. It excels in both sweet and savory guises and, if problems with its fragile skins were to be solved, many believe it could have greater international success than the kiwifruit.

The golden flesh between the skin and seed-pulp belies what happens when the fruit is chopped, pureed, or heated; it magically creates the most vibrant blood-red juice that survives cooking beautifully. The name has nothing to do with its origins, but was invented as a marketing ploy. **GC**

Naranjilla

Deliciously refreshing, with striking pale emerald pulp, the naranjilla (*Solanum quitoense*) thrives in the tropical heat of Peru, Colombia, and, in particular, Ecuador, where it is the national fruit. In contrast to the leaves, which are large and covered with a velvety purple down, the fruit of the naranjilla (or *lulo*) measures only 2½ inches (6 cm) or so across and has a bright-orange skin and a hairy coating, which can easily be scuffed off when the fruit is ripe.

Inside, a fleshy membrane divides the pulp into quarters, each studded with tiny seeds, and the flesh is so juicy the easiest way to eat a freshly picked naranjilla is to remove its stem and five-point calyx, rub off the fuzzy coat, cut the fruit in half, and squeeze the pulp straight into the mouth.

Rich in minerals and vitamins A and C, naranjilla can be made into ice cream or jam, added to pies, distilled as a wine, or mixed with banana, piled back in the shell and baked, but it is most popular served as a drink. The pulp is pureed and strained, then sweetened and poured into long glasses over plenty of ice for a foamy, pastel-green cooler. **WS**

Taste: *Outstanding poached, in pies or crumbles with or without apple, and in ice creams and sorbets, tamarillos also make unique savory chutneys, relishes, and sauces.*

Taste: *Fully ripe naranjillas combine the sharp tang of lemon with the mellow sweetness of fresh pineapple. The flesh is soft, very juicy, and has a slightly acidic taste.*

The hairy coating protects the naranjilla until it is ripe, after which the fuzz can be rubbed off. »

Comice Pear

Nashi Pear

The mid-nineteenth century was a golden age for pomologists. In 1838, the Comice Horticole (Horticultural Association) was founded in Angers, central France, to develop new strains of fruit and flowers. By 1842 it had organized the first exhibition of roses in the country. Seven years later it produced a pear variety that has outlasted the multifarious and many-flavored pears other nurseries offered, and that has stood the test of time as one of Europe's best-loved fruit.

The Comice is a large, rounded pear with a distinct neck. The skin is thin and greenish yellow, sometimes with a rosy blush, and the white flesh is extraordinarily juicy. It forms a favorite partnership with cheese—aged Parmigiano Reggiano or ripe Gorgonzola especially—and retains its shape and taste well when cooked. Pastry chefs bake it on a bed of frangipane for their *tartes aux poires*, and it is also suitable for the popular dessert "pears in red wine." Like other pears, it must be consumed perfectly ripe. It is hard and uninteresting when underripe; when overripe it is mushy. **MR**

The nashi (or Asian) pear originated in China and has been known in Asia for millennia, in many different varieties and under many different names: nashi is its Japanese name. Unlike Western pears that have to be picked while underripe, Asian pears ripen on the tree and can remain there for several weeks, still firm, before being eaten straight after picking.

Nashi pears (*Pyrus pyrifolia*) come in a range of colors, shapes, and sizes. Japanese markets display them lined up individually in protective foam wrappers, often at extortionate prices for gift purchasers. Popular varieties include Kosui (water of happiness), a small, flat bronze russet; Hosui (water of abundance), which is bronze-skinned, but larger, juicy, and sweet with low acidity; and Shinseiki, which is round, yellow, and medium to large in size.

The skin on nashi is always thick and a little rough, so the fruit is peeled. A popular dish in Korea is *yukheo*—shredded nashi pear mixed with raw meat and an egg. In China, the fruit are filled with honey and jujube, steamed, and served as dessert; the Japanese eat them chilled with a dusting of salt. **SB**

Taste: *Strikingly sweet and juicy with an almost buttery texture; its characteristic flavor note is ratafia-almond. The fruit bruises easily, but this does not mar the taste.*

Taste: *Combining the juiciness of pears and the crispness of apples, nashi pears are exceptionally sweet and crunchy, but dripping with juice.*

Valuable as gifts in China, nashi pears are carefully wrapped before transportation. ❯❯

Cox's Orange Pippin

Cox's Orange Pippin is widely regarded as the finest English table apple. Although closely related to the Ribston Pippin, a variety introduced from France in the seventeenth century, the Cox takes its name from a retired brewer who is credited with raising it in about 1825. According to the fruit farmer, David Atkins, "It is like a fragile English girl who can only be pollinated with loving care, a warm bed, and gentle handling." Its survival is a testimony to the skill of British growers.

Medium size and 2 to 3 inches (5–8 cm) in diameter, the yellowish green skin is flecked with reddish brushmarks; the flesh is creamy, firm, and very juicy; and the aroma is often described as "spicy." In season, freshly picked, the Cox's Orange Pippin is unbeatable, although some connoisseurs believe it should be left until winter to allow the complex flavors a chance to develop. However, fruit held in storage for sale throughout the year loses the edge that makes it so special. Cox's apples make a delicious monovarietal apple juice, but the fruit is not ideally suited to cooking. **MR**

Taste: *"Mango", "melon," and "freshly squeezed Florida orange," are experts' terms that do not adequately describe a fruit so juicy, sweet, complex, and distinctive.*

In season and freshly picked, the Cox's
◈ *Orange Pippin has unbeatable flavor.*

Reine de Reinettes

Despite its status as the most admired table apple in France, it is likely the Reine des Reinettes, in fact, originated either in Holland or the German state of Hanover. According to André Leroy's *Dictionary of Pomology* (1873), its original name derives from the daughter of a Hanoverian duke—Louise von Mecklenburg-Strelitz—who became queen of Prussia in 1793. It is probably, he suggests, the same apple as an earlier Dutch variety: the Kroon Renet.

A very pretty round apple, its smooth skin flecked with red and orange, the Reine des Reinettes is harvested late, from October to the end of November, but can be stored naturally until Christmas and beyond. Although eaten raw, it is suited to cooking: slices that are quartered or cut for a *tarte aux pommes* keep their shape well.

The term "reinette" is often used indiscriminately, but there are dozens of different related reinettes, notably the Reinette du Mans, Reinette d'Orléans, and Reinette du Canada. Many of these are delicious, but difficult to find outside of private gardens or scattered localities where they survive. **MR**

Taste: *A crisp, sweet apple with white, juicy flesh. It does not have a marked fragrance, but when cooked it gives off a seductive, honeyed aroma, almost like that of quince.*

Quince

Babaco

Lumpen and yellow, ripe quinces have one of the most delightful fragrances of any fruit: historically, they were sometimes used to scent rooms. The fruit of a small, deciduous tree, *Cydonia oblonga*, it is closely related to the apple and the pear, but was popularized internationally long before the apple: its botanical name derives from Cydonia, now Chania in Crete, where the Greeks developed a superior strain.

The quince has been cultivated for at least 3,000 years and, like other ancient fruits, has acquired layers of cultural symbolism along the way. It was most likely the "golden apple" that Paris awarded to Aphrodite, the Greek goddess of love, sparking the Trojan War; it figures in the Song of Solomon; and it was thought to be the fruit with which the serpent tempted Eve in the Garden of Eden.

Despite the promise of its honeyed, musky, and floral perfume, most varieties of quince are too sour and astringent to be eaten raw. Quince preserves are popular throughout much of Europe, and the fruit is cooked as an accompaniment to meat in many Middle Eastern cuisines. **FC**

Unknown in the wild, this unusual tropical fruit probably originated as a naturally occurring hybrid of two different types of papaya. Indigenous to Ecuador, babaco (*Carica pentagona*) is now grown commercially elsewhere, but, despite its striking, pentagonal profile and unique flavor, it is farmed only in small quantities, and is considered a rare fruit.

Probably size is part of the issue. At 8 to 12 inches (20–30 cm) long and 4 inches (10 cm) in diameter, it is a substantial fruit that generally weighs about 2 pounds (900 g): a size and price that discourages impulse buying and makes it difficult to find except in specialty markets.

The babaco turns from green to yellow, and becomes very fragrant when fully ripe. Both the skin and the seedless flesh are edible. Because its flesh has an effervescent quality, babaco is sometimes referred to as "champagne fruit." It is best eaten raw, cut into thick, crosswise slices and sprinkled with lemon juice and sugar. Babaco juice has long been a refreshing breakfast drink in Ecuador. Mixed with ice cream or yogurt, it makes delicious milkshakes. **SH**

Taste: *Cooked with sweeteners, the flavors develop into a supercharged blend akin to an abstract essence of apples and pears, while the colour becomes rich sunset.*

Taste: *The riper and softer the fruit, the better the flavor. Slightly acidic and not too sweet, babaco's unique taste blends notes of papaya, strawberry, and pineapple.*

*Quince is delicious made into a paste, dusted
❾ with sugar, and served in cubes as a confection.*

Crabapple

Cicely Mary Barker's Crabapple Fairy hymned her trademark flower thus: "Crab-apples, Crab-apples, out in the wood, / Little and bitter, yet little and good!" And these tiny sour apples, when cooked, far outperform their distinctive sourness when raw.

Species of crabapples, wild or cultivated, are found in North America, Europe, and Asia, although it is Anglo-Saxons who seem to like them best. In Britain, they can be found growing wild in woods (mostly oak woods) and fields. In Northumbria, they are known as "scroggs." They can vary in size from that of a plump cherry to that of a golf ball, and tend to have long stalks, which makes them look rather like cherries. Their color can vary from deep pink to yellow-green, depending on the variety. Because the Latin word for apple tree is *malus* and the Latin word for evil is also *malus*, the apple has long been associated with Adam and Eve and their exit from paradise. Yet alongside these sinful associations, the apple has also been considered the fruit of health: according to rhyme, an apple a day keeps the doctor away.

Crabapples are extremely tart, but have a high content of pectin (a natural setting agent). Combining them with low-pectin fruits is a way of ensuring jam has a good set. In medieval England, crabapples were cooked with honey and spices for use as a pie filling. They make a delightful jelly that is delicious spread on scones or toast, and which also pairs beautifully with savory foods such as roast game and meats. They can be added to pies and chutneys, or made into a potent crabapple wine. In the United States they are spiced and preserved whole to serve alongside pork and poultry. **LF**

Taste: *Raw crabapples are an acquired taste: pleasantly crunchy but distinctly acerbic. Crabapple jelly is wobbly, lustrous, sharp, and fantastic with roast pork.*

Often considered purely ornamental,
❷ *crabapples make a delicious jelly.*

Ber

Also known as Indian jujube or Chinese date, ber is one of the subcontinent's most ancient and highly prized fruits. Ber trees can grow to a height of 40 feet (12 m), and the fruits vary in color from green to reddish purple to dark brown. The fruits' size and shape vary, too: wild fruits tend to be small, around 1 inch (2.5 cm) in length, whereas cultivated fruit grow to 2 inches (5 cm) long, and they can be round, oval, or oblong. The fruits ripen at different times, even those growing on a single tree.

Believed to be native to tropical India, ber has migrated to other parts of the world, being cultivated in Australasia and Africa, where it is an important crop. In China, it has been cultivated for more than 4,000 years. American explorer David Fairchild encountered the fruit for the first time in 1938 on a boat leaving Shanghai, observing that "Ripe jujubes when eaten raw are amusing rather than delicious and have a crisp, sprightly flavor different from other fruits."

Most Indians believe that ripe ber fruit is best eaten fresh, but it can also be boiled with rice or millet and stewed or baked. Ber is also used in sweet dishes, drinks, butters, and spreads, or candied as confections. Sour, unripe fruit is not allowed to go to waste, although it has to be pickled to make it palatable. The fruit is easily digestible, but it can act as a mild laxative. The leaves from the ber tree can be eaten as a vegetable with couscous.

Ripe ber has a high sugar content, is rich in carotene, vitamin A, phosphorus, and calcium, and has one of the highest levels of vitamin C of all fruits. Ber fruits have a short storage life and should be kept in a cool, dry place. **WS**

Taste: *A ripe ber fruit is rich, juicy, and deliciously sweet with a hint of mild acidity. Some varieties of ber have soft pulp, whereas others have crisp, firm flesh.*

Jabuticaba

Some see the jabuticaba as an extravagance of nature, a fruit bequeathed from father to son. It takes more than a decade for the tree, a native of the Brazilian Atlantic rain forest, to reach sufficient maturity for the delicately flavored, small fruit to sprout from its trunk and branches, colored from violet to black and little larger than a grape. And, in the manner of the ancient grapevines from which the Brazilian grape tree takes its name, the older the tree, the better the fruit.

After picking, the jabuticaba has a life of no longer than thirty hours before it spoils, becoming sour and inedible. Brazilians from the state of Minas Gerais use it to make jams, compotes, a liqueur, and a spirit that is not distilled industrially, but created and recreated using household recipes passed on from mother to child. The jabuticaba also has its place in haute cuisine. French chefs living in Brazil such as Claude Troisgros, son of the legendary Pierre Troisgros, have used it to create sauces to accompany *magret de canard* and game. This is a perfect combination. **AL**

Kyoho Grape

In Japan, Kyoho grapes are considered the essence of grapes. The short season, exceptional flavor, and regal appearance of these large, dark purple fruits mean they come with a hefty price tag. This makes them more desirable to the Japanese, who prize exclusivity and cost in their gifts. The grapes are given during the traditional August gift season.

A cross between the varieties Campbell and Centennial, Kyohos originate from Kyushu, Japan's southern island. The name means "great mountain" and the best still grow in the region of Tanushimaru on the fertile Chikugo Plain, at the base of the Mino Mountains. The best Japanese Kyoho grapes are the size of small plums with a thick velvety skin, spectacularly sweet flesh, and large, bitter, and inedible seeds. Served cold, peeled, and unadorned, they make a luxurious dessert. They are also at the heart of the exclusive Kyoho wine.

Kyoho grapes are now cultivated outside Japan, notably in Korea, Taiwan, California, and Chile, which means they are available outside Japan, for a longer season, and at less phenomenal prices. **SB**

Taste: *The white pulp around the large seed is fabulously sweet, and the skin deliciously tannic. The aroma and flavor of the whole is reminiscent of red grapes.*

Taste: *The flesh is very sweet with a strong "grapeyness." The high sugar content means the texture is soft and slightly sticky; the scent is like supercharged Muscat.*

Muscat Grape

Muscadine

These honeyed fruit might be the world's oldest cultivated grape variety. They probably originated in Greece, but passed via the Roman Empire to what is now France. During the reign of the Emperor Charlemagne, Muscat grapes were being exported from the Frankish port of Frontignan. The name could be linked to the Islamic port of Muscat, once a part of Arabia, now part of Oman, or simply be a reference to their distinctive musky aroma.

There are more than 200 cultivars of Muscat—and counting. Different types are grown around the world both for eating and for wine making: fruits can be colored "white," black, green, red, and amber, can have thinner or thicker skins, come with seeds and without. Some, notably the famous Belgian Muscats that are delivered to Buckingham Palace, are grown under glass, while others are ripened by the sun. Although the vast majority of table grapes are grown for convenience rather than flavor, Muscat varieties are always recognizable as such, regardless of the strain or the provenance, so long as they are harvested ripe and eaten at once. **MR**

When European navigators explored the coasts of North Carolina, they remarked on the many grapes that grew there. In 1584, Walter Raleigh's juniors remarked that "In all the world, the like abundance is not to be found." The native muscadine, however, is a very different species from the European grape. *Vitis rotundifolia* is larger and sturdier, with a thicker skin: it loves heat and humidity, and dislikes cold weather. Once part of the diet of Native Americans, who some say knocked grapes from the vines with a stick rather than harvest them, the grapes have a musky, intense flavor, which lends them to eating out of hand. Also known as scuppernong, they were used for wine as early as the sixteenth century, although vintages tend to the bland and sweet.

Home cooks usually turn the purple, bronze, or pale gold fruit into sauces, jellies, and preserves, but chefs use them in soups or relishes, or as garnishes for meats, poultry, and fish. Varieties of muscadine are known as "southern fox," and commercial products often return home as souvenirs with visitors to the South. **SH**

Taste: *Muscat grapes are always honeyed, sweet, and floral, yet with a distinctly musky air. They often have nuances of attar of roses or orange-flower water.*

Taste: *Muscadine pulp tastes more like wine than other grapes. It is juicy, sweet, and intense. The thick skin is tart: when eaten out of hand, the pulp is squeezed from the skin.*

Honey Jack

Durian

Although many varieties of jackfruit can be found growing throughout Southeast Asia and in other tropical areas of the world, it is the honey jack or *peniwaraka*, as it is also known, that is the most highly prized for its sweet flavor.

The largest of all tree fruits, jackfruit can grow to a staggering 3 feet (90 cm) long and sometimes weigh up to 90 pounds (41 kg). They are thought to have originated in the rain forests of the western Ghats, a mountain range running down the southwest coast of India. In southern India, jackfruit are an important part of the local diet, being eaten both unripe as a vegetable and ripe as a fruit.

The ripe fruit has a noxious scent of rotting onions and is best prepared outdoors. When the fruit is cut open, copious amounts of sticky gum flow out and coat the knife and the hands of the person preparing the fruit unless both are first rubbed with vegetable oil. Because of this, jackfruit is often sold ready to eat, canned, or in shrink-wrapped plastic trays. Inside the honey jack, small, yellow-gold bulbs enclose a seed that is edible when boiled. **WS**

Known by many as the "king of fruits," the durian is the fruit of a tall tree, *Durio zibethinus*, which is native to Malaysia and cultivated in other Southeast Asian countries. The name derives from the Malay word for spike, *duri*, and this exotic-looking creature is coated in them. The large, thorny shell that encases the creamy fruit looks for all the world like a spiky football. It is never picked, but instead is left to ripen fully and then collected once it has fallen from its branches into the canopy nets below.

The durian is known primarily for its offensive and confronting odor, which is often compared with the stench of spoiled meat and has resulted in its prohibition from hotels and public transportation systems in its home territories. Yet, this remains a fruit that inspires devotion, and its flesh is highly valued for its unique flavor. It is used in both sweet and savory dishes across Southeast Asia.

Some Western countries import flash-frozen durians for immediate consumption, although nothing compares with cracking open a fresh durian at a roadside stall in the blazing tropical heat. **JN**

Taste: *Ripe jackfruit are soft and sweet with the honey jack being the sweetest and most aromatic of all— a luscious cross between a pineapple and a banana.*

Taste: *The flesh is eaten off the seed like ice cream from a cone. The texture is creamy and reminiscent of custard, with a subtle sweetness that offers hints of rum and raisin.*

Most hotels in Southeast Asia ban durian because of its pungent odor. »

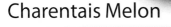

Charentais Melon

Shizuoka Melon

What is in a name? In France, the terms "Charentais" and "Cavaillon" are almost interchangeable as a signifier of quality. They refer respectively to melons grown in the Charentes, a *département* in the west of the country, and those from northern Provence. Both are direct descendants of muskmelon, or cantaloupe melon, introduced from Italy by monks during the sixteenth century, although the word cantaloupe was not used until the fruit had developed from a rare epicurean treat into a more widespread delicacy some 200 years later. By the early 1800s Charentes was recognized as an area that produced some of the best crops.

Round and 6 to 10 inches (15–25 cm) in diameter, the Charentais was once recognizable by a coarse irregular network of lines on its surface. Modern hybrids, however, have a smoother skin with stripes running down the side. The flesh varies from orange to pink, but is always soft and very juicy. Choosing a ripe melon requires a good sense of smell, and those in the know press around the peduncle in search of the subtle give that indicates ripeness. **MR**

Renowned for its precious muskmelons grown under glass, Shizuoka is a Japanese prefecture west of Tokyo. Only the costly price tag is likely to deter people from trying the delectable Shizuoka melon (*Cucumis melo*). In Japan, fruits such as melons, grapes, cherries, peaches, and pears are especially grown and given as luxury gifts, mostly at the two peak gift-giving seasons, at the end of the year or midsummer, to friends, family, and business clients. They are often elegantly presented in wooden boxes.

Shizuoka melons are meticulously cultivated in high-tech, air-conditioned greenhouses to insure their perfectly formed appearance. The melon vines are then planted in soil bedding that is separated from the ground to regulate moisture levels, and temperatures are carefully and continually monitored to optimum levels. The vines are trimmed so only three melons grow on each plant; when the baby melons reach the size of a human fist, two are removed to allow the most promising melon to take all the nourishment from the vine, and mature into the juicy delicacy that is Shizuoka melon. **CK**

Taste: *More than other kinds of melon, a Charentais at its peak has an exotic, sweet, almost musky perfume. The flesh stays tender right down to the rind.*

Taste: *Shizuoka melon has a sweet taste that is finely balanced with a slight hint of sourness. The melon has an appealing musky aroma and a perfectly round shape.*

The Japanese give Shizuoka melons in elegant wooden boxes as presents. »

YOKOHAMA MIZUNOBU **Fruit gift**

静岡県産

温室マスクメロン

2個

税込 ¥20000

Cassabanana

Few plant species have a fragrance as distinct as cassabanana. Its deep, involving aroma emanates not just from the fruit but from the flowers of this perennial creeper. Of Brazilian origin, *Sicana odorifera* is now found in almost all of tropical America. Long, cylindrical, and reminiscent of a giant cucumber—hence its alternate name "musk cucumber"—it comes in festive colors of orange, red, purple, or indigo, and assails the nose with an aroma like super charged fresh melon.

The fruit shares a number of characteristics with its pumpkin relatives: it is protected by a hard skin and has orange, fleshy pulp with strips of flat seeds. Due to its refreshing taste, the cassabanana should be enjoyed pure, either in its natural state or chilled; cut into small pieces with the seeds removed, it eats well in a fruit salad. Brazilians prefer to add sugar, even at the fully ripe stage. A versatile ingredient, cassabanana can be found in jams, chutneys, and other compotes, as well as a variety of candies. When underripe it works well as a vegetable, simply sliced and added to soups and stews. **AL**

Taste: *Nothing beats eating the cassabanana fresh and ripe. The potent fragrance leads to a clean taste with melon to the fore and banana nestled discreetly behind it.*

Watermelon

Mark Twain called watermelon "chief of this world's luxuries . . . When one has tasted it, he knows what Angels eat." Native to central Africa, *Citrullus lanatus* was cultivated and eaten in Egypt long before 2,000 BCE. It probably came to Europe when the Moors invaded Spain; it reached the New World on slave ships. Although in most of the Western world watermelon is considered a dessert, in arid countries it has long been used as a source of water, as well as a vessel for carrying water.

In general, the watermelon is a large fruit: most varieties come to market weighing 10 to 25 pounds (5–11 kg), although some, such as Sugar Baby and Bambino, are considerably smaller. The flesh can be red, pink, or yellow. The rind, which can be striped or plain, is completely edible and often pickled; the seeds, which can be brown or black, can be toasted and eaten out of hand.

In 1981, a farmer from Zentsuji, in Japan, developed a square watermelon for easy storage where space was at a premium. These curios are now beginning to be available elsewhere. **SH**

Taste: *Sweet but somewhat bland, with a grainy texture that collapses refreshingly in the mouth. When chilled, it seems as much a beverage as a fruit.*

Watermelons can grow in arid terrain such as deserts, providing a welcome source of refreshment. »

Lacatan Banana

Red Banana

When the first bananas reached Europe, in the sixteenth and seventeenth centuries, they acquired names such as Adam's fig or *figue du Paradis* (Paradise fig), raising the intriguing possibility the banana was the fruit of the Tree of Knowledge, and Adam's modesty was preserved with a comfortably large banana leaf rather than the more delicate fig. But, despite its apparent resemblance to a small palm, the banana plant is not a tree, but rather a herb that dies back at the end of the growing season and must produce a new trunk each year.

Today, numerous varieties of banana plant grow in the tropics, but many consider the Lacatan from the Philippines one of the best in the world. On the small side, or at least to North American and European eyes, the Lacatan is a delicate yet disease-resistant hybrid now also grown in Jamaica, other Caribbean islands, and parts of Latin America. Like other bananas destined for export, Lacatans are picked when two-thirds ripe: while bananas ripen well off the stem, the flavors of those picked fresh from the "tree" are the best. **WS**

In 1889 an advertisement for bananas informed the U.S. public "there are two kinds, the yellow and the red. The latter is considered the best." Despite their price being twice that of ordinary bananas—a fact that caused detractors to mutter darkly about "customers paying for their color"—red bananas soon became popular and by the early twentieth century *The Boston Cooking School Cookbook* was recommending them for a "Tropical Snow" dessert.

Red bananas continue to be prized above yellow-skinned varieties, and are still found in the United States, although most are so frail and short-lived they stay in the Caribbean and Asian regions where they grow. They can replace yellow bananas in any cooked dish, but their superior flavor means most people prefer to eat them raw. Red bananas range in color from orange or reddish brown to maroon or purple—some are variegated, with green stripes. As they ripen, like other bananas, they give off ethylene (a gas that helps some fruit develop color and ripeness) in such large quantities they can help a hard avocado ripen overnight. **WS**

Taste: *Highly fragrant, the Lacatan banana has sweet firm flesh that is equally delicious eaten raw or baked. The flesh turns a golden orangey yellow when ripe.*

Taste: *When fully ripe, the luscious flesh of red bananas is a creamy pink and very sweet. The rich flavor combines classic banana notes with strawberry.*

Banana plantations have spread over vast areas of tropical lowlands. »

Abacaxi Pineapple

Azores Pineapple

Long, long before Columbus arrived on the continent, the indigenous people of the Brazilian lowlands were already enjoying the delights of a tough-looking fruit with a seductive, citric aroma: the pineapple. It was soon domesticated and spread from Brazil to the hotter parts of South and Central America, getting as far as Mexico, where its allure was immediately noticed by European colonizers.

The Abacaxi is a particularly succulent, fragrant type of pineapple, with white or pale yellow flesh and only a tiny core. A tall and beautiful fruit, from the same family as many of the world's most beautiful flowers, it grows as a cluster of individual fruitlets amid a crown of sharp, pointed leaves.

There is no substitute for an Abacaxi served fresh and perfectly ripe. It makes fine desserts, from tarts and cakes to bonbons. Its well-balanced acidity makes it an ideal garnish for roasted meats, either pure or in a sweet sauce. Although discarded by many, the skin is used to make an excellent drink in Brazilian homes, simply boiled in water, strained, sweetened, and served chilled. **AL**

taste of the past, the Azores pineapple (DOP) is grown with great care under glass, like the fruits so lovingly tended in the hothouses of grand homes during the eighteenth century. The Azores, a cluster of nine volcanic islands stranded in the mid-Atlantic, belong to Portugal and have been inhabited since the fifteenth century. Until 250 years ago, the principal export crop was oranges: when these were ravaged by disease, the islanders switched to growing pineapples, especially for the luxury English market, where they were the most fashionable fruit. This unique, year-round harvest is still valued today.

São Miguel is the main producer of a type of Smooth Cayenne pineapple called St. Michael. The Gulf Stream flows past the islands, so the climate is temperate all year around, but there are differences in sweetness between winter pineapples and those that ripen in summer. The latter are eaten as a dessert, whereas those harvested in January or February are served mostly as a vegetable to accompany broiled beef or the lightly smoked blood pudding served in the *tascas*, or bars. **MR**

Taste: *The Abacaxi has an intense citric perfume and a sweet flavor. Best enjoyed au naturel, it is also excellent broiled and sprinkled with sugar and cinnamon.*

Taste: *Large, juicy, and tender Azores pineapples are sweet-and-sour in winter and sugary in summer. Both kinds have a potent scent and are never sold underripe.*

The English named the pineapple after
❰ *the pine cone, a reference to its bumpy skin.*

Kumquat

Yuzu

In China, just before the start of the Lunar New Year, small kumquat trees are positioned at the doors of homes and businesses to bring good luck and prosperity. For the Chinese, it is impossible to think of New Year without kumquats: the little, glossy orange citrus is as essential to the festival as lion dancers, peach blossoms, and children waving their scarlet packages of "lucky money."

The small fruit rarely reach more than 1¼ inches (3 cm) in diameter, and have a bittersweet flavor that is the reverse of most citrus fruits: rather than the pulp being sweet and the peel bitter, it is the kumquat's skin that is sweet, and the flesh that is sour. Round varieties tend to be sweeter than the oval ones.

Fresh kumquats are usually eaten whole so the sweet-and-sour flavors balance one another. They are delicious candied or preserved in syrup, and make vibrantly colored marmalades. They can also be used in relishes or pickles. In China, a powder of salt-cured kumquat is dissolved in hot water and sipped to soothe sore throats; some bartenders infuse the fruit in vodka to use in cocktails. **KKC**

The most cold-resistant of all the citrus fruits, yuzu is about the size of a mandarin, and some believe it originated as a hybrid of one. It grows wild in Korea and Tibet, but is most associated with Japan, where it was introduced more than 1,000 years ago.

Yuzu is mainly used in Japan for its uniquely fragrant peel, which is added at the last minute to soups, salads, and simmered dishes. Sweet white miso flavored with yuzu is a popular dressing for *aemono*; while the well-known dipping sauce ponzu is made with the juice of either yuzu or the sour green fruits *sudachi* (*Citrus sudachi*) and *kabosu* (*Citrus sphaerocarpa*). Koreans make a sweet yuzu marmalade that is diluted with hot water to create an aromatic and vitamin C–laden tea. Western chefs have also discovered the joys of yuzu, and both the juice and the zest are used to flavor ice creams, brûlées, cookies, and all manner of dishes, both Japanese and fusion.

It is traditional in Japan to put a whole yuzu, or its skin, in the bathtub on the day of the Winter Solstice to protect against winter colds and flu. **SB**

Taste: *Popped into the mouth fresh, the bittersweet aroma of the thin, honeyed skin gives way to a satisfying and extremely sour citrus burst of pulp and seeds.*

Taste: *Although lime and lemon are often prescribed as substitutes for this sharp, acidic fruit, yuzu has a distinctive, highly fragrant aroma. This is released on gentle heating.*

The kumquat tree's size made it a table-top dessert ❽ *for the Victorians, and a staple of Chinese New Year.*

Clementine

It is unclear precisely how this delicious little citrus fruit originated: some believe a priest named Père Clément crossbred it from a mandarin orange and a sour orange in Algeria some time about 1900. Others think it is just a type of tangerine.

Unlike other citrus fruits, such as oranges, limes, and lemons, clementines have a fleeting season: they are usually only available for a few months in the winter. They are small, generally a little larger than a golf ball, with a bright orange hue and very thin skin, which, as with tangerines, satsumas, and other mandarin oranges, is loose and easy to peel.

The clementine is generally too expensive to use as a common source for juice, and has a low yield compared to oranges. Cooking with the juice destroys its elusive flavor, while the thin skin is unsuitable for marmalade. The clementine is, however, delicious when the peeled fruit, broken apart into segments, is frozen for about thirty minutes—just long enough for the membrane to freeze so it turns shatteringly crisp and delicate, creating a fine contrast to the juicy flesh within. **KKC**

Taste: *The sweet, juicy, refreshing flesh has a delicate membrane and is usually seedless. Both the skin and the flesh are wonderfully fragrant. It is a pure pleasure to eat.*

Sorrento Lemon

Sunshine yellow, egg shaped, and distinctively knobbly, Sorrento lemons (IGP) have been appreciated for their exceptional flavor and aroma for centuries. Known to the locals as *sfusato amalfitano*, wall paintings and mosaics uncovered at Pompeii and Herculaneum suggest these most-prized lemons were being cultivated as long ago as the first century CE. Like other lemons, the parent stock most likely originated in northern India, and arrived in Italy by way of the Middle East.

The fruits' pronounced lemony flavor, highly scented skin, and juicy, sparsely seeded flesh ooze vitamin C, and this exceptional combination has earned them a shining reputation worldwide. Traditionally, they were grown along steep terraces, and matured under straw mats known as *pagliarelle*. Today, it is nets, not mats, that insure the fruit are protected from the elements. Their IGP status requires Sorrento lemons to be grown within a restricted designated geographical area, and only fruits weighing 3 ounces (80 g) or more can be sold under the name. **LF**

Taste: *Fragrant, thin-skinned, sweet, and tangy, with concentrated citrus oils in evidence, the raw fruit is often eaten dusted with confectioners' sugar, skin and all.*

A Sorrento lemon grove in Campania, southern Italy, shares its territory with brilliant red poppies. »

Key Lime

Finger Lime

Widely grown in tropical regions around the world, the Key lime (*Citrus aurantifolia*) is the lime that started it all. But despite its association with the Florida Keys and the Caribbean, it originated in Malaysia. It was most likely the Arabs who carried the fruit into Europe: it was known and cultivated not only in Spain but also in Italy and possibly France by the middle of the thirteenth century. European colonists brought it to south Florida and other parts of the New World three centuries later, although the Miami hurricane of 1926 wiped out commercial Key lime production in Florida, and today Mexico and Malaysia are two of the bigger producers.

About the size of a golf ball, these neat little fruits are more yellow than green when ripe. They are most prized for their juice, which can be used as a marinade, in cooking, or as a beverage, whether paired with salt, as in the classic margarita formulations, or sugar, in limeade or cordials. Key lime pie is the most famous dish made from the juice: a creamy pie topped with a dollop of whipped cream and garnished with a lime slice. **SH**

Named because of their resemblance to chubby digits, these Australian native citrus fruits are gaining popularity among chefs, as much for their flavor as their appearance, which ranges in color from purple or black to green, yellow, and bright pink. Yet, the fruit have not always been so highly regarded. Although we can assume Aborigines ate the species known as *Citrus australasica*, and the early settlers to Australia used them for marmalade, farmers in the fertile Northern Rivers region of New South Wales and southeast Queensland worked hard to rid their lands of the spiny, sprawling tree that interfered with their cattle grazing.

Dubbed "caviar lime," the fruits have jewellike, colorful vesicles that burst from the skin upon cutting like tiny citrus bath balls. These are housed in about six equal-size loculi, and make an attractive addition to dressings and drinks, and a flavorsome contribution to curd, sauces, jams, or chutneys. The aromatic skin has a glossy appearance and a slightly greasy texture due to surface oil cells; it can be dried and used like any other citrus peel in cooking. **SC-S**

Taste: *Extremely fragrant and pale in color, Key limes have a delicate citrusy lime flavor that is slightly acidic. They are tart, but with an underlying hint of sweetness.*

Taste: *The vesicles have a citrus tang with a subtle hint of turpentine. The slightest pressure from the teeth pops the casing and delivers a refreshing burst of juice.*

Calamansi

Citron

Most likely descended from a mandarin-kumquat cross of old and obscure origins, the calamansi barely reaches 1 inch (2.5 cm) in width, but its small form hides a citrus flavor that combines the sourness of lime with the sunny notes of tangerine.

A popular, easily grown tree across Southeast Asia, *Citrofortunella microcarpa* are enjoyed for their fragrant flowers and glossy foliage as well as their fruit. In Indonesia, Malaysia, Singapore, and the Philippines, calamansi is treated as a type of lime. It harmonizes well with other key Asian ingredients, such as coconut milk, fish sauce, soy sauce, shrimp paste, and chile. Broiled or barbecued seafoods, especially if doused in spicy sambals, are often served with calamansi on the side, and it works wonderfully in the Filipino marinated fish salad *kinilaw*. Calamansis are juiced to make drinks, squeezed over cut fruit, and are often a default garnish for street food such as fried noodles, whose rich ingredients require a sour foil. Modern chefs are increasingly harnessing calamansi's palate-cleansing power in sorbets and other desserts. **CTa**

Unusually for a fruit, the citron is valued not for its flesh, which is very dry and difficult to separate from its outer skin, but for its peel. It looks like a large, very knobbly lemon, but was popular long before its rival, finding its way from the perfumeries of ancient India to the household altars of China and Japan. The earliest written reference to citron is in the Indian *Vajasaneyi Samhita*, from before 800 BCE: Kubera, the Hindu god of wealth, often carries the fruit in his hand.

Most citrons are roughly egg-shaped—some can reach as much as 1 foot (30 cm) long—but one variety has a particularly spectacular appearance. Grown mainly in Japan and China, the Buddha's Hand Citron sprouts from its stem many separate, or nearly separated, lobes. Although highly fragrant, it contains little pulp.

While the juice and flesh found uses in older times, today it is the peel that is most utilized. Candied, it is used in confectionery and baking: it can be an ingredient in fruitcake, plum pudding, and similar products, and makes a delicious addition to *panforte*, the Italian confection from Siena. **SH**

Taste: *Calamansi juice rounds out the tart zip of lime with fruity notes of tangerine and musk. Its aromatic zest has a similarly wonderful fragrance, but with bitter notes.*

Taste: *The peel of the citron is thick and aromatic, almost resinous, with bittersweet, citrusy, and lemon zest flavors that respond well to candying. The flesh is unremarkable.*

Jaffa Orange

Some say this is the only orange in the world worth eating. Called Shamouti or Khalili in the Near East and Jaffa in the Western world, this extremely fragrant fruit appeared near Jaffa in the mid-nineteenth century—some say in 1844—when the area, part of the then Ottoman Empire, was known as Palestine. Although cultivated elsewhere in the eastern Mediterranean today, it is most closely linked with its original home in what is now Israel.

A medium-to-large orange, the Jaffa is believed to have first appeared as a "limb sport"—a mutation whereby one branch of a tree bears different fruit from the rest—on a type of local orange. It was exported to England early on, during British rule in Palestine, and became very popular. In the 1930s, it gave its name to cakelike dark chocolate and tangy orange creations still sold as Jaffa cakes.

Nearly seedless with a thick, easy-to-peel skin, the Jaffa is a good orange for eating by hand. In Israel, the peel is candied, dipped in chocolate, and served as a sweet snack. The intense orange flavor makes it work well in desserts, such as cheesecakes. **SH**

Taste: *The Jaffa orange has light, firm flesh that is juicy and sweet. The flavor is authentically and intensely "orangey" and comes across beautifully in juice.*

The Jaffa orange is the crowning glory of centuries of citrus cultivation in the eastern Mediterranean.

Blood Orange

Citrus fruit aficionados consider the blood orange to be one of the world's most superb dessert oranges. Generally smaller than its other cousins, it derives its red-colored flesh and faintly blushed peel from anthocyanin, a pigment commonly found in many flowers and red fruits, but not typically in citrus fruits. The first mutations were probably discovered in Sicily in the seventeenth century and most still grow in the Mediterranean area today.

Each of the three main varieties—Tarocco, Sanguinello, and Moro—has its own unique qualities. Seedless Tarocco is the sweetest, and its lightly flushed pulp contains more vitamin C than any orange in the world, largely due to the fertile soils around Mount Etna on which it grows. The sparsely seeded Sanguinello is the oldest, whereas the Moro has the deepest hue: its pulp can vary from scarlet through to burgundy, or even almost black.

Blood oranges can be used in most recipes that would contain regular orange juice, such as cakes, ice creams, and sorbets, but are particularly special simply squeezed and served as a drink. **LF**

Taste: *The tender flesh yields a glorious juice with a well-balanced flavor, oozing the sweet mouthwatering spirit of the orange, but hinting of sun-ripened raspberries.*

Pink Grapefruit

More attractive to some because of its color, pink grapefruit is very similar to white or golden varieties in both quality and taste, yet richer in nutrients. All colors of grapefruit (*Citrus paradisi*) derive from the pomelo, but precisely how is not known.

The grapefruit arrived in the United States via Florida in 1823. In 1907, a pink bud shoot (a branch or flower distinctly different from the rest of the plant) was discovered and subsequently propagated. All of today's pink grapefruit varieties are descended from a single sport that appeared in 1913.

So named, some say, because the fruits grow in clusters like grapes, most grapefruits are eaten in their raw state. For breakfast, grapefruit halves are sprinkled with sugar and eaten with a special serrated spoon that easily removes the segments. Pink grapefruit, in particular, is an attractive addition to salads, either combined with other fruits or on top of greens with seafood. Grapefruit are rarely used in cooking because their flavor can easily come to dominate, but they are delicious topped with sugar, cinnamon, and butter, then broiled. **SH**

Taste: *A tangy, tart-sweet flavor a little reminiscent of orange, with a distinctive bitterness that is increased by the bitter pith and membrane that encases the segments.*

Pomelo

The pomelo is often called a Chinese grapefruit and the two fruits are related, but it is widely accepted the pomelo came first. As its botanical name, *Citrus grandis*, suggests, it is the largest fruit in the citrus family: some grow to larger than 8 inches (20 cm) in diameter.

Like the grapefruit, the flesh of the pomelo can range from pale yellow to light ruby, with a flavor that can vary from mouth-puckeringly tart to sweet with hints of strawberry. The spongy skin is much thicker than a grapefruit's, and it is best peeled by scoring almost to the flesh: the segments inside are divided by a tough, inedible membrane that also needs to be removed. The segments are composed of myriad juicy "beads," which are beginning to find favor as a garnish with Western chefs.

As with many other citrus fruits, the skin of the pomelo is edible, although it takes time and effort to make it delicious. In Cantonese cuisine, it is often steamed or braised in superior stock with Chinese ham or dried shrimp roe. It can also be candied in the same way as orange and lemon peels. **KKC**

Taste: *There are many pomelo cultivars, but all share aromatic skin. The taste is similar to grapefruit, but the beads separate easily and burst satisfyingly in the mouth.*

Pomelos often arrive at market in the nets that help support their weight as they grow. »

Champagne Rhubarb

Although grown in the United States, Europe, and parts of Asia, rhubarb is perhaps quintessentially English. As a fruit, this vegetable reaches its apex in the form of "forced" rhubarb, rebranded by modern marketers as "champagne" rhubarb.

The stem of a leafy plant whose leaves are mildly toxic, rhubarb was introduced to the British Isles as a medicinal plant during Tudor times (1485–1603). Champagne rhubarb is grown indoors, out of the light and away from the cold, so it matures in winter. Its stems turn a bright lipstick pink rather than a fibrous green.

Victorian gardeners used straw and overturned buckets, or cloches, to blanch conventional rhubarb as it emerged from the ground. While home gardeners use this method today, commercial crops are grown in Yorkshire in heated barns. Forced rhubarb needs sweetening and has special affinities with orange zest, strawberries, and star anise. In England, it is used in pies, crumbles, and fools, while Anglo-Saxon chefs are also reinventing vegetable treatments popular farther east. **MR**

Taste: *The stems are slender, tender, and nicely sour when cooked. The aroma, like the taste, is green, but lightly perfumed. After poaching, the stems should remain intact.*

Sugarcane

Humankind's natural love of sweetness carried sugarcane around the world many thousands of years ago, but the wild ancestor of *Saccharum officinarum* probably originated in New Guinea. Cultivation began in parts of Asia and spread throughout the ancient world and eventually to the New World. Today, it is grown in temperate regions around the globe and, despite the rise of the sugar beet, remains the world's main source of sugar.

A gigantic fibrous grass, sugarcane looks a bit like bamboo. Its middle, though, is not hollow, but filled with a sweet sap or juice that can be pressed or sucked out. In South Asia, it was originally grown for chewing. It is still enjoyed that way in parts of Asia, Hawaii, and the Caribbean, optimally picked fresh from the field and eaten out of hand.

Fresh sugarcane juice, sometimes mixed with fresh ginger, lemon, or lime juice, is considered a delicacy and often used in cocktails in Latin America. The stalks can also be peeled and used as skewers for cooking, as in Thailand, where they impart a subtle sweetness to meat and dumplings. **SH**

Taste: *The best part of sugarcane is the juice or nectar. Not excessively sweet, it has a refreshing, grassy flavor. The fibrous stalk is usually chewed rather than swallowed.*

A worker harvests sugarcane by hand in Brazil, one of the world's biggest producers. ❯❯

Moscatel Raisin

While humans have almost certainly eaten grapes that have withered on the vine for hundreds of thousands of years, these crumpled gems, the flavorful dried fruit of Moscatel (Muscat) grapes, are without a doubt the royalty of the raisin world.

Large in size and a plummy brown in color, they come complete with seeds: the best are Málaga raisins, grown in an area of Andalusia that runs from southwest Axarquia through to the foothills of the Montes de Málaga. The countryside around this 39-mile (62 km) stretch of land—known as "The Route of the Raisin"—is speckled with traditional drying beds for the fruit that has changed little since nineteenth-century travelers praised it.

Málaga raisins follow a traditional drying process and are trimmed by hand; the finest, known as Málaga clusters, are dried on their stems. These are served as a dessert rather than used as a cooking ingredient, and have a great affinity with cheese. Soaked in sweet Málaga wine, ideally one made using Moscatel grapes, lesser grades of Moscatel raisin also make the most divine ice cream. **LF**

Taste: *Aromatic, lightly chewy, and sweet with a delicate crunch of seeds, Málaga raisins are deliciously rich with flavors of dark taffy, chestnut honey, and figs.*

Spread out on slanted beds called paseros,
⊘ *Moscatel grapes are dried in the sun.*

Prune d'Agen

Dark bluish-violet plum trees were introduced to France by crusaders returning from the Holy Land. They became known as the *pruniers d'Ente* (grafted trees), and the name has endured for centuries. Agen, a medium-size town east of Bordeaux, was never an important growing area, but its port on the River Garonne made it a major distribution center.

Originally the prunes—dried plums—were sun-dried. Now they are dehydrated at a low temperature for twenty-four hours. It takes 4 pounds (1.8 kg) of fruit to make 1 pound (450 g) of the large, black, wrinkled Pruneaux d'Agen. "Giants," the largest of the three official sizes, weigh just under ½ ounce (15 g).

Whereas Anglo-Saxons often treat the fruit as little more than a laxative, the French regard them as a jewel in their gastronomic crown. Steeped in Armagnac, stuffed with almond paste, flavoring the batter puddings called *fars,* and as the basis of a world-beating ice cream, they figure in many classic desserts. They also figure in savory recipes like *lapin sauté au pruneaux,* a rabbit stew thickened with gingerbread and a hint of bitter chocolate. **MR**

Taste: *Larger and more succulent than most prunes, pruneaux d'Agen share the dark, glutinous sweetness of others of their species.*

Hachiya Persimmon

One of the most spectacular sights of a Japanese winter is the leafless persimmon tree, its laden branches bending under the weight of shiny orange fruit, bright against the snow. And persimmons or kaki (*Diospyros kaki*)—both *shibugaki*, the astringent type that are inedible when merely ripe, and the sweet type known as *amagaki*—have been cultivated for many centuries.

The Hachiya persimmon is a kind of astringent persimmon characterized by its oval, acornlike shape and a mouth-puckering quality so intense, as haiku poet Issa remarked a number of centuries ago, only a mother's love can bear it. Yet, once "bletted"—or rotted in a controlled fashion—the tannins in Hachiya persimmons give way to a rich, honeyed sweetness. In Japan, it is most often eaten dried, and strings of persimmons, covered in their white, powdery sugar coating—drying in the winter sun—used to be a common sight in rural areas. Another rather pleasing way of removing the astringency of *shibugaki* is to soak them in the alcoholic drink known as *shochu*. **SB**

Taste: *Fresh but "bletted," the Hachiya persimmon is sticky, sweet, and so soft it needs to be eaten with a spoon. The flavor is like apricot with echoes of pumpkin.*

Pala Manis

Native to the Molucca Islands in Indonesia, nutmeg was so prized by both the Dutch and Portuguese, who colonized the islands in the early seventeenth century, their rivalry led to bloodshed. The British, who later occupied the Moluccas, took the nutmeg tree to the West Indies, where it is now cultivated, particularly on the island of Grenada.

The fruit of the nutmeg tree, pala manis looks like a large apricot. When split open, it reveals a shiny, chestnut-brown oval kernel encircled with lacy red arils. Both are dried to produce spices: the tendrillike arils become mace and the hard inner kernel, nutmeg. In Indonesia, the fruit's outer flesh is crystallized to make a popular sweet called *manisan pala*. In Sri Lanka, a jam is made from the fruit.

Serious cooks like to grate their own nutmeg kernel, which has a superior flavor to the packed, ground version. Only a little nutmeg is needed in both sweet and savory dishes—using too much overwhelms other flavors. Also, as the English herbalist Nicholas Culpeper (1616–54) warned, it can induce delirium in those who overindulge. **WS**

Taste: *Dried pala manis is a little like crystallized ginger in appearance and taste. Freshly grated nutmeg is warm, nutty, and sweet, and adds an exotic lift to milky puddings.*

A pala manis splits open on the branch, revealing the red arils that are dried as mace. ❯❯

Hunza Apricot

Quandong

High up in the Karakoram Mountains, in northern Pakistan, lies a land of lofty peaks and terraced valleys, of isolated villages and snowy winters: Hunza. The Hunzakuts who live here are renowned for their good health and longevity, which some attribute to the magnificent Hunza apricot. So revered is the apricot, in fact, a family's economic standing can be measured in apricot trees.

The Karakorams are at the western end of the Himalayan massif, and on the silk road that distributed Chinese silk across the continents: it might have been silk traders who brought the apricot from its Chinese homeland. The Hunzakuts enjoy their apricots fresh in season, but also dry vast quantltles of them. Dried, they can be eaten as they are, cooked into savory or sweet dishes, or pureed and mixed with snow to make a type of ice cream.

Fresh apricots are highly difficult to transport, so in the West the dried Hunza is the one to look for. Vastly different from the squishy, neon-orange types that are typically treated with sulfur as a preservative, the Hunza apricot is dark brown. **LF**

The scorched, parched wilderness of central Australia seems an inhospitable place for food to grow, but the desert yields delicacies that have been harvested by indigenous Australians for centuries. The quandong—also known as the "wild" or "desert" peach—is so high in vitamin C many early Australian explorers would have died of scurvy had they not stumbled upon this rich native food. Its English common name derives from *guwandhang*, the word used by the Wiradjuri people of the Lachlan River, in New South Wales.

As traditional "bush tucker" becomes a popular sustainable food source, the farming of quandong is growing. The fresh fruit is about the size of a small apricot, colored brilliant red, with white or pale yellow flesh. Indigenous communities dry it in the sun to preserve it for later use: frozen or dried it can last up to eight years without loss of flavor. The kernel is rich in oil and can be baked to give an almondlike nut, but some are bitter and unpalatable. The wood of the quandong tree releases a pleasant sandalwood scent when burned. **RH**

Taste: *The dried Hunza apricot is pleasantly chewy with a deep, slightly bosky, honeyed fruit aroma and a flavor that hints at dark toffee on the finish.*

Taste: *Acidic when fresh, quandong has a slight peach and apricot flavor, with rhubarb notes. Preparing it as a confit or preserving in brandy and sugar offsets the tartness.*

Hunza apricots flourish in the awe-inspiring surroundings of the Himalayan massif.

Guarana

Tamarind

Of all the fruits of the Amazon, the guarana berry is probably the best known, thanks to the fizzy sodas and "energy drinks" that are made from its fruit. The pretty fruit, which resembles an open eye colored in red, white, and black, is a legacy from indigenous people, whose origins are lost in time. Portuguese colonizers learned of it from the Sateré-Maués tribe as early as the seventeenth century.

From then until today, drinks made from guarana have been produced in the same way. Harvested from *Paullinia cupana*, a creeping shrub, the fruit is dried, toasted, and crushed to form a smooth paste. This is molded into rods that are then grated into a powder and diluted with water, creating a liquid with a high caffeine content.

Guarana began to appear on the shelves of health-food stores and drug stores marketed in various forms—from syrups, concentrated extracts, and capsules, to traditional rods for grating. Its followers see it as the perfect remedy for everyday stress; some see it as the ideal pick-me-up; other enthusiasts even claim aphrodisiac effects. **AL**

A world without tamarind would be bereft of Worcestershire sauce, the British staple HP sauce, countless chutneys, and innumerable curries from almost every tropical region, which is ample reason for venerating this tall, shady tree. Originating from Africa, *Tamarindus indica* has grown in India since prehistoric times and is now widely cultivated in tropical parts of the world.

Filipino cooks simmer the unripe green pods in soups and stews, while Indian cooks turn them into pickles and preserves. The brown pulp of mature pods is blended with water and strained of its seeds and fibers to make a paste, or "juice," that brings tamarind's delicious souring qualities to South Indian and Southeast Asian kitchens. As it is one of those rare ingredients at home in both savory and sweet dishes, tamarind is included in drinks and sorbets, as well as relishes, braised meats, and soups. In Vietnam and Thailand, an uncooked sweet-sour cultivar is eaten as a snack, or cooked with sugar and chile into spicy sweetmeats: this is sold in some Western markets as "sweet tamarind." **CTa**

Taste: *Guarana is best tried as a drink, hand-prepared with the concentrated extract. It has hints of vanilla and orange flavors, wrapped up in a fabulous sweetness.*

Taste: *Ripe tamarind has a fruity sourness with notes of apple, plum, quince, and carob: in sweet cultivars, the flavor is also tangy and sherbety. Young pods taste sharp.*

As the tamarind ripens, the fruit dries naturally within its brown husk. ❯❯

Honeyed Jujube

Dubbed "food of harmony" because they are reputed to strengthen the body and cleanse the blood, jujubes have been cultivated in China for more than 4,000 years. Also known as honey dates or red dates, they are not, in fact, true dates. Their size varies from small and round to long and thin; they can be cherry size or larger, more like plums.

Jujubes have creamy white flesh, a hard, single seed, and thin skins that turn from green to red as they ripen. Eaten fresh, the fruits are considered to be at their best before they become fully ripe, when they start to dry out and lose their succulence.

As well as eating jujubes fresh, the Chinese also dry, pickle, and smoke them. It is as a candied bonbon, however, they become an irresistible treat, capable of satisfying the sweetest tooth. The fruit is first boiled in syrup and then dried for up to two days. This boiling and drying process is repeated twice more, the skins being slit for the final boiling which is done in a more-concentrated syrup often flavored with honey. The candied fruits are then dried until they are no longer sticky. **WS**

Taste: *Fresh jujubes have crisp, sweet flesh with a flavor and texture similar to a dessert apple. Candied they are soft and mellow, with a luxurious honeyed sweetness.*

Khalasah Date

"Khalasah" is the Arabic word for quintessence, and date connoisseurs the world over consider this famous beauty exactly that. The epitome of date perfection, its gorgeous glossy skin shrouds sticky, irresistible, bright amber flesh. This cultivar of the date palm is grown in the Al-Ahsa province of Saudi Arabia, near one of the largest oases in the world.

The date palm (*Phoenix dactylifera*) is thought to have originated in the Persian Gulf, and has been cultivated since at least 5000 BCE, even before the Sumerians and Babylonians made the date palm their sacred tree. The ancient Romans loved dates, but imported them from North Africa; it was the Moors who brought the fruit to Spain, and Spaniards who then took them to California and Mexico. Today, a huge number of different varieties of date are grown around the world, but the Khalasah is routinely pronounced top of the crops.

Dates are best eaten like good chocolate, that is, left on the tongue so the outer skin simply slips off and the soft flesh slowly melts, releasing a glorious complexity of flavors. **LF**

Taste: *Dissolving slowly on the tongue, the Khalasah surrenders a complex swirl of honey and caramel, with notes of fresh sugarcane and hints of honeycomb toffee.*

Khalasah dates mature on the palm for many weeks before being carefully harvested. ❯

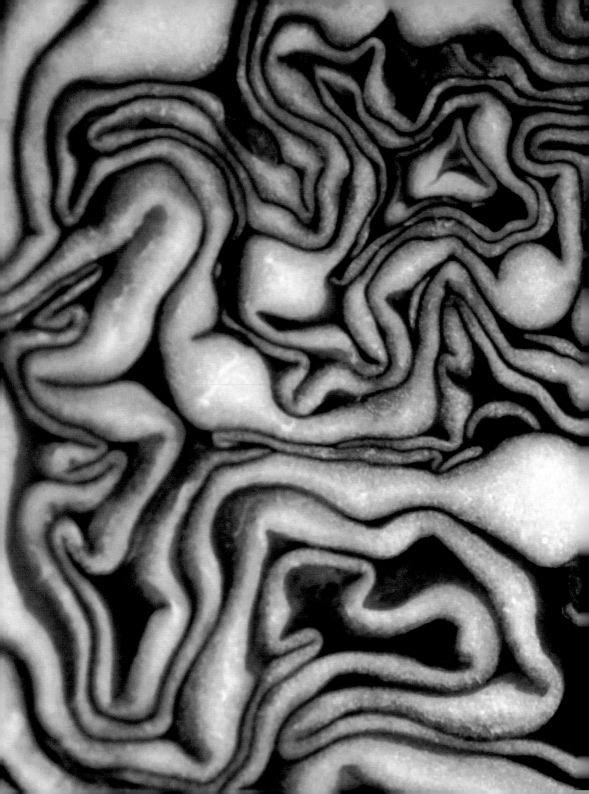

Nasturtium

Nasturtium, or *Tropaeolum majus,* is a completely edible plant prized both in the garden and in the kitchen for its brilliant red, orange, and yellow flowers. It is native to the jungles of Mexico and Peru, where the Incas grew it as an ornamental and cultivated a relative for its roots, hence its alternate name of Indian cress. Spanish conquistadores took the plant home with them in the sixteenth century. It was widely grown in colonial America.

Among the most common of edible flowers, nasturtium blooms are used both fresh and dried as garnishes, in salads, and on open-faced sandwiches. A delicious salad combines dried flowers with fresh radicchio, chives, and spinach under a dressing of Champagne vinegar, Dijon mustard, olive oil, salt, and pepper. Fresh, the blossoms make a striking and flavorsome casing for everything from cheese spreads to Mediterranean vegetable blends. The flower buds, when pickled, are an inexpensive substitute for capers, while the spicy leaves are good used sparingly in salad, and even the stems can be served boiled in soups. **SH**

Taste: *Mildly pungent and peppery, nasturtium blossoms have a sweet-spicy flavor similar to watercress. Those grown in full sun and picked later taste more intense.*

Zucchini Blossom

The zucchini blossom is the pretty yellow flower of the zucchini, also known as the courgette, a young summer squash (*Cucurbita pepo*), from the same family as cucumber and melon. Stuffed and fried or simply sizzled in a crisp golden tempura-style batter, the blossoms were once a specialty of Italian and French restaurants, but are now seen as a delicacy all over the world. The blossoms are very fragile and must be used within a day or two of being picked.

Interestingly, zucchini can be male or female, and both duly flower. The female blossom opens first, but once fertilized, crinkles and collapses as the fruit grows; by the time the zucchini is ready to be picked, the flower has wasted away. The male, however, blooms vigorously from a single thin stem, but never develops into a zucchini.

Typically, male flowers are larger and stay open longer than their female counterparts. Once the bees have done the job of collecting the pollen and transferring it to the female flower, nature has no farther use for the male blossom, and so it is the preferred flower for stuffing. **LF**

Taste: *Zucchini blossoms are mild and sweet in flavor and can be stuffed or eaten raw in salads. The smaller female flowers are favored for deep-frying in batter.*

A male zucchini flower awaits a bee to carry its pollen to the female flower nearby. »

Palm Heart

These prized ingredients are the tender, creamy cores of a number of different types of palm: the very top and middle of the green shoots of a brand new tree. With many varieties of palm, this excision kills the parent plant, making the heart a true luxury—hence its role in dishes with titles such as "millionaire's salad," a specialty of Mauritius.

The hearts of the cabbage palm, *Sabal palmetto*, which grows around the Caribbean and Central America, are known as "swamp cabbage" in Florida. There they are traditionally sliced thin, simmered in water with salt pork or bacon, and served with pepper vinegar. Because harvesting kills this palm, it is now a protected species in Florida.

Instead, hearts are harvested from *Bactris gasipaes*, the peach palm or *pejibaye*, which is native to the Amazon. In the wild, it was a staple in the lives of Indians in the region; today it is cultivated for its hearts, which, as it produces multiple shoots, can be harvested without killing the parent trees. In Brazil, the Assai palm is cultivated for its hearts, which are often are used as a filling for empanadas. **SH**

Taste: Soft, yet with a many layered texture, palm hearts have a sweet, nutty flavor, often described as a blend of artichokes, asparagus, and mushrooms.

The cabbage palm is the state tree of Florida, where harvesting of its heart is prohibited.

Cardoon

Like its close relative, the globe artichoke, the cardoon (*Cynara cardunculus*) belongs to the thistle family and originated in the Mediterranean, where it has been eaten for millennia. Unlike the artichoke, however, the cardoon is generally appreciated for its edible stalk, which Roman aristocracy stewed in fish sauce, and peasants apparently ate raw.

Today, cardoons are grown in a similar way to most celery plants, with banks of earth raised around the growing stalks to lighten their look and flavor. Unlike celery, however, these stalks remain too bitter to be enjoyed raw, although once cooked they become tender and take on an exquisite delicate flavor. They are especially popular in Spain, southern France, and Italy; although they arrived in England to a mixed reception, they were popular with the early New England colonists across the Atlantic. In Provence, cardoons are a favorite dish at Christmas. In northern Italy, they are served with the hot dip of olive oil, anchovies, and butter known as *bagna cauda*. They are roasted, used to make soup, or fried in a crisp, light, tempura-style batter. **LF**

Taste: Eaten raw, cardoons have spicy, celerylike aspects that hint of fennel. Cooked until tender, the bitterness subsides to reveal a fine artichoke flavor.

Pacaya

The edible flower bud of a tropical palm tree (*Chamaedorea tepejilote*), pacaya grows in Central America. The fleshy yellow flowers of the male plants resemble long thin ears of corn and are harvested while young and tender, and still enclosed in the spathes. Grown in Guatemala for the past two centuries, pacaya is harvested in the wild and from cultivated plants, often for export to North America. The tricky process of flower collection provides vital income to people living in poor, rural communities.

Also known as vegetable squid because of the snaking tendrils coiled in its large petals, pacaya can be eaten raw in salads. It is also often boiled and eaten as a vegetable; fried in an egg batter and served with tomato sauce, black beans, rice, and tortillas; or added to scrambled eggs and stir-fries. Pacaya is one of the fifty-odd ingredients found in *fiambre*, a salad served in Guatemala at the beginning of November for *El Día de los Muertos* (the Day of the Dead), when people honor their ancestors at cemeteries. In El Salvador, it is eaten stuffed with cheese as *pacaya rellena de queso*. **CK**

Flor de Izote

With an impressive flower spike reaching up to 3 feet (0.9 m) high and, in summer, covered in a stunning mass of fragrant, white flowers, flor de Izote is a yucca plant belonging to the agave family. The edible, bell-shaped flowers of this plant are considered a delicacy in Mexico, Costa Rica, Guatemala, and especially El Salvador, where it is the national flower. When the plant is semimature, bell-shaped flowers appear that can be harvested for eating, either as they open or just before they open. The ancient Maya boiled the flowers to make an energy-boosting herbal tea.

Rich in calcium, the flowers need soaking for twenty minutes or washing and blanching before cooking, to remove some of their bitterness. Locals use the flowers in *huevos revueltos* (scrambled eggs), tamales, and in dishes containing tomatoes, onions, or garlic, and even in barbecue sauce. They can also be a welcome ingredient in a salad, casserole, soup, or just fried in butter with a little salt and pepper. In El Salvador, the flowers are used to stuff *pupusas*, which are similar to a corn tortilla or pita bread. **CK**

Taste: *The tender petals of pacaya enclose chewy inner tendrils. The flower buds have a hearty, slightly bitter flavor a little like asparagus.*

Taste: *After careful soaking and blanching flor de Izote has a pleasantly bitter flavor. Even after cooking the flowers should still be slightly crunchy in texture.*

A single yucca flower spike bears a substantial crop of edible blooms. ⟫

Banana Flower

Bullet-shaped, heavy, and sheathed in ridged outer leaves of crimson purple, the banana flower or banana bud looks formidable. Yet, its tough exterior hides an ingredient of surprising delicacy, often compared to artichoke. The thick outer leaves unfold to reveal tightly packed softer leaf bracts, pale pink or burgundy in hue, interspersed with small fingerlike blossoms that are immature bananas. Both taste faintly earthy and astringent, and the blossoms bear a hint of bitterness.

Banana flowers are a common sight at markets in Vietnam, Thailand, the Philippines, and Cambodia, where they are eaten raw or lightly blanched in salads dressed with vinegar or citrus, cooked until tender in soups or coconut milk sauces, or shredded as a garnish for noodle dishes and the fondue-style sharing dishes known as "steamboats."

Small, rounded flowers are said to taste better than larger, more pointed specimens. They can discolor to a muddy brown extremely rapidly when sliced, and, therefore, are usually soaked in acidulated water immediately after being cut. **CTa**

Taste: *Banana flowers have the crisp texture of a palm heart, fortified by more fiber; their lightly nutty flavor is reminiscent of raw artichoke, mushroom, and zucchini.*

The heavy flower weighs down the shoot,
◉ **and the young bananas sprout upward.**

Roman Artichoke

The *carciofo romanesco del Lazio* (IGP), or Roman artichoke, is an exquisite type of globe artichoke with a large, spherical, tightly packed head and green leaves tinged a rosy violet color. A native of the Mediterranean, the exact history of *Cynara scolymus* is a little hazy: some think it was developed in ancient Sicily, others that the plant the ancient Greeks and Romans knew was a type of cardoon. It then disappeared, only to reappear in Italy during the Renaissance; many varieties grow there today.

For the most part, the Roman artichoke is cultivated along the Lazio coast around Rome and on toward Civitavecchia. Artichokes thrive in salty climes and the coastal soil offers ideal growing conditions. The season is from late winter to early spring, and, as with so many things edible and Italian, its arrival is a signal to party. Every April, the coastal town of Ladispoli holds a festival that sees the town's restaurants vying to produce the best Roman artichoke dish; at the Velletri festival, the artichokes are cooked over a fire fueled by their own dried shoots. **LF**

Taste: *Prized for being more tender than its cousins, the Roman artichoke has a smooth, creamy flavor followed by a slightly metallic aftertaste with patches of sweetness.*

Lumignano Pea

Snow Pea

Around Lumignano in the Berici Hills of the Veneto region in northern Italy, a wonderfully succulent and sweet variety of pea has been cultivated for hundreds of years. Production is tiny, but anyone fortunate enough to be in the area in spring should certainly seek them out.

It was apparently Benedictine monks who brought the peas to the hills, about 1,000 years ago. By accident or design, they selected an ideal microclimate: the sheer rock faces hold the warmth of the sun as if in a storage heater, reflecting it back onto the plants, while sun shines down from high above, meaning the peas ripened sweet and early. Over the centuries, farmers have carried on what the monks had started, adapting growing methods, and building steep terraces to access the best positions: everything, from the stones to the harvest, were hauled up and down on the farmers' backs.

The peas are harvested between April and May, and a festival—the Sagra dei Bisi—is held every May to celebrate. The peas perform wonderfully in the Venetian soup *risi e bisi* (rice and peas). **LF**

One of the pod peas—so named because both the pod and the immature peas are edible—snow peas, or mange-tout, one expression of *Pisum sativum*, are picked in early spring, when many regions still have snow on the ground. They are even younger than the sugar-snap varieties designed to be eaten pod and all: snow peas are eaten so flat and so young the seeds have barely had time to develop.

Legumes, including peas of many varieties, were harvested in the wild many, many millennia ago. Peas probably originated in western Asia, not far from where the ancient Greeks were cultivating them about 400 to 500 BCE, and *Pisum sativum* was well established in China by the seventh century CE. More than 1,000 years later, snow peas were one of thirty-odd varieties of pea Thomas Jefferson cultivated at Monticello, in Virginia.

Snow peas can be eaten raw or slightly cooked. In addition to their role as an ingredient in stir-fried dishes throughout Asia, they add color and texture to salads, soups, rice, and pasta dishes, or make an ideal accompaniment to meat or fish. **SH**

Taste: *Crisp, but tender, the fresh-flavored pods reveal juicy, small, vivid green peas that surrender a delightfully clean sweetness on the tongue.*

Taste: *Snow peas taste similar to garden peas, but are less starchy and have a sweeter flavor. Raw or quickly cooked, they have a clean, sweet, slightly grassy taste.*

French Bean

Despite their English name—in French they are *haricots verts*—these green beans are native to Central America, where they have been domesticated for more than 5,000 years. (The name *haricot* is a corruption of the Aztec word *ayecotl*.)

The parent plant, *Phaseolus vulgaris*, grows in a frankly bewildering range of varieties that make it the most cultivated type of bean in the United States and Europe. It was originally grown for its seeds alone, and many varieties—such as those that produce flageolets, or dried haricots—still are. The bean reached Europe during the sixteenth century, but it was probably Italians who were the first to eat the whole pods, a century or two later. Today, these slender beans have been carefully cultivated to produce tender pods with tiny seeds.

Fresh from the garden, French beans are crisp eaten raw. Steamed or boiled until crisp and tender, they have a starring role in *salad niçoise*, and make a good accompaniment to simple meat or fish dishes. More elaborate French recipes pair them with bacon, tomato sauce, or a rich cream sauce. **SH**

Taste: *French beans are at their best fresh, young, and straight from the garden—or at least a local supplier. Then they are sweet and crisp with a clean, "green" taste.*

Green Flageolet

Sometimes referred to as the "Rolls-Royce" of beans for their smooth texture and subtle flavor, green flageolets—*flageolets verts* in French—are small beans with a low starch content, grown for their light green seeds. In nineteenth-century France, bean seeds were colored red, white, yellow, or even black. It was not until the 1870s, however, that Gabriel Chevrier of Arpajon, a little town just south of Paris, developed a variety whose seeds stayed green long enough to be dried and sold while green. The "new" beans were very popular, and even today are sometimes known as *chevriers* in their creator's honor. Chevrier's original variety is now a heirloom breed and difficult to find, but both it and its descendants remain a great delicacy in the kitchen.

Fresh green flageolets, when available, should be cooked in very little water over low heat for a brief time. The dried ones can be cooked like any dried bean. They pair especially well with braised or roasted lamb, which is the traditional way to serve them in France; slow-cooked lamb shanks and flageolets is a popular dish in England. **SH**

Taste: *The beans have a very mild, very creamy flavor somewhat similar to but more delicate than edamame or small lima beans, with gentle chlorophyll notes.*

Edamame

The vegetarian influence of Buddhism means the soybean has long been an important food in China, Japan, and Southeast Asia. It is known as "the meat of the fields" for its high protein content, but because it is tough and indigestible when dried, it is usually processed into products, like tofu and soy sauce.

Immature beans, however, are a different matter. In Japan, where they are known as edamame, large bunches of the fuzzy green pods appear in food stores from May to September. Boiled in the pod they make a delicous accompaniment to drinks, particularly sake, and a basketful of edamame, warm from the pot and tossed in salt, is one of the joys of a visit to any *izakaya* (drinking establishment) in Japan.

Edamame have become fashionable in parts of the West, where they are increasingly available both fresh and frozen. Chefs use the bright green beans as an ingredient in many dishes, while edamame mash is a popular Pacific Rim side dish. In Japan, the Tamba region of Hyogo is known for its *kuromame*— a larger, darker variety that is particularly delicious. **SB**

Taste: *Sucking the salt off an edamame pod while squeezing the beans into your mouth is a real pleasure. The beans are tender, juicy, and subtly sweet, with a firm texture.*

Broad Bean

For centuries these flat, green, grayish, or pink seeds were a major source of protein both in Europe and in parts of Asia and Africa. Also called fava beans— their botanical name is *Vicia faba*—broad beans have been cultivated for so long and so widely any wild predecessors have been lost in antiquity.

Not everyone ate them, however. In ancient Egypt, the upper classes considered the beans unworthy, although today a local variety is dried and used in the popular dish *ful medames*. The sixth-century BCE philosopher Pythagoras called them the "beans of the dead," conceivably because for a very small percentage of the population broad beans can be toxic. The Romans held them in higher regard, which might explain their use fresh and dried in Italian stews and casseroles. In the spring, tender broad beans are eaten raw with pecorino cheese.

In China and Thailand, the beans, called "open mouth nut," are fried and served salted as a snack. Elsewhere they are used in everything from frittatas and risottos to soups and salads, and as an accompaniment to meats, such as cooked ham. **SH**

Taste: *Broad beans have a robust, meaty, earthy taste somewhere between a lima bean and an edamame. In young beans this taste is muted by a delicate sweetness.*

A staple for millennia, broad beans still exist in European gardens today. ❯❯

Petai Bean

Horseradish Pod

These beautiful spiraling pods—twist bean is a colloquial name—of petai (*Parkia speciosa*) look like something straight out of Tolkien. If their appearance is elven, however, their flavor is surely dwarven, with something of the sulfur mines about it: their other common name of stink bean is deserved because of the way their scent lingers about one's person after consumption, rather like garlic or asparagus.

The beans crunch softly between one's teeth and have nutlike nuances to their taste, and indeed they resemble jade-green marcona almonds, gently curved and ridged. In southern Thailand, where petai are called *sataw* or *sator*, two different varieties are eaten: *sataw kow*, which has twisted pods and sweeter beans, and *sataw darn*, which has straight pods and larger, stronger-smelling beans that are often pickled. Both there and across the border in Malaysia, petai are popularly stir-fried with shrimp and a spicy chile paste. Malaysians also enjoy petai as part of a typical meal centered on an assortment of herbs and vegetables eaten with sambals. **CTa**

Sometimes known as "drumsticks," the long, narrow pods of the horseradish tree contain seeds with a delicate, slightly hot flavor. The horseradish tree (*Moringa oleifera*) is not related to the horseradish of the mustard family. Rather, the tree received its name because its pungent root is used as a substitute for horseradish. The tree is grown in semi-arid tropical and subtropical areas, and is native to the southern foothills of the Himalayas, Africa, and the Middle East, although it is also cultivated in Latin America, Sri Lanka, Malaysia, and the Philippines.

The outer part of the pod is inedible, but the young, triangular seeds inside can be cooked as a vegetable similar to a green bean, and have a delicate flavor. They can be prepared in a variety of ways: fried; boiled; steamed; or made into a pickle. They are frequently made into soup and added to curries, dals, and stews. The mature pods can be stewed and eaten like an artichoke, by scraping away the inner pulp and discarding the remainder. When the mature pods are cooked, the flavor is similar to okra. **CK**

Taste: *Petai have an appealingly nutty, subtly sweet earthiness that brings to mind fava beans, but with an aura a little reminiscent of garlic.*

Taste: *Young horseradish pods are tender when cooked, and have a delicate flavor that has been compared to a combination of horseradish, asparagus, and peanut.*

The exotic appearance of twist beans is ⊗ *matched by their remarkable pungency.*

Silver Queen Corn

Ackee

For more than a half century, Silver Queen set the United States standard for corn that was eaten from the cob. But, although prized by celebrity chefs such as Thomas Keller, this corn with its delicate white kernels is becoming more difficult to find each day as growers turn to newer hybrids that hold their sweetness longer after picking.

Developed in 1955, Silver Queen can most likely trace its ancestry back more than 7,000 years to *teosinte*, a plant that grew wild in Mexico. Cultivation spread southward to Peru and northward into what would become the United States. Columbus found it in the New World and brought it back to Spain, although it was grown in Europe as a grain. Americans began cultivating sweet corn—varieties of corn to be eaten when immature and still sweet— about 1800. Silver Queen remains a prime choice. Like all sweet corn, it is best eaten within a day or so of being picked, before its sugar turns to starch. It is delicious boiled and slathered with butter, salt, and pepper, or grilled and seasoned with herbs or spices such as cumin. **SH**

Ackee, also spelled akee, takes its Latin name *Blighia sapida* from the infamous Captain Bligh. The red pear-shaped fruit, which grows in clusters on an evergreen tree, is indigenous to the forests of the Ivory Coast and Gold Coast of West Africa, and Bligh is said to have brought it on slave ships to Jamaica about 1793. Today, it is Jamaica's national fruit and figures alongside salt cod in the country's national dish, ackee and saltfish.

Ackee must only be picked when it has turned completely red and has split fully open in the distinctive "yawn" or "smile" that reveals its black seeds and the creamy yellow, pulpy aril around them. Only the pulp is eaten. The rest of the ripened ackee and all unripened ackee are toxic and can be fatal. (Canned ackee is available in many parts of the world and is completely safe to eat.)

Ackee looks, tastes, and feels very similar to creamy scrambled eggs. Some say it also looks like brains, hence its alternate name, vegetable brains. It is sometimes curried and used as a filling for patties, and can form part of a soup or a vegetarian stew. **SH**

Taste: *Silver Queen is the standard by which corn-on-the-cob is measured. It has a well-balanced sweetness that remains "corny," not sugary, and a creamy, milky flavor.*

Taste: *Ackee has a mild flavor that picks up the taste of other ingredients in the dish. Its texture is smoother and more melting than that of scrambled eggs.*

Ackee displays its "yawn" or "smile" when it is ripe for harvest. »

Tomatillo

Tomatillos are a fruit related to the ground cherry and Cape gooseberry, although like their close relative the tomato, they are used as a vegetable. Smaller than a regular tomato, tomatillos are encased in a papery calyx or husk that is removed before cooking. Usually green and mild flavored, they can be eaten raw, but their flavor grows with cooking.

Tomatillos (classified as *Physalis ixocarpa* and *P. philadelphica*) are also known as husk tomatoes and, although they are sometimes called green tomatoes, too, they should not be confused with green, unripe tomatoes. They originated in Mesoamerica and are still found in the wild and cultivated from the cool highlands of Guatemala to southern Texas. Tomatillos also grow in Australia, India, and East Africa. There are many different types of tomatillo prized throughout Latin America and distinguished by their color and size.

A common ingredient in Latin American cuisines, they are cooked or pureed into sauces, especially *salsas verdes* that go with grilled or roasted meats. They are also sometimes added to guacamole. **SH**

Taste: *Similar in texture to tomatoes, tomatillos have a refreshing acidic flavor with hints of apple and lemon that blends well with the heat of chiles.*

Green Tomato

Green tomatoes might be unripe, but they are not inedible. In fact, the immature state of this fruit, generally served as a vegetable, has a culinary culture all of its own. Green tomatoes take center stage in the United States when summer gives way to fall, and unripened tomatoes must be picked from the garden. Widely known and appreciated throughout the southern states, the fruit achieved worldwide notice in the film based on Fannie Flagg's novel, *Fried Green Tomatoes at the Whistle Stop Café*.

Fried green tomatoes are a delicacy. Thick slices of green tomato are dipped in egg, coated with flour and bread crumbs, and then fried in oil, to produce an appetizer or side dish. Green tomatoes are also used in soups, jams, relishes, salsas, and pickles.

Although most closely associated with the South, green tomatoes also feature in Indian cooking. Prepared with mustard seeds, cumin, and other spices, they can be served over rice as a vegetarian main course or used as a side dish. They are also used to make chutney. Green tomato tarte tatin is an American take on the French classic. **SH**

Taste: *Green tomatoes are best when they are truly green. Although the flavor is reminiscent of ripe tomatoes, they are much tarter. In their prime, they are firm and tangy.*

Cherry Tomato

As cherry tomatoes only became fashionable in the late twentieth century, it is easy to mistake them for a development of modern plant breeders. *Lycopersicon esculentum cerasiforme* was, in reality, cultivated by the Aztec civilization in Central America before the Spanish conquistadores took it back to Europe. Like other tomatoes, it probably evolved from wild Peruvian ancestors.

Even though tomatoes were not generally eaten by Old World gourmets (who remained suspicious of the fruit's deadly nightshade lineage) until the end of the nineteenth century, many kinds of cherry tomato were being grown. The cultivars developed today have usually been conceived with the needs of multiple retailers in mind (thicker skins, long shelf life). Bright red "Gardener's Delight," however, is a delicious English variety and the golden Japanese "Sungold" is very mellow and sweet.

Cherry tomatoes are generally eaten raw, although they are increasingly being cooked. Lightly pan-fried in olive oil and mixed with fresh herbs they make an instant summery pasta sauce. **MR**

Taste: *The sweetness and acidity of cherry tomatoes should be in balance. Juicy, with mellow acidity, and full of sweet flavor, they should have a subtle savory scent.*

San Marzano Tomato

When it comes to plum tomatoes, the San Marzano tomato has long carried the vote. Tomatoes have been cultivated in the southern Italian provinces of Naples, Salerno, and Avellino since the sixteenth century. When the San Marzano tomato arrived a couple of hundred years later, the volcanic ash from nearby Mount Vesuvius and the rich earth of the pre-Apennine hills combined with the sea air and created growing traditions to create a prized fruit.

Lauded for its intense flavor and vibrant color, the San Marzano's skin is easy to peel, its pulp is firm, and it has few seeds, making it perfect for tomato sauces. Since 1996, the Pomodoro di San Marzano has carried DOP certification, which distinguishes it from San Marzano tomatoes grown to less strict standards in other parts of the world. Pomodoro di San Marzano tomatoes grow on especially trained vines and are picked by hand over multiple harvests. They are washed, peeled, and canned without any additives or preservatives. The unmechanized process makes them expensive in comparison to other varieties, but they are without doubt worth it. **LF**

Taste: *San Marzano have a robust flavor that combines a complex sweetness with slightly acerbic notes. Canned, they exhibit a juicy excellence that is deliciously intense.*

Water Chestnut

After you taste fresh water chestnuts, the canned version will never seem the same again. Fresh water chestnuts have a lively, crisp, juicy texture and a subtly sweet taste; after canning, the experience is just a pale ghost of itself. The crunch remains, but the flavor vanishes into thin air.

Fresh water chestnuts (*Eleocharis dulcis*) have an unassuming appearance. Being the tubers of an aquatic plant, they are usually covered in mud. Rinsing reveals a shiny, dark brown, hard shell, not dissimilar to its namesake chestnut, which is peeled to reveal the white flesh inside. When buying, look for unwrinkled specimens that are completely firm; the ones with soft spots are moldy inside. Unpeeled water chestnuts can be stored for several weeks in a plastic bag in the refrigerator; after peeling they can be frozen without any loss of texture or flavor.

Water chestnuts are ground into a lumpy flour that makes a beautiful, crisp, delicate crust when fried. This, combined with fresh water chestnuts, makes a chewy steamed pudding that is traditionally eaten at Chinese New Year. **KKC**

Taste: *Water chestnuts can be eaten raw or cooked. They are often used in dishes where their crisp texture contrasts with softer ingredients, such as steamed ground pork.*

Water chestnuts feature in some Chinese stir-fries. ❯❯

Asian Eggplant

Eggplant

Browse the stalls selling eggplants in an Asian market and none of the varieties on offer are likely to resemble the shiny, deep purple beauties so ubiquitous in the West. Despite its starring role in Mediterranean cuisine, the eggplant is native to tropical Asia, where many varieties come in a host of different shapes, sizes, and colors.

The tiny, bitter variety popular in Thailand and known as *makhua puang* grows in clusters and is the size, shape, and color of a large pea. Other eggplants in Southeast Asia are small, round, and range in color from white to pale green, and yellow to purple. In Japan and China, eggplants are long and slender with pale purple skins, sometimes streaked with white. These are good for stir-fries.

Asian cooking rarely calls for eggplants to be salted to rid them of bitter juices. Small, round eggplants are added whole or halved to Thai curries to contrast with coconut sauces, whereas pea eggplants add astringency. Japanese eggplants (*nasu*) make fine tempura. In India, eggplant is used in the hot pickle *brinjal*. **WS**

A member of the diverse family that encompasses potatoes, tomatoes, and deadly nightshade, eggplant (*Solanum melongena*) is eaten as a vegetable, but is botanically a berry. Although some Asian, African, and Spanish varieties have a color and shape that explains their otherwise mystifying name, the classic Mediterranean varieties have shiny, smooth, dark purple skin and light flesh with pale brown seeds.

Probably originating in India, the eggplant traveled with the Arabs to Europe during the thirteenth century. Now a mainstay throughout the Mediterranean, eggplant makes its most celebrated appearance in the Turkish dish *imam bayildi*, stuffed with onions and cooked in copious quantities of olive oil. It is a key ingredient in Provençal ratatouille and in Greek moussaka, where it is layered with ground meat and white sauce. Roasted, it becomes the basis for numerous Greek and Middle Eastern dips, among them *baba ghanoush*. It can be served battered and fried, stuffed, pickled, in stews, as a relish, or in myriad other ways. **SH**

Taste: *Tart pea eggplants are used to balance sweeter ingredients in Thai dishes. Long, thin Asian eggplants have less seeds and, therefore, the most mellow flavor.*

Taste: *When cooked, eggplant has a subtle, creamy taste, often with a smooth bitterness from the skin that adds something indefinably extra to other ingredients.*

This vegetable display includes just a few of the ☻ *eggplant varieties grown in Southeast Asia.*

Hass Avocado

Plantain

The fruit of a subtropical tree, the avocado (*Persea americana*) has been cultivated in Central and South America since about 7000 BCE. The Hass variety is smaller than many others, higher in oil, easier to peel, and richer in flavor: it is a hybrid of species originally from Mexico and Guatemala.

Developed by Rudolph Hass of California during the 1920s and patented by him in 1935, the Hass has pebbly skin that darkens as it ripens from green through to indigo or almost black. It is the most widely cultivated avocado in the United States and is also grown extensively in Mexico. (All Hass avocado trees trace their lineage back to a single mother tree that died in 2002, aged seventy-five.)

Although no longer used as a butter substitute, as it was by seventeenth-century sailors—hence its names of midshipman's butter and butter pear—the avocado is still most often used raw. Guacamole, the simple mash that dates back to Aztec times, is by far the best-known dish. But the avocado also has a starring role in Cobb salad, a blend created at Los Angeles's Brown Derby restaurant. **SH**

A staple in East and Central Africa and parts of Asia, plantains are, essentially, kinds of banana that can only be used for cooking: they are generally larger than dessert bananas, with a tougher skin, and a starch level that renders them unappealing until heat converts it into sugars. Edible plantains start green, turn yellow, get black spots, and when fully ripe are all black. They were probably known in Southeast Asia as early as the sixth century BCE.

When green and unripe, plantains have a starchy, potatolike flavor: they can be sliced and fried into fries or chips. Once the interior is sweet and ripe, they lend themselves to mashing, sautéing, baking, boiling, sun-drying, and dishes from curries to the gloopy West African *fufu*. It is frying, however, that suits plantains' glutinous sweetness best, and *platanos maduras fritos*—fried slabs of juicy, golden plantain—is a Latin American and Caribbean side dish, commonly served with rice and beans, meat, fish, or even breakfast. *Pazham pori*—plantain fritters—are popular in India, while crunchy plantain chips are in vogue on several continents. **SH**

Taste: *Avocados have a sweet and nutty flavor. The Hass variety is especially rich. It has the subtle taste of room-temperature butter with a creamy aftertaste.*

Taste: *When green, plantains have a bland, starchy taste. Ripe plantains are sweet and have a distinctive flavor, with banana notes overlaying an almost carrotlike base.*

Women take unripe plantains to the open-air market in Mwika, Tanzania. »

Okra

Cucumber

Okra, or *Hibiscus esculentus*, is the only vegetable in the mallow family, which includes cotton and the hibiscus flower. Native to tropical Africa, it traveled with the slave trade—to Brazil in the seventeenth century, and also to the southern states of America. The okra plant can grow as high as 7 feet (2 m) tall and is cultivated for its pointed pods, which work as a thickening agent as well as a vegetable.

Also known as lady's fingers for its elegant shape, okra is famously combined with tomatoes, onions, spicy seasonings, and meat, shellfish, or both to make gumbo, the traditional dish from Louisiana. (The word "gumbo" is African in origin, and originally meant okra.) It is also served deep-fried after being soaked in buttermilk and battered with cornmeal. Okra's mild flavor and slippery texture means it complements acid ingredients, such as tomatoes: in Israel, it is served with tomato sauce and rice, in the United States it is cooked with tomatoes and corn, and in Greece it is prepared with tomatoes, oil, and vinegar. It appears in many curries and Middle Eastern stews. **SH**

Cucumber, one of the oldest cultivated vegetables, very possibly originated in India about 4,000 years ago. It appears in the Old Testament and was known to Charlemagne; the Roman emperor Tiberius and the French king Louis XIV ordered *Cucumis sativus* grown indoors in winter. Still, it generally grew outdoors until the nineteenth century when the English began cultivating it in greenhouses.

While Samuel Johnson believed "a cucumber should be well sliced, and dressed with pepper and vinegar, and then thrown out as good for nothing," sandwiches of thinly sliced cucumbers on buttered white bread make a quintessentially English treat.

The cooling, but discreet, bitterness means cucumber pairs well with other dairy foods, too, particularly sour cream or yogurt: thinly sliced cucumber with yogurt is popular in the United States, a cold cucumber soup with *smetana* is a traditional Russian dish, and the Indian raita and the Greek tzatziki both pair yogurt with cucumber. In salads, cucumber works well with ingredients as diverse as dill and tomatoes. **SH**

Taste: *Okra has a slightly fuzzy texture that is prickly when raw. Cooked okra has a pleasant mild flavor that is a cross between eggplant and asparagus.*

Taste: *A member of the melon family, the ridge cucumber has a juicy, sweet, airy taste similar to honeydew melon, yet more dilute, with a pleasant bitterness from the skin.*

Bitter Melon

Gnarled, covered in warts, and shaped like a rather pointy cucumber, bitter melon or bitter gourd, grows throughout India (but especially in Kerala), China, and Southeast Asia. *Momordica carantia* is picked when green, before it ripens, while it is still hard. All food cultures that enjoy its intense flavor scoop out the seeds in the middle to stuff it, but bitter melon is more commonly chopped.

While Vietnamese palates are hardy enough to consume slices raw, in India and China cooks attenuate the bitterness either by presalting it and squeezing out the excess juice or by parboiling. Chinese cooks work to balance its taste with other sweet, sour, and salty flavors, for example by pairing it with beef and black-bean sauce. In Sri Lanka, coconut milk tempers the bitterness. Malaysians slice it very thinly and coat it, whether fried or raw, with lime juice, while the southern Indian curry dish *pavakka theeyal* tames it with the gentle acidity of tamarind juice. Bitter melon is not often blended with other vegetables, but it makes an excellent spicy pickle with asafoetida and mango. **MR**

Taste: Bitter melon belongs to the same genus as gherkins, and it is easy to identify those biting, underripe flavors, but the bitterness is much more intense.

Silk Squash

Traditionally eaten during the summer months when its cooling, high water content can aid hydration, silk squash is one of the "three sisters." Along with corn and beans, squash was one of the three main indigenous plants cultivated by Native Americans thousands of years ago.

A member of the Cucurbitaceae family, silk squash goes by various names but the most common are dishwater gourd, angled luffa, and Chinese okra. Known botanically as *Luffa acutangula*, however, silk squash is most accurately called angled luffa because it is related to the tropical climbing plant that yields the loofah sponge.

Grown to be harvested before maturity, silk squash is long and tapered, with skin ranging from pale to dark green. It has watery flesh, lots of seeds, and edible skin that is tougher in larger specimens. Like zucchini, silk squash is good at absorbing the flavors of the other ingredients it is cooked with. If quickly stir-fried, silk squash maintains its crisp texture; longer, slower cooking gives it the silky consistency the name suggests. **KKC**

Taste: Silk squash's bland, but vaguely sweet, flavor and crisp, tender texture is like cucumber. Smaller silk squash are sweeter, more tender, and less seedy than larger ones.

Butternut Squash

With its tan skin, long neck, and bulbous base, butternut squash looks like nothing so much as a very large pear. One of the most popular of the myriad varieties of squash grown around the world, it is a winter squash—the fruit is left to ripen on the vine until it develops a hard, thick rind.

Squash have long been eaten in their New World home: archaeological evidence shows that varieties were consumed at least 12,000 years ago and cultivated more than 9,000 years ago. Butternut belongs to the *Cucurbita moschata* family of squashes: remains of cultivated relatives dating back to 5000 BCE have been found in Mexico. Colonists and Europeans adopted members of the family as early as the seventeenth century; today it is grown anywhere with a long, warm growing season.

Butternut squash is an extremely versatile vegetable that pairs particularly well with allspice, cinnamon, cloves, ginger, and other warming winter seasonings. It makes creamy soups and purees, is baked and served with brown sugar, and can even be turned into puddings and pies. **SH**

Taste: *Slightly sweet with nutty notes, yet with a dilute, gentle flavor, butternut squash tastes somewhat like a pumpkin and a bit like sweet potato or yam.*

Spaghetti Squash

Weight Watchers International put spaghetti squash, known as vegetable spaghetti in England, and also called noodle squash, on the culinary map when it introduced this low-calorie alternative to pasta to its members. A member of the extensive winter squash family (*Cucurbita pepo*), spaghetti squash is loosely cylindrical, like a jumbo zucchini. When ripe it has bright yellow skin and yellowish-white flesh.

The spaghetti squash is generally believed to have been developed about 1930 in North America, but its history is uncertain, especially since it is known and grown in Japan. It takes its name from the ease with which the cooked flesh can be forked into strands resembling spaghetti. An orange-fleshed variety, called Orangetti, was developed in the later twentieth century.

Spaghetti squash can be boiled, baked, or microwaved. As its name implies, the strands are often treated like spaghetti and dressed with sauces, or butter, fresh herbs, garlic, and Parmesan cheese. When treated like a squash, the vegetable is often served stuffed. It can also be used in soups. **SH**

Taste: *The fun of this rather bland vegetable is in its tendrilly texture. The taste is slightly sweet and nutty with a hint of lemon; the orange variety is slightly sweeter.*

Spaghetti squash becomes a fibrous mass when cooked. »

Pumpkin

Winter Melon

At the stroke of midnight, Cinderella's carriage most likely turned into a *Rouge Vif d'Estampes*, a large French pumpkin, or *potiron*, colored an orange so bright it is almost scarlet. But this stunningly flexible vegetable—which is technically a fruit—had its origins in Central America thousands of years ago.

When the first English explorers arrived in North America, they found Native Americans turning pumpkins into soup, stews, and other dishes. Centuries later, chefs have made pumpkin soup into a gastronomic classic, while pumpkin stews are popular from Africa to the Caribbean. The pumpkin's blandness means it can be treated both as savory and sweet: in the Thanksgiving classic, pumpkin pie, it is blended with molasses, sugar, and spices.

In the United States and England, freakishly large pumpkins are grown for festivals and contests: some have reached more than 220 pounds (100 kg) in weight. Neither these nor the types that are sold for carving into lanterns at Halloween make good eating: the fibrous texture makes them easy for children to cut, but militates against flavor. **SH**

The large, waxy-skinned gourd known as winter melon is actually a misnomer, being neither sweet nor a winter fruit. It is, in fact, a squash harvested during the winter months. It is also sometimes called wax gourd and ash gourd.

The winter melon (*Benincasa hispida*) is thought to have originated in Japan or Indonesia and is now popular all over Southeast Asia. Its white, waxy coating means it can be stored for many months as long as it remains uncut. It can weigh up to 100 pounds (45 kg). The smallest melons are sold whole, whereas larger ones are cut and sold in slices. The winter melon looks a bit like an oblong watermelon and its color varies from pale to dark green, although the flesh inside is white.

Winter melon is used in soups, curries, stir-fries, pickles, and preserves. At banquets, winter melon soup is served in a hollowed-out, whole small winter melon. Although commonly eaten as a vegetable in Southeast Asia, the flesh is also candied and is used to make a paste, along with almonds and sesame seeds, inside a popular pastry called wife's cakes. **KKC**

Taste: Pumpkins taste earthy and sweet, a cross between butternut squash and sweet potato. The flavor intensifies with cooking, but also forms a good base for other flavors.

Taste: Winter melon has a mild, delicate taste, a little like zucchini. Crisp and tender when cooked briefly, its texture becomes almost melting when cooked for longer.

 Pumpkins are grown on an agribusiness scale across North America.

Amaranth

Microgreen

Known to some as pigweed, to others as love-lies-bleeding, or Joseph's coat, amaranth in its various forms is a weed, a dye, an ornamental plant, a cereal, and a vegetable—not to mention an ingredient in Aztec blood rituals in Mexico. With more than fifty varieties, some of which can grow taller than a man, *Amaranthus* has been endlessly adapted as a food. In India, the spinachlike leaves, *chawli*, are mixed with dal, in a *bhaji* (a kind of fritter), or into dry curries. The Chinese stir-fry the leaves or add them to soups. In Africa, under the name *morogo*— a generic word for vegetables—freshly picked leaves go straight into the pot. It is also one of the greens of the Caribbean soup or side dish, *callaloo*.

The shot-size seeds are rich in protein and have been used as a cereal since Mayan times. In Mexico, they are popped like popcorn and mixed with honey or sugar syrup to make a chewy confection called *Alegria* (meaning happiness). In the Himalayas, crushed grain is compacted with raw sugar to make the snack known as *chikki*. Amaranth flour does not contain any gluten and is made into flatbreads. **MR**

The most delicate leaves of lettuces, herbs, and other greens, microgreens—or microleaves as they are also called—do not come in one variety, but many, ranging from arugula and mustard to celery and radish. Other popular varieties include spinach, ruby chard, beet, and cilantro.

Microleaves were "discovered" by enterprising chefs, who, after sampling the intense flavors of tiny plant leaves, incorporated them into salads and used them as seasonings and garnishes. Many vegetables and herbs are grown specifically as microgreens and valued not only for their flavor, but also for their color. They can be bought individually or in mixtures, and many cooks grow their own.

Because there are so many different varieties, there is a microgreen to suit most dishes. Several varieties make good salads when topped with a light vinaigrette and they can replace lettuce in sandwiches or wraps. Quickly sautéed, they make a delicious base for salmon and other fish. They add flavor to soups when dropped in at the very last minute, and make a flavorsome garnish. **SH**

Taste: *Amaranth leaves cook like spinach, but are milder tasting and not generally astringent. The grain is bland tasting with a texture similar to quinoa.*

Taste: *Microgreen arugula is mildly spicy and nutty; beet is earthy; broccoli is mildly peppery; mustard is tangy with a bite reminiscent of horseradish.*

According to Greek mythology, the amaranth flower
Ⓒ *never faded no matter how little light or water it had.*

Wild Arugula

Corn Salad

Arugula, *Eruca sativa*, is also known as rugola, rucola, Italian cress, and rocket, was valued by the ancient Romans not only for the small, serrated leaves, but for its seeds, which they used to flavor oils. (These were used in aphrodisiac mixtures as far back as the first century CE, and the plant was subsequently barred from monastery gardens.)

Long popular in Mediterranean Europe, particularly Italy, and in Egypt, where the numerous favored varieties are bland and cooked as a vegetable, it was in the 1990s that nations including Italy, India, Egypt, Turkey, and Israel pooled their resources of native strains to develop varieties that include the green now somewhat misleadingly sold as "wild arugula."

Aromatic and with an assertive flavor, wild arugula is often combined with milder greens: its superb pairing with shaved Parmesan cheese has become a culinary cliché. Prepared in the style of a pesto, it makes a good accompaniment to pasta or boiled potatoes. Either raw or lightly sautéed in olive oil it complements roast beef or broiled steak. **SH**

Under its French name *mâche*, corn salad (*Valerianella locusta*) or lamb's lettuce was a trendy ingredient in the warm mixed salads popular in the 1980s. Although cultivated commercially in France, the wild plant is treated as a weed by many other gardeners. It grows as a small, spreading, tufty sprig of elongated, dark green leaves, and will produce small clusters of flower heads if left unpicked.

The wild leaves make an autumn or winter salad when lettuces are unavailable, but for cooks, lamb's lettuce has one mild inconvenience. Traces of grit tend to lodge at the base of each plant, and can be tricky to remove, even with careful rinsing. The sprigs then need careful drying or trapped water can spoil the dressing.

Although lost to Anglo-Saxon kitchens until a generation ago, corn salad was a regular salad ingredient in seventeenth-century Britain. King Charles II's chef, Robert May, recommended it, as did John Evelyn in *Acetaria: a Discourse of Sallets* (1699). Nowadays, corn salad can be found in vacuum-packed salad mixtures and whole-food stores. **MR**

Taste: *This attention-getting leaf is spicy, peppery, and somewhat mustardy in flavor, with intense, lightly bitter, green back notes and a deliciously tangy flavor.*

Taste: *Corn salad is tender and mild without bitterness or astringency, and delivers an accessible, mildly sweet flavor alongside an almost velvety mouthfeel.*

Watercress

Pea Shoot

Watercress is one of nature's most lovely greens. Mostly eaten raw, the bunching small green leaves make a refreshing, colorful addition to everything from soups to salads. Originally native to Europe and Asia, it now also grows in the ponds and brooks of North America, and is widely cultivated elsewhere.

Watercress gets its name in part from the fact it grows in cold running water and, in general, the fresher and purer the water, the better the wild leaves. Despite its botanical name, *Nasturtium officinale*, it is a member of the same family as mustard, an entirely different genus from the nasturtium flower. Historically, watercress has been valued for its medicinal properties: the Greek general Xenophon made his men eat it as a tonic.

The British include watercress and/or cucumber sandwiches as part of afternoon tea. Watercress also makes a delicious salad, either alone and seasoned with fennel and balsamic vinegar or in combination with other greens such as arugula. In France, *potage cressonnière* is a creamed watercress and potato soup garnished with blanched watercress leaves. **SH**

This delicate vegetable, with its complex, elegant pea flavor, is the tender top leaves, stems, and tendrils of the young pea plant, and such a delicacy that from Shanghai to southern England plants are cultivated solely for their shoots. They can be eaten at stages varying from a threadlike stem only 2 inches (5 cm) long with leaves the size of a little fingernail, to young plants 6 inches (15 cm) long with leaves 1 inch (2.5 cm) in diameter.

It was probably the Hmong people of southern China and Southeast Asia who introduced pea shoots to a wider world. In China, where they are known as *dou miao* (Mandarin) and *dow miu* (Cantonese), they are served stir-fried, in soups, in salads, or in dumplings. In Japan and much of Southeast Asia, they are used in many contexts where other young greens might be.

Pea shoots are making an increased appearance in the West, where chefs harness the baby shoots as a pretty, surprisingly flavored garnish to fish and meats, transform them into salads dressed with lemon, or sauté older shoots with garlic. **SH**

Taste: *Raw watercress has a pungent, spicy taste reminiscent of peppery radishes. When cooked, it loses some of its bite, but releases a heady, flowery aroma.*

Taste: *Young pea shoots have a vegetal sweetness like fresh petits pois. Older shoots have a stronger flavor, with hints of baby spinach, watercress, and snow peas.*

Purslane

Purslane (*Portulaca oleracea*), also known by its Spanish name, *verdolaga*, is a succulent spreading herb with clusters of jadelike leaves that grows wild and is also cultivated. Found in the Americas, parts of Europe, southern Africa, and Asia, it has slipped in and out of favor as a culinary ingredient. It was once very popular throughout the Arab world and, more recently, was adopted by French chefs during the nouvelle cuisine fashion of the 1980s. Although most commonly eaten raw, it can also be cooked, when it gives a mucilaginous texture, rather like okra, to a sauce or soup. In Mexico, it is often served with hard cheese.

Purslane is enjoying a revival among the health-food lobby because it contains significant amounts of omega-3 fatty acids and vitamin E. The plant is also used in traditional Chinese medicine as a treatment for diarrhea, a strange choice since, eaten in quantity, it is an effective laxative. In Malawi, purslane's name translates as "buttocks of the chief's wife," a reference, no doubt, to the firm but springy texture of its leaves. **MR**

Taste: *The flavor is very bland, but gains characteristics from the soil where the purslane is grown, which can make it taste either lemony or salty.*

Long considered a weed by gardeners, purslane
⊘ *is gaining favor as a salad leaf.*

Sorrel

There are several kinds of sorrel that have been eaten as a vegetable since ancient times, however they share one common feature: they are all sour. Round-leafed or French sorrel (*Rumex scutatus*) is now the most commonly cultivated kind. It has long been used to offset rich food and was the key ingredient of one of the most famous nouvelle cuisine dishes, *escalope de saumon à l'oseille*, a fillet of salmon lightly cooked with a cream and sorrel sauce, that was created by the chefs, the Troisgros brothers.

Sorrel, often grown as a potherb, has a long growing season and is available from early spring until early winter. In old English cooking, a green sorrel sauce was served with roast goose. A handful of the leaves transforms a soup made with onion and potato. In French cuisine, sorrel puree traditionally accompanied a pot-roasted rolled veal round. Cultivated sorrel leaves dissolve with prolonged cooking. They should not be chopped with carbon-steel knives or stewed in iron pots, which will turn them black and bitter. **MR**

Taste: *Wilted for a few moments sorrel will turn from green to khaki. The level of sourness depends on the variety and the soil, but is always pleasant and lemony.*

Arrowhead Spinach

Spinach (*Spinacia oleracea*)—once called the "prince of vegetables" by the Arabs—has been cultivated since ancient times. Arrowhead or arrowleaf spinach is one of the prestige choices among gourmet chefs and is very popular in the United States, which is one of the world's biggest producers of spinach. In the 1920s, the vegetable was famously promoted as the strength-building food of the cartoon character Popeye the Sailor. (In fact, the absorption of spinach's high nutritional content, particularly iron, is inhibited by its oxalic acid levels.)

Often grown as a "baby" variety, hybrids of arrowhead spinach include Razzle Dazzle and Bordeaux. The latter has red stems that turn green with cooking. Some takes on the classic French *mesclun* or spring mix of green leaves include arrowhead spinach. It is also excellent on its own. New World chefs unite the leaves with any number of ingredients, including cherries, Mandarin oranges, cashews, and even wasabi dressing. Wilted arrowleaf spinach is also a popular base for any number of other ingredients from venison to shellfish. **SH**

Swiss Chard

This tall leafy vegetable with thick, crunchy red, white, or yellow stalks and wide green fan-shaped leaves is grown widely throughout France's Rhône valley and used in many Mediterranean cuisines. This ancient plant, however, has no known connection to Switzerland.

Swiss chard is a member of the beet family, as shown by its scientific name, *Beta vulgaris cicla,* and is probably the plant that Aristotle wrote about in the fourth century BCE under the name of beet. Other names include chard, leaf beet, seakale beet, white beet, and spinach beet.

The vegetable has a long history in Arab cuisines—it was quite possibly grown in the hanging gardens of ancient Babylon—and was an ingredient in many ancient Roman dishes. Today, it is widely used in Italy, sometimes as part of the filling in *tortelli di erbette*. The French use it to make *tourtes des blettes*, a sweet or savory tart. Swiss chard, raw or quickly sautéed, pairs well with beets and carrots in salads and can successfully be used in most recipes calling for greens. **SH**

Taste: *Unlike older variants of spinach with a stronger edge, arrowleaf spinach has a delicately sweet flavor. The Razzle Dazzle hybrid is especially mild tasting.*

Taste: *Spinach lovers adore Swiss chard. The leaves have a mild, sweet flavor that is reminiscent of spinach, but slightly bitter. The stalks can be compared to asparagus.*

The stems of rainbow chard might even tempt vegetable-shy children to try them. ›

Shungiku

The chrysanthemum is Japan's national flower. In autumn, chrysanthemum shows are held all over the country, while outsize dolls made entirely of the flowers used to be a common sight. Nevertheless, this does not deter the Japanese from eating a particular variety. Shungiku, the young leaves of the garland chrysanthemum (*Glebionis coronarium*) add a taste of the East to any food. As with arugula, there are two types: a smaller, stronger, "wild" style with serrated leaves, and a milder type with broad leaves. Most varieties fall somewhere in between.

Young tender leaves can be eaten raw, or used in tempura, but mostly they are boiled and then refreshed in cold water. They are a key ingredient in *sukiyaki* and other stewed dishes, to which they are added at the last minute. Boiled, they can be served *o-hitashi* style with soy sauce or vinegar. In China, under their Cantonese name, *tong ho*, they are used in soups, stir-fries, and salads. The flowers are also edible and often used as a garnish. The petals, the best of which come from Aomori prefecture, are also dried and sold in thin flat sheets called *kikunori*. **SB**

Uzouza Leaf

Harvested from a wild evergreen climbing plant in the rain forest, the uzouza leaf is one of the most popular green leafy vegetables in Nigeria. It is also eaten in other Central African countries, where it is known by various names; in English it is sometimes called wild spinach. The leaf is collected in the wild by rural communities, rather than cultivated, and then sold in markets across the region. The leaves are also exported to the United States and Europe for sale in African grocery stores.

Before being cooked, the leaves are cut into thin strips by rolling them and using a sharp knife to shave the ends into thin strips. The leaves are light green when fresh, and darken when dried or frozen. In Nigeria, the leaves are eaten raw in vegetable salads mixed with palm oil. The finely shredded leaves are also a common ingredient in hearty stews and soups such as the spicy fish and meat soup *ofe-owerri* and melon seed soup or *egusi*. In Cameroon and the Central African Republic, the leaves feature in a stew made from beef and greens in a peanut sauce. **CK**

Taste: *The earthy, tangy taste has a slight bitterness like the scent of chrysanthemums. Both taste and texture are coarser than spinach, for which it can be substituted.*

Taste: *Aromatic and almost sweet smelling, pale green uzouza leaves have a delicate taste similar to that of spinach.*

Chrysanthemums flourish in the shade of snow-capped Mount Fuji, Japan.

Bok Choy

Celtuce

Bok choy belongs to the large brassica family of plants, which includes other vegetables popular in Asian cooking such as mustard greens and Napa cabbage, as well as broccoli, Brussels sprouts, and kale. It has as many different spellings—*pak choi* and *bak choi* are two of the most common—as it boasts different varieties. Trying to figure them all out can confuse even a botanist. Some have lighter green leaves and thicker stems; with others the leaves are heavily veined with white, and the sizes can range from just over 1 inch (2.5 cm) up to 8 inches (20 cm). Bok choy, however, generally has a distinctive appearance: green, ruffled leaves contrast sharply with the smooth, juicy white stems that give the vegetable its name (the word transliterated *bak*, *pak*, or *bok* is Cantonese for "white").

The attractive white-green contrast means the vegetable is often cooked whole, while slightly larger ones are halved or quartered lengthwise. The stems are juicy and crunchy, whereas the thin leaves wilt quickly when cooked. Bok choy can be boiled, steamed, stir-fried, and used to fill dumplings. **KKC**

Also known as stem lettuce and asparagus lettuce, celtuce (*Lactuca sativa* var. *asparagina*) originated in China and is sometimes called Chinese lettuce. It is grown mainly for its thick, tender stem, but its romainelike leaves can also be eaten. In spite of its name, it is not a cross between lettuce and celery. In China, it is known as *wosun* or *woju*.

When peeled to remove the bitter, milky sap in its outer edges, the stem can be sliced or diced and eaten raw in a salad or cut into pieces and served with a dip. In China, the stems are broiled or boiled, added to soups and used in stir-fries with meat, poultry, or fish. The Chinese also pickle celtuce. The stem can also be cooked and served like broccoli. Young, tender celtuce leaves can be added to salads or lightly sautéed. Once the plant has matured, the milky sap makes the leaves bitter and inedible.

Celtuce is grown as a commercial crop in China. It is believed to have been brought to the United States in the 1940s by a missionary. In the rest of the world, it is not widely known and is grown mostly in home gardens. **SH**

Taste: *The flavor of all bok choys are subtle compared to many other types of brassica—mildly sweet and sometimes with a faintly bitter undertone.*

Taste: *When cooked the stem tastes like a cross between squash and artichoke. Raw, it is crisp, moist, and mild flavored. The young leaves have an endivelike bitterness.*

Pristine, freshly harvested bok choy on
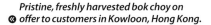 *offer to customers in Kowloon, Hong Kong.*

Melokhia

Although the leaves of the melokhia plant are eaten as a vegetable in many parts of the world, including the Middle East and South America, it is in Egypt that melokhia has been an important staple of the national diet since the time of the pharaohs.

Made into a wholesome soup called simply melokhia, the dish is still prepared in the same way as depicted in ancient tomb paintings. For centuries, generations of Egyptian women have balanced pots of the popular dish on their heads, carrying it out at lunchtime to their menfolk toiling in the fields.

In street markets in Cairo, the serrated-edged leaves are sold fresh, but for any expatriate Egyptian longing for a taste of home, they are exported dried, canned, and frozen. Fresh leaves need to be washed, dried, and finely chopped before simmering in water for about ten minutes. The most basic soup is simply melokhia leaves cooked in a light vegetable stock, but in Syria and Egypt a thicker version is made using chicken stock. Bread is put in bowls and piled with rice and small pieces of boned chicken, before the thick melokhia broth is spooned over. **WS**

Taste: *Melokhia leaves have a slightly bitter flavor similar to sorrel. When cooked they become glutinous, and have been described as a cross between okra and spinach.*

Turnip Green

The turnip (*Brassica rapa rapifera*) is one of the earliest cultivated vegetables. Traditionally, turnip greens, or turnip leaves, were a seasonal vegetable, available only when the turnip crop was thinned out in spring. Plants are now cultivated exclusively for their leaves both in the United States and Europe.

Typically light green, thin, and hairy, turnip greens feature in many traditional soul food dishes of the South, such as when they are cooked in a broth with a small portion of ham hock or salt pork for seasoning. They are also a feature of southern European recipes, particularly in the cooking of northern Portugal's Trás-os-Montes e Alto Douro region. The rustic cuisine of this mountainous area is characterized by strong flavors; here turnip greens are combined with *alheira*—a type of sausage made from meat other than pork—and with cod. In neighboring Galicia, in Spain, the leaves are served with pork, while farther south in Portugal they appear in soup and rice dishes, and as a side dish for fried mackerel. In the Apulia region of Italy, turnip greens are included in pasta dishes. **DM**

Taste: *Generally served boiled, the pungent leaves have a slightly bitter flavor, rather like mustard greens, which becomes milder with cooking.*

Turnip leaves flourish under protective netting on a farm in Suffolk, England. »

Rock Samphire

Marsh Samphire

Rock samphire (*Crithmum maritimum*) grows in nooks and crevices along the seashores of Europe. Edgar in Shakespeare's *King Lear* described harvesting it as a "dreadful trade," presumably because it involved dangerous clinging to cliff edges. In fact, it grows in more accessible areas, too.

In the seventeenth century, rock samphire was hugely popular in England. During the eighteenth century, it was used mainly as a pickle: in *Food For Free* (1972) author Richard Mabey described it being covered in spiced vinegar and left in a cooling baker's oven over the weekend. It was still popular in the nineteenth century, but dropped out of fashion, despite enjoying a brief revival in the late twentieth century.

As with other wild plants, it is best gathered early in the season when the pointed leaves are still tender. Later the texture becomes coarse and the resinous odor overpowering. The leaves are mainly used as a garnish, a side dish, a pickle, or in a mixed seafood salad. The unusual flavor requires discreet handling to prevent it from dominating a dish. **MR**

Very different from its rocky namesake, this bright green vegetable, shaped like lots of miniature Arizona cacti, flourishes in the mud of salt marshes around the coastlines of England, France, and the Low Countries. Collecting and cleaning it is a messy and time-consuming business, but as soon as the first shoots emerge in June the foraging begins.

Marsh samphire (*Salicornia europaea*) probably takes its name from the old French term, *l'herbe de Saint Pierre*, but is also known as glasswort, and was once used in glassmaking. Today, samphire and its relatives are seen as plants of the future because they will grow in salty conditions.

At the start of the season samphire can be eaten raw, but the saltiness is too much for many. It can be pickled, but this destroys the subtle green salinity. Blanched, it works well in light salads, and is the perfect seasonal partner to summer trout. In places where demand for samphire outstrips the local harvest, cultivated varieties are imported from Israel and the Gulf; *Salicornia virginica*, a related species, is harvested in the United States. **AMS**

Taste: *Lightly cooked, rock samphire is crunchy, but also, despite its saltiness, juicy. Its vaguely perfumed taste has been compared to carrots, but is individual and powerful.*

Taste: *Blanched without salt, dressed with butter, and eaten by pulling the succulent flesh off with the teeth, this briny delicacy lives up to its nickname "sea asparagus."*

Resilient to salt and drought, samphire is likely to have greater economic importance in the future. ❯

Dandelion

The French name for dandelion, *pissenlit*, echoes its seventeenth-century English name, "piss-a-bed." Its contemporary English name derives from the French *dent de lion* (lion's tooth), a reference to its serrated leaves. This edible weed (*Taraxacum officinale*), a relative of endive, is, of course, popularly known as a diuretic, but it is also a salad green. The white dandelion was cultivated in Flanders in the dark, in the same way as the poetically named endive *barbe de capucin* ("monk's beard"). It is a seasonal specialty at its best in March. Both the wild and cultivated kinds occur in salads, particularly *salade aux lardons*, where the leaves are mixed with just-fried bacon and a dressing of hot fat and vinegar.

The difference between wild and cultivated dandelion lies in the flavor. Except in the case of the youngest, most tender leaves, wild dandelion is bitter, to the point where it becomes unpleasant, whereas blanched leaves are much milder. Dandelion flowers, picked in spring, can be made into a golden, sweet preserve: *cramaillotte*, halfway between a honey and a jelly. **MR**

Taste: Dandelion leaves have a bitterness that blends well with other, gentler salad leaves. The leaves can also be cooked in much the same way as spinach.

Wild dandelions attract many insects due
❀ *to their high levels of pollen and nectar.*

Nettle

Widespread and abundant in northern states and throughout Europe, the leaves of stinging nettles, with their serrated edges and hairy surfaces, are among the most common sight in the wild and along roadsides. The sting derives from formic acid, and it is this that makes nettles so difficult to treat as a vegetable: gloves are essential during harvesting and preparation, although cooking destroys any chance of being stung.

Nettles flourish throughout the spring and summer, dying down in autumn, but are only edible in the spring when the leaves are tender. Then, they can be boiled or wilted or made into a soup—such as those enjoyed today in Ireland, Scandinavia, and Tibet. Later they turn bitter. (When the English diarist Samuel Pepys wrote of eating "nettle porridge" in 1661, he was probably describing a thick soup.)

The use of nettles in ethnic cuisines is often disguised by the generic term "wild greens," for example in Greek cooking where the term *hortes* often includes nettle and dandelion leaves. In Italy, nettles are added to rustic risottos or frittatas. **MR**

Taste: Although likened to spinach, nettles have a marked tang reminiscent of iodine. Freshly blanched, they have a bright green color unlike any other leaf vegetables.

Wild Garlic Leaf

Fiddlehead

Wild garlic, also known as ramsons, appears in early spring over much of Europe, usually in damp woodland. Its Latin name, *Allium ursinum* (bear garlic), might reflect the fact that it appears around the time when bears emerge from hibernation.

Wild garlic bulbs are edible, but better left in the ground. Although the starry white flower spikes that appear once the leaves are past their best are flavorsome and beautiful, it is the young, slender leaves that appeal to cooks, including renowned chefs, such as Marc Veyrat and Michel Bras. In Italian cuisine, wild garlic leaves flavor frittatas, are pounded to make a type of pesto, and appear in stuffings and soups. Belgians chop them finely and mix them with fromage blanc. The tender leaves can also be added in small amounts to green salads.

What makes wild garlic leaves so attractive to cooks and chefs is their intense bright green color after they have been blanched in boiling water. Some chefs also dry them, grind them to a powder with a little salt, and utilize the results as a versatile seasoning year-round. **MR**

Fiddleheads are a herald of the long-awaited New England spring. Tightly coiled, the bright green early shoots of the ostrich fern (*Matteuccia struthiopteris*) make their brief appearance each April and May. They take their name from their remarkable resemblance to the scrolled neck of a violin.

Although increasingly available in grocery stores in the northern United States and Canada, fiddleheads remain a wild plant and are foraged rather than farmed. Harvesting must happen before the tightly coiled head unfurls, making the plant inedible, and the perishable young shoots are best eaten as soon after picking as possible.

Caution should be taken when foraging: some varieties of fern are dangerous and bracken shoots, although eaten as *warabi* in Japan, have been considered carcinogenic. Fiddleheads should not be eaten raw. They are traditionally boiled or steamed and then blanched, after which they are often sautéed in butter and served as a side dish: they are frequently added to salads or soups. In New Zealand, koru shoots are a similar delicacy. **CLH**

Taste: Pureed wild garlic leaves taste less assertive than cultivated garlic bulbs, with a hint of chives. While garlicky, they do not have the strong odor of garlic.

Taste: Fiddleheads are best eaten on the day they are picked. They have a gentle taste with hints of asparagus and earthy artichoke, and are tender to the bite.

Fiddleheads take their name from their close resemblance to the scrolled neck of a violin. »

Bean Sprout

Wild Rice Stem

The young, tender sprouts of germinated beans have long been used in Chinese and Southeast Asian cuisines. Two types are preferred: those grown from mung beans, and those from soybeans. The former, which are usually shorter and stubbier, will have a little green "head" from the sprouted mung bean; soybean sprouts are longer and fatter, and the bean at the end is pale yellow.

Mung bean sprouts, which have a more delicate flavor, are more common; like soybean sprouts, they have a high water content and keep for only a few days in the refrigerator before they start to turn limp, brown, and mushy. Chefs remove the head—and often, the thin, tendril-like tail—leaving only the straight, white shoot to be cooked.

Bean sprouts are highly nutritious, making them an important part of the vegetarian diet in China and other parts of Asia. In some Western countries, a rainbow of different types of sprouts are available from whole-food stores—from alfalfa and radish to chickpeas and azuki beans—along with "sprouters" that enable the beans to be cultivated at home. **KKC**

There are four species of wild rice (*Zizania*) that are common to Asia and North America. The grass grows in swamps, stagnant shallow water, shallow water at the edges of small lakes, and slow-flowing streams. Its flowering head is visible above the water and it is traditionally harvested by canoe.

Manchurian wild rice (*Zizania caduciflora*) is cultivated in China for its round, crisp, white stem that is eaten as a vegetable. The stem is tough and requires the cultivation of a parasitic smut fungus (*Ustilago esculenta*) to turn it into the delicacy *chiao-pai* meaning "sticky shoot." The rice is harvested from 120 to 170 days after planting, when the stem starts to swell and before the fungus turns it black and the rice begins to deteriorate.

Wild rice stems have a nutty flavor reminiscent of coconut. They are usually served parboiled and then sautéed with other vegetables. They are also popular when served with soups and rice wine: the stem is cut into pieces, crushed, scalded, and soaked in cold water before being added to the soup and rice wine, and then simmered. **CK**

Taste: *Raw bean sprouts have a slightly grassy nuttiness. Overcooking makes them soggy, but cooked to perfection they are crisp, slightly earthy, and delicately sweet.*

Taste: *Wild rice stems have a mild, nutty flavor that tastes similar to coconut. They absorb flavors well and are commonly served with shredded meat.*

Hop Shoot

Bamboo Shoot

The hop (*Humulus lupulus*) is native to Europe and its flowers flavoured beer long before they became central to the business of brewing. The tender vine shoots of wild hops, tipped with buds like asparagus tops, were prized by the Romans and have been eaten as a vegetable since the Middle Ages. The first shoots are now grown as a luxury crop, and are the most expensive vegetable sold today. The British nickname "poor man's asparagus" is, therefore, somewhat inappropriate for this green spring truffle.

The season is extremely short, limited to the early spring when the new shoots poke their tips out of the ground. They grow rapidly, up to ½ inch (1 cm) an hour in warm conditions, and are pruned when they reach about 8 inches (20 cm) long. With their passion for good beer, the Belgians have a wide repertoire of dishes centred on hop shoots. In the past these tended to be quite heavy, involving elements such as a thick onion sauce (*sauce soubise*) or gratination. In modern cuisine, the shoots have been treated more simply or as a garnish. **MR**

It is strange that a plant that provides scaffolding for construction is, when young, delicate enough to be eaten as a vegetable. It is not only pandas that value bamboo shoots. The tender stems of the family of giant grasses are highly prized in China, Japan, Korea, Southeast Asia, and the Himalayas, and appear in dishes from curries to salads. They may be sold fresh, pickled, salted and dried, or canned.

Freshly harvested, bamboo shoots range from thinner than a pencil to about 3 inches (8 cm) in diameter. Bought fresh, they must be peeled of many layers of husk to reach the pale, edible core. Because some varieties contain a toxin that is destroyed by cooking they should never be eaten raw: blanch for several minutes in lightly salted water.

In many places with large Chinese communities, fresh bamboo shoots are available year-round: the best ones are the winter shoots, followed by spring varieties, then the summer kind. All canned shoots should be rinsed to rid them of their "tinned" taste. Whole pieces are preferable to sliced, and those labelled as winter shoots are best of all. **KKC**

Taste: *Lightly boiled, they have a texture reminiscent of spaghetti. Their taste has a note of the bitterness that hops give to beer, but is tempered by a pleasant sweetness.*

Taste: *The texture of blanched fresh bamboo shoots is moist but with a pleasant crunch, and the taste is slightly sweet, with subtle grassy, chlorophyll notes.*

Vaucluse Green Asparagus

Set in the heart of Provence, the Vaucluse enjoys an unique status for the quality of its fruit and vegetables, due partly to tourism, but also to a climate that has adapted to growning outstanding raw materials. As a species the green Vaucluse asparagus is no different from those grown elsewhere and its production is relatively recent. In his autobiography, written in the early twentieth century, the great chef Auguste Escoffier noted that in Provence all asparagus were white until he persuaded the farmers in Lauris to switch to green.

Green asparagus from the Luberon area of the Vaucluse is mainly grown in greenhouses or polytunnels so it can be brought to market early in the year—the season can start in February. The spears (the French refer to the stems as *turions*) are left to grow out of the ground to a height of no more than 1 foot (30 cm) before they are cut off just below the surface of the soil. The secret of their taste lies in eating them (boiled in a steep-sided pan that allows them to stand upright) within a day of picking, after which they start to loose their sweetness. **MR**

Bassano White Asparagus

In the spring, asparagus fever hits the pretty town of Bassano del Grappa, in northern Italy. The wonderful white asparagus grown here has a unique flavor: so much so it carries a DOC.

A member of the lily family, asparagus has been grown in Bassano for many years: it was valued as a delicacy before Roman times. In the early sixteenth century, or so the story goes, a devastating hailstorm destroyed the town's asparagus crop. Faced with such destruction, the farmers had little choice but to harvest the part of the plant that remained underground. The shoots were white because they lacked exposure to sunlight, but the asparagus was tender and flavorsome. The thrilled farmers decided to cultivate the whole plant underground from that point on.

In late May every year, Bassano hosts its a festival to celebrate its most prized crop. Farmers present their asparagus on the streets, while restaurants compete in *A Tavola con l'Asparago DOC di Bassano* to create a spectacular succession of courses involving the beloved white asparagus. **LF**

Taste: *Green asparagus should be firm and veering toward al dente in texture. Its color should be intense. Its characteristic taste is slightly sweet with a hint of sulfur.*

Taste: *The long, chubby spears have a notable succulence. The elegant, restrained sweetness is very remarkable: it opens up over the entire tongue with each mouthful.*

These shoots of green asparagus illustrate
❸ ***how the tips and scales can deepen to red.***

Angelica

Purple Sprouting Broccoli

Tall, waving fronds of musky-scented angelica (*Angelica archangelica*) line the banks of the ancient waterways that crisscross the swampy wilderness of Marais Poitevin, a marshy area close to Niort, in France's Poitou-Charente region. This land provides the damp soil essential for the plant's growth. For centuries the people living there relied on the healing powers of angelica as an antidote to poisons.

A member of the parsley family, angelica is also grown in Italy, Scotland, Germany, Scandinavia, Russia, and parts of North America, although it is mainly cultivated in France. It is one of the few plants to withstand the harsh climates of Iceland, Greenland, and the Faroes, where it is still cooked and eaten as a vegetable. The fresh leaves can also be shredded in salads and used in omelets and fish dishes, whereas the stems are often stewed with rhubarb or made into preserves and jams.

The most common use of angelica today, however, is as a candied confection for use in cakes, sweet breads, cheesecakes, or cut into diamond shapes as a decoration for sweetmeats. **WS**

A sturdy and substantial brassica, broccoli is a traditional winter vegetable in many countries: yet, it reaches its peak when young and newly budded in the spring. Like the cauliflower—to which it is botanically related—broccoli is a type of cabbage, topped with clusters of tiny buds that can range in color from yellowish white to a very deep purple through various shades of green. The vegetable was almost certainly developed in Italy (the Italian name means "little shoots"). As its early French name of Italian asparagus shows, the stems were enjoyed along with the flower heads.

Today, popular varieties are grown to produce the largest, most compact, and most consistently colored flowering head, although the varieties that were historically popular are returning to favor. With their small, dark flower heads, crisp but tender stems, and relatively delicate upper leaves, purple sprouting broccolis provide infinitely more flavor than blander mass market varieties, and are enjoyed whole, perhaps with butter or a dipping sauce, such as the Italian *bagna cauda*. **FC**

Taste: *Fresh angelica leaves and stems taste of licorice. The leaf stems can be blanched and eaten like celery. After crystallization the stems turn a glorious acid green.*

Taste: *The blanched heads of purple sprouting broccoli have a meaty flavor, crisp texture, and slightly bitter, ferrous aftertaste. The tender stems are slightly sweeter.*

Immature flowers form the heads of purple sprouting broccoli. »

Brussels Sprout

At their most flavorful and most widely available from September to March, Brussels sprouts (*Brassica oleracea*) are one of those foods you either love or hate. A member of the same family as cabbage, kale, broccoli, and other strong-flavored vegetables with an equally assertive aroma, their tightly packed leaves make them look like tiny cabbages. Most are green, although a few varieties are purple.

Probably brought to Belgium by the Roman legions and most likely served at the medieval Burgundian court at Lille, Brussels sprouts have been grown near Brussels for more than four centuries. Today, they are also cultivated in the United States, England, and across northern Europe.

Brussels sprouts lend themselves to many cooking methods—steamed and dressed with balsamic vinegar and Parmesan cheese, or served with cream or cheese sauces. They are a traditional Christmas dinner dish in England, and are often paired with chestnuts along the lines of the French and Belgian *bruxelloise*, a garnish of stewed Brussels sprouts, braised endive, and potatoes. **SH**

Taste: *Brussels sprouts are best fresh and cooked until they are tender. Then, they have a sweet taste like young cabbage. Smaller is best as large ones can be bitter.*

Kohlrabi

Although considered in many countries an Asian vegetable, kohlrabi originated in northern Europe, and the unusual name is German in origin. It means cabbage-turnip and, like the common cabbage, broccoli, and Brussels sprouts, this curious vegetable is a subspecies of *Brassica oleracea* (var. *gongolydes*). Kohlrabi is grown for its swelling, globe-shaped stem that resembles a turnip, yet appears just above the ground: it can be greenish-white or purple. The few cabbagelike leaves grow off long shoots above the globe. Those of young plants are edible, although mature leaves, like mature globes, are more traditionally used as animal fodder.

The globe can be diced and used in a stir-fry. It is often added to soups in China, and in Italy is sometimes made into a soup with rice. It is good mashed with potatoes, or pureed with butter. The youngest bulbs can be eaten raw, simply peeled and cut into matchsticks to add to a salad or a slaw. When very fresh and green, the leaves can be removed from their stems, blanched, sauteed, and dressed with a little lemon juice or vinegar. **SH**

Taste: *Kohlrabi bulbs that are no larger than a tennis ball are the mildest and sweetest, and taste like broccoli stems with a hint of radish. When raw, the taste is peppery.*

Red Cabbage

It is hard to imagine the cooking of the Scandinavian countries, Germany, Hungary, Poland, and other Eastern European states without red cabbage. This heading cabbage, much like its green and white cousins except in color, has been a long-standing staple in the cuisines of these countries, in part because it grows in cold weather. In the past, it was a survival food for many during the long and difficult winter months. Although perhaps peasant by reputation, with its shiny, dark magenta leaves, red cabbage actually makes for an elegant presentation. Since the color is only in the outer skin and stem, when cut it makes a pretty picture of red and white.

Red cabbage can be cooked just like green cabbage, but It has developed a group of recipes particular to itself. In the Ukraine, it is combined with apples, raisins, sugar, vinegar, and other vegetables to make a sweet-and-sour soup. Sweet-and-sour cabbage is a staple throughout Eastern Europe. *Rotkraut*, as it is called in Germany, is served with *sauerbraten*, a savory beef dish. A red cabbage preparation is served with ham in Sweden. **SH**

Taste: *There is little difference in flavor between red and green cabbage. Both are tender and juicy, although red cabbage is slightly more peppery.*

Braganza Cabbage

One of the more ancient vegetables that are still grown today, cabbages (*Brassica oleracea*) have most likely been cultivated since before recorded history. With its thick, chardlike stem and large, delicate, flaccid green leaves, Braganza cabbage is somewhat like the sea cabbages that grow wild along European coastlines. It has crinkly leaves that are loose, rather than forming a head, so it belongs to the group of cabbages known as Savoy.

Braganza cabbage goes by several other names: sea kale cabbage, Portugal cabbage, or (in Portugal) *couve tronchuda*. Its flavor is sweet, and its leaves hold up well to cooking, retaining both color and texture better than other varieties. Braganza cabbage is delicious steamed or braised, and it is the preferred choice of the Portuguese when they prepare their national dish *caldo verde*—a soup of vegetables, spicy linguiça sausage, and shredded Braganza. Many people associate the soup with kale, but the flavor of Braganza is much more distinctive. The young leaves can be served raw in salads, while the stems are often stir-fried. **LF**

Taste: *The fleshy leaves of Braganza cabbage have an exquisite, slightly sweet flavor, avoiding the sulfuric undercurrents often found in compact-headed varieties.*

Elephant Garlic

Jersey Shallot

Even folk who have never heard the name of this jumbo bulb might have certain expectations of its taste. Each head can reach half a pound (250 g) or more in weight, while the name suggests a flavor that will trample tender taste buds like a herd of pachyderms. But *Allium ampeloprasum* contradicts every expectation, with a milder character that sits comfortably between the intensity of garlic and the subtlety of leeks. Botanically speaking, in fact, the fist-size bulbs are more closely related to leeks than garlic. Their origins can be traced to Eastern Europe and Asia, although current development is centered on the West Coast of the United States.

Perhaps the best use of these garden giants reinforces their mild character: gentle, slow roasting mellows and sweetens the taste yet further. Roasting also softens the flesh so it can easily be spread on toasts or used as a dip. Because of their size, the whole cloves can be sliced and sautéed in butter, allowing gentle caramelization of the natural sugars into faint memories of its overbearing common garlic cousins. **TH**

Like onions and garlic, shallots belong to the *Allium* family, but they are smaller and sweeter than an onion, much less pungent than garlic, and often the unsung heroes of the kitchen because of their ability to add a subtle but delicious flavor to all manner of savory dishes.

The Jersey shallot is one of two main varieties of shallot; the other being the gray shallot. Whereas the gray shallot is also referred to as the "true shallot," the poor Jersey shallot has been saddled with the rather unflattering alternative name of "false shallot." Fortunately, this is less about flavor and more about the fact that the pinky colored Jersey shallot has a more rounded bulb than its slightly milder cousin and was initially thought to be an onion simply impersonating a shallot.

Shallots are believed to have originated in central Asia more than 2,000 years ago. Crusaders returning from the Holy Land introduced them to Europe in the Middle Ages, where they became particularly prominent in French cuisine, flavoring such classic sauces as *beurre blanc* and *béarnaise*. **LF**

Taste: *Cooked, the mild garlic and onion character in both flavor and aroma is complemented by a marked sweetness. Raw, it is similar to common garlic.*

Taste: *Jersey shallots fuse the gentle flavors of sweet, red onion with suggestions of garlic. They are heavenly oven-roasted until caramelized and served as a vegetable.*

Elephant garlic grows near Gilroy in California,
⊙ *home of the annual Gilroy Garlic Festival.*

Rosé de Roscoff Onion

Maui Onion

So special are the fragrant, rose-colored Rosé de Roscoff onions (AOC) that they have not only a museum dedicated to them, but also their own two-day festival—the *Fête de l'Oignon Rosé*—to celebrate them, held every August in Roscoff, Britanny, when the pretty pink onions are harvested.

The onions first appeared on the shores of Brittany in the mid-seventeenth century, when monks brought seeds by boat from Portugal. The local microclimate—created by the combination of sandy soils, mineral-rich seaweed, and warming Gulf air streams—meant the onions flourished and before long a blossoming onion industry was born.

The good keeping qualities of these onions led agricultural laborers known as "onion Johnnies" to travel to Britain to sell the unique pink onions door-to-door. Dressed in berets and striped shirts, and riding bicycles strung with the onions, they helped create the stereotypical image of Frenchmen.

Mild and fruity enough to be eaten raw, Rosé de Roscoff onions are also superb cooked in many dishes, including in soups, tarts, and breads. **LF**

Among the sweetest of onions, the Maui is white to golden yellow, juicy, and grown only in the rich, red earth of Haleakala, a dormant volcano on the island of Maui in Hawaii. It is one of the smallest of the sweet onion species and the earliest to mature, usually coming to market from April to June. It has a flattened spherelike shape and a crisp texture.

First grown commercially by a cooperative of local farmers in 1943, these delicately flavored onions are harvested by hand and then left to cure in the fields and dry in the mild trade winds. They were known only on the island until tourists began taking them back to the United States mainland. However, they are still not as widely available as other sweet onion varieties.

Maui onion ponzu dressing for salads and meats is produced commercially in Hawaii. Reflecting the strong Japanese influence on Hawaiian cuisine, it is citrus based and made with Maui onions and soy sauce. The onions are a good addition to many Asian stir-fries and fish dishes. They are also excellent cut into rings, battered, and deep fried. **SH**

Taste: Mild and sweet and delightfully crisp, Rosé de Roscoff are especially tasty when they are slowly cooked or roasted, causing the natural sugars to caramelize.

Taste: All onions become sweeter when cooked, but Maui onions have a sweet, delicate flavor and none of the "hotness" of many other onions, even when raw.

Uprooted Maui onions are allowed to dry on the red volcanic soil. ❯❯

Scallion

In the lily family, the genus *Allium* represents onions as well as leeks and garlic. There are many types of onions, but scallions, also known as green onions or spring onions in Britain, are not one of them. They are the immature plant of many different kinds of globe or bulb onions.

Scallions were probably first used in China as long ago as 100 BCE and they remain an important part of many Asian dishes. They are prized not only for their white roots, where the bulb is just beginning to form, but also for their long, straight green leaves. In Asian cooking, scallions add a bite to stir-fries and are mixed with very finely chopped fresh ginger to make a condiment for seafood.

In the West, scallions are generally eaten raw, either on their own or incorporated into salads. When sliced, the bulb of a scallion separates into nearly transparent rings, and is often used as a garnish for salads and soups. Called *ciboules* in France, whole scallions often appear as crudités. They are also an integral ingredient of mixed antipasto platters. **SH**

Taste: *Sweet to spicy and sometimes slightly hot, scallions are less pungent than mature onions and have a savory onion taste. The leaves are milder than the bulb.*

*Spring onions, like most members of the **Allium***
*❸ **family, produce highly ornamental flower heads.***

Calçot

The party animals of the *Allium* family, these delicious Catalan onions that look like giant spring onions or undersized leeks are traditionally grilled or roasted over vine cuttings and served with punchy garlic-laden sauces at fabulous local feasts known as *calçotadas*. The original festival, held in January in the town of Valls, southwest of Barcelona, plays host to about 30,000 revelling onion enthusiasts: a must-do for any visiting onionophile.

Calçot de Valls are a special variety of onion— *Blanca Gran Tardía de Lleida* to be precise. They were created in Valls in the late nineteenth century by an enterprising farmer who planted white onions and, as the young bulbs started to appear, dug them up, then repeatedly replanted them, each time keeping them covered with a protective layer of earth. This process, known in Spanish as *calzar* or "putting their boots on," blanches the onions and gives them their sweet flavour. Those first humble beginnings developed into an industry that now produces more than 20 million calçots every year, and has earned European Union recognition. **LF**

Taste: *Eating calçots is a delicious ritual. Pull away the charred outer leaves to expose the tender, sweet onion within, then dunk quickly into garlic-laced sauces.*

Ramp

Bleu de Solaise Leek

Ramps, also known as wild leeks, wild onions, or wild garlic, are, like other onions, members of the lily family. They are highly prized for their combination of garlic and onion flavors.

Native to the mountains of eastern North America, ramps (*Allium tricoccum*) are among the first edible plants to appear in early spring before the forest canopy turns green. As one of the harbingers of spring, they were fêted by the early settlers who used them medicinally, and in the Appalachian region festivals still celebrate their arrival. Highly aromatic, ramps can be foraged for only a brief seasonal window, and so they are often frozen or pickled for later use.

Ramps can take up to seven years to mature, and are found in patches or colonies at heights over 3,000 feet (900 m). With their white bulbs they look a little like a scallion, albeit one with a purplish stem and broader leaves: all parts of the plant are edible. The plant's growing popularity has caused over-harvesting in some areas, where ramps are now protected by legislation. **CLH**

The Bleu de Solaise leek (*Allium porrum*) is a chunky, Goliath of a leek. It is highly prized for both its fabulous flavor and its resistance to frosts, the latter of which is a valuable characteristic given it is a winter vegetable. Despite its very hefty dimensions, it has attractive, blue-gray-green swordlike leaves that turn violet in cold weather. A slow-growing heirloom variety, it originated around the French town of Solaise, near Lyon, on the eastern side of France, in the nineteenth century.

Tomb drawings indicate that leeks were grown in ancient Egypt. Nero, the artistically bent but much troubled Roman emperor, was given the nickname *Porrophagus*, or leek eater, because he believed eating leeks would improve his singing voice. The Romans introduced leeks to England and Wales, and although they are widely linked with those countries, France is one of the most important growers. Leeks are not really suitable for eating raw, but cooked they become tender and have a delicious flavor not as pronounced as the onion, although they belong to the same family. **LF**

Taste: *Sweet, but with pronounced flavors of both garlic and onion, ramps can be substituted for either in recipes. They are known for their strong and lasting aroma.*

Taste: *Bleu de Solaise leeks have a sweet yet mildly astringent flavor, similar to chives. A great base for soups, they are also exquisite teamed with cream and cheese.*

Early ramps push through the previous ⊗ *season's leaf fall after the snow has melted.*

Celery Heart

Florence Fennel

These slender, almost white inner ribs of celery are valued for their crunchy stalks, their fragrant leaves, and, in some quarters, their low caloric content. *Apium graveolens dulce,* the cultivated version of a white-flowered plant that grows wild in Europe and Asia, is a dieter's delight. Consuming and digesting a single rib generally burns more calories than the food itself contains.

Cooks, though, have long valued celery for its aromatic properties and, until half a millennium ago, it was a bitter, potent plant used more as a potherb than as a vegetable. The ancient Greeks used celery in garlands for their dead; the Romans wore celery garlands during drinking bouts for their strong fragrance, which masked less appealing aromas.

It was most likely the Italians who discovered celery's potential in the sixteenth century and began cultivating milder varieties. Today, these are a staple in stockpots and roasting pans, and widely cultivated in temperate regions throughout the world. The hearts are prized for their fresh, clean taste, and are less stringy than outer ribs. **SH**

Florence fennel, one of the three key manifestations of *Foeniculum vulgare,* is sometimes called bulb fennel. But it is not a bulb and it probably originated far from Florence in the Azores, volcanic islands stranded in the middle of the Atlantic.

The compact layered white or green fist that pokes out of the soil, with stalks protruding every which way, forms a versatile, licorice-flavored vegetable that developed from the wild herb. It is eaten both raw and cooked, in salads and braised, by itself and in composite dishes—it is often mixed with pasta. Perhaps on account of its sweetness, Florence fennel has an affinity with citrus flavors: many recipes call for a squeeze of lemon juice.

Although identified with Italy, where it is called *finocchio,* it is grown and eaten throughout Europe and the Americas. The wispy leaves are used as a herb, while the stems can be added to the barbecue and charred while grilling oily fish, such as sardines or mackerel. In fashionable restaurants, slender, tender "micro" fennel is served, simply split, boiled, and brushed with oil or butter. **MR**

Taste: *When raw, celery has a slightly, but pleasantly, bitter taste, reminiscent of parsley and anise. When fried, sautéed, or steamed, its flavor becomes a little milder.*

Taste: *The texture of raw fennel is crunchy, but long stewing renders it soft like celery. Its aniseed taste is distinctive yet mild and refreshing when eaten as a crudité.*

Fennel roasted in olive oil and balsamic vinegar is served as a side dish or added to soup recipes. »

Beauty Heart Radish

Chioggia Beet

Although the swollen stems of *Raphanus sativus* have been eaten the world over since prehistory, the origins of radishes are obscure. Historians tend to place them in western Asia. After the fall of the Roman empire, radishes disappeared from European literature, but they probably continued to grow.

Radishes come in many sizes, shapes, and colors. Among them the beauty heart radish—with its red flesh, white skin, and greenish shoulders—is one of the most distinctive. Known as *shinrimei* (meaning "beauty in the heart") in China, its other names include rose heart, Asian red meat, and red daikon. While related to the Japanese radishlike vegetable, the beauty heart is not a true daikon. It is also sometimes called watermelon radish, an apt name for when cut the radish looks like a slice of watermelon.

Because of their exceptional good looks, beauty heart radishes are valued sliced in salads and on sandwiches and as part of hors d'oeuvres platters. They can also be cooked like turnips and served with cream, or braised and sliced and added to stir-fries. In China, they are often pickled. **SH**

This heirloom variety of beet is strikingly pretty. Its magenta outer skin conceals an interior made up of concentric rings of alternating rose and white— hence its alternative names of bulls-eye beet or candy stripe beet—rather than the near-black color common to most beets. This arresting appearance is lost when cooked, so the beets are most often served raw. Beet (*Beta vulgaris*), or beetroot, evolved from wild sea beet, which grew around coastlines from Europe to India. Although in classical times the plant was valued more for its leaves than its roots, which were small, by the sixteenth century the spherical, bulbous root vegetable we know today had come into being, probably in Italy.

This beet takes its name from Chioggia, the coastal town on an island at the southern entrance to the Venetian lagoon, where it originated. Chioggia beet looks eye-catching when sliced crosswise and served raw in salads. When boiled, the colors bleed; roasting is a better alternative, but again affects the color. Cooking of any kind intensifies the sweetness, which is rather high. **LF**

Taste: *Unlike other radishes, beauty hearts get milder, not hotter, as they mature. Crisp, sweet, and mildly pungent, their outer edges are hotter than the colorful flesh inside.*

Taste: *Raw young Chioggia has a sweet, but faintly earthy, flavor with a crisp, juicy texture, and a subtle radishlike tang. Older roots have a more pronounced earthy flavor.*

Candy-striped and candy pink, Chioggia beets make a striking addition to any salad. ❯❯

Turnip

A European staple before potatoes had reached the Old World, turnips (*Brassica rapa*) were well established as a crop in early Greece and Rome. Later they were popular in Britain and northern Europe, whence they came to the United States in the early seventeenth century. They still account for considerable acreage in the United States, southern Europe, and Asia.

Small young turnips have always been more favored than their older, coarser siblings, and the current popularity of baby turnips is an extension of this trend. A member of the same family as cabbages and radishes, these crisp white roots are very different from the matured root vegetable.

Throughout the world, turnips are a flavorful addition to soups and stews. It is mostly in French and Asian cuisines, however, that they escape the pot of boiling water in favor of braising, roasting, sautéing, and stuffing. Tetlow turnips, named after the town in Germany where they originated, are considered a delicacy. *Kaku*, or Japanese turnips, are hotter, like radishes. **SH**

Jicama

A member of the legume family and native to Mexico and Central America, jicama (also known as the Mexican potato, yam bean, and Mexican turnip) is a versatile vegetable that until recently has been limited in popularity to only the regions of its origin. Now it has also found favor with North American and Chinese cooks, who appreciate its neutral flavor profile. In China, in particular, it is often an ingredient in stir-fries, although it can be used instead of water chestnuts in almost any Asian-style recipe.

In Mexico, its traditional home, the pleasingly crunchy jicama is regularly cut into matchstick-size pieces and used in salad. It is delicious eaten raw with a squirt of lime juice, a sprinkling of salt, and dash of cayenne pepper or dried chile flakes. It also goes well with fruit, and street vendors mix it with different melon chunks as a fruit salad.

Brown-skinned and shaped like a cross between a turnip and a beet, it can grow to weigh up to 50 pounds (25 kg), although most come to market no more than about 2 pounds (900 g). **SH**

Taste: *Baby turnips have a sweeter, more delicate taste than mature ones, which are harvested in autumn and can be musty. Raw, the texture is crisp and refreshing.*

Taste: *Jicama's crunchy and juicy white flesh has a bland flavor with a light sweetness similar to an apple or a pear. Although it looks starchy, there is no strong starch flavor.*

The edible part of a turnip root protrudes above the
⊘ *ground; a long taproot supplies it with nutrients.*

Celeriac

Arracacha

This winter vegetable, also called celery root or celery knob, is a type of celery (*Apium graveolens rapaceum*) that is grown solely for its tan to brown knobbly root. When peeled, it reveals an ivory white flesh with a firm, but not necessarily hard, texture. Believed to be derived from wild celery, celeriac was first cultivated in the Mediterranean area and gained popularity as a vegetable in the Middle Ages. Today, it is grown worldwide, although France, Germany, Holland, and Belgium are the main producers.

Related to carrot, parsnip, and fennel, celeriac should be peeled before using. Its leaves are usually discarded, but can be used as seasoning much like the leaves of its parent plant. Celeriac is popular in Europe, especially northern Europe, where it is cooked and combined with potatoes to serve as croquettes or a mashed dish. The French julienne the vegetable and sweat it with a little butter and sugar, but much of the European crop is pickled.

Celeriac is mostly underutilized in the United States and Great Britain. When a part of the menu, it is most often shredded or grated raw into salads. **SH**

Native to the New World, especially the Andes Mountains region, arracacha (*Arracacia xanthorrhiza*) was once a food of the Incas. It belongs to the same family as carrot, parsnip, and celery, but has never been widely cultivated because of its susceptibility to disease and its short shelf life once harvested. Nevertheless, this tasty tuber is grown in Brazil and in other parts of South America and the Caribbean.

Sometimes called a Peruvian carrot, arracacha looks like a large, white carrot. Although the young green stems can be boiled or eaten raw like celery, it is mainly used for its starchy root, which has a similar crisp texture to potato. The flesh ranges in color from white to light yellow or purple and emits a fragrant aroma when being cooked.

Arracacha is almost always cooked before it is eaten. The yellow-fleshed variety turns orange when cooked, making it a colorful ingredient. The roots can be boiled, baked, fried, or added to soups and stews. It is a common component in the hearty Andean stews known as *sancochos*, which are very popular in Colombia and Venezuela. **SH**

Taste: *Celeriac tastes like a cross between strong celery and parsley. The roots can be as large as a cantaloupe. The smaller the root, the milder the flavor.*

Taste: *Arracacha has a pleasantly mild, slightly sweet flavor that is a combination of celery, carrot, and parsnip with subtle hints of roasted chestnuts.*

Celeriac has great flavor and versatility, and makes a useful non-starch substitute for potatoes.

Chantenay Carrot

Parsnip

An heirloom carrot widely grown up until the 1960s, Chantenay or Chantennay carrots later lost favor commercially in the United Kingdom to larger mass-produced carrots. Fortunately, this squat sweet tasting variety has since made a strong comeback.

Wild carrots have grown throughout Asia and southern Europe for thousands of years. Early varieties were yellow, white, purple, or black, and the bright orange kind—a fine source of beta-carotene—was not developed until the seventeenth century by the Dutch. Chantenay carrots originated in France, probably in the late 1800s, when there are references to their medicinal use. Varieties include Royal Chantenay and Red Core Chantenay, and both are good for home growing.

Chantenays are shorter but thicker in girth than other carrots, but are not a "baby" carrot. Some have purple "shoulders." Although they are not always uniform in size and are sometimes gnarled and knotty, they always taste good. As versatile as any root vegetable, they can be boiled, steamed, or roasted, as well as eaten raw or juiced. **SH**

An old root vegetable, the parsnip was the potato of Europe before the potato came along—and at times its sugar, too. A member of the same family as parsley, carrots, and celery, the sweet root of *Pastinaca sativa* was used in medieval Europe both as a vegetable and as a starchy base for puddings.

The wild plant was probably native to the eastern Mediterranean and areas to the northeast, including the Caucasus, and was cultivated by the ancient Greeks. Although the Romans generally preferred carrots, it was probably they who introduced the parsnip to Britain. From there it spread to North America and Australasia in turn, although it is hardly grown at all in southern Europe.

Parsnips can be boiled, or added to soups and stews. (In Ireland, they were once used to make beer.) They make a nice alternative to mashed potatoes when boiled and mashed with butter, or pureed with cream and spices such as cinnamon or nutmeg. Added to the pan when roasting meat or poultry, the sugars caramelize to distinctive effect. Unlike carrots, parsnips are not eaten raw. **SH**

Taste: *Arguably the best tasting carrots grown, the Chantenay carrot is very sweet and is excellent for making carrot juice. The Red Core variety are the most delicious.*

Taste: *Parsnips taste a little similar to carrots, although they are more sugary with "rooty" undertones that are slightly reminiscent of turnips.*

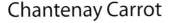

Sweet-tasting Chantenays need only to be scrubbed, not peeled, before eating.

Hamburg Parsley

Mooli

Ask a seasoned cook what they know about parsley and they will probably come up with two kinds: "curly" and "flat" leafed. Yet, Hamburg parsley (*Petroselinum crispum tuberosum*), although closely related to the latter, is more about the roots than the foliage. It originated in Germany during the sixteenth century and has been used there and in the Low Countries ever since. It is the magic ingredient in both the Flemish freshwater fish stew *waterzooi* and the Austrian boiled beef dish *tafelspitz*, a favorite of Emperor Franz Josef.

Hamburg parsley needs scraping or peeling before cooking, when it smells similar to lovage. While less aggressive than, say, horseradish, it is noticeably more potent than the parsnips or carrots it visibly resembles, with a taste that can be compared to celeriac, yet so strong it is better used as a flavoring rather than as a vegetable. Cooking softens the taste, but flavors the liquid in which it has simmered. Its ideal use is roasted in combination with other root vegetables, where it lifts their flavors without dominating them. **MR**

Most often found in Asian supermarkets or specialty food stores, daikon (also called mooli, or winter, Chinese, or Japanese radish) is a long, white root vegetable that looks something like an overweight carrot. It is a member of the radish family and can be used raw in much the same way. An important ingredient in the cooking of Korea, China, Japan, Vietnam, and India, where it is served raw, pickled, or cooked, daikon is believed to have originated in the Mediterranean. From there it traveled to China and then on to Japan.

The vegetable is grated and used in a variety of ways, including as a garnish for sashimi. Slices are also included in many stir-fries. In Japan, it is cooked with rice and fish stock as part of a piquant stew. *Muuch'ae kimchi* is a Korean pickled condiment made from daikon slices and seasonings. Often quite spicy, Westerners sometimes wash daikon down with a cold beer. Western chefs frequently use it as a garnish or ingredient in Asian-style dishes. It is also popular with vegetarians who value it for its low calorie content and high levels of vitamin C. **SH**

Taste: *The texture of cooked Hamburg parsley is very creamy, like overboiled carrot. The taste is a subtle amalgam of baby turnip, parsley, and celeriac.*

Taste: *Daikon has a crunchy texture similar to that of a radish, with a cool, sweet, and mildly peppery flavor. It has a pungency that resembles that of watercress.*

Salsify

Salsify, or *Tragopogon porrifolius*, is related to the daisy. The first part of its name, *Tragopogon*, refers to its species, goat's beard, while *porrifolius* alludes to its leeklike leaves. Native to the eastern Mediterranean, it is popular as a vegetable in Belgium and northern France, and often confused with its cousin *scorzonera*. True salsify looks a bit like a carrot, except that the skin is light gray or yellow, while scorzonera is dark gray and somewhat slimmer. Both are available from autumn to late spring.

Known as the "poor man's asparagus" because of its resemblance to white asparagus, salsify's chief drawback is its skin, which can be difficult to peel unless precooked. For this reason it is often sold already cooked in jars, then heated in butter before being served in French or Belgian *bistros* as an accompaniment to braised meats.

In Italy, both the leaves and shoots occasionally figure in salads. Meanwhile the Spanish, in addition to eating it, have traditionally held that salsify is an effective treatment for snakebites. **GM**

Taste: *Salsify has a vaguely smoky, nutty flavor and creamy texture; similar to the taste of white asparagus, but with a slight bitterness. It can cause flatulence.*

Golden Needle

Peering into almost any pot of soup in China is like looking into a culinary kaleidoscope. Names such as "Twelve Delights" or "Dragon's Dance" promise a host of different shapes, colors, textures, and flavors. One of the least familiar ingredients to Western eyes is golden needles or tiger buds, the fanciful names given to the long, thin buds of the fresh lily.

Traditionally harvested in the spring just before the flowers open, the buds of several species of *Hemerocallis* are now being force-cultivated over longer seasons to meet demand both in Asia and around the world. They range in color from a pale gold or orange in fresh sources to dark amber in dried versions. The latter require a brief soak before use, but excessively dry, brittle versions lack flavor.

The fresh buds can be tied into delicate knots to prevent them opening. They are often added to noodles and meats prepared over high heat, which releases their full aromatic potential. Their heady flavors complement fungi, particularly woodears and enokitake, and misos as well; these often appear together in recipes across China and Japan. **TH**

Taste: *Lily buds are faintly sweet with a musky flavor and aroma much like wild mushrooms. The pleasantly chewy texture is nearly as important as the taste.*

Bellflower Root

Lotus Root

Korean people describe the taste of their food as "pleasingly sour, sweet, hot, burning hot, salty, bitter, and nutty." The agreeable bitterness of their cuisine comes from ginger, ginseng, herbs, seeds, and certain vegetables, including a staple ingredient in Korean kitchens, the bellflower root. The root is also used in Japan and China, but mainly medicinally.

Called *toraji* in Korean, this long, milky white, earthy-looking root is in the same family as ginseng and looks similar. It has a crunchy, fibrous texture, and is available both fresh and dried. The raw roots need parboiling and rinsing to expel any excessive bitterness. The dried form is easily reconstituted in water and works equally well in cooking.

Bellflower root is most often prepared as one of the cooked or raw seasoned vegetables served at traditional family dinners. Bellflower root salad, a popular spicy cold dish, combines peeled strips of bellflower root along with salt, vinegar, red bell pepper, sesame oil, and seasonings. The root is also pickled, used in stir-fries, added to rice and noodle dishes, and pureed as a tasty pancake topping. **SH**

The lotus is revered in many parts of Asia. Although it grows in muddy ponds and lakes, the plant produces graceful, delicate flowers that rise proudly above their humble, less-than-pristine home: this represents the enlightenment one can achieve through spirituality.

The beautiful flowers and large, flat leaves of *Nelumbo nucifera* conceal long, thick segments of root—actually a rhizome. This has air chambers running through its length that form a delicate pattern when thinly sliced. Combined with its snow-white hue, this makes it an artistic ingredient for serving in salads or as a garnish; the holes can also be used to advantage during cooking, by chefs who stuff them with meat or glutinous rice.

Lotus root is eaten raw and cooked, in sweet and savory dishes; it can be dried, candied, ground into flour, or infused as a tea; it can be simmered for a long time without disintegrating, so it is often added to soups and stews. In Japan, lotus root is served in salads, stews, and as tempura; in Kashmir, under the name of *nedr*, it is often fried. **KKC**

Taste: *Korean cooks often flavor bellflower root with intense seasonings. Alone, it is earthy, faintly sweet, and a little bitter. Raw, its texture is crunchy and celerylike.*

Taste: *When raw, lotus root has a subtly sweet yet starchy taste like raw potato. The flavor becomes starchier as it cooks, but candying intensifies the sweetness.*

Lotus petals fall away to reveal the large seedhead. The dried seeds are important in East Asian cuisine. ❯❯

Gobo

In Japanese vegetable markets, the long brown taproots of great burdock (*Arctium lappa*) are piled high, encrusted with soil, and it is chiefly in Japan that burdock is eaten as a vegetable. Burdock tolerates a range of temperatures, so is available all over Japan under the name of gobo: Oura gobo, from Oura near Tokyo, has shorter, thicker roots with a hollow center, whereas Horikawa gobo, from the Kyoto region, has long thin roots.

Young, tender, tiny roots can be found in the pickle section of Japanese supermarkets. Although vacuum packed and colored a somewhat artificial orange, they are crunchy and delicious. Mostly, though, gobo is cooked. Do not peel, but scrub or lightly scrape the skin, to retain maximum flavor and goodness, then place it in acidulated water to keep the flesh white and lessen any bitterness.

A common method of preparation is to shave pieces from the tip of the root as if you are sharpening a pencil. These can then be sautéed in sesame oil and flavored with soy sauce and other aromatics to make the popular dish *kinpira*. **SB**

Taste: Gobo tastes earthy like Jerusalem artichoke. It softens on cooking, yet keeps just enough bite. A salad of cooked gobo, mayonnaise, and sesame is a revelation.

Sweet Potato

The root of a vine in the morning glory family, *Ipomoea batatas,* the sweet potato seems to have been eaten in Peru at least 10,000 years ago, and cultivated in its homeland of the tropical Americas since before the time of the Incas. Like other American tubers, it began its ascent to global popularity at the end of the fifteenth century.

Sweet potatoes come in a range of styles, with skin that varies from white to purple via orange, red, and brown, flesh along a continuum from white to red via orange, and texture that can be mealy, waxy, or simply mushy. Probably the most interesting kind are the sweet varieties with dark skin and bright orange flesh, such as Beauregard.

These nutrient-dense vegetables are always eaten cooked, and many like to accentuate their sweet, nutty flavor with cinnamon or nutmeg. Sweet potatoes are a Thanksgiving tradition and are also served sweetened in desserts, such as sweet potato pie. Roasted whole in their skins, they are a popular street food in parts of China and Japan. They are good baked and served with a little butter. **SH**

Taste: All sweet potatoes have a sweet, starchy taste, but Beauregards seem sweetest because of their softer, moister texture. Slightly nutty notes are evident.

Small plots of sweet potatoes, farmed by the Dani people of Indonesia as their staple food. ❯❯

Jerusalem Artichoke

Crosnes

Despite its name, the Jerusalem artichoke is not a member of the artichoke family and did not originate anywhere near Jerusalem. Native to the New World, *Helianthus tuberosus* is a tuber, and a member of the sunflower family, hence its alternative name, sunchoke. Some say its name originates from a mispronunciation of *girasole,* the Italian word for sunflower, coupled with the observation that its flavor resembles the globe or true artichoke. Its curious French title, *topinambour,* is a memento of a group of Brazilian Indians of the Topinambous tribe who were brought to France in 1613, creating a national sensation.

Packed with nutrients and relatively easy to grow, these awkward-shaped tubers have creamy white flesh. Their skin color varies, and most are knobbly, although varieties have been developed that are easy to peel. Jerusalem artichokes are good roasted, or in soups, or braised and served with butter and cream. The starch in Jerusalem artichokes is different to potato starch and not easily digestible by everyone. **SH**

About as long as a finger, these beady little tubers look somewhat like a caterpillar or a mismatched string of pearls. Although sometimes called Chinese artichokes, these are absolutely no relation of either globe artichokes or Jerusalem artichokes. They can also be known as knotroot or by their Japanese name, *chorogi.* The roots of *Stachys affinis,* a member of the mint family native to China and Japan, crosnes found their way from Beijing to France in the 1880s, when a man named Pailleux began growing them in his garden in the village of Crosnes. They retained some popularity until the 1920s, usually cooked in butter and then dressed with *fines herbes* or cream, but are now something of a curio.

Crosnes are still cultivated in China and Japan, where they are popular pickled. They had a renaissance in the United States at the beginning of the twenty-first century, where chefs serve them alongside everything from lobster to pork cheeks, and they are regaining some popularity in Europe. Their crunchy texture makes them a delightful snack when eaten raw and a good addition to salads. **SH**

Taste: *Raw, they are crisp like radishes, with a sweet and nutty flavor. Cooked, their texture is between Irish potatoes and roasted onions, and their flavor intensifies.*

Taste: *Not really an artichoke at all, crosnes (Chinese artichoke) has a sweet, nutty taste. Crisp, juicy, and a little peppery, the flavor offers hints of parsnip and apple.*

The Jerusalem artichoke's bright flower
◐ *accounts for its alternative name of sunchoke.*

Japanese Yam

Known in Japanese as *yamaimo* (mountain potato), and also as "mountain eel," the Japanese yam has been revered for its medicinal qualities in the Far East for thousands of years. In the past the Japanese have seen the long, juicy root as an aphrodisiac, suitable only for men.

A member of the large and sprawling yam family, *yamaimo* is unusual for a yam in that it is most often eaten raw. Grated into the form of *tororo*, it is served on top of a bowl of noodles or with rice, and eaten on the third day of January after the excesses of the New Year, apparently to aid digestion.

In Japan, there are two main varieties: the long, thin *nagaimo* and the fist-shaped *ichoimo*. The latter is slightly denser and less watery than *nagaimo*. It grows wild both in Japan and in the United States, but Japanese varieties are now widely cultivated, and harvested in winter. They can be found in Japanese markets, sometimes packaged in straw or sand to protect the delicate flesh during transport. *Yamaimo* flour is sometimes used as a binder in other foods. **SB**

Taste: *Raw, grated yam is very sticky—an acquired taste, but one worth acquiring. Thinly sliced, with soy sauce and wasabi, it is crisp and juicy. Cooked, it is gluey and soft.*

Taro

Also commonly called taro root or eddo, this ancient tuber might have been cultivated in India or Southeast Asia as early as 5000 BCE. It then spread to China, Japan, Egypt, and eventually Africa. Today, it is an important crop in all those places, as well as in Hawaii, the Caribbean, and other subtropical and tropical regions. Taro has many varieties and numerous names, but generally can be recognized by its dark brown hairy skin, which is similar to that of a coconut. Its flesh, colored white to light gray and sometimes pink, is very filling and highly nutritious, and must be cooked before eating.

In Hawaii, the purple-fleshed variety is pounded into a thick paste to make *poi*, and used as a side dish or cooking ingredient. Vegetarians like to thinly slice taro and fry it into chips. In the Caribbean, taro is made into soups and stews, including cream of taro soup. There and in Africa, the leaves from the taro plant are cooked and used like greens. Taro can be boiled, steamed, baked, deep-fried, or pureed and made into fritters. It must be eaten hot, because it gets very sticky when it cools. **SH**

Taste: *Taro has much more flavor than many other tubers. Its texture is similar to that of a white potato, but it has a nuttier and more earthy taste.*

A Hawaiian grinds taro into thick paste, poi, for use during the Establishment Day festival. »

Jersey Royal Potato

Ratte Potato

By the middle of the nineteenth century, Jersey, the largest of the British Channel Islands, was exporting 20,000 tons of potatoes to England. These potatoes were not, however, the variety for which the island is famous today. Around 1880, a farmer, Hugh de la Haye, acquired two outsize potatoes of uncertain origin from a store; he divided them into sixteen pieces, planted each piece, and exhibited the results at a local agricultural show. The editor of a St. Helier newspaper dubbed them the "Royal Jersey Flukes," implying the role luck had played in their discovery. The name stuck and the variety has never changed.

Small, kidney-shaped, and waxy, with a skin so thin it rubs off, the potato originally owed some of its quality to the rich Jersey soil, which was cultivated in the past with plentiful applications of seaweed, sometimes with additional guano. Today, the pressure to produce two crops a year and the use of chemical fertilizers mean not all Jersey Royal Potatoes (PDO) taste as good as they used to. They are best eaten immediately—freshly dug up and popped straight into the pot. **MR**

Rattes apparently earned their name from a shape that looks, arguably, like an earless rodent. When first introduced around 1872, however, these waxy potatoes had a more sympathetic name, Quenelles de Lyon. Like other French varieties they have evolved, and the finest quality is now identified with the Normandy strain, Rattes du Touquet. Produced in sandy soil along the coast from Calais to Abbéville, these small, elongated, yellow-skinned potatoes with firm, creamy flesh are planted in spring and harvested in late August and September.

Rattes are often identified with the buttery *purée de pommes de terre* of the chef Joël Robuchon, but show to best advantage in two classic recipes: sliced potatoes sautéed from raw with onions (*pommes lyonnaise*) and *gratin dauphinois*, in which thin slices are baked in cream with a hint of garlic. In these dishes their ability to keep their shape when cooked, allied to a depth of flavor, gives them an edge over other potato strains. Rattes, as a commercial variety, nearly became extinct a generation ago, but they are now grown in both North America and Europe. **MR**

Taste: *Boiled and then tossed in melted butter, Jersey Royals have a sweet taste and a distinctive firm texture. With their skin left on, there is a more earthy flavor.*

Taste: *The texture is dense, firm, resistant to breaking down, and yet smooth. Not sweet like new potatoes, rattes have a nutty taste, often likened to chestnuts.*

Pink Fir Apple Potato

Elongated, often knobbly, with pink skins and yellow, waxy flesh, these salad potatoes were developed in England in Victorian times, and are closely related in size and appearance to American fingerlings. In the nineteenth century English potato salads were considered sophisticated, mixed with red cabbage and beets, or cucumber, gherkins, and pearl onions or snipped chives, capers, and hard-boiled eggs.

The pink fir apple's origin is uncertain; there are suggestions it was already being imported into America in 1850 by British settlers, but it was only officially recognized as a variety there about 1870. During the twentieth century, it was not grown commercially, but survived precariously in private gardens, notably the country home of André Simon, president of the Wine and Food Society, in England.

Best enjoyed with its skin on, this potato owes its revival to the charitable organization now known as the Henry Doubleday Research Association or Garden Organic, also in England. This charity works to restore heritage crops by collecting plant seeds and making them available to the public. **MR**

Taste: *Thickly sliced, pink fir apple potatoes are nutty, earthy, and full of flavor. They taste significantly better when eaten freshly dug from the ground.*

Peruvian Purple Potato

The versatile spud has a humble appearance, except when it is garbed in royal colors. Peruvian purple potatoes—purple both inside and out—are a food fit for royalty, and, indeed, legend has it that when harvested, they were kept for the Inca kings.

Some believe Peruvian purples are the grandfathers of all potatoes. Potato cultivation in what is today southern Chile is thought to date from 5000 BCE. Europeans did not encounter potatoes until the sixteenth century, when Spanish colonists in the New World described them as "truffles."

Peru has been dubbed the potato capital of the world, for its array of different sizes, shapes, and colors. Peruvian purples get their color from the same antioxidant that makes blueberries blue. They are an heirloom member of the fingerling family of potatoes. Not to be confused with Okinawan or Hawaiian purple potatoes, which are actually sweet potatoes, Peruvian purples bring a touch of the exotic to the table. They can be cooked as other potatoes, but are impressive sliced into salads, made into french fries, or served as a colorful mash. **SH**

Taste: *Similar in taste to round red, round white, or other waxy potatoes, but with more complexity and depth of flavor, Peruvian purples have an earthy, creamy texture.*

Black Périgord Truffle

White Alba Truffle

Although synonymous with them today, the Périgord region of southwest France was never the main source of the famed "black diamonds"—*Tuber melanosporum*. It was more of a processing hub for those found elsewhere, mainly in Provence around Carpentras. Like its sister fungus, the white Alba truffle, a symbiotic relationship with a host tree is essential to the truffle's slow ripening underground. The hunting season lasts from November to February.

Rossini called truffles the "Mozart of the kitchen" and they are a key flavoring and aromatic tool in haute cuisine. Gnarled and black on the outside, not unlike shagreen to the touch, gray and veined on the inside, they should not be confused with cheaper, less-perfumed varieties such as *Tuber indicum*.

Freshly picked black truffles are infinitely better than processed ones, and when cooking with them it is unwise to skimp. They might not be the aphrodisiac some have claimed, but truffles can create an emotional response—eating them can be a complex, mystic experience. They make powerfully aromatic sauces and the finest of omelets. **MR**

White Alba truffles, the *tartufi bianchi* of legend, sit near the top of the league of luxury, expensive foods. Smooth, yellowish or ochre outside, grayish yellow on the inside, these wild fungi take their name from the Piedmontese town that has done so much to raise their profile. (Although strongly identified with this northern Italian province, *Tuber magnatum Pico* is also found in Croatia.)

Truffles have so far defied all efforts to grow them commercially, and because of increasing scarcity, truffle hunting is heavily regulated. During the season, which runs from October to December, trained dogs nose out the hidden tubers that grow up to 1 foot (30 cm) underground.

Unlike black Périgord truffles, white truffles are never cooked. Instead, they are shaved over food using a special cutter—an *affetta tartufi*. They have a special affinity with eggs and simple pasta dishes, such as the Piedmontese *agnolotti*. The intensity that distinguishes fresh truffles diminishes fast: oils, pastes, and cheeses sold under the name often contain chemicals rather than the real thing. **MR**

Taste: *Scientists have identified more than 100 aroma components in black truffles, ranging from nutty and grassy to sulfurous with hints of vanilla, rose petal, and bergamot.*

Taste: *The aroma, more than the taste, which can be likened to Parmesan cheese, is unique. The white Alba smells unforgettably intense and sulfurous.*

In most regions the truffle-hunting pig has been replaced by specially trained dogs. ❯❯

Huitlacoche

Iwatake

With a name that includes the Aztec word for dung, and a mode of life that involves growing on corn crops as a blight, huitlacoche (*Ustilago maydis*) is many, many times more delicious than a picture or description might lead one to believe. Also known as corn smut, and by more recent, market-friendly coinages such as Aztec caviar, Mexican truffle, and corn mushroom, this naturally occurring fungus disfigures growing corn. The neat white, yellow, or golden kernels swell and mutate into distorted silvery blue lumps with black interiors.

Mexican farmers have long embraced huitlacoche, but for years their American counterparts—and some legislative bodies—regarded it as a pest to be eradicated. Increased demand has prompted farmers in Mexico, the United States, and Canada to find ways of cultivating it. Chefs prize it for its rich umami flavor and the way it adds an exotic black or gray color to dishes. It can be difficult to source fresh huitlacoche outside Mexico, but specialty food stores in the United States and Canada frequently stock flash-frozen or canned versions. **CLH**

The Japanese delicacy iwatake (*Gyrophora esculenta*) takes it name from *iwa* meaning "rock" and *take* meaning "mushroom." Yet this is misleading, in that iwatake is a lichen that grows on rocks high In the mountains of Japan, China, and Korea. It has been collected as a prized culinary delicacy for hundreds of years and is said to enhance longevity.

Iwatake is also a rarity because lichens are notoriously slow growing, and it can take up to 100 years for iwatake to grow to a size worth harvesting. The harvesting itself is a precarious process and not for the faint-hearted. Harvesters need considerable mountaineering skills to rappel down mountains to gather iwatake by prizing it from the cliff face with a sharp knife. The process is made even more dangerous because iwatake is best harvested in wet weather because moisture makes it less likely the lichen will crumble when being removed.

In Japan, it is used as an ingredient in deep-fried tempura, soups, and salads. In Korea, rock mushroom is used in *kimchi* cabbage and radish soup, served with noodles or rice. **CK**

Taste: *Huitlacoche has a mushroomlike flavor with hints of corn and licorice. It is usually sautéed with garlic and onion and used to flavor traditional Mexican dishes.*

Taste: *Raw iwatake has a slimy, slippery texture and virtually no flavor. It can be somewhat chewy and is at its best when made into a delicate tempura.*

North Americans have had some difficulty in accepting that huitlacoche is edible.

Enokitake

Although to many these delicate fungi are Japanese mushrooms and called by their Japanese name, they grow wild in both North America and Europe. Because they grow throughout the winter—or at least during its warmer spells—they are sometimes called winter mushrooms in English and *yukinoshita* (under the snow) in Japanese.

The wild and cultivated forms of *Flammulina velutipes* appear somewhat different. The cultivated kind, grown on sawdust in cylinders and shielded from the light, are characterized by their thin and spindly white stems, up to 5 inches (12 cm) long, on top of which sits a sticky, cream-colored cap about the size of a button—½ inch (1 cm) across. Wild specimens are thicker and bigger with darker colored caps. In Japan, they are traditionally found on the wood of the Chinese hackberry tree, or enoki; in Germany, they are also much appreciated in season.

In Japan, enokitake are a common ingredient in sukiyaki, and other *nabemono* (one-pot dishes). Outside Japan, they are often eaten raw in salads, where their shape shows to advantage. **SB**

Taste: *Enokitake taste very mild and fresh, with a texture that is crisp for a mushroom yet also chewy, and long stringy stems that can get caught between the teeth.*

Matsutake

In Japan, the matsutake is prized every bit as much as the truffles of Alba. It grows only in certain pine forests, and defies cultivation: those found in undisturbed mountain forests of Japanese red pine are deemed the best.

A potent symbol of autumn, *Tricholoma matsutake* has been depicted in haiku, painting, and other decorative arts since at least the Heian era (794–1185 CE); Matsuo Basho, the seventeenth-century haiku master, devoted a poem to it. Up until the 1940s, Japanese mushroom hunters were finding 12,000 tons a year, but by 2005 this had declined to under 40 tons, a fact reflected in the exorbitant price.

For a short period of two or three weeks in autumn, Japanese stores enter a kind of matsutake frenzy. Specimens are arranged on fronds of bracken; store assistants shout the virtues of matsutake rice or bento; sweet cakes are crafted into mushrooms. The best matsutake are eaten before the dark cap that tops the white stem is fully open. Served lightly broiled with a squeeze of the *sudachi* citrus, matsutake is one of the pinnacles of gastronomy. **SB**

Taste: *Pungent and fragrant with the scent of pine woods, the texture is meatily dense. The taste is earthy and nutty with an aftertaste that is almost spicy but never peppery.*

Presentation boxes of matsutake at a street market in Kyoto, Japan. ❯

Maitake

The Japanese name of this remarkable mushroom—maitake or "dancing mushroom"—apparently arose because when mushroom hunters come across a particularly good specimen they dance with joy. In feudal Japan, the maitake is said to have been worth its weight in silver, so with specimens known to grow to as much as 45 pounds (20 kg) in weight, dancing with joy would seem entirely appropriate.

Known in English as hen-of-the-woods (but not to be confused with the unrelated chicken-of-the-woods), the maitake forms a round mass of curly, overlapping, leaflike fronds sprouting from a single thick white stem on hardwood, including oak. It has been used in Asian medicine for centuries, and in recent years an extract has been marketed worldwide as a food supplement.

Fresh maitake makes superlative tempura because the batter clings nicely to the fronds. It is good in miso soup, with noodles or rice, in simmered dishes, and stir-fried; it can also be sautéed in butter or oil, Western style, or added to soups, omelets, and risottos. **SB**

Taste: *Maitake has a mild mushroomy taste, a pleasant fragrance, and a robust but succulent texture with a little resistance to the bite, which is pleasing to most palates.*

Oyster Mushroom

More flavorsome than their cultivated relatives, the best oyster mushrooms (*Pleurotus ostreatus*) grow in clusters on tree stumps and decaying broadleaf wood. Unlike many other wild mushrooms, they have the advantage of being easily recognized and quite distinct from any of the toxic species.

Oyster mushrooms do not look or taste exactly like their namesake, but there is a similarity. Their flattened, lopsided caps in muted shades of gray and brown look a little like the oysters known as "natives" in England and *belons* in France, and may reach up to 5 inches (12.5 cm) across. When they are fried, their surface becomes slippery.

In England, at the turn of the twentieth century, these mushrooms were battered and fried, but the fashion has lapsed. Few cooks would look beyond cutting off the stubby, tough stems and frying the sliced caps in butter or fat. In France or Italy, parsley, garlic, and lemon juice will be added, whereas an oyster mushroom goulash with paprika, onion, and tomato is a Hungarian specialty. Greek cooks grill them over charcoal and baste with olive oil. **MR**

Taste: *Some people can pick out a faint anise smell, but it is mixed up with a pleasant, musty woodland aroma. The texture delivers more bite than a field mushroom.*

Oyster mushrooms are often used in stir-fried Japanese and Chinese dishes. »

Oronge Mushroom

Saffron Milk Cap

This rare, yet delicious, mushroom is found in many parts of the world, but particularly France and Italy: it is especially prized in Italian cooking. The name comes from the Provençal dialect word *ouronjo*, which means orange and refers to the mushroom's distinctive color. It is also known as Caesar's mushroom, or botanically *Amanita caesarea*.

The oronge mushroom has a firm, elliptical cap atop its yellow stem and gills, and is found in oak and chestnut forests from June to October. Great care must be taken to distinguish it from its deadly relatives in the Amanitaceae family, such as the death cap mushroom. (Agrippina, wife of the Emperor Claudius, probably laced a plate of delicious oronge mushrooms with poison extracted from the death cap to kill him.)

Lethality aside, oronge mushrooms have a firm texture and are superb eaten raw in salads. Pan-fried in a little oil or butter, they will ooze delectable juices. Washing leaves the mushrooms waterlogged and compromises their flavor; with good-quality specimens, a light brushing should suffice. **LF**

In Poland's national epic poem *Pan Tadeusz* (1834), the exiled romantic bard Adam Mickiewicz recalls a mushroom-picking outing back in the Napoleonic era: "But all hunt for milk caps which, though not very tall / And largely unsung, are the tastiest of all . . ." Even today, shawl-clad grannies hawking wicker baskets full of mushrooms are a common sight at rural roadsides in autumn.

Saffron milk caps are orange mushrooms (*Lactarius deliciosus*) that take their name from the milky reddish orange liquid they exude. Young specimens have a slightly convex cap, which becomes concave as they mature: they can measure up to 5 inches (12.5 cm) across. They grow most abundantly in the clearings of pine forests, and are most highly valued in fungophile eastern Europe, notably in Poland, Russia, Ukraine, and Slovakia.

Saffron milk caps can be pickled, used in soups, stewed in sour cream, or strung up to dry for future use. But connoisseurs—some of whom prefer them to ceps—insist pan-frying in butter is the only method that truly does them justice. **RS**

Taste: *Served raw, oronge mushrooms have a crisp, fresh earthiness and a deep, savory-sweet flavor. They work particularly well in dishes with chestnuts or chestnut flour.*

Taste: *Fried in butter, saffron milk caps taste rich and mellow with faintly peppery undertones. They are delicious eaten straight off the pan with rye bread to sop up the juices.*

Saffron milk caps are available in the United States and Europe during fall. ❯❯

VARIETY: *Lactaire*

COUNTRY: *Spain*

PRICE: 20— Per KG

Chanterelle

Cep

One of the great culinary wild mushrooms, *Cantharellus cibarius* and its relatives—the family is found across North America, Europe, China, and in parts of Africa—are often sold in France under the name *girolles*. They emerge in small clusters, and the cream- to apricot-colored caps form ruffle-edged trumpets beneath which the gills stretch down to the stems. Although the gathering season is said to be autumn, they start appearing in Mediterranean markets as early as May. Freshly gathered, they should be crisp and dry, never viscous or blotchy.

Chanterelles figure on most gastronomic menus as a garnish and are at their best sautéed rapidly in hot butter. Care has to be taken that they do not stew in their own juices. Even more than with other mushrooms, it is important not to wash them; simply wipe or brush them, or pick off any detritus.

Chanterelles' close relation, the tasty trompette de la mort (*Craterellus cornucopioides*), looks similar but for its black color. Mushroom hunters, however, should be wary of confusing true chanterelles with a different, toxic chanterelle-type mushroom. **MR**

The gastronomic term cep (*porcino* in Italian) most often refers to a variety of mushroom, *Boletus edulis,* that is commonly called king boletus in North America and the penny bun in England. The name apparently derives from a Gascon word, appropriate since many of the best recipes such as *cèpes à la Bordelaise*, fried with garlic, shallots, parsley, and bread crumbs, come from southwest France.

Ceps grow in broadleaf woodland, often in small clusters, emerging from late summer until autumn. They have thick stubby stems and tan to dark brown caps with pores—not gills—on the underside that are white and quite firm when young. They are at their best when small, firm, and rounded.

In northern Italy, dried *porcini* are used in many dishes, especially risotto and pasta, and there is a long tradition of preserving them in oil. Such pantry products have a place in the kitchen, but cannot match the fresh mushroom, so cep hunting expeditions are a popular hobby. Other varieties of *boletus* are equally good to eat, but need picking with care: the Satan Boletus is deadly poisonous. **MR**

Taste: *The intensity of the perfume, both sweet and musty, accords perfectly with the taste, and a chanterelle's texture has the right amount of bite.*

Taste: *Freshly foraged, ceps are strongly perfumed and meaty. The aroma differs from common mushrooms in its persistence: stews and sauces retain this distinctive note.*

The delicate flavor of chanterelles is best
❮ *preserved by quickly sautéing them in butter.*

Shiitake

Morel

Easy to cultivate and full of flavor, the shiitake has spread from Asia all around the world. Known botanically as *Lentinula edodes,* the shiitake grows in the wild around or on a type of chestnut oak called *shii,* from which it takes its name. In both Japan and China, mushrooms harvested with the cap not quite open, during winter, are considered the best. When served fresh, a decorative cross is often cut into the cap and the stem removed.

Unusually, the dried shiitake is more than just a preserved version of the fresh mushroom: it is a food in itself. The process of drying creates the amino acid sodium guanylate, which intensifies the aroma and taste of the flavorsome fresh mushroom, creating more of what the Japanese call "umami"—tastiness. The soaking liquid used to rehydrate the mushrooms has a sweet, earthy aroma, similar to dried porcini, that makes it an important element in *shojin ryori,* the strict vegetarian cuisine developed in Japanese Buddhist temples. It adds flavor and goodness to the diet, and is used in a vegetarian version of dashi, the basic stock used in all Japanese cooking. **SB**

Prized in North America, Asia, and throughout Europe, the *Morchellus* tribe of fungi includes several edible varieties, some crinkly, others conical, some brown, and some black. All are spongy—the familiar Italian name is *spugnola*—with white funnel-like stems, and all grow in the spring.

Fresh morels are velvety to the touch, yet almost brittle as mushrooms go. Because of their commercial value, they are often exported dried from developing countries, the Indian subcontinent especially. Reconstituted morels lack the delicate scent of the fresh ones, and the caps can be leathery and uninteresting. Eaten raw, morels can cause stomach upsets, because they contain traces of toxic helvellic acid: this is destroyed by cooking.

The honeycomb texture of the mushroom's cap traps finely diced shallots, ham, and other ingredients beautifully during cooking. In the classic French dish *morilles à la crème*, the sauce clings to the mushroom, enhancing the flavor. Chefs have stuffed morels with fine mousses or paneer, but this interferes with the texture and taste. **MR**

Taste: *The fresh mushroom is meaty with a mild, earthy taste. Dried and reconstituted shiitake is chewier, with a stronger mushroom taste, which is also sweet and aromatic.*

Taste: Morchella esculenta, *the best eating variety, has a fragrant mushroomy smell that grows in intensity when cooked with cream. The taste is delicate but persistent.*

On this typical shiitake farm in Japan, logs inoculated
⊗ *with shiitake spores produce a wealth of mushrooms.*

Kalamata Olive

Nyons Olive

This famous table olive, one of the oldest varieties in the world, comes from Greece where olives have grown since very early times. In fact, Greek mythology tells of a contest between the goddess Athena and the god Poseidon: Zeus promised to give control of Attica to whoever provided the most useful gift. Athena produced an olive tree and won.

Kalamata olive trees grow on the Greek mainland, and around the town in the Peloponnese Peninsula after which they are named. They are graceful and willowy in shape, and the fruit is oval with a small pimple at the end. When fully ripe, these olives are as dark as an eggplant. Their high fat content, around twenty-five percent, makes them suitable for table use, but few are pressed for their oil.

The ripe olives are laboriously harvested by hand, washed, and then placed in barrels to be cured naturally in brine. They are ready to eat after seven to eight months. Some are pitted and stuffed, the best with fresh ingredients such as almonds, cloves of garlic, cubes of cheese, or cooked and chopped pimientos. **JR**

The medieval fortress town of Nyons, in Provence, has been a center of excellence for olives for many years, and gained its own *appellation d'origine contrôlée* in 1968. Olive trees, *Olea europea,* were first planted in this part of Provence by Roman settlers as Julius Caesar conquered Gaul during the 50s BCE. They have grown here ever since.

The local olive variety is La Tanche, a hardy tree that can withstand the winter frosts. Indeed, the cold extracts the moisture from the olive, wrinkling the skin and concentrating the flavor just before the harvest, which falls after the middle of November but before January. When they are fully ripe and black in color, the olives are picked by hand.

The best olives are cured in a mixture of fresh brine and brine from the previous year. This method eschews the chemicals used to manufacture cheap "pizza" olives, and it takes six to eight months before the olives are fully cured. So seriously does the town take its olive trees that it is home to the *Musée de l'Olivier* (Olive Museum) and the *Institut du Monde de l'Olivier* (Global Olive Institute). **JR**

Taste: *Kalamata olives are very large and juicy and the flesh easily leaves the pit behind. The flavor is rich and strong, but very sweet in style without much bitterness.*

Taste: *Nyons olives are large with lush, juicy flesh and slightly crunchy skin. They are not very salty, but have an attractive bitterness underlying the full fruity flavor.*

Bella di Cerignola Olive

Sometimes known simply as Cerignola, these olives are prized for their size: the largest are as big as the top joint of the human thumb. Oval in shape and green or black in color, they come from the Gargano Promontory and other parts of Puglia in the "heel" of Italy, as specified in their *Denominazione di Origine Protetta* (DOP).

Green Bella di Cerignola are picked before the fruit becomes ripe and dark on the tree; those that will become black olives continue to mature before harvest. Both types are hand-picked in small baskets carried at the waist and delivered to the processing plant as soon after harvesting as possible, which helps keep quality high.

Both the green and the black olives are cured in a saltwater solution that has had a small amount of vinegar added to it. They remain in this solution for six to seven months until they are ready to eat. Unlike Spanish Gordal olives, for example, they are never cured in caustic soda or pasteurized before bottling. Both green and black olives are often served with local goat or sheep cheeses. **JR**

Taste: *Green Bella di Cerignola olives have a good crunchy but juicy texture, much like fresh nuts. The black Cerignola are softer with a more meaty taste.*

Moroccan-style Olive

"A taste older than meat, older than wine" is how writer Lawrence Durrell described the olive, a tree fruit native to the eastern Mediterranean. Indeed, olives have been gathered from wild trees since prehistoric times. The olive tree began to be cultivated, in or near Syrla, before 3000 BCE, and it probably reached North Africa via trade routes.

Olive trees still thrive on the arid North African plains and Morocco is a major olive producer. Masters in the use of spices, Moroccans preserve their olives in exquisitely aromatic marinades. As olives are harvested at each stage of ripeness, Moroccan markets feature huge bowls of gleaming green, pink, red, brown, and black fruit, all preserved in spicy blends including hot peppers, cumin, garlic, coriander seeds, preserved lemons, and fennel.

Olives can be marinated either by first briefly heating the olive oil and spices until fragrant and then adding the mix to the olives along with other ingredients such as garlic and / or preserved lemon, or by just combining all the ingredients. The longer the olives are marinated, the better they taste. **WS**

Taste: *Moroccan olives are juicy, with a deliciously nutty flavor. Depending on the marinade ingredients, the taste ranges from savory to sweet and pungent to aromatic.*

Frozen Pea

Freezing has been used to preserve food since time immemorial—since whenever the first human being dug a hole in the snow and left some meat to keep—but mechanical freezing of food did not come about until the 1840s. Even then, it took the best part of a century before the Brooklyn-born inventor Clarence Birdseye discovered the necessity of quick freezing, meaning vegetables could be preserved without destroying their taste and structure.

Birdseye's frozen foods were first marketed as "frosted." Freezing has never had much cachet, yet garden peas benefit especially from the freezing process. Peas lose their quality soon after picking, as sugar turns to starch—and for industrially farmed "fresh" peas, which can travel thousands of miles before they reach the consumer, the consequences to both flavor and texture can be dismal. By contrast, peas that are blanched and then flash-frozen within hours of leaving the field keep their natural sweetness, resulting, probably uniquely among frozen vegetables, in a taste and texture that is fresh and lively. **SH**

Taste: The best peas are grown in home gardens or bought fresh from the vine. But good-quality frozen peas offer a spring and summer flavor all year-round.

Row upon row of pea plants bask in the California sun. »

Pickled Silverskin Onion

Also known as "cocktail" onions, these little things—often as small as ½ inch (1 cm) in diameter—are the delicacies bartenders spear with a pick, transforming an everyday martini into the more exotic Gibson. They are small silverskin onions from varieties such as Pompeii and Paris, harvested young and then pickled, often in malt vinegar, sugar, salt, and spices.

The British are particularly fond of their pickled onions. Jars of onions as much as 1½ inches (3.5 cm) in diameter were once essential behind the bar of any self-respecting pub and de rigueur in every fish-and-chip shop. Their pungent flavor and sharp malt tang still pairs extremely well with full-flavored cheese, freshly made bread, and a glass of ale, and they also figure alongside ice cream as a pregnancy craving. Today, however, smaller onions, lighter vinegars, and sweeter cures are becoming the norm.

Rakkyo onions, although a different species from Western onions, are similar. Pickled in vinegar, mirin, soy sauce, or some combination of the three, they are widely used in Japanese cuisine. Some are cured in salt before pickling. **SH**

Lampascioni Onion

Muscari comosum, a type of hyacinth, grows wild in the woods and meadows of Apulia, southern Italy, and blossoms each spring bearing beautiful purple-blue flowers. When grown to eat, however, the plant is harvested long before its blooms appear: the little russet bulbs known as lampascioni onions, or *vampagioli,* are the heart of the culinary experience. The ancient Greeks knew them as an aphrodisiac.

During the Middle Ages, lampascioni were considered a food for the poor and were consumed in large quantities by peasants and farmers. Now, however, they are considered a delicacy and are prepared locally in a range of ways. Around the Murgia region of Puglia they are typically cooked under hot wood ashes before being dressed with olive oil and salt; they are also particularly delicious when stewed simply in extra virgin olive oil.

Outside Italy, lampascioni can be bought in jars, preserved in oil and balsamic vinegar (pictured above); Sapori del Salento produces a delicious *lampascioni alla brace*—grilled lampascioni preserved in extra virgin olive oil. **LF**

Taste: *Fresh silverskin onions have a mild onion flavor. Pickled, they are deliciously crunchy, with a sweet-and-sour tang. The precise taste is determined by the pickle.*

Taste: *The bitterness of raw lampascioni can be an acquired taste. Cooking brings out a mellow pairing of savory and sweet, with a hint of almonds.*

The tassel grape hyacinth, whose bulbs are sold as "wild onions," a somewhat misleading term. »

Pantelleria Caper

Zesty and piquant, capers (*Capparis spinosa*) are the unopened buds of a flowering bush that has grown wild in the Mediterranean, and in particular Italy, since Roman times. Pantelleria in Sicily is considered to produce some of the very finest, thanks to the black lavic soil that intensifies their distinctive aroma and flavor, and only capers from the region can be sold as Pantelleria capers.

The buds are harvested by hand between May and August. In their natural state they are hugely bitter, so a process of salting and rinsing is used to remove the harsh flavor. The buds are dried in the sun and then packed in salt and left for eight days. After rinsing, the operation is repeated twice more.

As capers are sold preserved in salt or brine, they need to be thoroughly washed before being eaten. They can be served alone with aperitifs, but are also typically used in sauces, particularly in the tomato-based *puttanesca* sauce and the tuna and caper sauce that is a feature of the delicious Italian veal dish *vitello tonnato*. Capers also marry incredibly well with anchovies. **LF**

Caper Berry

Bud brothers of the better-known caper, caper berries are the mature fruit of *Capparis spinosa*. While the lively little morsels known simply as "capers" are the unopened buds of the white flower the shrubs produce, caper berries are the actual fruit. Like most fruit, they are much larger than their flower buds, and look somewhat like a small green olive in size and color, albeit with muted white lines along the surface. They have a lightly seeded interior and are usually sold with the stems intact.

Caper berries are particularly popular in Spain, but are nowhere near as high-profile globally as their piquant younger siblings. Most often found in jars, pickled or preserved in brine, they have a milder flavor than capers, so do not usually make a good substitute in recipes. However, they are wonderful eaten in much the same way as olives, as part of a tapas plate or an antipasti course, or as a nibble with drinks: their stems make the perfect tool for easy handling and elegant eating. Caper berries make a good accompaniment to a plate of cold cuts, particularly beef, game, or rich pâtés, and fish. **LF**

Taste: *Piquant and salty with a pungent, saliva-inducing, citrusy tang, capers are reminiscent of a tiny gherkin. They deliver a welcome punch to salads, sauces, and pizzas.*

Taste: *Spirited and tangy, yet slightly more restrained than its better-known sibling, the caper berry delivers pizzazz without pucker. Size matters, and small is best.*

Caper plants grow well in arid areas. In Syria, nomads
❷ *collect them by hand to supplement their income.*

Pickled Gherkin

Cornichon

These small cucumbers from the Cucurbitaceae family—the same family as pumpkins, gourds, and watermelons—are possibly one of the oldest pickles on the planet. Eaten all around the world, they are very popular in the United States and are considered a delicacy in much of northern and eastern Europe. They are also enjoyed, perhaps partly for their salt-replenishing qualities, in parts of the Middle East.

In the colder climes of northern Europe, the pickling liquid tends to be a full-flavored concoction of vinegar laced with peppercorns, mustard seeds, dill, horseradish, salt, and spices such as chile, cinnamon, cloves, and gingerroot. In Russia, salty, pungent slices often appear as part of the traditional appetizer selection known as *zakuski* that is served alongside shots of vodka. In warmer climates, such as Turkey and Lebanon, brine-cured variants appear with olives, pickled root vegetables, and pickled peppers as a meze. On this side of the Atlantic, the main flavoring is dill seed, the preference is for a sweeter, milder taste, and the results are more likely to be known as dill pickles. **LF**

Cornichons are often translated as gherkins, but these diminutive pickled members of the cucumber family (*Cucumis sativus*) are somewhat different from the large sweet-and-sour sausagelike gherkins popular throughout the United States and central Europe. The species of ridge cucumber is the same, but the fruit is picked before it is fully developed, normally when smaller than a little finger or less than 2 inches (5 cm).

In France, the two preferred varieties for pickling are the Vert Petit de Paris and the Cornichon Amelioré de Bourgogne. Good-quality brands of cornichons are available, such as Maille, but some commercial brands can be overly tart. Homemade cornichons can be made using good white wine vinegar with shallots, onions, peppercorns, and possibly garlic and herbs. They take about two months in the mixture to reach their full potential.

Cornichons are a traditional partner to simple charcuterie such as *pâté de campagne* because they add contrast to the pork's fattiness. They also feature in the original recipe for tartare sauce. **MR**

Taste: *Crunchy on the outside, soft on the inside, a great gherkin delivers a perky, tongue-tingling balance of sweet and sour. Flavors depend on precise recipes.*

Taste: *Cornichons give a neat and satisfying crunch in the mouth. Flavors vary according to the pickling ingredients, but should always balance tart and sweet.*

Stallholders in Majorca display a tempting appetizer of crunchy and juicy pickled vegetables and olives. »

Sun-Dried Tomato

For centuries, across the southern Mediterranean—
in Italy, Spain, and Greece—plum tomatoes
(*Lycopersicon esculentum*) have been sliced in half,
sprinkled in salt, and dried in the sun for several days
before being packed into glass jars or clay crocks
and covered with olive oil for use when fresh
tomatoes are not in season.

Calabria is particularly associated with this
intensely flavored delicacy. There the rugged,
mountainous terrain can make growing conditions
difficult, and the preservation of fruit and vegetables
has long been traditional. Calabrians season their
sun-dried tomatoes with garlic, basil, and oregano
for use in antipasti, risottos, and stews.

Although the age-old method is still used by
home cooks and small producers, today most sun-
dried tomatoes are preserved in dehydrators,
a method which, although quicker, cannot match
the flavor of those dried naturally in the sun: the
technique was perfected in California in the mid-
1980s. As a result, what was once seen as a gourmet
item became highly popular across the globe. **MR**

Taste: *Sun-dried tomatoes are chewy and sweet, with
an intense tomato flavor. Those packed in olive oil should
be tender, delicate, and deep red, ready to eat.*

*The superior quality of tomatoes dried naturally in
the Calabrian sun justifies the heavy work involved.*

Navarra Piquillo Pepper

Fire-roasted and hand-peeled piquillo peppers—
Pimientos del Piquillo—are the specialty of an area of
Navarra in the Basque region of Spain. These small,
bright red bell peppers are named after their
uniquely curved point, or *piquillo*. They grow in the
fertile soils of the hills just north of the Ebro River,
and are picked between September and November.

The best are immediately roasted over embers
to loosen the outer skin while retaining the firm flesh
inside. Up to sixty percent of the weight is lost at this
stage, concentrating and intensifying the flavor.
They are skinned, cored, and seeded by hand, and
then trimmed and packed in jars in only their own
natural juices. The Lodosa *Denominación de Origen*,
granted in 1987, guarantees not only the peppers'
origin, but also this artisanal mode of preparation.

Drizzled with a little olive oil, and maybe some
garlic or parsley, these peppers do not need any
additional attention. Their ability to retain their
shape even after cooking has led Basque chefs to
stuff them with a variety of ingredients: crab, shrimp,
salt cod, chorizo, and mushrooms among them. **JAB**

Taste: *Sweet and only mildly spicy, these peppers have
an initial sharpness followed by a sweet, rounded flavour
from the natural oils and a smoky tang from fire-roasting.*

Piquanté Pepper

Chuño

What is small and red, and sweet and spicy at the same time? Answer: the sweet and spicy pickled peppers known as piquanté or sweet piquanté peppers, but also marketed worldwide as Peppadew™. These peppers—which look like a cross between a cocktail tomato and a small, plump bell pepper—were discovered growing wild in a vacation-home garden in the Eastern Cape in South Africa in the 1990s. Their discoverer, Johan Steenkamp, trademarked the name and patented the secret preparation recipe.

The capsicum from which the peppers are prepared is thought to be native to Central America. Extensively farmed in the provinces of Limpopo and Mpumalanga, Peppadew™ come ready to use in jars, in either a hot or mild version. Their unique crisp texture is attributed to the brining process that does not use any preservatives.

Fantastic in all types of cold salads, piquanté peppers add zing and brightness to numerous dishes, including pizzas and pasta sauces. They are also good stuffed with cheese as an appetizer. **HFi**

For at least 1,000 years, people living in the Andes of South America have been preserving potatoes as *chuño*, both to protect against crop failures and to provide lasting sustenance that can be easily stored and transported. Possibly the world's first dehydrated food, *chuño* allowed the ancient Incas to fuel the workforce behind their sophisticated empire in Bolivia and Peru—and, subsequently, enabled the Spanish invaders to feed their troops and laborers.

Making chuño is a lengthy process that can take up to four weeks. Potatoes are exposed to frost overnight, which causes them to lose moisture. The frozen tubers are then trodden on to squeeze out the excess water before being dried in the sun. To make chuño *blanco*, the potatoes are peeled and soaked in running water. (Chuño *negro* is left in its dark brown skin.) The resulting chuño will keep for ten years or more without refrigeration. Chuño are rehydrated in soups and stews, or prepared with cheese as a side dish. Chuño *blanco* are made into a dessert with molasses and fruit, *mazamorra*. **GR**

Taste: *Thin fleshed but tantalizingly crisp, piquanté peppers taste peppery and pleasantly astringent with definite sweet, spicy undertones.*

Taste: *Like a fresh potato only lighter as it contains less water, chuño is bland and easily assumes other flavors. It can be bitter if it is not properly washed and peeled.*

The piquanté pepper is better known under
❮ its trademarked name of Peppadew™.

Ja Choy

In Chinese and Southeast Asian cuisines, the range of varieties of mustard greens cultivated—some for their leaves, others for their stems—is dazzling. Ja choy is one of the most addictive and mouth-watering versions, although, as a khaki-colored lump of mustard stem covered in chile paste, it is hardly the most attractive.

Ja choy (Szechuan pickled vegetable) is made by salting the fresh mustard stem to draw out excess moisture, covering it with chile paste, and leaving it to ferment in a sealed earthenware jar about 2 feet (60 cm) high. The jar is cast as a single piece, and to get at the vegetable, the top of the jar must be painstakingly broken off. In supermarkets, ja choy is often sold sliced or julienned and wrapped in vacuum-sealed bags, ready to eat; if buying from traditional Chinese grocers, tongs or long chopsticks are used to select the most tender pieces.

Ja choy can be eaten on its own or cooked with other ingredients: rinse off excess chile paste that stains, then pat dry before using. Take saltiness into account when seasoning. **KKC**

Taste: *The preserved vegetable is a good balance of salty, tangy, and spicy: the best is soft and tender. It stimulates the taste buds and helps increase the appetite.*

Mui Choy

As with other preserved Chinese vegetables, mui choy tastes much better than it looks. The shriveled light brown stems and floppy dark green leaves are salted, dried mustard greens—botanically *Brassica juncea*, and in Cantonese *gai choi* or *gai choy*.

There are two types: sweet and salty. Although the sweet type is also strongly salty, the other variety is so salty it is heavily covered in salt flakes: in some dishes the two are used together so their flavors balance each other out. Both types are available as whole pieces in plastic packages, or chopped in cans: they should always be soaked and rinsed in water to get rid of excess salt.

Because of its chewiness, mui choy is usually finely chopped before being used in dishes: to soften and hydrate the vegetable, it can be steamed for about ten minutes and then soaked and rinsed. When cooking with mui choy, take its saltiness into consideration before seasoning the food.

Mui choy is frequently paired with braised pork belly or duck because the salty, sweet, and bitter flavors cut the fattiness of the meat. **KKC**

Taste: *Mui choy has an intense salty-sweet flavor— whether the salt or the sweet dominates depends on the type—and a slight bitterness like fresh mustard greens.*

Mustard greens in California, where they are eaten raw or cooked more often than preserved . »

Wakame

Wakame (*Undaria pinnatifida*) is a brown saltwater-dwelling marine algae native to the waters around Japan and Korea, although a similar plant, alaria, occurs in North America and Europe in the Atlantic Ocean. The cultivation of wakame, where the spores grow on rope, was introduced relatively recently.

Wakame grows well in fast-moving waters, where it produces tender plants. It is usually harvested in March and the fresh leaves are blanched and then chilled. This preserves the green color and inhibits growth of undesirable microorganisms, so it stays fresh for longer. In Japan, fresh wakame is on sale at harvest time, where it is piled high in salt-covered stringy mounds in stores and markets. Dried wakame is widely available in Japan and overseas. A dull gray-green color when dry, it magically regains its vibrant green hue when soaked in cold water.

Used extensively in miso soup, wakame is frequently combined with seafood or cucumber in vinegared salads. *Ita* wakame is dried pieces of wakame pressed into a flat sheet rather like nori, and is used as a condiment with rice. **SB**

Taste: *With a mild flavor of the ocean, wakame is slightly slippery, but not off-puttingly so. It is a bit like lettuce yet has a tender, melt-in-the-mouth texture.*

Wakame is an invasive seaweed as well as an important food. »

Hijiki

Nori

A user-friendly introduction to the world of sea vegetables, hijiki *(Hizikia fusiforme)* grows wild on the coasts of China, Korea, and Japan: the best is said to come from the Boshu peninsula in eastern Japan. It appears just below the tide line in dense clumps of black, cylindrical strands. Young shoots picked early in the season—in February and soon after—are most tender and the highest grade: they grow to thicker strings, like shoelaces, as they mature.

The harvested hijiki is cooked, which turns it an attractive deep black, and dried, ready for sale. When reconstituted it expands to five times the dry volume. Hijiki's somewhat coarse texture lends itself well to sautéing in sesame oil together with root vegetables, while its color is often used to create contrast, especially with carrots and lotus root. Cooked and flavored with a little sugar and soy sauce, it keeps for several days, making it a perfect ingredient for a bento box. In 2004, there was concern over the levels of naturally occurring arsenic in some hijiki, although the Japanese and Koreans have been eating it for centuries to no obvious detriment. **SB**

The Japanese have been eating nori, the name for various seaweeds and, most famously, the wrapping used for sushi rolls, for at least 1,300 years, and farming it for four centuries or so. Yet its survival in cultivation is down to a Dr. Kathleen Drew, who brought her understanding of laver—the Welsh name for various members of the nori family—to Kyushu in the 1940s. She is commemorated by a bronze monument near the Bay of Shimbara, where nori is still seeded the way she suggested.

Nori is harvested in winter from inlets near the shore, where fresh water and seawater meet. To make sheet nori, it is washed and chopped to produce a thin sludge, which is pasted onto bamboo mats and dried. The different types of nori have various names depending on what species they come from and what they are used for: aonori, for example, is dried green laver sold in small flakes.

In Wales, laver has been eaten for centuries, but prepared very differently from the Japanese method: boiled to a sludge, combined with oatmeal, and made into little patties of laverbread. **SB**

Taste: *Coarse and chewy with a texture more like land vegetables than slippery sea vegetables, hijiki is satisfyingly nutty and tastes strongly of the ocean.*

Taste: *Nori is mild, with only a faint taste of the sea, as it grows near estuaries. Crispy and savory, it is a perfect accompaniment to soy sauce and, surprisingly, cheese.*

On the Japanese coast, clumps of hijiki
🅚 *are pegged out to dehydrate in the sea air.*

Sauerkraut

It is difficult to find two words that are less likely to have anyone clambering to get to the dinner table than "fermented cabbage," but that is exactly what sauerkraut is. Love it or hate it, this traditional preserve has fans the world over, from China to Chile, and from the United States to Europe. Although frequently deemed a German invention, the fermentation of finely shredded cabbage actually goes back to ancient China.

Sauerkraut literally means "sour cabbage" and it is made by a very simple procedure involving wild fermentation, that is to say, it does not need a live starter to begin the process. Salt is added to finely shredded cabbage and this draws out water from the vegetable. Naturally occurring bacteria in the cabbage react with the resulting brine and this causes the cabbage to ferment and take on its sour flavor. Although it can be purchased in jars and cans, fresh sauerkraut has a superior flavor and texture.

Sauerkraut makes a refreshing side dish to salty meats such as sausages, ham, and bacon. It can also be eaten cold in salads and sandwiches. **LF**

Taste: *Crunchy and pleasantly tart, sauerkraut has a clean but pleasantly sour flavor that is good at cutting through the fattiness of some meats.*

Natto

The place of soy in Japanese culture is confirmed during the Setsubun festival marking the start of spring, as soybeans rattle onto the streets, chasing away bad luck and evil spirits. High in protein, yet generally indigestible, soybeans have inspired almost as much culinary ingenuity as milk, and one of their many fermented products is natto.

Natto is one of those foods that divides people. Popular in Tokyo, yet far too vulgar a taste for the refined folk of Kyoto, it is made of cooked soybeans. These are fermented, not with mold but with bacteria, into a pungent, sticky, and highly nutritious mass, where the beans retain their shape amid a viscous goo that forms fine threads like a sticky spider's web when stirred. Although claims that natto is a weight-loss panacea made on Japanese television have proved unfounded, modern natto is not only high in protein but an important vegetarian source of vitamin B_{12} and B_2. In eastern Japan, it is a popular breakfast food, mixed with soy sauce, mustard, and sometimes a raw egg or chopped scallion, and eaten with rice. **SB**

Taste: *The smell is highly pungent, like Gorgonzola with a whiff of ammonia; the texture is sticky and slightly slimy. Wrapped in a leaf and deep-fried, natto loses its stickiness.*

Silken Bean Curd

As its name suggests, silken bean curd is light, soft, and delicate. Unlike other types of fresh bean curd, which are pressed with weights to rid them of excess water, the coagulated soybean liquid used for silken bean curd is poured into molds and allowed to set, giving it a soft, moist, wobbly texture that is like the most fragile of custards. Because it is so delicate, silken bean curd is rarely cooked beyond being gently heated through; stir-frying, even if done with great care, will break the bean curd into small, unattractive lumps. Even slicing it can be difficult.

Commercially made silken bean curd comes in small blocks, but if you find it freshly made in Chinese markets, the vendor will use the edge of a shallow metal or porcelain plate to both cut it and scoop it out of its container. In Japan, silken bean curd is usually eaten "as is" with a dash of soy sauce and chopped scallions. It can also be made into desserts (usually served with sugar or ginger-flavored syrup), steamed with a light sauce, or cut into small cubes and poached gently in clear but flavorsome broth. **KKC**

Stinky Tofu

Never was there a food that better illustrated the saying that smell is nine-tenths of taste. Stinky tofu, known as *ch'ou doufu* in Mandarin, has a mild, faintly sour, beany flavor, but its aroma is monumental in stature, usually encountered before the doufu is within visual range.

To make it, assorted vegetables, herbs, shrimp, and sometimes other seafood items are fermented to produce a pungent brine, an initial step that takes days, if not weeks. Into this trenchant liquid, fresh bean-curd cakes are added. After marinating for several hours, followed by a brief rest period out of the brine, they acquire a spongy texture. Regional variations abound in China, Taiwan, and Hong Kong, their color and flavor varying with the makeup of both bean curd and brine.

Stinky tofu is often eaten as street food, perhaps for the sake of ventilation. Deep-fried until crusty on the outside, then dressed with spicy sauces, it is topped with chili oil and garlic in Hunan, while Taiwanese vendors also add vinegar and pickles. It also appears in steamed and soup preparations. **CTa**

Taste: *Silken bean curd has a soft, smooth texture and a delicate flavor. As with other bean curd, it is a good source of protein and is popular in vegetarian cuisine.*

Taste: *Stinky tofu seethes with hints of other microbe-enhanced foods, mainly tempeh and natto, with notes of Stilton and cider, plus a mushroomy dankness all its own.*

Goma Dofu

Yuba

Although goma dofu resembles tofu, it is actually made from sesame milk thickened with kuzu starch. Part of the Zen Buddhist vegetarian tradition known as *Shojin ryori*, it is often served at Japanese temples and monasteries at the start of a meal. Sesame seeds are high in calcium, and contain iron and vitamin B_1, making it is an important food for those on a dairy-free, no-meat diet, such as the Buddhist monks.

To make goma dofu, the sesame seeds are first dry roasted and then ground. The paste is then combined with water and thickened with kuzu. Another important ingredient, kuzu is also used as a thickener for sweets and jellies. Unlike other starches, it does not give off water when it sets, which makes it a superior, if expensive, thickener. Kuzu is added to the sesame milk, simmered for thirty minutes, and stirred vigorously until large elastic bubbles appear.

Goma dofu is usually served in a small square, anointed with a dab of wasabi and a drizzle of soy sauce. It is sometimes available ready-made in Japanese food stores. **SB**

It has been said that the fourteenth-century warlord Masahige Kusunoki used this high-protein food to sustain his people during the long siege of Chihaya castle. Fresh yuba is a delicacy in Kyoto cuisine and plays an important role in *shojin ryori*, the vegetarian cooking of Buddhist monks. The Buddhist monks of Rinnoji Temple in Nikko developed dried yuba as a portable, nutritious food to sustain them on retreats into the mountains. As tofu skin, yuba is still an everyday food in China, where it is known as *doufu*, and that is probably where it originated.

At Yuba Han, one of the few remaining original shops, they still prepare yuba daily by heating large rectangular pans of soymilk. The delicate protein skin that forms is scooped off and hung up to air-dry on long wooden rails. As it is so labor-intensive and highly perishable, fresh yuba is now a gourmet food. In Kyoto, restaurants specializing in yuba cuisine use both dried and fresh yuba in a variety of ways—as a wrapper for vegetables, as a garnish for soups or sushi, or, best of all, freshly made yuba, just as it is, with a dab of wasabi and a little soy sauce. **SB**

Taste: *Goma dofu is nutty and creamy with a texture halfway between jelly and custard. It has a rich, satisfying flavor that is rather addictive.*

Taste: *Fresh yuba is slightly nutty with a faint taste of bean. It has a creamy, unctuous texture, with a little resistance to the bite. Dried yuba needs reconstituting.*

Iru

Tempeh Murni

When fermented, this African locust bean makes a powerful condiment for flavoring dishes such as soups and stews. It is particularly popular with the Yoruba people of Nigeria, and in neighboring countries whose cuisines are noted for their love of strong flavors. Similar to *ogiri* (fermented melon seeds), iru is an ingredient in two of Nigeria's most pungent national dishes: *egusi* soup, made from seafood, bush meat, and ground melon seeds, and the fiery *ogbono* soup, made from the kernels of the wild mango tree and hot chiles.

Iru is available both fresh and dried, the fresh usually being wrapped in *moimoi* leaves, large, shiny, oval leaves similar to banana leaves. When dried iru is flattened into cakes, the drying process causes the fermented beans to lose some of their strong flavor, although when the dried iru is fried, much of this flavor is restored. High in protein, fat, and vitamins, iru is an important part of the diet of many West African people, particularly when meat is scarce. Fermenting the beans makes them easier to digest and increases their nutritional content. **WS**

This protein-rich soybean cake comes originally from Indonesia, but is now produced all over Southeast Asia. Tempeh is as versatile as meat and often replaces it in recipes as a cheaper alternative.

Tempeh can be cooked in all kinds of ways, being added to soups, stir-fries, braises, or salads and is even used in sandwich fillings. Like tofu, tempeh absorbs other flavors well so it is often marinated and broiled the same way as a steak or hamburger. When sliced and deep-fried, its outer skin becomes golden and crisp, which makes a satisfying contrast to the creamy-white inside.

Many different types of tempeh exist: *murni* indicates that the soybeans have been fermented in a plastic bag. The whole beans are first soaked overnight and then skinned before being cooked. They are then packed into a plastic bag and left to ferment for two to three days in a hot, humid place. Tempeh is widely available in blocks, both fresh and frozen. Home cooks in Indonesia also prepare their own tempeh, the tropical climate being ideally suited to the fermentation process. **WS**

Taste: *Iru is much more pungent than other fermented bean products and an acquired flavor. It is often compared to strong cheese, miso, and even stinky tofu.*

Taste: *Firmer than tofu with a denser, chunkier texture, tempeh has a slightly tart, nutty flavor, best described as a cross between red meat and a large field mushroom.*

Saikyo Miso

Miso, a paste made of fermented soybeans with, often, other grains, too, has existed in Japan since at least the eighth century CE, and comes in a wide range of colors, textures, and tastes. At the gentler end of the taste spectrum stands Saikyo miso, a sweet, smooth, white miso that lends itself almost as well to Western desserts as to classic Japanese dishes.

It is a specialty of Kyoto cuisine, or *Kyo ryori*, a style of cooking that developed under the twin influences of the imperial court and the vegetarian monks of the city's many Zen temples. In this refined and delicate cuisine, appearance is even more important than usual for Japan and lightness of color is favored: white miso, like light soy sauce, is preferred because it does not discolor the food.

Like almost all miso, Saikyo miso is made using soybeans mixed with either rice or barley, then fermented with *koji*—the moldy starter used in making soy sauce and sake. But the recipe contains more rice and less salt than is standard, meaning that Saikyo miso is high in natural sugars, so it ferments in weeks, rather than months. **SB**

Taste: *With a smooth and runny texture similar to lemon curd, and almost as sweet, Saikyo miso tastes delicate, fruity, and nutty with buttery caramel notes.*

Hatcho Miso

Probably the polar opposite of Saikyo miso—which has, in fact, been taken on all six Japanese expeditions to the South Pole—this rich, firm, savory miso has an equally lofty pedigree, being a daily favorite of the late Emperor Hirohito.

Unlike other miso, it is made only from soybeans and salt. It also stands apart for being produced using a naturally occurring mold, *Aspergillus hatcho*, which is unique to the Hatcho area of Okazaki. It is fermented for two to three cycles of the hot humid summers and mild winters of Aichi prefecture in central Japan.

Using organic soybeans, the Hatcho Miso Company in Okazaki has been making its miso for more than 500 years. It is fermented under the weight of 3 tons of river stones in cedar vats that are 7 feet (2 m) tall and can hold about 12,000 pounds (5,000 kg) miso. The pressure from the stones effectively blocks oxygen, creating an ideal growth environment for the microorganisms that make Hatcho miso a nutritional powerhouse. Perhaps it is one reason the Emperor lived so long. **SB**

Taste: *With a chunky texture so firm you can cut it with a knife, a rich brown color, and a deep, savory aroma, Hatcho miso gives a satisfying flavor to soups and stews.*

Huge vats turned on their sides wait to be filled once more at a Japanese miso factory. »

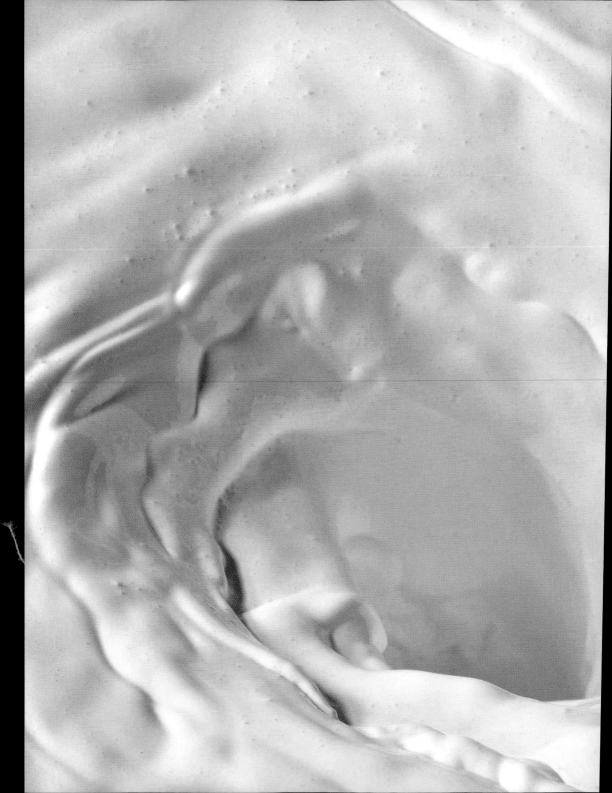

Cornish Clotted Cream

Crème Fraîche d'Isigny

In England's traditional Cornish farmhouses, this ultrarich cream was made in the kitchen, not the dairy, when the milk was at its richest and most abundant. The milk was heated without boiling to a gentle simmering temperature, then left to cool overnight. The next day, the cook would skim off the cream that had set on the surface: a skilled maker would be able to roll up the blanket like a jelly roll.

Nowadays the process is more mechanized. The cream is skimmed off the fresh milk and scalded in trays to achieve the desired consistency. With a minimum butterfat content of fifty-five percent or even more, clotted cream is very rich. At its best, the surface has a rough, partly crystalline, golden crust.

Clotted cream is the cornerstone of the famous English cream tea when it is traditionally served with warm scones and strawberry jam. *The Oxford Companion to Food* suggests that because of its similarity to the Near Eastern cream *kaymak*, it might have been introduced to Cornwall by Phoenician traders 2,000 years ago, but there is no evidence to support this attractive theory. **MR**

IIn 1932, forty-two dairy farmers around the town of Isigny-sur-Mer, in Normandy, formed a cooperative that has since expanded to represent farms in almost 200 communes along the English Channel. From their milk it manufactures fresh and ripened cheeses including Camembert and Mimolette, and two AOC products under its brand name Isigny Sainte Mère: butter and crème fraîche.

The latter, as its title suggests, could once refer to any cream from freshly milked cows. Its richness varied with the time of year or the quality of animal husbandry. Its thickness, sweetness, or acidity depended on how it was handled. Nowadays, the term describes a specific kind of pasteurized cream, produced in a factory, that is thick, rich (Isigny contains forty percent butterfat), and lIghtly acidulated as a result of controlled ripening. In France, crème fraîche is the workhorse of many classic cream sauces, particularly *sauce Normande*. Whipped and sweetened, it is the basis of Chantilly cream. To taste the difference from ordinary cream, however, it is best sampled fresh. **MR**

Taste: The key to its taste is in the name—"clotted." The dense texture is unique, while the farmhouse product has a rich flavor that far exceeds that of commercial variants.

Taste: Smooth textured, thick, and rich, crème fraîche d'Isigny is not cloying on the palate, and the hint of acidity gives it a taste that is refreshing, yet never sour.

The distinctive crust on clotted cream is produced
⊗ *by first ripening, then heating the cream.*

Smetana

Cottage Cheese

This sour cream is an essential ingredient of cultured Russian cuisine. It is left on the table as part of the mixed hors d'oeuvres called *zakuski* that are eaten with shots of vodka. It accompanies blinis and caviar, enriches soups, dressings, and sauces, and figures in the many recipes for pashka. It spread with Russian influence across eastern and central Europe and through the former Soviet states, although it was not known in the West until the Crimean War (1853–56).

Just as cream in western Europe ranges from clotted cream to crème fraîche, so eastern European smetanas vary widely. Some are sweeter, while others are more sour; some have a butterfat content of around twenty percent, others more than forty percent. A visit to the covered Besarabski market in Kiev gives a sense of this diversity, as ladies ladle out portions of smetana from behind a long counter.

The best smetana is produced on an artisanal scale, and soured and thickened by natural bacterial action, as it was in the past. The industrial product is made with a stabilizer additive to give the cream body and, though thick and sour, is less rich. **MR**

To most consumers cottage cheese is a generic term for industrially processed fresh curd made from skim milk or dried milk solids. Tasting mild with very low acidity, this lightly compacted mass of small, moist, rubbery gobbets is used for both salads and sandwiches, as well as dips.

Its origins, however, begin as a fresh, unpressed curd made either from naturally soured raw milk or with renneted fresh milk. Known in England as "green" cheese, because it was new (or "pot" cheese), it probably acquired the name "cottage" to point up the distinction between cheeses made from whole milk and those made from skim milks.

According to John Ayto's *The Diner's Dictionary* (1990), the usage first appeared in print in Bartlett's *Dictionary of Americanisms* in 1848. Artisan cheese-makers in the United States (among them Cabot Creamery, Vermont, and Sweet Home Farms, Alabama) still produce cottage cheese for sale in farmers' markets. Under craft conditions, the cottage cheese can be made "sweet" or "soured," in the latter case by the addition of buttermilk. **MR**

Taste: *Artisanal smetana looks smooth and velvety white. The sourness is always apparent and contrasts with the creaminess, but not aggressively. It has a refreshing taste.*

Taste: *The bland taste allied to its texture makes cottage cheese a good mixer, rather than a cheese worth eating in its own right. It is partnered with foods such as pineapple.*

Russian dairy workers are celebrated by this
 Soviet-era mosaic mural on Sakhalin Island.

Labneh

Islamic cookbooks from as early as the fourteenth century call for a "Persian milk" that might well be the forerunner of labneh. Also spelt "labne," "lebne," and "laban," this creamy, spreadable dairy product is closer to a yogurt than a cheese, and still home-made throughout the Middle East, especially in Syria and neighboring Lebanon.

Labneh can be made from cow's, goat's, or sheep's milk that is either whole or skim. Fresh yogurt is strained through a cheesecloth for four or five hours until it reaches the desired texture, when it is generally salted. The results vary from a smooth dipping product to one that can, after extra straining, be shaped into small balls and preserved in olive oil. Spread on warm pita bread and rolled up, labneh is called *arus* ("the bride"). As a meze, it is served with olive oil, lemon juice, and a sumac and thyme seasoning known as *za'atar*. For dessert, it is eaten with cinnamon and honey. In the Middle East labneh is prepared from whole milk, but Western countries now produce low-fat versions. These lack the suave mouthfeel of the genuine item. **MR**

Taste: *The texture of labneh is always smooth with none of the furriness on the palate that is typical of manufactured dairy products. It should taste of clean, fresh milk.*

Sheep's Milk Yogurt

Whether you term it "Greek," as is popular in most Western supermarkets, or "Bulgarian," as a homage to the discovery of the *Lactobacillus bulgaricus* bacteria that ferment the milk, sheep's milk yogurt is a delightfully creamy, rich dairy product.

Yogurt is, in fact, a pan-Balkan specialty. In *The Melting Pot* (1999), Maria Kaneva-Johnson describes the sheep's yogurt freshly made by Macedonian shepherds on Mount Bistra: "This mountain yogurt was the finest that I have ever eaten—thick, rich, and delicately flavored under its pale-golden crust of cream." There is special affection for yogurt produced late in August when the sheep's milk is at its richest. In the Rhodope Mountains of Bulgaria, one yogurt is famous under the name "gathered mad milk" because it ferments wildly and is made with milk from several milkings.

Export of commercial Greek yogurt goes some way toward explaining its status today. More just renown is earned by the sublime coupling of the farmhouse yogurt with Hymettus honey enjoyed by millions of visitors to Greece each year. **MR**

Taste: *The finest sheep's milk yogurt is silky smooth and unctuous in texture. Faintly sweet, it should have no harshness or unpleasant acidity.*

Sheep grazing in Bulgaria's Rhodope Mountains produce milk for the local yogurt **kisselo mlyako.** ❯❯

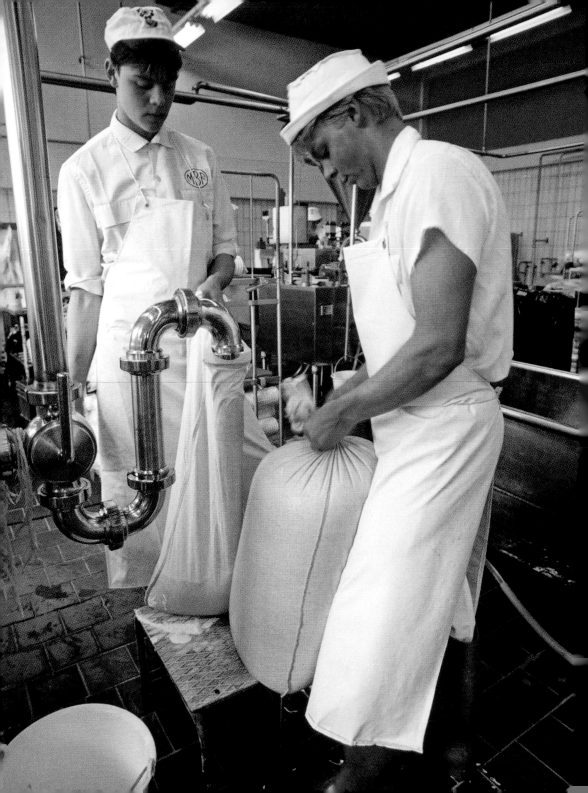

Skyr

Cuajada

This ancient dairy product was introduced to Iceland by the Vikings, who settled the island more than 1,000 years ago, and it remains a source of pride to Icelanders, who consider skyr a national specialty.

Although similar to yogurt, and often marketed in a similar way, skyr is not, in fact, a yogurt. Yogurt is a form of soured milk containing bacteria that alter its texture while adding a measure of acidity. Skyr is a fresh, low-fat cheese, made from milk that has been curdled using rennet and drained a little; it also has added bacteria similar to those found in yogurt. Like yogurt, it is also digested far more quickly and more easily than milk: about ninety percent of it is assimilated within an hour, as opposed to thirty percent for milk. For this reason, and because of its low-fat content, it is considered to be a genuinely healthy food, and contains neither stabilizers nor the skim milk powder used in the manufacture of factory-produced low-fat yogurts. It is usually sweetened and softened with milk or cream to taste. Icelanders traditionally eat skyr at breakfast or alongside a dessert. **MR**

Cuajada (meaning "curds") is a Spanish version of junket, the old-fashioned dessert, and is made by adding rennet to fresh milk. To make this wobbly wonder, the milk is heated gently, the rennet is added, and the mixture is poured into small earthenware or terra-cotta pots where it is left to set before being sweetened to taste.

Cuajada is popular in northern Spain, in the Basque Country and around the Navarra and Castilla y León regions, although it is possible to find it all over Spain these days. Traditionally, it was made with ewe's milk and set with a vegetable rennet, giving it a delightfully loose set and delicious mild flavor. The milk was heated using a red-hot poker, which gave it a pleasant, vaguely burnt aftertaste. Now it is more likely to be made from cow's milk and set with animal rennet, but artisan-made versions of the dessert are certainly worth seeking out.

Cuajada is typically served as a dessert and sweetened with honey or sugar, often accompanied by walnuts. It is also eaten for breakfast, again with honey and often alongside fresh fruit. **LF**

Taste: *Skyr is creamy but not smooth, quite dense, with a clear, clean taste of freshly soured milk. Softened with other dairy, it resembles a slightly grainy fromage blanc.*

Taste: *Light and silky with an engaging quiver, handmade cuajada has the lemony tang of ewe's milk. Distantly yogurtlike, the consistency is somewhat more graceful.*

Most skyr is made in Iceland, where
⊗ *flavored versions are also available.*

Beurre d'Échiré

Goat's Butter

Darling of Michelin-starred chefs, Beurre d'Échiré (AOC) comes from a creamery in Deux-Sèvres (a *département* of the Loire valley) that has run as a cooperative for more than a century. The milk is supplied from sixty-six farms, all no more than 20 miles (32 km) away. Strict controls insure the traditional practices of butter-making continue. The fresh milk is kept between 46°–50°F (8°–10°C), rather than at a chill temperature, to enhance the ripening of the cream, and is not pasteurized. The dairy has a dispensation from the European Community to churn the butter in two giant teak butter-churns. The wood, chosen because it does not taint the cream with tannins, also contributes to the butter's texture. It is more fibrous than the smooth butters found on supermarket shelves, and is packaged in *bourriches*, elegant boxes made from poplar wood.

Beurre d'Échiré finds its main use at the table, but is the key ingredient of a good *beurre blanc*, the sauce made by reducing finely diced shallots and dry white wine to a glaze and then whisking in small cubes of butter to form a warm emulsion. **MR**

The production of goat's milk in increasingly large herds on an agro-industrial scale is a recent phenomenon in both North America and Europe. Proponents claim fewer people are allergic to goat's milk than to cow's milk. Although similar to cow's butter in its fat level and caloric content, goat's butter is, indeed, more digestible. The fat globules cluster differently than those in cow's milk, are more easily assimilated, and contain types of fatty acids that are more readily digested by intestinal enzymes.

The milk is marginally richer in fat than the average cow's milk, so lends itself to butter-making, particularly in those dairies where the cream is automatically separated and returned to the milk. Goat's butter leaves the churn white, yet producing farms often use annatto or carotene colorings to give it a pale yellow tint. Like other butters, it can be salted or unsalted, and is spreadable at room temperature and firm in the refrigerator. The level of "goaty" taste changes from producer to producer, but is significantly different from cow's butter. **MR**

Taste: *Beurre d'Échiré is distinctive in taste and texture. Spread on bread it seems more waxy than normal butter, while the taste of ripened cream lingers in the mouth.*

Taste: *The suggestion of goat cheese in the taste is what makes goat's butter special. It spreads as easily and melts as fluently as more conventional butters.*

Aficionados of goat's milk products insist that the quality is superior from farms where goats roam free. »

Vologda Butter

Lying 250 miles (400 km) northeast of Moscow, the Russian town of Vologda is famous for three things: flax, lace, and butter. With a butterfat content of eight-two and a half percent, Vologda butter is truly a gourmet product. Only three dairies in the region have been making this exceptional butter since 1881.

With its roots in the mid-nineteenth century, Vologda butter owes its special qualities to Nikolai Vereshchagin, the founder of modern Russian dairy farming. Noticing the sour taste of some butter, he separated the sweet cream from the milk twice, instead of the usual once. This resulted in increased butterfat and a richer flavor. The butter was dubbed "Parisian butter" after it won a gold medal at the Paris Exhibition. Its name changed after the Russian Revolution and production declined under communism. But since the 1990s the world has rediscovered this fine butter, despite scurrilous attempts to pass off old government surplus butter under the Vologda name. An oval portrait of a milkmaid symbolizes the authenticity of the genuine butter, as does the name *Vologodskoye maslo*. **FP**

Taste: *Clean and fresh on the palate, Vologda butter has a creamy taste with a hint of walnut, and a melt-in-the-mouth texture. The best butter is sold in birch wood casks.*

Cadí Butter

Cadí butter (DOP), or Mantega de l'Alt Urgell i Cerdanya, is the sweet butter made by the Cadí cooperative in Catalonia, in Spain. The breathtaking landscapes of the Pyrenees and the Cadí mountains protect vast expanses of leafy woodland and verdant meadows, thus providing a unique home for the cows whose milk produces this extraordinary butter. The cold, dry winters, spring rains, and hot, arid summers react with the flora and fauna and create lush grazing that gives a distinctive flavor to the milk, and is captured perfectly in the butter.

The Cadí cooperative was set up in 1915 by a group of forward-thinking producers who wanted to farm in a way that was most compatible with the environment. Production began with just 420 pints (200 liters) of milk a day and, although the quantity has increased significantly over the years, output is limited to insure only the best milk is used. Cadí butter now carries a DOP certificate, which means that every stage of the production has to adhere to strict criteria, including the diet and geographical habitat of the cattle. **LF**

Taste: *Cadí butter has a silky consistency, a creamy, sweet flavor, and a penetrating aroma of lush green pastures and mountain air. Particularly good with dark rye breads.*

The milk of cows that graze in the Cadí mountains produces a unique butter. »

Obatzda

No visit to a Bavarian beer garden is complete without a bowl of this hearty cheese spread. It might come piled high on German rye bread, topped with radishes, olives, and slices of red onion, or served alongside chunks of crusty pretzel. Yet however obatza is served, most agree it makes the perfect partner to the tall, foaming steins of local *weissbier*.

Obatzda recipes vary, but most are based on first chopping and squashing a ripe Camembert cheese and then whipping it with softened butter or a soft cheese, such as Romadur, and a good shot of German beer until it is spreadable. Finely chopped onion, black pepper, sweet or hot paprika, and caraway seeds are then stirred in. The spread is then left for several hours to let the flavors to develop.

Lovers of strong flavors can replace all or part of the Camembert with Limburger, a soft cow's milk cheese with a traffic-stopping aroma. Similar is the Austrian-Slovakian spread *liptauer*. Made using the same mix of spices and flavorings, the Camembert and butter are replaced with a curd cheese produced from sheep's milk. **WS**

Mascarpone

Mascarpone is one of Italy's most distinguished cheeses: some believe its name originates from the words for "better than good." It is particularly well known because it features as a major ingredient in tiramisu, the much-loved Italian dessert.

Originally thought to have been produced around the turn of the sixteenth century in an area to the southwest of Milan, mascarpone is a cream cheese, made from the milk of cows grazed on rich pastures of grass, herbs, and flowers. The cream is heated, then mixed with citric or tartaric acid, which cause it to separate. The solids are then drained through cheesecloth and the result is mascarpone.

Mascarpone is highly versatile and complements a variety of both sweet and savory dishes. It is often used to add a luxurious finish to risottos and pasta sauces, and has a particular affinity with delicate vegetables and fish. Mascarpone makes a great companion to fresh fruit when served chilled, straight from the tub, and creates a delectable base for homemade ice creams in place of the more commonly used egg-enriched mixture. **LF**

Taste: *Flecks of pepper and onion counter the spread's creaminess. The sharp, savory taste of Camembert adds a pungent edge and caraway seeds give a hint of licorice.*

Taste: *Mascarpone has a dense, velvety consistency and rich, creamy flavor with very slightly sweet overtones. It delivers a pleasing layer of creaminess to the palate.*

Ricotta Romana

Brocciu

Ricotta cheeses are produced from the whey remaining after the process of traditional cheese-making: Ricotta Romana (PDO) is made from the whey of Pecorino Romano, both cheeses that have been made since Roman times.

Like its parent cheese, Ricotta Romana is made exclusively from the fresh milk of sheep raised in the Lazio region of Italy. Following removal of the curds used to produce Pecorino Romano, the leftover whey is reheated. This causes the proteins in the whey to solidify and form another curd, which is skimmed off and left in special conical baskets to drain. The result is a pure white cheese with a soft, slightly crumbly texture and a special sweet flavor that reflects the lush pastures on which the sheep initially grazed. After draining, it is wrapped in paper parchment and sold to be eaten as soon as possible.

Whey cheeses are used as an ingredient for the most part, especially to fill pasta and when making desserts, but the fine flavor and light creaminess of Ricotta Romana make it especially delicious when eaten with fruit or drizzled with honey. **LF**

Brocciu (AOC) is Corsica's national cheese. According to one story it dates from the time of King Solomon, who taught the island's shepherds how to make it. This assertion might stretch history almost as much as it stretches geography, but the comment made by the nineteenth-century writer Émile Bergerat—"Whoever hasn't tasted it doesn't know the island"—is not wide of the mark.

Like ricotta, Brocciu is prepared from the whey that is drained off during the manufacture of other cheeses. Some fresh milk is added to sheep's or goat's whey, then the liquid is heated almost to simmering point and emptied into molds. The unripened Brocciu, sold in reed baskets, can be eaten fresh (*frescu*) like fromage blanc—sometimes within hours of draining. After maturing for three weeks, when it is still soft, but covered with a thin skin, it is sold as *passu*. It can also be aged for up to six months. In Corsican cuisine, the various forms of Brocciu appear in everything from contemporary desserts to warming, rustic soups, and can be found stuffing pasta, vegetables, or even fish. **MR**

Taste: *The light, fresh, milky flavor has a clean, sweet essence and a finish that is creamy but not cloying: a million miles from the tubs of ricotta in the supermarket.*

Taste: *The texture is like cottage cheese and the taste is similar, but characteristic of the goat's or ewe's milk from which it is made. With age it becomes more savory.*

Mozzarella di Bufala Campana

Mozzarella di Bufala Campana (DOP) is easily recognizable by its green and red logo bearing the black face of a buffalo. The origins of this cheese can be traced back to the introduction of the buffalo to Italy, probably during early medieval times.

Fresh, soft textured, and porcelain white, Mozzarella di Bufala Campana is made from buffalo milk using age-old techniques and traditions in only seven provinces in the southwest of Italy. It has a barely noticeable rind and a delicate milky taste. When cut, it oozes a chalk-colored, watery fluid with a gentle tang of milk enzymes.

Mozzarella belongs to the "stretched curd" family of cheeses and takes its name from the Italian word *mozzare*, which means "to cut off." The cheese-maker kneads the curd with his hands, in the same way that a baker kneads dough, until the stretched paste is smooth and shiny. He then pulls out a strand and "cuts" it with his finger and thumb to form a ball of cheese, a process known as *mozzatura*. The cheeses are put into brine baths and soaked until they take on a fibrous and elastic consistency. **LF**

Taste: *Mozzarella has a cool, sweet, milky flavor, melt-in-the-mouth texture, and fresh, delicately balanced herbal qualities. It combines well with juicy fruits.*

Kneading mozzarella by hand gives the cheese its elasticity. »

Crowdie

Brillat-Savarin

True crowdie is a Scottish cottage cheese made with naturally soured raw skim milk. Traditionally it was made by crofters who left the milk by a warm peat fire or, in summer, in the sun, until it curdled then strained off the whey through a cloth. This process, however, has all but died out, except on the most isolated farms. The freshly fermented cheese mixed with thick, rich cream is known by its Gaelic name—*gruth is uachdar*—and has formed the basis for a family of flavored fresh cheeses.

In the past crowdie was eaten with a spoon, but it is more commonly served at the end of a meal with a plate of crisp oatcakes. Served alongside a bowl of cream, and dishes of toasted oats, whisky, honey, and seasonal fruit, typically raspberries, it was traditionally part of a unique Scottish delicacy, cranachan. Guests sitting at the table could mix their own cocktail from the ingredients. Modern recipes tend to dish up ready-mixed versions that can taste delicious, but lack the charm of the original dessert; nowadays, crowdie is almost always left out in favor of thicker cream. **MR**

Jean-Anthelme Brillat-Savarin was the author of a classic work on gastronomy—*The Physiology of Taste* (1825)—and famously observed that "a dessert without cheese is like a beautiful woman without an eye." His eponymous cheese, however, has a more recent origin. It was first sold under that name about 1930 by a Parisian cheesemonger, Henri Androuët, whose son would become president of the Guilde des Fromagers and author of the *Guide du Fromage* (1971), the French cheese bible. It is classed as a *triple crème* because extra cream is added to the whole milk, delivering additional richness and a butterfat level of seventy-five percent, meaning three-quarters of the cheese's dry matter is fat.

Produced as a thick disk that weighs roughly 1¼ pounds (500 g), Brillat-Savarin can pass as a fresh cheese, but is probably at its best when left for two to three weeks. By then it has a silky smooth, spreadable texture. Brillat-Savarin is produced in a few craft factories in different regions of the country, but it originated in Normandy, where the milk can have an extra richness. **MR**

Taste: *Handmade fresh crowdie is moist but compact, rather than granular like cottage cheese. The taste is lactic and lemony, and more refreshing than rich.*

Taste: *The cheese has a pleasant aroma like that of heated fresh cream. Its acidity is very light and the taste mild. The mouthfeel is creamy and melting, rather than pasty.*

Sakura Cheese

Époisses

The most successful cheese a traditionally non-cheesemaking nation has ever produced, sakura is made in Hokkaido, Japan's most northern island. The soft cow's milk cheese has been winning prizes since 1998, including a gold medal at the Mountain Cheese Olympics, in Switzerland. Handmade at the Kyodogakusha Shintoku cooperative, sakura is the creation of farmer Nozomu Miyajima, who began making cheese in 1989.

The milk, taken from the morning milking, comes from Swiss Brown cows that graze on the steep slopes of the Hidaka Mountains. The production of sakura is similar to that of goat cheese, using a small amount of rennet and strong acidification. After three days of fermentation, the cheeses are covered with the white *Geotrichum* mold and placed on the salted leaves of the Sakura cherry tree. They are then left for an additional eight days to ferment, during which time the cheese absorbs the fragrance of the leaves. Finally, a salted pink cherry blossom flower is placed on the top of each cheese before they are packed into boxes. **SB**

"Look, see the amber patina; See the thick tears running down its sides; Smell this subtle scent adored by epicures . . . " These lines might come from a poem by Georges Patriat (1900), but lovers of strong cheese continue to wax lyrical about the delicacy he celebrates. Époisses is often classed (erroneously) as a monastery cheese because, like some close cousins—Pont l'Evêque and Maroilles—which do have links with medieval cloisters, it is washed in alcohol during its ripening phase. In fact, its origin is attributed to farms in western Burgundy. The number of farms producing it fell after World War I and for a short period in the 1950s it ceased to exist. Since then it has enjoyed a healthy rebirth.

Époisses de Bourgogne (AOC) is washed in Marc de Bourgogne. The cheeses have a thin orange rind and come in two sizes, one about 10 ounces (300 g) in weight, the other as large as 2¼ pounds (1 kg). They are beige in color, gently supple when pressed, and smooth but not quite spreadable; sold in wooden boxes from about five weeks old, they reach their peak after two months' affinage. **MR**

Taste: *Mild, with a soft creamy texture similar to French St. Marcellin, Sakura's yeasty, fermented aroma is counterbalanced by its cherry blossom fragrance.*

Taste: *The aroma is tangy with hints of damp woodland in fall. The flavor is pronounced, rounded, and lingering, although not sharp, overly acid, or harsh.*

Vacherin

There is nothing like food, perhaps cheese in particular, to bring out a veritable rash of patriotism. Vacherin, a deliciously soft winter cheese from the mountains that form the border of France and Switzerland, is such an example. Once upon a time, Vacherin (du) Mont d'Or could be either Swiss or French, thanks to a shared E.U. appellation: today Vacherin Mont d'Or can be made in Switzerland alone, and the French must sell their cheese as Mont d'Or or Vacherin du Haut-Doubs. Folk from either side of the border take great pride in their cheeses.

Both Vacherins are produced only during the cooler months of the year. The curd—which in France is made using the raw milk of specified cows—is poured into thin spruce hoops. These stay in place throughout the initial maturing process, during which the cheese can be washed in a light brine solution; it undergoes its final affinage in the pine box in which it will eventually be sold.

Ripened to perfection, Vacherin has a wavy orange skin that contains a silky, almost runny inside, which is usually dished up with a spoon. **MR**

Langres

Steven Jenkins put it well in his *Cheese Primer* (1996): "Langres is excruciatingly delicious—it just shocks your tongue with its intense, spicy, creamy flavor."

A rich cheese that takes its flavor from the Marc de Champagne in which it is washed during the ripening process, Langres (AOC) has a unique appearance. Cylindrical in shape, the top forms a bowl into which, at one time, it was fashionable to pour *eau-de-vie*, an unnecessary practice that, like the one of pouring port into Stilton, has died out. The bowl originates with the earthenware molds (*fromottes*) in which the curds were left to drain. These were shaped rather like the top half of a wine bottle; the whey would drip out through the "neck," leaving a hollow in the curd. But the critical part of the process takes place during the washing phase. Over several weeks, the immature cheeses are washed in a cocktail of brine and alcohol.

Langres should be supple but soft. Because it is unpasteurized and relatively young when eaten, it cannot be exported to the United States and is rarely found outside France. **MR**

Taste: *Maturing in spruce gives Vacherin a faintly resinous aroma. The cheese has a flavor that is deep rather than strong. The texture is soft enough to drop from a spoon.*

Taste: *Like many monastery cheeses, Langres has an in-your-face smell. Its aroma is matched by a texture that is denser than clotted cream, and a powerful flavor.*

Langres, like many French cheeses, has a texture that is as well-liked as its flavor. ❯

Limburger

Herve

Brick shaped and brick colored, this cheese has emigrated from its lowland Belgian home to Germany and, once firmly established there, crossed the Atlantic to create an outpost in Wisconsin.

It belongs, like Maroilles and Munster, to the family of Trappist cheeses that were first devised by monks. These are washed and wiped during their maturing to develop a tacky brownish or reddish coat. In Germany, where it is also known as *Backsteinkäse*, Limburger is made to both full-fat and skim-milk recipes. The potent aroma comes from bathing it up to eight times in a brine solution inoculated with *Corynebacteria*. During this period the blocks are turned until they develop an even skin. This should be sticky, but not slimy.

The version in the United States, made by the Chalet Cheese Cooperative in Monroe, Wisconsin, is indistinguishable from its European counterpart. It is served in a traditional deli sandwich on rye bread with raw onion. Although Limburger is often the butt of jokes about its pungent smell, it is not actually a strong-tasting cheese. **MR**

This small, bright orange washed-rind cheese has a venerable history. Although there are references to cheese being produced in the Pays de Herve (a corner of Belgium that abuts the Dutch and German borders) before his time, Herve owes its existence to a law passed in the sixteenth century by Charles V, Holy Roman Emperor, forbidding the export of grain from the region. Peasant farmers converted their land from cereals to pasture and Herve was a by-product of the enforced switch.

To make Herve (AOC), the fresh curd is lightly pressed into bands between wooden boards. These are turned for four or five days before they are firm enough to be cut into blocks. The surface color, known as *morge,* is obtained by washing the surface with a liquid containing the bacteria *Brevibacterium linens.* Thereafter the texture and the taste depend on affinage. Cheesemongers might ripen Herve until sharp and spicy, keep it mild, or sell it at a degree of maturity between these two extremes. Locally, it is enjoyed with *sirop de Liège,* a sweet, sticky, black syrup made from boiled apples. **MR**

Taste: *The texture is very springy, softer in the case of the full-fat cheese. The smell is reminiscent of dampness and decay, but the taste is round, sweetish, and mellow.*

Taste: *Like other washed rind cheeses, such as Munster, which it closely resembles, Herve has a strong aroma of decay that belies a fruity flavor and a smooth texture.*

An ornately tiled panel from the renowned
◉ *Pfunds Molkeri cheese shop in Dresden, Germany.*

Camembert Fermier

Camembert fermier is an increasingly rare product whose taste outshines all its imitators. Its creation is often credited to Marie Harel, a Normandy dairymaid, helped in some versions by a curate from Brie in 1791. However, there are references to Camembert cheese from at least a century before then, although no one is sure how it was made. Pierre Androuët observed in his magisterial *Guide du Fromage* (1971) that the crucial moment in Camembert's history occurred in 1891, when the wooden cylindrical box used to package it was invented. Until then it had been distributed in straw and was often spoiled.

Camembert fermier is an AOC, mold-ripened cheese from Normandy, made with unpasteurized milk on a farm. There is only one surviving farmer–producer, François Durand, still making the cheese in Camembert. The 9-ounce (250 g) disk is fatter than most factory cheeses. The white mold has hints of gray, brown, and orange. It has the usual aroma, but is more complex, mixed with the smells of fruit and chanterelles. It should not be runny when cut open but should have a smooth texture akin to Brie. **MR**

Taste: *The flavor of ripe farmhouse Camembert is milder than the factory-made products. One is conscious of the fresh milk from which it is made and the taste lasts longer.*

The flavors of Camembert fermier develop
⊘ *during an aging period of up to twenty-one days.*

Brie de Meaux

Brie de Meaux has a long pedigree and can claim with some justice to be the "king of cheese and the cheese of kings," since it traces endorsements back to the reign of Charlemagne in the eighth century.

This famous, mold-ripened cheese has various elements affecting its quality. The primary reference is its AOC status, which means it must originate from one of three *départements* near Paris: Seine-et-Marne, Meuse, and the Loiret. The second criterion is the use of unpasteurized milk: although some factories do use pasteurized, heat treatment alters the microbial flora in the milk. A third factor is the use of the *pelle à brie*—a hand tool—to ladle the curds into the hoops. This gives a more delicate texture.

Affinage, the process of ripening the cheese, is as important as its making. Over a period of a month, mottled white-to-russet mold forms on the surface of the disks and the yellowish curd becomes more supple. Brie is ready to eat when there is no longer a chalky thread running through the middle, but aficionados prefer it not to be runny because it develops an ammonia smell when overripe. **MR**

Taste: *A perfectly ripe Brie bulges slightly but does not flow. It is almost fruity, but more tangy than the pasteurized factory-produced versions.*

Harzer Roller

The beautiful mountainous region of Harz lies deep in the German countryside, south of the town of Braunschweig, in Lower Saxony. The area is best known for breeding canaries and producing a strong-smelling, sour milk cheese, both of which are known as Harzer Roller.

Made from low-fat curd cheese or quark, Harzer Roller is a small, cylindrical cheese often flavored with caraway seeds. It is famed for its extremely strong smell that develops after maturing for only a few days. The distinctive aroma is considered pretty offputting by some, but belies its mildly piquant taste. It can be kept in the refrigerator or at room temperature, and lasts up to six weeks. The younger the cheese, the whiter it is at the core, which still contains the quark, and so the more delicate it is in flavor. As the cheese ripens, the core turns a golden yellow and the flavor strengthens.

Harzer Roller is high in protein and contains only one percent fat, and is therefore loved by those on a low-calorie diet. It is typically eaten with bread, pickled cucumbers, or mustard. **CK**

Crottin de Chavignol

Crottin de Chavignol has been made in the village of Chavignol since the sixteenth century and is probably the most famous cheese from the Loire valley. It is still produced on at least two dozen farms from raw goat's milk. The French word *crottin*, which means a small animal dropping, gives a clue as to its size: a small cylinder that fits snugly in the palm of the hand and weighs, according to its ripeness, somewhere around 2 ounces (60 g).

Chavignol's vigorous maturation is a key to why this cheese is such a gem. When still fresh, a week or so after draining and salting, it is pleasantly acid. As molds start to develop on the surface, it grows drier and the flavors balance out. When the molds turn blue and the crottins continue to dry out, the cheese becomes harder and more strongly flavored. Finally, and these are not found outside the region, aged cheeses stored in earthenware jars develop a creamy texture allied to a powerful taste. In its early stages of maturity Crottin de Chavignol is delicious thickly sliced, broiled, and served with a leafy salad dressed in old vinegar and hazelnut oil. **MR**

Taste: *Harzer Roller cheese has a powerfully strong aroma and a slightly spicy flavor. It can be eaten young and firm, or ripe and runny according to preference.*

Taste: *Even when dry and strong, these wonderful cheeses have a clean taste of goat's milk that is never musty. Their natural accompaniment is a glass of Sancerre wine.*

The village of Chavignol makes Sancerre white wine as well as the eponymous cheese. ❯❯

Rocamadour

Picodon

A place of pilgrimage to the Black Madonna, the village of Rocamadour clings to the tall cliffs that channel the Alzou River in southwestern France. It is a mysterious and romantic location, and the farmers and cheese-makers of the surrounding *départements* who produce the small, roughly 1-ounce (30 g) disks of goat cheese trade on this reputation.

Its full title—Cabécou de Rocamadour—places it in a family of *fromages de chèvre* that take their name from a patois word for goat. Although it was once sometimes made with sheep's milk during the winter, its manufacture has been standardized by AOC regulation. Today, it is a seasonal *chèvre* that must be made only from raw milk between April and November. Goats must get eighty percent of their food from natural grazing and cannot be stocked at a greater density than ten animals per hectare.

Fresh cheeses appear for sale within a week of being made. They have a grid pattern on the surface from the racks on which they are stored. As they age, cabécous develop a blotchy skin, while the creamy heart hardens and develops from soft to chewy. **MR**

In summer, the aroma of Picodon goat cheese wafts through the village markets of the Drôme and the Ardèche, two French *départements* separated by the river Rhône. Small cylinders weighing less than 3½ ounces (100 g), they begin life fresh, white, and innocuous, but will become hard, sharp, and pungent with full maturity.

In the local Langue d'Oc patois, Picodon bears the name Picaoudou, but the cheese was not considered a specific named variety until the mid-nineteenth century. Although it has benefited from an AOC since 2000, it remains very much a local cheese whose taste and quality depends on the husbandry and dairying skills of individual farmers.

There are two basic variations of the cheese. The Picodon de Dieulefit is washed during the ripening process and develops a blue-yellow mold on the rind, whereas other Picodons are left to dry out. Both are seasonal, in their prime from April to August. Connoisseurs prefer them when the smooth texture is allied to a pleasant goatiness, but has yet to develop the fiery quality appreciated by some habitués. **MR**

Taste: *Young Rocamadour has a soft texture and a clean, pleasant taste, reflecting the goat's diet of dry grass. As it ages, the cheese becomes more goaty, nutty, and sharper.*

Taste: *Fresh Picodon is similar to many other small goat cheeses, but as it ripens it develops a marked earthy taste that should, optimally, include the scent of wild herbs.*

A Drôme dairyman adds another rack to his stock of freshly formed Picodon cheeses. ❯❯

Chabichou

A goat cheese from Poitou in central France, Chabichou du Poitou (AOC) has an etymology that links it to the Moors, who were driven out of France during the eighth century by Charles Martel. The "chabi" of its name derives from *chebli*, an Arabic word for goat.

The farmhouse (*fermier*) version is prepared with raw milk and is seasonal, made between the end of spring and the fall. Currently, only six farms make the artisanal cheese, although factory-produced Chabichou is available all year round. It is made with fresh curd from whole milk, and left for at last ten days before salting: it matures for an additional ten days before it is ready to eat as a young cheese.

Chabichou's shape—small, cylindrical, and slightly truncated at the top—is referred to as a "bonde" in the local patois: each weighs 3½ ounces (100 g). The mold that covers the surface can be white, blue, gray, or all three, while the bottom of the cheese is embossed with the initials "CdP." During affinage Chabichou continues to develop, becoming first supple, then slightly crumbly. **MR**

Taste: *Chabichou fermier has a pronounced goaty smell. When young it is quite mild with an unctuous mouthfeel. It becomes sharper with prolonged affinage.*

Tiroler Graukäse

Tiroler graukäse (PDO), or Tyrolean Grey Cheese, is a form of aged ricotta made in the Zillertal valley in the Austrian Alps, northeast of Innsbruck. The cheese has been made from the milk of Tyrolean cows for centuries and was once a key part of the peasant diet. Made from raw or pasteurized skim milk, the cheese is extremely low-fat (half a percent). It takes between ten to fifteen days to mature, during which time it is washed with a bacteria mold; rennet is not added during the process. Tiroler graukäse has a thin, blue-gray rind with slight cracks; inside the cheese is marbled with gray-green mold veins. The paste is dry with a gooey, white core that turns yellow as it matures. The cheese needs to be eaten within twenty-five days, because if left too long it can develop a sour aftertaste.

Tiroler graukäse is often served in slices on rustic bread, or with vinegar, olive oil, and marinated onions. It is also used in salads and to make a sauce for dumplings. Locals add small cubes of it to a soup base of meat broth, flour, and whipped cream, which is then eaten with black bread. **CK**

Taste: *Dry at the edges, Tiroler graukäse has a fattier texture toward the middle. It has a strong aroma and a tart flavor that is slightly spicy and mildly acidic.*

A Tyrolean dairy cow greets visitors by means of its flowered headdress. »

Stinking Bishop

This modern British cheese was developed by the Gloucestershire cheese-maker Charles Martell in the 1990s. It takes its name from a Worcestershire pear that was, in turn, named after a cantankerous farmer called Bishop, who once shot a kettle of hot water when it failed to boil. In appearance and style this cheese is modeled on the French monastery cheeses such as Époisses and Pont l'Evêque.

Martell, a committed conservationist, is both a collector of pear trees and the main force behind saving the heritage breed of Gloucester cattle. Initially, he experimented with their milk to produce the unpasteurized flat disks of cheese that are washed in a brine and perry solution as part of the ripening process. The growing notoriety of the cheese (it featured in an Oscar-winning Wallace & Gromit film animation, *The Curse of the Were-Rabbit*) has meant Martell now uses bought-in pasteurized milk. His own small herd of rare-breed cattle, however, continues to supply the raw material for traditional wheels of unpasteurized Single and Double Gloucester. **MR**

Taste: *Stinking Bishop lives up to its name. A significant part of this smooth cheese's attraction is the contrast between the subtle, creamy taste and the aggressive nose.*

Pears for the cheese's perry solution are sorted by hand. »

Torta del Casar

Made from the milk of the Merino and Entrefina breeds of sheep that graze on the harsh, steppelike plains of the province of Extremadura, in central Spain, this organic unpasteurized cheese is so soft when ripe that it is almost runny. Its size—from about 1 pound (450 g) up to more than 2 pounds (900 g)—makes it awkward to serve, so the top is normally sliced off and the contents dished out with a spoon or with a hunk of crusty white bread.

Once a seasonal cheese only produced at the end of winter and in early spring when the ewes were lambing, Torta del Casar (PDO) is now available throughout the year. The first half of its name refers to the shape—like a cake—the second to the town where it was originally produced, Casar de Cáceres. Today, it is made only by eight artisan dairies from whole milk curdled using the *cuajo* plant—a type of wild thistle, specifically *Cynara cardunculus*—as a flavorsome, vegetarian rennet. After ripening for at least sixty days, the paste becomes smooth and then unctuous. It is best left for some time at room temperature before being eaten. **MR**

Serra da Estrela

The highest region of Portugal, Serra da Estrela, a mountainous spine running down the middle of the country, produces an eponymous DOP sheep's milk cheese. The predominantly black-coated, Bordeleira sheep is an autochthonous Iberian breed that would be in danger of extinction but for its link to the "king of Portuguese cheeses."

Similar to the Torta del Casar, Serra da Estrela is a soft, runny cheese. Because there are not any cattle in the region, the milk is curdled with rennet from the cardoon thistle, which is infused in the warm milk and then removed so the curds can be stirred and broken by hand. These are then poured into cloth-lined hoops and the extra whey is squeezed out by hand. Formed into cylinders, the fresh cheeses are wrapped in cheesecloth and left to mature for up to three weeks. Taken from the ripening room, they continue to mature until the paste inside turns to a fatty, tacky cream. When ready to eat, the rind on top of the cheese is sliced off and the contents are spooned onto a plate or the traditional cornmeal bread of the region, *broa*. **MR**

Taste: *The rich buttery paste of Torta del Casar has a dropping consistency. The sweetness of the sheep's milk is tempered by the herbal, vaguely bitter taste of the* cuajo.

Taste: *Mildly herbaceous, Serra da Estrela has a sweet taste with undertones of burnt toffee. Its aroma is intense and its soft, creamy texture is perfect for spreading.*

Portugal's black Bordeleira sheep is now rare, so milk from other species is increasingly used. »

Reblochon

Munster

This wonderful cheese from the Savoyard mountains in southeast France has an interesting name. It derives from a patois word, *reblocher*, which means to squeeze the cow's teat a second time. This second milking would extract a richer liquid that could then be set aside, if in abundance, for cheese-making.

Coming from high alpine pastures, Reblochon (AOC) has a strong seasonal connotation, and is at its best in summer and fall when the cattle graze extensively. *Reblochon fruitier* is produced in several hamlets using milk from cows that have not fed on silage, whereas the word "fermier" (farmer) on the label is an additional sign of good provenance.

Reblochon is made as a 1-pound (450 g) disk and as a smaller "petit Reblochon" from whole and, at its best, untreated milk. During the ripening process it develops a rind about the color of latte— possibly with hints of pink—which can, in turn, be covered with a light bloom. Ready at about two months old, the Reblochon cheese is smooth and velvety with a color of aged ivory. It is resilient to the touch, almost elastic. **MR**

There are cheeses called Munster produced all over the world, but the Munster (AOP) made in and around Alsace stands out from the crowds. In this part of eastern France the food and the wines—like the names of towns and the language—are influenced by the proximity of the German border and by a history during periods of which the region was under German control.

"Munster kaes" is a monastery cheese (the word is itself a contraction of the Latin *monasterium*) whose pedigree goes back to the Middle Ages. It is sold as a small, flattish disk that must weigh at least 4 ¼ ounces (120 g), or in a larger version that weighs somewhere about 1 to 3 pounds (450–1500 g).

Munster—also known as Munster Géromé—is ripened in warm, very humid conditions, normally for only two or three weeks. During this time it is regularly wiped with a light brine. The surface develops an orange tinge, the inside of the cheese turns a buttery yellow, the texture changes to a soft consistency not unlike clotted cream, and the aroma builds to its characteristic intensity. **MR**

Taste: *The smell alone of Reblochon is enticing. Its taste is not aggressive but full, with a touch of grassiness. With fifty percent butterfat, the finish is long and satisfying.*

Taste: *Ripe Munster has a decaying aroma, mixed with an appealing fruitiness. The taste is strong and tangy, but not in a harsh, acidic way—in fact, it is almost meaty.*

Postel

Azeitão

Handmade by the Trappist monks at Postel Abbey in the Belgian municipality of Mol, Postel is a dense cow's milk cheese. To a certain extent the cheese has a French character, largely because the monks fled to Postel from France during Napoleon's antichurch campaign during the mid-nineteenth century. Today, the monks continue to make several cheeses at the abbey. Aged for a minimum of twelve months, Postel is a hard cheese that is suitable for grating. The paste is dark, slightly open, mustard yellow in color, and tinged with brown toward the edges. It has a distinctive loaf shape that resembles a flattened barrel. It makes a delightful table cheese, but it is also excellent for cooking, too.

Belgium now produces about 300 cheeses and, as with the country's beer, the monasteries have had a clear influence on the development of its cheeses. During the Middle Ages, there were fifty abbeys in Belgium making cheese to sell to the public, but now only the one at Postel continues to do so— other abbeys associated with cheeses do so simply by licensing their name. **LF**

Nestled in the lush, herbaceous foothills of the Arrábida Mountains, the Portuguese village of Azeitão produces a lovely semisoft cheese made from unpasteurized ewe's milk. Local legend places its origins in the nineteenth century, when a homesick farmer sent for a Serra cheese from his old flock of sheep and Azeitão adopted the cheese as its own. The cheese has PDO status and is made by artisans in Setúbal, Sesimbra, and Palmela.

Rather than animal rennet, wild cardoon thistle flowers (*Cynara cardunculus*) are used to separate the curd from the whey. It is left by an open fire to curdle in huge clay pots lined with the thistle flowers, and then molded into cloth-covered wheels. Azeitão varies in texture from soft and buttery to chewy and firm as it ages, with few or no holes. It has a strong, earthy aroma and the flavor intensifies as it matures. Azeitão is often eaten by cutting open the top, and scooping out the runny cheese with a small spoon. It is usually served with rustic nutty bread, or with pine nuts and honey, and a glass of the local *Moscatel*. **CK**

Taste: *Postel cheese has a firm texture, an agreeable aroma, and an initial rich, nutty flavour that releases hints of warm spices, such as cloves and nutmeg, on the palate.*

Taste: *Azeitão has a tangy, slightly salty flavor with undertones of creamy sour milk and herbs. Ripe and at room temperature, it has a runny unctuous texture.*

Maroilles

Taleggio

One reason why Maroilles (AOC) produces such a buttery-tasting cheese is that the milk is sourced from the Bretonne Pie Noire, a cow that has Jersey and Guernsey strains in its genetic inheritance. The cheese, however, comes not from Brittany, but from Pas-de-Calais, on the northern rim of France, next to the border with Belgium. This is a true monastery cheese, possibly first produced at an abbey (where St. Hubert is said to be buried) near the eponymous village. According to the French cheese bible, *Guide du Fromage* (1971), it was first known as Craquegnon. By the eighteenth century, it was a heavily salted cheese made on farms for sale in large towns such as Lille, where it was washed to desalt it.

In its classic incarnation today, Maroilles is a washed-rind cheese with an orange skin, shaped like a flattened brick roughly 5 inches (12 cm) square. However, there are a number of different sizes: the Monceau, the Mignon, and the Quart. Maroilles has a more elastic texture than some other "smellies," perhaps because it is washed only in a brine solution without any additional alcohol. **MR**

Although one of Italy's more venerable cheeses and today protected by a DOP, Taleggio did not officially exist by name until 1918. Until then it was one of several Lombardy cheeses known as *stracchino*, a dialect word that relates to milk from cattle tired after their seasonal droves from the alpine pastures into the valleys. It is still identified with the valleys of Taleggio and Valsassina, but is made across the north throughout the year.

A square, flat cheese, Taleggio weighs about 5 pounds (2.25 kg). Its reddish brown rind is stamped with four rings, three of which enclose a letter "T," the fourth a band. A full-fat cheese, it develops the powerful aroma for which it is famous during a ripening process that lasts more than a month and sees the surface smeared with a brine solution inoculated with a mold and bacteria. When very ripe the surface of the cheese should bulge like an over-filled corset. The off-white paste should be smooth like a springy butter. If it has a chalky core it is underripe; if it is runny it is overripe. The rind is edible, but is better scraped off the cheese. **MR**

Taste: *Although strong smelling, Maroilles has a clean aroma. The taste is strong, more of a cheese to eat with pain de campagne than on its own.*

Taste: *Craft Taleggios from Valtellina, Valsassina, and Valtaleggio have a distinctive taste that can be meaty, beefy, mushroomy, fruity, nutty, and salty, all at once.*

Maroilles cheeses acquire their distinctive crisscross
❸ *pattern as they are turned on the wire rack.*

Tilsiter

Feta

Today Tilsiter (or Tilsit) is often thought of as a Swiss cheese, but it is much traveled. In the nineteenth century it was made at Tilsit in eastern Prussia by a Swiss, Otto Wartmann, who was possibly producing a cheese of Dutch origin. In 1893 he returned to his native Thurgau, set up the Holzhoff dairy in Bissegg, and returned to his profession as a cheese-maker, apparently after tinkering with the recipe he had borrowed. Made in 4-pound (1.8 kg) semihard wheels, Tilsiter is made in various versions, both raw and pasteurized, and may be aged for up to six months. The yellowish curd is pocked with pea-size holes. German Tilsit is another kind of cheese: loaf shaped, with a washed rind, its semisoft, springy paste is marked with small fissures. Although many are eaten sliced as a mild breakfast cheese, a strong farmhouse Tilsit can be similar to a Limburger.

The conflicting styles and confused history mean there are effectively two very different cheeses bearing the same name. Ironically, the town of Tilsit—renamed Sovetsk after the Russian Revolution—no longer exists. **MR**

Feta has been a staple part of the Mediterranean diet for centuries. In fact, some historians believe Polyphemus, the one-eyed Cyclops encountered by Odysseus in Homer, was preparing an early precursor of this salty, white cheese.

Although Bulgaria and Turkey have a long heritage of producing feta and it has been made more recently in many other countries, in 2005, after fighting a long battle, Greece achieved PDO status for its emblematic cheese. As of October 2007, a feta cheese must be made in Greece from the milk of sheep, goats, or both. The pressed, sliced curd is salted and dried for twenty-four hours before maturing in a brine bath for about a month.

While much feta is mass-produced and has little but salt to define its taste, the best examples are still made in the country from the intensely flavored, unpasteurized milk of animals that have grazed on the high, scrubby pastures of the mountains. Feta will keep almost indefinitely if submerged in brine but can dry out very quickly if exposed to air. Some soak it briefly in water to remove excess salt. **HFL**

Taste: *Swiss Tilsiter is always made from excellent milk. It has an earthier flavor than, say, Gruyère. German Tilsit is a mild slicing cheese that can become more pungent.*

Taste: *Taken direct from its brine bath and consumed at room temperature, this tangy, pure white cheese is solid and crumbly, yet creamy, with a milky acidity.*

Ardrahan

Tomme de Savoie

Like Cashel Blue, Ardrahan belongs to the family of modern Irish cheeses that were pioneered during the 1980s. Eugene Burns began the business in his farmhouse in County Cork to the south of the island, making cheese with milk from the family's herd of pedigree Friesians. His widow runs the farm today.

Ardrahan is made as a pasteurized, semisoft, washed-rind cheese, using vegetarian rennet to coagulate the milk. The small—11-ounce (300 g)—and medium—2-pound (900 g)—wheels owe their distinctive character to the bacteria inoculated into the brine with which they are wiped during early ripening, in this case *Brevibacterium aurantiacum*. Lightly pressed during making, the mild, springy cheese begins to bulge at the edges as it ages, at the same time developing both silkiness and potency.

Relatively low in both fat and cholesterol, it is a popular cooking cheese in its native Eire and has made waves internationally. Ardrahan's first outlet was a customer in Rungis, the celebrated Paris wholesale market, and it is regularly served at the White House on St. Patrick's Day. **MR**

With its light, sweet taste, Tomme de Savoie comes from the Savoy region of the French Alps. Originally a tomme was made from the skim milk left over after the cream had been removed for butter-making, often by farms working cooperatively. However, until 1996, the name was borrowed by French manufacturers and used to market factory cheese. An IGP label now guarantees its authenticity.

Today, Tomme de Savoie can be made using skim milk, full-fat milk, or something in between: the fat content of the finished cheese varies between twenty percent and forty-five percent. The cheeses are made in wheels that weigh 2½–4 pounds (1.2–2 kg), which are brushed regularly to prevent undesirable black mold forming and turned by hand every other day during an affinage that lasts from one to three months.

Invisible to the naked eye, hidden under the rind crust, tommes have either a red label (indicating dairy manufacture) or a green label (for farmhouse manufacture). A good-quality Tomme will also specify *fabrication traditionelle au lait cru*. **MR**

Taste: *When ripe, Ardrahan has a compact texture, more chalky in the middle than most other smeared cheeses. The earthy aroma is stronger than the silky smooth taste.*

Taste: *Tomme has an open texture, sometimes with small holes. The light flavor varies according to the fat content: cheese lovers will prefer the rougher, drier, higher fat kind.*

Olomoucké Tvarůžky

Olomoucké tvarůžky, or mature Olomouc (pronounced OH-la-mootz), is one of the Czech Republic's best-known traditional cheeses. It has been produced in the Haná region for hundreds of years, and is named after the town of Olomouc. It was first documented in the late fifteenth century, when it was reputed to be a favorite of Czech king Rudolf II, and the cheese was awarded a prize at the first Austrian Dairy Exhibition held in Vienna in 1872. It even has a museum dedicated to it in the town of Lotice. An application has been made for the cheese to be registered as an internationally Protected Designation of Origin product.

The cheese, which is very low fat at only one percent, is made according to an ancient recipe from skimmed sour curd, which is crushed and mixed with ripening agents. Salt is the only added preservative. As it matures, Olomoucké tvarůžky develops a distinctive, powerful aroma, which some people dislike. Its surface is covered with a golden to orange smear, and the cheese is semisoft in texture with a softer core. It is moist and slightly sticky, with a lustrous, translucent layer on the outside. The inside is firm and may be creamy white or pale beige. The cheese is usually molded into short rolls, rings, wheels, or sticks weighing approximately ¾ to 1 ounce (20–30 g) each.

Intriguingly, the cheese was included in a Czech-Chinese banquet some years ago when Olomouc cheese dumplings in ginger sauce were served as a dessert. This flavorsome and nutritious table cheese is commonly eaten with bread, but it is also a staple ingredient of Czech cuisine. It is a popular Czech bar snack, and can be fried in batter. **CK**

Taste: *Olomoucké tvarůžky has a yellowish color and a savory, piquant flavor. It is easily recognizable by its very distinctive pungent odor.*

Hoch Ybrig

The cheese Hoch Ybrig (pronounced hockh EE-brig) comes from the town of Kussnacht in the Swiss canton of Schwyz, high in the Swiss Alps. Created relatively recently, in the 1980s, the semihard cheese was modeled on Swiss Gruyère and shares its name with the picturesque alpine region.

The cheese is sold in wheels weighing around 15 pounds (6.8 kg); because of its limited availability it is expensive to buy. It is made in a single dairy during the summer months from unpasteurized milk from a number of herds of Simmenthal cows from small farms, where they graze on lush alpine pastures containing wildflowers and abundant herbs. The whey is removed from the cooked pressed curds, and the cheese is washed in a white wine brine once a week to help mold grow and to ripen the cheese, a process that gives the cheese its unique character and flavor. The wheels are brought to market after aging eight months to one year. Young cheeses are slightly reddish, whereas more mature wheels have darker, harder rinds with a dusting of white mold and a strong earthy aroma. Year-old cheeses will have developed a deep golden interior and more powerful flavor, with pleasantly crunchy protein crystals, similar to those that develop in aged Parmigiano-Reggiano.

Hoch Ybrig is best eaten after having been left at room temperature for about an hour, when the surface will glisten with drops of milk fat. It is delicious served with mostarda and a chunk of fresh baguette, and a glass of white wine or Amontillado sherry to enhance the nutty aroma of the cheese. It is also superb with crisp apple slices or grapes, and is an excellent cheese for fondue. **CK**

Taste: *Hoch Ybrig has a smooth, slightly granular texture similar to aged Parmigiano-Reggiano, a musty aroma, and an exquisite sweet flavor tinged with a rich nuttiness.*

The milk of Swiss Simmental cows is flavored by the rich flora found in high alpen pastures. ❯❯

Selles-sur-Cher

Fleur du Maquis

In the heart of Sologne, the region south of Orléans, the town of Selles-sur-Cher has lent its name to a goat cheese of distinction that stands comparison with other classic *chèvres* of the Loire valley: Sainte Maure, Valançay, and Crottin de Chavignol.

Selles-sur-Cher was recognized as a specific style of cheese in the 1880s, when the *coquetiers* who traveled around farmhouses to buy for resale began distributing it. Made from whole, unpasteurized milk, it achieves its own personality through the care with which the milk is produced, the delicacy with which the curd is formed, and the care taken in its affinage—a painstaking process for any cheese, but particularly for one as small as this.

Goats are mainly reared indoors on a diet of cereals and hay. Very little rennet is used to curdle the milk; the curd is ladled by hand into molds. After it has settled, the flattish disks are coated by hand with a solution of salt and ash. Left for several weeks to harden and mature, the cheeses become drier, finer, smoother, and denser, achieving a beautiful balance. **MR**

The name alone of this Corsican cheese would make it attractive, redolent of the flowers and herbs that scent the island's rocky plains. Coated in rosemary and savory leaves, sometimes flecked with chili pepper, it catches the eye on any counter or shelf.

Fleur du Maquis is a seasonal cheese, made between spring and late summer, most often using milk from the island's Lacaune ewes. It can be sold fresh or left for several months to ripen, by which time it will start to turn runny. Although it was probably conceived as a tourist cheese in the early 1950s, it has always been a craft product, made with raw milk, sometimes under its alternative names of Brindamour or Brin d'Amour.

When young, the outside leaves retain their silver-green color. As the cheese ages, they dry out and discolor, and mold forms under the surface. The best stage at which to sample Fleur du Maquis depends entirely on personal preference. Cheeses weigh from about 1 pound (450 g) and should be chosen with care. Check the label to see whether they have been made with sheep or goat's milk. **MR**

Taste: *On a ripe Selles-sur-Cher, the cheese under the ash coating is less than 1 inch (2.5 cm) thick. The flavor is distinctly, but not aggressively goaty, with extreme length.*

Taste: *Scrape off the herbs on the surface before eating. Texture and taste ranges from sweet, pleasant, and herby in fresh cheese to strong, intense flavors in older cheese.*

Milk from Lacaune ewes is used in both Fleur du Maquis and Roquefort. ❯❯

Afuega'l Pitu

Afuega'l pitu is a historic, traditional cheese, made in the Asturias region of Spain, an area noted for its variety of cheeses, many of them artisanal. Afuega'l pitu is a cow's milk cheese, made from raw or pasteurized milk. The cheese's striking, colloquial name translates as "choke the cockerel," thought to be a reference to the cheese's distinctive texture or to its strong flavor. One of the area's oldest cheeses, it has the distinction of being legally protected; it has been given a Protected Designation of Origin (PDO), a definition that recognizes the cheese's geographical origins and that restricts production to an area between the Nalan and Narcea rivers.

Afuega'l pitu has two authentic shapes, which may confuse some cheese aficionados. In the Atroncao form it takes the shape of a sawed off cone, which is obtained by ladling the curds into molds (*barreñas*). Alternatively, the fresh cheese may be hung up in small bags to drain, where it compresses and acquires a round pomelolike form. Furthermore, the cheese is also available *blanco* (white) or *rojo* (red), the latter given color and flavor by having either hot or sweet pimentón added to the curd.

The variety of forms afuega'l pitu can take also extends to its size and weight. The maturing time also varies, so the cheese ranges in texture and flavor from soft and mild when young to a stronger, more textured version when older. Some versions also feature molds on the rind, adding to the depth of the flavor.

In Asturias, where local cheese-makers show off their produce at an annual festival, it is traditionally washed down with the dry cider for which the region is well-known. **MR**

Casu Marzu

Squeamish readers may want to skip this entry. Casu marzu is a Sardinian cheese that, unless you hail from the island itself and consider it liquid gold as some older locals do, might politely be described as an acquired taste. (Indeed, it may rank as a food you would rather know of, than actually eat.) Casu marzu means "rotten cheese" and is literally riddled with live maggots. Banned even in its country of origin, it tends to be sold under the counter. In fact there is a large black market for the cheese and shepherds produce small quantities of it for niche markets, and also sell it to people who request it.

Casu marzu is an offshoot of Pecorino Sardo, a wonderful Sardinian cheese made from ewe's milk. In spring a few cuts are made into the rind, and the larvae of a cheese fly known as *Piophila casei* are introduced to the cheese. The grubs are allowed to grow inside the cheese paste to help encourage an advanced level of fermentation, one that most people would describe as decomposition. The developing grubs produce a spicy cream inside the cheese with a very soft melting texture, causing it to ooze beads of an aptly named liquid known as *lagrima*, which means "tears" in Sardinian.

The cheese is normally eaten with Sardinian bread (pane carasau) accompanied by Cannonau, a strong red wine. The translucent maggots (which should be alive when the cheese is eaten) are ⅓ inch (8 mm) long and can jump distances almost twice their length—diners might like to consider wearing eye protection. If the maggots are not wriggling, the cheese has become toxic. Some people prefer to remove the larvae before eating; others throw caution to the wind and devour the lot. **LF**

Taste: *Round afuega'l pitu is open-textured and granular, whereas the Atroncao, rich at first, becomes firmer almost brittle when aged. It is mildly acidic when young.*

Taste: *The maggots can be eliminated by sealing the cheese in a paper bag and waiting for them to die. What remains has a pungency that defies description.*

Before its exposure to maggots, casu marzu begins life as Pecorino Sardo cheese. ❯❯

Yarg

Caerphilly

A Cornish cheese created near the end of the twentieth century, Yarg is a kind of Caerphilly wrapped in stinging nettles. Allegedly it traces its pedigree back to an early seventeenth-century best-seller, *The English Housewife* by Gervase Markham, that describes how fresh cheeses were sometimes laid out on nettles while they aged.

Made only at Lynher Dairy, a boutique cheese-maker near Truro, using milk from its own farm, Yarg combines modern technology with handcrafting. After brining, each lightly pressed 6-pound (3 kg) cheese is coated by hand in a nettle layer before it goes to the maturing room to ripen. Generally the cheese is marketed young to multiple retailers and delicatessens, where the spinach-colored green leaves create an instant visual impact. For a handful of specialist cheesemongers, however, Lynher Dairy changes the recipe. It replaces vegetarian rennet with a traditional animal one. Extended ripening turns the leaves black and molds form on the surface. The cheese looks less appealing to some, but the flavor becomes more distinctive. **MR**

This crumbly white cheese was once thought of as unique to Wales. It was considered a coal miners' cheese; they took chunks of it down the pits wrapped in cabbage leaves. The hot conditions might explain why Caerphilly was often more salty than other British cheeses. Yet, Caerphilly was also made in Somerset, where dairy farmers found a use for excess milk. They exported it across the Bristol Channel because it never achieved much popularity in a county that had its own love affair with Cheddar.

During World War II the Ministry of Food banned Caerphilly in the false belief the cheese did not keep and when the war ended no Welsh cheese-makers were able to reestablish the craft commercially. An industrial version survived, but the handmade cheese almost died out. One Somerset dairy farmer, Chris Duckett, continues to make an authentic version. He, in turn, has trained Todd Trethowan, who has revived Caerphilly-making at Gorwydd in Wales. Duckett's Caerphilly is eaten at a few weeks old but Trethowan's is allowed to mature until it develops a rind. **MR**

Taste: Young nettle Yarg has a pleasant, lightly acidic taste with a mushroomlike aroma. The nettle taste is only marginal. Aged nettle Yarg has more length and depth.

Taste: Duckett's Caerphilly is a milky curd cheese, open textured, lightly flavored, and salty. The Gorwydd version is crumbly and lactic in the middle, but earthier under the rind.

Cheeses made in the Caerphilly style are aged for two to eight weeks. »

Schabziger

Gjetost

If the moon were made of green cheese, as folklore once had it, it would have to be made of Schabziger. Hard, green, and shaped like a neat truncated cone weighing about 3½ ounces (100 g), this remarkable cheese comes from the eastern Swiss canton of Glarus. It might have been created by monks more than 1,000 years ago and the first recipe dates to 1463.

Schabziger has a stunningly low fat content for a cheese—about three percent. It is made using skim cow's milk to produce a curd that is pressed, dried, ground into powder, then mixed with blue fenugreek (*Trigonella caerulea*), the herb that gives it its pale green color and flavor. It is then pressed into small molds and left to harden.

In Switzerland, Schabziger is traditionally grated and mixed with butter to make a kind of spread: premixed Schabziger butters are now available. The cheese can also be used as a flavoring for noodles and *rösti*. Its powerful and distinctive flavor, however, means it is more commonly used as a seasoning, particularly in the United States where it is known (and sold) as Sapsago. **MR**

Gjetost is an unusual and distinctive cheese from Norway, with the texture of fudge and a flavor reminiscent of sweet—but still cheesy—caramel. It is made with cream and whey from the milk of both goats and cows, cooked under pressure until the lactose, or natural milk sugars, caramelize and the cheese develops its characteristic flavor and color. It is then cooled in rectangular molds.

Like many foods, Gjetost was the result of a happy accident. Over 130 years ago, Anne Hov, a farmer's wife from Norway's Gudbrandsdalen valley, had the bright idea of adding cream to the whey cheese she was making. The cheese commanded higher prices than her regular produce, and so Gjetost was born. The story goes that the resulting income saved the valley from imminent financial ruin.

Gjetost is best served in wafer-thin slices using a cheese plane. Typically, it is eaten with Norwegian flatbreads or broiled until melting and served with toast. It is delicious melted over a number of dishes and into sauces to accompany meats such as game. It also makes a tasty addition to a cheeseboard. **LF**

Taste: *Schabziger is so hard it has to be grated or ground before it can be eaten. Then its strong herby flavor with undertones of romaine lettuce or sage surfaces.*

Taste: *After the first bite, the caramel nature of Gjetost gives way to a fresh, slightly sour-sweet edge, rather than the cloying qualities one might expect at first glance.*

Everyday life in Gudbrandsdalen, Norway, around the time Gjetost was first created. ❯❯

Tête de Moine

Halloumi

Created by Swiss monks and originally known as Bellelay, this cheese might have an 800-year-old history but today's producers recommend it is best served directly from the refrigerator. This is because it is served in a unique way—pared very thinly, so that the air brings out maximum flavor from the cheese. This was once done with a knife held at right angles to the cheese, but is now achieved using a *girolle*, a device invented in 1982 that scrapes the surface in circles to create frilly curls. The colder it is, the thinner the cheese can be pared, but it must be eaten quickly or the air will decimate the flavor and texture of the fine curls.

Tête de Moine, or "monk's head," has an AOC status and is made by nine dairies using raw unpasteurized milk in the Jura region. Ripened for four to six months, the rind of the cheese is brine washed, creating a sticky red coating that gives the cheese its characteristic spicy, fruity aroma. Fine shavings of the cheese are sometimes eaten with ground black pepper or cumin. It is also good with fruit and charcuterie, or shaved over salads. **GC**

A creamy white soft to semihard cheese with a fibrous, springy texture that is made from goat's and/or ewe's milk and a little mint. It was originally made by Bedouin in the Middle East, as its good keeping qualities made it ideal for their nomadic lifestyle. The popularity of the cheese led to its widespread production throughout Greece and Cyprus, where it remains a favorite cheese.

Halloumi is made in Cyprus using centuries-old methods. It is such a key part of the culture that halloumi "police" visit stores and dairies to ensure that the time-honored methods are being upheld. Halloumi can be eaten fresh or left to mature for one month. The finished cheese can be sliced but not crumbled, and it is at its best when cooked.

In Cyprus, thin slices of the cheese are cooked in a hot pan until the outside is crisp and golden and the inside is soft. Or it is grilled and drizzled with olive oil, and then served with salad and pita bread. In Lebanon, where it is known as kebab cheese, it is cubed, threaded on skewers, and grilled over charcoal, then sold as a popular street snack. **CW**

Taste: *Tête de Moine has a spicy, mushroomy, nutty flavor with an elegant sweet finish on the palate. Its supple texture ranges from semihard to hard.*

Taste: *Salty, but mild, with a tangy flavor. Some halloumi is saltier than others and needs soaking in warm water or milk for a short time to remove excess salt.*

Wafer-thin layers of a Tête de Moine cheese
⊘ *are sheared from its surface by a girolle.*

Raclette du Valais

Appenzeller

Like fondue, the word "raclette" has become synonymous with orgies of stringy, molten cheese. Yet, unlike fondue, there is no dipping involved. At a typical raclette party, diners consume quantities of potatoes cooked in their skins, hams, salami, and slices of freshly melted cheese, scraped from a slab that has been grilled in front of an open fire.

Raclette is a generic term that describes the scraping process, and Raclette du Valais—named after the eponymous Swiss canton—is the flag under which several cheeses fly, each called after the area of pasture on which the cattle supplying the milk grazed: the big three are Conches, Bagnes, and Simplon. To prepare raclette the rind is scraped to remove any dirt that might adhere to it, then the cut surface of the cheese round is placed about 2 inches (5 cm) from a heat source. As soon as a layer starts to melt it is scraped off downward onto a plate. There are currently various gadgets that make the task easier, although less atavistically satisfying. Raclette can also be aged for up to six months and offered with an aperitif. **MR**

Appenzeller is the sharpest and spiciest of the Swiss mountain cheeses, very different in character from Gruyère and Emmentaler. A hard pressed cheese, it is aged for at least six months before it earns the highest "Extra" rating. Made in the northeast Canton of Appenzell, its history goes back to the early Middle Ages when the parish was created and tithes were stored in the abbot's cellars. References to the cheese date from the late thirteenth century.

Appenzeller is washed in *sulz*, a mixture of cider or wine and spices. Some makers use up to twenty different ingredients in their *sulz*. Like other washed cheeses produced at Trappist or Benedictine abbeys, such as Pont L'Evêque, Herve, and Époisses, the process was probably introduced by monks. The wheel-shaped cheese has a brown rind and a yellowish paste that is pocked with small holes. It is made by about seventy-five dairies, but only three produce it from unpasteurized milk, recognizable by the thin bluish-gray line between the rind and paste. Appenzeller's spicy fragrance and elastic texture make it ideal for fondue. **MR**

Taste: *The distinctive taste of Raclette du Valais is sweet, aromatic, and mildly lactic. The texture of the toasted cheese is soft and runny, reflecting its rich, buttery curd.*

Taste: *With an aroma similar to burnt butter, Appenzeller has a semihard but creamy texture. Initially similar to Gruyère but spicier, it is tangy and pleasantly sharp.*

Emmentaler

Gruyère

Swiss Emmentaler has fought long and hard to protect its identity, obtaining an AOC in 2006. While good Emmentaler (or Emmental or Emmenthal) is also produced in France, the name has been used as a generic in other countries and not all of these copycat cheeses meet the highest standards. Produced in several Swiss cantons, Emmentaler can weigh as much as 250 pounds (115 kg). Sliced open, it is immediately recognizable by its famous holes, some the size of golf balls: these are caused by bacteria that emit carbon dioxide during ripening.

Emmentaler is made from partially skimmed unpasteurized milk, and is sweeter than many hard cow's milk cheeses. It is brined after it has been pressed and because of its size has a relatively low level of saltiness. Winter cheeses made when the cattle are kept indoors are paler than the summer ones when cows graze on alpine pastures.

Simply melted by itself, Emmentaler is very stringy, but for French and Swiss cooks it is the cheese of choice, as suited to soufflés and gratins as to partnering Gruyère in a cheese fondue. **MR**

Swiss Gruyère (AOC) originated amid the foothills of the Alps, in the eponymous district of the Swiss canton of Fribourg. The earliest record of it as a distinctive variety dates from 1655, but records show that cheese was marketed in the region at least as early as the mid-thirteenth century.

Made from unpasteurized whole milk, this close cousin of Emmentaler is a large cheese weighing up to 85 pounds (38 kg). It is aged for at least five months, more often eight or even ten; a two-year-old cheese is sold under the Fribourg name. Although a Gruyère can have small holes, these are rare and not a sign of quality; nor are the occasional rifts under the rind. It is smooth and most often ivory in hue, although it can tend toward a deeper yellow. It can be made in either salted or half-salted (*demi-sel*) forms. The most highly prized Gruyère is produced seasonally with milk from alpine pastures that can add luscious, even floral flavors. Used widely in cooking, Gruyère forms the key ingredient (alongside Emmentaler) of a Swiss cheese fondue, the dip of melted cheese, white wine, and kirsch. **MR**

Taste: *Emmentaler has a sweet, nutty, fruity flavor, like a less buttery Gruyère. Treat ready packed, sliced, or grated Emmentaler with caution unless backed by an AOC label.*

Taste: *The characteristic taste of semifirm Gruyère is its sweetness and fruitiness, but it is also nutty. Its taste is deep, although not strong, and lingers in the mouth.*

Mimolette Vieille

Aged Gouda

The name Mimolette hints it was dreamed up by a marketing guru. "Mi" equals half; "molette" implies a measure of softness. However, it was not. The story goes that Jean Baptiste Colbert, one of Louis XIV's ministers, banned cheese imports from Holland during one of the recurring wars between France and its neighbor. Dairymaids in northern France then took to making their own version of a popular Dutch cheese. Shaped like a large cannonball—hence its alternative name "Boule de Lille"—this impressive *fromage* weighs 9 pounds (4 kg).

Mimolette is a pressed cheese that varies from semifirm to hard. Its thick, crusty rind is attacked by mites. These tiny creatures serve to aerate the cheese, helping the bacteria and enzymes perform their flavor-giving miracle. Cheeses sold as Mimolette Vieille must be at least twelve months old, and Extra Vieille at least eighteen months old, although the cheese continues to develop taste beyond this. The principal manufacturer is Isigny-Sainte-Mère in Normandy. Its cheese benefits from the French quality mark Label Rouge. **MR**

This venerable cheese, like Cheddar, has a worldwide reputation. It has been made in the Netherlands for at least eight centuries and much copied by the dairy industries of other countries over that time. In its young form, Gouda is a bland, mellow cheese made from whole milk by a technique known as "washed curd," where the solid curds are washed before pressing. It is springy, with quite a waxy texture, and the Dutch eat slices of it at breakfast.

Yet when Gouda is aged—ideally for as much as six years—this rather mundane raw material takes on entirely new identities. After one year, it can still be sliced with a sharp knife, but is starting to become brittle. At five or six years old, it can be as hard as a Parmigiano-Reggiano, packed with a powerful, complex flavor and calcium lactate crystals that make it almost crunchy when chewed. When Gouda has reached this stage of maturity, the distinctive flavor and aroma is best savored on its own or with a well-made bread and a glass of good Low Countries beer. It should not be treated as an alternative to Parmesan and used for cooking. **MR**

Taste: *Mimolette's scent is often likened to butterscotch. The taste of Vieille is nutty, with a lot more edge than the young cheese. The texture is hard, brittle, and very waxy.*

Taste: *The aroma of aged Gouda ranges from honeylike to butterscotch or dark caramel. Its taste, which should not be too salty, is sometimes likened to old whiskey.*

Quite possibly related to the Edam family,
✖ *Mimolettes can undergo years of aging.*

Cheshire

In medieval England, Cheshire was the benchmark by which all other cheeses were measured. In the nineteenth and early twentieth centuries, Cheshire was the only British cheese, apart from Stilton, that the French knew by name. During the 1920s more than 1,200 farms were making Cheshire, and before World War II it accounted for sixty percent of British cheese consumption.

Today, this typical English hard cheese survives as a much-diluted factory product, and is made on a bare handful of farms. Only one of these, Appleby's of Hawkstone, still makes cloth-bound cylinders with unpasteurized milk from its own dairy herd. Cows graze on the Cheshire Plain, above mines that have produced rock salt for two millennia, which gives a saltiness to the cheese. It is usually eaten younger than Cheddar, rarely at more than six months old. Some Cheshire cheeses have an orange tinge due to the addition of annatto. Appleby's makes versions with and without the use of this natural dye. Their method delivers a cheese that is less sour and more buttery than other Cheshires. **MR**

Taste: *Appleby's Cheshire cuts easily and is open-textured and flaky, rather than crumbly. The taste is brightly sour, almost piquant, although never harsh or biting.*

Cheddar

In the eighteenth century, when Daniel Defoe (creator of *Robinson Crusoe*) visited Cheddar, the village on the Somerset levels was already known for the large wheels of cheese produced there. The distinctive "cheddaring" process, however, where the fresh curd is cut into blocks and stacked then restacked so that it drains under its own weight, was not described until the mid-nineteenth century.

Today, Cheddar is a generic term for a hard pressed cheese that is made in English-speaking countries around the world. It covers everything from young, industrial cheeses to small-scale, artisan creations. The finest English Cheddars still made in Somerset come from three farms: Montgomery's, Keen's, and Westcombe Dairy. These are the only ones to use unpasteurized milk from their own herds, animal rennet to separate the curds and whey, and a traditional starter to promote the acidity in the milk. The cheese wheels weigh more than 30 pounds (14 kg) each and are matured for between twelve and eighteen months. There is just one farmhouse producer based in Cheddar itself. **MR**

Taste: *Mature Cheddar has a typical nuttiness. Its compact texture is not too dense. It should never be harsh, hot, or acidic, but should cover the palate with its long flavor.*

At the start of the "cheddaring" process, fresh curd is placed on steel mesh to drain it of whey. ❯❯

Idiazabal

Ossau-Iraty

The fashion for Basque cuisine that began in the 1980s put the spotlight on a hard cheese produced with milk from the indigenous Latxa sheep, Idiazabal (DOP). In size and shape the cylinders resemble Manchego, but Idiazabal's character is all its own.

Traditionally, shepherds pastured their sheep in the Pyrenees in spring and summer, made their cheeses *in situ,* and brought them down with their flock at the outset of winter. They would, incidentally, store their cheeses in the open chimneys of their mountain huts. Today, outside the Basque country and Navarra where it is made, Idiazabal is thought of as smoked cheese, and is often gently smoked over beech, birch, or fruitwoods. This process gives the outer rind a patina of antique wood that transmits its flavor through the ripening curd.

Idiazabal is ready to eat at between two and four months old, but can be kept for much longer when it becomes hard enough to grate. Most Idiazabal is made in small factories from unpasteurized milk, but a handful of shepherds still make it in the time-honored way. **MR**

More than 100 shepherd-farmers, grazing flocks of between 200 and 400 ewes on the lower slopes of the French Pyrenees, still make this traditional French Basque sheep's milk cheese. Although protected by an AOC, Ossau-Iraty is less standardized in style than many other cheeses with a designated origin: in fact, its particular charm is that each cheese-maker will come up with a slightly different cheese from his or her neighbor.

It must be made using whole milk only from Basque sheep, during a season that generally runs from the New Year until the end of August. (It is illegal to make Ossau-Iraty in September or October.) The summer cheeses, produced when the sheep graze on high, wild pastures, are most desirable: during this time, farmers strain the milk over stinging nettles for extra herbaceous hints. The cylinders of cheese can weigh anything from 4 to 15 pounds (2–7 kg) and are matured—sometimes still in traditional cellars or caves—for more than three months. All have a minimum butterfat level of fifty percent, so are typically oily. **MR**

Taste: *Unsmoked Idiazabal is sweet, buttery, and firm with a nutty flavor. The influence of the smoking is subtle, rather than assertive, delivering an elegant complexity.*

Taste: *Ossau-Iraty is firm, but not hard, with a melting texture. The taste is fatty, sweet, and nutty: in its homeland it is paired with cherry jam, which enhances its flavors.*

Paški Sir

This Croatian sheep's milk cheese is a jewel of a hard cheese, bursting with both flavor and history. Pronounced pash-key seer, paški sir can be translated as "cheese of the island of Pag." Pag is one of Croatia's four Kvarner islands on the Adriatic Sea, and this quiet little island is becoming a popular tourist destination. Tourism apart, Pag is known for only four things: cheese, lamb, lace, and salt.

Paški sir is a delicacy seldom found outside Croatia. The cheese is made from the milk of seaside sheep whose origins date back to the eighteenth and nineteenth centuries, by the crossing of regional sheep varieties with imported merino sheep. These rugged sheep feast on salt-slaked grasses and sagebrush that give their milk a distinctly herbaceous flavor. This is enhanced farther through a curing process that involves brining the wheels in salt water, with some being rubbed with olive oil and ash. Young paški sir is aged for five months, while old versions are aged for a year or longer. Only about eighty tons of this cheese is produced yearly, from the island's 40,000 sheep. **JH**

Taste: *A hard cheese that can melt at high temperatures, paški sir offers a Parmigiano-Reggiano-like taste, only saltier and with a slightly more herbaceous flavor.*

São Jorge

The Azores, which belong to Portugal, are a group of volcanic islands in the middle of the Atlantic. São Miguel, the largest, has a significant dairy industry, but it is São Jorge that has lent its name to a cheese exported across the Portuguese diaspora. It is a semifirm cheese, generally eaten very young and, when produced commercially, it is easy-going enough for Azorean hotels to serve it sliced for breakfast. In local *tascas*, a cross between tapas bars and bistros, small wedges are eaten as an aperitif.

São Jorge is a narrow rib of a pasture-matted isle. The Gulf Stream insures a temperate climate that is ideal for dairying, and cattle graze all year around in small enclosures that shield them from Atlantic storms. Nowadays the cheese is made with milk from modern breeds of cattle, but the islands still have a few of the Ramón Grande breed that were brought here in the sixteenth century. Wheels of cheese weigh 12 to 22 pounds (6–10 kg) and have a yellowish rind. Aged São Jorge is still sold in the main market of São Miguel, but is generally exported at about four months old. **MR**

Taste: *São Jorge has a lactic taste, crossed with a touch of sweetness. Connoisseurs claim to detect a hint of grassiness. Its texture is compact with a smooth finish.*

Boulette d'Avesnes

It seems unkind to describe a cheese as antisocial, but Boulette d'Avesnes does make its presence felt and should be treated with respect. Cone shaped and paprika colored, it comes from the same corner of France as another "smelly," Maroilles, and is unusual in that it is both a washed-rind cheese and a flavored cheese. The first element of this pungent pairing derives from bathing in a beer brine during the early stages of ripening. The second is down to the pepper, tarragon, parsley, and, in some recipes, ground cloves stirred into the curd. Add a dusting of annatto and one has an item worthy of its nickname "the devil's suppository."

The first reference to Boulette d'Avesnes links it to the Abbaye de Maroilles in 1760. At that time farmers made it entirely with cooked whey. Today, it is a full-fat cheese made by artisans using the same basic process as for Maroilles, although it has to be hand-rolled to obtain its unique shape. A Boulette is 4 to 5 inches (10–12 cm) high and weighs about 7 ounces (200 g); it is matured for about three months before it is sold over the counter. **MR**

Tartous Shanklish

This unusual-looking cheese, which has been likened to a grubby tennis ball, is a specialty of the port of Tartous, 137 miles (220 km) northwest of Damascus. Aromatic shanklish cheeses, also known as *surke*, are made along the Syrian coast and into north Lebanon, either from cow's, goat's, or sheep's milk, but the Tartous version is the most famed.

The cheese is traditionally made at home. Milk is fermented into yogurt, then shaken in a ceramic container. Any butter is removed until a semi-skim yogurt remains. This is heated until it separates and the white residue is hung in a cloth for twelve hours. What remains is known as *arash*. This is salted, rolled into balls, and coated in spices such as Aleppo pepper or *za'atar* (although aniseeds or chiles can also add a kick). The balls are then left to dry in the sun for about ten days, scraped clean, immersed in dried wild thyme, and left to ferment for anything from a week to a month.

Tartous shanklish can be eaten as a meze dish or as a table cheese. Locals most often serve it in a salad of tomato with oil and minced onion. **CK**

Taste: *On a cheeseboard this is the last one to sample, as it is the most pungent. Apart from its assertive smell, the cheese will prickle the palate with added spice.*

Taste: *Tastes like an aged feta, but with deep herby notes and a spicy kick. Flavor does depend on age: mature cheeses are darker, harder in texture, and more pungent.*

The Tartous area of Syria; its cheese can be made from the milk of cows, goats, or sheep. ❯❯

Churpi

Travelers to the Indian subcontinent—particularly Tibet, India, Nepal, and Bhutan, where nomadic herdsmen in hilly regions have depended on the shaggy-haired yak for thousands of years—are likely to encounter churpi.

Mainly made by yak farmers from sweet, rich yak's milk, although it can be made from buffalo or cow's milk, churpi is an unusual type of hard, dried cheese. While most hard cheese can be cut with a knife, churpi needs to be broken with a hammer. It must then be sucked or chewed over a long period of time—from ten minutes up to an hour or more—to get the distinctive flavor of the cheese. At first, churpi has no taste, but after an hour or more a milky taste coats the palate. The indigenous people carry it while they accompany their grazing herds of goats or sheep. It is portable, nutritious, and energy-giving.

Prior to the 1980s, Nepal was the world's leading yak cheese producer and churpi remains important to the rural economy there. Production methods have changed little over the years; the cheese is traditionally made using a special cylindrical churn made of wood and bamboo, before being molded, pressed, and dried.

Churpi can be chewed as a snack, and is ideal for travelers. It is very popular in Nepal, where it is sucked and chewed rather like chewing gum. A Tibetan delicacy is made by lightly frying churpi with the young tendrils of a local fiddlehead fern called *ningro*. Yak cheese is beginning to be known across the world, thanks largely to China. There are varying styles of the cheese, and as the Chinese government puts its weight behind yak dairy initiatives in western China, more are likely to head west. **TB**

Moose Cheese

The moose (the American name for the European elk) has an important place in Swedish culture and food. Although the animal is valued for its meat, there is, however, no tradition of eating moose cheese in Sweden. In 1996 Christer and Ulla Johansson decided to try something new to breathe life into the sleepy community of Bjurholm in northern Sweden and adopted a couple of abandoned moose. Their dairy farm is now home to more than a dozen moose and is the only moose dairy farm in Europe. The usually wild animals have been domesticated, making it possible to milk them.

People not only make the pilgrimage to the Johanssons' "Älgens hus" (Moose House) to pat domesticated moose, they also visit to try the unique moose cheese that is made here. Moose only produce milk between May and September and the milking process can take up to two hours; each moose produces about a gallon (4–5 liters) of milk a day. The milk is kept refrigerated and curdling is done three times per year—yielding 660 pounds (300 kg) of cheese annually.

Moose milk is somewhat similar to cow's milk, but higher in protein and fat. It is very nutritious and reputed to have great health benefits. In Russia, moose milk is used to treat blood diseases and gastrointestinal ailments such as stomach ulcers. It is also becoming popular as a drink.

The extremely expensive price per pound means that moose cheese is for the lucky few. It is sold in upmarket restaurants and a few exclusive outlets in Sweden. The Johanssons make three different types of moose cheese, one of which is best described as a feta type, and is stored in rape oil. **CC**

Taste: *Rock-hard churpi, once patiently softened in the mouth, has a creamy texture that coats the palate. It has a distinctive flavor that is slightly sweet and mildly salty.*

Taste: *Moose cheese is less "crumbly" than feta and has a much smoother, broader, and deeper taste. The high price tag suggests it should be enjoyed on its own.*

Yaks produce sweet, richly flavored milk and ❰ *cheese-making preserves it in a portable form.*

Arzúa-Ulloa

Ubriaco

Traditionally known as "turnip-top cheese" and made in the provinces of La Coruña and Lugo in Galicia, in northwest Spain, Arzúa-Ulloa is a delightful cow's milk cheese. Hugely popular in Spain, it is also known as *queixo do pais* or "cheese from the countryside." Young Arzúa-Ulloa has a soft paste and a mild flavor, whereas the cured version has a salty edge and a harder texture.

Artisan Arzúa-Ulloa carries a DOP certificate that lays down strict criteria governing the entire production of the cheese. It must be produced from the full-fat milk of specified breeds of cow, in particular Rubia Gallega (also known as Galician Blonde), Friesian, or Alpine Brown—all of which yield a deliciously sweet, dense milk that contributes toward making the special flavor of the cheese.

To make Arzúa-Ulloa, salt is added to the milk and the mixture is heated to 33° C (91° F), at which point the milk curdles and the curds are poured into molds before being left to drain. Young cheeses are left to develop from six to fifteen days, but the cured variety matures for at least six months. **LF**

Ubriaco or "drunken" cheese comes from near the Piave River, in the Veneto region of Italy. It is so called because the young cheese is literally soaked in wine and then covered with crushed grape skins before maturation. Ripening cheese in wine and grape must is traditional in Italy, thought to stem from times past when oil was scarce and expensive.

Ubriaco is made between September and November by dunking pieces of Latteria, Asiago, Montasio, Marsure, or Fagagna—all cheeses made from full-cream cow's milk and already seasoned for between six and twenty-four months—in the fresh marc of red wine, mainly Merlot, Cabernet, Raboso, or Refosco. The cheese is immersed in the wine for between thirty-five and fifty hours, then dried and matured for between six and ten months. Consequently, the crust takes on a dark purple to light violet shade, depending on the wine used.

The taste of Ubriaco cheese varies according to the cheese and wine used. A fine cheese eaten on its own, it is best accompanied by a young red wine of the same variety as the marc used in making it. **HFa**

Taste: *Young Arzúa-Ulloa has a clean, milky aroma and a mild, buttery taste. The mature cheese develops a harder texture with flavors hinting of vanilla and walnuts.*

Taste: *The best Ubriaco has a firm, crumbly, open texture and is never rubbery. It has a nutty, slightly tangy taste with a characteristic hint of pineapple on the palate.*

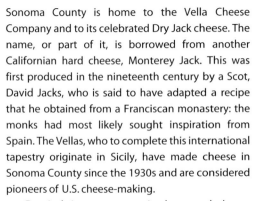

Dry Jack

Sonoma County is home to the Vella Cheese Company and to its celebrated Dry Jack cheese. The name, or part of it, is borrowed from another Californian hard cheese, Monterey Jack. This was first produced in the nineteenth century by a Scot, David Jacks, who is said to have adapted a recipe that he obtained from a Franciscan monastery: the monks had most likely sought inspiration from Spain. The Vellas, who to complete this international tapestry originate in Sicily, have made cheese in Sonoma County since the 1930s and are considered pioneers of U.S. cheese-making.

Dry Jack is an unpasteurized, pressed cheese made with whole Guernsey milk. It becomes hard and flaky with aging, rather like an Italian *grano*. Wheels of Bear Flag—the driest of their four "Jacks"—are aged for two years, weigh about 8 pounds (4 kg), and are coated in a mix of cocoa powder and oil to protect them from mites. Like Parmigiano-Reggiano, the aged Jack can be eaten with fruit, but it is generally used in Italo-Californian cuisine, flaked on pasta or over salads. **MR**

Taste: *Friable and dense, Dry Jack's texture is a little oilier than the Italian cheese with which it is often compared. The taste is rich and powerful with an acidic edge.*

Provolone Valpadana

Provolone Valpadana (DOP) belongs, like mozzarella, to the *pasta filata* family of cheeses, a name that refers to the practice of curd "spinning," which began in southern Italy during the Middle Ages. The high temperatures used for cheese-making would initially create an unstable curd that crumbled back into the whey. Yet it was noticed that if the curd was left to rest for some time, it tended to "spin"— develop a plastic texture, which could then, like wool, form threads if stretched. The end result was good, so the process was copied. The curds were left to rest on tables then stretched in hot water. The finished aged cheese became known as provolone.

In time, the cheese-makers moved north to the lush and fertile plains of Lombardy and Provolone Valpadana was born. Today, it is made according to strict DOP criteria, molded into various traditional shapes, bound with strong twine, and hung in special caves to age for between two and four years. The result is a tangy cheese with a hard texture, which is especially good served in flakes in a similar way to Parmigiano-Reggiano. **LF**

Taste: *Full flavored and firm, Provolone Valpadana has a tangy piquancy and a pleasing texture. Gutsy and with a clean edge, it makes an excellent table cheese.*

Karak Jameed

The time and care invested in making traditional cheeses is well known in Italy and France, but in the Middle East—specifically in the region surrounding the Jordanian city of Karak—cooks descended from Bedouin tribes practice the craft in their own unique fashion. Rather than the giant wheels seen in Europe, artisans there create small lumps of jameed, a pungent dairy product that straddles the line between cheese and yogurt. It is said that Karak produces the country's very best jameed.

To make this unique dried yogurt, goat's-milk yogurt, with added salt and sometimes herbs, is hung in cheesecloth. The cloth is repeatedly twisted to squeeze out any moisture so that it begins to form a ball shape. This flattens slightly as it dries until it is rock hard. If dried in the sun, the jameed acquires a yellowish hue; left in the shade it remains a milky color. Nowadays, jameed is also produced in a state-of-the-art dairy in the town of Ader

Jameed is famously used in the preparation of Jordan's revered rice and lamb dish, mansaf. This was originally a traditional Bedouin dish, made with the foodstuffs most plentiful to Bedouins: sheep or lamb meat and the yogurt produced from sheep's milk. Mansaf is eaten on celebratory occasions and is served on a large platter; according to tradition it should be eaten standing up using one's hands, and no more than eight people should collect around the platter. The balls of jameed are reconstituted in water and crushed to yield a wheylike liquid that is used to make the accompanying sauce. From recent times, liquid jameed has been produced to speed up the sauce-making process. Jameed is also used to lend its distinctive tart tang to soups. **TH**

Taste: *Jameed is essentially the distilled essence of tangy goat's milk in a creamy soft base. It is like an extremely intense and salty feta with an almost feral smell.*

Xynotyro

In Greek, "xyno" refers to anything sharp tasting, such as lemons or yogurt, that has an acidic flavor, while "tiri" means cheese. The name of this cheese, therefore, translates as "sour cheese," which does not accurately describe a flavor profile that includes both caramel and the sour taste of the whey. Like most Greek cheeses, it is made from ewe's or goat's milk, or a mixture of the two (but never from cow's milk as this would not produce the traditional flavor and color), and is produced in the Cyclades islands of the Aegean Sea, especially Mykonos and Naxos. Greece has a long tradition of cheese-making, dating back thousands of years. In the *Odyssey*, Homer mentioned putting curdled goat's and ewe's milk into baskets to make cheese.

An unpasteurized, rindless, whey cheese with the low content of twenty per cent fat, xynotyro is traditionally drained and then left to mature for several days in reed baskets. This process accounts for the distinctive markings on the cheese's surface, caused when the surface of the cheese comes into contact with the basket. The need to stack xynotyro in baskets also accounts for the fact that the resulting cheeses are distributed in assorted shapes and sizes. Traditionally, after xynotyro has matured for three months the cheese is preserved in bags made of animal skin.

Xynotyro can be eaten when fresh and young or as a mature cheese after ripening. It may be eaten on its own, but it is more often served with a salad of cucumber, tomato, and black olives. As it shreds and melts easily, xynotyro also works well in baked dishes such as tarts and pies, including *tyropitakia* (filo pastry triangles filled with cheese). **CK**

Taste: *Xynotyro is a white cheese with a hard, flaky texture. It has a distinctive sweet-and-sour flavor with an undertone of burnt caramel.*

Xynotyro can be used in a number of Greek baked foods, such as cheese and spinach–filled spanakopita. ❯

Fiore Sardo

Parmigiano-Reggiano

Sardinian pecorino, Fiore Sardo (DOP), has a number of unique selling points that make it different from other Italian ewe's milk cheeses. The race of sheep, *pecora sarda*, though widely distributed throughout Italy, is indigenous to the island. And the flocks graze on Mediterranean pastures that offer an unrivaled variety of wild grasses and herbs.

Fiore Sardo is the only Italian raw milk sheep cheese that bears a European *Denominazione di Origine Protetta* certification. The main zone of production is Gavoi, although smaller amounts come from Ollolai, Ovodda, Lodine, Fonni, and Orgosolo. The raw milk is coagulated with a natural lamb's or goat's rennet, and the curds are broken by hand in open vats. Freshly formed cheeses are dry-salted, then very lightly smoked using a combination of myrtle, wild oak, arbutus, and olive woods. They are left in maturing cellars for seven months, at which point they begin to approach their prime. By ten months, when they are usually marketed, they have turned into dry, hard cheeses with a butterfat content of about seventy-five percent. **MR**

Undisputedly known as the king of Italian cheeses, Parmigiano-Reggiano (DOP) has picked up an impressive array of fans. It was reputed to be Napoleon's favorite cheese, and the French playwright Molière was said to have a big soft spot for it—when stricken by the illness that eventually claimed his life, he apparently eschewed the more traditional broth in favor of Parmigiano.

Modern production techniques are still based on methods used during the Middle Ages. Parmigiano belongs to the family of cheeses known as *grana* (grain) in its homeland, and is produced from raw milk in magnificent wheels, each of which weighs in at more than 66 pounds (30 kg). The name Parmigiano-Reggiano is stenciled in small dots on the slightly oily, straw-colored rind of each cheese, signifying it has been produced by artisans in specified zones of Emilia-Romagna in northern Italy.

Parmigiano is fabulous shaved over salads, stirred into risotto, pounded in pesto, or grated on to soups and pasta, but it is perhaps best of all simply served in bite-size chunks before dinner. **LF**

Taste: *Sharp on the palate, Fiore Sardo has echoes of wild plants and a sweet taste reminiscent of dried fruit. A dense, hard cheese that can still be easily sliced.*

Taste: *Parmigiano-Reggiano has a wonderful complexity of flavor. Initially salty and nutty, the taste opens up into an intense rich tang with surprisingly subtle fruity notes.*

The method of making Parmigiano today is based on techniques used during the Middle Ages. ❯

Manchego

Pecorino Romano

The flat, dry region of La Mancha in central Spain takes its name from the Moors, who called it Al Mansha (the waterless land). Burning hot in summer, icy in winter, it produces some of the world's finest saffron and a great cheese, Manchego (DOP).

Made with whole milk from Manchega ewes, this hard, pressed cheese is made in cylinders that weigh about 6 pounds (3 kg) each. The rinds are distinguished by zigzag basket-weave indents that were originally a memento of the esparto grass moulds into which shepherds pressed their curd.

Manchego is produced both on an industrial and on a craft scale and so its quality ranges from outstanding to reliable. The color varies from white to a pale lemon-yellow, depending on the season it was produced and the quality of the milk. When sold at about two months old (*fresco*), it is mild and sweet. By a year old (*curado*), it is drier and more complex. Aged for two years (*añejo* or *viejo*), a farmhouse Manchego develops into a powerful savory cheese that marries perfectly with honey. Thin wedges are a basic part of Spanish tapas bar culture. **MR**

Probably one of the oldest cheeses in existence, Pecorino Romano (DOP) made its first literary appearance in the first century CE when the Roman agronomist Columella provided an account of how to make it, which still holds roughly true today. It is probably the most famous of the Italian Pecorino cheeses, all of which are made from sheep's milk, and take their names from the word *pecora* (sheep).

As the name would suggest, Pecorino Romano was created near Rome, but much production is now focused on Sardinia. It is matured for between eight and twelve months, and has an ivory-colored paste that darkens and develops a saltier flavor as the cheese matures into a typical *grana* cheese, with a hard, granular texture and piquant taste.

Like its siblings, for example Pecorino delle Crete Senesi and the Sicilian Pecorino Canestrato, Pecorino Romano is ideal for grating and is typically used in pasta dishes and salads. The mature cheese is shaved thinly and served with cured meats, fruits, or breads. It also makes a superb dessert cheese, drizzled lightly with a little full-flavored honey. **LF**

Taste: *The taste of Manchego is determined by its age and provenance. As it matures and hardens, a good farmhouse cheese develops fantastic intensity and length of flavor.*

Taste: *The fruity, zesty tang of the newly mature cheese develops into a well-defined piquancy. The potent flavor so typical of grana cheeses becomes more robust with age.*

Pecorino di Fossa

Leidsekaas

Italy offers literally hundreds of ewe's milk cheeses, but Pecorino di Fossa is absolutely unique. It is a *formaggio di fossa*, or buried cheese, which matures in a pothole covered with leaves or straw.

A specialty of Sogliano al Rubicone in southern Emilia-Romagna, the cheese was originally concealed to protect it during the internecine conflicts that were common before Italy became a single nation. Today, it is entombed during August, wrapped in canvas, and sealed in a communal *fossa*, or "grave," until St. Catherine's Day in late November.

Pecorino cheeses are always hard and "sheepy." After three months in humid, airless environments, they emerge with a powerful pungency. But what comes out depends on what goes in. Cheeses that were part-ripened will be harder and drier than those that were still young, and there is no conformity in size, shape, or color. The outsides can be russet, yellow, or dirty white; the paste can range from off-white to a pale straw hue. Although it is used as a cooking cheese, Pecorino di Fossa is best enjoyed by itself, accompanied by honey or fruit. **MR**

The arms of the southern Dutch town of Leiden, two crossed keys, figure on every authentic aged Leidsekaas. One of a family of large pressed cheeses including Gouda and, from Friesland in the north of the Netherlands, Kanterkaas, it can be eaten young as part of a typical breakfast collation or aged for many years: it is sometimes coated in reddish wax.

What gives Leidsekaas its special character is flavoring with cumin, caraway, and occasionally cloves, too. The spices are only mixed with a part of the fresh curd and sandwiched between two other layers that contain cheese only. Leidsekaas is made both by creameries and in dairies on cheese-making farms: Boeren-leidsekaas (PDO), the farmhouse variety, is usually prepared from unpasteurized milk.

Aging completely transforms these cheeses, making them even more interesting than their spice content might suggest. The wheels, which weigh about 17 pounds (8 kg), can easily be sliced at first, but a six-year-old cheese will be harder than an aged Parmigiano-Reggiano. The taste and appearance will also reflect changes brought about by time. **MR**

Taste: *In general, Pecorino di Fossa is sharp and tangy with a hint of bitterness that contrasts with the sweetness of ewe's milk, giving a complex taste experience.*

Taste: *The young cheeses are springy, yellowish, and pleasantly flavored by the raw spices. With age the color darkens to burnt orange and the texture hardens.*

Roquefort

Bleu d'Auvergne

One of the world's "big three" blue cheeses, Roquefort (AOC) has acquired its fair share of legends. The most popular is that a young shepherd left his lunch of bread and ewe's milk cheese in a cave in southwest France while he visited his girlfriend. When it was later discovered, the bread had gone moldy, as had the cheese, but the results were delicious. What does have a historical basis is that Charles VI gave a monopoly to the inhabitants of Roquefort-sur-Soulzon to make this cheese.

Between fact and fiction we have the main elements of what Roquefort is: ewe's milk cheese with a characteristic blue marbling, matured most often in caves. This marbling comes from an eponymous form of bacterium, *Penicillium roqueforti*, which has since been used as the base for diverse blue cheeses. Roquefort is a seasonal cheese, matured for at least three months, and available from the end of winter. It should have an ivory ground with even marbling; when cut it should not crumble. Seepage of serum from the cheese is not a bad sign. In fact, some experts prize it. **MR**

Often described as a cow's milk Roquefort because its veining was once achieved with the help of moldy rye bread, Bleu d'Auvergne (AOC) is one of France's most widely eaten blue cheeses. It is also the first to have been manufactured industrially.

Auvergne was already known for its Cantal cheese in 1854, when a cheese-maker, Antoine Roussel, discovered he could induce blueing in his large Cantals by spiking them as they matured in his cellars. The taste of the marbled cheese was new and different, meaning he could sell it at a premium. (The link between *Penicillium roqueforti* bacteria and the blue veins was not understood scientifically until the early twentieth century.) As with other "blues," the milk is inoculated with bacteria and the fresh cheeses are pierced around their circumference to aerate them. During ripening, molds form on the hand-salted rinds and an even network of marbling develops inside. A similar cheese, Bleu des Causses (AOC), is produced to the same recipe, always with unpasteurized milk, farther south in the *départements* of Hérault and Gard. **MR**

Taste: *The smell of Roquefort is a pointer to the taste of this salty, powerfully flavored cheese. The sharpness, paired with a subtle sweetness, is its main attraction.*

Taste: *Firm and fatty, Bleu d'Auvergne has a strong cheesy scent. The taste is potent and very salty, with hints of sourness alongside subtle grassy, wildflower notes.*

Natural draft passages—fleurines—ensure
✪ *that Roquefort maturing in caves is well ventilated.*

Stilton

Curiously, this celebrated English blue cheese might never have been made in the town from which it takes its name. The association derives from the landlord of the Bell Inn in Stilton, Cooper Thornhill, who agreed in 1730 with a dairy farmer from Wymondham, in Leicestershire, that he would market his blue cheese. As Stilton was on the main stagecoach route between London and the north of England, word of the inn and its cheese spread. Blue cheese had been popular in the Midlands for generations, however, and Stilton (PDO) might have developed from a family recipe produced on the Quenby Hall estate for Lady Beaumont.

Today Stilton is one of very few English cheeses to benefit from a Protected Designation of Origin. It is produced by six creameries in the counties of Leicestershire, Nottinghamshire, and Derbyshire, using whole pasteurized milk from local cows.

Stiltons are unctuous and richly flavored. Today the blue veining that made its name is controlled by inoculation with *Penicillium roqueforti*, the mold with which Roquefort is made. **MR**

Taste: *As it ripens, Stilton develops a buttery, nutty smoothness with a hint of sharpness from the marbling. The texture is creamy and the finish clean but lasting.*

⊗ *A "cheese iron" is used to extract a core from a Stilton in order to check its flavor and texture.*

Smokey Blue™

Marketed as Smokey Blue™ and created in 2005 by the Rogue Creamery in Central Point, Oregon, this award-winning cheese is believed to be the world's first, and only, smoked blue cheese. Established in the 1930s in Oregon's Rogue River valley, the creamery is dedicated to producing artisanal cheeses and was the first to make blue cheese in caves west of the Missouri River.

The creamery specializes in blue cheeses and only uses milk from Brown Swiss and Holstein cows, which graze along the Rogue River on wild grasses, herbs, and flowers. The creamery took one of its own blue cheeses and cold smoked it for sixteen hours over hazelnut shells. This bold move resulted in a nutty-flavored cheese that is less sharp and tangy than most traditional blue cheeses.

Made from full-cream milk, this unique cheese is best eaten at room temperature. It is good simply on a baguette with fresh tomato and basil, sliced or melted atop a broiled burger, or tossed with chives into a warm, new potato salad. It is also a good conversation starter on a cheese plate. **SH**

Taste: *This semifirm buttery cheese has sweet caramel and hazelnut flavors, tempered with a sharp, saltiness and an understated smokiness.*

Cashel Blue

The Rock of Cashel stands high above Ireland's Tipperary plain, topped with the twelfth-century chapel of King Cormac. When Louis and Jane Grubb started making Cashel Blue on their family farm in the 1980s, they borrowed the iconic outcrop's name. Theirs was the first blue cheese to be made in Eire and its success helped inspire a string of new Irish cheeses—notably Milleens, Gubbeen, and Durrus.

The Grubbs intended Cashel to be a cheese for the local market, using milk from their Friesian herd to make something similar to Danish Blue. But it turned out closer to softer, creamier blue cheeses, and has grown into an internationally known brand that is exported to Europe and the United States. Today, Cashel is made from pasteurized milk, in wheels weighing 3¼ pounds (1.5 kg), which are ripened for about four months. The best cheeses are made between April and early fall when the cattle feed on the lush Irish pasture: these can be aged for longer. Another branch of the family produces a similar cheese, Crozier Blue, which is made from ewe's milk, like Roquefort. **MR**

Gorgonzola

Alongside Stilton and Roquefort, Gorgonzola (DOP) is one of the three greatest blue cheeses in the world today. Made from whole cow's milk, it belongs to the family of white "uncooked" cheeses known as *stracchino*. Around the eleventh century, however, or so the story goes, a fortunate accident occurred when an innkeeper left a white cheese out in his kitchen and it became veined with mold. The results tasted so good that the idea stuck and Gorgonzola became a *stracchino verde*, with its characteristic marbling of green or blue mold. Today cheesemakers rely on *Penicillium* spores to create their mold, and use metal rods to create channels that insure its even spread and growth.

Gorgonzola takes its name from a village near Milan, where the cheeses were originally thought to have been made. Today it has a DOP certification, which limits production to regions of Piedmont and Lombardy. Gorgonzola makes a wonderful table cheese, but also lends itself to cooking, having a particular affinity with walnuts, pasta, and peppery leaves like spinach and arugula. **LF**

Taste: *Milder, less salty, less sharp, and less blue than many blue cheeses, Cashel Blue stands out for its melt-in-the-mouth creaminess, to the point of being spreadable.*

Taste: *Semisoft and creamy with a subtle salty edge, Gorgonzola develops a firmer texture and gathers a flavorful spiciness and peppery pizzazz as it ages.*

Making air holes in a cheese containing Penicillium spores promotes the characteristic "blue" veining. »

Cabrales

Given its name and its reputation for pungency, the casual observer can be forgiven for thinking Cabrales (DOP) is a goat cheese. Although goat's milk is sometimes used in its recipe, mixed with cow's and even sheep's milk, it is its "blueness" that dominates Cabrales, not the creature that produced it. It is made in spring and summer in the Asturias region of northern Spain, and matured in limestone caves. The best is ripened for about four months. High, inaccessible pasturage gives the milk, which is generally unpasteurized, its special quality.

The cylinders of cheese, weighing 5 to 9 pounds (2.5–4 kg), are not dissimilar to Roquefort, but Cabrales lacks the latter's sweaty texture and salty taste. The rind is crustier, the texture a little crumbly, and the veining a vivid blue, rather than the greenish persillage of the French cheese. Cheese deity Steven Jenkins waxes lyrical about the taste. "[The] flavor immediately electrifies the tongue with . . . blackberries and currants; bittersweet chocolate; grass and hay; leather and woodsmoke, walnuts and, yes, beef . . ." **MR**

Taste: *The white paste contrasting with clear blue veins points to the taste that is intense and sharp-edged. The texture is open and crumbly, but smooth and rich.*

Cabrales matures in natural limestone caves. »

Fynsk Rygeost

Danes are very proud of this smoked cheese, which is arguably the only one of all the Danish cheeses that was invented in Denmark without taking "inspiration" from somewhere else. Rygeost, both fresh and smoked, is believed to date back to a sour-milk cheese—one of the earliest sorts of cheese—that was first produced by the Vikings. Cattle have been raised in Denmark for centuries and butter, milk, and cheese have long been part of the Danish diet.

Rygeost traditionally comes from a small group of cheese-makers on the island of Fyn, Denmark's third largest island, which has a long tradition of producing foods. On the island, the cheese is only made at the Løgismose Dairy. As well as producing around 1,650 tons of commercial rygeost each year, islanders also like to make their own cheeses, smoke them in brick-built "ovens," and eat them as part of their picnics on lazy summer evenings. The cheese is made with whole cow's milk, buttermilk, and rennet, and is traditionally smoked quickly (in about thirty seconds) over nettles and oat straw, which gives it its characteristic smoky flavor. The straw is cut in a special way to prevent it from snapping, as this would spoil the smoking. The cheese rests on a grid during smoking, causing the large white disks rapidly to become crisscrossed with brown marks. Often, the cheeses are sprinkled with caraway.

Rygeost is usually eaten with radishes and chives on a piece of Danish rye bread, but it is also good on white bread with black-currant jam. It is often included in *sommersalat* (summer salad) with toasted rye bread, and is eaten around a bonfire on Midsummer's Night, which is always celebrated in Scandinavia, along with copious quantities of beer. **CTj**

Leipäjuusto

The name of the Finnish cheese leipäjuusto, also known as juustoleipä, literally translates as "bread cheese," and derives from its manufacturing process, which can include baking to give it its characteristic golden brown color. Other dialects have various names, such as *narskujuusto*, that refer to the way in which the cheese "squeaks" while being eaten.

Leipäjuusto is a cheese steeped in centuries-old tradition and owes its high quality to the richness of Finnish cow's milk. Traditionally the cheese was made from cow's beestings, the rich yellow milk first taken from a cow that has recently calved. In the old days it was considered a festive food and was a common "repayment" to people who had helped with the harvest.

To extend its longevity, the cheese was left to dry and harden in rye bread. It could last for several years in this form, which most likely instigated the habit of dipping it in coffee to soften it. In Sweden, a few pieces are put into a cup and hot coffee poured over them to make *kaffeost*. The cheese can also be served with cloudberry jelly or fresh cloudberries. It is also sliced, with a little cream poured on top, followed by a sprinkling of sugar and cinnamon, and then grilled or baked for a few minutes and served with cloudberry jelly.

Today's leipäjuusto is typically soft and lasts for about a week in the refrigerator. It is round and flat with a slightly wheat breadlike surface derived from the oven. Leipäjuusto has a "squeaky" consistency and is eaten cold or warm. Most connoisseurs prefer the homemade variety, although the ready-made product is more common today. Popular brands include Juustoportti, Valio, Ingman, and Arla. **CC**

Taste: *This creamy, crumbly cheese has a distinct and distinctive smokiness. The taste remains smooth and aromatic, combined with a slightly acidic finish.*

Taste: *Somewhere in between unsalted halloumi and mozzarella but with a sweeter, more buttery flavor, leipäjuusto is popular served with cloudberry jelly.*

Milk from Finnish cows has a richness that derives from their lush pastures. »

Oscypek

Parenica

This delightful smoked sheep cheese comes from the Tatra Mountains, which form a natural border between Poland and Slovakia. It is traditionally made by Góral (highlander) shepherds from unpasteurized milk, using hand-carved molds that create distinctive rustic, geometric patterns on the spindle-shaped cheeses. Afterward, it is soaked in brine and smoked in tiny rustic smokehouses.

In the days before refrigeration, the cheeses could then be indefinitely suspended from a cottage rafter, protected by their brownish crust. They were mentioned in an early fifteenth-century chronicle and the first recorded recipe appeared in 1748. Polish officials are currently campaigning to have oscypek recognized with a European Union PDO, a project challenged by the existence of a similarly named Slovak cheese called ostiepok.

Oscypek is a favorite breakfast and supper food for many Poles, served with rye or black bread and butter. "Trendies" might add it cubed to salads in place of feta or bread it, fry it, and serve it with cranberry jam. **RS**

Parenica (PDO)—which means "steamed cheese" in Slovakian—has been made by shepherds in a mountainous region of the Slovak republic, close to the borders of Poland, the Czech Republic, and the Ukraine since the early 1800s. It is a semifirm cheese made from unpasteurized sheep's milk produced by the Wallachian, Cigaya, and East Friesian breeds, although sometimes cow's milk is added. The cheese is sometimes lightly smoked.

To make parenica cheese, the curdled cheese is molded by hand into lumps, which are then left to ferment before being placed in wooden churns and steamed in hot water. Steaming darkens the color of the outside of the cheese. The cheese is then pulled out of the water, stretched, and folded into strips. These are skilfully wound into two rolls connected in a distinctive S-shape and bound with cheese string. These distinctive spiral shapes were a popular decorative motif used by the ancient Slavs and parenica cheese always featured at the *jarmoks*, or annual fairs, traditionally held throughout the Slovak Republic. **CK**

Taste: *Oscypek is a mild, slightly salty cheese with faintly smoky undertones. It is cream colored and springy with a pleasantly squeaky texture on the teeth.*

Taste: *Parenica cheese has the odor of sheep's milk, a stringy, elastic texture, and a delicate, pleasantly salty flavor. The smoked version has a mildly smoky aroma.*

Oscypek is piled on a stall selling traditional
◉ *foods at a Christmas market in Krakow, Poland.*

Quail Egg

Until the twentieth century, quail were thought of as small wild game birds. But a combination of over-hunting and, in Italy, netting—a practice nineteenth-century sources claimed could capture 100,000 birds in a day—means the species is rarely found outside farms in Europe. They are reared commercially in large flocks both for their meat and for their eggs, which, with their pretty mottled shells, were once a rare delicacy.

Small enough to sit on a teaspoon, a quail egg is ideally suited as a garnish in restaurant cooking, and during the nouvelle cuisine era professional chefs dished them up in miniature versions of established dishes as an entrée or amuse-bouche. The fashion was bolstered by a range of recipes on how best to cook the eggs themselves. Soft-boiled eggs need three minutes, hard-boiled five. Vinegar in the boiling water makes the shells easier to peel.

Setting aside the mechanics of their cooking, quail eggs tend to be distributed through the food chain fresher than hen eggs. They are also richer, as well as being higher in cholesterol. **MR**

Taste: A quail egg tastes like a good free-range egg, although the quality, richness, and depth of flavor can vary depending on the bird's diet.

Gull Egg

The Vikings considered gull eggs to be a delicacy and they remain a traditional pleasure during the spring breeding season in northern regions from Alaska to Siberia via Scandinavia. In England, where the eggs were a staple hors d'oeuvre in Edwardian gentlemen's clubs, they are regaining their status as a delicacy today. Just as a century ago, they are served in their pointed, speckled shells, albeit today they are more often soft-boiled than hard-boiled.

Today the collection of wild bird eggs is strictly controlled in many countries. In Britain, collectors must have a license and are limited to a narrow seasonal window. However, independent research for the *Journal of Environmental Monitoring* (2005) appears to show that gull eggs are increasingly being contaminated by toxic pollutants. It concluded children and nursing mothers should not eat them and that healthy adults should reduce their consumption to a minimum. Given this unequivocal warning, it might be that gull eggs will soon become the northern hemisphere's answer to Japanese fugu—a gastronomic matter of life and death. **MR**

Taste: Despite a diet of fish, gull eggs do not taste remotely fishy. They have a strikingly rich, intensely flavored yolk and a fragile, creamy white.

Pheasant Egg

Goose Egg

Although the pheasant spread from its home in the Caucasus into Asia, into Europe, and thence into the Americas, its eggs have rarely been harvested for anything but breeding, although Anthimus, the Byzantine gourmet who was also an ambassador to the Franks, referred to them in the sixth century CE.

Today, pheasant eggs are usually a neglected by-product of field sports. On country estates pheasants are bred and released into the wild in order to supply game birds for managed shoots. The wild hen pheasants are caught in traps in February and kept in laying pens. Between April and June they will lay about thirty-five eggs each, and, although most will go to the hatcheries to provide the birds that will be released during the following hunting season, some eggs are kept as a luxury.

Larger than quail eggs—they weigh about ¾ ounce (22 g)—pheasant eggs are rounded at one end but more pointed than a hen's at the other. Rarely sold outside of farm shops, they are hard to find and expensive, each one costing up to three times the price of a larger chicken egg. **MR**

It would be easy to assume from its appearance—which, just like hen eggs, can vary from breed to breed—that a goose egg is a large version of a chicken egg. Size is, of course, an issue. Goose eggs can weigh up to two or three times as much as hen eggs, which typically tip the scales at around 1¾ to 2½ ounces (50–70 g), although there are other differences, too.

Even allowing for the fact that the bird's diet will influence the composition of its eggs—as will its age—geese lay much richer eggs than hens. A typical goose egg contains a far higher level of cholesterol and saturated fat than a typical hen egg.

Strangely, goose egg whites will not whip to a stiff foam, so it is not possible to make a soufflé or a zabaglione. Nor do goose eggs respond well to boiling. They will, however, produce extremely well-flavored, rich custards, scrambled eggs, and cakes that use a chemical raising agent. When breaking a goose egg shell, it is advisable to crack it first with a blunt-edge kitchen utensil to avoid damaging the yolk. Goose yolks have a bright color. **MR**

Taste: *Hard-boiled and shelled, a pheasant egg might be mistaken for a gull egg, except that the white is less translucent. The yolk tastes similar to the best hen eggs.*

Taste: *Used in cooking, goose eggs give the impression of more body. Sauces are thicker, glossier, and taste as though they have been enriched with butter.*

Burford Brown Egg

Pei Dan

Burford Brown eggs take their name from the pretty town of Burford in the Cotswolds, in England. The eggs acquired their name early in the twentieth century, partly on account of their location and partly for their thick, rich brown shells. That said, both breed and shell have a rather minor influence on the quality of an egg: freshness, feed, and animal welfare are much more important.

There is no pedigree breed of hen called a "Burford," but the eggs are marketed by a specialist free-range egg supplier, Clarence Court, a brand created by farmer Philip Lee-Woolf in 1990. Although based in Cornwall, he has adopted the name and story, and uses hybrid hens that will lay eggs with the special character.

Compared to most other eggs sold through British multiple retailers, Burford Browns have the character that those familiar with eggs from traditionally reared barnyard fowl recognize. In cooking, the advantages of the eggs over factory-farmed ones is marked: thicker custards, stiffer mayonnaise, better cakes, and lighter soufflés. **MR**

Pei dan—or good pei dan—looks as if it belongs in a museum rather than on a plate. The "white" ranges from golden amber to an unusual translucent black; the yolk contains merging rings of soft green, yellow, and gray; the middle is soft, dark, and oozing.

People unused to these wonderful preserved eggs tend to view them with horrified fascination, and, if they bother to taste them, are frequently repulsed. Perhaps it is names such as "thousand-year-old eggs" or "century eggs" that scare off the novices. In fact, most mass-produced eggs take less than two weeks to "cure," while the better, more traditional eggs are cured under their coating of ash, tea, slaked lime, salt, and often earth for about three months.

Pei dan is usually eaten peeled but uncooked, often with pickled spring ginger. It can also be simmered with congee and salted dried pork or steamed with spinach, garlic, and another type of Chinese preserved eggs—salted eggs. You can smell "bad" pei dan from across a room—the strong ammonia scent will make your eyes water. **KKC**

Taste: *Burford Brown eggs have a thicker yolk than standard free-range eggs, with a deep, orange-yellow color and a much richer flavor.*

Taste: *A good pei dan tastes rich, complex, and pungent, like ripe blue cheese with a very faint hint of ammonia. The texture of the white is slightly rubbery, but the yolk is soft.*

Salted duck eggs are sold in colorful nets at the annual Duanwu Festival in China. »

Unagi

The eel (unagi) has long been a valued food and a legendary source of "stamina" in Japan. The rich, fatty flesh of this fish is indeed high in proteins and vitamin A. In Japan, eel consumption traditionally rises during the period known as the "days of the bull," the two days after the rainy season in June, when the enervating humidity of summer creates a lethargy known as *natsubate*. This condition demands the consumption of energy-giving food, with a consequent rush on eel restaurants. Such is unagi's popularity in Japan that eels are farmed on a large scale. Historically, the farmed eels were housed in artificial ponds, but now they are raised in indoor tanks in temperature-controlled conditions. Natural eel populations are currently under threat and the food should be obtained from sustainable sources.

In Japan, the most popular way of eating eel is in the dish *kabayaki*, in which the eel is basted with sweetened soy sauce and then grilled over charcoal, resulting in deliciously contrasting crisp skin and succulent flesh. Japan has many restaurants offering only eel dishes, especially *kabayaki*. True unagi enthusiasts opt for *shirayaki*, eel grilled without sauce. *Unagi donburi*, a convenient, tasty, one-pot meal where the cooked eel is served on steamed rice, is said to have been invented to enable kabuki audiences to eat without interruption during the famously long performances.

In Japan's eastern Kanto area, the fins, tail, and head of the eel are removed before grilling; Kansai folk in the west prefer to leave them on. A common and delicious accompaniment everywhere is the tongue-numbing pepper and citrus *sansho*, which is commonly served with fatty foods. **SB**

Elver

Thinner than a pencil, as long as a finger, and almost transparent—hence their alternative name "glass eels"—elvers are fragile creatures. These immature eels cluster in shoals near the mouths of tidal rivers, visible mainly as a wriggling disturbance in the water. Mature eels spawn in the Sargasso Sea, in the middle of the North Atlantic, and it takes two or three years for the Gulf Stream to carry their leaflike larvae (*Leptocephalus*) toward Europe. On arrival, the little creatures shift shape again and transform into what are recognizably miniature eels. Today, elvers are an expensive, highly prized delicacy.

In Britain, the tradition of eating both eels and elvers dates back to medieval times. The River Severn was long noted for its abundance of eels. Elvers there are trapped at night in fine-meshed nets placed across the river as they make their way upstream. Today, much of the elver catch is sold abroad to supply eel farms. English ways of eating elvers include elver pie (a type of pasty), frying them in bacon fat, and flouring and deep-frying them.

Elvers are also treasured in Spain, a country with a rich tradition of seafood dishes; the writer Ernest Hemingway wrote appreciatively of *angulas* "as tiny as beansprouts." A favorite Spanish way of preparing *angulas* is to fry them briefly in olive oil with garlic and a touch of chile, and serve them sizzling hot to be eaten with a wooden fork. When the live elvers hit the hot pan, they lose their glassiness and turn an opaque cream hue; their eyes are seen as two black dots.

Sadly, with European eel populations at a historic low, consumption of this traditional delicacy cannot be justified at present. **MR**

Taste: *Cooked* kabayaki-*style, unagi is sweet and unctuous, with a pronounced fishy taste, and an underlying smokiness. It has a rich, creamy texture.

Taste: *The delight of elvers is in their texture, which is rather like that of pasta, but creamier and with a little more bite. The taste is mild and delicate, not fishy.*

Unagi, cooked in the **kabayaki**-*style as here, is costly in Japan but highly valued for its nutritional content.*

Tilapia

Mojarra

Tilapia has become one of the most farmed fish around the world, although it is not a new practice: records indicate that tilapia farming existed more than 2,000 years ago in ancient Egypt. Tilapia is the common name for about 100 different species worldwide, and it is becoming more and more popular as an eco-friendly fish. Both *Sarotherodon mossambicus*, also known as Mozambique tilapia, and *S. niloticus,* the Nile tilapia, are good for eating.

Tilapia have a hardy, adaptable constitution, thriving in fresh, brackish, and salt waters, as well as in crowded farming aquariums. Tilapia carefully farmed in controlled environments have more flavor than wild hybrid varieties. Tilapia is now popular in the United States, where most of the supply comes from farms in Central and South America.

A versatile fish, tilapia can be broiled, baked, fried, blackened, stir-fried, or added to a fish soup. Its mildness offers a blank canvas on which cooks can overlay a multitude of other flavors. It is particularly suited to Chinese cuisine, which allows seasonings such as garlic and ginger to really shine. **BF**

The mojarra is a tropical fish from the Gerreidae family, found in the Caribbean. It lives predominatly in shallow coastal areas to avoid larger predators, although it is also known to occasionally venture into rivers inland. There are many different species of mojarra and they can be difficult to identify unless very closely examined.

A silvery fish with a compressed body and a highly protruding mouth, it grows up to 13½ inches (35 cm) long. It is highly prized throughout Central America, and is popular in Colombia, Ecuador, Puerto Rico, Costa Rica, and Mexico, where it is widely found in markets and restaurants.

Mojarra is served in a number of ways throughout Latin America. Fried as *mojarra frita,* it has a tasty crusty skin and is eaten with white rice and *tostones,* or flattened fried plantain. It can be roasted whole, including head, tails, and bones, and served with white rice, avocado, lettuce, tomato, and lime juice. It is also simply grilled over smoking coals, then eaten with hot chipotle pepper sauce and sautéed onions. **CK**

Taste: *Tilapia has lean, white flesh. Its mild, slightly sweet flavor makes it perfect for marinating and partnering with sauces and other ingredients.*

Taste: *The mojarra is a bony fish with flaky, meaty, white flesh. It has a mild, satisfying flavor that is a cross between tilapia and snapper.*

In a 1400–1390 BCE tomb painting, an official of Thutmose IV spears tilapia in marshland.

Spotted Sorubim

Sterlet

Few freshwater fish from south of the equator possess both the size and the supreme flavor of the spotted sorubim (or *pintado*), a native of the São Francisco, Prata, and Paraguay river basins in Brazil. The undisputed king of sorubims in South America, it has distinctive skin covered in black spots and can exceed 5 feet (1.5 m) in length and 176 pounds (80 kg) in weight. Despite feeding on crustaceans and small fish, which it ingests along with mud and thick sand, its white, fatty, bonefree flesh has a pleasant flavor, as well as a consistent texture. Either cut into thick slices or roasted whole, the spotted sorubim reigns in *churrascarias* (barbecue grill restaurants) all over Brazil; its qualities are enhanced by the effects of charcoal grilling.

With its flat head and round body covered in skin instead of scales, the spotted sorubim lends itself to many other culinary delights. It is often cooked in an oven with only a coarse salt seasoning to bring out the taste of the flesh, or in a clay pan, with the resulting juice used to make *pirão*, a salty paste thickened with fine cassava flour. **AL**

Of the twenty-five species of sturgeon, sterlet is one of the smallest. It can reach about 20 inches (50 cm) in length and is about the size of a farmed salmon. The river-loving sterlet (*Acipenser ruthenus*) is found as far north as Siberia. It was once abundant in the estuaries that feed into the Black and Caspian Seas. But sturgeon numbers have been decimated in the hunt for caviar and even the most ardent fisheater should think twice before sampling a wild sterlet.

In times when sterlet was plentiful, it was valued both for its taste and texture. Recipes for it appear in early Russian and Turkish cooking manuals. Although sturgeon farming has been developing in North America and Europe, mainly with a view to supplying caviar, the smaller sterlet has only recently been targeted by aquaculture industries.

The whole fish was served grilled to Presidents Putin and Bush when the U.S. leader stopped over in Moscow. Barbecued, baked, stewed, fried, in soups, and even raw, it often figures on the menus of Russia's new generation restaurants, but many of these have originated in fish farms. **MR**

Taste: *As a fish rich in "good" fat, the spotted sorubim reveals its full glory when flame-grilled; its oil softens the flesh and the flames confer a delicious burned aroma.*

Taste: *Praised as the "queen of sturgeons," wild sterlet is often compared to veal. Firm and meaty, it has a compact, flesh with a mild taste, reflecting its freshwater origin.*

This fish market stall in Astrahan, southern Russia, is entirely devoted to various forms of smoked sturgeon. »

Pike

Zander

"A long, fast, very savage fish," pike has been described as a freshwater barracuda. It can empty a lake or pond of other fish—even take aquatic birds. So far as its reputation as a food goes, *Esox lucius* has had a reputation both as a delicacy and as inedible.

In the Middle Ages, it was much admired. A recipe by Taillevent from the fourteenth-century *Le Viandier*, for pike dressed with ginger and saffron, begins with the advice to the cook to slap it on the broiler. Today, Lyon has a particular liking for this fish, especially those that are caught in the historic fishponds of the neighboring Dombes. Pounded and mixed with cream, they are the basis of the celebrated *quenelles de brochet*, which are served with a crayfish-based *sauce Nantua*.

Although specimens weighing up to 45 pounds (20 kg) have been caught, the preferred size for cooking is 2 to 4 pounds (900 g–1.8 kg). Pike has a thick layer of scales and sharp, pointed bones, so presents as much of a challenge to the cook as to the game fisherman. Opponents argue that it can taste very muddy if it has lived in stagnant water. **MR**

A much-prized fish gracing the tables of restaurants and riverside inns throughout Europe, zander (*Stizostedion lucioperca*) is a voracious predator known to grow to 3 feet 3 inches (1 m) in length. It has exceedingly sharp teeth, and enjoys a diet of smaller fish, which gives it a full and meaty flavor.

Also known as pike-perch, zander is often incorrectly thought to be closely related to the other "wolf of the river," the mean and snappy pike. Zander also has a similar fin pattern to freshwater bream, but it is, in fact, not a hybrid of either of these fish. It is native to the fresh and brackish waters of Central and Eastern Europe and much of the fish landed there finds its way to the restaurants of the Netherlands, where it is considered to be a delicacy.

It was introduced into the United Kingdom, specifically East Anglia, primarily as a sport fish, but proved to be so damaging to other fish stocks it was culled. It is also imported there in small quantities, but demand in Europe is so high that zander is a rare find in English markets. In flavor, it is often compared with the North American walleye. **STS**

Taste: *Pike has white, firm, flaky flesh. Its taste lacks the sweet mineral aromas of some sea fish, but at its best has a flavor comparable to that of grey mullet or sea bass.*

Taste: *Zander flesh is very firm and meaty with a full herbaceous flavor quite similar to carp and almost indistinguishable from that of a walleye.*

A plentiful catch of young pike—known as ❸ kawakamasu *in Japan—is dried in the sun near Chiba.*

Carp

Elephant Ear Fish

Widely esteemed in Asian, Eastern European, and Jewish cuisine—whether steamed, roasted, or poached in a seasoned stock—carp is served at family meals on high days and holidays. The fish is a delicacy particularly in Poland, where it is roasted and served as a traditional festive dish on Christmas Eve. Carp is also beautiful cooked *au bleu*; that is, cooked immediately after being caught, usually by simmering in white wine with herbs, or in water containing salt and vinegar. Muddy water leads to muddy-flavored fish, so if possible the best choice will be fish farmed on gravel.

The common carp has a dark bronze back with gold sides and a yellow belly, and the body is fully covered with large scales. All members of the carp family have a thick natural slime that needs to be rinsed away prior to scaling; this is best done by a gentle soaking in acidulated water.

Species of carp are native to the Danube and Asia, but various types have been introduced to many countries worldwide. Carp is one of the most widely farmed freshwater fish in the world. **STS**

Given that Vietnamese cuisine is somewhat notorious among Westerners for delicacies such as dog or still-beating snake heart, the idea of elephant ear fish might not instantly be considered appetizing. In fact, elephant ear fish is a type of butterfly fish (*Chaetodon*) most noted for its flat shape, similar to bass.

The fish is popular throughout the Mekong River Delta. What is most notable about it, however, is how it is presented. Roughly the size of a large platter, the fish is drawn, fried, and then propped up between wooden chopsticks, sometimes dressed with fresh herbs and sculpted vegetables. Chopsticks are used to peel off the crispy, curling scales, and prize away the soft, white, flaky flesh. The flesh is then layered, along with local herbs such as mint, cilantro, basil, and sometimes noodles and cucumber, in thin rice-paper wrappers. These are then rolled up and dipped in *nuoc cham* fish sauce. The result is a wonderfully sweet and succulent dish, as the texture of the meaty, earthy, soft flesh is balanced by the light, but chewy, wrapers, and given a kick by the salty-, hot chili-, garlic-, and lime-fish sauce. **CK**

Taste: *Carp are best known for their herbaceous, murky, almost woody flavor, but this will depend primarily upon the habitat in which they live.*

Taste: *The elephant ear fish is known for its wonderfully sweet and succulent taste; its notoriety comes from its appearance and name.*

Cooking simply with herbs and seasoning
Ⓚ *preserves and enhances the flavor of carp.*

Copper River King Salmon

Arctic Char

For a period that begins in mid-May and lasts a mere four weeks, hundreds of thousands of king salmon (*Oncorhynchus tshawytscha*) grapple their way upstream through 300 miles of Alaska's Copper River, from the Pacific to their spawning grounds. This huge effort translates into flesh that is firm, yet packed with extra stores of flavor-bearing fat.

The first major wild Alaskan fish to come to market each spring, and the largest of the five Pacific salmon species, king salmon's fleeting availability and steep retail price catapult it into the realm of luxury, but salmon groupies swear the annual splurge is worth it. This was not always so.

While Copper River salmon had been fished for canning as early as 1889, the king salmon began its rise to prominence almost a century later. This was when former fisherman Jon Rowley convinced his peers salmon could fetch a much higher price if they improved their onboard processing and brought the fish to market fresh. Today, king salmon are sustainably harvested using methods approved by the respected Seafood Watch Program. **CLH**

A close cousin of both salmon and trout, Arctic char (*Salvelinus alpinus*) is one of the most northerly freshwater fish. Slow to mature, it thrives in the icy polar regions of North America and Europe, including Canada, Iceland, and Russia: in the wild it rarely reaches more than 12 inches (30 cm) in length or 10 ounces (300 g) in weight.

Arctic char are unusual in that they can flourish both as resident populations or as anadromous, meaning some fish live permanently in land-locked lakes—notably in Scandinavia, the Alps, and the northern British Isles—while others reside in salt water, returning to freshwater rivers and streams to spawn and spend the winter.

The fish has a long history in Inuit culture, where it provided an integral food source for indigenous people. In England during the eighteenth and nineteenth centuries, Arctic char was highly prized and a status symbol of the wealthy. While abundant in the wild, its extreme habitat makes it difficult to economically bring to market, so much of what is found in restaurants and markets is farmed. **CLH**

Taste: *High in omega-3 oils, Copper River king salmon is packed with flavor. Its large stores of fat deliver a velvety texture, without the mushiness of much farmed salmon.*

Taste: *Arctic char can range in color from deep orange to pale pink. It has a delicate, mild flavor that resembles salmon or trout. It should be tender, but not mushy.*

A woman with her catch of Arctic char in the North Slope of Alaska, where rivers flow over frozen tundra.

Rainbow Trout

Ishkan Trout

This sparkling, eye-catching fish is native to the rivers of the Pacific west coast, Alaska, northern United States, Canada, and Asia. Straight from the water, pan-fried or poached in a light *court bouillon* over a campfire on the riverbank, a wild rainbow trout is a gastronomic sensation.

Rainbow trout is a round fish with a deep body, a small head, and beady eyes. The skin color is predominantly spotty, light green across the back shading down to a white belly and a striking pink stripe running parallel to the lateral line down the flank of the fish, giving the rainbow appearance. The color of the flesh depends on the diet of the trout. A wild fish might feed on a freshwater shrimp diet, creating a pale orange-pink flesh. Farmed fish, on the other hand are fed a dye (from both natural and synthetic sources) that gives the flesh a deep orange color.

The wild migratory rainbow species, caught in the Pacific, is the steelhead trout, but, like salmon, it spends only part of its life cycle at sea, returning to fresh water to spawn. **STS**

One of the largest high-altitude lakes in the world, picturesque, alpine Lake Sevan in Armenia, is home to a unique fish prized for its subtle flavor. Contrary to its name, ishkan trout (*Salmo ischchan*) is actually a member of the salmon family. In this land-locked country ishkan trout is referred to as the "prince of fishes," reputedly because the spots on its head resemble a crown. Records show that the fish was served at a state banquet in 1919 surrounded with its own caviar and accompanied by a sauce made with the cream of water-buffalo milk mixed with freshly peeled walnuts and a touch of horseradish. The fish is still served today with a walnut sauce.

Sadly, the ishkan trout is endangered due to the introduction of competing fish such as common whitefish and Danube crayfish into Lake Sevan. However, it is now legally farmed locally, and it was also successfully introduced into Kyrgyz Republic's Issyk-Kul Lake in central Asia during the 1970s.

Ishkan trout is delicious broiled or poached. In Armenia, it is often stuffed with tender fruits such as prunes or apricots before being baked. **CK**

Taste: *The flavor of fresh trout depends on its habitat, but it often has a slightly earthy note. The flakes of a wild fish have a delicate flavor reminiscent of herbs and fungi.*

Taste: *Ishkan trout has a mild, delicate flavor similar to trout. Its pink flesh is virtually boneless. The broiled fish is excellent served rolled up in the local lavash flatbread.*

Baking does not spoil the beautiful pink
ⓚ *coloring on the skin of rainbow trout.*

Sardine

Sea Trout

All around the world silvery, soft-boned sardines have long provided fresh, barbecued suppers. Straight out of the water, still in rigor mortis, with bright convex eyes, and few loose scales, sardines are, at this stage, at their very best.

Although they have many fine bones, for which they are often criticized, sardines also offer lovely cream-colored fillets when cooked. A quick scaling and gutting can easily be achieved with thumb and finger in place of a knife. They are best broiled, barbecued, or marinated and can also be eaten raw as an hors d'oeuvre. Traditional flavor partners include oregano, extra virgin olive oil, and lemon.

The term sardine varies depending on where you are in the world. In Europe, it is used to describe a young European pilchard, under about 4 inches (10 cm) in length. Any longer and it is just a pilchard. In the United States, it refers to any small, saltwater fish such as sprat, young pilchard, and herring.

Portugal, Spain, and France produce high-quality canned sardines, packed in extra virgin olive oil, which are a useful store cupboard staple. **STS**

Sea trout (*Salmo trutta trutta*), or salmon trout, are sleek, gleaming fish considered by many to outrank salmon both in looks and flavor. Like salmon, the flesh is soft-pink because of a diet of crustaceans, which contain the distinctive carotenoid pigment. The flavor, too, is similar, although sea trout is more creamy. The whole fish is often stuffed before cooking, but its taste is enhanced by simply poaching it in a lightly acidulated *court bouillon* and then being served with a creamy hollandaise sauce.

The migratory form of the widely distributed brown trout, sea trout are found in the streams and rivers of northern Europe. They spend between one to five years in fresh water and their middle life at sea, where they feed and grow, before returning to fresh water to spawn. Sea trout have been introduced to Chile, Argentina, New Zealand, Australia, and the eastern seaboard of North America.

Good brown and sea trout needs little flavoring and suits poaching, broiling, or frying. It is deliciously sweet and spicy broiled with honey, butter, salt, and plenty of freshly ground black pepper. **STS**

Taste: *Although sardines are high in omega-3 oils, they are not overly "fishy" in taste. They are best eaten very fresh and are delicious grilled and simply lightly seasoned.*

Taste: *Sea trout is herbier than rainbow trout, but less earthy then the nonmigratory brown trout. It is delicious fried, poached, or cooked* en papillote.

Freshly caught sardines, cooked over charcoal and
❸ *served with lemon, are popular beach fare in Spain.*

Shisamo

Whitebait

A small, saltwater fish, about 4 to 6 inches (10–15 cm) long, shisamo is common to the northern Pacific Ocean and the Atlantic Ocean, although it travels to fresh water to spawn. Indeed, it is traditionally caught in Japan at the Kushiro river mouth as it swims upstream in October and November. A rare and expensive delicacy, the roe-carrying female fish are most prized, and those from Kushiro City and Mukawa particularly so. For a short period in the autumn, shisamo is served locally in Mukawa as sashimi and sushi.

Most usually, however, shisamo are salted, dried, and threaded, side-by-side with their mouths gaping open, along a bamboo skewer for char-grilling. This makes an impressive, if somewhat unnerving, sight in the street markets. The process not only preserves the fish, but salting followed by sun-drying breaks down protein, creating amino acids that create the delicious flavor known as *umami*. The aroma of charcoal-grilled shisamo wafting though Japanese streets, as late night drinkers sip their sake, is a never-to-be-forgotten memory. **SB**

Small, silver-white, and translucent, whitebait are the young fry of various fish, caught during the first year of their life. In England, they are usually young herring or sprat; in New England, they are the fry of silverside or sand-eel; whereas in New Zealand, they are young freshwater fish such as inanga. In France, whitebait are known as *blanchailles,* and in Italy as *bianchetti* or *gianchetti*, although the latter are usually the spawn of sardines and anchovies.

The culinary history of whitebait in England goes back to the early seventeenth century, when small fry swarmed the tidal waters of the Thames. These delicate little fish did not travel well, so diners had to go to them. Taverns along the river in Greenwich and Blackwall started to serve special whitebait dinners that proved highly popular.

Then as now, whitebait were fried whole. To prepare these delicious small fry, wash fresh whitebait in cold salt water, drain, toss in beaten egg, and lightly dust in well-seasoned flour before deep-frying in oil until golden. Simply serve with lemon wedges. **LW**

Taste: *Char-grilled shisamo are crispy, smoky, salty, and deeply savory, with a slightly bitter and burnt aftertaste. Their texture is chewy and meaty.*

Taste: *A mound of tiny silver fish, lightly battered, deep-fried to crispness, and doused with lemon juice delivers the intensified taste of a whole fish in one small mouthful.*

In Japan, reusable wooden crates are used to ✪ *transport the catch to Tokyo's Tsukiji fish market.*

Hong Kong Grouper

A delicacy in China and Southeast Asia, Hong Kong grouper (*Epinephelus akaara*) is found in shallow seas and around coral reefs throughout the Far East. This exotic fish is regarded as a gourmet food and since the region—and in particular Hong Kong—has become more prosperous, so has demand for the fish increased. This is threatening the survival of one of the oldest fish living on coral reefs.

Fishermen sometimes use cyanide to stun their catch of wild Hong Kong grouper. The fish are then packaged in bags of water before being delivered to seafood restaurants where they are sold to eager locals at exorbitant prices. The endangered status of wild Hong Kong grouper has led to much effort being channeled into encouraging the local population to opt for farm-reared Hong Kong grouper instead.

In China and Hong Kong, grouper is believed to bring good luck and have medicinal value. The fish can be baked, fried, or broiled. In China, it is often served steamed and eaten whole. In Southeast Asia, it is also delicious wok-fried with lemongrass and stuffed with *belachan*, a local shrimp paste. **CK**

Hiramasa Kingfish

Plucked from the waters encircling the South Pole, immediately killed by *iki jimi*—a Japanese method, where a spike through the brain minimizes pain and stress, and drains the blood, resulting in whiter fillets—the most-prized kingfish sashimi starts its journey north cooled in a slurry of ice.

In Tokyo, *Seriola lalandi* (a.k.a. yellowtail kingfish, or gold-striped amberjack) is welcomed at the tables of the best restaurants and on the plates of the most discerning diners. Biodynamically farmed in a cool climate, off the south coast of Australia, it is firmer and tastier than that farmed in subtropical waters. Served as sashimi, hiramasa kingfish is firm, rich in oil, and sweet; its flesh is a pretty pale pearl pink.

Hiramasa cooks to a moist opaque ivory, but the broad flakes can easily become dry and tough with overcooking. It stands up well in Southeast Asian curries and casseroles, where the flesh holds together firmly, yet benefits from the moisture of a sauce. Although more delicate in flavor and texture, cooked hiramasa kingfish can be compared to a gentler tuna. **RH**

Taste: *The Hong Kong grouper is prized for its tasty, firm flesh. It has a magnificent fresh flavor when steamed. Farmed fish is an acceptable substitute for the wild.*

Taste: *Hiramasa is at its best raw. In sashimi it is firm to the bite, with a fresh, marine aroma. Cooked, it has a meaty mouthfeel, with a taste that is mildly sweet and briny.*

Grouper sold in Hong Kong's busy night fish markets ⊘ *is now more likely to be farmed than wild-caught.*

Coral Trout

In the aerated tanks of Cantonese restaurants, thick-lipped, fire-engine-red fish sprinkled with iridescent blue spots swish slowly up to the glass through the bubbly water. Coral trout (*Plectropomus leopardus*), also known as leopard fish, flourish in subtropical waters around the reefs of Australia and throughout the Indo-Pacific. Their spectacular skin, which varies from red or bright orange to dark olive or brown, conceals a most succulent meat, with a mild sweet taste and gentle aroma.

While the fish can grow to more than 50 pounds (23 kg), it is small-to-medium fish, weighing upward of 2 pounds (900 g), that make the best eating. The pale pink flesh cooks to a brilliant, almost ultraviolet white and forms large, mouthwatering flakes. Coral trout belong to the same family as sea bass and groupers, which gives an indication of the general taste and mouthfeel. While they suit many cooking styles—including steaming, sautéing, and deep-frying—broiling the fillets simply with lemon and butter beautifully highlights both the taste and the texture of this sublime fish. **RH**

Taste: *The large, firm flakes are sweet in taste, velvety in texture, and devoid of a "fishy" taste or aroma. The skin can sometimes taint the flesh with a bitter flavor.*

Silver Pomfret

Shaped like a plate with aerodynamic fins and a forked tail, silver pomfret (*Pampus argenteus*) swims off the Indian subcontinent, around the China seas, and as far as coastal Japan. Like many other fish prized for their taste, it risks extinction from over-exploitation, in part because its natural habitat is the muddy seabed of inshore waters. It belongs to a small genus of fish commonly known as "butterfish" (Stromateidae), a name that provides a clue as to its cooked texture. Also known as white pomfret, it should not be confused with the black pomfret that belongs to a different species, and fetches less than a quarter of its price in Asian markets.

Chinese and Southeast Asian chefs generally cook it whole (they eat the soft fins, too), but it fillets and skins easily, producing lean, boneless strips of flesh. Down the west coast of India from Mumbai to Goa it is baked in a tandoor, while Thais prefer to fry theirs. Chinese and Malays like it best steamed with ginger and scallions. To date silver pomfret has defied all attempts to farm it, so it remains an exclusive and increasingly rare luxury. **MR**

Taste: *Silver pomfret has an ivory white flesh. Its texture when steamed is soft and melting. It is very fatty, too. Freshly caught, it is almost sweet, and not at all fishy.*

In South India, foods such as pomfret are served on banana leaf, which may also be used as a flavoring. ❯❯

Barramundi

Barracuda

Succulent, sweetly flavored, healthy, inexpensive, easy to cook, available fresh locally all year-round, and it leaves your environmental conscience clear. Impossible? No, it is barramundi.

Native to tropical northern Australian waters, the barramundi (*Lates calcarifer*) is one of the world's finest eating and sporting fish. To sample the mouthwatering delights of wild "barra"—the name is an Aboriginal word meaning large-scaled fish— aficionados travel down-under during the peak February to April season and battle these silver monsters, which can weigh between 65 to 130 pounds (30–59 kg).

Luckily modern aquaculture, and an eye to sustainability, provides an alternative for the rest of the planet. Fresh and saltwater farmed barramundi is available in the Asia-Pacific region, Europe, and United States. Packed with heart-healthy omega-3 and omega-6 fatty acids, barramundi is also light on bones and the fat content helps it stand up to most forms of kitchen abuse, consistently producing a luscious, succulent result. **RH**

Positioned near the top of the seafood chain, the barracuda is as good an eater, as it is eaten. It is renowned as a voracious predator and with its scary mouthful of fang-like teeth it is easy to see why. It has a sleek aerodynamic body similar to the European freshwater pike and is extremely fast, possessing a characteristically forked tail to give it turn of speed. Barracuda swim in shoals and hunt in packs, and they corral their prey into a huge cylinder near the surface of the sea and then dart into the column to snap up their victims.

The barracuda has something of a reputation for attacking humans, although this probably has more to do with its aggressive appearance than actual fact. Of course, humans have the culinary advantage more frequently: pan-fried or barbecued, the excellent quality of the barracuda lends itself to rich and bold flavors.

In general, the barracuda's color is dark bronze or steely gray above, chalky-white or silver along the belly, often with a row of darker cross-bars, chevrons, or black spots on each side. **STS**

Taste: *Wild barramundi has a sweet flavor, robust flakes, and an al dente mouthfeel, suggestive of an active life in open waters. Farmed barra is milder and finer textured.*

Taste: *Rich, meaty, and well-textured, the barracuda has a distinctive gamy flavor. Eitherer filleted or cut into meaty steaks it is excellent for cooking.*

People associate the barracuda with Australia, but this is the Mediterranean species, Sphyraena sphyraena. ❯❯

Luvar

Dubbed the "Cadillac of fish" and the "best fish in the ocean," the only downside of the elusive luvar is its rarity. It is almost never seen in fish markets and seldom forms part of a fisherman's catch; when it does, it is most often instantly cooked and eaten as a treat by its lucky captor. Once or twice a year, fish suppliers on the west coast of the United States are able to offer luvar to their customers. The fish is also found in the Gulf of Mexico, where it is called the "emperador." Back in 1997 an especially fine specimen went on sale in Sydney, Australia, and a few years ago one was caught in Newlyn in Cornwall, only to be stuffed for posterity.

The luvar, a large solitary fish, has been known to grow to almost 10 feet (3 m) long. It lives in the deep waters of the Atlantic and Pacific Oceans. While similar to members of the tuna family, the luvar is not directly related to any other species. It is the sole species in its family, Luvaridae.

Luvar is a beautiful, eye-catching fish, silver colored with a brilliant pink lower body and a deep blue, dark-spotted upper body with scarlet fins and tail. The fish has a huge, bulging head similar to that of a Mediterranean dorade, with small, low-set eyes. Females produce huge numbers of eggs; one fish, 5 ½ feet (1.7 m) long, was estimated to contain 47.5 million eggs. The adult is entirely different from the young fish and goes through several characteristic stages of development. These changes have led to several of the stages being claimed at one time or another as distinct species of fish. For such a large fish, it has a tiny, toothless mouth that limits its diet largely to jellyfish and other gelatinous, planktonic animals. **WS**

Taste: *Similar in color and texture to turbot and halibut, the flesh is white with big flakes that are firm, sweet, and succulent. A sublime fish by most fish lovers' standards.*

Flying Fish

Despite their striking name, flying fish, which belong to the family Exocoetidae, do not actually fly. Rather, they glide through the air, using their extremely large, wing-shaped pectoral fins and vibrating tail to help them. This striking action is achieved by the fish swimming very fast up to the surface of the sea and launching themselves upward through the air, sometimes for 55 yards (50 m) at 30 miles (50 km) per hour. Found in warm tropical and semitropical seas, the fish rising out of the waves and soaring through the air make an arresting sight. Their distinctive gliding through the air is a strategy to evade underwater predators such as swordfish.

The flying fish is highly valued in the Caribbean, where it is associated particularly with the island of Barbados, nicknamed "the land of the flying fish." Something of an island mascot, the fish features on Bajan stamps and coins. The flying fish industry has long been an important part of the island's economy and is a popular food. With its many tiny, fine bones, it is best eaten in fillet form. The national dish of Barbados is flying fish and *cou cou*—flying fish fillets, flavored with lime juice, garlic, and pepper sauce, fried or steamed, served with cornmeal and okra. Most visitors to Barbados experience it fried in breadcrumbs with a squeeze of lime juice or as "fish and chips." Sadly, overfishing has made the flying fish a rarity in Barbadian waters, leading to fishing disputes with nearby Tobago. There are now conservation initiatives to try and preserve flying fish stocks.

In Japan, the fine-grained, orange-red roe of the flying fish (*tobiko*) is used in sushi, often as garnish, valued for its crunchy texture. **MR**

Taste: *The texture is quite compact and dry for a small fish, not woolly as might be expected. Once the little bones have been negotiated, the taste is sweet and meaty.*

The long, wing-like pectoral fins of flying fish are seen in this catch, photographed off the coast of Barbados. ❯❯

Parrotfish

One of the most decorative and prettiest fish in the sea, parrotfish (so named because of its beaklike head and bright coloring) make a colorful splash. The fish requires scaling prior to gutting and cooking, and while the removal of the scales takes some of the gloss off the skin color, it takes away nothing from the unique flavor. Parrotfish are often offered as a delicacy in the Caribbean, where they are pan-fried, broiled, or served with a rich coconut curry sauce. The small blue parrotfish from Sri Lanka, meanwhile, has a very delicate white flesh and is generally considered by fans to be the best flavored.

Despite their appeal, parrotfish should perhaps be tried only once in a lifetime. They are known to graze on certain seaweeds that are threatening to destroy coral reefs; it is because of this that some scientists believe parrotfish should not be on the menu at all. If you like the taste, a good option would be to try another close relative, such as the wrasse or scaly fish, or perhaps farmed barramundi or grey mullet. **STS**

Taste: *Parrotfish flesh is white and soft in texture with the subtle flavors of herbs. Fillets are best broiled or barbecued to create a seared and seasoned exterior.*

Gilthead Bream

The sweet, delicate, white flaky flesh of the gilthead bream is sometimes likened to that of sea bass, although in Mediterranean countries the flavor is judged to be far superior. It is considered the most-prized of the bream family. Found in the wild, in shallow water over sand or mud, where it mainly feeds on molluscs and crustaceans, it can tolerate brackish conditions in river estuaries, but migrates to deeper water to spawn in winter. It is also one of the most important saltwater farmed fish, especially throughout the Mediterranean.

The gilthead has a round deep body that is flattened on the sides, making it easy to fillet. The back of the fish is a dark gray-blue and it has a silver belly. It has a golden spot on each cheek, and a bright golden bar runs across the forehead between the eyes, hence its common name.

The fish requires scaling prior to filleting, although care needs to be taken to trim the sharp fins, particularly the dorsal and rear fins first, as they can inflict a nasty wound if touched. The whole fish is delicious broiled or stuffed and baked. **STS**

Taste: *The fish can be filleted, but the best flavor is obtained from cooking it whole, on the bone. The cheek, or "pearl," is the sweetest and most delicate morsel of all.*

Golden Kingklip

A member of the eel family, the golden kingklip is found in deep waters off the coasts of Chile, Argentina, South Africa, New Zealand, and Australia, where it burrows in the sand and mud. Also known locally as golden conger, pink ling, and congria dorado, it is particularly popular in Latin America. Golden kingklip (*Genypterus blacodes*) has an orange-pink, eel-like body that tapers to a point at the tail and can grow to more than 5 feet (1.5 m) in length and up to a weight of 55 pounds (25 kg).

Golden kingklip can be found fresh, frozen, or smoked. It is high in protein, rich in calcium, iodine, and iron, and has high levels of omega-3 and omega-6 oils. In South Africa, where it is known as *koningklip* in Afrikaans, it is often used along with other local fish, such as *geelbek* and *katokel*, to make excellent pickled and curried fish, a culinary process to which its firm, mild flesh is well suited. Golden kingklip is a versatile fish for the kitchen—excellent for baking, poaching, broiling, and frying. Its texture also makes it ideal for adding in chunks to flavorsome fish stews. **HFi**

Taste: *The pink-to-white flesh of golden kingclip is free of bones and has a sweet, light flavor. The mild-flavored flesh of this eel-like fish has a firm, moist texture.*

Lamprey

A very primitive fish that mostly survives by clamping itself to other fish and sucking their blood, the lamprey is slimy, muscular, and unprepossessing. It is also very good eating, too much so for one King Henry I, of England, who, according to legend, died in 1135 after eating too many of them.

Out of fashion in some European countries, lamprey is still consumed with gusto in Portugal and Galicia, in northern Spain. Arbo, or "Villa da Lampreas" (Village of Lampreys), holds a spring festival in its honor. It has protected status in some countries because of overfishing and pollution.

In size they can grow to over 3 feet (1 m) long and they would doubtless be more popular were it not for their rather repellent appearance, allied to the difficulty of preparing them. The live fish has to be bled first and the outer slime removed before cooking. In the classic *lamproie à la bordelaise*— Bordeaux is perhaps the only part of France where lamprey is still enjoyed—chunks of the fish are stewed in red wine with Bayonne ham and the reserved blood is used to thicken the sauce. **MR**

Taste: *The texture of lamprey is very chewy, closer to monkfish or lobster than other seafood. Its meaty flavor is similar to eel, but with a pleasantly earthy aftertaste.*

Black Scabbard Fish

The black scabbard (*Aphanopus carbo*) is a sinister-looking fish with large eyes, needlelike teeth, and a long, elongated body resembling a scabbard. Although widely found in the northeastern Atlantic from Iceland to the Canary Islands, this fish is inextricably linked with the Portuguese island of Madeira, where it is known as *espada preta*, not to be confused with the *espada branca* (white scabbard) which is also fished off Madeiran shores.

Captured mainly by Câmara de Lobos fishermen, the fish measures about 3¼ inches (1 m) long and can live from four to ten years. Due to its deepwater habitat it is a dark fish with big eyes, different from the scabbard fish captured in mainland waters and requiring careful handling because of its sharp teeth. Madeiran fishermen first encountered the inky-black fish in the fifteenth century when they were line-catching mackerel. Because black scabbard lurk at depths of around 3,280 feet (1,000 m), where nets are next to useless, fishermen had to develop special hooks and very long lines—usually 5,250 feet (1,600 m) long—to increase their chances of catching them. Their work is one of the deepest types of deep-sea fishing in the world.

The finless fish are marketed whole, but minus their stomachs, which are forced out of their mouths by pressure as they are hauled up from the depths. The firm-textured fish has a fatty layer under the skin and is served simply fried or broiled; in Madeira, it is also paired with fruits, such as banana or passion fruit, to add sweetness to its fine white flesh. The fish is also available smoked. *Espada* should not be confused with *espetada*, a popular Madeiran dish of barbecued beef skewers. **STS**

Taste: *The flesh of black scabbard fish is sweet, rich, and buttery. The meaty texture pulls away easily from the bone. The delicate skin cooks away and need not be removed.*

Despite its looks, the deep-sea black scabbard is surprisingly delicious. »

Red Snapper

Red snapper is one of the most popular white fish on the market and in many countries of the world "white fish" simply means red snapper. Lightly spiced and baked in banana leaves, or blackened with Cajun spices, red snapper goes perfectly with the flavors of its tropical origins.

Red snapper is a member of the huge Lutjanidae family of fish, of which there are more than 200 species worldwide, with colors varying from light pink to deep rosy red. Warm, tropical oceans around the world are home to these striking species of fish, which feed on crab, squid, shrimp, and small fish. Species that have a red or pink skin include Bourgeois, Malabar, Vara Vara, yellow tail, and B-line snapper, and many of these also have regional names depending on the locality in which they were landed. Most commercial red snapper is harvested in the Gulf of Mexico and Indonesia.

Red snapper is a versatile fish, superb filleted, stuffed, or baked whole. And it is, of course, fantastic broiled or barbecued whole, especially wrapped in a banana leaf to seal in the beautiful flavor. **STS**

Taste: *Red snapper has a firm texture and a sweet, nutty flavor. It suits seasonings from all around the world, from chiles to herbs, including basil and rosemary.*

In the tropics, red snapper may be barbecued with
fresh herbs and other seasonings on a banana leaf.

Red Mullet

Crimson-colored and often streaked with gold, red mullet (*Mullus surmuletus* and *M. barbatus*) are among the most treasured of Mediterranean fish, although they are also found in the Atlantic. They are easily recognized by their color, which can change from red to pink both while the fish is alive and on the slab. Romans during the first century CE were fascinated by this phenomenon and frequently kept the fish in captivity for observation.

There are other species of red mullet throughout the world, such as *Upeneus sundaicus,* which lives in Australian waters. Outside Europe, red mullet is often known as goatfish. Mediterranean red mullet supplies are currently under pressure and it is best to avoid eating immature fish less than 9 inches (22 cm) long, and fish caught during the spawning season from May to July.

Red mullet is usually cooked whole (the liver is considered a delicacy), either grilled, fried, or baked *en papillote*. For a perfect taste of summer, simply grill over hot coals with some olive oil and fresh herbs; it needs little other adornment. **LW**

Taste: *Firm in texture and delicate, but satisfying, in flavor, the taste of this elegant fish is sometimes compared to crab, on which the red mullet feeds.*

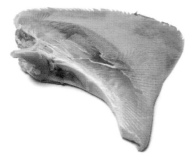

Skate

Unlike many other classic dishes that have been given a facelift over the last few years, poached skate with *beurre noisette*, parsley, lemon, and capers has (thankfully) remained unchanged on most restaurant menus. The parts of this fish commonly eaten are the wings (fins), although skate "nobs" (cuts from the muscle on the back and head) are sometimes available.

As with many popular fish, there have been concerns over the sustainability of some skate species. Unfortunately, skate (some of which are threatened) and ray (some of which are still plentiful) are difficult to tell apart on the fishmonger's slab: their skin, which is the distinguishing feature, is removed prior to sale. Skate are slow growing, taking five to ten years to mature, and only lay a small number of eggs. They are, therefore, vulnerable to overfishing. In common with other cartilaginous fish they excrete urea through the flesh and if not stored correctly will smell of ammonia. Avoid purchasing such fish (and, indeed, any seafood smelling of ammonia), as it is an indication it has deteriorated past consumption. **STS**

Taste: *The delicate-textured flesh of the wings lies in strands over a weblike cartilage and can be steamed, roasted, or fried. The unique flavor includes just a hint of aniseed.*

Looped over poles, skate dry on the beach at Ericeira, Portugal. »

Yellowtail Flounder

Native to the eastern seaboard from the Canadian province of Labrador to Chesapeake Bay, the yellowtail flounder (*Limanda ferruginea*) is among the most popular saltwater fish in North America. The species is also encountered in the northeastern Atlantic, where it is referred to as yellowtailed dab.

Very low in fat, yellowtail flounder is a flatfish that has both eyes on one side of its head, usually on the right side. It has a yellow tail and its skin, which is usually reddish-brown or blue-gray, is dotted with rust-colored spots, hence its alternative name rusty dab. American or Canadian plaice are sometimes mistakenly identified as yellowtail flounder, but they are, in fact, a different variety.

Yellowtail flounder can be cooked whole or as fillets. Care should be taken not to overcook this delicate fish, although it is adaptable to most cooking methods, such as baking, steaming, poaching, or cooking *en papillote*. It is also well suited to stuffing, and especially good with crabmeat. Aïoli, hollandaise, and Creole-style sauces are good matches to flounder. **SH**

Taste: *Yellowtail flounder is much admired for its natural, subtle flavor and its very fine texture. Its spotted skin is also edible and pleasant-tasting.*

Dover Sole

Dover sole (*Solea solea*) is famed for its superior flavor and culinary versatility. It is a dextral flatfish, meaning that both eyes lie on the right side of its body. Long, narrow, and sepia-colored on its upper side, like all flatfish it dwells on the seabed, only venturing to the surface at night when it is best fished. It ranges from the Mediterranean to northern Scotland and the south of Norway. What is sold as Dover sole in the United States is, in fact, flounder.

The fish is so named because Dover on the south coast of England once provided the best supply of sole to London. Dover sole has suffered from overfishing; in the United Kingdom, fish certified by the Marine Stewardship Council shows it comes from well-managed fisheries. Avoid eating sole less than 11 inches (28 cm) long or fish caught during the breeding season in spring and early summer.

Delicate Dover sole can easily be overpowered by rich sauces. It is best prepared simply—brushed with melted butter and broiled on each side for about five minutes. However, the classic mild green grape sauce of *sole Véronique* works admirably. **LW**

Taste: *Dover sole delivers one of the finest flavors of all white fish: the flesh is thick, white, and slightly sticky, with a delicate, lingering flavor. It is best cooked on the bone.*

Lemon Sole

Like all flatfish, the lemon sole lives on the seabed, dark side up, light side down and, chameleonlike, changes color to suit its surroundings. But this delicious member of the Pleuronectidae family is not a true sole: it has both eyes on the left side of its body, and rests on the sand on its right side, unlike other soles, which have their eyes on the right side of the body, and rest on their left sides.

Microstomus kitt has a pointed nose and looks rounder, more like a plaice than the true sole. The back is generally dark brown with irregular blotchy markings of orange and yellow; the underbelly is pale. It can live for seventeen years and reach up to 26 inches (65 cm) in length.

Lemon sole can be found in all the northern seas on the coastal banks of Europe from Iceland and Norway down to France, and is fished by trawlers. Fisheries are largely unregulated, although quota is restricted in both the Norwegian and North Seas. Only choose fish over 10 inches (25 cm) in length and avoid eating them during the breeding season (April to August). **LW**

Taste: *Lemon sole is smooth, light, and melts in the mouth, leaving a buttery aftertaste. The thin, tender skin is also tasty. Fry or broil in butter and serve with lemon juice.*

John Dory

The decidedly odd-verging-on-ugly appearance of John Dory belies the flavor of its excellent fillets. Particularly valued in the Mediterranean countries and Australia, John Dory (*Zeus* spp) can also be found off the coast of England, in the eastern North Atlantic, and in the northwest Pacific. It has a thin, olive-yellow body, massive head, large retractable jaws, and long, spiny sculptural fins.

The presence of dark spots near its gills thought to resemble a finger and thumb print has led to its association with the Galilean fisherman, St. Peter. Legend has it that when the apostle caught a John Dory it made such pitiful noises he threw it right back, leaving an imprint of his finger marks on its body. The fish is, therefore, often known as St. Peter's fish; in French it is called *St. Pierre*, whereas in Spanish it is known as *pez de San Pedro*.

John Dory tends to be expensive because the head and gut alone make up two-thirds of its body weight. A distinctively flavored fish, it is good steamed whole or, if using fillets, allow 5 ounces (140 g) per person, and simply broil or pan-fry. **LW**

Taste: *As good as those flavorsome heavyweights Dover sole and turbot, the firm, dense flesh of John Dory comes off the bone easily and has a sweet, succulent flavor.*

Turbot

Supremely prized in Europe and Asia for its firm, white flesh, turbot (*Psetta maxima*) is almost circular in shape, with a mottled skin that, instead of scales, is studded with knobbly spots that look like nail-heads. Part of a small family of left-eyed flatfish, turbot ranges from the Black Sea, through the Mediterranean to the North Atlantic coast of Iceland. It is farmed in Europe, Chile, Norway, and China.

Turbot have been known to grow to more than 3 feet (1 m) in length, but the normal adult size is about half that. Avoid eating turbot from the North Sea, where it has been overfished. In other areas choose line-caught fish or those caught in dolphin-friendly nets. It should not be caught during spawning, between April and August.

Midsize turbot are best, weighing 4½ to 6½ pounds (2–3 kg), and fillets from the top of the fish yield the plumpest flesh. The thickest part of the fins is regarded as a delicacy, having an unusual gelatinous texture. Turbot is often steamed and served with rich sauces, such as lobster or hollandaise. It is also excellent fried or broiled. **LW**

Halibut

Popularly once eaten on holy days, halibut used to be spelled "holibut." Indeed, the word "holy" forms part of its name in several languages. The largest flatfish in the sea, halibut (*Hippoglossus hippoglossus*) has both eyes on the right side of its body. Found in the cool, temperate waters of the Atlantic, halibut can grow to a whopping 8 feet (2.3 m) in length and weigh more than 650 pounds (295 kg). Not quite so hefty, the Pacific halibut (*H. stenolepis*) lives in waters from California through Alaska to northern Asia, and is less vulnerable to overfishing than its Atlantic cousin.

In many parts of Scandinavia, halibut has always played a strong part, both fresh and dried, in the national diets. In Western Europe, it has been less popular, at times only eaten when nothing else was available. Immortalized in a poem by William Cowper in 1784, it was not until the twentieth century that halibut's star began to rise in England.

Fillets or steaks are often poached and served with a hollandaise sauce, although it is a fish suited to all cooking methods. **LW**

Taste: *The bright white flesh is rich and moist with the bite of a fleshy sautéed mushroom. It has a supremely refined flavor. Even the skin, nailheads and all, is thought tasty.*

Taste: *Not unlike turbot, but less expensive, halibut has a fine, but firm, texture with few bones and a clean, delicately sweet flavor that requires little seasoning.*

Halibut fillets cook on the barbecue within ten minutes per inch (2.5 cm) of thickness. »

Cod

Cod is the king of the Gadidae group and it is loved in many countries around the world. However, its enduring popularity has also led to its downfall, as Mark Kurlansky chronicled in his moving book *Cod: A Biography of the Fish That Changed the World*.

As there is such demand for it, cod stocks have been overexploited for many years. Limited supply, especially from the North Sea, has pushed up market prices. There are, however, sustainable quantities available from the waters around Iceland and the Arctic and, additionally, cod is now being successfully farmed in northern Europe and is of excellent quality.

The best part of the cod is the thickest section around the loin or the top part of the fillet. Cod can be salted, dried, and smoked. It lends itself to most cooking methods and can be baked, broiled, fried, or poached. Cod is still top of the league tables with fish fryers. Although the newspaper of yesteryear has been replaced by plain paper, deep-fried cod in crispy batter and chunky fried potatoes, doused in salt and malt vinegar is a British institution. **STS**

Taste: *The chunky white fillets cook to a pure white with large open flakes and a delicate and distinct flavor that resonates with the highlights of its diet of small shellfish.*

Gulls feast on offal from gutted cod and other fish
❂ caught off the coast of Newfoundland, Canada.

Monkfish

In his classic *North Atlantic Seafood*, food writer Alan Davidson noted monkfish (*Lophius pescatorius*) has a variety of local names: "belly fish and goose fish (because it stuffs itself), allmouth (North Carolina), and the cognate 'lawyer' (parts of New England), and bellows fish." Its other name, anglerfish, points to a dangling fleshy-tipped spine above the voracious jaws it uses as a bait to lure its prey. This odd-looking fish has a number of seaweedlike fringes around its head that, along with its mottled skin, make it an expert in camouflage.

It is a grotesque fish, related to sharks, that can grow up to 6 feet (2 m) long. With a cartilaginous spine, but no bones other than those of its fins, it is meaty and firm-fleshed, highly regarded by some culinary cultures. Until a generation ago, it was considered by many cooks to be a cheap substitute for lobster or scampi, because of its color and texture. In Italy, *coda di rospo* (monkfish tail) is fried, broiled, and baked. Cooked through, it can be dry, bland, and chewy, but when it is perfectly cooked, it lives up to its name of "poor man's lobster." **MR**

Taste: *The texture of monkfish tail changes according to its size, but is always dense and very juicy. It only becomes dry with overcooking. The taste is mild, but sweet.*

Chilean Sea Bass

Swordfish

Chilean Sea Bass is the name, in the United States, for Patagonian toothfish or icefish, so named because the Chileans were the first to market it here. The fish is a favorite among American chefs because the fillets are pure white, succulent, and flavorsome, lending themselves to a myriad of flavor combinations. It is particularly popular on the West Coast, where it is most commonly sold prepared as steaks or thick dense white fillets, and is either pan-fried or roasted.

The fish feed largely on squid and shrimp, which goes some way to explain why it has such a wonderful flavor. It is found in the cold deep waters of the southern Atlantic, southern Pacific, Indian, and southern oceans around the continental shelves. The average weight of a commercially caught fish is 20 pounds (about 9 kg) with large adults occasionally exceeding 440 pounds (200 kg). They can reach a length of 8 feet (2.3 m). The fish is endangered by overfishing, although the Marine Stewardship Council has certified as sustainable a South Georgia fishery in the South Atlantic. **STS**

A predator at the top of the food chain, this mighty blue-gray fish with its dramatic bill, or "sword," cuts a dash in fish markets the world over. Found globally, the swordfish (*Xiphias gladius*) generally migrates between temperate or cold waters in summer and warmer waters in winter. It can reach up to 13 feet (4 m) in length, including its sword, which it uses to slash or stun its prey.

The swordfish has been an easy target for the harpoon since classical times as it often basks near the water's surface. Today, it is under huge fishing pressure: many swordfish stocks are unmanaged and overfished. Catches include immature swordfish, as well as a bycatch of other species, such as marine turtles. Swordfish populations need to be managed internationally; those in the North Atlantic are recovering well due to the efforts of U.S. authorities.

Swordfish is popular in most world cuisines, especially in Sicily, where the fishermen are renowned for their skill in catching them. Marinated swordfish steaks are delicious char-grilled. In Turkey, thin slices of smoked swordfish are a delicacy. **LW**

Taste: *The flavor is stronger and more robust than other white textured fish, although it is often cooked and treated in the same way as cod.*

Taste: *Slightly pink, compact, and juicy, swordfish has a veal-like texture. Its flavor is mild and meaty, but not as fishy as tuna. Cook 'til the flesh is opaque, but still moist.*

A swordfish adorns the side of a pirogue, a West African flat-bottomed fishing boat. »

Sea Bass

One of the most highly prized fish in Europe, the sea bass (*Dicentrarchus labrax)* is found all the way from Norway to West Africa. It is a beautiful, streamlined silver fish with a pointed head, which grows to a maximum length of 40 inches (1 m) and a maximum weight of 26 pounds (12 kg).

Although a saltwater fish, the bass has a penchant for fresh water. Most young bass spend their early lives in estuaries and return home from time to time even when mature. According to the poet Horace, gourmets in ancient Rome used to say they could tell the difference between a sea bass caught in the sea at the mouth of the Tiber and one caught between the bridges of the city. (According to Juvenal, the bass that lurked between the bridges fed on the city's sewage.)

Trawlers target spawning and prespawning fish, so if line-caught bass are not available pick the smaller fish that are farmed in salt lagoons and sea cages throughout the Mediterranean and beyond. Simple to cook, roast or broil whole with herbs and serve with a dash of olive oil and lemon juice. **LW**

Striped Bass

Early settlers highly praised the taste and flavor of this American species of bass, regarding it as an excellent proposition for the table and never tiring of its delicate flavor. The pearl in the cheek was especially savored, as it is sweet and particularly flavorsome. Striped bass (*Morone saxatilis*) remains highly popular today, and is thought by many to be best served lightly fried and garnished with lemon.

There are several species of bass found in the United States, so called because they resemble the popular European sea bass in shape and size. They have slightly deeper bodies than the European species and are commonly known there as striped sea bass, rock, and rockfish. They are found in both fresh and salt water: like the salmon, they breed in fresh water. The body of the bass is long and silver with dark stripes running from the gills to the base of the tail. It is thought to live up to thirty years, and it can grow to 6½ feet (2 m) in length and more than 110 pounds (50 kg) in weight. Highly regarded as a sport fishing species, striped bass are also farmed in Turkey, Mexico, Iran, and Ecuador. **STS**

Taste: *The thin, crisp silver skin of sea bass splits open to reveal firm, fragrant, flavorful flesh—like ultrasoft, ultramoist chicken breast with a sticky bite.*

Taste: *In its raw state the flesh has a gray translucency that cooks to firm, meaty, white fillets. It has a fine rounded flavor, not dissimilar to that of sea bass.*

People shop for fish in Bologna, Italy; serving
❮ *sea bass at Passover is an Italian-Jewish tradition.*

Blue Marlin

Famed as the "big fish" in Ernest Hemingway's novella *The Old Man and the Sea*, the blue marlin (*Makaira nigricans*) is one of the most impressive ocean dwellers. It is distinguished by a powerful, long, spear-shaped jaw or bill, and is known to attain 14 feet (4.3 m) in length and to weigh up to 1 ton (910 kg). With its vivid, deep-blue coloring fading to a silvery-white flash across its flanks and belly, the blue marlin is a spectacular creature. It is found in the tropical and temperate waters of the Atlantic, Pacific, and Indian oceans, where it can be readily identified by the pronounced dorsal fin running along the full length of its back.

The blue marlin is thought to use its long, spear-shaped upper jaw, or bill, to slash through dense schools of fish, before returning to eat its stunned and wounded victims. The predator fish prefers the warmer temperatures of surface waters, feeding on pelagic species such as mackerel, but it also eats squid and is known to dive deep to obtain them.

The blue marlin's amazing size and appearance, coupled with its legendary capacity to fight hard when hooked, have made the species a popular game fish, much coveted by sporting fishermen and trophy hunters. The firm flesh is also used in Japan for sushi and sashimi.

Like other long-lived, top-level ocean predators, warnings of high mercury levels in the meat are attached to consumption of blue marlin. The fish is slow-growing and slow to reproduce, and conservationists are concerned that the population is in decline. An excellent alternative is mahimahi, a smaller fish but one that has a similar, densely textured flesh and rich flavor. **STS**

Kanpachi

In Japan, kanpachi is known as an "ascending fish," which means that its name changes according to its size and age. Kanpachi is the Japanese name for the most mature stage of *Seriola dumerili*, or greater amberjack, when it is over 4 feet (1.2 m) long. The fish is found in the Indo-Pacific, Mediterranean, Caribbean, and along the South and North American east coasts. Its name comes from the yellow (amber) streaks that run down its sides, and a close relative, *Seriola lalandi*, is known as the yellowtail amberjack. Kanpachi is a deep-sea fighter that will test the will and strength of the most experienced of fishermen. It is a carnivore that feeds on smaller fish and can achieve a length of 6 ½ feet (2 m) and weigh 198 pounds (90 kg).

In Japan and elsewhere, kanpachi is often commercially farmed; the fish are fed a special diet to optimize the flavor of the meat, which is popularly used for sushi. Wild adult fish caught in the spring or summer at about half their fully mature size (called *shiogo* or *akahana* in Japan) are considered best for this purpose. Reputedly, the fish is best eaten before it is three years old and not in the fall (after the spawning season), when it has developed an unpleasant odor.

Kanpachi is an extra lean, dense fish. Kanpachi fillets can be 1 inch (2.5 cm) or more thick and can be served as carpaccio. In the United States, kanpachi from the Gulf of Mexico is sometimes known as Gulf tuna and the fillets are usually broiled or fried. In Japan, however, it is most commonly used in sushi, especially *nigiri*, a type of sushi made with rice and raw fish. Sushi chefs in Japan undergo extensive training to learn to make *nigiri*. **SH**

Taste: *The steaks of this fish are firm and dense with a similar flavor to swordfish, as well as that of mahimahi. It is easily overcooked and generally suits char-grilling.*

Taste: *The pale white flesh is firm and creamy and melts in the mouth. Stronger in flavor than flounder, grouper, or snapper, it has a slight taste of the sea, but is still mild.*

The writer and sports fisherman Ernest Hemingway ⓚ described the blue marlin as a formidable foe.

Hake

Hake is a deep-swimming member of the cod family found in the Atlantic and northern Pacific oceans. The European hake (*Merluccius merluccius*) ranges from the Mediterranean to Norway. One North American species is the silver hake (*Merluccius bilinearis*), so called because it has a silvery sheen when freshly caught. Adult hake grow to a length of 40 inches (1 m) and weigh up to 11 pounds (5 kg). The fish is available fresh—whole or as fillets, steaks, or cutlets—and frozen, salted, and smoked.

Hake is much loved on the Iberian Peninsula, where it is known to the Spanish as *merluza* and the Portuguese as *pescada*. It was introduced to Iberian cuisines by the Basques, who call it *legatz*. It often appears in casseroles with other types of fish, as well as shellfish such as lobster, prawns, and mussels. In France, hake is known as *saumon blanc*.

Hake has few small bones and is easy to prepare. The lack of bones makes it suitable for fish soups, stews, and casseroles, and the flesh's subtle, delicate flavor makes it a successful substitute for any recipes that specify cod or other white fish. **FR**

Taste: *Hake's lean flesh is soft and creamy in texture. It is white to pink in color, and flakes easily. The delicate and unobtrusive flavor lends itself well to light poaching.*

Freshly landed hake is packed on ice in Peterhead, Scotland. »

Black Cod

Black cod, which gained fame through renowned chef Nobu Matsuhisa's Black Cod and Miso, is fast becoming a popular and sustainable alternative to the overexploited Atlantic cod. This sleek fish is more blue-gray than black, and like many other species, it has a string of regional names, including butterfish (United States and Australia), candlefish (United Kingdom), and coal fish (Canada). But be careful: confusingly, many of these names can also refer to other species, making it easy to buy the wrong fish. True black cod has a firm, meaty texture, although there is a fibrous element to frozen fillets.

Black cod is caught in the cold and very deep waters of the Pacific Northwest, from as far south as Baja California through to the Bering Sea. Canadians tend to fish it in traps that not only preserve the quality of the fish, but have also virtually eliminated the by-catch of smaller fish and, therefore, help sustainability. To experience black cod at its best, buy it fresh; much of the fish caught for the European market is frozen on landing and then subsequently transported. **STS**

Bluefin Tuna

The most highly prized species of fish in Japan, bluefin tuna is considered a must for the very best platter of sashimi, due to its fine quality and delicate but rich oils. The Japanese have a distinct preference for the belly area, or *otoro*, due to its high oil content, whereas in the West, bluefin tuna is filleted, and the lean loin section along the back is the favored cut.

Northern bluefin tuna is the most valued of the tuna family, used primarily for sashimi; tuna steaks and canned products come from other members of the family. They are the largest of all the tuna species, adults being typically 6½ feet (2 m) long when caught, but they can reach in excess of 13 feet (4 m). The largest recorded specimen weighed a massive 1,500 pounds (680 kg), although adults usually average around 550 pounds (250 kg).

In Japan, where it is a particular delicacy, a single giant bluefin tuna fetches an astronomical price. The fish's high status has put enormous pressure on stocks and the northern bluefin is under threat from overfishing. A more sustainable option is the excellent yellowfin tuna. **STS**

Taste: Black cod has a strong and unique flavor, which complements the distinctive flavors of wasabi, miso, and shoyu particularly well.

Taste: Bluefin tuna has a similar texture to a beef fillet, but with a subtle, understated flavor. It is very lean and has large, open flakes.

Old and new nets for tuna fishing dry in the sun on Isola San Pietro, Sardinia, Italy. ❯❯

Rollmop

Fugu

These sweet-and-sour delicacies take their distinctive name from the German word *rollen*, which means "to roll." Herring fillets (complete with skin) are first marinated, then rolled around a pickle—usually an onion or a gherkin—before the whole thing is secured with a small wooden stick. Rollmops are popular in many northern European countries, notably Germany, Scandinavia, the Czech Republic, Slovakia, and parts of Scotland—and have even made their way to South Africa. The recipe for the marinade varies from country to country, but usually includes white wine or apple-cider vinegar, onion, peppercorns, mustard seeds, salt, and sugar.

The development of rail transport during the first half of the nineteenth century meant herring could easily be carried inland from the ports of the North Sea and the Baltic Sea, so the method of pickling evolved. The results became particularly associated with Berlin, where they had a starring role in the displays of ready-to-eat foods that adorned old Berlin pubs. They still have a reputation as a hangover cure. **LF**

Fugu is a spiny fish with a habit of blowing itself up into a round ball if threatened, hence its popular name of puffer fish. It is a renowned delicacy in Japan, where it has been eaten for centuries in spite of (or perhaps because of) the fact a lethal toxin is found in its gut, liver, ovary, and skin.

Tingling lips are a normal reaction. But if anything more than a minute amount is eaten the poison attacks the nervous system, leading to creeping numbness, followed by the clatter of chopsticks as the diner loses his grip... However, preparation of the fish in restaurants has been licensed since 1949, and deaths almost always occur as a result of untrained preparation at home.

The gourmet's Russian roulette that is a fugu dinner is always an occasion. The flesh is served as sashimi, cut in wafer-thin slices and ostentatiously presented on a huge platter in overlapping slices resembling a flower. It is eaten with a dipping sauce of soy sauce, sudachi citrus, scallion, grated daikon radish, and red bell pepper. A one-pot dish of fugu and vegetables usually follows. **SB**

Taste: *Soft, with a glossy appearance and a silky, melting texture, rollmops have a tasty sweet-and-sour flavor. They are particularly good with dark rye and sourdough breads.*

Taste: *The sashimi is light and astringent and the cooked fugu-chiri rich and meaty. Many say, however, its taste is surpassed by the thrill of the experience of eating it.*

The Shinsekai blowfish restaurant in Osaka, Japan, attracts diners with a large model of the fish. ❯❯

Cantabrian Boquerone

A superstar among anchovies, the Cantabrian Sea on the northern Atlantic coast of Spain has long been considered the world's best source for these silver-skinned gems.

Rather than being preserved in swathes of salt as many anchovies are, Cantabrian *boquerones* are usually packed in olive oil or a light cure of oil and vinegar. The fish tend to be plumper and meatier than their Mediterranean cousins, and have a delicious, full flavor. Fresh anchovies deteriorate fast, so processing must take place within hours of landing the catch. The anchovies are trimmed and filleted by hand before being salted, washed, and packed in olive oil or oil and vinegar.

Unfortunately, their popularity comes at a price. Despite regulations governing fishing in the area, reserves have plummeted and, at the time of writing, a total ban has been placed on anchovy fishing in the Cantabrian Sea, so stocks are allowed to replenish naturally. However, anchovies cured in the Cantabrian-style, although prepared elsewhere, are still available. **LF**

Taste: *Cantabrian boquerones are meltingly tender and silky in texture. They have a mouthwatering flavor with a hint of sweetness and are not in-your-face fishy.*

Collioure Anchovy

The delicate texture of freshly caught anchovies makes them poor travelers and it is for this reason that they are usually canned, salted, cured, or marinated. Collioure, a small Mediterranean fishing port in the Roussillon region of France, is widely held to produce the ultimate salted anchovy—plump, flavor-packed, and with a unique aroma.

Anchovy fishing was well developed in Collioure by the nineteenth century, although the salt-curing of fish there dates back to the Middle Ages. Today, despite cheaper competition from producers in Morocco, several salting houses in Collioure continue to prepare their fine product, which now has PDO status. Local women, known as *anchoïeuses*, hand pick the freshly caught fish, which are cleaned, drawn, and sandwiched between layers of salt in vats. They are then left to mature at least 100 days.

Collioure anchovies are produced from the *Engraulis encrassicholus* species of anchovy. Populations of European anchovies are fluctuating and the fishing season currently runs from April to May, and again from September to October. **STS**

Taste: *Collioure anchovies have dark brown, firm-textured fillets. They have a distinctive, slightly perfumed scent of mountain ham, and a salty, rich, lingering taste.*

Roque Anchois is just one of the establishments in Collioure, France, that specialize in anchovies. ❯

Seki Aji

A specialty of the southern island of Kyushu, seki aji, or horse mackerel, is caught in the Bungo Suido channel, where the strong currents of the Pacific Ocean meet the sheltered water of the inland sea. This results in strong tidal currents that lower the fat content of the fish, because it has to swim so hard against them, and gives it a mildness of flavor esteemed throughout Japan. Seki aji is an example of what the Japanese call *hikari mono*—shiny things— such as herring and mackerel. Although eaten as sashimi, it is always washed and marinated in vinegar before serving. As well as helping to preserve the fish, this also firms up the flesh and makes slicing it easier. Seki aji is caught only by the traditional pole-and-line method, using a single hook, and not with nets. This practice, together with the local technique of *ikejime*—a method of draining the blood from the fish very quickly—preserves the flavor.

Eaten as sashimi, often with grated ginger and onion, seki aji also goes well with the citrus kabosu. Local dishes include *Matsuoka zushi*, when it is served as *nigiri* sushi then wrapped in a bracken leaf. **SB**

Taste: *Somewhat milder than mackerel with a sweet and fresh taste, seki aji has a slightly crunchy, pinkish flesh with a mild fattiness.*

Isle of Man Kipper

Kippers are a form of smoked herring. The process was adopted in nineteenth-century Britain after John Woodger decided to borrow a technique that was being used to cure salmon—and also finnan haddock. The fish were split, brined, hung in a smokehouse on wooden rods or "tenters," and cold smoked. This method was once widespread along the northeast coast of England, but has now almost died out, except at Craster, in Northumbria, and, off the west coast, in the Isle of Man.

During the twentieth century kippers were a common breakfast dish. Their popularity was due partly to the abundance of the catch, partly to the fact that processing was industrialized; however, their quality suffered as herring in poor condition were cured and colored with coal tar dyes. To make Manx kippers, normally sold in pairs, the fattest, freshest herring are smoked over oak chippings. The best way to cook them is in simmering water. To remove the many tiny bones, lay them skin uppermost, peel that off, then rub butter over the flesh and pull it away from the backbone. **MR**

Taste: *The rich flavor from the oak smoking is key to a good kipper, but so is the freshness and oiliness of the fish. A kipper should be succulent, never "fishy," and not too salty.*

Kippers take on their distinctive rich color and flavor during their time in the smokehouse. »

Maatjes Herring

A herring is referred to as a "virgin" when it has not produced either sperm or eggs: it has the unique privilege of becoming a virgin again after spawning. The word "maatje" used to describe the delicious new-season herring of the Netherlands is derived from the term for a virgin—*maagd*.

Each year at the end of May, when the fish are in peak condition (with a minimum sixteen percent fat content), the season begins. In the past, the first barrel of fish landed was offered to the queen. Today, it is auctioned and sold for charity in the port of Scheveningen, as part of the *Vlaggetjesdag* (Flag Day) festivities. From then on until July, maatjes herring are known as *hollandse nieuwe*.

Although there are recipes for cooking maatjes herring, the Dutch like to eat the fillets raw, from street stalls. The fillets can be sampled either simply sprinkled with a little salt or with the addition of chopped raw onion, maybe on a slice of bread. The key to quality is their freshness: they should be eaten within hours of catching and filleted to order before oxidation mars the taste. **MR**

Taste: *The flesh is white and soft, with all but the tiniest bones removed, and the skin is a bright gunmetal blue. It has a sweetish, seaweedy taste allied to a touch of oiliness.*

Maatjes herrings have been packed into wooden barrels for centuries; salted herring was a ship's food.

Surströmming

Neither the name, which means "sour herring," nor the pungent, clinging smell, reminiscent of a mix between rotten eggs and sewage, deters the faithful from this traditional Swedish delicacy. In northern Sweden, devotees celebrate its annual premiere, traditionally on the third Thursday in August, with outdoor parties and orgies of consumption.

Until recently a staple in some parts of Sweden, surströmming is made with fermented (not rotten) herring. In the old days, quite possibly from as early as the fifteenth century, fermentation was an alternative to curing with salt or smoke. Today, the treatment is most popular in northern Sweden, where most surströmming is produced on the island of Ulvön. Slightly more than one million cans are produced annually, and although a growing number make their way abroad to countries such as Japan, many palates remain unconvinced of its appeal.

Surströmming is eaten with almond potato, finely chopped onion, and a type of flatbread known as *tunnbröd*. It is preferably accompanied by beer and *snaps* (schnapps), but some prefer milk. **CC**

Taste: *Surströmming has an unusual sweet, yet mildly salty, taste with an overpowering pungency, reminiscent of a well-matured cheese that lingers on the palate.*

Smoked Eel

Smoked eel is eaten around the world—they were once popular with the Maori of New Zealand—but today it is most highly prized in the Netherlands.

Eels living in European rivers and lakes travel to the Sargasso Sea, a calm patch of the Atlantic rich in sargasso seaweed, on an extraordinary journey to spawn. The best time to catch them is just before they start to migrate, when they are at their fattest and largest. They should be kept alive until the moment they are processed to retain their taste and succulence.

Once killed, the eels are drawn and brined or dry salted before being hot-smoked in a kiln over hardwood, typically oak or beech. To eat the eels, known as *gerookte paling*, the Dutch peel away the golden, oily skin and eat the flesh directly off the bones. In less atavistic circumstances they might eat the fillets with a creamed horseradish sauce as do their neighbors in northern Germany and Scandinavia. European eel populations are currently under intense pressure and fishing of wild stocks is under regulation by the industry. **MR**

Taste: *Smoked eels are oily, smoky, and rich, almost fatty, under the skin. Their texture is firm and compact—they should not flake—and their taste should not be fishy.*

Smoked Mackerel

The smoking of fish to enable long-term storage goes back thousands of years. Fishermen might well have accidentally discovered the effects of smoking fish when drying their catch over a fire. Since the advent of refrigeration, however, fish tend to be smoked for their enhanced flavor and texture, rather than for preservation.

The oily-fleshed, torpedo-shaped mackerel is perfectly suited to smoking as a culinary treatment and responds to it incredibly well. Mackerel is typically hot smoked, which helps give the fish its characteristically flaky texture. (In general, cold smoking tends to impart the flavors of smoking without affecting the nature of the fish's flesh, because no actual cooking takes place.)

Smoked mackerel is usually sold in vacuum packs or canned in oil: the best brands use extra virgin olive oil. One very special product to look out for is the Beech Smoked Mackerel from the Spanish company Don Reinaldo; softly smoked and packed in olive oil, they offer smoked mackerel at its irresistible best. **LF**

Taste: *Smoked mackerel has a full, but rounded, almost buttery flavor with a light, balanced smokiness. Its moist, juicy texture comes from the fish rather than the oil.*

Gutted mackerel are suspended directly over the heat of the smokehouse to ensure that they cook. »

Tallinn Kilud

Small, silvery, and piquant, kilud are the celebrated preserved Baltic sprats (*Sprattus sprattus balticus*) that hail from Estonia. They are a particular specialty of Tallinn, the capital city. Too small to be filleted, kilud come with head and guts intact, packed tightly into small cans and spiced with up to twenty spices, including nutmeg, cloves, cinnamon, and black pepper. Each of the bright blue pocket-size cans traditionally contains a bay leaf.

Salted sprats have long been a staple food in Estonia. The poorer people who lived farther inland would come to the coast to trade their grain for fish, which would be salted and cured in huge wooden barrels. Modern methods of preparing kilud are thought to be based on those used as long ago as the sixteenth century, when the sprats enjoyed a reputation for being especially sweet. With the advent of canning, the legend of the Tallinn Kilud was born; the cans carry a picturesque image of the medieval skyline of Old Tallinn, which inspired the phrase "sprat-can skyline," an expression now used to describe the view of Tallinn from the sea. **LF**

Taste: *Deliciously sweet, with warm spicy overtones, kilud have an overall softness with the pleasant, slightly crunchy texture of tiny yielding bones.*

The Tallinn skyline, familiar to all purchasers of canned kilud.

Arbroath Smokie

Smoked Snoek

The dramatic seascape dominates the east coast of Scotland, and for centuries the villages that scatter the cliff tops and the harbors were built on fishing, most often of haddock. Like other smoked fish, Arbroath Smokies (PGI) originated as a method of preservation in the days before refrigeration.

Arbroath Smokies are unusual in two ways: the fish are smoked whole, complete with bones, and they are smoked in pairs. The haddocks are drawn, beheaded, and dry-salted for two hours to draw out excess moisture from the skin. Then they are tied in pairs, hung over wooden rods, and washed to remove the salt before smoking over oak or beech. The method was first developed in the village of Auchmithie in the early nineteenth century, but the fish acquired its name as people moved to the larger town of Arbroath farther south.

The best way to eat an Arbroath Smokie is "hot off the barrel"—still warm from the smoking process. Otherwise it can be split open and the bone removed before eating cold or warming with a chunk of butter in the cavity. **CTr**

Smoked snoek is a genuine South African national treasure that should have as much *Appellation Contrôlée* street cred as prosciutto. It is important, however, not to confuse smoked snoek with its inexpensive cousin, salt snoek.

A cousin of the mackerel, snoek (*Thyrsites atun*) is found in the temperate waters of the southern hemisphere. It should not be mistaken for a type of bass found in the Gulf of Mexico known as "snook." In New Zealand and Australia, it is called barracouta, but is not related to the fierce barracuda (though, in the seventeenth century, some of the men of Jan van Riebeeck, the founder of Cape Town, apparently lost fingers to the fish). Highly popular in South Africa, snoek has even made its own contribution to Cape slang: "Slat my dood met 'n pap snoek," which literally translates to "kill me with a soggy snoek."

Snoek can be cooked in numerous ways. In South Africa, smoked snoek is usually made into pâtés and spreads, but it is also served flaked with tomatoes and peppers in a type of kedgeree dish called *smoor-snoek* (smothered snoek). **HFi**

Taste: *The texture is soft, melting, and flaky. The fresh fish flavor is nicely balanced with a touch of salt and rich smoke. Each component should enhance the other.*

Taste: *Salty in taste, but wonderfully textured because of partial drying and smoking, smoked snoek flakes off the astounding number of vicious-looking bones very easily.*

Bombay Duck

Salt Cod

Although the name conjures up a creature of the feathered variety, Bombay duck (*Harpadon nehereus*) is, in fact, fish, not fowl. Also known as bummalow, it is found in Asian waters, especially in the estuaries and coastal waters of India, including those around Mumbai (formerly Bombay).

In India, the fish is sometimes served fresh, but the vast majority of it is filleted, salted, and dried in the sun. After drying, the fish has an incredibly powerful smell. One story connects its name to during the British Raj when the fish was transported by train and the compartments would reek of it. Brits nicknamed the odor "Bombay dak," after the train.

Diehard Indian food fanatics consider Bombay duck a culinary delight, especially when it is ground and sprinkled over curries. Once commonly served at Indian restaurants in the United Kingdom until the European Union banned it because it was not made in a factory, it is available again.

Fry Bombay duck for a few minutes and serve hot with poppadoms or a curry. It can also be prepared as a pickle. **LF**

In Portugal, salt cod is known as *bacalhau*; in Italy, *baccalà*; in Spain, *bacalao*; in France, *morue*; in English, it is simply salt cod. Whatever the language, with modern technology and refrigeration, salting foods to preserve them is no longer a necessity, although for hundreds of years, salting and drying was the main method used for fish preservation. But, because salting actually changes the flavor and texture of the fish so superbly, salt cod now belongs in the luxury league.

Overfishing in the North Atlantic has driven cod stocks to near collapse, so prices have rocketed. It is possible now to find salted Pacific cod and some processors have started to substitute other species of fish, such as ling, haddock, and pollock.

Supermarkets in Portugal and Spain have whole counters selling huge, flat pieces of salt cod. It looks somewhat shriveled and unappetizing, but after soaking for one to two days, it can be used in a host of fabulous recipes; it makes a great match with the best olive oil. It is superb in crisp batter and irresistible in garlic-laced *brandade de morue*. **LF**

Taste: *Dried bombay duck has a brittle texture that crumbles in the mouth and a love-it-or-loathe-it piquancy, with salty overtones of which anchovy lovers will approve.*

Taste: *Reconstituted and cooked, salt cod has a firm, but moist and flaky texture and gloriously gutsy, savory flavor with faintly brackish overtones.*

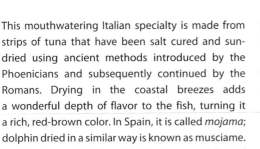

Mosciame del Tonno

Bottarga di Muggine

This mouthwatering Italian specialty is made from strips of tuna that have been salt cured and sun-dried using ancient methods introduced by the Phoenicians and subsequently continued by the Romans. Drying in the coastal breezes adds a wonderful depth of flavor to the fish, turning it a rich, red-brown color. In Spain, it is called *mojama*; dolphin dried in a similar way is known as musciame.

Mosciame is thought to have originated in Liguria, although it is now associated with Carloforte, an island off the south of Sardinia. It was introduced by Ligurian fishermen who settled there in the 1700s. The tuna loins are first cleaned and then cured in sea salt. After rinsing, they are hung out to dry in the Mediterranean sun and air, causing the tuna to dehydrate and lose up to half its weight.

Mosciame looks very like the cured Italian beef bresaola, and it is often served in much the same way—in paper-thin slices, drizzled with extra virgin olive oil and a squirt of lemon. Also delicious grated into pasta or salads, mosciame is sometimes used in the traditional Genoese dish *cappon magro*. **LF**

Bottarga di muggine is the roe of the female grey mullet. The finest comes from the salty waters of Lake Cabras, in western Sardinia. Sometimes referred to as "the poor man's caviar," this is a fantastic creation in its own right and deserves to be recognized as such.

The roe, which is extracted in one whole piece, is cleaned and salted before being lightly pressed, then washed and dried in the sun. The resulting product is shaped like a long tear drop 4 to 7 inches (10–18 cm) long and is golden amber in color. Traditionally enclosed in wax and sold in pairs, today bottarga di muggine is more likely to be vacuum-wrapped in plastic.

After removing the thin surrounding membrane, the bottarga can be cut into wafer-thin slices and dressed with good extra virgin olive oil and lemon juice. But, possibly the most delicious and typical way of serving it is to shave or grate it over freshly cooked spaghetti. Ideally, bottarga di muggine should not be bought already grated, and it should never be cooked. **LF**

Taste: *Extremely lean and tender, mosciame responds well to good olive oil. It has a pronounced, almost meaty flavor like cured ham, but with subtle fishy overtones.*

Taste: *Bottarga di muggine has a delicately briny, but not overly fishy flavor that opens up on the palate, energizing the taste buds and hinting gently of spice.*

Beeswax is traditionally used to preserve the freshness of the cured roe—bottarga di muggine. ❯❯

Monkfish Liver

A traditional delicacy in Japan, where it is called *ankimo*, this alluring ingredient is beginning to appear in a growing number of kitchens—both in homes and restaurants—around the world. Naturally rich, monkfish liver achieves a silky, melt-in-the-mouth texture when cooked, which has earned it the nickname of the "foie gras of the sea."

The typical monkfish liver weighs in at over 1 pound (450 g). Before cooking, it is often lightly seasoned and marinated—traditionally salted and soaked in sake or mirin—then wrapped into a cylinder and steamed or simmered. Sometimes the liver is battered and deep-fried, to be served with layers of minced or sliced tuna meat. It lends itself best to presentations that include light, fresh, crisp flavors that complement the liver's richness, while allowing its delicate taste to prevail. Presentations initially tended toward "fusion" treatments in which the liver was sliced in small portions and paired with ponzu sauce, perhaps also with seaweed salad or shredded daikon. More recently, U.S. and European chefs have favored preparations similar to those for duck or goose foie gras.

At the time of writing, monkfish populations are under threat from overfishing for the huge Chinese and Japanese markets and, latterly, also the European and North American markets, where demand is increasing specifically due to greater appreciation of the liver, rather than the meat. To conserve world stocks, all forms of the fish are best avoided. A ten-year plan to rebuild New England and mid-Atlantic monkfish stocks was implemented in 1999, and in time will hopefully result in better controlled, sustainable fisheries. **CN**

Taste: The rich texture of classic foie gras pairs with the fresh, briny flavor of simply steamed shellfish, creating a delicacy that more than justifies its gourmet status.

Potted Shrimp

A delicacy in England, potted shrimp is identified with Morecambe Bay, a treacherous expanse of intertidal mudflats off the northern Lancashire coast. The small brown shrimp are netted by fishermen who cook their catch by dropping them briefly into boiling seawater to guarantee freshness. (People who live around Morecambe Bay believe that shrimps taste sweeter and juicier when simmered in fresh rather than salted water, but this is a privilege only available to those who go shrimping for their own account, rather than commercially.) Local fishermen drive tractors over the flats at low tide trailing nets through the shallow water instead of using fishing smacks.

The "potting" stage of the process is done on land. First the small crustaceans are chilled. The head and carapace are pulled off and the flesh is squeezed and twisted out of the tail. Removing the shrimp flesh is a labor-intensive operation because no machine can perform the work; a good picker extracts no more than 1 pound (700 g) of meat in an hour.

The shrimp are then packed in pots with butter, seasoned with pepper and nutmeg, then coated with a second layer of clarified butter that insulates the food from the air, helping to preserve it. Shrimps cost more than butter, and so the higher the proportion of tails in the product, the better the quality will usually be.

Potted shrimp is eaten with hot brown toast or crusty wheat bread, sometimes served with a wedge of lemon, or in cucumber sandwiches in which the potted shrimp takes the place of butter. It is also served as a starter with green salads. **MR**

Taste: The sweet shellfish taste balances the salty iodine flavor and the fattiness of the butter. Spices add an extra piquancy. Potted shrimp taste best eaten with hot toast.

In Morecambe Bay, England, shrimp are cooked as soon as they are caught to preserve their freshness. »

Taramosalata

Icre

The stridently pink, fishy slurry sold very cheaply in supermarkets is a travesty of this subtle and delicious meze. The custom of eating mezes is rooted in Greece, Turkey, and Lebanon, and taramosalata is to be found in all three countries, although most commonly associated with Greece.

Historically the salted, cured roe used to make taramosalata was from the grey mullet. Carp roe has also been used, but both these have become scarce and so more expensive, leading to widespread use of cod roe instead. The roe is pounded with olive oil, lemon, a small quantity of minced onion (but never garlic), and either bread or mashed potato, which makes it go farther and softens the flavor of the very strong-tasting roe.

Now available all year-round, taramosalata was traditionally a Lenten fasting food, as it does not contain any meat or dairy products. Properly made, its color varies from pale pink to pink tinged with coral. It is often served as a meze, or with alcoholic drinks, as the Greeks consider it decadent to drink without eating something at the same time. **AMS**

Today we think of caviar as a Russian contribution to the world's list of gourmet foods, but history suggests it was the Chinese who first made caviar— not with sturgeon roe, but with the eggs of the river fish carp. Genghis Khan took Chinese caviar with him when he invaded Russia, and sturgeon soon took over there as the roe of choice because of its attractive color.

Although taramosalata made with cod roe has become a national dish in Greece, it has long been produced in southeastern Europe using carp roe. Carp plays an important part in Balkan cuisine, especially in Romania, where their version of taramosalata has the unfortunate name (at least to English language-speakers) of *icre de crap* (*crap* being Romanian for carp). After removing the membrane on the carp roe, it is salted and left until the roe turns orange. It is then pounded with fresh bread crumbs and blended with oil so it emulsifies with the roe. Seasoned with lemon juice, salt, and sometimes finely chopped onion, it is eaten on crackers or rye bread for a tasty snack. **WS**

Taste: *Often served decorated with ripe olives, taramosalata is eaten in its home countries simply with bread, which enables appreciation of its delicate taste.*

Taste: *Icre has a soft, creamy texture and a delicate fishy flavor that is less salty and strong than commercial taramosalata. Naturally cured, it has a warm orange hue.*

In the eastern Mediterranean, taramosalata and
❸ other meze dishes are commonly enjoyed al fresco.

Kazunoko

The salted and preserved eggs harvested from the ovaries of female herring, kazunoko is an expensive delicacy in Japan, where it is known as "yellow diamonds." Although available all year-round, especially in sushi shops, it is during New Year festivities that most kazunoko is sold, as it is an essential part of the New Year cuisine known as *osechi ryori*. The ingredients used to make *osechi ryori* are chosen for their symbolism; the abundance of eggs (one ovary can contain 100,000 of them) in kazunoko symbolizes prosperity and fertility, both of which are hoped for in the coming year.

There are two types: *hoshi* kazunoko is slightly harder as it is more dried than salted, and *shio* kazunoko is more salted than dried, and, therefore, softer. Both should be soaked in water before using, to remove some of the saltiness, although ready-to-eat versions are also available. In sushi stores, kazunoko is served thinly sliced as a topping for *nigiri zushi*, or marinated in a mixture of sake, mirin, dashi, and soy sauce. Kazunoko keeps refrigerated for a couple of weeks, and freezes well. **SB**

Taste: *Kazunoko is crunchy, hard, salty, and satisfyingly savory; comparable to a crunchy bottarga, but with a touch more bitterness.*

Salmon Roe

A brilliant deep, glassy orange and bursting with sweet, rich, salmon fish oil, these impressive eggs are not for the faint-hearted. But anyone who enjoys caviar will love them.

Salmon roe eggs are juicy and inviting, and are used extensively as a stand-alone hors d'oeuvre or to finish canapés and *nori maki* sushi. Eggs harvested from the Pacific species of chum or dog salmon are considered to be the finest, although other salmon roe can also be used.

After gutting the "hen" (female) fish, workers remove the eggs, which resemble a small pea in size. The eggs are rinsed and tenderly separated from the delicate membrane that holds them in place, before being packed in a salt solution.

Like caviar, salmon roe is best served simply, so it can be seen and admired. Sour cream and blinis make a fantastic accompaniment, it stands out beautifully on canapés, and in Japan it is most often used as an outstanding decorative finish to sushi. In that country, the orange-colored spheres were once favored as fish bait, too. **STS**

Taste: *The flavor is a mix of honey, the sea, and the rich oils of raw salmon. The initial mouthfeel is a soft, yielding ball that releases the oil-rich fish contents with one bite.*

The red color of salmon roe, here on sale in Kyoto, contributes to the visual appeal of Japanese cuisine. »

Crab Roe

Wasabi Tobiko

The decadent unctuousness of crab roe has earned it luxury status throughout Asia, where it is used to garnish steamed dumplings and seafood dishes, enrich soups and sauces, or is simply enjoyed *au naturel*, scooped out of the cooked crab shells. (When present, male crab milt is often referred to as roe in Asian restaurants, probably because "crab sperm" does not sound quite as appealing.)

Shanghai cuisine's seasonal hairy crabs (named for their furry claws) are beloved for their abundant sticky orange roe. In Hong Kong, a particular crab species is named yellow oil crab.

Around Southeast Asia, large mud crabs are the most popular source of roe. One unusual southern Chinese dish cures raw mud crab in a bath of soy sauce and spices for a couple of days: the marinating process transforms the roe into a vivid vermilion paste. In the Philippines, the roe of small crabs is a delicacy known as *taba ng talangka*. It is cooked with garlic and calamansi juice and eaten with rice. In the southern states, crab roe appears in She-Crab Soup, a cross between a bisque and a chowder. **CTa**

Wasabi tobiko, the processed eggs of the flying fish, is becoming increasingly popular outside of Japan for its striking appearance and versatility. Tobiko comes in various colors and flavors, including bright-green wasabi flavor, dark green with a jalapeño kick, and black flavored with squid ink. Tobiko is popular as a topping for *gunkan maki*, or "battleship sushi," where ingredients are placed on top of an oblong of rice and held in place with nori seaweed. Farmed capelin roe (*masago*) from Iceland and Denmark is sometimes passed off as tobiko.

Tobiko is valued more for its texture than its flavor. In its natural state it has a pale yellow color and is rather tasteless, but perhaps its best quality is its resilience. Hard and crunchy, these tiny eggs, smaller than caviar, do not fall apart when handled. The eggs are first removed from the fish and washed in a centrifuge to free them from their membrane. They are then frozen and sent for more processing. The eggs are salted and, in the case of ordinary tobiko, colored orange, or with wasabi tobiko, colored vivid green and flavored with wasabi. **SB**

Taste: *Roe flavors vary, but have in common a pure, sweet distillation of crab character and umami, melded with the tongue-coating richness of every kind of yolk.*

Taste: *Crunchy and refreshing as the small, loose eggs burst open in the mouth, they have a salty sweetness and a hint of brininess, followed by the heat of wasabi.*

A crab boat laden with crab pots and their bright ❮ *marker buoys approaches Newfoundland, Canada.*

Beluga Caviar

Caviar d'Aquitaine

A king's ransom is the price paid for this exceptional and exquisite caviar—the lightly salted roe of female sturgeon from the Caspian and Black Seas—and it must be the ultimate luxury food. Although other countries now produce fine caviar, Russian and Iranian caviar retains its historically high status. Beluga caviar comes from the grandest, oldest, largest, and rarest sturgeon (*Huso huso*). The Beluga sturgeon takes twenty years to reach maturity, hence, the hefty price tag on the roe.

Beluga eggs are steely gray in color and larger than sevruga or osciotr (osetra), both of which come from other species of sturgeon, and with beluga make up the caviar "holy trinity." The eminence of caviar has led to all three species being severely overfished, especially in the Black Sea; those in the Caspian Sea are now protected. (Caviar d' Aquitaine, left, makes a sustainable and delicious alternative.) Beluga caviar is best served simply, with thin toast or with blinis and sour cream. Caviar should never be served with a metal spoon or from a metal bowl, which alter the taste of the eggs. **STS**

Think of the origins of caviar and most will pinpoint Russia, Iran, and the Caspian Sea. Since the first half of the twentieth century, however, caviar produced from wild sturgeon caught in the estuaries of the Gironde and Aquitaine has fast gained recognition.

Exploitation and destruction of habitat are increasingly bringing many species to the brink of extinction. But, there is now an excellent, guilt-free caviar coming from Aquitaine, where the Siberian baeri sturgeon is being farmed very successfully. The baeri sturgeon thrives in the warmer French waters. In Siberia, sturgeon take between fifteen and twenty years to reach maturity, whereas in Aquitaine it takes half the time.

The young male sturgeon are identified using ultrasound technology. They are culled at the age of three to four years and then sent to the wet fish trade as exceptional sturgeon fillets. Meanwhile, the females are nurtured until their eggs are considered to be a sufficient size and quality to harvest. The eggs have a deep gray color and release a pale yellow oil when pressed. **STS**

Taste: *Soft and creamy in texture, the oil in the middle of the eggs delivers a hint of walnut. Premium caviar labeled "Imperial" is from the largest, lightest colored eggs.*

Taste: *The caviar from Aquitaine is perfumed with a light, delicate, almost smoky, flavor with a long, lingering taste of cream cheese, likened by some to a ripe Brie.*

These cans of Russian caviar cans are color-coded:
🅚 red for sevruga, yellow for osetra, and blue for beluga.

Mantis Shrimp

The marine equivalent of the praying mantis, this peculiar crustacean is so called because of its enlarged pair of grasping forelimbs. Fast moving and difficult to catch, mantis shrimp can grow to about 8 inches (20 cm) in length. Solitary creatures, they burrow themselves into the sand or live in crevices in reefs and rocks.

There are about 400 species of mantis shrimp, which vary from nondescript shades of brown and gray to glowing neon colors. Known as "thumb splitters" by divers, mantis shrimp aggressively use their incredibly strong claws to either smash or spear their prey. They have even been known to crack aquarium glass.

Mantis shrimp are best eaten when their ovaries are full and the flesh is firm. They are popular in Mediterranean countries, especially Italy's Romagna region, where they are simmered, peeled, and dipped in a seasoned batter before being fried. They can also be stewed or used in fish soups. In Japan, where they are known as *shako*, mantis shrimp often appear on sashimi menus. **STS**

Taste: *Their sharp shells make them tricky to open, but the tail meat rewards the effort: fine in texture and superbly sweet in flavor, they are more like lobster than shrimp.*

The insectlike appearance of the mantis shrimp's
tail accounts for its alternative name of sea locust.

Arctic Prawn

As the name would suggest, these crustaceans take their distinctive essence from the icy and unpolluted waters of the far north. Also known as northern or deep-water prawns, they are harvested in the Arctic—particularly around Canada and Greenland—but also in the North Atlantic and North Pacific.

The low temperatures mean *Pandalus borealis* grows much more slowly than its relatives in warmer climates. The prawns take five or six years to reach maturity, which intensifies the flavors of their meat and improves its texture. There have been concerns regarding overfishing, and efforts began in the 1990s to stabilize stock levels. Controls and licensing have delivered results, but the impact of global warming on cold water stocks remains to be seen.

Arctic prawns are enjoyed around the northern hemisphere, especially in Scandinavia, where they are traditionally eaten cold at midsummer with an aquavit chaser. These sweet, versatile crustaceans absorb flavors easily and lend themselves to simple, fresh, unfussy Scandinavian dishes, as well as retro favorites such as a seafood cocktail. **AME**

Taste: *The Arctic prawn is smaller, juicier, sweeter, and more succulent than many of its relatives, the texture less stringy and more meaty, with a satisfying density.*

Marron

Pattes Rouges Crayfish

Probably the best eating crayfish in the world, the marron's only natural habitat is in and around the Margaret River, in Western Australia. Both *Cherax tenuimanus* ("hairy" marron) and *Cherax cainii* ("smooth" marron) exist in the wild in a very limited area, so recreational fishing is tightly controlled, but farming has made this luxury more available. Farmed marron thrive in Australian waters, especially around Kangaroo Island: the best are exported alive, and frozen is not recommended.

The name, from the local Aboriginal language Nyungar, means something equivalent to "bread" or "food." The world's third largest crayfish, with a weight of up to 4 pounds (1.8 kg), and a high meat-to-shell ratio, marron are dark brown in color when mature, but turn an incendiary vermilion when plunged into hot water.

The tail meat is best served simply, as medallions with a good mayonnaise or aïoli, lemon, and freshly ground pepper; a deft chef can leave the meat of the whole claw intact. The hepatopancreas or "mustard" is prized for its sweetness and consistency. **RH**

These make a fantastic addition to a seafood platter, but take care not to leave live crayfish unguarded in the refrigerator, as these feisty little crustaceans will find their way out of the bowl and into anything else they fancy. Pattes rouge crayfish, also known as signal crayfish, originate from the western United States. Take care when handling them too, as they have a punchy nip.

These crayfish can grow up to about 6 inches (15 cm) in length. They look like small lobsters, but are, in fact, freshwater crustaceans and can survive for long periods of time out of water. This allows them to move between waterways across land. Crayfish are solitary animals and will eat anything from plants to meat, including smaller crayfish. Alive, they have greenish-brown bodies, with large claws, and a deep orange undershell. As a mini lobster, their body is wide, but short at the tail. The claws reveal a very small morsel of meat, but generally it is only the tail that is eaten. (The claws can make magnificently flavored shellfish stock, so should be kept.) **STS**

Taste: *Marron flesh is a stark white, tinged red at the edges. The sweetly perfumed flavor offers mild hints of vanilla and nut. The claw meat is particularly stunning.*

Taste: *Once you have managed to crack open the shell, which can be tricky as it is not brittle, the meat in the tail is beautifully sweet and succulent.*

Wooden crayfish traps; the crayfish are lured inside by a variety of baits. »

Corryvreckan Langoustine

Audresselles Lobster

The Corryvreckan "whirlpool"—which lies between the west coast of Scotland and the Inner Hebrides—is the second largest in Europe. Below the surface, tidal currents converge around a pillar of rock that juts from a seabed broken by a deep pit, the result of which is a maelstrom.

The langoustines that inhabit these cold and strenuous waters, at depths of up to 660 feet (200 m), grow to an extraordinary size. Whether known as scampi, Dublin Bay prawns, or simply (in Scotland) prawns, most of the langoustines that are caught off the coasts of Europe are fished with nets at a weight of about 1 to 1½ ounces (25–40 g). Off Corryvreckan, where they are captured in traps like lobsters, they can reach as much as 1 pound (450 g) in weight.

Like other crustaceans, *Nephrops norvegicus* must be cooked fresh out of the water and from live to be eaten at their best. Those prepared in seawater and seaweed at the Crinan Hotel in the tiny port of the same name where they are landed are the finest of all. Live langoustines are shipped around the world in tubes, but are never quite so delicious. **MR**

Beloved of French and Dutch aristocrats since the sixteenth and seventeenth centuries, the Audresselles lobster encapsulates the very finest elements of the European lobster. Known in France as *homard bleu*, the exquisite "royal" Audresselles is found off the coast of Brittany.

An uncooked European lobster can vary a little in color, depending on its habitat, however, the Audresselles lobster is renowned for its stunning dark Prussian blue shell fading to a cream underside, and white freckles along the side of the tail shell and carapace. It is also famed for the sweet flavor of its meat and was once the highlight at banquets.

Lobster meat is always served cooked, whether it be in lobster thermidor or simply boiled for a salad. The meat also makes excellent bisques. The claws are of a particularly delicate nature and it is worth hunting for the meat in the small legs, too, because it is sweet and succulent. When buying a cooked lobster it is important to check the body feels solid and that the tail is tucked tightly under the body, because this shows the animal was cooked fresh. **STS**

Taste: *Only the tail of the Corryvreckan langoustine is usually eaten. The firm meatiness coupled with the sweetness of the tail meat are utterly unique.*

Taste: *Audresselles lobster encompasses everything good about seafood. The tail meat has a fibrous, dense texture with a sweetness of flavor that is difficult to beat.*

Langoustines that survive the turbulent seas below
❸ the Corryvreckan whirlpool grow to an impressive size.

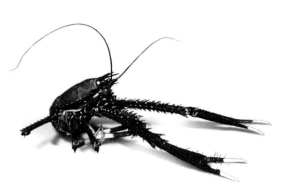

Moreton Bay Bug

Neither the name nor the appearance of the Moreton Bay bug are calculated to appeal to dinner guests: it looks somewhat like an alien trilobite, or a creation out of *Jurassic Park*. Yet this delicious type of lobster yields a sweet, versatile flesh that is equally good boiled, barbecued, or incorporated into a variety of sauces. Biologically *Thenus orientalis*, the Moreton Bay bug goes by a range of names throughout its Indo-Pacific hunting ground, but takes its Anglo-Saxon moniker from the bay outside Brisbane. Along with its good, but less-good, cousin the Balmain bug (*Ibacus peronii*), it often appears as a by-product of shrimp and scallop trawling.

Commonly found in local fish markets already cooked to a vibrant orange, the tail meat is the only edible part. Uncooked or live bugs are a muddy olive gray with a weedy aroma that advertises their seagrass habitat, although fresh meat from uncooked bugs has excellent applications in sauces, ravioli, or other dumplings. Tossed with ginger and Chinese greens or sautéed in butter and served over fresh egg fettuccine, Moreton Bay bug meat is sublime. **RH**

Taste: *Freshly cooked Moreton Bay bug is firm and sweet with background notes of ozone and nutmeg, much enhanced by cooking on an open barbecue.*

Squat Lobster

Squat lobster can be a confusing title since it is used fairly indiscriminately around the world to describe many kinds of crustaceans that look like lobster, but are not. So North Americans often call langoustines this, and stubby, clawless slipper lobsters are also referred to as "squats." True squats are members of the Galatheidae family that includes over seventy species, of which only a few are fished commercially.

Galathea squamifera thrives off the northwest coast of Scotland and the Orkney Isles. It was overlooked for years because of the flourishing langoustine fishery. Caught in creels, and about the size of a crayfish, up to nearly 2 inches (4 cm) long, it contains little meat in the tail, but this is well worth prizing out of the shell. Chestnut brown or red and blue in its natural habitat, it turns reddish-orange when boiled. It is only at its very best when cooked from live. The most efficient way of preparing them is to make a bisque with the carapace and serve the shells separately. Because the fishing industry has only begun to exploit squat lobsters, they are considered to be a sustainable species. **MR**

Taste: *It takes two or three squat lobster tails to make a mouthful, but their taste and texture has the characteristic crustacean flavor: very sweet, quite juicy, and chewy.*

Lobster creels wait on the quayside at Stromness, the second-largest settlement in the Orkney Isles. »

Maine Lobster

Cool ocean water and plenty of rocky shoreline helped cement the iconic relationship between Maine and its beloved lobster (*Homarus americanus*).

Although the first recorded Maine lobster catch was in 1605, it is believed humans consumed the crustacean long before then. Once so abundant it was considered poor-man's food, today lobster is a dish of luxury, often served on special occasions. There is some debate over the sustainability of lobster though, prompting lobstermen to establish conservation methods and minimum size limits. It is one of the few foods still sold live in U.S. markets.

Most lobster is sold in its hard-shell form, though soft-shell lobster can be found. Some claim soft-shell lobsters produce sweeter meat and are easier to break open. Generally boiled, steamed, or broiled, meat from the tail is white in color. Its bite is more firm and dense than the tender claw and knuckle meat, but both have a deeply rich flavor. Although usually a dark brownish color, rare blue, yellow, or even two-toned lobsters have been caught—all turn bright red when boiled. **CLH**

Pitu

With its impressive pair of claws, its exceptional meat, and its remarkable size, the pitu, or camarão, is the king of freshwater shrimp. It frequents the rivers and estuaries of Latin America, but is most commonly associated with Brazil. The pitu's color varies depending on where it is fished. At times almost translucent, it can range from terra-cotta to cinnamon-brown. It is also referred to as *poti*, *canela* (cinnamon), and *camarão verdadeiro* (real prawn).

This shrimp is more mildly flavored than its marine cousins and can reach a length of 10½ inches (27 cm) and a colossal 14 ounces (400 g) in weight. Its meat is wonderfully delicate and is perfectly cooked after only a short time, when it turns a pinky color. It is commonly found in traditional stews, such as *moquecas* and *escaldados*.

When Portuguese colonizers first landed on the Bahian coast of Brazil during the 1500s, pitu was one of the foods that the indigenous people brought them as a gift. A staple of the Brazilian dining table for centuries, it is gaining increasing popularity among the country's top chefs. **AL**

Taste: *The sweetest, most succulent meat is found in the tail and claws. Maine lobster can be dressed lightly with mayonnaise for a summertime favorite—the lobster roll.*

Taste: *Similar to a lobster in flavor, the pitu is fantastic when broiled. Only a few drops of Sicilian lime and a drizzle of olive oil are needed to bring out its qualities.*

These buoys in Ellsworth, Maine, enable fishermen
⊘ *to locate their traps and collect their harvest.*

Dungeness Crab

Yellow Oil Crab

The Dungeness crab (*Cancer magister*) is one of the most iconic foods of North America's Pacific Coast. This large, plump crab with sweet, delicious meat is sustainably harvested from California to Alaska, but takes its name from a tiny spot on the shores of Washington State: Dungeness, so named by the eighteenth-century explorer Captain Vancouver, after Dungeness on the English Channel.

What sets Dungeness apart from other crabs is its size—typically about 2 pounds (900 g). One crab is ideal for a single serving, and both the body and legs are packed with meat. Most crab lovers prefer to enjoy Dungeness in its simplest form: steamed or boiled and eaten straight from the shell, warm or cold. Many like it plain, untouched by melted butter, mayonnaise, or cocktail sauce. In-shell crab portions can be quickly stir-fried with seasonings, such as ginger root, garlic, and scallions for added flavor, or added to a pot of cioppino, the Mediterranean-style seafood stew from San Francisco. The meat can be used in countless dishes from the classic crab Louis salad to the ubiquitous crab cakes. **CN**

In these days of global cuisine, when ingredients from all over the world seem to be available practically everywhere, those rare, truly seasonal foods are all the more special. Yellow oil crab is available for only a few months each year, from May to August, and to taste it you will have to travel to Hong Kong or southern China.

Yellow oil crabs are female mud crabs that are literally sunburnt. The scorching heat and high humidity melts the roe of the crabs into a yellow oil that permeates their entire bodies down to the tips of their golden claws. Wild crabs are considered by connoisseurs to be the best because the rich, yellow roe is said to be sweeter than that of farmed crabs. Farming, however, extends the season from just two weeks to up to three months.

The crabs must be cooked carefully so the roe does not spill out of the body. They are usually steamed (plain or with rice wine) or simmered as a congee or soup (a decadent version is made with shark's fin). Some chefs remove the crab roe and make it into dumplings or cook it with noodles. **KKC**

Taste: *There is a delicacy to Dungeness crab meat that includes a tender texture. The sweet meat has only the subtlest hint of briny sea flavor when steamed or boiled.*

Taste: *Yellow oil crab roe is as rich and soft as room-temperature butter. After harvesting the crabs only live a few days. Restaurants require they be preordered.*

Moleche

Visit Venice in spring or fall and the little crabs known as moleche will be a common sight at the famous Rialto market, and *moleche frite* (fried moleche) will feature on the menu of every self-respecting restaurant. Crisp on the outside, but capturing the essence of the sea within, these are a delicacy well worth pursuing.

The crabs, known in English as "green crabs," or biologically as *Carcinus mediterraneus*, are at a stage in their life cycle when they are changing shells and are so soft it is possible—and, more than that, utterly delightful—to eat them whole. They are harvested in nets between February and late April or early May, and then again in October and November, along the natural channels in the lagoons of Venice.

Typically these tiny delights are soaked in beaten egg, dusted with flour, and deep fried. The act of soaking appears to purge them of their excess brine and gives a glorious crisp finish. In the Murano region, the legs are generally removed before cooking, whereas in Venice the crabs are more often than not both served and eaten whole. **LF**

Hairy Crab

Shanghainese hairy crabs are rarely found outside Hong Kong and China. And anyone who does achieve this will pay a premium for doubtful quality. Like other types of crabs, hairy crabs should be cooked alive, and the quality deteriorates the longer they are out of the water.

Hairy crabs are distinguished by the long, fine hairs on their claws. They are eaten primarily for their abundant roe, rather than for the small amount of meat. What is eaten from a male crab is, in fact, its sexual organs and sperm. Male "roe" is softer and creamier than that of the females.

Yang Cheng Lake, in Jiangsu province, is the best source for hairy crabs due to the quality of the water, which gives them lighter hair and sweeter meat. The lake produces only a small percentage of the crabs on the market. Unscrupulous sellers give their crabs, sourced from other lakes, a quick dip in Yang Cheng Lake and claim it the provenance. Genuine producers are fighting back with methods such as laser tatoos, but the counterfeiters copy these tactics as quickly as they are created. **KKC**

Taste: *Salty, crunchy, succulent, all at once briny and sweet, moleche should be devoured hot immediately after serving with a generous squeeze of lemon.*

Taste: *These deliciously sweet, succulent crabs are traditionally eaten steamed, with a dipping sauce made from Shanghainese brown vinegar and shredded ginger.*

Stone Crab

These flat-bodied, oval-shaped crabs with extremely hard claws prized for their meat began their rise to culinary fame in 1921 when Joe Weiss, who owned a small fish shack on Miami Beach, was asked to cook a bag filled with them by a marine researcher. Weiss tossed them in a pot of boiling water, then served them chilled with mustard sauce, coleslaw, and hash brown potatoes. And so a Florida tradition was born.

Found mainly off the Atlantic coast from North Carolina to Florida and around into the Gulf of Mexico, stone crabs are believed by scientists to be right-handed since the claw on the right side is usually the largest. They have the ability to regenerate their claws. For that reason, the crabs caught usually have one claw carefully removed and are then put back into the water to grow a new one. They can regenerate claws up to three or four times.

Stone crabs are often cooked soon after harvesting; they are sold frozen, but this can make the meat tough and stringy. Best eaten chilled, they are delicious with melted butter, but are also perfect in any dish calling for crabmeat. **SH**

Taste: Paired with Champagne or sparkling wine, stone crab claws are a delicacy for seafood lovers. The sweet, flaky meat has a slight saltiness and taste of the sea.

Stone crabs are as much a part of summer
◊ *on the Florida Keys as boats and sunshine.*

Goose-necked Barnacle

Unsurprisingly, the goose-necked barnacle gets its name from its resemblance to the head or neck of a goose. In Spain, where it is known as *percebe*, there is an annual festival devoted to it in Galicia. It is also prized in parts of Latin America, and grown commercially in Canada.

A type of crustacean, the goose-necked barnacle lives on rocks and flotsam in the ocean intertidal zone. It has a foot that attaches the barnacle to the rock, a long soft body like the neck of a goose, and a hard shell at the top. To feed it needs the motion of the sea to bring it nutrients, so it only survives where there is considerable current or wave action.

Goose-necked barnacles are much sought after as a delicacy in several Mediterranean countries. They can be eaten raw, but they are usually steamed in their shells over a seafood stock and then served immediately. This simple recipe best preserves their sublime, clean taste. The soft body has a thick skin that is easily removed after cooking by pulling the hard shell and the skin with a nail. Be prepared for squirting juices; it can be a messy affair! **STS**

Taste: Often served in clusters, algae and all, goose-necked barnacles taste similar to lobster or crab claws. But the texture is very different—moist, soft, and chewy.

Telline de Camargue

Tartufo di Mare

One of the most delicious small clams in the world, the telline (*Donax trunculus*) is just one of the many native gourmet wonders of the Camargue region of France. These little delights are found just beneath the surface of the wet sand along the shoreline of the Mediterranean coast, particularly the stretch between Arles and Montpellier. They became one of the gourmet "finds" of the 1960s and have been marketed in the region ever since.

The traditional method of harvest is a carefully regulated art that takes place in the morning: a net mounted onto a frame is strapped to the *tellinier*, who works back and forth along the shore gathering the molluscs in each sweep. Once harvested, the tellines are soaked in water for between twelve and twenty-four hours before being served.

Popular in risotto and pasta dishes, Tellines de Camargue are traditionally enjoyed raw, cooked à la Provencal, or garnished with the powerful parsley and garlic mix *persillade*. A steaming bowl of tellines cooked *en persillade* can contain up to fifty little shells per serving. **STS**

You can be forgiven for staying with the rather romantic Italian name of tartufi di mare, or truffle of the sea, for this fabulous variety of shellfish; its other commonly used name is warty clam!

Tartufi di mare are similar in shape to common *vongole*. They have a chunky, solid-looking shell that is beige to brown in color, with a distinctive covering of prominent, concentric warty ridges. The species *Venus verrucosa* is found in temperate water in parts of the Atlantic and Mediterranean; it is considered a particular delicacy in the provinces of Puglia and Friuli and around the Gulf of Naples. Like all bivalve molluscs, the clams should only be consumed during months that contain an "r" because in the summer months they are breeding. Today, many of the waters around Italy are subject to a closed-fishing season in late summer, therefore allowing fish stocks to replenish naturally.

Frequently served raw, tartufi di mare are exquisite when prepared in pasta sauces, often in a similar way to the classic *spaghetti alle vongole*. They also eat well in risotto and salads. **LF**

Taste: *With a sweet delicate flavor and a subtle taste of the sea, these molluscs are relished by locals and tourists alike. These are an absolute must for shellfish aficionados.*

Taste: *Tartufi di mare are silky soft in texture and pleasantly brackish on the tongue, suggesting hints of fresh sea air without being overpoweringly fishy.*

Fresh tellines are offered for sale at
◐ *a fish market in Aix-en-Provence, France.*

STEWKEY

STIFFKEY

1975

Stewkey Blue Cockle

Littleneck Clam

The English North Norfolk village of Stiffkey—once pronounced "Stewkey"—is perhaps as famous for its disgraced vicar, as for its seafood. (Harold Davidson was defrocked in 1932 for consorting with London prostitutes and died after being mauled by a lion.)

Stiffkey's harbor silted up toward the end of the nineteenth century and the muddy edges of the village became an excellent breeding ground for cockles with a distinctive dark gray-blue shell. Stewkey blues (*Cerastoderma edule*) were originally only those harvested from Stiffkey, but is now a generic term for all Norfolk cockles.

Until shortly after World War II the women of the village harvested cockles throughout the year. Cockling is heavy and dangerous work, as the tide comes in very fast, and the Stiffkey women had Amazonian reputations. Traditionally, the cockles were boiled and eaten with vinegar, and were a popular treat for tourists. Indeed, they can still be bought like this a little farther along the coast at Wells-next-the-Sea. They can also be used instead of clams in dishes, such as *spaghetti alle vongole*. **AMS**

Each coast of the United States stakes a claim to its own littleneck clam. The one on the Atlantic coast is not a distinct species. Instead, it is the smallest of the region's hard-shell clam species known as the quahog (*Mercenaria mercenaria*).

This clam is often referred to as the Little Neck clam. It is named after Little Neck Bay on Long Island, in New York, which was once the region's most-popular source for half-shell clams. In raw bars along the eastern seaboard, littlenecks sit perched on beds of ice, raw on the half-shell ready for slurping. It is also a favorite for the baked clam treat clams casino, steamed with white wine, or tossed with pasta and fresh herbs.

Not quite as highly prized, the Pacific coast has the common littleneck, or native littleneck (*Protothaca staminea*). Found along the sandy shores from California to Alaska, this littleneck has a chewier texture and is usually cooked—steamed, roasted, or in a chowder. Both Atlantic and Pacific littleneck clams are farmed today, a recommended choice of sustainability watchdogs. **CN**

Taste: *The plump, fishy, succulence of Stewkey blues is best experienced by cooking them in wine, garlic, salt, and pepper until they open, and eating them immediately.*

Taste: *The tenderness of wild Atlantic littlenecks makes them ideal for eating raw on the half-shell. They are sweet and scrumptious, with a briny hint of Long Island waters.*

This sign at the Norfolk village of Stiffkey helpfully ❮ *also supplies the original pronunciation of the name.*

Toheroa

This iconic New Zealand speciality is regarded as one of the finest tasting fish, but one you are unlikely to taste fresh. *Paphies ventricosum*, a member of the clam family, is famed for having a highly developed digging tongue, and is native to only a few beaches on both the North and the South Islands. Fresh water from lagoons in the dunes results in an inshore concentration of plankton, food for the toheroa.

Toheroa can grow up to 6 inches (15 cm) long and live in the soft sands between high and low tide; their position is only detectable by a blowhole. At the least disturbance they frantically dig themselves deeper and many a hunter has been defeated by their amazing speed. Disease and overharvesting in the past, particularly for the canning industry (there were three toheroa canning factories in New Zealand at one time), have resulted in strict prohibition of toheroa-gathering for most seasons: the last season was one solitary day in 1993. An exception is made for Maori who have traditional fishing rights, that is, who have proven toheroa is basic to their lifestyle—yet even they have limits on how many they can gather, may dig only with their hands or wood (no metal), and must gather toheroa that are at least 4 inches (10 cm) long. When permitted, New Zealanders flock to dig for the succulent creatures. In the 1950s, toheroa fritters fried in oil were a popular dish.

The smaller, more prolific tua tua clam is used as a substitute, particularly for toheroa soup. It is good, but does not equal the real thing, and also lacks the distinctive green color deriving from the plankton in the toheroa gut. Khaki-green toheroa soup was the traditional start to the Christmas meal in New Zealand and has a wonderfully delicate flavor. **GC**

Taste: *Generally chopped and made into soups, pâtés, or fritters, the meat is a grubby green and has a rich flavor, like that of mussels but creamier and more pronounced.*

Geoduck

One of the strangest creatures to be eaten from the sea, the geoduck (pronounced gooey-duck), *Panopea abrupta*, is the world's largest burrowing clam. A slow-growing clam, it is among the longest-living creatures in the world, living for over 100 years in some cases. Its name is thought to derive from a Native American word meaning "dig deep." Indeed, this oversized clam can burrow more than 3 feet (1 m) into the sand. The average weight of a geoduck is around 2 pounds (0.9 kg), although it can weigh as much as 7 pounds (3 kg). The most striking aspect of the clam's appearance is the thick, long, ivory-colored neck or siphon, which protrudes outside the hinged shells.

The geoduck is indigenous to Pacific waters from northern California to southeast Alaska, with the largest harvest coming from Washington's Puget Sound. With geoduck meat highly esteemed in Asian cuisines, particularly those of Japan, Taiwan, and China (where it is called the "elephant trunk clam"), there is a profitable market in live geoducks shipped to those countries. In the regulated market, geoducks are harvested at twelve years old by divers who use a directional water jet, called a "stinger," to wash away the sediment and reveal the lurking clam, which is lifted out. Wild harvesting of geoduck is increasingly closely regulated, which has led to a marked growth in geoduck aquaculture.

In Japan, the firm, sweet neck meat is prized for use raw in sushi or sashimi, blanched and served with a dipping sauce, or stir-fried. The dried meat is used in China for broths. In the United States the neck meat is used in chowders, whereas the more tender body meat is simply pan-fried. **CN**

Taste: *Meat from the neck (siphon) of the geoduck is typically eaten raw. It has a firm, almost crisp texture and briny sea flavor. The body meat is richer and more tender.*

Given that the long neck is eaten, a geoduck provides much more meat than most clams. ❯

Razor Clam

Increasingly popular in the United Kingdom, the European razor clam (*Ensis ensis*) has only recently begun to be commercially exploited. It is found from Norway to the Atlantic coasts of Spain, as well as parts of the Mediterranean.

It is a burrowing bivalve mollusc with an elongated narrow shell shaped like a cut-throat razor, hence the name. Both halves of the shell are curved, with a smooth olive-green or brown outer surface. The inner surface is white with hints of purple. The large muscular edible part known as the "foot" almost entirely fills the shell.

When carefully cooked this sweet and textured mollusc has a flavor somewhere between scallop and lobster meat. The long strand of flesh extracted from the shell resembles a peeled lychee both in appearance and texture. Cooked from live, razor clams can be steamed open over a ginger-infused stock or broiled with a generous helping of garlic butter; overcooked, they become a chewy disappointment. Other popular recipes include clam chowder, fritters, and pasta sauces. **STS**

Taste: *Razor clam meat has a sweet, succulent seafood flavor. Although the whole clam is generally eaten, the stomach contents should be avoided.*

Date-Mussel

The most highly prized of molluscs, this tiny member of the mussel family takes eighty years to grow to a length of 4¾ inches (12 cm). Long, dark, and cylindrical, it looks similar to the fruit of the date palm, hence its name. It is also known as date-shell.

Native to the Mediterranean, the European date-mussel (*Lithophaga lithophaga*) secretes a liquid acid that enables it to soften and then bore into limestone rock and coral where it lives. Its destructive powers were displayed for all to see when the columns of a Roman temple at Puzzuoli, long submerged in the Bay of Naples, were brought to the surface by an earthquake.

Because the date-mussel tunnels through rock, harvesting it disturbs the habitat of other marine life. This slow-maturing mollusc has become so sought after that it has become endangered. Restaurants have had to take it off their menus and any harvesters of illegal date-mussels risk prosecution. Trade has shifted from western Europe, where its collection has been banned or limited, to northern and Eastern European countries **WS**

Taste: *Similar in flavor and texture to a mussel, it is usually eaten raw. In many countries, especially Italy, it is mixed with other shellfish in soups and added to risottos.*

Mont St. Michel Mussel

Green-Shelled Mussel

Mussels grown on *bouchots* (wooden pillars) in France have long been a well-loved shellfish, whether it is those from Île de Ré, where the mussels are roasted over flaming pine needles, or those that are harvested from the northern Brittany coast, and Mont St. Michel in particular, and cooked in cider and cream. It is the Mont St. Michel mussels (AOC), however, that command the highest prices and have an exceptional reputation among chefs.

The mussel is a bivalve mollusc, with two bluish-black shells and a pointed wedge-shape at one end. Mont St. Michel mussels are relatively small, but the succulent cream and orange flesh provide a satisfying mouthful compared to smaller, more traditional shellfish such as cockles. Mussels are best enjoyed from fall through to spring, because they spawn in the warmer months and the flesh becomes thin.

Traditional recipes such as *moules marinières* and *moules frites* are arguably still the best. Some say female mussels are better than the pale creamy male, but this is personal taste! **STS**

These delectable shellfish were known as green-lipped mussels until interfering officials observed it is the shells, not the creatures themselves, that glisten emerald green. Traditionally New Zealanders ate the huge blue-shelled mussel, a daunting culinary task to those used to smaller, European molluscs. The more elegant, green-shelled mussel, *Perna canaliculus,* became a commercial export crop because it was closer to European expectations.

There has been much discussion, but little proof, of the health-giving properties of green-shelled mussels. However, this has sensibly been superseded by greater interest in their flavor. They come in two flesh colors, an important distinction if you are a mussel on the prowl—the orange ones are boys, the cream are girls. Like blue-shelled mussels, they are sometimes served with vinegar and raw onion, but this overwhelms their delicacy. In New Zealand, they can be purchased cool, wet, and alive from dedicated dispensers in almost every supermarket. Exports tend to be on the half-shell and have "added-value" flavourings or sauces. **GC**

Taste: *Mont St. Michel mussels are at their best when the weather has been very cold. Steamed open, the shells reveal large, meaty mussels with a sweet and juicy flavor.*

Taste: *Best enjoyed simply steamed, where the melting texture of all but the lips tastes elegantly sweet and creamy, with a distinct, tangy aftertaste of the sea.*

Spéciale Gillardeau

Sydney Rock Oyster

Oysters are an iconic food. They have a clean simplicity of taste that expresses the essence of the sea, with elements that reflect the unique area where they are grown, just as a wine reflects its *terroir*.

The French take their oysters very seriously, and have a labeling system with a complexity to match. Gillardeau oysters belong to an elite subset of *fines de claire* oysters, known as *spéciales de claire*. They are named for the celebrated family of oyster farmers that produces them.

Gillardeau oysters are sent to market in wet wooden baskets, often with seaweed to keep them damp and cool. As with all oysters, it is important they are alive when opened for consumption. If the shell is open, it should close when tapped at the hinge end. If it does not, the mollusc is dead and should be discarded. As living things, oysters must never be sealed in airtight containers, and should not be allowed to get too cold. They are best stored at the bottom of the refrigerator, with the more bowl-shaped half of the shell at the bottom, and a damp cloth over the tray. **STS**

Endemic to Australia, these bivalve molluscs have been commercially cultivated since the 1870s. They breed in saltwater and estuarine habitats along the coasts of Victoria, New South Wales, and Queensland, and at Albany, in Western Australia.

Compared to other oysters, the Sydney rock (*Saccostrea glomerata*) is medium size. They reach harvesting size in about three years, but selective breeding trials have developed a "super Sydney rock" that can be harvested in two years. Although they are the most common edible oysters in Australia, they command a high price because of the strict environmental conditions surrounding production.

Sydney rocks are plump and briny with a sweet and creamy taste. They have a starring role on the Sydney dining scene, which is awash with bijou oyster bars and classy seafood restaurants, and many a diner has been tempted to try a Sydney rock as their first oyster. Although most oysters are eaten raw, they are also magnificent in recipes, such as oyster mornay or vichyssoise, for those who cannot stomach them live. **SCS**

Taste: *A strong marine flavor without the metallic zing many associate with oysters. Crush them in the mouth to maximize the nutty aftertaste and briny tang.*

Taste: *Chewed or not, these oysters are sweet on the front palate, then salty with a rich aftertaste. Their delicate characteristics are best enjoyed when served* au naturel.

A farmer checks a rack of Sydney rock oysters on the Hawkesbury River, New South Wales. »

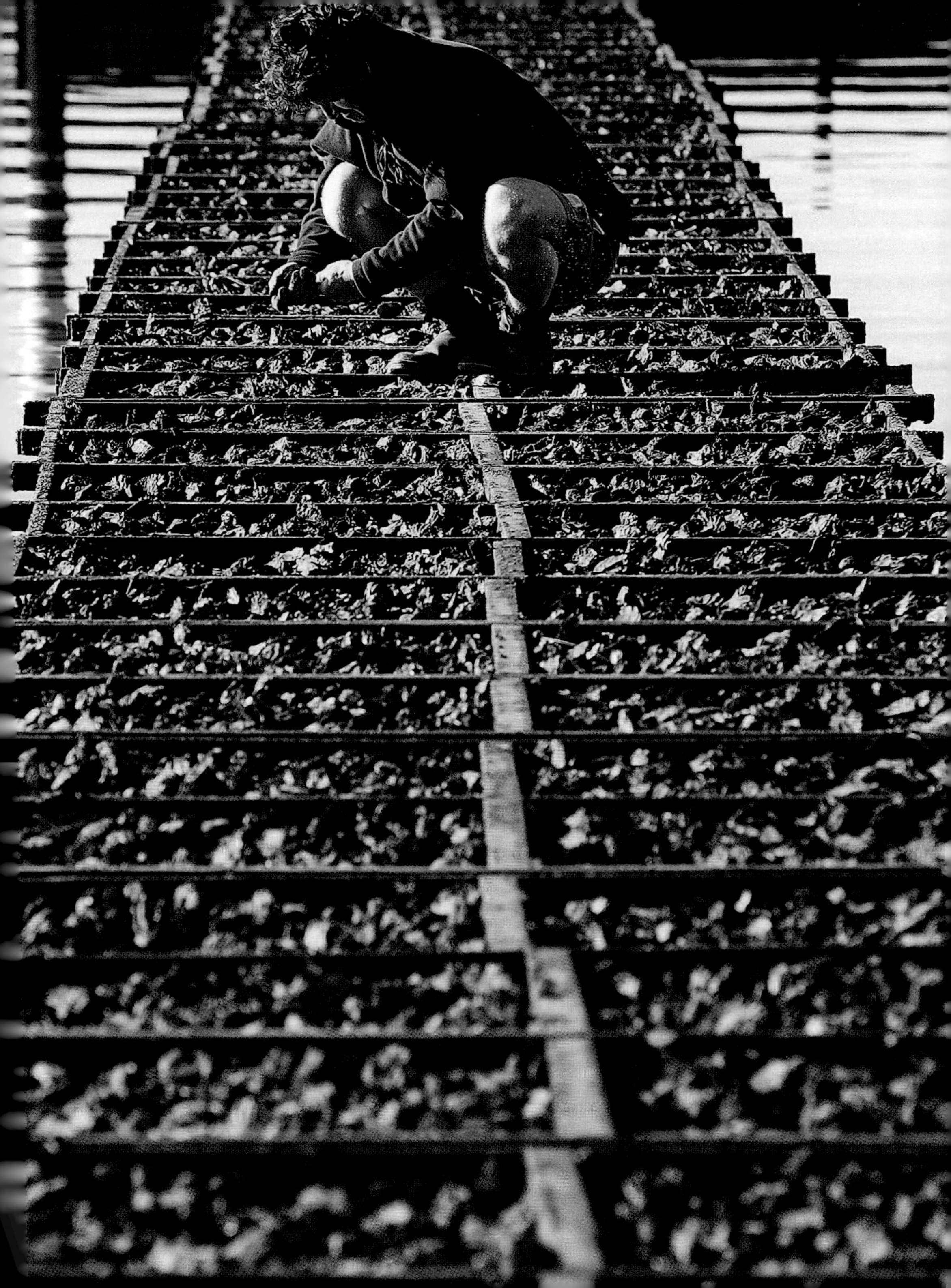

Hiroshima Oyster

Aptly nicknamed "milk of the sea," Hiroshima oysters (*Crassostrea gigas*) can grow up to 10 inches (25 cm) long, and are said to contain more glycogen, iron, and phosphorus than those from other areas. Together, Japan, Korea, and China produce ninety percent of the world's oysters, but with consumers in Japan concerned over the quality of imports, Hiroshima oysters are increasingly prized.

The oyster is celebrated throughout Hiroshima, and nearby Miyajima hosts an oyster festival each year, where visitors can taste Hiroshima oysters fresh on the half-shell with a selection of dressings, such as sudachi citrus and soy sauce, or the Hiroshima specialty *dote nabe*—a one-pot stew, cooked at the table, of oysters, tofu, and vegetables simmered in a miso-based broth.

Oysters are also used to make *kaki meshi* (oyster rice) and *gunkan maki* (battleship sushi), in which soft, runny ingredients are placed on top of an oval of sushi rice, encased and supported by a "wall" of nori sea vegetable. *Kaki furai*—breaded and deep-fried oysters—are eaten all over Japan. **SB**

Kumamoto Oyster

The Kumamoto oyster (*Crassostrea sikamea*) has a niche market all of its own. However, it is also a stark reminder of the consequences of overfishing.

Taking its name from the large bay on the southernmost Japanese island of Kyushu, this small Pacific oyster is a wonderful delicacy. But, although they are now grown around the world, they are extinct in their place of origin, Kumamoto Bay. In the United States they are farmed in Humboldt Bay, California, but take a number of years to reach a marketable size, making them one of the most costly oysters on the restaurant menu. They are only available in small quantities and are in high demand for their fabulous taste.

Kumamoto oysters have a sweeter, more delicate taste than other Pacific oysters. One reason for their popularity, especially in the United States, is that they are considered to be an excellent year-round oyster remaining firmer and meatier in the warmer months than other species. Their deep shell retains their liquid beautifully, making them ideal for serving on the half-shell. **STS**

Taste: *A giant among oysters, the Hiroshima oyster is creamy, shiny, and supple, with a velvety, milky, yet slightly minerally, taste. The texture is firm.*

Taste: *Delicately salty, this is an excellent "first timer," the perfect introduction to the joys of eating live oysters. The meat is firm, with a sweet taste, and fills the shell well.*

Japanese oyster farmers work beds outlined ❧ *by buoys near the Amakusa Islands, Kumamoto.*

Bay Scallop

Diver King Scallop

Native to the Atlantic coast of the United States—and so emblematic of the East Coast the scallop is the state shell of New York State—bay scallops (*Argopectens irradians*) grow in shallow coastal waters from New England as far south as Florida. As with other scallops the edible part is the adductor muscle that opens and closes the iconic shell.

There is still some wild harvest of bay scallops in the northeastern United States, although scallop farming is on the increase, and a large proportion of bay scallops sold in the United States actually originate with Chinese aquaculture operations. Most are shucked immediately upon harvest: scallops in their shells—while harder to come by—are infinitely more rewarding.

Scallop aquaculture throughout the world has gained a green light from watchdogs for its low environmental impact. Incredibly versatile, bay scallops adapt well to most cooking methods. Their small size means that they cook in a flash. Sweet little nuggets of maritime meat, they can tempt even finicky eaters. **CN**

The magnificent diver king scallop (*Pecten maximus*) is caught in the relatively deep waters of the eastern Atlantic, from Norway to the south of Spain, and also around the Azores. As the name suggests, these shellfish are harvested by hand by divers who will select the biggest ones available to get the highest market value. Dredged scallops are also available; they are usually much cheaper because they are of variable size and can contain sand and grit from the dredging process.

Seared in a hot pan so they are brown on the outside but barely cooked in the middle, diver king scallops are a most delicious shellfish and they quite literally melt in the mouth. In Europe, both the white adductor muscle meat and the orange/cream tongue or coral (roe) is eaten, whereas in the United States the white muscle is favored and the roe is usually discarded.

Popular in both classic and contemporary cuisine, mouthwatering recipes include the heavenly *coquilles St. Jacques à la Parisienne* and seared scallops in a saffron *beurre blanc*. **STS**

Taste: *Eaten raw, their texture is tender, but toothsome, and their flavor slightly buttery and sweet. They are best cooked simply, such as sautéed with butter and lemon.*

Taste: *Sweet, succulent, and rich, the intense flavor of the meat takes on a certain nuttiness when seared in butter. Avoid overcooking to preserve the delicate texture.*

Scallops cook quickly, either on the grill as here ***or barbecued on skewers with other ingredients.***

Baby Squid

Prized along the Mediterranean coast of Europe, these tiny members of the cephalopod family are oval little creatures that measure 1¼ to 2½ inches (3–6 cm) long. Mother Nature judiciously furnished them with pearly opaque bodies because they swim near to the surface of the water and are prone to attack from below.

They are firm and slightly flattened in shape, with eight arms and two long tentacles, and their soft exterior surrounds a central body cavity with a bony cartilage that is removed before cooking. This provides a perfect natural receptacle for stuffing, although baby squid are also delicious grilled, marinated, fried, frittered, or served in salads.

In Spain, baby squid are known as *chipirones* and are a highly valued delicacy. *Chipirones* "Los Peperetes" are poached baby squid that have been canned in olive oil—a particularly delicious treat not to be missed. Succulent and delectable, these are caught in Galician estuaries and, like other baby squid, pair wonderfully with top-quality olive oil and freshly squeezed lemon juice. **LF**

Taste: *Tender, juicy, and sweet, with a smooth, silky texture, baby squid taste subtly of the sea, but are never overly "fishy."*

Ika

The Japanese love squid. While there are many species of ika in oceans across the world, and squids of their various kinds are valued from Korea to the Mediterranean, half of the world's catch is consumed in Japan. The most popular species are *surume ika* (Pacific flying squid), *yari ika* (spear squid), and *kaminari ika* (cuttlefish). All ika have a central bone inside the body cavity that is easy to remove.

Different species are suited to different recipes and are prepared in a variety of ways, notably raw in sashimi, deep-fried in tempura, and broiled in teriyaki. Light cooking preserves the soft texture; overcooking renders it chewy.

Ika somen is a specialty of the town of Hakodate. Raw ika is sliced into long, fine strips that resemble *somen* noodles. These are then eaten like noodles, with a raw quail egg, some wakame sea vegetable, and a soy-based dipping sauce. Whole raw squid are sometimes stuffed with sushi rice to make *ika zushi*. *Ikayaki* are whole broiled squid basted in a sweet soy sauce and broiled teriyaki style—a popular festival food in summer. **SB**

Taste: *Ika somen is slightly sticky while being smooth and velvety, with a mild, creamy, but not fishy taste. Surume ika is rich, sweet, chewy, and deeply satisfying.*

Squid are laid on a rack to dry; in Asia, dried squid is used in many recipes as well as eaten as a snack. »

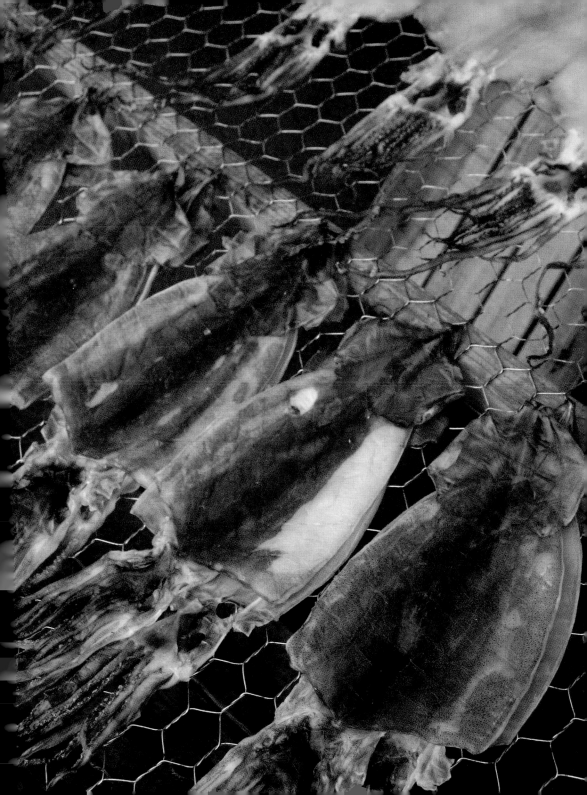

Octopus

There are hundreds of different species of octopus, enjoyed by some cuisines, rejected by others. Unlike cuttlefish and squid, the tentacles, rather than the body, make for better eating.

Although it is a solitary animal, octopus is still more abundant in the Mediterranean than squid, which helps to explain why so many recipes for cooking it exist. Baby octopus is delicious fried whole as in the Italian *fritto misto*, but larger ones might need prolonged simmering before they become tender. Slices marinated with lemon juice and olive oil are a typical meze. Stewing octopus in its own ink is popular in Greek-island cooking, and also around the Iberian coast.

While the sight of Greek fishermen tenderizing octopus by beating them against the side of a boat can seem repulsive—although the animal is already dead—it stands little comparison to the Japanese habit of eating octopus as sashimi while still alive enough to wriggle. John Ashburne observes "The sensation, as the suckers attach to the roof of your mouth, is impossible to convey." **MR**

Taste: *Octopus offers a whole range of different textures. Thin slices can be rubbery or chewy; whole fried baby octopus is crisp. Large tentacles with suckers are meaty.*

Akashi Tako

Akashi tako (*Octopus vulgaris*) is eaten enthusiastically by the Japanese who, unlike most of the rest of the human race, are not repelled by its eight legs and strange appearance, but find it positively cute. But this does not stop them eating it—sometimes alive.

A nutrient-rich diet of shrimp, plankton, and crab, along with a fast-moving current, is said to make the tako caught in Akashi the best in Japan. The importance of the octopus to the town is apparent, with octopus nets and clay pots in store windows and tentacles hanging to dry in the sun. The local fish market, Uo no Tana (meaning fish shelf), displays its fresh fish on wooden planks under running water, and has become a tourist attraction.

Rich in protein, low in fat, and high in amino acids, tako can be eaten raw, but is more usually lightly boiled; it is also traditionally tenderized by kneading the flesh in finely grated daikon pulp. Popular ways of eating Akashi tako are in *takosu*—thinly sliced boiled tako served in a sweet vinegar, combined with cucumber and sometimes miso, and *takonikomi*—or simmered in sweet soy sauce. **SB**

Taste: *Akashi tako is creamy, soft, and velvety with a light chewiness and a mild sweet taste of the sea. It is particularly good battered and served as* akashiyaki.

Japanese **takoyaki** *consists of pieces of octopus grilled in a pancake mixture with ginger and scallion.* ❯

Sea Urchin

Prickly as hedgehogs, these round, spiky balls litter the floors and rocks of all the world's oceans, concealing a rounded body with neither head nor tail. Like starfish, sea urchins are echinoderms, and their bodies are symmetrical across five axes. Their edible parts, therefore, are also five in number: roe-like yellow-to-orange lobes that form the creatures' gonads.

Across the many culinary cultures of the globe that appreciate sea urchins, there is a general consensus they are best eaten raw. In Japan, "uni" is eaten as a sushi and there are several grades available in the fish markets. The most sought after are bright golden and firm; the paler ones are softer and less sweet. While the same degree of refinement is not found in the West, sea urchins are still considered a luxury and, particularly in the Mediterranean, are becoming scarce as a result of overconsumption. Most species are not currently farmed: Canadian fisheries are generally acknowledged as the most sustainable source of the wild delicacy. **MR**

Sea Cucumber

Also known as the sea slug, the sea cucumber's name seems an appropriate one for this ugly creature that slowly crawls the ocean floor in search of food. In Chinese cuisine, it is boiled, salted, and dried before sale, a treatment that turns it ash gray and makes it capable of being stored almost indefinitely: it has to be cleaned, rehydrated, and cooked for hours before it is tender enough to eat.

Like many Chinese delicacies, sea cucumber is appreciated not for its taste but for its texture: this is gelatinous, slightly chewy, and extremely distinctive. Because of its high cost, it is a popular inclusion on Chinese banquet menus, when it is often braised in a superior stock flavored with rice wine, ginger, soy sauce, and oyster sauce. Populations are endangered in many parts of the world, although Australia operates sustainable sea cucumber fisheries. Very different sea cucumbers are eaten in Spain, where they are known as *espardeñas* or *espardenyes*. Small, white, and tender, they provide a completely different eating experience from their Pacific cousins. **KKC**

Taste: *The taste is always of the sea, but never "fishy." It varies species to species, from an intensely salty, seaweedy explosion of the ocean to sweeter, creamier flavors.*

Taste: *Chinese sea cucumber has a neutral taste that absorbs the flavors it is cooked with. Spanish sea cucumber tastes mild with a chewy, squidlike texture.*

The Japanese term uni *refers to the edible portion of a sea urchin; here, more than 100 are displayed.*

Violet

Despite its name, this curious creature is not a flower but an edible sea-squirt (*Microcosmus sulcatus*). So little valued is it in English-speaking cultures that its name is French, and pronounced as such. On the Mediterranean coast, where it is prized, it is also called *figue de mer* (sea fig) or *uovo di mare* (sea egg).

The barrel-shaped adults are attached to underwater rocks, piers, boats, and the sea bottom. The violet feeds by siphoning seawater through its body and using a basketlike internal filter to capture plankton and oxygen; gnarled in appearance, it is the size of a large oyster. It projects two siphons, one for inhaling and one for exhaling seawater. Although the exterior looks shell-like, it is actually leathery.

To reach its edible parts, you must slice the violet in half through the middle, a process that reveals a yellowy mush, similar in appearance to scrambled egg (some may find its appearance off-putting). The yellow pulp has a strong salty flavor with a tang of iodine. The pulp is spooned out and may be eaten raw or alternatively cooked in a soup. Smaller violets have a sweeter flavor than the larger specimens, which have a stronger tang of iodine.

Violets are especially popular in Provence, France, and stalls that offer them as an expensive shellfish snack are still found intermittently in the side streets of Marseille. While occasionally added to the famous fish stew, bouillabaisse, they appear more often as part of a *plateau de fruits de mer*.

Different varieties of sea-squirt are prized in Chile, Korea, and Japan, where they are considered to be a delicacy and served raw. Salted and seasoned sea squirt is especially popular in Korea as a side dish and is widely available in bottles and jars. **MR**

Taste: *Oyster lovers might well like the salty, iodine tang of violets, but their soft, mushy texture makes them an acquired taste for those who prefer firm seafood.*

Squid Ink

As the name would suggest, this viscous ebony ink comes from squid, which, like their fellow cephalopods cuttlefish and octopus, have eight arms and two tentacles arranged in pairs. More relevantly, they have no shell or bone on their exterior, so are very susceptible to attack from predators.

Instead of providing external armor for the squid's self-defense, nature has endowed the squid with the ability to discharge a thick stream of black liquid that clouds the water. This diversion tactic is thought to confuse predators, and at the same time the ink cloud alerts other members of the same species and provides them with cover for escape.

Squid ink is entirely edible and delicious to boot; it adds a wonderful tang of the sea and a unique, eye-catching black tint to sauces, pasta, and rice dishes. In Hokkaido, Japan, a summer squid festival takes place, and among the many savory squid dishes there is also on sale a squid ink ice cream, *ikazuri aisukurimu*. An ice-cream stall near the famous Tsukiji fish market in Tokyo also sells grayish-black, soft, whipped squid ink ice cream. In Europe, the ink is the defining ingredient in the famous Spanish black rice dish *arroz negro*, and is a popular ingredient in Catalan cuisine in rice and pasta dishes. It features prominently in Italian cuisine, where it is a particular favorite for coloring and flavoring pasta that is then served with shellfish. Squid ink risotto is a traditional Venetian dish. The ink is also good in sauces, the slight downside being that it tends to color everything it touches—including teeth.

Fresh squid ink should be used immediately or refrigerated for a short time in a non-porous bowl as, like squid, it will begin to smell if left to stand. **LF**

Taste: *Squid ink adds a pleasing salty punch to sauces and a restrained fishy flavor and appealing color to pasta dough. Look for the natural sac inside fresh squid.*

*Italian **pasta nero** takes its black coloring from squid ink mixed in with the pasta dough before cooking.* ❯❯

Conch

"Conch" is a generic name used for the many kinds of large, single-shell molluscs found in tropical waters around the globe. However, it is the Queen conch (*Strombus gigas*), with its graceful, pointed shell, and iridescent rosy pink interior "lips," that is sought out by seafood gourmets. The name of conch may seem unprepossessing compared with the flamboyance of the shell, but it becomes even less so in Florida, the Bahamas, and some other Caribbean islands, where it is more bluntly pronounced konk.

Inside the shell is a large, snail-like mollusc. This creature lives on sandy, sea-grass beds and among the coral reefs of warm shallows, growing to a length of 12 inches (30.5 cm) on a diet of aquatic plants. A slow-moving animal, it is easily harvested by fishermen who can sell both the shellfish and the beautiful shell. For centuries, the molluscs have been prized in the Caribbean, where they are a common source of food, and where their shells are also used for horns, as containers, to make fish hooks, and as ornaments. Today, however, there are major concerns that *Strombus gigas* is being exploited at a rate that is unsustainable worldwide.

Despite this, conch is a hugely popular food in the Caribbean and its surrounding countries. In order to tenderize the meat of this large mollusc, the flesh is often beaten (as with octopus) or marinated in lime juice to tenderize it. It can be grilled whole as a steak or diced and turned into fritters, chowders, or gumbos. It can also be eaten raw in salads, cooked in a tasty stew with red kidney beans, marinated in wafer-thin slices with lime juice as ceviche, or tossed with onions, tomato, and fresh cilantro along with a good measure of lemon or lime juice. **WS**

Taste: *Conch meat needs tenderizing or steeping in an acidulated, usually lime juice-based, marinade. It then has a mild brininess and sweet flavor similar to clams.*

Great heaps of conch shells are left by fishermen
ⓧ of the Netherlands Antilles in the Caribbean.

Frog

It is not just the French who enjoy eating frogs. Outside Europe, particularly in Thailand, sacks of live frogs are a feature of food markets, where they are prepared on the spot and eaten whole in a green curry. In the West, it is usually, though not exclusively, the legs that are consumed. Frogs' legs have been eaten in France since medieval times, particularly during the fasting period of Lent.

In the Italian region of Pavia (Lombardy), frogs' legs are eaten in risottos, frittatas, and tomato stews. In one celebrated recipe, whole frogs are stuffed with spinach. In French regional cuisine, they are preferred sautéed in butter with garlic and parsley. The menus of famous French chef Escoffier euphemistically referred to frogs as *nymphes*. In one of his recipes, *Chaud-froid a L'Aurore*, poached nymphs' legs are steeped in a fish sauce, then layered in a bed of Champagne jelly. The French colonial influence means that frogs also feature in the cusines of Louisiana in the United States and French-speaking parts of the West Indies.

It is often assumed that frogs are caught in the wild, but they are increasingly being farmed in Asia and the Americas. Commercial frog ponds were quite common in France during the nineteenth century, and the region of Dombes, in particular, is famous for its frogs. Overexploitation combined with the loss of the frog's natural marshy habitat, means that *Rana esculenta* is now a protected species in France. The frogs that appear on French restaurant menus are now generally Asian bullfrogs, imported from Southeast Asia. There are, however, major animal welfare concerns regarding the international trade in frogs' legs. **MR**

Taste: *It is very often claimed that frogs' legs taste like chicken. Actually, the slightly gelatinous texture is more akin to young farmed rabbit.*

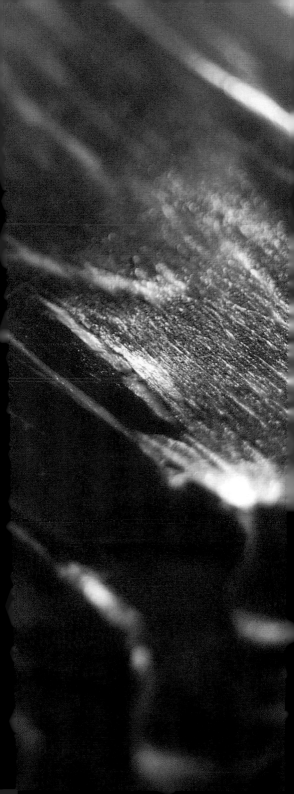

Akita Hinai-jidori Chicken

Described as "the ultimate free-range chicken," Akita Hinai-jidori birds are reared on small organic farms with clover pastures and mountain streams, and fed throughout the breeding period on apples, vegetables, and tomatoes. This special chicken is the result of crossbreeding the Hinai-dori, which is native to the mountainous Akita prefecture of Japan, with the Rhode Island Red (*Gallus domesticus*) from the United States. A similar quality chicken has been developed since 1991 in California by Dennis Mao for the Los Angeles restaurant market.

In Japan, the chicken is famed for being served raw, sashimi-style. For this preparation, the chicken needs to be exceptionally fresh (that is, alive on the same day it is served) and not previously frozen. Tokyo restaurants also serve the liver, gizzard, and brain of this esteemed bird. In the Wakayama prefecture, the chicken is seasoned with sea salt and then grilled over *binchōtan*, a traditional oak charcoal. The exceptional breast meat is also delicious grilled or broiled and served simply sliced with steamed vegetables. **CK**

Taste: *Akita Hinai-jidori chicken yields lean, moist meat with a creamy, firm texture, and a natural chicken flavor. Its renowned quality and flavor make it ideal for sashimi.*

Guinea Fowl

Originally thought to be from Guinea, in West Africa, these resilient birds have been domesticated and bred throughout the world. Guinea fowl were introduced into China in the seventeenth century and are referred to in India as Chinese fowl.

Having been raised in captivity as far back as 2400 BCE by ancient Egyptians, guinea fowl are today found in the United States in various colors and breeds, ranging from 12 ounces (350 g) to about 4 pounds (1.8 kg). In South Africa, they mostly still roam wild, which contributes to the quality of the dark meat, and low fat (around five percent) and cholesterol levels. The lean meat benefits from some form of barding such as bacon. Such a delicate meat deserves to be cooked with tender loving care, which will result in a moist, succulent poultry dish.

Males mate for life and young guineas are called "keets." Since it is difficult to distinguish between young males and females by appearance alone, the tell-tale two-syllable call of the female, sounding like "buck-wheat," helps those in the know. Guinea eggs are nutritious but difficult to come by. **HFi**

Taste: *Prepared in the same way as chicken, but with reduced cooking times on account of the smaller weight, the meat is rich and gamy with plump poultry juiciness.*

The magnificent vulterine guinea fowl, with its striking blue plumage, is found wild in northeast Africa. ❯❯

Volaille de Bresse

Red Grouse

In translation, "Bresse chicken" implies a single product, but the French name covers three equally fine types of poultry: *poulet*, a smallish bird that weighs about 3 pounds (1.4 kg); *poularde*, which weighs 4 to 5 pounds (1.8 to 2.3 kg); and *chapon*, a capon, or neutered male, that can tip the scales at as much as 9 pounds (over 4 kg). All are covered by an *Appellation d'Origine Contrôlée* and it is the capon, here, as elsewhere, a luxury for the festive season, that fetches the highest price by weight.

A Bresse chicken must not only come from the Bresse region, near Lyons, but must also belong to the eponymous breed whose pedigree was established early in the twentieth century. There are three separate strains, with white, gray, and black feathers, but all have the distinctive blue feet.

The *poulet* is a supreme spit-roasting bird, succulent, tender, and well flavored. It is the base of many chicken sauté dishes, especially those associated with *cuisine lyonnaise*. The *poularde* is often braised—in one famous *poularde en demi-deuil* recipe, with truffles under the skin. **MR**

Unique to the British Isles, the red grouse (*Lagopus lagopus scoticus*), which is a subspecies of the willow grouse, lives on moorland, where it feeds almost exclusively on heather. Smaller than the black grouse, it is reddish-brown with a plump body and a hook-tipped bill. These wild game birds cannot be successfully commercially reared. Their habitat is managed by gamekeepers and the birds can only be shot during the grouse-hunting season that begins on August 12th, if their population is high enough. Wet weather during the first two weeks of May, when the chicks hatch, or diseases like stronglyosis, can greatly deplete their numbers.

When preparing grouse, the cook needs to identify whether the bird is young or old because older birds are tougher. The easiest way to do so is to hold the bird by its lower beak and if it snaps, it is young, whereas if it does not, it is old. Young birds are good for roasting and braising, whereas older ones are best kept for the casserole. Grouse is often paired with sweet flavors, such as mashed potatoes flavored with parsnips, or fruit sauces. **MG**

Taste: *The flavor of Bresse poultry is neither strong nor bland; it is fine and delicately flavored, with toothsome flesh and thin, crisp skin when carefully roasted.*

Taste: *The unique flavor of red grouse begins on the palate with a rich gamy taste that gives way to the subtle sweetness of heather and the scent of wild herbs.*

The start of the hunting season for red grouse in the United Kingdom is known as the Glorious Twelfth. »

Imperial Peking Duck

Challans Duck

Except as pork, animal fat is in short supply in the Chinese diet, but fattened duck helps to fill the gap. Semiwild ducks are used to control small land-crabs that can devastate rice paddies, but the Chinese accidentally discovered they also ate rice.

The Imperial Peking Duck breed dates from the Ming Dynasty (1368–1644). Grain being shipped by boat to the capital, Peking, was inevitably spilled on riverside wharves and ended up in the stomachs of the waterside ducks. Peasants, noticing that these ducks grew inordinately fat, began to rear them in cages and force-feed them to develop an even plumper bird, perfect for roasting. Now popular in the United States and England, large Imperial Peking ducks can weigh up to 12 pounds (5.4 kg) and might carry a third of their body weight in fat.

One of the most famous duck dishes is Peking duck. The recipe involves pumping the bird with air and then hanging it up to dry. The characteristic crispy mahogany skin associated with the dish is achieved by coating the duck in a syrup and soy sauce mixture before roasting. **MR**

Close to the Atlantic coast in the heart of the Breton marshes, Challans is a region where wild-fowling has always flourished. According to folk history, Challans ducks are a cross between wild birds and ones introduced from Holland during the seventeenth century. By the nineteenth century, under the name of *canard nantais*, they were sent (from Nantes railroad station, hence the name) to Paris, where they were much admired.

The reputation of the duck owes much to the Parisian restaurant La Tour d'Argent. It created a recipe for a pressed duck in which the sauce is thickened with the duck's blood. The restaurant has kept a record of every duck sold and who ate it for more than a century: the Prince of Wales (the future King Edward VII), for example, ate No. 328 in 1890. Since then the figure has passed the million mark.

In the Loire valley, nearer its home, Challans duck is eaten simply roasted with fresh peas. Those in the know say the female of the species (*la canette*) is tastier than the male, however, both carry plenty of subcutaneous fat over the breast. **MR**

Taste: *The tender, fatty flesh of roasted Imperial Peking duck provides a perfect foil to the crispness of the skin, creating a tantalizing balance of sweet and salty flavors.*

Taste: *Served in thin slices with a sauce of cherries, black currants, or orange, the light, gamy flavor of tender duck contrasts wonderfully with the fruit.*

A window display of duck roasted in a mixture of soy and syrup identifies a restaurant in Shanghai, China.

Kelly Bronze® Turkey

Bourbon Red Turkey

Although around ninety percent of the turkeys reared in the United Kingdom are industrially produced in barns containing up to 20,000 birds, all Kelly Bronze® turkeys range free in woodland and pastures. At the beginning of the twentieth century, British turkeys, although bred for size, were much slimmer than they are now: they looked, when roasted, like angular giant pheasants. However, these breeds were superseded by modern "double-breasted" varieties—often so encumbered by their unnaturally bloated bosoms that they can only be bred using artificial insemination.

In 1984, Derek Kelly, an English farmer in Essex, revived an old strain of Bronze turkey that combined the yield of meat found on large-breasted breeds with the depth of flavor associated with traditional poultry husbandry. Today, Kelly's son rears his flock semiwild in woodland, without additives or drugs. Kelly Bronze turkeys take twice as long as most commercial birds to mature. They are plucked by hand and left to hang for up to two weeks to develop their characteristic gamy taste. **MR**

Benjamin Franklin once argued that the wild turkey might make a better symbol of America than the bald eagle, and the bird retains a prominent place in American culture. It is not only the beloved centerpiece of Thanksgiving celebrations, but the pride of many holiday feasts—in several European countries as well as in the New World.

Turkey has been an important food source in the Americas for thousands of years: it is thought to have first been domesticated as early as the second millennium BCE. The Bourbon Red, a bird of dark, rich mahogany color with white feather accents on the wings and tail, arrived on the scene relatively late: in Bourbon County, Kentucky, where it was established in the late nineteenth century. The breed was valuable during the first half of the twentieth century, but lost favor over the years with breeders who preferred larger-breasted birds. But recent efforts to conserve heritage foods have helped return attention to the Bourbon Red and other varieties that are less buxom but often have more distinctive flavor than their modern cousins. **CN**

Taste: *The smell of a roasted Kelly Bronze is clearly gamy, like partridge. The breast meat is moist, but denser than a chicken's and the leg is similar in texture to young lamb.*

Taste: *The Bourbon Red turkey, like many heritage breeds, offers a more richly flavored meat. Roasted whole, the crisp golden skin contrasts with the juicy meat beneath.*

On their respective Thanksgiving Days, U.S. and Canadian families enjoy a roast turkey dinner. »

Squab

Pigeons have been bred for the table since ancient times, when their meat was valued as a delicacy to be enjoyed by pharaohs, emperors, and kings. The art of raising pigeons for the table began in ancient Egypt, where pigeon stew featured on the menu.

A member of the Columba family and known as *pigeonneau* in France, a squab is any young pigeon on the point of leaving the nest; true squabs have never flown. It must be around four weeks old and weigh less than 14 oz (400 g). The young flesh is plump, delicate, and very fat, but the fat is under the skin and renders down in cooking, making it one of the most easily digestible of all meats, unlike either domestic poultry or wild game birds.

The best way to cook a squab is to split it open and fry it in extra-virgin olive oil or butter, or a mix of both. It can also be stuffed and roasted whole, when the breast still needs protection with bacon or fat. It can be cooked as pigeon, but the delicacy of the meat calls for the simplest of methods. Squab pie is a traditional dish, although it sometimes contains mutton or pork, rather than pigeon. **LW**

Quail

This dainty game bird is beloved both by the hunter and the epicure. It is also known across the world as blue quail, bush quail, and mountain quail. Despite being rather dumpy, seeming almost to strain itself when taking off, the quail is a migratory bird, its long wings enabling it to cross high mountains and seas. It has a distinctive call of three sharp notes that has led to a nickname in England of "wet-my-lip."

Quail is reared commercially in Europe for its meat and its eggs, which are also considered a delicacy. This highly regarded bird (*Coturnix coturnix*) belongs to the same family as the partridge and has a similar appearance, although it is much smaller. In parts of the United States, the terms quail and partridge are interchangeable.

Like most game birds, quail is best prepared simply to appreciate its sweet, gamy flavor. Cooked *en papillote*, with the cavity stuffed with a few fresh herbs and garlic or cloves, quail is superb. As the parcel is opened the full fragrance of this delicate bird meets your olfactory senses, preparing you for the luxurious feast within. **LW**

Taste: *What little meat there is on these young birds is perfect: half duck, half chicken, it is dark, flavorful, and extremely tender. Prepare in the same manner as chicken.*

Taste: *Pleasing in shape, taste, and color, quail meat is rich, uniquely fragrant, soft, and moist. When roasted the skin is crisp and juicy, like crackling on pork.*

Quail is best simply prepared; here it is served grilled on skewers with a tahini and lemon sauce. ❯❯

Toulouse Goose

Graylag Goose

The most commonly reared breed of large gray goose in France, the Toulouse (also known as *L'oie grise des Landes* or the Gray Landes goose) is often used for the production of foie gras. It can weigh up to 20 pounds (9 kg) after fattening, but will normally reach maturity at about 12 pounds (5.4 kg).

Although classified as poultry and, therefore, white meat, goose has a dark colored flesh and the flavor is stronger and more pungent than most poultry. The Toulouse goose is central to the cuisine of southwest France. The meat is often reserved for *confit d'oie* (goose meat preserved in its own fat), which is a basic ingredient of the white bean and Toulouse sausage stew, cassoulet, but it has other uses. Accompanied by potatoes sautéed in goose fat, garnished with diced black truffles (*à la sarladaise*) it is a specialty of Périgord. The neck can also be stuffed with a forcemeat and braised.

The Toulouse goose is considered to be the best meat bird in Europe and is frequently roasted whole at Christmas, although in France turkey is the more popular choice. **MR**

According to the historian Livy, a flock of noisy geese at Capitoline Hill alerted Rome to invading Gauls in 390 BCE. Geese were first domesticated in Egypt, and both the Egyptians and the Romans prized them for their liver. The graylag goose (*Anser anser*)—the ancestor of domestic geese in North America and Euope—Is bigger and bulkier than other gray geese, and can weigh up to 11 pounds (5 kg).

A migratory bird, it is found in parts of northern Europe and Eurasia stretching across to Russia. Its plumage is pale gray with a white belly, and it has a large orange bill. During the breeding season it is found in fens, marshes, lakes, and damp moorland. The draining of marshland has led to the decline of the graylag goose in Europe.

Goose is common Christmas fare in parts of Europe, although it vies with turkey in popularity. In the United Kingdom, it was once traditionally eaten at Michaelmas (Sept. 29). Mrs. Beeton recommends cooking it with a glass of port or wine to which mustard, salt, and cayenne pepper are added. In China, goose is often air-dried. **CK**

Taste: *The dark reddish flesh of goose has a strong farmyard flavor. Baked in the oven, the fatty skin turns crisp, giving a unique contrast with the melting meat.*

Taste: *Graylag goose meat is very rich in flavor and lean, with most of the fat concentrated in the skin. Tart fruit sauces offset the fattiness of roast goose meat.*

The Toulouse goose is the prime choice for roasting
❈ *whole, but its fat is also valued for its use in cooking.*

Partridge

Of the many varieties of partridge, the two most esteemed for the table in Europe are the common grey partridge (*Perdrix perdrix*) and the red-legged partridge (*Alectoris rufa*); both have been introduced to the United States, although the chukar partridge (*Alectoris chukar*), which is native to Turkey, is most popular on game farms.

As with other game birds, modern farming methods are affecting the creatures' natural habitat, although the birds are reared extensively for sport shooting. The grey partridge can be found all over Europe as far north as Sweden and Russia, and in parts of Asia; the red-legged partridge is found mainly in Spain, Portugal, and southwest France. Both are small plump birds that are strikingly good to eat, although the red-legged partridges are fleshier and milder in flavor. Young partridges require little or no hanging, and are best cooked simply, either roasted or broiled; their flesh is full of flavor and easily digestible. Older birds are very flavorsome indeed. They should be hung or marinated before slow cooking. **LW**

Taste: *It is tantalizing to be presented with this plump little bird. The flesh is moist and mildly gamy, like the taste and texture of liver, especially when served pink.*

Pheasant

According to legend, Jason and the Argonauts brought the pheasant back with them when they returned from the Caucasus with the fabled Golden Fleece; from Greece it went to Rome; and from Rome to Europe. Today, this important and most hunted game bird is found as far east as Siberia and China. A huge population of common pheasant (*Phasianus colchicus*) is sustained artificially in the United States and in Europe; in the former it is also known as the ring-necked pheasant or Chinese pheasant.

The male pheasant is magnificently handsome, but it is the smaller, plainer hen that chefs seek out for her plump, tender meat. Traditionally, pheasant is hung by the neck for up to ten days before being cooked, to heighten the flavor and texture. Young pheasants are wrapped in bacon or larded to keep the meat moist and then roasted. Older birds are sautéed in butter, and then cooked slowly in wines, alcohol, and rich stocks. Fruit is often used in the cooking to offset the meat's gamy flavor. Many chefs prefer to cook the breast portion on its own, using the rest for pâtés, terrines, and pies. **LW**

Taste: *Pale, lean, and firm, pheasant has the most delicate meat. The breast is creamy, yet crumbly, with a hint of walnut; the darker leg meat is more sinewy, but still succulent.*

Pheasants need hanging before plucking because having survived in the wild their meat is tougher. »

Gadwall

Widely distributed across Europe, Asia, and North America, the gadwall (*Anas strepera*) is a gray dabbling duck that feeds in both saltwater and freshwater marshland. At the end of summer it leaves its breeding ground in the Arctic Circle to winter in southern Europe.

The gadwall is often mistaken by both shooters and butchers for a mallard because it has similar feathers and is a similar size (albeit a bit smaller), but the main distinguishing factor is its white rear wing feathers, which are visible in flight. Gadwall are shot by shooters who either wait at the tide edge for the birds to fly past or sit alongside where the birds are feeding. The gadwall is considered to be one of the easiest ducks to shoot as it tends to fly in a straight line and is more trusting than other wild ducks. It is commonly seen in large flocks, which makes it easier to shoot in bigger numbers.

The first mention of its name is found in *Merrett's List of Birds* (1666) but its exact origin is uncertain. Said by some to be derived from *quedul*, the onomatopoeic Latin word for quack, the gadwall also has a number of local variants and is known variously as the gray duck, rodge, or sand widgeon.

Gadwall is akin to most forms of farmed duck, but being wild it is naturally leaner than its farmed counterpart. It has a coarse-grained meat that works well with traditional duck sauces such as orange. The lack of fat means that the gadwall is best roasted and larded with bacon, or cooked in the classic French style, with turnips, or even boiled in a *court bouillon* and then roasted in a hot oven to keep the flesh moist. Roast gadwall are also excellent stuffed with a veal and wild mushroom forcemeat. **MG**

Teal

The teal (which belongs to the genus *Anas*) is a small, wild dabbling duck, much prized by wildfowlers. The European teal (*Anas crecca*) is partly migratory, overwintering in southern Europe in the wetlands and marshes that form their preferred habitat. The male of the European teal is a handsome bird, with a chestnut head and a broad green eye patch, while both the male and female show bright green wing patches when in flight. There are several species of teal in North America, including *Anas carolinensis*, the green-winged teal, and *Anas discors*, the blue-winged teal. A gregarious bird, the teal arrives at wintering sites in large flocks.

Teal are considered one of the most difficult of wild ducks to shoot, due to their small size and their ability to change direction quickly and unpredictably while flying. Unlike other ducks, they do not respond to calls or to decoys, which adds to their sporting challenge for hunters.

When it comes to eating this flavorful but small wild bird, at least one teal per person is required. They are often eaten as a starter, but when prepared as a main course they are served on a large plate, sometimes with up to three teal per person. The bird's exceptional flavor comes in part from the generous levels of fat found on it. However, the meat is fine-grained and appears to be completely smooth when cut. On the whole, teal, like most wild duck, are enjoyed best when they are served pink, as they can dry out and toughen if cooked for too long. Excellent when cooked with aromatic spices or flavorful herbs, teal can be cooked in a variety of ways, from simply wrapping in bacon and roasting to grilling, frying, or braising with wine. **MG**

Taste: *Gadwall has a flavor very similar to that of mallard. Like most duck, it has a pleasant covering of fat, which is fantastic to eat when cooked to a crisp.*

Taste: *The rich, buttery flavor of teal comes from the fat that the bird acquires on its diet of barley, samphire seeds, and grasses, which contribute to its wonderful flavor.*

Duck breasts are best sautéed over a high heat, long enough to seal the outside but so that the inside is pink.

Golden Plover

Sometimes referred to, rather unfairly, as "poor man's partridge," the golden plover (*Pluvialis apricaria*) spends its summer on breeding grounds in the Arctic Circle and migrates south for the winter. Many gourmands consider the flavor of this small game bird to be superior to that of the French partridge. The bird is so named because of the golden spots that adorn its plumage.

The golden plover lives predominantly on inland, freshwater marshy areas and is seldom encountered in the salt marsh. It uses its short beak to unearth and eat grubs and small water-borne invertebrates. Golden plovers commonly fly in large groups. When a group is shot at from below, the shooter can mistakenly think he has downed the whole group becauses the birds descend rapidly on hearing the sound of the shot.

Tradition had it that plovers "live on air" and therefore they were among the relatively few gamebirds served without having been drawn—in other words, with their guts intact. A golden plover usually provides just about enough meat for one person. Quickly roasted, the birds were often served on toast—famously, golden plover on toast featured on the dinner menu of the *Titanic*. The breast meat is noted for being covered by a large amount of tasty fat, which makes it particularly juicy, particularly in early summer when the birds fatten themselves for the breeding season.

The first eggs of the season were once offered to the ruling British monarch and reached very high prices. They were also much sought after to prettify fashionable set pieces made of aspic, their color and shape being said to resemble large opals. **MG**

Taste: *The meat is lighter than that of a snipe, but would not fall into the category of a dark meat like pigeon. It has a delicate flavor, less liverish than most marsh birds.*

Ptarmigan

A member of the grouse family, the ptarmigan (*Lagopus mutus*) is larger than the famous red grouse and can be found in high, snowy, mountainous terrain and in subarctic countries around the globe. In North America, it is known as the rock ptarmigan. Its thick feathers, which, unusually, extend down over its feet, ensure that it can survive in these cold regions. The ptarmigan burrows into the snow for shelter and to escape predators, such as the Arctic fox. Famously, its plumage alters with the seasons to enable it to blend in with its surroundings. In the winter, when the landscape is covered by snow, the plumage turns pure white, but once the snow has melted the bird develops a mottled, brown plumage, affording it perfect camouflage in the barren rocky terrain.

An edible game bird, the ptarmigan has long been valued equally for eating and hunting, and pursuing it is a popular sport in those parts of the world where it lives. The flavor of the meat depends on the mountain food, such as shoots, leaves, berries, and insects, that has been available to the bird, but is compared to the rich taste of red grouse or hare. Restaurants often serve ptarmigan with sweet potatoes or a port jus because the sweetness brings out the exceptional flavor of the bird. The liver and hearts are often mashed into a pâté and served as a starter with bread cooked in goose fat. Carpaccio of ptarmigan is a real delicacy, served thinly sliced and dressed with capers, a touch of olive oil, and lime juice. In Iceland, ptarmigan is highly regarded, especially when well hung, and is popular as a Christmas dish accompanied by red-currant jelly and pickled red cabbage. **MG**

Taste: *Similar to red grouse, the dark meat of ptarmigan is rich and full of flavor. It combines the smell of heather, the scent of juniper berries, and a hint of Iberian ham.*

The ptarmigan is native to the Canadian Arctic, where it is still hunted and eaten by the Inuit. »

Snipe

Woodcock

As one might expect from a bird that lent its name to a sharpshooter, this little creature is extremely hard to target as it zigzags at high speeds through the wetlands and waterways where it winters. It is noted and prized by hunters in North America, Europe, and beyond; while the season varies from country to country, it can generally be shot from the latter part of summer to late winter or early spring.

Less popular now than during their nineteenth-century heyday, snipe are still held in high regard by many chefs and gastronomes. Both because they are tricky to hunt and because of their tiny size, they tend to be sold mainly by specialists: most weigh only 4 ounces (115 g), with only a third of that weight as meat. Like woodcock, they are traditionally cooked with the entrails left in, and sometimes using their own beak as a skewer; they are often served with toast, brioche, or bread cooked in goose fat so the diner can spread the "trails" on them as a pâté, which is excellent accompanied by a glass of port. Snipe should never be overhung or overcooked, because they will become incredibly tough. **MG**

Prized wherever it is found, from Scandinavia and northern Asia through to Italy and southern Spain, the Eurasian woodcock (pictured here) is valued not only for its taste but, particularly in Britain, as a test of the hunter's skill. It roosts in the trees and bushes of wetlands by day, flying out to feed through the night, and uses its long beak to probe the marshy ground for grubs and worms. Like snipe, woodcocks' fast, twisting flight makes them very difficult to shoot. In Britain and Ireland, it is considered a sign of great sporting prowess to shoot two woodcock with two shots—one from each barrel of the gun.

Woodcocks are valued not only for their meat but for their entrails: they are always cooked with them in, although the gizzard is removed. American woodcock are smaller, but also highly prized. In France, the birds are seasoned with lemon juice, salt, and spices, and combined with brandy and foie gras or fatty bacon; in the Italian *beccacce alla norcina*, they are made into a delicious stuffing with sausages, butter, herbs, and, when in season, black truffle. In Britain, the entrails are eaten on toast. **MG**

Taste: *Prized for the rich, light meat on the breast, the flavor of snipe is unique: the best comparison is to that of woodcock. Enjoy the smooth, creamy entrails on toast.*

Taste: *Woodcock meat is darker than snipe, with a rich, lightly gamy flavor. The entrails are surprisingly mild: creamy, rich, and smooth, with slightly liverish notes.*

Although snipe does not yield much meat, it is still
⊗ *enjoyed as a delicacy in many top restaurants.*

Tinamou

Shy and solitary, the tinamou is a bird native to the tropical lowlands of Latin America. In the 1800s it was marketed in Europe as the South American quail until it became rare in the wild. The size of a plump chicken, it does look a little like a quail. There are forty-seven species of tinamou; some are hunted for sport in Argentina, but the Argentine tinamou (*Rhychotus rufescens*) is also popular for the table.

Low in fat and high in protein, the bird is famed for its tender meat, attributed to the fact that it rarely flies, preferring to walk. The meat has a curious opalescent quality, so the tinamou is highly regarded as a table bird. In the wild the tinamou lives an average of five years, but in captivity it reaches its mature weight at twelve to sixteen weeks, and is best eaten at thirteen weeks when its meat is most tender. The breast meat is ideal as an appetizer, when it is battered and pan-fried, but it is also a good meat for use in stews flavored with tomatoes and garlic.

The tinamou's eggs are edible and taste similar to chicken eggs. However, they are most prized for their glossy green, turquoise, purple, or red shells. Several females may lay eggs in one nest, or one female may lay eggs in several nests. In either case, it is a male tinamou that builds the nest and sits on the eggs, and later tends the chicks. It is the female tinamou that courts the male.

Attempts by enthusiasts to introduce the tinamou into the European repertoire of game birds came to nought when it was discovered that the bird flew only very reluctantly. Its tolerant behavior toward other birds had led many to believe it would be a successful companion to the pheasant. **CK**

Taste: *The incredibly tender, white flesh of the tinamou is semiopaque in appearance. It has a mild, gamy flavor and can be prepared in the manner of partridge.*

Tinamou can be prepared in a similar way to
✷ *quail and partridge such as pan-fried in butter.*

Paca

The paca (*Agouti paca*) is a large, brown, white-spotted rodent found in forests, swamps, and jungles from east central Mexico and Cuba southward to northern Paraguay, Brazil, and Argentina. Resembling a guinea pig in appearance, an adult can weigh up to 30 pounds (14 kg). Pacas are, despite their rather rotund appearance, remarkably fast on land and in the water; they are generally nocturnal animals.

The paca's tender meat is regarded as an exquisite delicacy, so much so that it was considered to be a gourmet food fit for Queen Elizabeth II of the United Kingdom, who was served paca when she visited Belize on a royal tour in 1985. Unusually for a forest animal, the flesh and skin can be almost white; in flavor and texture they are like chicken.

In the wild pacas mainly survive on fruits and seeds, but they are hunted by farmers because they eat crops such as corn, yam, cassava, and sugar cane. Some governments have banned paca hunting because the animal has been overculled in some areas. Attempts have been made to raise it in captivity, although the meat of the domesticated animal is said to be inferior.

In its region of distribution, the meat is cooked in various ways. In Panama, it is grilled on a skewer, or roasted after being marinated in a black pepper sauce. In Mexico, it is boiled unskinned, or it is barbecued over hot coals and eaten with tortillas and a spicy salsa. Indigenous Latin American peoples often smoke the flesh of the paca, which preserves it from deterioration, while the Guyanese stuff the paca's stomach with a mixture of meat and grain before roasting it. **CK**

Taste: *Paca has beautifully tender meat that cuts easily and melts in the mouth. In flavor, it is a cross somewhere between chicken and pork.*

Hare

These beautiful, intelligent creatures, from the *Leporidae* family, feature in folklore and myth from the Hindu *Panchatantra* to *Aesop's Fables*. Hare was the most common game animal in Greek and Roman times, whereas in England their exuberant behavior over the mating period is responsible for the expression: "mad as a March hare."

Various species of hare are found worldwide, from Europe, China, and India to Africa, the Americas, and Australasia, and the line between rabbit and hare is fairly blurred, although hares, unlike rabbits, have never been domesticated. Generally, hares (a category into which Europeans would place the Californian jackrabbit) are larger than rabbits with long ears, the eponymous hare lip, and strong hindquarters. A young hare is known as a leveret until it is a year old, at which point its lip becomes more pronounced and its smooth coat turns wiry.

Hare should be hung for six days to develop its flavor and texture, head downward over a bowl to catch its blood for later use in the cooking pot. **LW**

Taste: *The meat is lean and dry, the flavor strong—half chicken, half venison. Young hares are best roasted or jugged. Older specimens reward lengthy cooking.*

Rex du Poitou®

While the name Rex du Poitou® would not have been familiar to epicures even a generation ago, it is gaining currency today. It refers to a strain of rabbit that was bred by French geneticists to have a commercial value not only for its Orylag fur, but for its excellent meat.

In France, rearing rabbits in cages for the table is traditional in the countryside. The meat is sweeter and more tender than that of wild rabbits, and the creatures can reach up to 5 pounds (2.3 kg) in weight, much larger than most of their wild peers.

The Rex du Poitou®, now a registered trademark, began to make an impact on the food world in 1996, when it won the Coq d'Or prize for the best French food product awarded by the *France Gourmande à Domicile* guide. Since then the meat has become more readily available and is sold in Paris at a premium. Farming is carried out on an artisanal scale and the Rex du Poitou® remains an exclusive meat comparable to, say, Bresse chicken. It has been featured by several Michelin-starred chefs and is growing in popularity. **MR**

Taste: *Smooth-textured Rex du Poitou® has a plump, fleshy appearance. Its mild taste is less gamy than wild rabbit. Unlike other farmed rabbits, it does not dry out when cooked.*

The mild sweet flavor of rabbit meat is enhanced here by marinating the legs in olive oil, garlic, and thyme.

Moose

Roe Deer

The largest member of the deer family, the moose, or European elk (*Alces alces*), can weigh up to 1,500 pounds (680 kg). Found in the far north of Europe and Asia, it has played an important role in Scandinavia as a source of protein since the Stone Age, and is known as "king of the forest" in both Norway and Sweden.

For many Swedes and Norwegians moose hunting is one of the highlights of the year. When the season begins, hunters from all walks of life gather—in northern Sweden, schools and factories actually close for the day. Yet despite this active hunting tradition and culture, which sees over 100,000 animals shot each year, the region maintains the world's most dense population of moose.

Thanks to its natural diet of leaves and twigs, moose is lean and full of minerals and vitamins. This healthy meat is not only served as tenderloins and steaks, but widely used in the ground form. The Swedish astronaut Christer Fuglesang treated his astronaut colleagues to some dried moose meat on his first trip into space. **CC**

One of the smaller species of deer, the roe deer (*Capreolus capreolus*) has long been regarded as providing the finest venison. It feeds on a rich diet of shoots, leaves, roses, herbs, and berries that contributes to its exceptionally delicate flavor. Unlike most other deer species, roe deer is hunted all year-round in almost all northern European countries where it lives, insuring sport for the hunter and fine food for the gourmand.

Also found in Asia Minor and the Caspian coastal regions, roe deer have reddish bodies, a gray face, and a white rump patch. They are shy animals, solitary except for when mating, and live in dense forest and woodland. They are not farmed or seen in parks and need traditional stalking. Wild roe deer has to be hung for at least a week before cooking.

Roe deer provides a wonderfully tasty meat, more tender than most other venison. The lean meat simply requires frequent basting when roasting. Lean neck meat and rumps can be pan-fried. Roe deer venison is particularly good served with root vegetables and a robust gravy. **MG**

Taste: *Moose meat is less gamy than much other venison, and, in fact, is not unlike beef in its flavor and appearance, although leaner, with a fresher flavor.*

Taste: *The tenderloin has an incredibly smooth texture that is like cutting through butter. The subtle flavor is like cured meat, but with the venison taste still remaining.*

Roe deer are known to produce the best venison; in this preparation the steaks are coated in a pepper crust. ❯❯

Reindeer

This majestic Arctic animal has been a source of meat for the Sami, who inhabit the Sami region, which runs through Norway, Sweden, Finland, and Russia, for as long as it has lived alongside humans. Traditionally, they use every single part of the animal: the meat, blood, and internal organs are eaten; the fur is used for clothing and shoes; the bones and antlers are transformed into knives and decorative objects. Today, the Sami ranch reindeer in huge herds, with the help of snowmobiles and sometimes even helicopters.

While greatly reduced in numbers, the reindeer is not endangered. It grazes freely, making a very ethical choice of food. It is lower in fat than beef or pork, making it a healthy choice. Today, it is seen as a delicacy in many parts of Scandinavia, and is most commonly served simply sautéed. Many Sami still cook it according to the old recipes, cutting thin slices from a frozen joint or shoulder, then sautéing in its own fat. It also commonly appears in soups or stews, with the bones forming the base of the broth, as well as dried, or smoked. **CTj**

Springbok

A South African national symbol during white minority rule, and a mascot of many athletic teams, the springbok is also a culinary delicacy. A smallish antelope, *Antidorcas marsupialis*, its name means literally "jumping buck," because of its tendency to leap straight into the air when excited. During the displays known as "pronking" it can reach many times its own 30 inch (75 cm) height.

The springbok forages for grass in large herds in dry, inland regions, meaning its meat is organic and entirely free of chemical fertilizers and growth hormones. It leads a highly active lifestyle, and is adapted to survive both drought and low food availability. Consequently, its meat is high in protein, low in fat, and finely textured.

The extremely low fat content means the meat was traditionally viewed as dry, and larger cuts should always be well larded and cooked with care. Cooked, it is often used for pies, terrines, and pâtés, like other venison. Locally it can be salted, spiced, and dried to make biltong, or the dried sausage known as *droëwors*. **ABH**

Taste: *Reindeer has a clear gamy taste, not dissimilar to venison, but with a sweeter, smoother finish. It is lean and tender, especially when roasted slowly and not overdone.*

Taste: *Springbok is subtly gamy and is enhanced by the use of garlic and spices during cooking. Its dense texture benefits from partnering with sweet-and-sour flavors.*

Versatile reindeer meat is used in dishes ranging from soups to stews; it is excellent pan-fried and served rare.

Ostrich

Tuscan Wild Boar

Mostly solitary animals when wild, ostriches are once again being farmed in large ranches, as they were during the nineteenth century. By the early twentieth century, their fashionable feathers were ranked fourth on the list of South African exports after gold, diamonds, and wool.

A diet of seeds, leaves, flowers, and insects and strong legs that can produce a speed of 40 miles per hour (65 km/h) both contribute to the oxygen-rich, blood-red meat, which is between two and three percent fat, about twenty-six per cent protein, and low in cholesterol. Because of its low fat content, the meat can appear dry if not correctly cooked.

Steaks, tenderloins, and neck are the most popular cuts of meat, but almost the entire bird can be used, even the stomach. Schnitzels, goulashes, burgers, pâtés, and biltong are but a few of the dishes made using ostrich meat. Ostrich oil, high in omega-3, 6, and 9, is used to produce an excellent soap. Feathers and leather, as well as tourist attractions in the form of ostrich rides, continue to contribute to a growing industry. **HFi**

The rolling hillsides and woodlands of Tuscany have always been abundant in game, not least the brawny *cinghiale*, or wild boar. Its meat has a wonderfully intense depth of flavor helped by a diet rich in naturally foraged roots, herbs, acorns, chestnuts, mushrooms, and sometimes even truffles, so it comes as no surprise it has long been a specialty in the region. All manner of recipes have been handed down through the generations and various cuts form the base for some of Italy's finest sausage, prosciutto, and salami products. The meat of wild boar has a deeper, more pronounced essence than that of domestic pigs and the sausages and cured meat products generally have a more robust flavor and aroma.

The hunting season takes place during the winter months, and Tuscan wild boar respond well to slow cooking in some of the province's gutsy red wines, making rich, powerful stews and casseroles. A favorite with locals and tourists alike is *pappardelle al sugo di cinghiale*, or pappardelle pasta with a rich wild boar sauce. **LF**

Taste: *With a pleasant meaty flavor and a distinct difference from other game, ostrich meat can be used as a healthy alternative to beef in most recipes.*

Taste: *Wild boar has a deep red hue and an intense taste. The meat is aromatic without being overly gamy. The flavor is full-bodied with a sweet, but piquant, edge.*

Cinghiale porchetta *(roast wild boar) makes a tasty snack served on crusty rustic bread in Tuscany.* »

Sucking Pig

Gloucester Old Spot Pork

Sucking or suckling pig—a piglet slaughtered so young it has fed only on its mother's milk—is considered a delicacy in many countries. Spanish and Chinese cuisines value the animal highly, and in the Philippines, a place where these two cultures meet, the piglets are flavored with tropical herbs, spit-roasted over charcoal, and sold as *lechón baboy*. (The La Loma district of Quezon City has a special reputation for its sucking pigs.) In Portugal, sucking pig—*leitão assado*—is closely identified with the town of Mealhada, where it is stuffed with garlic and lard and baked in brick ovens.

Yet everywhere it is eaten the *pièce de résistance* is the skin. Carefully handled, it takes on a rich mahogany color and a texture so brittle it cracks when pressed. The flesh, naturally bland, white, and sweet, absorbs the flavors of both stuffing and, over an open fire, smoke.

Although the name implies a tiny creature, there are wide differences between a three-week-old animal weighing less than 11 pounds (5 kg) and one more than twice its weight and age. **MR**

A generation ago, Gloucester Old Spot pigs from the West of England were in serious danger of extinction. They have recovered partly as a reaction against factory farming, partly on merit. Popular at the turn of the twentieth century, they were also known as orchard pigs or cottager's pigs, folksy names that probably described the humble environments where they were reared.

For a period the "Old Spot" was the most valuable British pig, but it fell from favor partly because it has more fat on it than was fashionable, partly because modern crosses can be produced more economically. Yet in the serious business of cooking, it performs far better than its replacements. The fat need not be excessive with good husbandry, just sufficient to protect and baste the meat. The lean meat has intramuscular fat and shrinks less than other pork when roasted.

The belly has thick layers of fat and lean. A handicap in the past, this is now seen as an advantage to produce a roast with excellent flavor. The Old Spot also makes an excellent bacon pig. **MR**

Taste: *The crackling skin on a well-roasted sucking pig is as crisp as caramel on a fresh toffee apple. Under it, the meat is beautifully creamy and lightly gelatinous.*

Taste: *The texture of Old Spot is more open than factory-farmed pigs: the fibers of the meat are tastier, softer, and juicier. The fat delivers a rich taste of pork dripping.*

In the Philippines, spit-roasted sucking pigs are eaten ⊗ *on special occasions, often with a liver-based sauce.*

Aveyron Lamb

The Aveyron is a region of France on the edge of the Massif Central renowned for its Roquefort cheese, made with milk from Lacaune sheep. Farmers in the region joined together to create high-quality lamb, Agneau Allaiton d'Aveyron, by evolving a Lacaune meat breed.

The young lambs are kept in barns from birth and fed exclusively on their mothers' milk for the first two months. They then remain enclosed until slaughter, receiving additional cereals in their diet; the ewes graze on pasture during the daytime, which enriches their milk.

The objective of this husbandry is to produce a kind of meat that parallels the finest veal, whose texture and taste depend on a diet centered on milk. It produces a carcass of a size sought after by chefs in particular, but which has the characteristic tenderness, color, and taste of spring lamb, which is smaller and only available for a limited season. Untypically, starred gastronomic restaurants are happy to put this lamb's variety meats—particularly liver—and secondary cuts on their menus. **MR**

Gower Salt Marsh Lamb

The Gower Peninsula, on the south coast of Wales, is characterized by its sandy bays, farmland, and salt marshes. Because the marshes lie at sea level, the vegetation—cordgrass, sea lavender, and sorrel—is impregnated with the brackish, iodine aromatics of seawater. Sheep grazing here produce lambs whose meat has a distinct flavor from that of the surrounding hillsides. It has always paired well with the local seaweeds known as laverbread (*Porphyra*) that are cooked and then fried in small cakes.

Until recently, lambs reared in the area were marketed without any attempt to distinguish them from other livestock. Early in the millennium, however, two sheep farmers started a small cooperative to promote their meat: at the time of writing it handles about 1,500 lambs each year.

There are other sheep that benefit from a similar diet. In the Orkneys, off the north coast of Scotland, a semiwild breed on the island of North Ronaldsay provides excellent meat; in northern France, on the flats around Mont St. Michel, *mouton de pré salé* has enjoyed a similar reputation. **MR**

Taste: *When roasted or broiled, the underdone meat of Aveyron lamb has a pale pink color. They are very juicy with the sweetness characteristic of spring lamb.*

Taste: *Leaner and darker than meat from the Welsh hills, Gower Salt Marsh lamb has a taste that is closer to a yearling than a young lamb, but sweet and juicy.*

Strong flavors like rosemary and anchovy season lamb well; here pungent caraway seeds are used. ❯❯

Fat-tailed Sheep

A striking example of selective breeding, the fat-tailed sheep appeared around the fourth millennium BCE. Today, the many different varieties account for around a quarter of the world's sheep population.

The astonishing tail of the fat-tailed sheep is a large, portable lump of fat that can weigh over 25 pounds (12 kg) and is, like the camel's hump, an energy storehouse for the animal. The appearance of the tail varies according to the breed, ranging from a wide flap to a broad, pendulous tail; some are so long that they drag along the ground. Fat-tailed sheep are common in Africa, the Near and Middle East, northern India, Mongolia, and western China.

Mentions of the fat from fat-tailed sheep as an ingredient occur in early Arabic cookery books. As far back as the Middle Ages, recipes for clarifying this fat, *alya*, coloring it, and using it as a cooking ingredient in desserts, pastries, and savory dishes were already popular. Traveling through Persia at this time, Marco Polo described the tails as "fat and excellent to eat." The smell of the fat being rendered is rank, but the flavor is noted for its delicacy, partly accounting for the fragrance of many Iranian, Syrian, and Lebanese dishes. The Lebanese use the fat in a dish called *qawarma*, in which minced lamb is preserved in fat from the tail of the fat-tailed sheep. A traditional food of Lebanese mountain tribes and once a staple of the winter months, *qawarma* is increasingly seen as a delicacy.

An important aspect of the fat-tailed sheep's continuing popularity is that the meat is lean, since most of the fat of the animal is localized in the tail. In Lebanon, the lean meat is used in *kibbeh nayeh*, while the liver is eaten raw. **MR**

Taste: *Eaten as halal meat, fat-tailed sheep are bled and not left pink when cooked. The meat is firmer and meatier than Western lamb. The fat is mild rather than tallowy.*

Goat

Goats are thought to have been domesticated alongside sheep around 10,000 years ago in southwest Asia. The domestic goat (*Capra hircus*) is probably descended from the wild *Capra aegagrus*. The long history of domestication has yielded many breeds of goats, reared for their milk, meat, and hair. Goats are valued for their ability to thrive in harsh environments and to traverse difficult terrain.

Although goats are reared for their meat as well as their milk in many countries—including subsaharan Africa, southern Asia, southern Europe, Latin America, and the Caribbean—the meat, especially from the adult male "billy goat," has an unfavorable reputation for being scrawny and tough. The meat from young goats (kids) is preferred by many for being the most tender and mild in flavor. In Mediterranean countries roast kid is a traditional festive dish.

Curried goat is the de facto national dish of Jamaica, where the animal was probably introduced by the Spanish. The spices with which the goat is seasoned there are in part based on indigenous produce, whereas the recipe's origin may owe more to immigrant labor from the Indian subcontinent. Traditional flavorings for Jamaican curried goat are the fierily hot Scotch Bonnet pepper and fragrant allspice berries. Its popularity has spread across the Caribbean and through the West Indian diaspora.

Goat's milk, with its small, easily digested fat particles, is a popular drink in many parts of the world. In countries with a dairy tradition, such as the United Kingdom, it is also increasingly used to make cheese, easily distinguished from other cheeses by its bright white appearance. **MR**

Taste: *Long, slow cooking tenderizes goat meat. Lean and similar in color to mutton, it is strongly flavored without the tallowy taste associated with mutton.*

Free-ranging goats, such as these on a Norwegian hillside, search widely for food and yield lean meat. ❯❯

Villsau Mutton

Isard

The ancient breed of sheep known locally as Villsau (wild sheep) or Gammel Norsk Sau (old Norwegian sheep) live and graze mainly around the cold and windy western coast of Norway. Although bred for meat, they spend their lives outdoors in freedom, using the natural resources of the rugged landscape to supply food and shelter all year round. It is this diet, rich in wild shrubs, heathers, herbs, grasses, and even seaweeds, that helps give Villsau mutton its unique and spectacular flavor.

Although small in stature, the Villsau's hardy way of life results in a distribution that is very different to that of more standard breeds. Their fatty tissue is concentrated around the internal organs—hence their round bellies—and the marbling of fat on the flesh between the muscle fibers is very fine, making the meat extremely tender. The meat of the Villsau sheep is often used in the traditional Nordic delicacies *pinnekjøtt*, a dish prepared from salted, dried ribs, which are then steamed over birch twigs, and *fenalår*, cured leg of mutton. Both dishes are traditionally served at Christmastime. **LF**

The Pyrenean chamois (*Rupicapra pyrenaica*), known as *isard* in French, is a mountain antelope that inhabits both the French and Spanish sides of the Pyrenees and was so popular among gourmets it had almost been hunted to extinction by the 1960s. The establishment of the first national parks has enabled the population to recover; hunting is still strictly controlled, although isard are now bred commercially. Isard inhabit rocky high pastures, feeding on grass, lichens, and the young shoots of trees and bushes, which give it the delicate flavor for which it is so highly prized.

Modern chefs prefer younger isard as the meat is more tender and the flavor less gamy. It is often served simply grilled over embers. Mature isard can be treated similarly to venison. In the Spanish region of Catalonia, isard is traditionally marinated for hours in red wine with rosemary, sage, and thyme and then prepared in a stew. The broth is made with the bones and the sauce is enriched with a small amount of chocolate. Isard is good partnered with chestnuts, apples, and mushrooms. **RL**

Taste: *Soaked and steamed until falling off the bone, Villsau mutton has a tender texture and a rich flavor with hints of herbs and grass and a whisper of saltiness.*

Taste: *Lean and firm in texture, the subtle gamy flavor has aromatic nuances of mountain herbs, which distinguish it from the less complex flavors of kid goat.*

Piedmont Veal

Limousin Veal

Veal has long been prized in European gastronomic culture for its tender eating qualities and sweet flavor. And in Piedmont, northern Italy, a specific strain of cattle has evolved to become world renowned for the fantastic quality of its meat. Broad shouldered and chunky, the *razza piemontese* is a gentle giant of a breed with characteristic double muscling that means it produces lean, concentrated meat with less fat and gristle than normal. A diet rich in natural grasses creates a unique flavor.

Veal was first introduced as a way for the dairy industry to make use of surplus male calves and did not take long to catch on. Today, the rosy, relatively mature veal of Piedmont, raised without antibiotics or hormones, has become the basis of various regional specialties. *Carne cruda all'Albese* (or *carne cruda*) is a dish of raw veal, hand-chopped using two knives, then dressed in a simple mixture of extra virgin olive oil and lemon juice, seasoned with salt and black pepper. Occasionally it might be served with shavings of Parmesan; in the autumn fresh truffle makes a decadent embellishment. **LF**

The calves that will produce Limousin veal (IGP) are raised in much kinder conditions than many of their peers: *sous la mère* (with their mothers), and nourished on their mothers' milk. They are raised in the Limousin region of west-central France, which centers on the city of Limoges, hence their name.

The title, however, can be confusing. "Limousin" cattle are a prime beef breed. But "Limousin" veal can come from other breeds, provided it is reared in the region and according to the criteria laid down in the IGP. The French Label Rouge quality mark specifies that the veal should be reared to between 90 and 160 days old, it should only be given food supplements during the last couple of months before slaughter, and the carcass should weigh no more than 375 pounds (170 kg).

The flesh of Limousin veal is paler than that from calves reared by agroindustrial methods, and more succulent because fat from the mother's milk is deposited in the muscle fibers. During cooking, this meat retains its body, whereas lesser veal tends to shrink and dry out. **MR**

Taste: *Raw Piedmont veal is succulent and juicy with savory, grassy notes; cooked, its flavor remains more meaty than milk-fed veal, yet is still tender and juicy.*

Taste: *The prime cuts of Limousin veal—loin, ribs, and rolled top round—are lightly, but cleanly, flavored, with a juicy, firm texture when broiled or fried.*

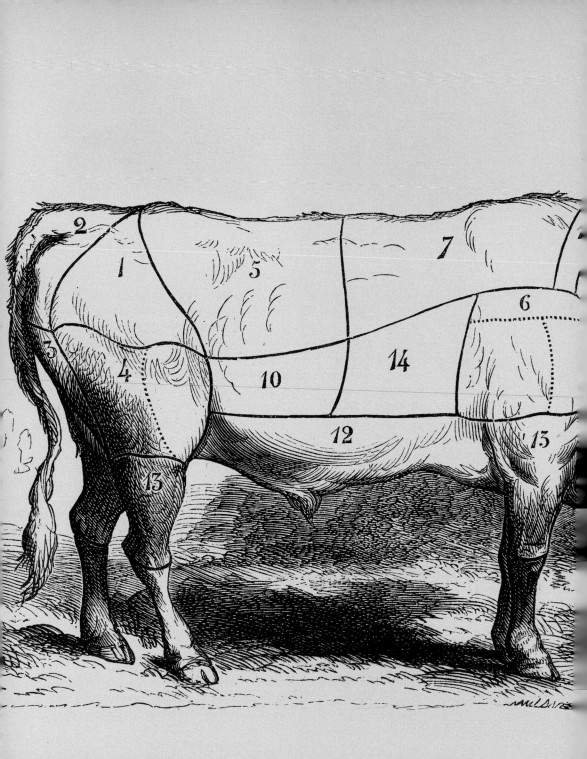

Aberdeen-Angus Beef

The most widely known breed of Scottish cattle originated in the early nineteenth century. A pioneer breeder, Hugh Watson, from Keillor, in the county of Angus, developed a strain of cattle that William McCombie, from Tillyfour, in Aberdeenshire, bred closely—hence the name Aberdeen Angus. The breed's success came from its strong genes: its characteristic black color, hornlessness, rapid growth, and excellent meat are all easily inherited.

Adaptability has helped keep the Aberdeen-Angus at the top of the table of beef breeds. Today, worldwide there are more than 50 million Aberdeen-Angus type cattle, and the breed is still developing to produce cattle that fit the current trend for larger, leaner meat, such as Charolais and Limousin, but with better flavor. The results have fat marbled through their meat. Although available worldwide, most still believe the breed is finest in Scotland, thanks to the climate and husbandry. Wherever it is produced, Aberdeen-Angus has a certification trademark, which guarantees quality and allows breeders to command a premium. **CTr**

Taste: Aberdeen-Angus is distinctive by its dense texture and deeply colored fat. Cooked, it has a broad flavor and good texture. Its density also makes it excellent eaten raw.

An 1855 French illustration informs beef buyers of the cuts available.

Bison

Kobe Beef

What is often referred to as buffalo or American buffalo is, in fact, bison (*Bison bison*). This woolly, humped member of the Bovidae family, is only a distant relative of the African buffalo and the Asian water buffalo. Bison was a mainstay of the diet of the Native Americans and the pioneers who settled on the western plains of the United States and Canada. At one time, millions roamed the plains, but overhunting reduced their numbers to about 1,500 by the late 1800s. Since the late twentieth century, however, there has been a revival of interest in bison as a source of flavorsome meat; herds are now carefully managed and there are about 2,000 bison producers in the United States.

Bison produces lean, tender meat, higher in iron and lower in fat than most beef. Chefs have eagerly embraced the more costly cuts, like tenderloin, strip, and rib eye. Care must be taken not to overcook bison—cook slowly on low heat. Less tender cuts need braising. Cattle and bison have been cross-bred to produce a new meat known as "beefalo" in the United States and "cattalo" in Canada. **SH**

What foie gras is to liver, Kobe beef is to steak. It comes from any of several related breeds of native Japanese cattle, known collectively as Wagyu, and so the terms Wagyu and Kobe have been used almost interchangeably. The export of Wagyu cattle from Japan to around the world, however, has led the Japanese to protect the denomination Kobe beef so it can now only be applied to homegrown meat.

The cost and the folklore surrounding Kobe cattle's husbandry give it epic status. The diet of grain and beer, allied to regular massage—which both tenderizes the beef and relaxes the bullock—is said to turn Wagyu cattle into a uniquely fatty animal. (Incidentally, the meat is low in cholesterol.) All this is true, but the central difference relates to the breeds themselves. They are genetically disposed to produce much more intramuscular marbling than any Western beef cattle. When seared, the surface of a Kobe beef steak caramelizes rapidly and crisps. It should be eaten rare, or "blue." Otherwise the benefit of texture and taste leech out, leaving it dry and uninteresting. **MR**

Taste: Bison has a deeper red color than beef but without any marbling. Not in the least gamy, it tastes similar to good beef, but slightly sweeter, richer, and fuller in flavor.

Taste: The marbled fat makes Kobe beef so special. This creates a smooth, velvety feel, rather than the juiciness of, say, an Angus steak: the light taste lingers on the palate.

For centuries, the Japanese have been selectively breeding cattle for their high level of fatty marbling. »

Horsemeat

Rattlesnake

The concept of eating horse is abhorrent to many Anglo-Saxons "who would rather eat the rider than the horse," but is relatively common in Belgium, France, Austria, Iceland, Italy, Japan, and parts of Canada. While much horsemeat comes from breeds such as carthorses, which might otherwise have become extinct except for their role as food, any kind of horse can be sold for its flesh.

Proponents claim horsemeat is healthier than beef: it is leaner, and contains fewer calories and less fat. Specialist butchers might take more care in handling the carcass, and, because horses are generally reared on a small scale, there are few of the problems linked to factory farming practices.

The difference between beef and horsemeat is In the tenderness. Nearly all cuts of the latter can be eaten by rapid cooking rather than the slow cooking necessary for tougher cuts of beef. Connoisseurs of steak tartare claim horsemeat is essential to the recipe and the name of the dish itself may have connections to mounted Tartar warriors: horsemeat remains a significant part of the Mongolian diet. **MR**

Snakes elicit reactions of fear in most Western minds. Those anxieties might best be traded with visions of gourmet delight, as have the residents of America's arid southwest deserts on discovering rattlesnake to be a flavorful source of food.

Ranchers in the Southwest have adopted the western diamondback rattlesnake (*Crotalus atrox*), as an exotic food. The species is very thick and meaty, with the skinned snake fillets almost always remaining on the bony skeleton. The meat flakes off more easily after cooking, but is usually served up with the numerous pinlike bones intact.

Rattlesnake is available fresh, frozen, and canned in various sauces and smokes, which can overpower the flavor of the meat. Dried and smoked forms of rattlesnake are also traded in the southern states and Mexico. Care is advised with sourcing uncooked meat as it can carry harmful parasites. Rattlesnake is most commonly deep-fried in a cornmeal coating, much like catfish. The canned meat is used in a wide array of recipes, ranging from dips to barbecue. **TH**

Taste: *High levels of glycogen in the meat explain why horsemeat tastes sweeter than beef. Its texture is tender enough to fry. Enthusiasts prefer eating it rare, even raw.*

Taste: *More like a strong white fish with gamy overtones than the archetypal comparison to chicken, the chewy texture has been compared to alligator.*

An old Parisian sign advertises horsemeat. Special
⊗ *stores were set up to ensure the quality of the meat sold.*

Mississippi Alligator

Kangaroo

Mississippi alligator, or American alligator, is native to Mississippi and southeastern areas of the United States. Primarily found in marshes and freshwater swamps, the high demand for its skin and meat put it on the endangered list in the 1960s and it remains a species of concern. The alligator population has since recovered with the help of captive habitats. These farms meet the demand for alligator products without depleting the species.

Eating alligator is nothing new. Native Americans were smoking and eating alligator when Spanish explorers came to Florida in the 1600s. Because alligators are large, they provide a variety of cuts of meat, both tender and more tough. Alligator takes well to marinades and can be broiled, fried, or grilled. Often the tougher cuts are simmered in a stew.

Alligator jambalaya with hot sausage, tomato, rice, green bell pepper, garlic, and other seasonings is a popular dish, as is spicy alligator sausage. Restaurants along the Gulf Coast serve grilled or fried alligator tail. Spicy Creole and Cajun seasonings go particularly well with this meat. **SH**

Kangaroo has long been a favorite meat among Australian Aborigines, but the idea of eating an animal from the national coat of arms (as well as a fondness for the TV character, Skippy) has been enough to stop many nonindigenous Australians from even trying it. Less squeamish Aboriginal Australians would, and still do, shoot or spear and gut their catch, singe its hair, scrape it off, then bury the animal under earth and hot coals for cooking. The generic term "kangaroo" encompasses several species including wallabies and wallaroos, all marsupials native predominantly to Australia. White settlers ate the meat, which is the same color as liver, in the early years of the colony because it was much cheaper than imported salt pork and was often the only fresh meat available.

An increase in beef and mutton production saw kangaroo meat disappear from the table and relegated to pet food status until the late 1970s. As interest in native foods grows, so too does the demand for kangaroo, which is a versatile meat as well as low in fat (two percent) and cholesterol. **SCS**

Taste: *Alligator meat is a firm-textured white meat that tastes like chicken, only with a richer, slightly fishy flavor. Depending on how it is cooked, it can have a swampy taste.*

Taste: *Kangaroo should be lightly cooked and well rested to preserve moisture. Young meat tastes very like beef and becomes pleasantly gamy and venisonlike over time.*

Five of the forty-eight species of Australian kangaroo— prepared here as kabobs—are harvested for meat. »

Escargot de Bourgogne

There are many edible varieties of snail, from infant *petit gris* to the giant African land snail that can grow up to 10 inches (25 cm) long, but few have any special appeal. Their attraction lies in the extraction of an unusual meat that was, historically, kept for times when food was scarce. Medieval monasteries added snails to the menu during Lent; sailors carried them on board ship; and purged on rosemary, they are a traditional component of paella.

The French are voracious eaters of snails, devouring some 40,000 tons per year. Today, the snail most often eaten in France is the common garden snail (*Helix aspersa*) which is mainly imported from farms abroad. Until quite recently, the escargot de Bourgogne (*Helix pomatia*)—a close relative of the common garden snail—was synonymous with a traditional style of French cuisine and figured on every bistro menu. But it is a species that does not like to be farmed, and the modern-day scarcity of wild snails in France means that the dish escargots de Bourgogne is increasingly rare.

Although subtly flavored, the snails require a good deal of preparation. Gathered alive, they are purged to eliminate plant toxins and grit. This is achieved either by starving them for five to seven days, or by keeping them in a shaded place, such as a bucket, for around two weeks and feeding them herbs. They are then drowned, blanched, and simmered, before they are ready for a final cooking. In the classic recipe, the snails are put back in their large, pale shells with a *beurre d'escargot*—a parsley and garlic butter—and baked in a very hot oven. This high cholesterol dish tastes delicious and is a traditional New Year's specialty in France. **MR**

Taste: *Escargots de Bourgogne have an indefinable meatiness. They are chewy, but owe their fame as a delicacy to the garlic butter, which should be bubbling.*

Although snails are in many cultures a protein source of last resort, the French have elevated their status.

Bee Larva

Eating insects is a strange concept for Westerners, although many different cultures around the world from Asia to Central America have eaten them both as a staple and a delicacy. Humans often turn to insects when there is a scarcity of fish and meat, and alternative sources of protein are needed.

Bee larvae are eaten in Mexico and the Far East. In Japan, China, Thailand, and Vietnam they are usually served as an appetizer, sometimes together with the honeycomb. The yellow larvae look similar to fat maggots or mealworms and are very delicate. They can be eaten live, fresh from the hive, but they are also prepared in a number of different ways. Fried in oil with a little salt and pepper, perhaps a touch of chile, the larvae take on a crispy texture.

For a sweeter taste, bee larvae are fried with soy sauce and sugar, while in Mexico they are sometimes seen served covered in chocolate. In Japan, bee larvae, *hachinoko*, are sold preserved and canned in soy-bean oil. The Chinese marinate the larvae with onion, lemongrass, and coconut cream. Once they are fully marinated, the larvae are wrapped in linen, steamed for twenty minutes, and served with boiled rice or noodles.

When societies become more urbanized, their eating habits change and there develops a growing dependency on fast food and Western ingredients. In such circumstances, people come to associate their insect consumption with underdevelopment and the past. In Japan, bee larva consumption is said to be declining among the young, while the old still appreciate the nostalgia of their *hachinoko*. Insect secretions such as honey remain almost universally popular, however. **CK**

Taste: *Raw, live bee larvae wriggle, and have a milky, honey taste. When fried, the larvae have a crunchy, crisp texture with a subtle flavor of honey.*

Giant Water Beetle

Thai people are fairly adventurous when it comes to food. Tucking into a bowl of authentic *pad thai* noodles is only touching the tip of the Thai culinary iceberg. Insects such as roasted, spiced crickets and fried bamboo worm larvae are also regular fare. However, it is the giant water beetle (*Lethocerus indicus*)—known as *maeng daa*—that locals devour with a passion. The beetle is considered a delicacy and is prized for its subtle "fishy" flavor.

The water beetle, which can reach almost 4 inches (10 cm) in length, is particularly valued in the rural Isaan region of northeast Thailand. At night locals use lights and vibrations to attract the best specimens that inhabit Thailand's watery rice fields. Such is the demand for the giant water beetle that it is now being farmed.

Water beetles are best prepared fresh as the taste deteriorates fast. They can be stir-fried with straw mushrooms, scallions, chile, and garlic, or ground into a paste with chile and eaten with sticky rice. But the most popular method of cooking is to deep-fry them whole. Cracking into one takes practice. First the legs are removed and the exoskeleton is prized open to access the meaty interior. The body holds a flaky meat the consistency of tinned tuna and the head contains a gelatinous combination of parts. Beetles laden with eggs—the consistency of tiny caviar—are a particular delicacy.

In the Canton province of China, giant water beetles are dropped into boiling salted water then seasoned with a little oil. In the Far East, insects are often eaten for medicinal purposes, but no health benefits have been ascribed to the giant water beetle. They are eaten solely for culinary pleasure. **TH**

Taste: Water beetle tastes like whitefish that stayed out all night. Even when prepared with chile the mild, shrimp flavor shows through with nutty overtones.

Fried until crispy, the giant water beetle is Thailand's number one edible insect.

Leaf-Cutter Ant

Leaf-cutter ants are so called because they use their jaws to cut away portions of leaves to be carried to their nest. Perhaps surprisingly, the ants are appreciated as a food item, particularly in Brazil's Amazon basin. They are at their best at the beginning of the rainy season when females leave the nest in huge numbers, moving sluggishly enough to be easy prey. They are caught by the basket load, and eaten either raw or roasted with salt. Their taste is nutty and highly appreciated.

In Brazil, the leaf-cutter ant now has an extensive urban following, too, with trays of the cooked ants being hawked through the streets of São Paulo. One of the country's most famous authors, Monteiro Lobato, who was born at the end of the nineteenth century in the Paraíba valley, called leaf-cutter ants the peasant's caviar, the ultimate delicacy for someone from that upstate region. Passed on from generation to generation, the ancient legacy is still alive in the valley today. It is customary to eat ants between the months of September and November, when they grow wings and leave their nests to mate. Only females are eaten, known as *içá* or *tanajura*.

Care is needed in preparing the insect for eating. The head, thorax, legs, and wings are removed, and the back is pan-fried in oil until crispy. The result is best when pork fat, rather than vegetable oil, is used for this process. Once fried, the *içá* is dusted with cassava or cornstarch and is ready to serve. Many ant fans crush this mixture with a pestle to obtain the famous *paçoca de içá* (*içá* mixture). Some São Paulo chefs have compared the taste of leaf-cutter ants to that of a strongly flavored home-made butter, as it consists of pure protein. **AL**

Taste: After frying, well-toasted leaf-cutter ant is intensely crunchy in the mouth and leaves behind a taste similar to a strong butter.

Veal Sweetbread

The term "sweetbreads" covers two internal organs: the thymus gland in the throat and the pancreas near the stomach. Of these, the latter attracts more gastronomic interest. When raw, it is rounded, but of irregular shape, off-white to pink in hue, and not dissimilar to a blancmange—at least at first blush. When cooked it becomes firmer and smoother.

Until the latter part of the last century, the pancreas was soaked, blanched, trimmed, and pressed before being braised in a sauce and served as an intermediate course—after the hors d'oeuvre and the fish, but before the main roast. Now chefs prefer to trim and then roast the sweetbreads, basting them with butter, and leaving them still juicy in the middle. They are popular on the menus of luxury restaurants. A specialty of Alain Ducasse, arguably France's most highly regarded chef—pasta with sweetbreads, coxcombs, cock's kidneys, truffles, lobster, and a cream sauce—gives a sense of how this simple ingredient can be presented, although in Argentina and Uruguay you will find them grilling on the traditional *asado*. **MR**

Taste: *Smooth and tender, sweetbreads make an able and attractive catalyst for other ingredients. Consumed solo, neither their scent nor their taste is especially marked.*

Lamb's Kidney

A lamb's kidney reflects the age at which the creature was slaughtered: they can be anything from a few weeks to ten months old. In Spain, where baby, milk-fed lamb is grilled over an open fire, the kidneys are a tiny pink delicacy. But the deviled kidneys that were once served from silver chafing dishes as part of the great British breakfast, like the skewered kabobs that are still part of everyday Turkish street food, are generally larger.

Fully developed, a lamb's kidney weighs more than 1 ounce (25 g). They have a characteristic shape: rounded on the surface and slightly turned in on the side. Just cooked through, or slightly underdone, a kidney is juicy and tender. Overdone, it becomes unpleasantly hard and rubbery, yet returns to softness after prolonged cooking, as in the British steak and kidney pie, where its taste and texture improve on the more usual ox kidney. Because older kidneys have an assertive taste, they are often combined with sauces enriched with sherry, Madeira, port, or mustard, with which they have a natural affinity. **MR**

Taste: *Kidneys should have a rich, fresh, meaty taste when cooked, ranging from the delicacy of young pink flesh to the dark, velvety flavor of fully developed organs.*

The filling for steak and kidney pie is cooked separately in order to judge when the meat is tender. ❯❯

Bull's Testicle

The Montana Testicle Festival, held each year in the United States, is most definitely not for everyone, but those who attend always say they "had a ball." The culinary focus there is breaded and deep-fried bull's testicles, commonly referred to as Rocky Mountain oysters or "cowboy caviar."

Although talking about testicles—let alone eating them—may offend some twenty-first-century sensibilities, people have been eating animal testicles for many centuries. Not surprisingly, they have aphrodisiac associations. Testicles from sheep (lamb), bulls, calves (sometimes called prairie oysters), pigs, buffalos, turkeys, and roosters have long been considered a delicacy, often a seasonal one, eaten during the spring after male animals have been castrated so they can be retained and raised for meat. In North America, the tradition of eating "Rocky Mountain oysters" is found in those parts of the country that have a history of cattle ranching.

As is apparent, there are many culinary euphemisms for testicles. "Stones" was the historic word for testicles in England. The term "fry" is often used to denote testicles, as in lambs' fry or bull's fry. In France, the term *animelles* is used for testicles from sheep and other animals.

In Spain and Portugal, testicles, known as *criadillas* and *criadilhas* respectively, are considered a delicacy, cut into strips and fried, sometimes flavored with garlic and parsley. They can also be sautéed, stewed, or served with a variety of sauces. Although North Americans, the British, and the French have become squeamish about this meat, others parts of the world, such as the Middle East and the Philippines, serve it regularly. **SH**

Lamb's Brain

Long accounted a rich delicacy, lambs' brains are very much a food lover's food. In the United States, where animal internal organs are often lumped together as "variety meats," and the United Kingdom, where animal disease, notably BSE (bovine spongiform encephalitis) has made consumers nervous and the government cautious, they are barely tolerated. In other parts of the world, however, including Hungary, Turkey, much of the Middle East, Italy, and France, they remain a popular, indeed esteemed, food.

Low in fat and rich in iron, the two joined, pale pink lobes contain more than the minimum daily requirement for an adult of vitamin B_{12}. Preparation involves washing the brains, removing membranes and blood vessels, soaking, and washing once more.

In France, lambs' brains are cooked in a wide variety of ways: poached in a *court bouillon* then pan-fried with browned butter and capers; *en matelote*, where they are poached then served with onions, mushrooms, and a red wine sauce; or served as the sophisticated *beignets de cervelle*, brain fritters with a herb mayonnaise. In *tartare de cervelle* they are poached, then combined in a patty with capers, cornichons, hard-boiled eggs, and mustard mayonnaise. In Italy, lambs' brains are eaten in dishes including *cervella alla Napolitana*, baked with olives, capers, and breadcrumbs, and *cervella fritta alla Milanese*, where they are blanched, cut into morsels, breaded, and fried until golden-brown. In Lebanon, Jordan, Syria, Hungary, and elsewhere in the former Ottoman Empire, they are fried and served cold as a salad with olive oil, lemon juice, and often seasoned with parsley and spices. **MR**

Taste: *Testicles resemble chicken in that they take on the flavor of the sauce served alongside. Basically, they are bland, with a chewy, sometimes gristly texture.*

Taste: *Brains have a very faint aroma compared to most meats and the taste is mild and delicate. The texture can be soft or curdlike, depending on the duration of cooking.*

A food stall vendor in Marrakesh prepares traditional baked lamb's head and brain. ❯❯

Calf's Liver

Food cultures that put a high value on variety meats consider calf's liver a luxury. Calf's liver figures all over central Europe in Jewish Ashkenazi cuisine and forms the basis of a famous Venetian specialty, *fegato alla veneziana*, strips of liver sautéed with onions until sweet, and of *foie de veau à la lyonnaise*, another liver-and-onion pairing. The flavor of onions is thought particularly to enhance that of the liver.

Although similar on paper, these dishes reflect different culinary approaches. Italians cook their variety meats right though, whereas the French tend to prefer them a little underdone. Both ways are delicious, because calf's liver has a texture and taste that responds to rapid pan-frying. Liver is rich in iron and minerals—a 4-ounce (100 g) slice supplies good amounts of vitamins A, B_2, B_{12}, and folate, which helps to account for its depth of flavor.

Even from a young calf the liver's taste is upfront, although it is milder than most lamb or pig livers. It should be rosy pink, with a fine grain. The finest comes from animals fed with mother's milk. The quality also depends on skilled butchery. **MR**

Taste: *Calf's liver should have a clean, distinctive taste much sweeter than other forms of liver, allied to a smooth, almost melting texture and a pleasant smell.*

Ox Cheek

The tangle of muscle and sinew around the jaw of an ox works harder than any other part of its body. By its nature it is a tough meat requiring gentle, long cooking—a fact that also, counterintuitively, explains its delights. For a long time, the ox cheek was a cheap cut of meat. French tripe butchers sold it for the poor man's *pot au feu*; Victorian household manuals recommended it as an indulgence for the industrious poor. Inside the cheek is a muscle—the masseter—that weighs about 8 ounces (200 g), and it is this that is increasingly attracting top chefs. Like the shin of beef, it combines lean meat with collagen, a connective tissue that becomes tender after prolonged cooking. In classic dishes, such as a *daube de boeuf* or *boeuf bourguignon*, these nuggets of ox cheek give unique richness and body to the sauce in which they are simmered.

France led the ox cheek revival, thanks to the large, hefty cattle breeds developed from working animals. Both their heads and the muscles within them are larger than those on breeds like the Aberdeen-Angus. **MR**

Taste: *The texture of a slow-cooked piece of ox cheek is tender, gelatinous, and succulent. It has a strong beefy taste, perhaps less pronounced than oxtail.*

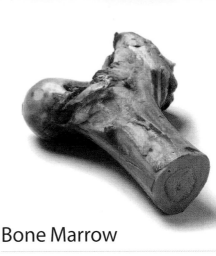

Pig's Feet

Bone Marrow

Until the second half of the twentieth century, pig's feet were treated as rustic food. They might be braised slowly for up to ten hours and coated in bread crumbs or dished up with a split pea soup. They were used by charcutiers to prepare the jellies that decorated their terrines. Then, with the advent of nouvelle cuisine, pig's feet took on a new lease of life when chefs began to turn them into a luxury product. The feet were braised, boned, filled with creamy mousselines, sweetbreads, and truffles, then reformed and dished up with wine sauces.

The foot itself contains little flesh, but the outer pig skin is gelatinous and tender when cooked. It has to be carefully scraped before it can be stuffed. In Cantonese cuisine, pig's feet are a specialty, often eaten at the start of New Year celebrations for good luck. Traditionally, the feet are blanched in water from springs in the Bai Yun mountain and served crisp-skinned with a sweet-and-sour sauce. Also popular in Hong Kong, pig's feet are regularly eaten smoked or accompanied by a ginger and black vinegar sauce. **MR**

Archaeologists believe in prehistoric times our cannibal ancestors enjoyed eating the marrow from their victims' bones. More recently, beef marrowbones in a white napkin were served at the tables of the wealthy together with a silver scoop for exracting the warm, rich, jellylike fat.

Bone marrow is high in monounsaturated fat and protein. Its function in the body is to produce blood cells. But not all bones contain marrow: some are almost solid. Marrow is found in the limbs, especially in the leg bones. To obtain it, the whole bone can be cut into short pieces and roasted, or the raw bones can be sawn up before the marrow is extracted and poached.

In the Italian dish *osso buco* a sliced shin of veal is braised with the marrowbone; in French classic cuisine a garnish of poached marrowbone was essential to the composition of an *entrecôte bordelaise*. Italians have a high regard for beef bone marrow, and many recipes insist on it being used alongside butter at the start of a risotto. It is also included in a variety of bean soup recipes. **MR**

Taste: *Simply braised, pig's feet have little to offer, but as a base they actually attract other flavors, enhancing them by helping them to stick to the palate.*

Taste: *The taste of marrow, like that of a good beef dripping, is smooth and subtly meaty, but never "red." The texture is fragile, like a lightly set pudding, and very greasy.*

Sheep's Head

Sheep's head is a delicacy that harks back to the days when truly no part of an animal was wasted, although it is still enjoyed by several cultures.

In Norway and Iceland, one sign of fall was traditionally the treat of smoked sheep's head. This was offered when the sheep were brought down from the hills where they had been fattening over the summer. Some sheep would be culled, according to demand, and the rest used for both their wool and meat throughout the winter.

Icelanders still enjoy singed sheep's head at Thorablott, the spring festival renowned for unusual food consumption. In Scotland, boiled sheep's head broth was the traditional Saturday night fare for dutiful Christian ministers sitting down to write the Sunday sermon, and would also be served cold the next day for dinner (the recipe in *The Cook and Housewife's Manual*, published in 1828, begins with the instruction, "Choose a large, fat head"). In Italy, fewer people are partaking of the dish, although it appears on the menus of traditional restaurants, such as those in Little Italy in New York City.

In the Middle East, however, sheep's head remains popular, appearing at celebratory banquets where the split roasted head is typically served with the eyes. In Iraq, it is slowly cooked into a meat broth with the stomach and feet for the traditional dish *pacha*, while in both Kazakhstan and Kyrgyzstan boiled sheep's head is consumed during the elaborate ceremonial feast of *Beshbarmak*. In the ceremony, the head is offered as mark of great respect to the honored guest. Brains and tongues are mostly served with the head. Kazakhs offer the ears to young men to encourage attentiveness. **BF**

Taste: *Grilled, the flavor of the meat is that of mutton. The cheek meat can have more texture when grilled (as opposed to slowly stewed). Brains, if served, are buttery.*

Tripe

Usually from an ox or calf, although also from sheep or deer, tripe is a hold-all term for the stomach, or, to be accurate, for the four separate stomachs that together form a production line to digest the ruminant's food. The first (the rumen) holds the food that is swallowed. This food is regurgitated, chewed again, and swallowed as cud to pass via the second, honeycombed stomach (the reticulum) into the third (psalterium), and ultimately the fourth (abomasum). Each tripe has its own texture and taste. All require scrubbing to make them edible.

Tripe forms the foundation of warming soups in cuisines from Jamaica to Turkey. The four different tripes, simmered together slowly for up to ten hours with calf's foot, onions, and carrots, produce the Normandy specialty of *tripes à la mode de Caen*. (Veal tripe is generally considered the finest for this dish.) In the Spanish *callos a la madrileña*, tripe is stewed with ingredients including spicy chorizo sausage and morcilla. In England, honeycomb tripe eaten with onions and a white sauce was once a pauper's food, and is still a nostalgic dish in the north.

During the 1960s a chain of tripe restaurants took northern England by storm. They were run by United Cattle Products and were known as UCPs. More than 150 outlets, mainly in northwest England, were characterized by serving tripe in unexpectedly refined surroundings. Sparklingly clean tablecloths were used, and the food was served by silver service. The business was not to survive the arrival of fast food, however, and in the 1970s it was sold, eventually to be bought by the burger chain Wimpy. Tripe is still seen as a working-class food in England, but elsewhere it is regarded as a regional food. **MR**

Taste: *Stewed together, the flavor of the four tripes is rich, gelatinous, and robust. The texture of tripe depends on which one is used and how it is prepared.*

In France, tripe was traditionally prepared at a triperie. It is especially enjoyed in Normandy and Auvergne. ❯❯

TRIPERIE

Fraise de Veau
Pieds-veaux.agn.porc
Paté de tête

Tripes { maison
cuites-crue

museaux cuits

Foie Gras de Canard

Hungarian Goose Liver

Cramming ducks with corn to fatten their livers until the organs weigh about 1 pound (450 g) each produces the luxury that is known the world over as foie gras de canard. On small farms in southwest France, the ducks are left to grow and range freely most of their lives. It is only during the last two or three weeks they are force-fed the diet; cruelty lies in the abuse of the system where industrial manufacturers produce foie gras from caged birds.

Experts can distinguish different styles of this luxurious delicacy. Those from the Landes, south of Bordeaux, are the creamiest or silkiest; from Béarn, in Gascony, they are rustic, with a farmyard flavor. Eating a thin sliver of raw, fresh foie gras is the ultimate way of appreciating its taste and texture, but slow cooking under vacuum, usually after marinating in Madeira, port, Armagnac, and/or truffle juice, produces the smooth, intensely perfumed terrines that make the reputations of chefs. Strict legislation protects the use of the name, and terms such as parfait, mousse, or pâté on foie gras products indicate added ingredients. **MR**

According to historians, Egyptians in pharaonic times were the first to fatten their geese and produce the bloated, but delicious, livers now known as foie gras. The technique spread across Europe during the Middle Ages, probably by way of Jewish communities, and to nowhere more than Transdanubian Hungary, where rearing geese for their livers is an art form. The birds are bred for their large size, the variety of corn is especially selected for its influence on the fattening process, and the drinking water is mixed with a solution of white clay. Overeating raises the level of fat in the blood, from where it transfers to the liver. (Hungarians prefer the Oroshaza goose, which can supply fattened livers that weigh more than 2 pounds (900 g) each.)

In Hungary, roasted goose liver, *sült libamáj*, is often soaked in milk before cooking, colored in hot goose fat, and seasoned with paprika. The liver is an omnipresent ingredient on Hungarian restaurant menus, dished up fried, used as a stuffing, accompanied by fruit, sweetened with honey, or simply served on bread with peppers. **MR**

Taste: *More than its taste, the texture of foie gras is unique: unctuous, smooth, melting, velvety, and creamy. The taste of the liver is never strong or overly assertive.*

Taste: *The liver taste is mild, but has a faint metallic zing in the raw state that disappears with cooking. The texture is similar to that of duck's liver, but seems more compact.*

An old Sarlat shop sign signals the availability of foie gras and truffles in the French Dordogne.

Confit

This apparently decadent food—meat gently slow-cooked in its own rendered fat until melting and then stored in the fat, which acts as a seal—in fact originated with the most pragmatic of purposes: to preserve meat against the coming winter. The word "confit" is a French term that denotes preservation, and this is an ancient way of preserving food, associated particularly with the southwest region of France. The process tenderizes the meat used—usually goose, duck, or pork—and in sterilized jars (or canned) the meat keeps for several months.

Goose meat is particularly suited to confit. Slow-grown geese, especially those that have been used for foie gras, lay down large amounts of fat, not only underneath their skin, but also inside their carcass, around the vital organs. The leg thigh is highly prized, while wings are valued for their tenderness. Other delicious savory confits are made using game, rabbit, turkey, and offal ranging from gizzards to tongues. Chefs are now creating versions using less traditional fatty meats, such as lamb and oxtail. When served cold in France, a confit is traditionally accompanied by a bitter salad of dandelion or endive to cut through the fattiness.

A confit is often added as an ingredient to flavor another dish. Confits of both goose and duck are optional but much-employed ingredients of cassoulet, a French dish made with haricot beans and assorted meats, and the Alsatian *choucroute garnie*. The confit technique can be found elsewhere in the world, too; in the Lebanon, for example, *qawarma*, a traditional winter food of Lebanese mountain tribes, consists of minced lamb preserved in fat from the tail of the fat-tailed sheep. **MR**

Qalaya

This preserved meat, sometimes written as *khlea* or *khelea*, forms a key part of Lebanese, Moroccan, and Algerian cuisines. Before the days of refrigeration, peoples of the eastern Mediterranean and North Africa prolonged the life of meat in a similar way to the French confit. The long, slow cooking in fat softens the meat's texture and retains its flavor.

The meat most commonly used is beef, which is cut into manageable pieces and rubbed generously with salt and garlic. It is then rubbed again with a mixture of spices—coriander seeds, ground cumin, paprika, dried mint, and occasionally saffron—before being left to marinate in a crock in the cool air, or overnight. The meat is then taken out to dry in the hot summer sun. The qalaya is not left out at night because dampening in the cool dew hastens putrefaction. The meat is now ready for cooking.

The marinated pieces of meat are then fried until crisp in either mutton or beef fat, often with the addition of olive oil. After cooling, the meat is placed in jars and covered completely with melted fat from the pan. The sealed jars are stored until the meat is required for a meal, when the contents are lifted out, the fat scraped off, and excess salt rinsed away.

Qalaya is added as a flavoring for tagines, couscous, and stews. It is sometimes used with beans, lentils, barley, and pumpkins. With the cost of fresh meat in the Maghreb becoming ever steeper, many families are now obliged to buy their qalaya ready-made from nearby souks, but purists prefer the taste of the real thing: qalaya made in the home. For many, however, the cost of a year's supply of home-made qalaya represents a considerable financial outlay. **WS**

Taste: *The taste and texture of a confit depends on its end use. In a cassoulet, it may fall off the bone. Roasted, the skin should be crisp, and the meat unctuous and melting.*

Taste: *Warm and spicy, with the rich, earthy taste of mutton and the fire of chile, qalaya evokes the vivid aromas and flavors of the souk.*

Cooked and then covered in a sealed jar with its own fat, which acts as a preservative, confits keep well.

Rillette

Pâté de Campagne

These delicious examples of charcuterie originate in the late Middle Ages: the name is derived either from an old French word for an ear (*rille*) or, possibly, from the term for a strip of fat (*reille*). Essentially, slow-cooked pork—sometimes combined with other meats—is stewed in its own natural dripping until the fibers of the meat are tender enough to flake into the juices by hand. Cooled, the mixture forms a soft, spreadable emulsion, roughly two parts of lean to one of fat.

The two iconic styles of rillettes are those of Tours and Le Mans. Rillettes de Tours, from the Loire valley, are the darker and smoother, taking their color from the searing they undergo at the outset of cooking. (For the sister recipe *rillons*, chunks of lean pork, stewed until crusty, are left to set in the cooled dripping.) Rillettes du Mans are paler, but contain small pieces of pork. Both versions owe their quality to the individual charcutier's skill. The art lies in blending the flecked meat with its reduced cooking juices and the dripping, which will have absorbed the flavor from the seasoning. **MR**

Leaving aside its rustic title, pâté de campagne, is the Adam and Eve of an endless line of French pâtés and terrines. It is a balanced blend of the darker and lighter meats and the harder and softer fats, usually with the addition of some pig's liver that gives it a softer, almost spreadable texture. Ground, or better still chopped, blended with pickling salt, herbs, and spices, sometimes marinated with wine or finished with brandy, it can be baked, steamed, or simmered in a bain marie. Found in every French market and charcuterie, its quality reflects the traditional craftsmanship of its maker. In contrast with the anemic pâtés de campagne sold both outside of France and by some chain stores inside it, it is a hearty, nourishing tribute to free-range pigs that have been reared slowly and expensively.

By adding game in place of the lean pork, a pâté de campagne can be changed into a partridge, hare, or wild boar version. The basic difference between a pâté de campagne and one baked in pastry—*en croûte*—is that the latter rarely includes liver and is, in consequence, firmer. **MR**

Taste: *Typically prepared from sows that have given birth to just one litter, rillettes are always delectably rich and fatty, but should taste of the finest artisanal pork.*

Taste: *The aroma of fresh pâté de campagne is both meaty and spicy. The robust flavors should blend into a harmonious whole with no one ingredient dominant.*

A stall sells rillettes at a farmers' market. They are
usually served cold, spread on slices of bread or toast.

Nduja

This fabulous, peppery hot, spreadable salami comes from Calabria, the part of Italy at the toe of the big boot. Made with pork meat, fat, and salt, it has a very high content of Calabrian red chile pepper—hence the vivid scarlet color and the kick. Bizarrely, this fiery-red chile explosion is also supposed to have aphrodisiac properties.

The term nduja apparently derives from the French specialty *andouille*, which is believed to have been introduced there in the Middle Ages during a period of French supremacy. The seasoned pork is forced into natural pig casings and then smoked over aromatic wood, before being left to mature for several months.

Fantastic as part of an antipasti offering, nduja makes great party food and a versatile and delicious seasoning aid. It can be scooped straight out of its casing and spread over bread, or eaten just as it comes. Stirred into pasta sauces it adds oomph and body, although one favorite Calabrian way to serve it is to heat it in little terracotta pots and keep it warm over a candle to use as a dip. **LF**

Taste: *Moist and meaty, hints of smoke and a spicy zing dance deliciously over the tongue. Fans of fiery food will love it. Add a little ricotta to temper the heat a touch.*

The Calabrian chiles used to spice nduja dry out in the warm open air. »

Chorizo Ibérico de Bellota

Chorizo Riojano

Along with the fabulous jamòn Ibérico de Bellota and lomo Ibérico de Bellota, chorizo Ibérico de Bellota comes from the unique breed of bristly, black-footed pig known as cerdo Ibérico. Ibérico pigs wander free in an area known as the *dehesa*, a bio-network of eye-catching beauty spanning Spain's Aracena and Extremadura regions. An abundance of oak and cork trees are found there and the pigs gobble greedily at the acorns until they reach the stipulated weight for slaughter.

Whereas *jamòn* is made from the legs of the pig and *lomo* is whole tenderloin, chorizo is made from selected cuts of the remaining meat. In keeping with the whole Ibérico de Bellota production philosophy, the chorizo is hand crafted. The pork meat is seasoned with salt, garlic, herbs, and paprika; the latter gives it the smoky flavor and rich red color typical of chorizo. The mixture is then forced into natural casings and cured for two months.

Chorizo Ibérico de Bellota should be served in thin slices, at room temperature. It is typically served as a tapa dish. **LF**

Spain classifies its fantastic range of artisan chorizos into the regions in which they were traditionally made. Chorizo Riojano (IGP) is a specialty of La Rioja, in northern Spain. Handmade, using prime-quality pork, salt, paprika, and garlic, chorizo Riojano is a soft-cured sausage suitable for cooking and is traditionally used to add a smoky, peppery depth to soups, stews, and paellas. Like most chorizo, it is available sweet (*dulce*) or hot (*picante*).

Chorizo, in its present form, does not have as long a history as most other Spanish sausages and cured meats. Pimentón, the Spanish version of paprika produced from pimentos or capsicums, did not arrive on the scene until the sixteenth century. Prior to this, chorizos were a fairly pale affair. Originally the pimentón was added to help prevent the pork from spoiling, but it is now hard to imagine chorizo without its signature paprika flavor.

Chorizo Riojano is encased in natural skins, in either a string or as a characteristic horseshoe shape. It can be broiled, grilled, boiled, sautéed, barbecued, or added to give a kick to many cooked dishes. **LF**

Taste: *Unctuous and meaty with a glorious flavor that is a skillful balance of piquancy and sweet smokiness. The rich marbling of fat surrenders beautifully on the tongue.*

Taste: *Chorizo Riojano has a complex, full flavor, and juicy texture. It has prominent garlic notes and a well-balanced smokiness, enlivened with a distinct piquancy.*

Chorizo is sold hanging in strings along with other dry-cured sausages and meats throughout Spain. ❯❯

Salchichón de Vic

When it comes to cured pork products, the Spanish really know their stuff, and salchichón de Vic is a fine example of their expertise. Pepper-speckled and temptingly rich, it is made from prime cuts of pork from pigs raised on a natural diet, and cured in the abundant, undulating landscape of La Plana de Vic, an area between Spain's Catalan Pyrenees and the coast that benefits from altitudes of 1,310 to 1,970 feet (400–600 m). This superb microclimate plays a key role in the salchichón's exquisite flavor.

Lean pork meat is mixed with back bacon and seasoned with salt and pepper, then macerated for a minimum of forty-eight hours before being forced into natural hog casings. The salchichón is then hung to allow the characteristic flavors to develop and the meat to dry out. The typical finished product is about 3 inches (7.5 cm) in diameter and between 20 and 24 inches (50–60 cm) long, although a smaller version can be found. Production is limited to twenty-eight villages and salchichón de Vic carries an IGP certificate to insure strict criteria governing all aspects of manufacture are adhered to. **LF**

Taste: *Full flavored with a well-balanced mixture of fat to meat, salchichón de Vic delivers deep savory notes and a prolonged aftertaste. Serve thinly sliced.*

Felino Salami

Felino salami is so well regarded in Italy it even has its own museum inside the eighteenth-century cellars of Felino Castle, in the province of Parma. But the production of salami in Felino can be traced back earlier than then, to the fifteenth century. It is made from pork taken from native Italian pigs, using proportions of seventy-five percent lean meat to twenty-five percent fat, ground and blended with salt, pepper, and little else, although some recipes can include a little wine. It is then forced into pig intestine and left to hang for at least three months, where it develops its distinctive shape: long, with a slightly bulbous end.

While salami contains a high percentage of salt to aid preservation, the area's microclimate allows the salami to mature in conditions that enhance the flavor and texture without the need for such heavy salting. Ideally, salami should be stored in the refrigerator, but removed several hours before eating to allow its full flavors to come out. It should be cut into slices no thicker than a peppercorn, at an angle of 60°, to appreciate the optimum flavor. **LF**

Taste: *Thinly sliced and served at room temperature, Felino salami is tender and succulent. Garlic tends not to be used in the seasoning, producing a delicate, sweet edge.*

After maturing for at least a month, Felino salami assumes its characteristic white-gray exterior. »

Chinese Sausage

The so-called wind-dried meats are an important feature of the Chinese winter diet. Long strings of reddish *lap cheung* (Chinese sausage)—a kind of sweet and salty salami made from pork—and *yuen cheung* (liver sausage) were traditionally made at home during the winter months, when the air was cool and breezy enough for the sausages to be hung outside to dry without fear of spoilage. Like other Chinese cured meats, they are now made year-round on a large scale by vendors who specialize in them. A base of pork meat, pork liver, or both is lubricated with pork fat, and flavored with rice wine, five-spice powder, soy sauce, and sugar.

Chinese sausages are always cooked before being eaten. One of the easiest and best methods is to steam them on top of rice: the delicious fat in the sausages renders out and adds flavor to the rice. The sausages can also be steamed on their own, then sliced, and fried until crisp. They are often served accompanied by bitter greens because the strong flavors of the vegetables balance the fatty richness of the meat. **KKC**

Taste: *Flavor varies depending on the choice of spice mix: some are very sweet, while others more savory. No fillers, such as bread, are used in Chinese sausages.*

An array of Chinese sausages await sale for New Year. »

Kabanos

Linguiça

Kabanos (plural kabanosy) is a firm, long, finger-thick sausage. Its low moisture content means it keeps indefinitely without refrigeration, so it became the preferred food of travelers, hunters, and soldiers in Eastern Europe, who would, quite literally, tuck the sticklike sausages under their belts.

Kabanosy are made from a combination of diced lean and fatty pork, seasoned with salt, pepper, garlic, caraway, and sometimes a pinch of ground allspice. A small amount of saltpeter is added to cure the mixture, which is then left to blend overnight in a cool place, before it is stuffed into thin sheep's casings and hung up to air-dry in the breeze. Next, the sausages are slowly smoked to an attractive reddish-brown, and air-dried once again for several days until they weigh roughly about half of what they did before processing.

Their longevity—a product of this smoking and drying—means kabanosy are still favorites of Polish and Ukrainian campers, hikers, anglers, and hunters; however, they are equally at home at elegant banquets and family celebrations. **RS**

This smoked pork sausage is seasoned with paprika, onions, garlic, herbs, and spices, to provide a distinctly Portuguese flavor. Although linguiça is not dissimilar to the milder types of Spanish chorizo, the Portuguese have been making pork and blood sausages for centuries. The meat is coarsely ground, mixed with the other ingredients, and forced into natural hog casings. The sausages are then smoked.

Linguiça have traveled pretty much anywhere the people of Portugal have settled. And, as a result, they have become very popular in areas with a high quota of Portuguese immigrants, most notably Brazil, but also places as diverse as New England and Hawaii, where linguiça are usually referred to simply as "Portuguese sausage."

Linguiça sausages are found in *caldo verde*, the Portuguese national stew of potatoes and greens, and in *cozido à Portuguesa*, another hearty stew of beef shin, pork, winter vegetables, and smoked sausages. They can also be grilled over charcoal, fried, or used on any of myriad occasions when a spicy, gutsy country sausage is required. **LF**

Taste: *Hearty and meaty, the texture of kabanosy vary from firm but supple to dry and brittle. The flavor is vigorous, with peppery, garlicky, and smoky notes.*

Taste: *Fried in good oil and served hot, linguiça has a gutsy, but not overly spicy, flavor that is both savory and smoky with piquant overtones.*

Linguiça, made according to an old recipe, is one of many traditional meats found at Portuguese markets. »

Saucisson d'Arles

Arles is a popular Provençal tourist destination so it is only to be expected that a local specialty should be dressed up with its very own myth. According to a nineteenth-century poet: "An Indian prince visited Arles and found so many beautiful girls there he lost his head. His arms and limbs dropped off, too, leaving behind his torso in a silver gown . . ."—the saucisson d'Arles. More prosaically, the combination might have been invented about 1655 by a charcutier called Godart, who is known to have sold a Bologna *socisol*. Whether the current recipe bears any relation to his sausage is uncertain, however.

Saucisson d'Arles is a dry, cured sausage, like Italian salami, but concocted from a mixture of pork, donkey, and bull beef, and seasoned with red wine and herbes de Provence. The donkey meat is what sets it apart, but today it is questionable whether this magic ingredient still finds its way into the mix. Putative saucisson d'Arles is sold by stallholders at the local market, but the most reliable source for this delicacy is Bernard Genin, a local charcutier who sells it from his store, La Farandole. **MR**

Taste: *Unsmoked and dried for three weeks, saucisson d'Arles is a classic example of the French-style saucisson sec. Thinly sliced, it makes an ideal baguette-filler.*

The well-known Provençal sausage looks much like salami. ❯❯

Soppressa del Pasubio

Soppressata di Calabria

Mount Pasubio is a mountain belonging to the Prealps, or "Little Dolomites," in northern Italy. A strategic site during World War I, it is now an area of great natural beauty, popular not only with hikers and bikers, but with the pigs whose meat makes the remarkable, elegantly textured salami known as Soppressa delle Valli del Pasubio.

Although raised on a diet rich in chestnuts and potatoes, the pigs are substantially free to roam, devouring wild roots and herbs, and drinking from streams rich in natural minerals, which gives their meat a very distinctive and delicious flavor.

A carefully balanced mixture of finely chopped pork meat and fat is seasoned with salt and pepper, then forced into natural casings. It matures for anything from five months to more than two years in cool, dry cellars, acquiring its downy layer of natural white mold. Soppressa del Pasubio is fabulous served thinly sliced as an antipasto offering, but in the Veneto area is often presented as a main course, cut into slightly thicker slices and served atop chunks of broiled, golden polenta. **LF**

Many regions of Italy have their own version of soppressata, but perhaps the most famous is Soppressata di Calabria (DOP), a wonderfully piquant pork salami. It must be made in Calabria from the meat of pigs born in southern Italy—specifically Calabria, Sicily, Basilicata, Apulia, and Campania—and slaughtered in Calabria.

Traditionally, prime cuts of pork shoulder and belly are coarsely chopped and seasoned with a mixture of peppercorns, fennel seeds, and chili pepper—a relatively high, yet balanced, ratio of added fat gives the salami a superb melting quality. The seasoned meat is encased in a natural hog casing, then pressed between weights into a flattened shape before its final curing phase.

There has been a tradition of cured meats in Calabria since the ancient Greeks appeared on the scene, but the first confirmed written reference did not appear until the seventeenth century. A century or so later, the legendary lover Giacomo Casanova was apparently converted to its charms while traveling through Calabria. **LF**

Taste: *Soppressa del Pasubio has a perfectly balanced meat to fat ratio and a firm, dense texture; the flavor is intense and lively without being overly spicy.*

Taste: *Thinly sliced Soppressata di Calabria has a well rounded, warm, piquant flavor and succulent, velvety texture that sets it apart from inferior, leathery imitations.*

The spectacular scenery of Mount Pasubio is home to
☉ *the pigs whose meat make a renowned local salami.*

Finocchiona Salami

This full-flavored, even pungent, Tuscan specialty is made from pork seasoned with garlic, peppercorns, fennel seeds (or *finocchio*), and often Chianti wine. It has been a traditional local delicacy for so long its origins are lost.

One legend maintains a thief at a fair close to the town of Prato stole a salami and concealed it in a stand of wild fennel. When he collected it, he discovered the salami had absorbed the essence of the herb and taken on a superb flavor. Another story claims wine-makers added the seeds to their wine to help sell it. Fennel seeds have a slightly numbing effect on the taste buds, and so when potential customers called by to sample the wines, they would be offered finocchiona to inoculate their palates against poor-quality wine.

There are two types of finocchiona: a firm variety known simply as finocchiona, and a younger, softer variety known as sbriciolona. Macelleria Falorni produce a true gastronomic finocchiona, made to exceptionally high standards from the meat of a semiwild Tuscan pig known as Cinta Senese. **LF**

Taste: *Flavorsome, moist finocchiona salami has a piquant zing balanced with a whisper of fennel. Sliced thinly, it is particularly good with unsalted Tuscan bread.*

Salami di Cinghiale

Salame di cinghiale is one of the true kings of Italian cured meats. The best examples are made with the thigh meat of wild boars, which is usually mixed with pork shoulder and then seasoned with salt and pepper. Sometimes extra seasonings, such as garlic, chile, and red wine are added. The mixture is forced into natural hog casings and cured in conditions that can vary according to the climate of the region in which the salami is produced. Although generally regarded as a Tuscan specialty, salame di cinghiale is also produced elsewhere in Italy, including in Umbria and Sardinia.

The diet of the wild boar typically consists of chestnuts, beech nuts, acorns, herbs, roots, mushrooms, and occasionally even truffles. This richly diverse diet lends the meat an incredible, intense quality and the cured salamis produced from it tend to have a delicious, robust flavor.

Salami di cinghiale makes perfect eating when sliced and served as part of an antipasto course washed down with a gutsy red wine. It is also fabulous added to pasta sauces and stews. **LF**

Taste: *Salami di cinghiale has a chewy texture with an intense flavor displaying subtle gamy, nutty, and sweet nuances opening out to a gentle piquancy.*

A specialist butcher's store in Umbria proudly displays cured meat products including salami di cinghiale. »

Rügenwalder Teewurst

This soft, pink sausage is believed to have originated in 1834 in the small Baltic town of Rügenwalde (now part of Poland). Made from finely ground pork, bacon, and beef packed into short reddish-brown skins, teewurst are smoked over beechwood before being left to mature for seven to ten days.

Smooth-textured due to a fat content of between thirty and forty percent, teewurst (meaning "tea sausage" in German) probably gets its name due to the ease with which it can be spread on rye bread, crackers, and toast for a snack. It also makes a tasty addition to herby stuffings for goose, chicken, and other poultry, or rolled pork roasts.

In 1927, the companies producing Rügenwalder Teewurst were awarded a PDO, but by the end of World War II they had been forced to flee their homeland. Moving west, they established new businesses in the then Federal Republic of Germany. Today, it is only teewurst makers who were originally based in Rügenwalde that are allowed to display the protected seal of origin; others must label their produce "Rugenwalder-style teewurst." **WS**

Thüringer Leberwurst

A close relative of teewurst, leberwurst is another popular cooked German sausage and one that is soft enough to spread. Like teewurst, leberwurst is made all over Germany and Austria, with each region having its own particular recipes.

Thüringer Leberwurst (PGI) is one of the most highly regarded and gained Its Protected Geographical Indication in 2003. It is produced in a region of central eastern Germany that is renowned for the quality of its foods, especially its meat and sausage products; Thüringen also makes excellent rotwurst and rostbratwurst.

In German, leberwurst means "liver sausage." Although most are made using cooked pork liver, goose, calves', and lamb's liver can also be included. Different flavorings and seasonings are added to the ground variety meat, including onions, chives, spices, and sometimes even apple, so the texture of the finished sausage is either fine or coarse. The sausages can also be plainly cooked or smoked. Leberwurst is ideal generously spread on rye bread or crispbreads for breakfast, or for a snack. **WS**

Taste: *Teewurst is so soft it can be spread with a knife. It has a rich, creamy texture and the savory flavor of smoked ham spiked with pepper and other warm spices.*

Taste: *Leberwurst has a strong and savory flavor, offset by the warmth of onion and pepper. The depth of the flavor depends on the type of liver used in the recipe.*

Sausages such as teewurst and leberwurst create an attractive display in a German butcher's shop.

Merguez

Just as the color red can indicate danger in daily life, the bright hue of these small, thin link sausages indicates at a glance they are not for the faint-hearted: the color stems from the addition of the hot chile paste harissa. Merguez are particularly associated with Algeria and Tunisia, but have been favored by Arabs around the world since at least the thirteenth century, and are a versatile ingredient in North African and Middle Eastern cooking. As Islam prohibits the consumption of pig products, these are made with lamb, mutton, or beef, never pork.

About 3 to 4 inches (7–10 cm) long, merguez sausages can be spiced with a veritable Aladdin's cave of flavorings. Although harissa is the best-known ingredient, other common choices include preserved lemons, aniseed, cinnamon, sumac (for tartness), and even dried rose petals. They are usually sold fresh for grilling or broiling to serve alongside couscous or to be eaten on their own as a snack, although they can also be sun-dried and stored in olive oil. Fresh or dried sausages are also included in tagines and stews. **BLeB**

Mititei

A Romanian word meaning "small things," mititei is also the name of one of Romania's traditional dishes. Mititei are spiced, grilled meatballs or rolls usually made from ground beef, but they can also be made from a mixture of beef and pork, or beef and mutton. According to legend, mititei were invented at a Bucharest restaurant called La Lordachi, which was renowned for its sausages. The story goes that one busy evening the kitchen ran out of sausage casings and so converted the sausage mixture into small balls instead. These were then grilled, and so mititei were born.

The meat is combined with onion, garlic, olive oil, salt, pepper, and baking soda, which plumps up the meat. Paprika is often added, although other seasonings, including thyme, caraway, marjoram, allspice, cumin, chile, or cloves, can also be used. The kneaded mixture is then shaped into small balls and refrigerated for several hours, before being grilled until brown. Mititei are best served with pickles or mustard in a bread roll alongside a cold beer. They also good eaten with potatoes or a rice pilaf. **CK**

Taste: *Always spicy and flavorsome, merguez have a dense texture that makes them ideal for barbecuing or pan-frying. They pair well with lentils and couscous.*

Taste: *Mititei are juicy and tender with a piquant, spicy garlicky flavor that varies according to the seasonings used. Do not use too lean a meat or the balls will dry out.*

Spicy merguez sausages await grilling at a Moroccan 🔾 *market; they are also popular in France and Belgium.*

Alheiras de Mirandela

Jésus de Morteau

The best alheiras are considered to be the renowned alheiras de Mirandela from northern Portugal. They are a legacy of the Jewish community in the late fifteenth century when King Manuel I attempted to rid Portugal of residents who did not subscribe to the Catholic faith. Under Judaism, pork meat is forbidden and this made Jewish people fairly easy to identify because they were never seen preparing and smoking the traditional pork sausages in the local *fumeiros*, or smokehouses. The sharp-witted Jews realized that if they created a porkfree sausage that looked identical to the original variety, they could attend the *fumeiros* alongside other citizens.

Alheiras sausages are made from a wide variety of meats such as veal, duck, chicken, turkey, and rabbit; they do not usually include pork. To create this Portuguese specialty, a seasoned mixture of meats is mixed with bread, garlic, and paprika. The casings are stuffed in such a way that the sausages make a "u" shape, and they are then smoked slowly over several days. Typically alheiras are fried in olive oil, and served with a fried egg and vegetables. **LF**

How this sausage acquired its name is unknown; perhaps it was seen to resemble a baby Jesus in swaddling clothes. The Morteau part, however, is simple to explain: Morteau—"dead water"—is a town in the mountainous Jura region of France.

Jésus de Morteau (AOC) is an example of agricultural synergy. Pigs are fed with whey from cheese-making (Tomme de Comté is the local specialty), a diet that produces the rich pork that is the base of the sausage. Diced shoulder and neck meat is blended with a little fat from the back, the butcher's personal choice of seasoning is added, and the mixture is piped or filled into a natural casing with a distinctive wooden peg at one end. Then the sausage is smoked in the traditional Jura chimneys—*tuyés*—over resinous, coniferous wood.

Sold raw or cooked, Jésus de Morteau adds body to hearty peasant recipes, simmered in a wine-flavored court bouillon and served with potatoes or lentils. In a *gratinée de Morteau*, slices of cooked sausage are coated in sauce, topped with Comté, and glazed in the oven or under the broiler. **MR**

Taste: *Alheiras de Mirandela is a truly sassy sausage. A distinct smokiness and the obvious presence of garlic complements the well-defined and appealing texture.*

Taste: *Jésus de Morteau has a spicy, cured taste overlaid by the flavor of resinous wood smoke. It is dense with a firm texture that reflects it high proportion of lean meat.*

The finest alheiras (smoked sausages)
❖ *come from northern Portugal.*

Andouille de Vire

Zampone di Modena

As early as the fifteenth century, the French cooking tract *Le Mesnagier de Paris* described an andouille as intestines packed inside an intestine. It is distinguished from its little sister, the andouillette, by its size. The baby is usually eaten fresh off the grill; the grownup is served finely sliced and cold.

Unlike andouilles from other parts of France, which can include sheep or cow tripe, the andouille de Vire from lower Normandy is prepared exclusively from pork chitterlings. These are washed, brined, seasoned, and packed into a large pork casing. The best artisanal versions are then cold-smoked over beech chippings for about one month. At the end of this they are simmered for six hours in water or a flavored broth, shrinking from 5 pounds (2.3 kg) to just over 1 pound (450 g) in weight. Left to mature, the outer surface develops a dark skin, almost black, while the interior is pale pink and appetizing.

The andouille de Vire's integrity is protected by a charter from the local craftsmen who make the product. A genuine example is recognized by the length of cord embedded in its outer surface. **MR**

Zampone is an Italian pork sausage made from ground pork, fat, and rinds seasoned with spices and encased in a boned pig's foot. There are two types: an uncooked, authentic one that requires overnight soaking and careful, slow simmering for four hours, and a precooked, vacuum-packed type that needs no more than twenty minutes gentle cooking. Both versions are served hot, in slices, traditionally with lentils at celebrations.

Legend has it zampone was created in the early sixteenth century in a town called Mirandola, near Modena, when Pope Julius II, otherwise known as the Warrior Pope, invaded the town. The story claims townspeople slaughtered all the pigs to prevent them falling prey to the enemy, so they needed to preserve as much as they could.

Today, Zampone di Modena carries an IGP certification. Zampone is generally eaten rind and all; when cooked, it has a glutinous, melting consistency. For anyone not keen on foot's more unctuous qualities, Cotechino di Modena is an almost identical product in sausage skin. **LF**

Taste: *The andouille de Vire tastes clean, fresh, and only a little smoky. Slices should look meaty, without the spiraled appearance of some French tripe sausages.*

Taste: *Deeply flavored and aromatic, Zampone di Modena's tender, gelatinous, almost gummy, rind gives way to a uniform succulence throughout.*

The uniqueness of Zampone di Modena is that the filling is stuffed into a pig's foot rather than a casing. »

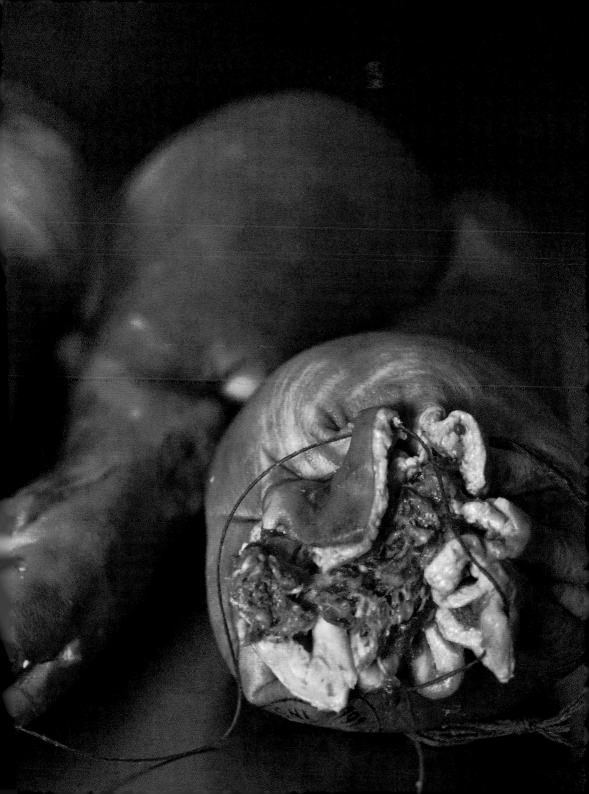

St. Gallen Bratwurst

Thüringer Rostbratwurst

Close to the German border in eastern Switzerland, the beautiful provincial city of St. Gallen is renowned for its colorful oriel windows, its lace embroidery, and for its take on the famous German bratwurst sausage. Bratwurst is made from pork or veal, or sometimes a mixture of both. St. Gallen bratwurst consist of finely ground veal that is seasoned, depending on the recipe, with spices such as ginger, nutmeg, coriander, and caraway. These pale, gently spiced sausages are available cooked and fresh, the latter requiring broiling or sautéing.

Made all over Germany, bratwurst is usually named after the place with which it is associated, and St. Gallen is justly proud of its own particular version of this German institution. People can be seen walking all over the historic center eating hot, juicy bratwurst fresh from street stalls with the bread known as *buerli*. The local firm Gemperli's make theirs with a mixture of veal, pork, bacon, and milk. St. Gallen bratwurst are delicious broiled and served with hot mustard, fried onions, and *rösti*. They are also excellent partnered with a rich, onion gravy. **FP**

Among Germany's many sausages, such as bierwurst, bockwurst, knackwurst, and weisswurst, bratwurst from the state of Thuringia is the one with the longest pedigree. References to it go back to the start of the fifteenth century and there are records of fines set for selling poor merchandise, such as rancid beef or meat infested with parasites, dating from 1432. With 365,000,000 pieces sold each year it is among the nation's favorites. In Thuringia itself, each person consumes an average of sixty bratwursts a year.

It is made from pork belly that is first ground and then slowly chopped to obtain a fine, compact mixture that is piped into natural casings. With no additives other than salt and spices it is a pure meat sausage. Sausages are between 6 and 10 inches (15–25 cm) long. Thüringer Rostbratwurst are roasted or more commonly grilled or broiled after being scored with diagonal cuts to help them cook more evenly. They are usually eaten smeared with mustard. As a snack, they are sold between a bread roll with the sausage poking out at both ends. **MR**

Taste: *Firm and lean, St. Gallen bratwurst have a mild veal taste, accented by light spices, which expands on the taste buds. Broil or fry to best seal in the flavor and juices.*

Taste: *As it contains no preservative and is sold soon after manufacture, Thüringer Rostbratwurst is a fresh-tasting, lightly seasoned sausage, with a dense, but juicy, texture.*

Rostbratwurst are usually served grilled; sweet German mustard complements their mild flavor. ❯

Weisswurst

Weisswurst is a tasty, traditional white sausage made from well-seasoned veal and pork meats that started life in Munich and is now famous all over Bavaria. According to legend, it was created more than 150 years ago, when a young butcher to a Munich inn was making veal sausages and found to his horror the skins for the casing had run out. In a bid to satisfy the customers, the quick-thinking butcher substituted a thinner hog casing. Concerned that the skin would burst if fried, he cooked the sausage in boiling water. The result was greeted with great enthusiasm, and to this day weisswurst is taken to the table in a pot containing its cooking water.

By tradition, weisswurst is a breakfast dish. The sausage is popped out of its skin and the meat sucked out and eaten with Bavarian sweet mustard and a pretzel, all washed down with white German beer. The sausages are very perishable and are best made fresh every morning. In Bavaria, the saying goes that weisswurst should never be allowed to hear the church bells' noon chime, hence they are eaten for the first meal of the day. **LF**

Taste: *This parsley-speckled specialty reveals a juicy, well-balanced combination of lean to fat, with a full meaty flavor that offers hints of lemon and spices.*

Figatellu

Figatellu (figatelli is its plural form) is a traditional form of Corsican charcuterie, a long, thin, dark colored sausage, of which the main ingredient is pig's liver. It is chopped or ground together with lean pork, mixed with red or rosé wine made from the local Niellucciu grape, and seasoned with garlic and sometimes cloves, before being funneled into sausage skins. It is then gently smoked for up to five days. Grilled over charcoal, it is eaten between slices of pain de campagne bread with *pulenta* (polenta) or a chestnut puree.

The tradition of killing a pig at the start of winter, the *tumbera*, is still practiced in Corsican villages, particularly in the northern region of Castagniccia, which takes its name from the chestnut woods growing there. Although often described as black, the island breed is, in fact, a long-snouted animal with a pink coat and mottled black spots that still roams semiwild, feeding on chestnuts and acorns. It is used for other cured meats—*prisuttu* (ham), *coppa* (loin), *lonzu* (fillet), and *panzetta*—whose names reflect their Italian mainland parentage. **MR**

Taste: *Due to its high blended liver content, figatellu has a texture and taste similar to blood sausage, enhanced with a smokiness from being charred over an open fire.*

Loukanika

Cumberland Sausage

This long, thin sausage from the Greek islands is traditionally made between mid-November and New Year's Day, when the farmers slaughter their hogs. The name comes from the Latin *lucanicus*, which is believed to have been a sausage eaten by the Lucanian people who occupied the area of southern Italy now known as Basilicata in the fifth century BCE, and where a long, coiled, chile-spiked pork sausage called *lucanica* is still popular today.

Loukanika has a high meat content, often a mixture of pork and lamb, although flavorings vary according to where the sausages are made. Cooks on the island of Simi, for example, put in lots of garlic, whereas those from Cyprus prefer cilantro, cumin, or oregano. The seasoned meat mixture is stuffed into casings and the resulting sausages soaked in red wine before being smoked. Fresh loukanika are also made.

Loukanika can be fried or broiled and served as part of a meze platter or with vegetables as a main course. They can also be casseroled with gigandes beans, potatoes, tomatoes, and peppers. **WS**

Instantly recognizable in a British butcher's window, Cumberland sausage is less easy to pin down with regard to its origin. Its appearance—a long tube of chopped or ground pork filling a natural casing of pig intestine coiled into spirals—is unique for an English sausage. What its ingredients are and how it is seasoned is another matter.

Locals in Cumbria, northwest England, say it used to be made with pork from the Cumberland pig, a fatty, lop-eared breed that died out in the 1960s. It is still made from pork, though, as is usual with many British sausages, it may contain up to twenty percent rusk. (Some Cumberlands have a ninety-eight percent meat content.) A generation ago, butchers ground the pork coarsely. Now the best sausages, prepared with meat from rare breed pigs, are chopped by hand. In either case, the coarseness of the mixture implies only better-quality cuts were used.

The seasoning varies from butcher to butcher, but the predominant taste comes from the blend of black and white pepper. Plans are afoot to try and get this regional sausage protected PGI status. **MR**

Taste: *Rich and meaty, the flavors of loukanika depend on individual sausagemakers. Smoked loukanika have a drier texture than fresh, with a hint of woodsmoke.*

Taste: *Usually fried or broiled, Cumberland sausage has a stretched, plump outer skin that is almost crisp and a peppery pork taste. The texture is succulent and chewy.*

Kaszanka

This hearty blood sausage, studded with buckwheat groats, is known as kaszanka in Poland; in North America, where it was introduced during the influx of Poles over a century ago, it is known as kiska. Kaszanka fanciers on both sides of the Atlantic are prepared to pay top money for it.

Like other blood sausages, kaszanka was traditionally prepared at pig-butchering time in early winter, when the frugal folk of yesteryear ensured that absolutely nothing was wasted. Blood spoils and coagulates very quickly, so blood sausage is found in many cultures where pigs are reared.

The Polish kaszanka is distinguished by the addition of buckwheat, as well as onion and spices. Together with hog's blood it contains cooked and coarsely chopped pork rinds, lungs, jowls, and trimmings, and golden-brown nuggets of fatback pork, fried until crunchy. The mixture is seasoned with salt, pepper, marjoram, and sometimes allspice, then packed into large pig intestines and boiled or baked. Some aficionados insist that the sausage is best when steamed. During cooking, a straw is inserted into the sausage to test it for doneness. If the straw is dry, the sausage is deemed to be cooked enough; if it is wet, more cooking is required.

Kaszanka can be eaten cold or hot, on its own or accompanied by mustard, prepared horseradish, or gherkin. Some people like it refried and smothered in onions, while others reheat their kaszanka in boiling water. Hot kaszanka served with mustard, a slice of rye bread, and a stein of beer is traditional street food and market-day fare in Poland. Like all blood sausages, kaszanka has a limited shelf life and is best eaten within three weeks of manufacture. **RS**

Taste: *The dusky groats blend with the meat and blood into a rich, hearty, harmonious whole, with fragrant marjoram providing the chief flavor accent.*

Kaszanka sausages provide a welcome hot snack at a busy Krakow winter market.

Botifarra Dolça

Botifarra dolça is a curious, cylindrical, Catalonian sausage characterized by the addition of lemon and sugar or honey. It exists in two forms: raw and dried, the latter being air-dried for no more than twenty-five days. Cinnamon may also be added to the pork mixture. The sausage meat is stuffed into natural skins and simmered gently in water that also contains lemon and sugar or honey.

Rumored to come from a Moorish recipe, botifarra dolça has its origins in medieval cookery, when honey and sugar were more frequently used in savory dishes. This was an alternative method of preserving meat to salting, drying, or storing it in lard. Botifarra dolça is found only around Girona and the Alto Ampurdan region of northern Catalonia, particularly around the three villages of Salitja, Sant Dalmai, and Vilobi d'Onya, which host an annual festival that celebrates the botifarra dolça. Production of the sausage is so localized that it is virtually unknown elsewhere in Catalonia.

The flavor combinations of botifarra dolça are so unexpected to the modern palate that chefs struggle to know when to use it. By tradition it should be prepared as a main course, accompanied by stewed apples or potatoes, but due to its sweetness (the skin caramelizes on cooking), it is often served erroneously as a dessert, often with sweet fried bread. A happy compromise is to offer it with an aperitif, when the aromatic sweetness of the sausage can satisfy initial pangs of hunger. Botifarra dolça is said to have been one of Salvador Dali's favorite foods, and in his honor the longest botifarra dolça in the world was made and measured just outside his birthplace. **RL**

Taste: *Botifarra dolça has the savory presence of a pork sausage overlaid with clear notes of caramelized honey and light, warm cinnamon undertones.*

Morcilla Dulce

Morcilla de Burgos

Blood sausage, otherwise known as black pudding, is a traditional food popular the world over. Its production goes back centuries, and even earns a mention in Homer's *Odyssey*: "As when a man besides a great fire has filled a sausage with fat and blood, and turns it this way and that, and is very eager to get it quickly roasted . . ."

Morcilla dulce is the Uruguayan sweet version of blood sausage, made from pig's blood with orange peel, walnuts, and sometimes raisins. In a nation that is said to boast more livestock than people—thanks to its vast grassy interior—locals eat a lot of meat broiled, fried, barbecued, or roasted. Along with grilled beef and lamb, morcilla dulce forms the staples of Uruguay's highly popular *parilladas*, or grill rooms, which serve mixed meats cooked over hot wood coals. It is also served at *asados*, or barbecues. Many of Uruguay's national dishes are indebted to European influences, in particular Spanish and Italian cuisines, and morcilla dulce is most likely to have its ancestry in the morcilla blood sausage made throughout Spain. **CK**

Blood sausage buffs will love morcilla de Burgos—the rather delicious blood sausage from Burgos, in the Castilla y León region of northern Spain. Morcilla is one of the most typical products in Spanish gastronomy and morcilla de Burgos is generally considered the best that Spain has to offer.

The sausage was created as a by-product of the ritual of *la matanza*—the slaughter of pigs that has customarily taken place all over Spain during the late fall or winter months. Whole families gather together, and the fattened pig is slaughtered and butchered to provide food for the winter months. No part of the pig is wasted—and that includes the blood, which is cooked until it thickens and congeals. In the case of morcilla de Burgos, spices and seasonings are added for flavor together with rice to give texture and bulk. The mixture is then forced into the cleaned guts or intestines of the pig.

Morcilla de Burgos is often served sliced and lightly fried as a tapa dish, but it is also used as an ingredient in stews and cooked bean dishes. Anyone traveling to Spain should give it a try. **LF**

Taste: *Morcilla dulce has a complex, crumbly texture that melts in the mouth while delivering a sweet and spicy tang of citrus, and a hint of nuttiness.*

Taste: *Served sliced and hot, dark, juicy, rice-speckled morcilla de Burgos oozes bold, lip-smacking flavors that are traditionally highly savory.*

A selection of locally made blood sausages features in the display of a butcher's shop in Burgos, Spain. ❯❯

Oak-Smoked Back Bacon

Bacon is meat from the side of the pig, cured with dry salt or steeped in brine. For many centuries it was a staple food for peasant families, who would keep their own pig and use the cured bacon (smoked and unsmoked) to flavor otherwise bland dishes during the winter months.

After maturing, bacon can be cold-smoked at around 104°F (40°C), popularly over oak or beech wood. Oak-smoked bacon is a firm favorite in the United Kingdom and is enjoyed for its earthy, yet mellow, flavor that will complement rather than overpower accompanying ingredients. It leaves a predictably smoky finish on the palate and the meatier back rashers are particularly succulent.

Oak-smoked bacon is extremely addictive; it is an iconic sandwich filling and a popular addition to salads and pasta dishes. Bacon is also at the heart of the cooked English breakfast, where it might accompany blood sausage, pork sausages, eggs, and broiled tomatoes. The "fry up" is a relatively recent development: in Victorian times Britons were more likely to eat cold meat for breakfast. **GM**

Taste: *Salty, smoky, and more intense in flavor than ham, smoked bacon provides a comforting taste sensation. It should be sweet as well as smoky and linger on the palate.*

Grilled simply, the flavor and quality of
Ⓚ *oak- smoked back bacon shines through.*

Peameal Bacon

To be Canadian is, for many, to understand that bacon comes in two forms: the popular "strip" or "streaky" bacon that forms part of the full English breakfast—not to mention the full Irish breakfast, or the full Scottish breakfast—and the pink, juicy, cornmeal-encrusted loin known from Newfoundland to British Columbia as peameal bacon.

Unlike imitations presented as Canadian bacon, true peameal bacon is never smoked. Sold both as the boned, rolled loin and, more commonly, in substantial slices that can reach up to ¼ inch (0.5 cm) thick, peameal bacon is trimmed of fat, brined, then coated in a yellowish cornmeal "jacket." This meal was once made from crushed, dried yellow peas, hence the name, but the precise origins of peameal itself remain unknown.

Although sold raw, the classic preparation, as ubiquitously seen in Toronto's St. Lawrence Market, is fried and stacked in the middle of a fresh kaiser bun. Mustard is occasionally offered, but spurned by traditionalists. Alternate preparations can include peameal roasts and barbecued-grilled slices. **SBe**

Taste: *Lean, salty, somewhat sweet, and faintly nutty tasting, peameal bacon is almost impossible to dry out, thus yielding a consistently moist and juicy meat.*

Guanciale

Hangikjöt

Guanciale is a specialty bacon product that originated in central Italy and is made from the single piece of meat that lies between the throat and the cheek or jowl (*guancia* in Italian) of the pig. As with many Italian cured meats, its history goes back centuries, and curing methods are still based on traditional recipes. The meat is covered in a mixture of salt, pepper, sugar, and spices and dry-cured for a month. It is then hung for another month before it is ready to be used. Guanciale is the bacon featured in the classic Italian pasta dishes spaghetti carbonara and *pasta all'amatriciana*, although many people mistakenly believe pancetta—belly bacon—has always been used. This is a very fatty bacon, but the fat renders down as the meat cooks.

Nowadays, guanciale is produced in many areas, and each regional variation has its own character: guanciale from Calabria tends to be spicy and fiery; whereas guanciale from Le Marche is sometimes lightly smoked; Tuscan guanciale is more mellow and aromatic. Guanciale has a particular affinity with fish, legumes, and dark green vegetables. **LF**

Hangikjöt, or "hanging meat" as the word translates, is a smoked Icelandic specialty now typically made from lamb, but has in the past also been made from mutton and sometimes even horsemeat.

The salting and smoking of meat as a method of preservation in Iceland stretches back to techniques practiced among the Nordic peoples in the eighth century. Short summers and long winters meant it was necessary to conserve food for sustenance during the colder months. What gives hangikjöt such a distinct flavor and aroma is the fact it is traditionally smoked for up to five days over dried sheep dung; however, this is sometimes mixed with juniper or birch wood shavings.

Although sometimes served as a topping for bread or the thick pancakes known as *skonsur*, hangikjöt is not generally eaten on a daily basis. It is considered a delicacy that is usually offered as part of the Christmas Eve festivities, when it is served hot or cold, accompanied by cooked potatoes with a creamy, béchamel-style white sauce, peas, and pickled red cabbage. **LF**

Taste: *Sliced into lardons and cooked, richly flavored guanciale adds glorious flavor and distinct savory notes to accompanying ingredients.*

Taste: *Salty, with a pronounced smokiness, and delicious savory flavor that kick-starts the gastric juices, hangikjöt has a unique, all-pervading, smoky aroma.*

Icelandic sheep are herded to pasture; the legs, thighs, and sides of lamb are ideal for smoking as hangikjöt. »

Yunnan Ham

As with some other types of ham, such as Black Forest in Europe and Smithfield in the United States, Chinese Yunnan ham is salted, smoked, and air-dried, and some countries prohibit its importation because it is technically considered raw. Smoking and curing the meat reduces its water content and intensifies the flavor. It can be eaten raw (sliced as thinly as Smithfield ham because it is tough in thicker slices), but often it is added in small quantities to other ingredients to add its sweet-salty richness to the dish. The bones are prized for flavoring broths.

Yunnan ham is expensive, although much cheaper than its European and U.S. cousins, and a little goes a long way. It can be purchased in chunks or slices, with or without the bone. Some houses in Yunnan (and in Hunan, where a similar ham is made) will have a ham hanging from the ceiling rafters so pieces can be carved off and used as needed. Sometimes mold appears, but if the ham has been properly cured, the mold will be scraped off and the ham underneath used as usual. **KKC**

Smithfield Ham

The little town of Smithfield, Virginia, calls itself "the ham capital of the world," and Smithfield ham is one of the more famous of the family of salt-cured and (often) smoked country hams that have deep roots throughout the southern states. Commercial production in Smithfield is said to date back to 1779. Smithfield hams gained their distinctive character from the hogs' traditional diet, which was rich in local Virginia peanuts.

Production is strictly regulated. The hams are dry-cured with salt, smoked long and slowly over hickory wood (often with fruitwood as well), and then aged at least six months. Smithfield connoisseurs often prefer hams cured for a year or longer, intensifying their flavor and character.

Smithfield ham is almost always cooked before serving. First, it is soaked in water for at least a day, then scrubbed and simmered in water until tender, when it can be finished in myriad ways: rubbed with brown sugar and baked whole, or sliced, pan-fried, and served, Southern-style, with red-eye gravy and buttermilk biscuits. **CN**

Taste: *Yunnan ham is beautifully balanced with sweet, smoky, and umami flavors. It is smooth-textured, slightly moist, and a little chewy.*

Taste: *Even after soaking and simmering in water, the dominant taste of this ham is salt. Serve it thinly sliced, or use it to flavor dishes like potato soup or sautéed greens.*

The lengthy process of curing and aging Smithfield ham in the right conditions contributes to its high price. ❯

Bradenham Ham

Black Forest Ham

Probably the rarest of British hams, Bradenham has crossed several counties in its peregrinations. Although known as early as the 1780s, when some believe it came from Buckinghamshire, in England, it was granted a Royal Warrant much later, in 1888. By then it was being made in the neighboring county, at the Royal Wiltshire Bacon Factory, Calne.

A long-cut haunch, taken from a fat bacon pig, Bradenham had an unlikely tar-colored surface, which came from immersion in a concentrated brine cure that included both juniper and coriander seed, but most importantly, molasses. The hams were dried for five to six months before they were considered mature, then soaked for up to three days, and finally poached at a low temperature.

In the late twentieth century, the factory closed and Bradenham production moved to Yorkshire. This factory also shut and the ham was in danger of extinction. The recipe, however, lightly modified, has survived in the form of Dukeshill Shropshire Black Ham, while London's Fortnum & Mason sells an organic version known as "Black Ham." **MR**

When it comes to the ham hall of fame, the mouth-watering specialty known as Black Forest ham (PDO) is up there with the best. The name carries a protected designation of origin certification, which means any ham bearing that label and sold within the European Union must come from a designated area within the Black Forest, in southern Germany.

Black Forest ham is made from prime legs of pork that are hand-rubbed with salt, herbs, garlic, and spices, such as coriander and juniper berries, although exact recipes are usually handed down through generations and are often closely guarded secrets. The mixture draws out the moisture from the meat, which is then smoked in special smoke chambers over brushwood gathered from the fir trees of the Black Forest. This process gives the hams a unique and delicious flavor. As a finishing touch, they are sometimes dipped in beef blood to give the outer surface a deep brown or black color. Typically served thinly sliced as an appetizer or snack, Black Forest ham also makes an appearance on breakfast tables in Germany and in cooked dishes. **LF**

Taste: *Bradenham ham has a noticeable sweetness. A firm, meaty ham, the current versions are less fatty than it once was, in line with current food trends.*

Taste: *Black Forest ham has a deep, complex flavor that delivers a pronounced, but not overpowering, saltiness, which then gives way to well-balanced smoky aromatics.*

Pig farming has long been associated with the Black Forest and wild boar are still found there. »

Culatello di Zibello

Coppa Piacentina

Culatello di Zibello (DOP) is a mouthwatering artisan prosciutto named for the town of Zibello, in Parma, Italy. Records show it was being produced in the area as long ago as the fifteenth century.

This is made from the large back muscle of the rear legs of pigs that must be bred, raised, and slaughtered within a specified region around the River Po. The river contributes to notoriously heavy winter fogs that contrast with the warm summer weather and create a unique humidity. This permeates the surrounding plains and, as the meat ripens in the moist, cool atmosphere after slaughter, it grows sweet and delicious.

Very soon after the pigs are slaughtered, the hind legs are skinned and boned, and the small, lean front muscle is removed. The meat is hand-salted, then trussed to create its typical pear shape. It is then left to rest. Some days later the meat is massaged again to help the salt penetration. Another period of resting follows before the hams are bound in pigs' bladders and left to mature in cellars for at least a year. **LF**

Coppa Piacentina (DOP) is an exquisite Italian cured pork product that uses meat taken from the upper neck part of *suino pesante italiano*, a particular breed of pig reared around Piacenza. With its temperate climate and lush vegetation, the area has proved an ideal environment for pig farming.

The production of coppa Piacentina is believed to have started during Roman times, but centuries later, in the farmhouses of the Po valley, curing and maturing techniques were perfected that have produced some of Italy's finest cured meats. Since 1997, coppa Piacentina has carried a *Denominazione di Origine Protetta*, which strictly governs the region in which the pigs are raised and the processes through which the meat is cured and matured.

The pork is covered with a dry mixture of salt and local aromatics, then left to dry for seven days before being rubbed down by hand, wrapped in pig intestine, and left to cure for at least six months. It is typically served in paper-thin slices that need little more than a drizzle of extra virgin olive oil and perhaps a squeeze of lemon. **LF**

Taste: *Culatello di Zibello has a glorious pink color and a fine marbling of fat that melts on the tongue to give a superbly structured balance of salty, sweet, spicy, and nutty.*

Taste: *Coppa Piacentina has a deep red color with a light veining of fat. The full, but balanced, spicy, grassy aroma gives way to a toothsome, subtle sweetness.*

Culatello di Zibello, instantly recognizable by its trussed pear shape, cures in a Parma cellar.

Jamón Ibérico de Bellota

Lomo Ibérico de Bellota

Connoisseurs consider jamón Ibérico de Bellota the king among cured hams. It is produced in Spain, and comes from a bristly, black-footed, acorn-munching pig known as cerdo Ibérico that roams freely in the *dehesa*, an incredible area spanning more than 5 million acres (2 million hectares) of the Aracena and Extremadura mountains. The *dehesa* boasts a diverse ecosystem of cork and oak trees, wild herbs, grasses, and aromatic plants, and this provides the biggest part of the animals' diet.

Bellota is the Spanish word for acorn and during the preslaughter fattening period the pigs must reach a specified weight on a diet of foraged acorns and grasses alone; to make the grade, their body weight must increase by at least one third. The resulting fat layer penetrates into the muscle fibers, giving the finished hams a fine, yellowy white marbling and an incomparable flavor. What adds to the magic of this extraordinary ham is that half of this fat is monounsaturated—the type found in extra virgin olive oil, rather than the artery clogging kind more often associated with pork products. **LF**

Just like the superb jamón Ibérico de Bellota, lomo Ibérico de Bellota comes from the distinctive breed of stubbly, black-footed pig known as cerdo Ibérico. Prior to slaughter, the pigs have a diet rich in *bellotas*, the acorns that have dropped from the abundant oak trees of the *dehesa*, a protected ecosystem in Spain's Aracena and Extremadura mountains.

Lomo is created using an entire section of the tenderloin that is dry-cured for three months after being rubbed with an enticing mixture of olive oil, garlic, salt, herbs, and spices—usually oregano, nutmeg, and Spanish paprika. An artisan-produced specialty, it is very different from the more mainstream Spanish sausages—such as salchichón and chorizo—as it is not a mixture of meat, but a whole piece of tenderloin in a natural skin casing. For this reason, it shows off the handsome swirl of yellow-white fat that is so characteristic of Ibérico de Bellota to beautiful effect.

It is typically served thinly sliced, and alone, as a tapa dish; it has such a fabulous flavor there is little need for any accompaniment. **LF**

Taste: *To capture its true essence, eat the ham unadorned and at room temperature. It has an exquisite nutty flavor, savory-sweet aroma, and melt-in-the-mouth texture.*

Taste: *Eaten at room temperature, the richly flavored, dark red meat has organoleptic qualities. Both salty and sweet, it has an intense flavor and silky smooth texture.*

Ibérico pigs roam freely in southern Spain. Jamón Ibérico
⊗ *comes from pigs that are seventy-five percent Ibérico.*

Pancetta

Pancetta is produced all over Italy. It is salted pork belly that is left to rest for anything between eight and fifteen days, depending on the type of pancetta being produced and, naturally, the weight. Cracked black pepper and spices such as cloves, nutmeg, juniper, and cinnamon are added to the basic salting mixture to enhance the natural flavor. In central Italy, fennel seeds and garlic are sometimes added. (Some varieties are also smoked.)

Pancetta usually has a dark, fleshy pink color with streaks of white fat, and is traditionally rolled, but sometimes flattened. Pancetta Piacentina (DOP), is produced exclusively in the province of Piacenza, and has a deep red coloring. Pancetta di Calabria (DOP) is produced only in Calabria and is left to cure for at least thirty days. The meat is rosy, with layers of white fat, and is dusted with ground chile pepper.

Pancetta is usually served thinly sliced or cut into lardons. It is used in much-loved pasta dishes, such as *pasta all'amatriciana* and pasta carbonara, and is often used in *soffrito* (the Italian equivalent of the French *mirepoix*) as a base for flavoring. **LF**

Taste: *Pancetta has a subtle sweetness that comes through the mouthwatering, salty tang of the meat. Additional cooking enhances its intense savory notes.*

Serrano Ham

Air-cured ham from white-foot pigs is produced in several of the mountainous areas of Spain. Some of the best serrano hams are said to come from Trevélez, in the Sierra Nevada and Teruel in Aragón.

Traditionally hams were ripened in cool, dry mountain sheds called *secaderos*. Nowadays, the meat is cured in high-tech *secaderos* in controlled conditions, monitored by the Denominacíon de Origen (DO) inspectors. Serrano hams are first salted for about two weeks to draw off excess moisture, then washed and hung to dry. Finally, they are air-cured, usually for between one and two years, during which time they can lose up to fifty percent of their weight. They are not smoked during the curing process, nor are any artificial flavorings or colorings permitted. Serrano hams contain less moisture than their French and Italian counterparts and the natural curing process gives rise to a unique aroma and flavor.

Cut into thin slices, it is usually served as a tapa, but can also be incorporated into soups and other dishes, such as croquettes with ham. **JAB**

Taste: *Deep pink in color, the ham has a salty tang and a sweet flavor, which increases the longer the ham has been cured. It must be eaten at room temperature.*

The low moisture content of Serrano ham—Spain's celebrated meat product—adds to its intense flavor. »

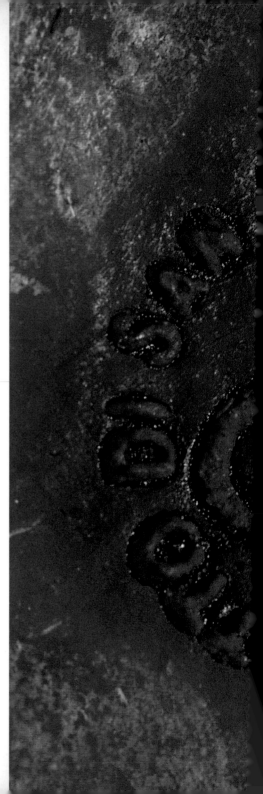

Prosciutto di San Daniele

Prosciutto di San Daniele is a mouthwatering cured ham from the town of San Daniele, in the beautiful Friuli region of northern Italy. The hams benefit from fresh mountain winds and warm Adriatic Sea breezes, which combine to create the ideal microclimate for curing. The high altitudes and dry air give the hams a wonderful, unique flavor and texture.

Salting and drying is a method of preservation that goes back to ancient times and prosciutto di San Daniele (DOP) is still made along those same lines. The thighs of Italian-bred pigs are trimmed and hand massaged weekly with a dry salt cure for a period of one month, before being washed and air-dried for between one and two years. During the drying period, the hams lose up to thirty percent of their original weight. Prosciutto di San Daniele carries a DOP certificate, which insures the hams meet strict criteria governing each stage of production.

Sliced wafer thin and served as antipasto with bread, the ham makes a superb accompaniment to juicy fruits such as melon and sun-ripened figs and is particularly delicious with pasta. **LF**

Taste: *Reddish pink in color, with a pronounced, deliciously savory aroma and glorious silky smooth texture, prosciutto di San Daniele melts in the mouth.*

Two digits stamped on prosciutto di San Daniele identify the ham-maker. ❯

Jambon d'Ardenne

Spalla Cotta di San Secondo

A sixteenth-century engraving by Peter Brueghel the Elder illustrates the virtue Prudence with peasant women preparing hams to be salted. In the Ardenne, the wooded region that extends across the borders of Belgium, France, and Luxembourg, hams were a central part of the rural economy. The pigs would forage in the woods in spring and summer, before being slaughtered and cured for ham in winter.

Famous hams are still produced in the region from carefully reared pigs, and the use of the name is protected. The best Belgian jambon d'Ardenne is prepared not only by salt-curing but by smoking. The curing mix always includes salt and juniper—"poor man's peppercorns"—and often garlic, shallots, and other spices. The hams are smoked over beech and oak from the Ardenne and allowed to ripen slowly. Although jambon d'Ardenne is normally eaten raw, it can also be desalted and poached to produce cooked hams that can baked in pastry afterward. This developed from the habit of serving a ham baked in sourdough at the *kermesse*, or carnival, before Lent. **MR**

The region of the pig par excellence lies north of Parma, Italy, embracing the towns of Brescello, Colorno, Zibello, Busseto, Polesine Parmense, and, specifically, San Secondo. There, during the last week in August, the annual *fiera della spalla* (fair of the pork shoulder) is celebrated. A delicacy that is little known outside the select circle of connoisseurs of typical niche products, spalla cotta is produced in relatively small quantities and traditionally eaten in the summer, after a period of maturing.

The composer Giuseppe Verdi was a discerning gourmet who loved the produce of his native region. He often served spalla to his publisher Giulio Ricordi. In two letters, one dated 1872 and the other 1890, the composer describes the way to prepare the meat. "Put it in lukewarm water for about twelve hours, which will remove the salt. Then put it in cold water and boil it over a low heat, so that it does not break up, for about three and half hours. To check when it is cooked enough, stick a toothpick in the meat and if it goes in easily, the shoulder is cooked enough. Leave it to cool in its own broth and serve." **HFa**

Taste: *When raw, the smokiness dominates Belgian jambon d'Ardenne. Cooked on the bone, it is firm textured and very salty, with complex, well-developed flavors.*

Taste: *Spalla is a particularly fragrant and very tender ham with a delicate warm spiciness. It is at its best served lukewarm, in thick slices.*

Spalla cotta, a speciality of the Parma lowlands, is found in delicatessens deboned and ready to serve. »

Lountza

Wędzonka Krotoszyńska

Lean and flavorsome, lountza is a smoked pork tenderloin popular in Greek and Cypriot cuisines. It is typically served cold in slices as an aperitif or as an appetizer, but is also delicious fried or broiled, and is often offered hot as part of a selection of traditional meats in Greek and Cypriot restaurants. Visitors to Cyprus should sample lountza alongside the circular sesame-coated bread *koulouri*.

To make lountza, pork tenderloin is marinated for about fifteen days in a mixture of local dry red wine with salt and spices, usually coriander, cumin, and black pepper. The tenderloin is then pressed and dried; with commercially made lountza this process is done by machine and then the tenderloin is transferred to special smoking rooms called *kapnistiri*. As the meat smokes, it dehydrates further. The home preparation of lountza, however, is still alive and well, using time-honored recipes that have often been kept a closely guarded secret within a family or village for generations. Artisan-made lountza is smoked over the aromatic branches and leaves of local Mediterranean herbs and shrubs. **LF**

The seven-syllable mouthful Wędzonka krotoszyńska refers to an uncooked, cured, smoked pork cut best described as the back tenderloin portion rimmed with bacon. Although the Polish town of Krotoszyn had a pork butchers' guild by the start of the fifteenth century, the term "Wędzonka krotoszyńska" was not coined until the 1960s.

To make these raw hamlike loins, the pork cuts are rubbed with salt and a sprinkling of saltpeter, snugly packed into barrels to cure, and then smoked. Hardwoods such as oak or beech are preferred, but some producers try other flavor twists by adding pine or fir logs to the fire, along with such herbs as juniper, rosemary, and nettle. The result is a luscious, fragrant marbled cut, reddish brown on the outside and a uniform pink on the inside, with a thin strip of white bacon fat.

This country-style delicacy, which has numerous devotees at home and abroad, is delightful eaten with rye or dark bread, pickles, and condiments, such as horseradish, *cwikla*, or mustard. It can also take the place of ham or bacon with fried eggs. **RS**

Taste: *Lightly smoked and deliciously tender, lountza delivers a savory, although not overly salty, flavor with a gentle spicy kick and a fragrant suggestion of herbs.*

Taste: *Wędzonka krotoszyńska has a lovely, deep, cured-pork flavor with smoky undertones. It has a firm, slightly resilient texture typical of most uncooked, cured meats.*

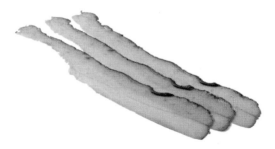

Lardo di Colonnata

Legend has it that when Michelangelo traveled to Colonnata to procure marble for his sculptures, he also treated himself to generous amounts of this once-forgotten, now world-famous *salume*. For centuries lardo served as a filling for bread and fed quarrymen excavating the Apuane Mountains. Later, nineteenth-century anarchist groups took their pigs with them to their mountain hideouts and carried on the traditional method of seasoning.

Shortly after slaughter, the lard is extracted from around the pig's spine, sliced into rectangular blocks, and stacked within porous marble basins (*conche*) that are left in the town's naturally humid caves. The walls of the *conche* are rubbed in garlic and the bottoms covered with sea salt, herbs, and spices; ground black pepper, rosemary, freshly peeled garlic, and sea salt are introduced between each layer of lard. Depending on which jealously-guarded family recipe is used, aniseed, coriander, nutmeg, cinnamon, oregano, or sage can also find their way into the *conche* before they are sealed. The seasoning process takes at least six months. **JM**

Taste: *Finely sliced lardo di Colonnata (IGP) is most delicious when served on bruschetta. The intense, salty meat contrasts superbly with the bread's crunchiness.*

Westphalian Ham

Westphalian ham might not be as familiar as the hams of Spain and Italy, but it is certainly up there with the best of cured pork. Succulent and flavorsome, with a lightly smoked edge, it comes from pigs that have been raised on acorns in the Westphalia Forest, in the far north of Germany. The production of Westphalian ham is still based on traditional methods and each stage is meticulously controlled to maintain quality. The variety of pig and their habitat are important criteria, and the acorn-rich diet gives the animals a particularly lean body mass and fabulous eating properties.

To draw out the excess moisture from the meat, the hams are hand-salted in a dry cure to which herbs and spices have been added. The hams are then washed and hung to mature in temperature and humidity-controlled chambers for anything from six to twelve months before being smoked slowly over beech wood and juniper branches.

Westphalian ham is delicious served in very thin slices as an appetizer and marries particularly well with sweet, juicy fruits such as melon and figs. **LF**

Taste: *With a compact texture and distinctive smoke and herb aroma, Westphalian ham has a pronounced saltiness superbly offset by a mild nuttiness and gamy overtones.*

Tiroler Speck

Speck is a delectable, juniper-flavored cured ham produced in the Alto Adige, an area often referred to as the South Tyrol because it lies to the south of the Austrian and Swiss Alps. An area of stunning natural beauty, it combines alpine landscapes with clear mountain air, and provides the ideal microclimate in which to cure Tiroler speck (PGI).

Like other cured hams, speck grew from the need to preserve meat for the winter months and it has been made since the fifteenth century in Italy and Austria. The especially selected legs are boned and trimmed before being immersed in herbs and spices, including salt, pepper, rosemary, juniper berries, bay, and pimiento, for about three weeks. The whole process is carried out by hand, and the hams are turned regularly to insure the flavors are evenly absorbed. The legs are then cold-smoked and left to mature in controlled temperatures and humidity levels for about twenty-two weeks.

Tiroler speck is more like German ham than Italian prosciutto. It is excellent with crusty bread and a glass of wine, but is also good in salads. **LF**

Taste: *Thinly sliced Tiroler speck has a mouthwatering, melt-in-the-mouth quality with slightly herby, savory notes that are balanced with a soft smoky edge.*

The Tyrol offers perfect conditions for curing ham. »

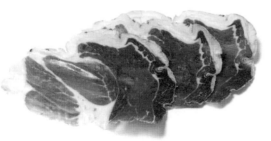

Bresaola dell'Ossola

Bresaola is the name given to an air-dried meat product that is mostly made in the Valtellina area of Lombardy, in northern Italy, from raw leg cuts of beef that are salted, spiced, and then hung to dry.

Its lesser-known but exceptionally distinctive and delicious cousin, bresaola dell'Ossola, comes from neighboring Piedmont. While the name might be similar, bresaola dell'Ossola utilizes salt veal rather than beef, flavored with a marinade of white wine, sugar, pepper, thyme, rosemary, bay leaves, cinnamon, and cloves. Following the ancient practice of preserving meat to eat throughout the year, bresaola dell'Ossola is traditionally made during winter. The veal is trimmed of fat, marinated, and sheathed in natural intestine before being hung up to cure in a cool, well-ventilated atmosphere.

At the end of the curing process, the meat has an appealing deep red hue and a gloriously piquant aroma. It is high in protein, low in fat, and rich in iron. Typically it is served in paper-thin slices, at room temperature or very slightly chilled, as part of the antipasto course. **LF**

Bündnerfleisch

Bündnerfleisch is a dry-cured beef from the Swiss canton of Grisons, whose origins lie in the alpine inhabitants' desire to preserve the best parts of their cattle to eat during the winter. Bündnerfleisch has also become a registered brand name, and is guaranteed as genuine only if marked with the label "zertifizierte GGA ABCert (SCES 038)."

Free from fat and sinew, it is made from the fascia (connective tissue) of beef and flavored with salt, spices, and alpine herbs. The meat is layered in containers and stored for three to five weeks at near to freezing point, with the layers rearranged weekly to insure even seasoning. The meat is then washed in wine before being kept for another five to ten days at a low temperature before the drying phase, which can take from five to seventeen weeks at temperatures of a maximum of 64° F (18°C). Bündnerfleisch's rectangular shape comes from it being pressed during the drying phase to distribute the moisture. It is usually eaten thinly sliced, sometimes with an oil and vinegar dressing, or diced and added to soups, fondues, and raclette. **CK**

Taste: *When thinly sliced, the tender texture of bresaola dell'Ossola has a melting quality and the rich flavor is redolent of the distinctive aromatics in the marinade.*

Taste: *Bündnerfleisch has a delicate texture and a deep, rich, full-bodied flavor with a hint of the Swiss Alps suggested by the subtle herb and spice seasoning.*

The maturing period of bresaola dell'Ossola gives the lean meat its characteristic deep red color.

Pastirma

What bresaola is to Italians, pastirma is to Turks. Air-dried beef, though sometimes made with buffalo meat, it is eaten across the region that once formed the Ottoman Empire. Legend attributes its creation to Turkish horsemen who carried meat in their saddlebags, which became pressed as they rode. Historians believe it was already being eaten in Byzantium (present-day Istanbul) when it was the capital of the Greek-speaking Roman Empire. Also known as *bastirma*, the Greeks call it *pastourmá*.

Since the seventeenth century, when it was praised in Evliya Çelebi's *Book of Travels*, the finest pastirma has been linked to Kayseri in Central Anatolia. Unlike bresaola, which is normally prepared with boned sirloin, up to twenty-six different joints of meat are used for the preparation. After boning, the beef is scored, salted, washed, and air-dried. During the process it is rubbed with a spicy paste of paprika, garlic, cumin, and fenugreek (*çemen*). Early in its maturation, the outer surface is reddish, but this turns brown with aging. Sliced finely, it is eaten raw, but it is also lightly broiled or added to bean stews. **MR**

Mocetta

This exquisite cured meat comes from Val d'Aosta, in Italy, a diverse and wonderful Alpine region that incorporates rugged mountains, glaciers, forests, and rivers. Originally, it was made from the leg meat of local wild goats, but now the animals are one of a number of protected species that roam the Parco Nazionale del Gran Paradiso. Instead, these days, mocetta is usually made from the meat of domesticated adult cattle, although at certain times of year venison is sometimes used.

The legs are usually prepared for curing by hand: the meat is trimmed of fat and the veins and sinews are removed. The legs are then cured in a mixture of aromatic mountain herbs and left to mature for anything from one month to a year. Dark and delicious, mocetta is typically sliced into thin strips and served as an antipasto dish, either simply on its own or with a drizzle of extra virgin olive oil. Although it works well as a filling for ravioli, it is not generally considered as a meat to cook with; subjecting mocetta to heat destroys its delicately balanced flavor and texture. **LF**

Taste: Freshly cured pastirma is like a spicy carpaccio with a paprika taste that is typical of Turkish food. The flavors tend to mellow and become rounder as the meat dries.

Taste: Lean and tender, mocetta has a fine texture and saltiness that gives way to a well-balanced gamy flavor. It combines well with walnut oil and dark rye breads.

Alpine cattle are now used to make the cured meat mocetta, which once came from the leg of a wild goat. »

Smoked Ox Tongue

In an epic, sixteenth-century Rabelaisian banquet of over 100 dishes, wedged between "calves fry" and a "cold roast loin of veal," the giant hero, Pantagruel, manages to find space for some smoked ox tongue.

Pickling ox tongues in brine and then smoking them, mirrors the process of making bacon. Adding nitrite, or in the past saltpeter, to the cure gives the tongue the vivid red color that accounts for its Gallic name *langue à l'écarlate*. The technique of curing and smoking it has been practiced from the eastern frontiers of the former Ottoman empire to the western edge of Europe and thence to the Americas. Jewish cooking also has many recipes for corned ox tongue.

In French cuisine, it is more often served hot with a rich sauce. But, it is sold cold in the northern town of Valenciennes, where charcutiers prepare *langue de boeuf Lucullus*, sliced smoked tongue held together with layers of foie gras. In Britain, pressed tongue was, along with the cucumber sandwich, an integral part of the polite institution known as afternoon tea, although not always smoked. **MR**

Taste: *The ox tongue itself has a firm texture, whereas the root is much softer. The smoke adds a piquancy to a taste that is reminiscent of corned beef.*

Zebra Biltong

When the Boer pioneers set out from the Cape of Good Hope on their Great Trek into the interior during the 1830s, they needed provisions to last on their journey. The salted, dried meat they produced from their cattle and from game they hunted on their way came to be known as biltong.

While most commonly made from beef today, during the hunting season biltong is also made from venison and other game such as ostrich, giraffe, and, more rarely, Burchell's zebra. The meat is rubbed with a salt mixture that generally contains crushed coriander seeds, vinegar, and sugar, often along with saltpeter (potassium nitrate). It is hung in a draft to air-dry. Once dry, it is rubbed again, then returned to dry more.

Good-quality biltong should be dark and dry on the outside, but translucently red on the inside when cut into thin slivers. If kept dry, it will remain good for months without losing its flavor. In days of yore, it was wrapped in cheesecloth once dry and hung inside a chimney for its flavor to be enhanced even further by smoke. **ABH**

Taste: *Biltong has a pungent, gamy scent and a savory, salty tang. Zebra biltong has additional flavor, while the interior has an unusually deep red hue.*

Biltong hangs to dry in the South African wind. When dried in the sun, biltong becomes extremely hard. »

Llama Charqui

Llama charqui is cut, pressed, salted, and dried llama meat. It is made in South America, where the llama roams across the high plains of the Andean mountains in Chile, Brazil, Peru, and Bolivia, and where the animal has long been prized for its wool, leather, manure, and as a pack animal.

Llama charqui's origins lie with the Incas—the word *charqui* is from Quechua, the ancient Inca language. This has been anglicized to become jerky, the term now widely used for various forms of dried meat The Incas stored rations in *tambos*, or inns, along the trails that stretched across their empire, such as the one leading to Peru's magnificent ruined city of Machu Picchu. The control of dried llama meat was essential to the success of the Inca civilization, which depended on a regular supply of protein to feed its growing urban population. After the Spanish conquest of the Andean peoples in the sixteenth century, the llama population declined drastically, and with it the consumption of llama meat. However, dried llama meat still provides nutrition for weary travelers, and continues to be traded in the coastal regions.

In South America, beef, sheep, and alpaca are also dried in the air and sun to make charqui. The slave populations of Latin America were largely fed upon dried meat and fish, so both have remained part of the culinary heritage over a wide area.

Eaten in flat, thin slices, llama charqui is high in protein and withstands storage for a long period of time. Indigenous peoples such as Bolivia's Aymara still make it, and the Aymara eat a traditional dish called *olluco con charqui* made from small, potatolike tubers cooked with llama charqui. **CK**

Taste: *Flaky sheets of dried llama charqui have a pleasantly chewy texture. The flavor is both salty and spicy with a rich gamy undertone.*

Suovas

The nomadic Sami people have been preparing suovas, the smoked meat of the Scandinavian reindeer (*Rangifer tarandus*), since ancient times. The Sami are an indigenous people living in Sapmi, an area that spans the northern regions of Norway, Sweden, Finland, and Russia. Their language and culture were shaped by the bitterly cold, harsh environment in which they live. The reindeer is central, indeed essential, to the Sami people's culture and cuisine. Historically the Sami people were nomadic, following the reindeer herd as they migrated annually to the mountains. Many traditional Sami foods, therefore, including suovas, had to remain edible for a long period of time. With winter lasting 200 days of the year in Sapmi, reindeer meat has always been a vital mainstay.

The reindeer herds are now domesticated to a very large extent, however, they still roam free on the open plains of the tundra and graze on a natural diet of grass, herbs, and lichen, so their meat is lean and full of vitamins and minerals.

Suovas means "smoke" in Sami. After salt-drying for at least three days, the meat is duly smoked in the kåta, a cone-shaped, closed timber hut, over a fire of alder, birch, or juniper wood lit directly on the hut floor. The rising smoke cures the meat, a process that lasts for around twelve hours, and it hangs for an additional day to cool down slowly.

After curing, the meat can be eaten either as it is or grilled; it has a delicate but distinctive flavor. This simple food is well known as a gastronomic experience and appears regularly on the menu at the prestigious Nobel Prize dinner. As a starter, thin slices of suovas are served with lingonberry jelly. **CC**

Taste: *The burgundy red meat is aromatic in taste and extremely tender. The smokiness does not dominate the fine and distinct gamy flavor of the reindeer.*

During the lengthy Sapmi winter, reindeer meat for suovas has to dry in very cold temperatures. ❯

Cilantro Leaf

Chervil

One green herb in the garden has become a base flavor in many of the world's cuisines: cilantro leaf (coriander to Europeans). In fact, some estimates rank it second only to basil in volume worldwide. *Coriandrum sativum* in its various forms appears in the records as far back as ancient Egypt, but the leaves have risen and fallen in popularity—perhaps because of a predisposition in some diners to taste a soapy character in the leaves. Yet kitchen use in ancient Greece and Rome and during the Middle Ages is well documented, and a resurgence in modern times has confirmed their culinary merit.

Stacked in bunches next to flat-leaf parsley in a store, the leaves can be difficult to distinguish from their neighbors, but one gentle rub and sniff soon differentiates the two. The larger, lower leaves of the plant are best in the kitchen, whereas the wispy growth on the bolting stems is less pungent and, therefore, less useful. Served raw in spring rolls and fresh salsas, the full brunt of the flavor is obvious. When cooked into curries or soups, it is often added last to preserve the pungent aromatics. **TH**

If tarragon is a pillar of French herb society, chervil is easily the grande dame of the ball. More intriguing and complex than common parsley, it delivers finesse where more boisterous herbs would simply overpower, yet achieves a unique signature. Even in the garden it looks dressed for polite society with its fernlike fronds and delicate white flowers.

Anthriscus cerefolium sits comfortably next to dill and parsley in the Umbelliferae family and the foliage resembles a cross between the two. The rather scrawny roots are occasionally consumed as a vegetable, but the main culinary benefit lies in the young green leaves. The Roman scholar Pliny praised their gentle, cheerful, and warming effects. Because the taste dissipates quickly with heat, the crafty French began infusing chervil into vinegar to preserve the character for cooking. Even with the fresh herb, addition toward the end of cooking is advised. An ideal potency for eggs and fish, chervil adds the right notes of flavor and a brilliant burst of green. It also balances perfectly with chives, parsley, and tarragon in the French blend *fines herbes*. **TH**

Taste: *The herbaceous character of parsley comes with bold citrus overtones and a slightly sharp character. The aromatics are a blend of pepper and mild rosemary or pine.*

Taste: *Faint fennel and licorice flavors come in slowly behind parsley impressions with very mild pepper tones. Fresh chervil is infinitely preferable to dried.*

Wild chervil (cow parsley) originated in the Middle East; it is used in Japanese vegetarian cookery. »

Rosemary

A rosemary bush left to its own devices can overtake whatever package it inhabits. A single brush against its rounded needles, thick with the aroma of pine and camphor, can suggest a similarly overpowering tendency on the palate, but this gnarly old man of the garden can become a gentle giant of the kitchen. *Rosmarinus officinalis* has spawned countless myths and legends. It has been grown to attract friends, valued for its stimulant properties, and worn at funerals as a symbol of remembrance: modern research shows antimicrobial effects that support more mundane historic uses as a disinfectant.

The tender new leaves are preferable to older stems, but even thick stems can be used as skewers on the barbecue to impart flavor. In Spain, bees forage fields of blue rosemary flowers to produce a scented honey. When using fresh leaves, very finely chop small amounts or use high heat to temper the pungency of entire branches. When paired with other strong components such as garlic or sage on a roasting spit of lamb, rosemary will hold its own, but the firing will calm the intensity greatly. **TH**

Taste: *Strong cedar comes through in the aroma and flavor. The palate is slightly oily, with notes of pine, camphor, sage, and hints of pepper. Avoid dried versions.*

Dill

A field of new dill is quietly seductive when first encountered. The light green fronds wave in the most gentle of breezes and invite touch with their delicate leaves. Iran, Turkey, and many European nations have fallen in love with this wisp of a plant and use it in the most delicate springtime cooking.

Easily cultivated, *Anethum graveolens* shoots a tall, fibrous stem upward before seeding. The delicate leaves that branch off this center, also called dill weed, are tender, feathery, and surprisingly tart when eaten fresh. Later in the year, however, dill offers more intensely sour flavors as the seeds develop and its alter ego comes forth: strong, robust, and ready to add a potent culinary punch.

In native northern climates, dill was embraced early and is now the quintessential flavoring for cold-water fish such as salmon. Many Scandinavian cooks use it to brighten sauces based on cream or yogurt almost as other cuisines use salt. Farther south, potatoes and cabbages and other brassicas are peppered with ground dill seed in the robust cuisines of Central and Eastern Europe. **TH**

Taste: *The fresh leaf is subtly sour with green herbaceous character. Dried versions are less complex. The seed tastes stronger with suggestions of licorice and fennel.*

In the Middle Ages dill was used in medicines and witchcraft; it was believed to have special powers. ❯

Moroccan Mint

Holy Basil

Fresh green mint is perhaps the purest distillation of spring. The sheer exuberance of the season seems embodied in this prolific perennial that can overtake garden space almost overnight. While easily grown worldwide, nowhere else has this buoyant leaf found the fame it receives in Morocco.

Most Moroccan growers have planted heirloom seeds gathered from previous crops for generations, leading to great individualistic pride in each farm's production, not to mention uncertainty as to which cultivars and hybrids of spearmint (*Mentha spicata*) and peppermint (*Mentha piperita*) are being produced. What is clear, though, is that the arid soil and intense heat of the North African *terroir* produces leaves that set a global standard for quality and pungency.

Yogurt stirred with mint complements almost any tagine and the mandatory couscous will have at least been steamed over vegetables simmering in a broth seasoned with mint. Fresh mint is also brewed with Chinese green "gunpowder" tea and copious amounts of sugar and then served in small glasses in the ceremony that welcomes every guest. **TH**

This bushy, aromatic plant, known botanically as *Ocimum sanctum*, is revered all over India under its local name of *tulsi*. Whether bright green (*Rama tulsi*) or purplish (*Krishna tulsi*), the divine prefixes underline their sacred place in the Hindu home. The plants are regarded as the earthly manifestation of the Hindu supreme being Vishnu and their leaves are traditionally offered to him during prayers. Often offerings to him are returned to the devotee after worship with tulsi leaves as a benediction. The woody roots of the plant are also used to make rosary beads.

Yet for all its cultural significance, in India tulsi is used medicinally and spiritually, rather than in the kitchen. In Thailand, however, where it is called *kaphrao*, its leaves sit alongside Thai basil and lemon basil as one of the trinity that underpins the national cuisine. Both "red" and "white" leaves are used in traditional curries and stir-fries, most famously *phat kaphrao*, and holy basil is so associated with Thailand in Southeast Asia that its Lao name (confusingly) means "Thai basil." **RD**

Taste: *Bright, sharp menthol notes and a long-lasting flavor are common to all species. The citrus and pepper scent and zing reveal themselves in varying intensities.*

Taste: *The leaves release a strong anise aroma and the juice has a peppery, almost mentholated flavor that is clovelike. It needs to be thoroughly cooked into a dish.*

In parts of India, holy basil is also sold as a tea, which is believed to relieve stress and impart energy. »

French Tarragon

Known as "the dragon herb," genuine French tarragon is a demanding plant. It refuses to grow from seed, must have precisely the soil it asks for, and will deaden the tongue if chewed directly. Perhaps unsurprisingly, it was used as a medicine in ancient times.

Artemisia dracunculus, a perennial that rarely flowers, will form a bushy mass of slender leaves over the hot summer months and recover well from even nearly constant harvesting. It has migrated and naturalized across North America and Europe, propagated by cuttings and division. A relative known as Russian tarragon grows from seed, but lacks flavor and has little value in the kitchen; an unrelated species called Mexican tarragon has similar but less complex tastes and should not be considered a substitute for the genuine article.

French cuisine best uses its namesake tarragon, adding it to bean and lentil dishes, béarnaise sauce, light vinegars, and classic herb blends like *fines herbes*. Beyond French borders, the herb appears in the fish and egg dishes of Scandinavia. **TH**

Taste: *Mint, anise, and licorice all merge with a mild numbing effect when tasting true French tarragon. All leaves, fresh or dried, should be a brilliant green.*

Lemon Thyme

Thyme really needs little improvement to gain status in the kitchen. Savory notes complement meats and sauces well with balanced hints of herbaceous sweetness. Mother Nature, however, is never one to rest on her laurels and gives us yet another permutation of thyme, with the distinctive essence of citrus: lemon thyme.

Thymus citriodorus looks almost identical to ordinary thyme, although it is usually variegated with leaves of pale yellow and green. Although naturalized widely across Europe and North America, lemon thyme is rarely grown commercially and almost never sold dried. What makes lemon thyme special is the strong citrus aroma that swells up from the foliage with only the slightest touch. The aroma crosses into the flavor, albeit not quite so intensely, and without the acidity of lemon juice.

The light flavors of the fresh herb are perfect for fish and shellfish. While roasting and high heat will destroy the lemon character, gentler processes such as steeping into cream sauces or a quick sauté will preserve the special essences of lemon thyme. **TH**

Taste: *Like ordinary thyme, the leaves are camphoraceous and sweet, but with pronounced citrus aroma. The lemon character infuses or evaporates quickly with heating.*

In summer, the variegated lemon thyme shrub has tiny pinkish flowers that are attractive to bees. »

Nepitella

Fenugreek

The lavender blue flowers of nepitella—an opportunistic member of the mint family also known as lesser calamint—have covered the coastal areas of the Mediterranean in summer since Greek and Roman times. Popular as a medicinal herb in medieval times, nepitella has only been cultivated as a culinary herb in the last few centuries.

Calamintha nepeta is a perennial with hairy leaves that look like a cross between spearmint and catnip. Tuscans have long grown the plants for ailments ranging from indigestion to insomnia. Although the leaves can be dried for use as a tea, there is no substitute for the fresh herb in the kitchen.

Since the plant thrives in coastal conditions, it has naturally evolved to complement seafood dishes in Italian regional cuisines. In Tuscany, shrimp and other shellfish often get paired with nepitella harvested wild from the countryside. The leaves are also often used with mushrooms and included in sweet sausage formulas across the entire country. Nepitella can substitute mint successfully in almost any recipe, albeit with more savory overtones. **TH**

Finds of ancient fenugreek seeds suggest that the benefits of the plant were known at least 4,000 years ago. However, rather than using them in curry powders and yogurt sauces, they were being grown to feed early domesticated herds. Over time, both the seeds and leaves successfully graduated from the barn to the kitchen.

Trigonella foenum-graecum was most likely cultivated from wild species in China and India but is now grown globally in almost any dry climate. While the hard, angular seeds are used widely for both flavoring and coloring, the gently rounded leaves are equally popular in India for their nutty, aromatic character. Commonly called *methi*, both the fresh and dried leaves appear in many different dishes.

Classically in India, *methi* is mixed into sauces or cooked into chutneys; it can also be blended into flatbreads like naan. Fenugreek leaves are also very popular in the cuisines of North Africa, Georgia, and southwest Russia, notably in the Georgian spice blend *khmeli suneli*. The seeds appear often in curry spice blends including Bengali *panch phoron*. **TH**

Taste: *Nepitella combines the flavors of sweet mint and savory oregano. A weak celerylike bitterness is present in older growth. It has a mild lemon aroma when first picked.*

Taste: *The fresh leaves taste spinachy with distinct slightly spicy notes of peanuts and caramel. Dried, the green essence is muted and nutty flavors dominate.*

Culantro

Take a handful of cilantro leafs and sprinkle it with pepper, then wrap it in lemon zest: the resulting flavor will be close to the impact of culantro. The name of this Caribbean leaf confuses folk from both sides of the Atlantic. But, although most of its sobriquets, from the English "long coriander," "sawleaf coriander," and "Mexican coriander" to the Hindi *bhandhanya* (broad coriander) or Thai *pak chi farang* (foreign coriander), suggest it is a type of coriander, it is "cilantro," which means coriander leaf. Popular in Thailand, Vietnam, Indonesia, Malaysia, and parts of Latin America, *Eryngium foetidum* has elongated leaves that look much like dandelion greens when growing in low clusters. Fields In very hot climates get shaded artificially to encourage tender growth and reduced flowering because older plants become less flavorsome.

Culantro is used raw in fresh salsas and garnishes or cooked into soups and noodle dishes. In much of the Caribbean and Central America, it anchors *sofrito*, the Hispanic blend of garlic, peppers, and onions, which is the base of countless recipes. **TH**

Ligurian Basil

Liguria sits perfectly poised on the Italian Riviera, where the Mediterranean breezes sweep up to the Alps, creating a funnel of swirling moist and salty breezes that create the perfect microclimate for the region's most desired product: basil.

Basil growing operations in Liguria are still largely the prerogative of the small farmer and have resisted the modernization that has cheapened much of the world's herb production. They mainly grow the Genoese basil strain, named after the region's capital, Genoa, and claimed by some to be a subspecies. The plants are painstakingly tended by hand and are now produced nearly year round with the help of greenhouses to extend the season. Most growers seed fresh crops two or three times per year to allow the leaves to be harvested relatively young: these are the most prized for their delicate flavour.

Other than the famous pesto, which relies on the mildness of the local basil leaves, Ligurian basil appears in recipes all over Italy. The mere fact that most Italians can agree Liguria produces the best basil speaks volumes about the quality of the crop. **TH**

Taste: *It has the flavor of cilantro leaves enhanced by citrus. Bitterness increases and bright notes fade if older leaves are harvested, so dried versions are nearly useless.*

Taste: *Liguria produces a nearly perfect template basil flavor: completely mild without any of the sharp or bitter notes or hints of mint or oregano found elsewhere.*

Chive

Where garlic, onions, or shallots are too strong, or where cooking is not required, chives provide a featherweight alternative. Hundreds huddle together in the herb garden, waving in the breeze like some sort of land-based sea anemone. Delicate, brilliant green tubular stems reach upward and ultimately burst forth striking purple-pink blossoms.

Chives are just one of many things Marco Polo supposedly brought back from his journey to the Far East, but evidence suggests they were cultivated in Europe long before his travels. A related species, *Allium tuberosum*, known as "garlic chives" or "Chinese chives," is, indeed, native to Asia and, as the name suggests, exhibits a stronger flavor in both its flat leaves and its white flowers.

Of all kitchen herbs, *Allium schoenoprasum* could be the easiest to cultivate. The edible flower exhibits all the flavor of the stem but with more pepper, although it is the stem that provides such a delicate accent to many European cuisines. Compound butters, eggs, and soufflés are all flavored with fresh chives. **TH**

Taste: *Fresh chives have a mild onion character and a delicately grassy taste. Although moist and papery thin, their pleasant texture comes close to a crunch.*

Chives are farmed commercially both for their stems and flowers. »

Kinome

Japanese efficiency lets nothing go to waste, and the prickly ash bush that provides sansho (in Japan) and Szechuan peppercorn (in China) as a spice is no exception to this rule. The young leaves of *Zanthoxylum piperitum*, and sometimes of other related species, are pressed into service as both flavoring and garnish, thanks to a mesmerizing combination of spice and citrus.

The leaves must be young and tender to be used as an ingredient: they provide a vibrant lime-meets-pepper character along with some of the signature shock to the palate that Szechuan peppercorns offer. In older growth, the texture is tough and the flavors dissipated. Individual leaves have a bright green color and wrinkled, serrated edges, and most commonly appear in markets as intact fronds on the stem or packaged leaves carefully plucked from the branch. Dry versions are nearly nonexistent and of little or no value to the chef. Preparations in Japanese cooking range from a fine shredding of leaves as a garnish in soups and sushi to flash frying in oil or using as a base for a paste. **TH**

Mitsuba

Of all the cuisines in the world, Japanese is probably the most artistic. Every element is placed with care and intent to emphasize the delicate nature of the craft, like a single long stem of mitsuba, tied into a decorative knot as a garnish.

Cryptotaenia japonica, sometimes called Japanese chervil, Japanese parsley, honewort, or trefoil, shoots forward long, spindly stems up to 18 inches (45 cm) in length terminating in a flat trefoil leaf. Both the leaves and stems are edible with the latter turning a delicate pale green as the plant matures. Farmers sometimes cover the stems with soil or straw as they grow or cultivate the entire plant in darkness to blanch it, producing nearly white stems and foliage known as *kirimitsuba*. The plant seeds easily, and seeds are sprouted as an edible.

Mitsuba's flavor is easily destroyed by heat so most recipes call for its use raw or as an addition at the end of cooking, like the leaves that typically float atop a bowl of miso soup. Mitsuba leaves and sprouts can impart a light, chlorophyll-laden taste to sushi rolls, salads, and noodle dishes. **TH**

Taste: *The citrus aroma is mirrored in taste along with pepper, mint, and mild chili on the palate. Slight numbing of the tongue is apparent when the leaves are served raw.*

Taste: *Mitsuba has a delicate flavor, reminiscent of parsley, with faint connotations of chervil and celery leaf. Harvest fresh only hours before use.*

Mitsuba leaf stalks resemble cilantro stems, although the flavor is much milder. »

Shiso Leaf

Nature has delivered to the Japanese an herb almost ideally suited to their cuisine. Shiso—perilla in the United States—has a bold flavor but is not so strong as to leave an otherwise balanced plate off kilter; the palm-sized serrated leaves, in hues of brilliant purple and intense green, could be considered art all on their own.

Although grown in Korea, China, Burma, and much of Southeast Asia, *Perilla frutescens* reaches much of the world painstakingly harvested as individual leaves and packaged with true Japanese elegance for export at a price. For the less particular chef who can suffer imperfect leaves, the plant, which is an annual in the mint family, can be grown from seed, and will yield edible flowers as a bonus. The seeds are also edible—fresh, dried, or pressed to extract their potent oil.

Both the leaves and seeds impart their unique flavor to pickles and marinades or are pounded into regional spice mixes. The large ornate leaves may be fried in tempura or included as part of sushi service; in Korea they are used as a wrap for food. **TH**

Taste: *Shiso leaf has strong citrus aromas much like grapefruit, which soften on the palate, accompanied by decidedly green herb tastes of chive and mint.*

Kaffir Lime Leaf

If there is a signature flavor that sums up Southeast Asian cooking, it is most certainly kaffir lime leaf. Any food stall of merit in the region will have a stash of fresh leaves on hand, if not a nearby tree for regular harvests. Pounding them into fresh green curries with cilantro, chiles, and lemongrass is a daily chore that is a cornerstone of the cuisine.

The bifurcated double leaves, the knobbly, almost juiceless fruit, and the long, spindly branches give an indication that *Citrus hystrix* offers something different from the citric norm. It is the thick, fresh leaves with their singular, pungent taste that are most commonly used in the kitchen, whether infused into stocks or minced into dishes. They are sometimes found dried, but the process turns them pale, and they should be used only as a last resort.

A technique common in Thailand is to flavor sea salt with minced kaffir lime leaves, in sealed jars to preserve the aroma. Kaffir lime leaf also makes a notable appearance in Vietnamese *pho*, a gently simmered broth that marries the taste with lemongrass and white pepper. **TH**

Taste: *Kaffir lime leaves must be steeped or abraded to release their flavor, which is reminiscent of tart lime zest. The aroma is strong and distinctive.*

In addition to its culinary uses, the kaffir lime is an attractive bush with fragrant white flowers. ❯❯

Lovage

Neapolitan Parsley

Lovage cannot decide whether to be a herb, a spice, or a vegetable. For chefs who have discovered its flavors, perhaps the correct answer is all three.

In Roman times, the likes of Apicius called for *Levisticum officinale* widely in cooking, while Galen, more prosaically, recommended it as a cure for wind. The foliage resembles celery leaf in both shape and taste and can be harvested regularly from the hollow, ribbed sems that easily reach 5 feet (1.5 m) in height. Both stems and roots can be used as a vegetable; the leaves can be used as a herb or added to salad; the seed-fruits that ripen on the umbrel of yellow flowers can be collected and dried as a spice, much like fennel.

The flavors of lovage in its different forms are well suited to an enormous variety of dishes; the leaves in salads, the seeds in pickles, and the stems simmered into soups, for example. For fans of the flavor, one traditional rustic Italian preparation calls for stems and roots sautéed as a vegetable to be spiced with ground seeds, making a trilogy of lovage on a single plate. **TH**

Often known as "celery-leaf parsley," this giant member of the parsley family can grow to just over 3 feet (1 m) in height, with stems so thick they can be eaten like celery. Like the well known flat and curly-leafed parsleys, and the lesser-known Hamburg (root) parsley, Neapolitan parsley (*Parsley Gigante di Napoli*) is one of the *Petroselinum crispum* species, and a member of the celery (Umbelliferae) family.

It is not to be confused with the more common flat-leafed variant that is often known as Italian parsley, and is also a key ingredient in many Middle Eastern cuisines. Neapolitan parsley looks very different. Its large, broad, glossy green leaves are smooth with indented edges.

Neapolitan parsley has long been grown in the areas around Naples and is particularly prized in southern Italy. The leaves have a lovely aroma and are much appreciated for their pungent flavor. The stems are generally eaten in much the same way as celery, added to soups and sauces or blanched and served as a vegetable. It has a particular affinity with salty and blue cheeses, beef, and fish. **LF**

Taste: *Celery leaf flavor dominates. The stems are like pleasantly bitter cabbage; the roots are dill-like; the seeds are mildly sweet; and the leaves have a light bitterness.*

Taste: *The sweet aroma and fresh but pungent flavor display well-defined essences of parsley that are gently enhanced by distinct celerylike eating qualities.*

Fields of lovage are common to Europe, where the shrubs grow equally well in sun or shade.

Rau Ram

Originally a wild perennial that tends to spread voraciously throughout any warm undergrowth it could find in the South Asian tropics, rau ram is one of the most interesting herbs found in the lush greenery of Vietnam. Despite this vigorous growth, it rarely escapes to kitchens outside the region.

Also known commonly as Vietnamese cilantro and Cambodian mint, *Polygonum odoratum* has slender, pointed green leaves are almost as valuable for their characteristic aroma as they are for their flavor. This has led to wider cultivation as an essential oil crop in Australia and India, and is contributing to wider availability as a fresh leaf herb outside the South Pacific. Dried leaves have almost no culinary value.

Malaysia, Thailand, and Indonesia all use rau ram, but Vietnam embraces the leaf most heartily as fresh spice, salad green, and culinary ingredient. Rau ram is such an integral component of laksa that it is known as laksa leaf in Malaysia. In addition to being added to soups, it can also be wrapped into spring rolls, or pounded into fresh curry pastes. **TH**

Taste: *The peppery taste of fresh cilantro meets sweet spearmint in rau ram. These flavors are complemented by mildly bitter components much like celeriac.*

Curry Leaf

Despite its English name, and European botanical name, the curry leaf has nothing to do with either Europe or that beloved British condiment, curry powder. *Murraya koenigii* takes its title from a pair of eighteenth-century European botanists, Johann Andreas Murray and Johann Gerhard König, but has an indispensable role in Sri Lankan and southern Indian kitchens under its respective names of *karapincha* and *karuveppilai.*

Although used in north India and in northern Thailand, too, the curry leaf tree is emblematic of South India. Here most homes grow at least one for the leaves that are plucked fresh for the day's menu. Daily a distinct citrusy, yet pungent, smell wafts through homes as curry leaves and spices sputter in heated oil. In South Indian cuisine, the leaves temper staple vegetarian food; in Sri Lanka, they add bite to dry meat dishes. The leaves perk up traditional soups (*rasam*), lentils (*sambhar*), and vegetable stews, plus coconut chutney, pickles, and even buttermilk. Recent research has indicated that the curry leaf might be beneficial for diabetics. **RD**

Taste: *Fried when fresh, the edible leaves release a spicy-citrusy aroma and a peppery flavor. Freeze or refrigerate rather than drying to preserve their subtle characteristics.*

The colors and aromas from the numerous bowls of spices make a most attractive market stall. »

Boldo Leaf

Smyrna Bay Leaf

Markets in the remote Andes of Chile and Peru are tiny bastions of economic opportunism. Merchants there can shift from selling parkas to potatoes within a week depending on what becomes available. One of the more frequent wares to arrive on their stalls is a native leaf called boldo.

While the leaves are the principal flavoring element of the evergreen tree *Peumus boldus*, which looks much like a large bay laurel, it also produces small green berries that are dried and consumed much like peppercorns. It is now cultivated more widely around the Mediterranean, particularly in North Africa, mainly for medicinal uses, although chefs are slowly discovering uses in the kitchen.

In its native regions, boldo is used both as an addition to slowly simmered dishes and as a wrapper to infuse flavor into grilled meats. Larger leaves are discarded after cooking, but tender young leaves can be shredded finely and consumed directly after wilting from the cooking heat. Boldo leaf is also brewed as a tisane by itself or added to the classic South American herb tea, *yerba mate*. **TH**

Bay leaf is a foundation of flavor across most modern cuisines. Its perfume can underpin more complex creations but, as with most foundations, you need to seek out the strongest base material you can find. With bay, that means a trip to Turkey, specifically the hills around the port of Izmir (formerly Smyrna), where the conditions are tailor-made to produce the perfect leaf.

Through the long Turkish summer the bay trees soak in the sunlight; in the fall, drying conditions perfectly concentrate the flavor. Batches of leaves are combed by hand to select the specimens that will become the top grade. Free of blemishes and still slightly pliable, these are intensely fragrant when fresh and remain so for up to a year.

Turkish bay seems able to remind cooks just why *Laurus nobilis* has gained such culinary prominence. Where more pedestrian sources seem weak and pallid, Smyrna produces a deep, rich character that could be a reference point for even the most demanding chefs: it is as likely to appear in classic French stocks as in American meat rubs. **TH**

Taste: *Like a blend of bay and mint, yet slightly more bitter on the palate, the larger fresh leaves have a strong resinous odor that cooks away slowly.*

Taste: *Smyrna bay leaves have the strong herbaceous taste of thyme and the bitterness of celery. An intense camphoraceous, sweet aroma wafts from fresh sources.*

Bay trees thrive in hot conditions and produce tough evergreen leaves that are usually dried in the shade. »

Rue

Salam Leaf

The human palate registers flavors as a mixture of sour, salty, sweet, and bitter. Naturally occurring ingredients rarely key just one of these receptors, but rather tempt several simultaneously. Not so with rue, a herb with an ancient history that could perhaps be the perfect reference point for bitter.

In ancient times, its medical and culinary virtues were highly praised. Pliny and Hippocrates made reference to rue, whereas Apicius used the plant in many of his recipes. Later, it was used for sprinkling holy water—hence its name "herb of grace."

A bushy evergreen that lends its name to its botanical family—which includes both lemons and oranges—*Ruta graveolens* has a foul aroma that is known to repel insects, animals, and some humans. While still cultivated for medicinal uses, culinary applications are rarer than in the past. In the Mediterranean it is cautiously used as a bitter component in salads, and flavors a bitter version of grappa, the Italian distilled spirit. Medical warnings exist against consumption in large quantities and skin rashes can appear after contact with the plant. **TH**

One of the signature flavors of Indonesian cuisine that bewilders Western palates, the scent of salam leaf (known locally as *daun salam*) appears in the whirl of aromatics that emanate from almost every door along the alleys where local restaurants cluster. A member of the myrtle family, *Eugenia polyantha* produces elliptical leaves about twice the size of bay leaves with a resinous feel when fresh. Despite their common name of "Indonesian bay leaves" and some similarities in usage to bay laurel leaves, there is little common ground in terms of flavor.

Leaves can be dried and transported outside growing regions for culinary efforts with reasonable, but very different results. Medicinal uses of leaves, berries, and bark can lead to confusion in the marketplace, but chefs use smell and taste to guide them to the fresher sources intended for the kitchen. Salam leaves feature in everything from stir-fries to sauces and are one of many spices used in the celebrated Balinese dish *bebek betutu*—a whole duck, stuffed, spiced, wrapped in leaves, and slow-cooked underground up to twenty-four hours. **TH**

Taste: *Almost unbearably bitter when tasted raw, cooking reduces rue's intensity. Bitter oranges, celery seed, and raw mustard seed only begin to approach the potent taste.*

Taste: *Fresh leaves have a lemon-meets-cinnamon scent that is mirrored in the flavor. Dried samples are muted versions of the fresh with additional nutty flavor.*

Savory

Epazote

Herbs often gain a reputation both for their abilities in cooking and in medicine. With a plant as fragrant and useful as savory, it is no wonder Pliny and Virgil sang its praises in ancient Rome as everything from aphrodisiac to bee attractant. Shakespeare also found its fragrance worthy of mention.

The genus of plants was named *Satureja* for a rumored affiliation with satyrs, the legendarily libidinous half-man, half-beast creatures. Summer savory, *S. hortensis*, is a more delicate annual, whereas winter savory, *S. montana*, is a hearty perennial. Both are members of the mint family and have slender, needle-shaped leaves that form on sturdy, stalklike stems. Both are naturalized across the Americas and Europe.

In Italy, both types of fresh savory are slowly stewed into bean and lentil dishes, but are also used in dry forms to create herb blends with oregano, thyme, and rosemary. In wider culinary circles, sweeter summer savory is paired with fennel seeds as a common sausage seasoning, and bolder winter savory gets rubbed and roasted on meats. **TH**

Opportunistic cooks in Mexico saw a chance to accent their bean-laden cuisine when they brushed past epazote. The plant both grows like and looks like a weed, and the strong scent of tar pours forth from its wiry, wispy leaves at the slightest touch. Yet, although *Chenopodium ambrosioides* might give chefs pause at first sniff, a long simmer delivers a unique undercurrent of taste that speaks of desert sunsets and Latin feasts.

A hallmark of Mexican cooking is taking plenty of time in the kitchen and nowhere is this more evident than when cooking with epazote. The pungent plant takes hours to mellow into something palatable and beans offer the perfect carrier. Truly a native of the region, it is this secret ingredient visitors often fail to identify in the slow-cooked beans that appear on the table in one form or another from morning through to night.

Epazote finds its way into corn and egg dishes as well, but must be used sparingly. The crushed leaves are often added to the local flour, *masa harina*, when making tamales and tortillas. **TH**

Taste: *Both savories have a peppery tinge with rosemary and thyme notes, but summer savory is more delicate. Winter savory has a sharper, tarragonlike character.*

Taste: *Epazote tastes like the adopted child of caraway and bay. Add a stem complete with leaves to the pot, then remove the stem once the leaves have detached.*

Lemongrass

Pandan Leaf

At a distance, clusters of lemongrass (*Cymbopogon citratus*) in their native habitat look deceptively plain. Long, skinny leaves of an unassuming green fan out from the stem, yet release at a single touch a profuse lemon aroma that has made this pungent plant a staple of kitchens across Southeast Asia.

In Thailand, Laos, and Vietnam, cooks pulverize lemongrass in tall mortars, combining it with garlic, kaffir lime leaf, and other herbs to create a thick curry paste that is integral to their cooking. Island cultures of the South Pacific also cultivate the crop with great success and include it in their cuisines.

Although the leaves have some use in teas and medicinal applications, the fibrous stems and slight bulb at the base of the perennial hold the bulk of flavor. Woody and tough, they are commonly macerated in oils and other spices and removed after infusion. (Similarly, a bundle can be tied and simmered in stock to impart the essence.) More rarely, the outer layers of fresh cuttings are separated to reveal tender young shoots in the middle that can be chopped finely and added directly to dishes. **TH**

One of the mysterious nuances of flavor that highlights Southeast Asian cuisines, this floral leaf has a taste and aroma so subtle it can almost be considered sneaky. *Pandanus amaryllifolius*, sometimes referred to by its family name of screwpine, is cultivated from Thailand to New Guinea for its fragrant leaves. Blade-shaped fronds up to 2 feet (60 cm) in length spread out from a central trunk and are harvested almost year round. When fresh, the leaves are crushed, torn, or even tied into knots before adding to simmering pots to help release their signature taste. In regions where fresh is not available, they might be sold frozen, blanched, infused in water, or as a paste.

Most common in Malay, Thai, and Indonesian cuisines, pandan is commonly found in rice dishes and is often married with coconut. It perfumes sweet treats from ice creams and cocktails to the classic Malay pandan cake, which attains its green color from the leaves. It also pairs well with chicken and fish, either infused into the region's simmering stews or used as wrappers to flavor the meats. **TH**

Taste: *The aroma can be stronger than genuine citrus, while the flavor is a rich lemon without the acidity. Hints of camphor and mint are present in the freshest sources.*

Taste: *Pandan has a floral character that is like a cross between mild jasmine and vanilla. Frozen leaves are often sold as wrappers, but have little flavor remaining.*

Lemongrass can often be seen growing along the edges of bogs or shallow water gardens.

Sweet Marjoram

Trying to navigate the complex family tree of marjoram is like trying to seat bickering relatives at a holiday table without starting an argument. Lamiaceae, commonly known as the mint family, includes potent siblings like oregano and exotic cousins, such as shiso, but it is marjoram, especially the sweeter varieties of *Origanum majorana*, that occupies the role of peacemaker and mediator.

Marjoram is one of the herbs that can easily anchor a garden with almost no effort, whether it be a country acreage or an urban window box. Perennial tendrils of numerous cultivars offer repeated harvests throughout the year. Sweetness seems to diminish from the moment of picking, and fresh is generally superior to dehydrated forms, so growing pots near the kitchen is recommended.

Marjoram marries with tomatoes famously: albeit not so potent as oregano, it provides both a savory and sweet foil for their acidity. All the cuisines that ring the Mediterranean have embraced the herb, either alone or in concert with some of its more rambunctious family members. **TH**

Taste: *Most species start with grassy flavors and finish with mild pepper. Anise, sage, and lemon notes appear midpalate, but tend not to linger as with stronger herbs.*

Greek Oregano

Greece is a nation with a long, proud history, and its gardens and wilderness seem to honor the past. Oregano, a popular herb since at least the fifth century CE, still flourishes amid ancient stones and hillsides. Unsurprisingly, given this long history, the Greeks benefit not only from their sandy soils and ocean influences, but from specific beneficial species, sometimes sold overseas as "wild oregano." The types known as *hirtum* and *kaliteri* gain most favor among locals, but when even individual cultivars from small producers are transported abroad, something is lost that cannot be duplicated.

Fortunately for the chef, bundles of the herb are dried and exported widely. Since the herb owes its flavor and scent to a high content of essential oils, this process does not do irreparable harm and dry sources are still good in the kitchen. Classically paired with tomatoes and other acidic ingredients, Greek oregano can withstand culinary pressure. Fresh pickings work well with rosemary and lemon, while dried bunches can simmer at length without being completely destroyed by the heat. **TH**

Taste: *With deeper herbaceous character than ordinary oregano, the notes of licorice, bay, pepper, and fennel can be individually identified on the palate.*

Greek oregano is a decorative addition to any herb garden and produces pinky purple blossoms. ❯❯

Dalmatian Sage

Lemon Myrtle

Of all the herbs in the kitchen, sage is perhaps the most powerful workhorse. But for the best and most complex version of this bold leaf you must seek out crops from the unique coastal region known as Dalmatia. The balance of sun and sea there elevates the taste well above ordinary garden varieties.

Sage has been credited with a wide range of healing powers over the centuries; however, its impact today is culinary. In Croatia, its earthy depths of flavor blossom to new heights thanks to the mists of the Adriatic Sea. Analysis of essential oils shows that the unique microclimate and historical cultivars have mutated ordinary sage into a herb that is mellower and slightly sweeter than the other *Salvia* species. The tender fresh leaves may be used whole but more commonly are dried then rubbed to remove the stems and create a soft, cottonlike down.

Prized across Europe, Dalmatian sage appears in sausages and cured meats to the north and in pastas and herb blends to the south. Like all sages it makes a perfect foil in compound butters and stronger sauces for roast meats. **TH**

Despite its delicious aromatics, this versatile east coast Australian flavoring is hardly a herb: the parent plant is a rain forest giant that can grow up to 65 feet (20 m) tall. However, in the plantations where cleared rain forest is being reforested, the trees are managed rather like tea.

This traditional Australian ingredient forms the basis of possibly the most widely used Australian flavoring (lemon myrtle sprinkle). It tastes similar to a blend of lemongrass, lime, and lemon oils—all popular flavors on their own—and it is often used instead of, or to enhance, these commodity ingredients. Lemon myrtle sprinkle is successfully used in both sweet and savory applications and its popularity is growing internationally. It appears in herbal teas, bakery goods, beverages, and nutritional supplements as both a functional ingredient and flavoring. In the kitchen, it is best used as a finishing herb in a similar way to cilantro (coriander) and basil. Citral, the active essential oil, boils just above blood temperature, so the flavors are best infused into warm foods. **VC**

Taste: *Mild pine flavors sneak through grassy base notes, hinting at rosemary and peppercorn. Use fresh leaves or find dried versions that do not crumble to the touch.*

Taste: *The palate is predominantly lime with a late hint of menthol, complemented by mild acid, faint anise, and green tea. Initial sweet notes of lemongrass oil.*

Salvia *is a small shrub native to Europe; its spiky flower* ⊘ *is vivid purple in color and most distinctive.*

Filé

Myriad scents permeate the air of Cajun bayous—from the smoke of andouille sausage to the brine of fresh shrimp—but sassafras trees cast a more delicate aroma. Locals dry and grind the multilobed leaves of this tree into filé, the powder chefs use as both flavoring and thickening.

When rubbed, most parts of *Sassafras albidum* will deliver at least a hint of the citrus-meets-earth aroma that first attracted chefs. This scent comes primarily from an essential oil that contains safrole, a substance which, although carcinogenic in large quantities, has appeared in everything from root beer to curative tonics.

Although the powdered leaf is industrially produced for the kitchen, it is small local producers who rub the carefully dried leaf into the delicate fluff most prized by Cajun and Creole chefs for finishing soups and stews. Most notable of these is gumbo, a slow simmer of fresh seafood, okra, and sausage thickened with filé. Experienced chefs stir the powder into a hot dish at service rather than simmer directly for fear of overly mucilaginous results. **TH**

Taste: *Used sparingly and away from direct heat, filé lends a unique base note to dishes. Hints of lime and overtones of sage tinge the palate and—when fresh—the aroma.*

Herbes de Provence

The *garrigue*, with its scented hillsides overgrown in flowers and herbs, is the wilderness at the heart of Provence. In the past—and still for some today—it was part of the culinary folk culture to pick bundles of fresh herbs from the *garrigue* and leave them to dry in the sun. During the 1960s, therefore, "herbes de Provence" came to mean a blend of dried herbs and lavender, harvested in the south of France.

Since 2003 a French Label Rouge denotes a blend that contains twenty-six percent each of savory, rosemary, and oregano, nineenteen percent thyme, and three percent basil, a mix that is adapted to char-grilled foods and also to some classic Provençal daubes and sautés. Unlike the original blends, however, these are cultivated herbs, with controlled levels of essential oils that are dried mechanically, rather than by the sun, and others, not covered by the quality denomination, can be equally or even more interesting. Look also for a gourmet mix of wild savory, thyme, and fennel seed with marjoram, rosemary, and lavender, which is close to the earliest herbes de Provence concept. **MR**

Taste: *The scent of herbes de Provence is in-your-face fragrant, with contrasting sweet and harsh aromas. They bring the perfumes of the garrigue to cooking.*

This classic blend is famous worldwide and is particularly popular packaged in traditional sacks. »

Bird's Nest

While it was almost certainly extreme hunger that drove the first person to eat bird's nest, it took great skill and imagination to turn it into a delicacy.

The nests are made by a species of swiflet that build their nests on the high walls of caves. Instead of building their nests from twigs, feathers and grass, as other birds do, these swiflets, which are native to Southeast Asia, use a gummy substance that has been variously identified as a regurgitated seaweed or the bird's own saliva. It hardens as it dries and helps the nests adhere to the sheer, cave walls. Harvesting is perilous as it involves scaling the high, slippery cave walls, but some entrepreneurs are enticing swiflets into empty buildings to build their nests, making collection much easier.

Bird's nest is considered highly nutritious and is central to the classic Chinese dish, bird's nest soup. As it is so easy to digest, it is often given as a tonic to the elderly. Whole nests that are almost entirely free of feathers and other foreign matter are the most highly prized, but even the broken nests are extremely expensive. **KKC**

Taste: *Bird's nest is virtually tasteless—it takes on the flavor of the ingredients it is cooked with. The nests are soaked and cleaned before being made into desserts and soups.*

A man collects nests for bird's nest soup in Thailand. ❯❯

Horseradish

Wasabi

For cooks, horseradish is one of the hardest ingredients to work with. When grated raw, this white potent root causes the eyes to run far worse than the most pungent onion as the volatile oils that deliver the intense horseradish "hit" are released into the air. These dissipate with exposure: the finer horseradish is ground, and the sooner it is used after preparation, the hotter its taste will be. (It also discolors quickly once cut, unless brushed with lemon juice or vinegar.)

The edible root of the plant *Armoracia rusticana*, horseradish is used in all European cuisines, but is probably most popular in northern, eastern, and central Europe. In Britain, it is rarely used, apart from in a cold sauce that is traditionally served with roast beef, but in Germany and Austria in particular, it appears in different sauces or grated by itself as an accompaniment to a range of meat and fish dishes. Mixed with cream, it is the ideal partner for hot-smoked fish such as eel or trout. Shredded and combined with apple, it serves as a spicy relish for cold meats. **MR**

Traditionally served as a fiery condiment to sushi and sashimi, this knobbly green root, or rhizome, is sometimes known in the West as Japanese horseradish. The largest producer of the precious fresh root in Japan is the Izu peninsula, where the mild climate and high annual rainfall create the perfect conditions for wasabi growing, and plants grown here are said to have the finest flavour.

Clean, flowing water is essential to the wasabi root's growth, which makes for a rare and expensive product. Demand far exceeds supply and most of the ready-prepared wasabi pastes and powders on the market are based on horseradish. Cultivation has, however, begun in the United States and Canada.

The heat of wasabi comes from the substance allyl isothiocyanate that is released when the root is grated. The best restaurants in Japan bring a grater made of sharkskin (its closely serrated surface creates a fine pulp) to the table for it to be grated immediately before eating, as the pungency of fresh wasabi decreases after only fifteen minutes. Wasabi pairs well with beef, raw fish, rice, and seafood. **SB**

Taste: *At first taste, horseradish has a flavor that is similar to hot mustard, but with a fresher, raw element. Texture depends on how finely it is shredded or grated.*

Taste: *Fresh wasabi has a creamy, fragrant, and peppery, yet crisp, vegetable taste with a touch of sweetness. It is surprisingly milder than the horseradish-based products.*

Although wasabi is largely grown for its root, the leaves and stems are also harvested and processed. »

Young Ginger

Myoga

Ginger is well known for its sharp, almost hot bite. The large twisted hands are peeled of their rough, leathery skin to reveal fibrous yellow flesh that howls with intensity. Yet this boisterous, gnarly root was once the tender delicacy known variously as "young," "spring," or "green" ginger.

China and Australia produce the most young ginger. The new growth of *Zingiber officinale* appears in China during March and April, and in Australia during September and October, and looks very different from older versions. It has pale, translucent, edible skin, tender flesh, and pink protruding shoots that would otherwise become the stems of a new plant. This form of gingerroot is delicate enough to create the best grades of preserved ginger, the version sold in syrup as a delicacy, and the candied variety known as crystallized ginger. In Japan, young ginger is also the basis for *amazu shoga*, the thinly sliced, pink, pickled ginger served with sushi and sashimi. In Chinese cuisines, the young root is often shredded like a vegetable for use in salads and spring rolls. **TH**

The plump, pink, immature flower buds of a member of the ginger family, picked before they open, just on the verge of emerging from the soil, make a very special vegetable. In Japan, they are eagerly sought after when the season begins, despite the belief that eating myoga makes one forgetful.

It was probably the Chinese who introduced *Zingiber mioga* to Japan, where it grows wild in damp, mountainous areas to the north. There the shoots are covered with a natural mulch of thick vegetation, which shields them from the light, meaning the buds are pale. In cultivation, they are grown under substances such as sawdust to achieve the same effect. The Japanese harvest is strictly seasonal, although growers in New Zealand and Australia are beginning to fill the gap in the market.

Myoga is eaten raw, usually very finely sliced as a garnish or part of a salad, or minced as an ingredient in dipping sauces. Not only the buds but the young stems, called *myogatake*, may be pickled: they are often served alongside grilled fish, much as spring ginger shoots might be. **SB**

Taste: *The sweet essence of ginger is very present, despite the absence of heat. Only look for fresh, young ginger in the spring and avoid any with signs of green growth.*

Taste: *Crisp and juicy, as crunchy as celery, myoga has none of the heat of true ginger, but is strongly aromatic. An attractive trace of bitterness makes it quite unique.*

Galangal

Any Southeast Asian market on the planet will have a giant pile of fresh gingerroot. If you look to one side of this old favorite, you will most likely find one of its lesser-known cousins, galangal, which is just as essential to their culinary sensibilities. It was widely used in Europe during the Middle Ages, only later falling into disuse as ginger became more available.

While a number of different rhizomes are sometimes sold as galangal, there are two varieties that matter—lesser and greater galangal (*Alpinia officinarum* and *Alpinia galangal* respectively). As they are named for size, not potency, it is lesser galangal that is the hotter of the two. The flesh of greater galangal is a light creamy yellow covered by a translucent skin, whereas lesser galangal has reddish skin and flesh of a darker, more amber hue. Both are fibrous much like common gingerroot.

Most southern Pacific cuisines use galangal extensively. The roots can be shredded for salsas and marinades or ground into a paste as part of a curry. Fresh forms are preferred, but dried galangal can be used in stock and soup seasonings. **TH**

Taste: *A cross between gingerroot, pepper, and mild mustard in flavor, the lasting impression is similarly hot with hints at horseradish and citrus.*

Turmeric Root

Fresh turmeric, shredded or pounded, adds a much more vibrant flavor to any dish than the cooked, dried, golden orange powder found in most spice racks. Thinner and darker than its common ginger cousins, one scratch of the thin skin reveals the bright flesh within, which deeply colors anything it touches, including the cook's fingers.

Fresh *Curcuma longa* draws its intensity from the curcumin in the root, a compound that has been studied extensively in recent years, although the dried version also has many culinary uses. A large part of the crop, however, is destined for use as a dye, both in and out of the food industry; K. T. Achaya, in *A Historical Dictionary of Indian Food* (1998), records its use as a depilatory in India.

In its homeland of Southeast Asia, fresh turmeric is used widely, particularly in Thai cooking, where it is treated not dissimilarly to its cousin ginger. It is also used fresh in season in many parts of India, although the vegetarian Jains forbid it to be consumed, because it grows underground and might, therefore, contain life forms. **TH**

Taste: *Fresh turmeric has intense, mustardlike overtones and a light peppery character. Dried forms exhibit these flavors when fresh, but are prone to lose potency over time.*

Gilroy Garlic

In California, the land of big surf and movie stars, laidback attitudes apply to almost every aspect of life. Not so in the small valley of Gilroy, just south of San Francisco, where garlic is a serious obsession. Annual summer festivals attract thousands with Miss Garlic pageants, garlic marathons, vendors hawking everything from garlic sashes to garlic juice, and veritable parades of people in garlic-shaped hats. Pickled, smoked, as a base, or as a topping, garlic is incorporated into every food imaginable—even ice cream.

Where less-desirable garlic can be bitter and flat in taste, Gilroy offers crops that seem to sing a medley taken straight from the California sun. Their sweetness and heady aroma dominate the palate, while their depth of flavor and richness of color excels. Numerous varieties of *Allium sativum*, ranging in color from pure white to pale purple, are grown for harvest and Gilroy processors offer it in forms from fresh peeled whole cloves to dehydrated powders. The bulbs work wondrously in the myriad cuisines where garlic is essential. **TH**

Taste: *Notably more pungent than other sources, Gilroy garlic can be sharp, almost hot, when eaten raw. The sweetness blossoms when roasted.*

An old-fashioned mural advertises Gilroy garlic. »

Borage

Crowned with a handful of star-shaped purple flowers, and covered in tiny hairs—almost as if it were wearing a poorly knitted sweater—borage stands in many gardens like a tall, fuzzy soldier. In Europe, it was once known both as a herb and as a vegetable, and credited with the capacity to relieve depression and impart courage. It was one of the first crops to reach the New World in the fifteenth century and is still widely cultivated in Spain.

The crisp, clean taste of raw borage leaves and flowers make them popular additions to salads. The leaves can also be blended into cold sauces, most famously, perhaps, the German spring blend of seven herbs, *Frankfurter Grüne Sosse* (Frankfurt green sauce), or cooked as a vegetable, as in the Italian *pottaggio alla rustica*, where they are parboiled and combined with olive oil, garlic, anchovies, salt, pepper, and wild fennel. The mature stems have a mild bitterness much like cabbage or celeriac when cooked, but still manage to maintain some of their fresh flavors. Hairs toughen with age and should be removed when possible. **TH**

Taste: *Curiously similar to cucumber in flavor, there are also hints of sweet mint and cilantro leaf in all parts of borage. The candied stems taste a little like licorice.*

The sun rises over a field of borage in Wiltshire Downs, England.

Lavender

From pantry to apothecary, lavender seems to evoke something deep and lusty in the mind, yet with playful, floral accents on the surface.

The French have historically adapted the heady tastes in the kitchen by including lavender flowers in Provençal herb blends and adding them to roasting meats. More recently in the New World, the coastal climates of the Central Pacific have hosted a burgeoning agribusiness with new cultivars entering the market in a wide range of potencies and flavor profiles, amid all the farmers' market pleasures that are a cliché of Mediterranean climes.

Numerous subspecies of *Lavandula officinalis* are easily cultivated in home gardens, but care should be taken with drying that concentrates the essential oils. Some people will register an unpleasant soapy taste if the essence is too strong or too much is added to a dish. Uses range from sweet and savory pastries to saucissons or jellies, whereas bakeries sometimes preserve whole flowers in sugar. When cooking, infuse flowers in cream or stock to temper potency. **TH**

Taste: *The intense savory character that underlies the floral scent is accented with faint pine and cedar flavors. Subtle sweetness is found only in fresh spring growth.*

Bolivian Rainbow Chile

New Mexico Chile

The color blue does not tend to suggest edibility. When it is accompanied by a full spectrum of other hues—red, orange, green, purple, and yellow—often on the same plant, and at the same time, wise gourmets tread gently. With the Bolivian Rainbow, this caution is well-placed. The searing heat of its vibrant fruit can stop almost anyone in their tracks.

After a dramatic bright purple flowering, small green peppers appear. They will ultimately mature to orange, then red, having turned purple, blue, or yellow, for the intervening period. The leaves, too, can morph from green into eggplant hues. Never more than 2 inches (5 cm) long, the tulip-shaped peppers look almost like strands of multicolored Christmas lights strung on the foliage of the parent plant, a botanical color explosion that has made the pepper almost as popular an ornamental plant as it is an edible one.

Like most heirloom varieties of chile, the Bolivian Rainbow is usually seen in the old cuisines of Central and South America where it is used sparingly in citrus-themed sauces and fresh salsas. **TH**

In the red deserts of New Mexico there is practically a civil war over who grows the most flavorful chiles—Chimayo to the north or Hatch to the south—and precisely what it is that makes them so distinguished. Scientists at New Mexico State University are studing these and other capsaicin questions, yet both villages serve up distInctive versions of *Capsicum annuum* with a flair that seems to engulf the entire culture at harvest time.

Local farmers arrive at regional festivals as if to a culinary rodeo, in a ragtag fleet of pickup trucks and tractors with huge burlap sacks of chile pepper bounty colored a rainbow of reds, oranges, yellows, and greens. Festooned in cowboy hats and snakeskin boots, they seem to come as much for bragging rights as the featured produce.

Small farmers extract the most from optimal growing conditions, and, whether fully ripened red or the prized new green chiles, the flavors have a brilliance and complexity not found elsewhere. Roadside stalls offer the braids of fresh or dried chiles known as *ristras* (strings) in most shapes or sizes. **TH**

Taste: *Fruit are ripe when dark red. Behind the intense heat, residual flavors suggest sweet plum. Even when underripe the heat is considerable: treat with respect.*

Taste: *A full range of heat can be found married to characteristic plum, apricot, and cranberry flavors. Color indicates ripeness but all are equally useful.*

Teardrop-shaped and vividly colored, the chiles ❮ *resemble a string of Christmas tree lights.*

Habanero Chile

Chipotle Chile

With all chiles, it is important to understand the difference between heat and flavor. Mild, fruity types—like ancho chiles with their notes of plums and raisins—have a very different place in the kitchen from sharp, hot species. But only the related Scotch bonnet chiles can even come close to habanero for delivering nature's hottest punch.

The chemical compound capsaicin registers as heat on the human tongue, and it is measured on a scale developed by Wilbur Scoville about a century ago: the hottest chiles run to about 300,000 Scoville units, and both habaneros and Scotch bonnets register near this point. While removal of the interior webbing and seeds can lessen the intensity, the flesh alone still packs considerable heat.

Despite the heat, habaneros develop unique flavors as the walnut-size fruits ripen from green to orange. Even small amounts can deliver spice to salsas and cooked sauces. The severe heat is also used in bottled condiments that combine the flavors with everything from vinegar to carrots. Use great care when handling all varieties. **TH**

When fairly pedestrian chiles like jalapeños meet vast quantities of charcoal and smoke, they take on a new life and a new name: chipotles, shriveled nuggets of heat and flavor that can transform even the most mundane dishes into dining that somehow expresses the essence of barbecue. Depending on the region, base chile, and smoking time, either the larger, brown *ahumado* or the smaller, deep crimson *morita* will emerge from days of smoking and drying.

Smoke, heat, and chiles have a natural affinity that takes little effort to cultivate, and can generate obsessive enthusiasm among fans, spawning legions of hot sauces, barbecue rubs, salsas—even sweets. Chipotles are sold either as smoke-dried whole pods or preserved in a tomato-based *adobo* sauce. Both offer the deep barbecue tastes, but the former seem more pungent, whereas the latter offers the benefit of the infused sauce. Heat levels vary widely, mirroring the range seen in the parent chiles, but canned versions are typically milder. When using dried chipotles, the seeds and stems should be removed to avoid bitter tastes. **TH**

Taste: *Sharp citrus notes manage to escape from behind the dangerous heat, with essences ranging from apricot to lime. Drying accentuates a mild smoky character.*

Taste: *The flavor of chipotle is almost pure smoke, which eliminates almost all of the original vegetal, sweet chile flesh tastes. The heat can vary from mild to severe.*

An age-old scene of smoking chipotles. Aztec markets sold smoked chiles five centuries ago. »

Barberry

There are not many cranberry bogs in Iran. But if chefs want a tart red berry to add punch to stews or rice dishes, they reach for barberries (*zereshk*): it is these that crown the top of *shirin polow*, the fruity pilaf known as "the king of Persian dishes."

The tiny berries cluster under round, waxy leaves protected by sharp thorns: they ripen to a deep red and are sun-dried by processors, which concentrates their tartness many times. Their many species were once to be found growing wild all over North America and Europe, where their high pectin content made them popular in jams and jellies.

But barberries can host a fungus known as wheat rust, which can decimate grain crops. This led to extensive eradication efforts in North America and Europe—most notably in the early twentieth century—and, although rust-resistant strains of wheat have been developed, wild barberries remain rare on those continents. In Asia, the berries are still cultivated as an inexpensive tart component for soups, stocks, and desserts. They can be powdered and used as a spice. **TH**

Taste: *Dried barberries are extremely tart and sour, but regain a slight sweetness when rehydrated and cooked. The tiny seeds can be gritty if not cooked thoroughly.*

Amchur

In deconstructing the flavor of almost any fruit, the tastes and textures that define it are to be found hiding behind layers of sweetness. Mango creates so much activity on the palate it begs such an exercise for sheer curiosity. Conveniently, therefore, chefs across India took the sour green fruit and dried them in the sun, creating amchur.

Long slices or fine powder made from dried green mangoes are sold in almost any Indian market. Commercial varieties, which can be spelled in a number of ways or simply sold as "mango powder," occasionally include preservatives and coloring agents. Whole unripe fruits are also sold in growing areas and home chefs can manufacture their own amchur with simple sun-drying, although care should be taken to avoid mold and bacteria.

Like fresh green mangoes, amchur is used in dishes across India. It acts in much the same way as citrus and tamarind: it is not only a souring agent, but a mild tenderizer and, as such, is used in marinades for meat and fish. Starchy vegetables also benefit from the lift sour amchur adds to regional sauces. **TH**

Taste: *Simultaneously sweet and sour, the taste is reminiscent of mild tamarind and bitter melon. The texture is always fibrous and sometimes tough.*

Black Lime

It was probably a happy accident in the desert that first gave the culinary world black limes. Where fresh citrus can be sparse or distant, necessity becomes the mother of invention and nothing is wasted, not even the heat of the day. Traded over long distances, black limes are perfectly preserved for the trip and have scattered themselves among the cuisines of North Africa and the Middle East.

Persian limes, *Citrus latifolia*, are briefly brined and then dried in the intense sun until the exterior turns a pale tan color. Inside, the process leaves them almost hollow and completely black. Here they transform from fruit to pungent spice: the dried peel and inner flesh retain their original piquant flavor, but have become intense with processing.

Moroccan tagines and Middle Eastern lamb stews will often call for whole black limes to be tossed in for the full cooking time to add acidity throughout the dish. Ground, the tart powder can be used as a table condiment in place of salt or included in dry rubs and more complex spice blends as a souring agent. **TH**

Taste: *A dry, tart character is concentrated well beyond normal citrus levels, but has little lingering taste or aroma. Black limes can be cracked and simmered or ground fine.*

Bush Tomato

Although Australian Aborigines once made this fruit flourish in fired ground, today the knee-high, prickly bushes sprout along the edges of dirt tracks. The term bush tomato, which is colloquial Aboriginal and dates back many years, is used in Australian cooking to denote one member of the Solanaceae, *Solanum centrale*, which is generally picked by hand as dried, blueberry-size fruits that are pale to dark tan in color.

Alongside another fifteen Solanum species, the bush tomato was a staple food for Aborigines in central Australia, who also call them "desert raisins." They make an exceptional chutney that transforms the classic bruschetta into the colloquially popular "bushetta." Always look for at least three percent bush tomatoes in the ingredients.

The fruit have a very strong taste that can morph from strong to unpalatable very quickly. For the forager, bush tomatoes growing in rocky ground in association with mulga (*Acacia aneura*) are a lot more bitter than those growing in sand: the bitterness can generally be balanced with a little salt. **VC**

Taste: *When picked dry, these are pungent berries with a flavor that resembles caramel without the sweetness, somewhere between tamarillo and beef stock powder.*

Fennel Seed

Fennel seeds are a culinary chameleon. The aroma is savory, like licorice, yet when bitten they deliver a surprising sweetness. Almost as confirmation of this dual life, they appear in many of the world's most balanced spice blends, notably Chinese five-spice and panch phoron, and seem able to bend to the will of whichever dish they inhabit.

In India, where they are known as *saunf*, they appear not only in curries, but coated with sugar and served as a breath freshener at the end of meals. In Europe, where they are still used occasionally in sweets, they play a starring savory role as the key spice in many sausages and cured meats.

Used widely in both cuisine and medicine since ancient times, this easy-growing perennial has since spread across most of the globe. The seed fruits form on broad umbels after a brilliant yellow flowering late in the season. They are ridged and distinctly green in hue when at their freshest, but mute to pale yellow or even brown with age. They are perfect candidates for dry toasting before use, which amplifies both their sweet and savory aspects. **TH**

Taste: *Characteristically dominated by licorice and anise, the freshest fennel has considerable sweetness in the finish. Stale samples will have a noticeable bitterness.*

Fennel grows wild and in abundance
◈ *on the arid Sardinian landscape.*

Fennel Pollen

Plants are wonderful machines. They pump the pure essence of their environment up from the earth, blend it with sun and rain, and distil all this goodness into their growing efforts. The most aromatic parts of this endeavor usually land in the flowers to lure insects, but something much larger than a bee has discovered the flavor benefits of fennel pollen.

The spice originated in Italy, where sausage makers wanted a lighter impression of fennel for their goods. Opportunistic farmers discovered it was the pollen and anthers that held the most interesting tastes. Harvested by hand and meticulously processed, this magic dust packs considerable punch and some have compared its potency and price with saffron. Although it is traditionally collected in only a few areas of Italy, the profit potential has given rise to new producers in the western United States and wider global availability.

The aroma of fennel pollen is almost as valuable as the flavor. When added at the very end of cooking—or even at the table—and gently stirred into warm dishes, it delivers a heady waft. **TH**

Taste: *This amber and green mottled powder is light, fluffy, and extremely potent. The sweetness is closer to anise than fennel, and there are subtle bites of clove.*

Hungarian Paprika

Pimentón de La Vera

The Habsburg kings certainly got several things right. Soaring architecture aside, it was during their era that paprika was introduced: the sweet pepper spice destined to become the "red gold" of Hungary.

For a few weeks in late autumn, the valley around Kalocsa becomes a hive of activity with the arrival of crates of fresh brilliant red pepper pods. They are destined to be dried and ground by local processors whose techniques have passed down through the centuries. Some focus on using only the most tender flesh, whereas others concentrate on balancing the flavors found in different batches. They produce a bewildering range of varieties and grades, ranging from honey sweet to noticeably hot, with a sheer cultural focus and dedication to taste that outclasses the rest of the world.

Besides the well-known Hungarian *goulash*, a paprika-laden stew, the crimson powder is key to several regional sausages and meat rubs, too. Care should be taken to find the freshest versions just after harvest, because shelf life diminishes over the year leading up to the next season. **TH**

Smoked paprika, or *pimentón*, made from ground red chile peppers, is one of the essential ingredients in Spanish cooking, used in everything from chorizo to soups, from octopus to fried eggs. There are different intensities of flavor depending on the variety of pepper used—from sweet and mild (*dulce*), to bittersweet or medium hot (*agridulce*), and hot (*picante*). The seeds are always removed so *pimentón* is never as hot as the original chile.

It seems that within a generation of Christopher Columbus's first voyage to the New World, chiles were established in Extremadura, Spain. Today, the descendants of those original peppers are cultivated throughout that region, in the alluvial soils along the river in La Vera. Each fall the small, round peppers are harvested manually, then placed in special drying houses where they are smoked over oak wood for about two weeks and hand-turned every few hours. They are then carefully stone-ground to create *pimentón de La Vera,* a regional specialty that has been granted a *Denominación de Origen* in recognition of its unique quality. **JAB**

Taste: *A base of sweet pepper can be pronounced or tempered with savory heat. The aroma of this intensely colored powder is a key indicator of freshness.*

Taste: *With an intoxicating smoky aroma, almost sweet flavor, and silky texture, pimentón adds color, depth of flavor, and a variable degree of spiciness to any dish.*

Even the spiciest smoked paprika is not as fiery as its vivid red color would suggest. »

Fresh Green Peppercorn

Tellicherry Peppercorn

Peppercorns add punch to almost every cuisine and the familiar dried kernels are an essential flavor on the modern palate. They grow, like miniature grapes dangling from the vine, in dense bunches under wide, waxy green leaves in subtropical climates. Picked and utilized while green and immature, the fresh berries of the peppercorn plant, *Piper nigrum*, deliver a flavor unlike any other.

Village markets sell the smooth green berries, still clustered on a vine 4 to 8 inches (10–20 cm) in length. Because they spoil so quickly, many nations brine or pickle them in an attempt to ship them overseas. Preservation, however, tends to mute the bright character of fresh fruit and the flavor is often overshadowed by vinegar and salt. Even air-dried and freeze-dried versions fail to deliver the incomparable taste of the spicy fresh fruit.

Thai cuisine has embraced the use of fresh green peppercorns in curries and other piquant sauces. The French have also taken up the banner of both fresh and preserved versions, but transportation difficulties tend to limit their global availability. **TH**

Peppercorns can be called the most important spice of all time. They have been the drive behind exploration, the focus of conquests, and the basis of trading empires: they remain a culinary essential.

Highly prized for its black pepper production is Tellicherry, a mountainous coastal region in southwest India. In the high, cool air, green berries are allowed to mature to the largest size achievable before they begin to ripen and turn scarlet, and are then plucked by hand. Oxidization turns them black; drying gives the characteristic dimpled texture; they are then sorted and graded. The auction houses here are some of the oldest in the world and their time-honored techniques serve as a guarantee of quality.

Sarawak in Malaysia and Muntok in Indonesia are particularly famed for their white peppercorns. These have had their outer husks removed before drying, producing a spice that lacks initial bite but lingers longer on the tongue. Although ripe red peppercorns are sometimes sold, either brined or freeze-dried, these should not be confused with the pink peppercorn, a wholly different species. **TH**

Taste: *Green peppercorns offer a sunny interpretation of pepper with little lingering on the palate. Strong herbs like rosemary and tarragon can be perceived in the aroma.*

Taste: *The freshest black peppercorns have a heat in the finish much like chiles and complex aromatics that range from clove to allspice. White versions are more mellow.*

Today peppercorns are plentiful and inexpensive.
In the fifteenth century they were a rare luxury spice.

Pink Peppercorn

Szechuan Peppercorn

Christmas trees decked in holly do not usually spring to mind in the blazing heat of South America or the Indian Ocean. Yet, the Brazilian pepper trees that flourish in both regions, covered in emerald foliage with clusters of tiny pink berries, easily conjure the name "Christmas berries" by color alone.

Despite their name and appearance, species of *Schinus terebinthifolius* are not related to true peppercorns and gentle crushing reveals the differences quickly. Not a hard solid, but rather a paper-thin shell around an inner seed, the berries disintegrate into flakes with little effort. (Some classify the species as mildly toxic, so care should be taken before random harvesting.)

Réunion Island is a French overseas territory and chefs there adopted pink peppercorns into their refined culinary art as beautiful dots of delicate flavor in true French tradition. The flavor is amazingly sweet, with only hints of their namesake peppercorn pungency. This makes them a natural addition to lighter sauces and delicate seafood, but also a perfect table condiment. **TH**

Spices easily manage to convey taste and aroma, but it is a much rarer feat to evoke an actual physical response. The heat of chiles is a well-known example of this, but so too is the remarkable Szechuan peppercorn, which has the unique effect of numbing the tongue when eaten directly.

The precise relationship between the Japanese spice known as sansho and the Chinese spice known as Szechuan peppercorns has been the subject of much debate, intensified by regional sensitivities. Both are made from the seed pods of the prickly ash bush, *Zanthoxylum piperitum*, or sometimes other *Zanthoxylum* species; both share a flavor profile; the only difference is that sansho is a more refined version than many Szechuan peppers. When buying, choose sources free of stems, seeds, and flecks of fruit.

The flavor and texture of Szechuan peppercorn is essential to classic Chinese five-spice powder and substitutions never quite match the original. As its name suggests, the fiery cuisine of Szechuan embraces the spice, utilizing it in hot-and-spicy dishes such as *Ma Po Tofu*. **TH**

Taste: *Pink peppercorns should be bought whole. They taste sugary sweet when eaten directly. There are mild camphor notes and a very faint peppery bite in the finish.*

Taste: *All the zest of lime is mixed with the aromatics of cardamom, the heat of pepper, and the feeling of chiles in a crescendo that climaxes in the unique numbing effect.*

The attractive berries of pink peppercorns do
◔ *not give off their sweet aroma until crushed.*

Sumac

Colorful piles of ground spices populate Middle Eastern bazaars, but visitors can be perplexed as to the source of the burgundy powder that tastes of salty lemons and cranberries. This spice is actually the ground fruit of the sumac shrub and has become the ultimate condiment from Istanbul to Morocco.

Wild crops of the clustered, tiny, berrylike fruit spring up all around the Mediterranean, but *Rhus coriaria* is most readily embraced in Arabic kitchens. Sumac is rarely found whole, although where chefs demand freshness some merchants will grind to order. Older berries become moist, so salt is required during grinding, resulting in tiny flakes. Occasionally the berries are pressed to form a potent juice that is used sparingly, like vinegar.

Used pure or in spice mixes like *za'atar*, sumac can often replace lemon or lime as the souring element in recipes. When rubbed on lamb or stirred into hummus, the bright flavor lifts otherwise heavy cuisine just as citrus might. The tart character lends itself to yogurt-based sauces and combines well with olive oil as a topping for flatbreads. **TH**

Ajowan

With its dry, arid flavor it is appropriate ajowan flourishes in desert lands: it can stand intense heat both in the climate and the kitchen. Set against the searing chile pastes of northeast Africa, its pungent taste and tarry aroma survive where lesser flavors, such as cumin, might disappear.

Trachyspermum ammi produces seedlike fruits shaped like a squat cumin seed with a characteristic hairlike "tail." The fruits are beige to brown with slight green hues in fresher sources. Produced and sold in Africa, the Middle East, India, and South Asia, they have yet to attain global popularity, probably because of their overwhelming taste. The key flavor in the seeds is thymol, also present in the herb thyme, which is sometimes extracted from the crop for use in toothpaste and digestive aids.

Most chefs toast or fry the seeds to temper the intensity into a mellower savory taste. Nan or poppadoms benefit from a small measure of ajowan, which relaxes in the high heat of baking. Also called Ethiopian cumin, ajowan appears in the country's famous berbere spice paste. **TH**

Taste: *The fresh spice is tart and puckering with hints of tamarind. Low heat preserves its intensity best, but larger amounts hold up to grilling and baking.*

Taste: *Somewhere between caraway and celery seed in taste, the thymol can create a domineering thyme flavor. The off-putting tarry aroma is lessened by cooking.*

The berries of some species of North American sumac ◊ *trees were once used to make a lemonade drink.*

Aleppo Pepper

Caraway

Aleppo, a plateau city in northwest Syria, has a secret that has escaped the fortress walls. The surrounding valley produces a mild fruity chile pepper many regard as the perfect balance of sweet, sharp, and heat. The microclimate benefits from the Mediterranean trade winds and has transformed what could otherwise be an uninteresting pepper into something brilliant and sublime.

Ancient trade routes first deposited the pepper locally in the late sixteenth century, but over time the local crop proved more mellow and interesting than original plantings. Often imitated in parts of nearby Turkey, the genuine article from Aleppo still offers an elusive taste that is only mildly hot and distinctly sweet. Even the crimson color seems oddly unique when compared to more pedestrian peppers.

Aleppo pepper was often sold ground with some salt added as a preservative, a practice that continues today. A dish of Aleppo pepper at the table for sprinkling over roast vegetables, hummus, or oiled flatbread will exemplify what has made the subtle flavor so popular across the Middle East. **TH**

An unassuming brown color with little aroma, you would never suspect some of the flavor antics caraway manages later in life. Even in the fields, the plants are reluctant to show their true intent. The feathery greens that look much like their relatives fennel and carrot take two whole years to produce their "seeds" (technically, fruit). The Netherlands, Germany, and Poland remain important producers of good-quality caraway, and significant crops also come from the central plains of Canada.

The tiny seeds are curved and ridged, and do not immediately release their pungent taste. Toasting dry or heating in oil solves this problem and most uses include this as a necessary step. Distillers have long used *Carum carvi* to flavor spirits, most notably brennivin in Iceland. More mildly, the seeds add an accent to cheeses, and even feature as a flavor note in preserved fish. In the hands of bakers, caraway helps define bold rye bread. It is a classic addition to sauerkraut and potatoes and is frequently credited as a digestive. More infrequently, the roots of the plant are enjoyed as a vegetable. **TH**

Taste: *Mild heat follows light fruit notes akin to apricot and cranberry. The ground form is a minuscule flake rather than a fine powder, and makes an excellent condiment.*

Taste: *Caraway has a dry, woodsy, anise-led character. Uncooked, it displays considerable bitterness and a lack of sweetness; intense heat alleviates these characteristics.*

Caraway plants produce their delicate white flowers in their second year of growth. ❯❯

Allspice

Restaurant perfection in the Caribbean is often little more than a grass hut and a fire pit perched on the beach. Tourists and locals sit side by side waiting to see what the chef can concoct from the local market offerings of the day. Whether fish or chicken, tomatillos or plantains, it is a sure bet that everything will be laced with the local favorite: allspice.

Native to the islands and a staple of Central and South American cuisine as far back as the Mayan empire, the deceptively plain brown berries of *Pimenta dioica* hold a sharp jolt that awakens the taste buds. Commercial cultivation began in Jamaica, and once Spanish traders brought it to the Old World in the seventeenth century, comparisons with clove and peppercorns began.

Paired with the local Jamaican chiles, allspice is most famous in "jerk," a piquant rub applied to fish, pork, and chicken before they are roasted over coals. Across the Atlantic, the spice became popular in mulling wines when paired with cinnamon, cardamom, and orange peel, and appears in recipes for steak sauces and other table condiments. **TH**

Taste: *Strong aromatics are obvious, similar to clove, but with slightly less potency and bite. Peppercorn notes infuse with menthol and cinnamon hints.*

Roadside stalls sell freshly cooked jerk ❸ *meat as well as the jerk seasoning itself.*

Coriander Seed

Coriander is a remarkable plant for the chef. Every part from its spindly roots to the tips of the leaves is consumed in some form or fashion. The seed-fruits that appear in late summer after a proliferation of white flowers ultimately become the basis for everything from curry to pickles.

The botany of *Coriandrum sativum* is unsettled at best with various cultivars grown for seed crops categorized by shape, size, and region. European and African versions are round and lightly ridged, with the Indian species being smoother and oval shaped. Biblical references and ancient husks found in the archaeological digs of Egypt show some form of coriander seed was cultivated for thousands of years.

Coriander seeds have entrenched themselves in almost every world cuisine. The rich gamut of foods using coriander seeds encompasses Indian spice blends, European sausages, American corned beef, and Asian curries. Often described as "warming," the citrus aroma is nearly as important as the subtle taste, and the prized "white" beers of Belgium rely heavily on that aromatic. **TH**

Taste: *Freshness is key to getting a good citrus aroma and taste from coriander seeds. Newly crushed seeds should exude considerable aroma. Sift out any residual husks.*

Guatemalan Cardamom

Cinnamon

India has been associated with the bold flavor of cardamom, a member of the ginger family, for thousands of years. Sweet and pungent in aroma, the prized sticky black seeds of the so-called "queen of spices" are encased in brilliantly green pods. Somewhat surprisingly, a New World country now rivals India as the world's largest producer of *Elettaria cardamomum*—Guatemala.

In the Middle East, cardamom has long had a symbiotic relationship with coffee. An aromatic brew of the two—known as *kahwe hal* in Arabic— welcomes guests in every home. Guatemala is a key producer of both cardamom and coffee beans, which thrive in the tropical conditions of the highlands, and plantations often mix the two crops. That New World crops can withstand this time-honored combination half a world away speaks to the impressive way in which Guatemala has entered the cardamom market.

Green cardamom can flavor savory stews, curries, and pilafs, as well as sweet dishes and hot drinks. Use sparingly, as a little goes a long way. **TH**

Just beyond the tree line of Sri Lankan beaches the faint aroma of cinnamon tempts spice traders and gourmands alike. Plantations peppered about the southern coasts produce this unique spice, frequently imitated, but never equaled by its more boisterous and severe cousin from overseas, cassia.

The shrublike trees, *Cinnamomum zeylanicum*, send out willowy, thin branches that are peeled of their bark, known as "quills," and rolled into fragrant bundles. Bark peeling approaches an art form, and the trade traditionally passes down the generations. Practiced hands use simple rodlike tools to loosen and cut the inner layers of bark, which are sun-dried, graded, and rolled into final shape. Auctions usher bundles of cut "sticks" into the time-honored spice trade destined for ports worldwide.

Praised by Egyptian embalmers and Roman emperors alike, true cinnamon has myriad uses. Not merely a staple of sweet pastry, it blends into savory dishes equally well. Sticks can perfume rice or curry exquisitely and are essential in classic Indian chai or mulled wine. **TH**

Taste: *Top-quality cardamom pods have a strong aroma of menthol and ginger. Simultaneously sweet and spicy on the palate, seeds are best preserved in their own pods.*

Taste: *True cinnamon exudes a delicate floral aroma, with sweetness and pepperlike heat. It is best infused gently to release essential oils and preserve the aromatics.*

One of the first spices to be used in the Mediterranean, cinnamon was initially only added to savory dishes. »

Anardana

In the Middle East, the heat of the desert often creates as much as it consumes. Reasonable conjecture would say this was the case with anardana, dried pomegranate seed, a spice whose origins are lost in the suns of the past, but whose pleasantly tart and bitter taste has stood the test of time. Wild species from the Himalayas are purported to give the best results because the fruit is so sour.

The juicy, crimson pomegranate segments, known as arils, are separated and laid out in the sun on large tarpaulins. Over five to ten days, their color changes from the brilliant red of the fresh fruit to a dull purple, almost black, and their firm shape withers to a dark smudge around the central seed. Masses of the sticky dried seeds are collected and used as a souring agent, both whole and ground.

In its native land, anardana is often sun-dried at home: because of its residual moisture, the quality can falter quickly. Most popularly found in chutneys and sauces, anardana is also used in baking, blended into a variety of spice mixes, and as a souring agent in curries and soups. **TH**

Taste: *The pronounced tartness, very much like dried sour cherries, is immediate, alongside bitter components from the inner seed. Anardana should never be completely dry.*

Juniper

Open a bottle of gin and inhale. Imagine those same aromas beside the sun-drenched Mediterranean. Now picture hillside cascades of spiked green foliage on twisted trunks and dusty blue berries scattered about. Finally wrap that scent around slow-roasted lamb from wood-fired rotisseries and you have the wonderful juniper of Italy's Amalfi Coast.

Perhaps because some junipers are mildly toxic, or perhaps because the fruits take more than a year to ripen from green to dark purple, the culinary species, *Juniperus communis*, is often overlooked. Not so in southern Italy, where it has been popular since medieval times, when common folk discovered the potent flavor of the berries.

Paired with similarly strong tastes, such as rosemary and garlic, juniper can withstand the intense heat of the grill, the long roasts of the oven, or the pungency of game. Pounded together with peppercorn and allspice, it makes a perfect trilogy of savory, sharp, and sweet. Crushing a few berries in a gin cocktail adds a bright lift that echoes the original distillation. **TH**

Taste: *Dry and arid on the tongue, the scent is distinctly grassy and slightly sharp like cloves. Some subtle bay character shows through. Look for whole, smooth berries.*

The juniper berries are sorted and checked by hand for their suitability for use in gin. ❯❯

Saffron

If you were to plant a few acres of pale purple crocuses, bet your annual salary on the weather, hire hundreds of workers to spend hours plucking the smallest bits from between the petals by hand, then risk the whole lot by drying it over a fire where one mistake could consume the whole affair . . . Well, you would be wasting your time, of course. Experts already do this in the course of bringing saffron, the most expensive of spices, to a wider audience.

This insane risk tends to breed a fair bit of national pride among the successful growers. Along with La Mancha in southern central Spain, Kashmir leads the pack in both product quality and bragging rights, but notable productions also come from Pakistan and Iran.

Although saffron can command extortionate prices even when sold in typically tiny portions, the stigma of the *Crocus sativus* are so potent that only a few pennies worth are needed per dish. Saffron is embraced in the cuisine of the key growing areas, whether as curries or paella, but has been an exotic delicacy outside their shores for centuries. **TH**

Taste: *Arid on the palate when sampled directly, the taste has a deep savory undercurrent reminiscent of bay, but with a persistent floral aroma akin to lavender.*

Traditionally entire families were involved in the harvest. »

Vanilla Bean

Star Anise

The perfume of vanilla envelopes the senses with floral sweetness and conjures images of the tropical forests from which it comes. A stroll through the island plantations of Madagascar is itself a sensory paradise as the large green vines blossom with the orchids that will give way to bunches of seed pods.

Vanilla planifolia thrives not only in the tropical humidity of its native Latin America, but also in Africa and Tahiti. Only the very best beans, or pods, are destined for the kitchen. The long, green fruit are cured slowly with careful drying, twisting, and massaging. Over many months they acquire a rich, black color and shrink to a third of their original size. Second only to saffron in price, the highest-quality beans are shipped around the globe to pastry chefs waiting to unlock their scent and taste.

The moist, plump beans need airtight storage. After splitting lengthwise, the inner pith with its thousands of minuscule seeds can be scraped into batters and sauces to gently infuse. The tougher outer husk still holds plenty of flavor that can be preserved in sugar for later use. **TH**

The dried fruits of *Illicium verum*, commonly known as star anise, are perfect little rust-colored stars, with a polished seed nestled inside each elegant carpel. They form in the middle of the year, after the evergreen tree's prodigious light pink or yellow flowering, and impart a flavor and scent that quite simply defines southern China.

Ancient Chinese herbalists utilized star anise long before modern pharmaceutical companies began harvesting the crops for shikimic acid to use in medicines. But recent battles against bird flu have led to shortages of the crop destined for the kitchen. Culinary star anise is almost exclusively cultivated in southern China, with sporadic production elsewhere in Southeast Asia; the trees take years to mature, which also hinders efforts to expand cultivation.

Chinese five-spice powder relies for its impact on star anise, as do many infused liqueurs, such as pastis. Whole stars are often included in dishes that require long, slow braising and meld their intensity with meat harmoniously. Buy whole, intact stars as a sign of top quality and grind only as needed. **TH**

Taste: *Beans should never be brittle. The rich, floral aroma and taste lean toward sweetness and can have overtones of orange or sherry.*

Taste: *Star anise derives its licorice flavor from the aromatic compound anethole. A strong licorice element with aniselike sweetness is obvious, even in the aroma.*

After harvest, the vanilla beans are spread
❖ *out to dry beneath the Tahitian sun.*

Annatto Seed

Mahlab

Some things in nature beg investigation, tempting us with unusual foliage, deep colors, or unique aromas. For the Mayan priests who used it as a colorant in ceremonials, annatto offered all these. It was probably no accident the brick-colored seeds that nestle within the pods of *Bixa orellana* quickly made their way from pigment to palate.

Handling the raw seeds turns fingertips red so many Central American cuisines impart not only the color of annatto, but, just as importantly, its flavor by means of an oil infusion. Farther north in Mexico, notably in the Yucatan Peninsula, the seeds are used to make a paste known as *achiote*. The taste can create a curious dry sensation on the tongue, but the color it gives to a dish lives up to its parent's nickname, the lipstick tree.

The complex *mole* sauces of Mexico often include annatto, but it can also stand alone as the main seasoning for pit-roasted pork. In coastal regions of Central America, fish are frequently sautéed using only annatto oil. Further inland, it flavors root vegetables and cooked grains. **TH**

The ingenious bakers of the Middle East and Turkey saw a quite literally golden opportunity in a small, wild cherry that grows across the region. Not in the fruit, as one might expect, but in the kernels at the middle that, when dried to a golden brown color in the sun, become the spice mahlab.

Prunus mahaleb, or St. Lucy's cherry, is a large, shrublike tree that is cultivated almost exclusively for mahlab spice production. The deep red fruit is cast off as bitter and inedible, and the pits are split to reveal the soft, inner seed. This will harden as it dries to form an almond-shaped spice with delicate ridges. Many alternative spellings are found on the labels of Middle Eastern markets, but all indicate the same aromatic spice: occasionally processors can miss discolored seeds or other debris so a quick inspection is worthwhile.

The freshly ground seeds are added to breads and pastries, most famously the celebratory Easter breads of Armenia and Greece. As a fine powder, mahlab thickens stews of lamb and grain, and flavors the Middle Eastern cheese *nabulsi*. **TH**

Taste: *Earthy and savoury in taste with a pleasantly mild bitterness, the aroma is of sandalwood or cedar. The red pigment releases easily by abrading or steeping in oil.*

Taste: *A nutty aroma gives way to bitter notes that hint at celery seed and bitter orange. Mahlab loses flavor easily so it is best to buy whole kernels with a consistent color.*

Asafoetida

Black Cumin

Growing in the dusty fields of India, giant fennel looks like it has seen better days. Spare leaves and wiry branches seem to barely hold together and about the only thing worse than the look of the plant is the overwhelming stench of the sap, a foul-smelling veil that hides a culinary treasure.

At harvest time, farmers slit the plant until it exudes a deep amber sap. This coagulates into a thick resin that is malleable at first, but soon hardens into brittle chunks that exhibit the aroma of sulfur. Slow to dissolve in normal cooking, the dried sap garners a litany of colorful pseudonyms, including "devil's dung" and "fetid sap," but is more commonly known as hing powder to local chefs, who utilize its pungency to flavor dishes in the same way Western chefs use garlic.

Whether sautéed in oil or flashed with the heat of a tandoor oven, asafoetida requires an intense heat to dissipate the acrid aroma and leave more mellow tastes and smells behind. Also grown in Iran, Iraq, Pakistan, and Afghanistan, it plays a supporting role in many Indian and South Asian dishes. **TH**

When going in search of this gentle expression of common cumin, the first thing to know is that it is not the completely unrelated nigella seeds often sold as black cumin. Nigella seeds (*Nigella sativa*) are black and angular, about the size of mustard seeds, while true black cumin (*Bunium persicum*) is crescent-shaped, and slightly longer and thinner than its common cumin cousins.

Black cumin's color is, indeed, almost black, tending toward dark brown, while the seeds have the distinct aroma of dried grasses. The plant originates in the wilds of Iran, Pakistan, and northern India, where its scarce nature has earned it the name "royal" cumin. Limited supply means the black stuff costs about triple the price of the more common "white" cumin. Due to its subtle sweetness, black cumin is preferred in the milder dishes of its native regions, especially when little or no heat is present in the spicing as with, for example, lamb korma. Ordinary cumin can be substituted in dishes, but a better solution would include a small measure of fennel seed to duplicate the sweetness. **TH**

Taste: *Asafoetida tastes like sautéed garlic with mildly bitter notes of caraway or fennel. The smell (sulfur, rotten eggs, and dirty socks) is nothing if not distinctive.*

Taste: *Black cumin is like a sweeter version of common white cumin with some slightly mild bitterness in the taste and aroma much like celery or thyme.*

Grains of Paradise

A merchant standing in fourteenth-century Venice literally had the world on his doorstep. With the rise of the city-state's importance as a trade center, all manner of exotica was landing daily. The merchant's task was to create a market for such wares and, in an early example of marketing, "grains of paradise" was coined as the name for these pungent little seeds.

Given the popularity and cost of peppercorns, not much effort was needed to convince chefs to try *Aframomum melegueta*, although elaborate tales of the dragons, elephants, or even Eden to be found at their source helped spur on sales. Almost pyramidal in shape, they arrived in pods about 2 inches (5 cm) in length with fibrous outer husks, so could easily withstand the overland journey from West Africa to the Adriatic coast.

By the eighteenth century, however, their popularity declined, and they had been displaced by peppercorns. Yet, as if to prove the value of a great name, grains of paradise have recently undergone a resurgence of popularity among modern chefs. Traditionally, they are used to flavor meats. **TH**

Taste: Fair peppery heat is mixed with essences of ginger, camphor, and cardamom on the palate. They are best ground only when needed to preserve their aromatics.

Blade Mace

Anyone lucky enough to live near a nutmeg grove knows that it is not merely the familiar nutmeg kernels that offer flavor. Inside the peachlike fruit of *Myristica fragrans*, lacy tendrils of a brilliant scarlet clutch the seed pod tightly in their web. Harvest these strands and you have blades of mace, a spice that captivates the taste buds every bit as well as its partner, nutmeg.

Nutmeg and mace provided the flashpoint for the spice races that initiated the age of exploration, as traders sought a route to the spice's native Banda Islands. Dutch, Portuguese, and English forces fought for supremacy until finally the crops began to spread across the tropics.

Blades of mace have the consistency of tough leather, however, they lose both this and their color fast, drying to a brittle pale orange in a matter of days. For this reason, most mace is processed into a fine powder for global export, but the prized whole blades can be found closer to the modern growing regions of Indonesia, Sri Lanka, and parts of the Caribbean. **TH**

Taste: Fresh blades offer a completely different experience from the pale impression powdered varieties provide. The flavor is similar to nutmeg, yet sharper and more intense.

Arils freshly stripped from the nutmeg fruit are laid out to dry before being processed as mace. »

Cubeb Pepper

As if to echo the tangled climbing vines that produced it, cubeb pepper had a long and convoluted path to follow before it reached the tables of medieval Europe. Traced backward through Venice via the Arabs, across Africa, past India and China, and ultimately to Indonesia, it is no wonder the pepper had an uphill climb.

Sometimes termed "tailed pepper," because of an identifying stem on the dried black berries, *Piper cubeba* originated in tropical Java, from which it was unwilling to stray. This made access to the spice difficult and it was ultimately supplanted by the more easily cultivated common peppercorn. Although popular in Indonesian cooking, cultivation is limited. Minuscule productions, blending with inferior *Piper* species, relegation to medicinal tinctures, and use in cigarettes make cubeb even more unpopular. The few culinary footholds cubeb has found are in Arabic spice mixes like ras-el-hanout and in complex recipes for distilled gin alongside juniper. But the taste is different enough to warrant exploration no matter what route you must follow to find a supply. **TH**

Taste: *Pepper meets ginger and allspice on the palate in a combination that is not as strong as common peppercorn. Cubeb has a bite similar to clove in flavor and aroma.*

Clove

So potent is the taste and scent of cloves that these tiny, unopened buds once divided the globe, as Spain, Portugal, Holland, and England rushed to reach their origins in Indonesia. Cloves were traded as far back as Roman times, via trails that snaked overland through Arabia and India. But these early supply lines were expensive and risky, so the naval powers of the fifteenth century sought an overseas route to the famed spice islands and beyond.

Until modern times *Syzygium aromaticum*, the evergreen tree that produces the clustered young buds that dry into cloves, was cultivated only in Indonesia. Since then it has spread to Sri Lanka, Zanzibar, and Madagascar, among others. Just after the buds turn a dull pinkish hue, they are collected and dried to a darker bronze. (In the freshest batches, the rounded tip is several shades lighter and unmarked by age or travel.)

Used whole, they infuse well and are seen in everything from rice to mulled wine. Ground, their gamut ranges from Indian spice mixes to European sausages and pastries. **TH**

Taste: *Similar to allspice, but with more sweetness and peppery character, the strong aroma is matched with a slight numbing effect from the intense oils.*

Growing on Mount Lawu, central Java, clove trees are used to make kretek, a type of Indonesian cigarette. »

Fleur de Sel de Guérande

Salt pans in the Guérande marshes on the Atlantic west coast of France supply the unrefined, damp, grey sea salt that chefs and bakers love for their cooking. A small fraction of this brackish harvest, like cream on top of milk, is Fleur de Sel (French for "flower of salt"). This is the fine crystal crust on the surface of the drying salt water that will only form if the wind blows from the right quarter. Freshly scraped off the surface, it may be a frosty flamingo pink, but it turns a dull off-white within a day. It has to mature for a year before it is ready for the table.

Refined salt (pure sodium chloride) tastes bitter to a trained palate, whereas unrefined salt contains a cocktail of minerals including iron, magnesium, and potassium. Cooks used to working with the latter put less into their recipes than they would of the refined product. Although chefs tend to prefer the unrefined, grey Guérande salt for cooking, the costly Fleur de Sel is handled with discretion, a final sprinkling on a finished dish to lift its flavor. In any Michelin-starred restaurant it is the condiment left on the table for customers to serve themselves. **MR**

Taste: *Crisp, crusty, crunchy grains of Fleur de Sel taste obviously of salt, but individual crystals melt on the tongue and linger, rather than giving an aggressive hit.*

Workers rake coarse salt into piles
from the man-made salt marshes.

Maldon Salt

Maldon lies at the tail end of the Blackwater Estuary in Essex, England, amid open water, mudflats, and salt marshes. Here salters harvest the brackish tidal water and transform it into crystalline flakes of salt.

The process starts with seawater collected twice a month, when the new moon and the full moon bring the highest tides, and, assuming there has been no rain, the water will be most salty. Stored in tanks, it settles into three layers: the salter only draws off the water sandwiched between the less salty top and the silt that sinks to the bottom. Simmered for a day in square, shallow pans, the liquid becomes a breeding ground for crystals. As the water evaporates, hollow, pyramid-shaped grains of salt, some microscopic, a few as large as postage stamps, form crazy patterns.

Unlike most table salt, Maldon retains significant traces of potassium, calcium, and magnesium. Chefs claim they need less Maldon salt to season food than common table salt. The Spanish chef Ferran Adrià has ordered consignments of the largest crystals to make them into a crunchy, crystalline "ravioli." **MR**

Taste: *The flakes of Maldon salt are brittle like miniature cornflakes and crumble when lightly crushed. The taste seems to be more lively on the tongue than grain salt.*

Smoked Sea Salt

Kala Namak

Something primeval stirs us to crave smoke around our food, and everything from chiles to cheese has taken a pass through smoldering embers to tempt our taste buds further. It seems natural, then, that porous sea salt crystals—which can absorb flavors like a sponge—would ultimately inhale the essence of the fire.

Smoked versions of salt have appeared almost anywhere there is an ocean and a forest, but thankfully modern times have refined the process greatly. In one method, cool smoke is generated and infused into the surface of salt crystals without melting. Another technique distills seawater over fires to produce delicate, crystalline forms completely permeated with smoke. In the United States, the diversity of woods available for the barbecue has seen salts smoked over everything from alder to mesquite; the Danes ascribe their method to the Vikings and use an exotic combination that includes cherry and juniper to impart deep smoke character. Both the smoke and the salt itself contribute to the finished flavor. **TH**

Naming confusion seems to be normal sport when translating from East to West. A particularly glaring example of this comes with kala namak, or black salt, which is neither black nor a salt. Actually a mined mineral blend from India, the color is more gray or brown than jet, and sodium chloride is only one component of its complex composition.

Hues of gray, pink, and beige can all be found in samples depending on their precise source and refinement. The aroma and taste can be off-putting to the uninitiated, recalling hard-boiled eggs and sulfur, but even modest heat tempers these components into a pleasantly earthy mix.

Kala namak is often blended with yogurt sauces and cooked into various chutneys. *Chaat masala*, a pungent spice blend commonly sprinkled on snacks in India, is dominated by black salt and asafoetida and certainly not for the faint of heart. In the fusion style, pure kala namak can be used as a simple dusting on fresh fruit with no cooking at all for maximum impact. When powdered, humidity can sometimes lead it to clump. **TH**

Taste: *Smoke intensity and residual wood flavors vary based on production sources. Colors range from charcoal to mottled amber and crystal sizes are similarly diverse.*

Taste: *The scent is suitably volcanic, with pungent aromas of asafoetida, sulfur, and garlic leading to a salty, sometimes metallic edge on the palate.*

Unrefined kala namak is sludgelike and is extracted from volcanic lakes using a special tool. ❯❯

Panch Phoron

Curry Powder

The number five occurs in spice mixes with a regularity that suggests an underlying pattern. According to one theory, the four key elements of taste—sweet, sour, bitter, and salt—are experienced in different places on the tongue. The fifth taste is a union of the five, a mysterious balance on the palate.

Panch phoron is a great achievement of the Bengali chefs of eastern India, a visually curious seed mix that generally comprises black or brown mustard, fenugreek, fennel, nigella, and cumin, perhaps with wild onion or celery seed as one element. These flavors developed as a natural bridge between the foods of Southeast Asia and India and add perfect depth to the largely vegetarian cuisine around Bengal. Roasted dry or fried in butter, panch phoron most often starts the potato and lentil dishes of Bangladesh with its blossoming aroma and the sound of searing seeds leaping from the pan. The intense heat of cooking opens and unifies otherwise closed flavors within the ingredients. Grinding is only advised after this stage; home chefs can easily mix their own using equal parts of each seed. **TH**

The mere mention of curry powder and its hundreds of interpretations will earn you a heated debate. This almost entirely inauthentic spice blend takes its name, like the dish it refers to, from the Tamil word *kari* and the Canarese word *karil*, both of which mean a sauce or relish served with rice. Although in India prepared powders are almost nonexistent and both chefs and home cooks use pure ingredients from the start, a dried ground mix was the simplest way for the British colonial power to transport a flavor back from the East and for tentative European cooks to begin to work with it.

Yet accepting the shortcut and forgiving history, well-crafted curry powders have merit. The permutations from a typical base of coriander seeds, peppercorns, turmeric, and ginger are endless. Cardamom, cinnamon, chiles, mustard seeds, and fennel are just a few examples of spices that round out formulas from countless vendors. Twenty ingredients is the norm, not an exception, and this flavorful head start in the kitchen can introduce an exotic culinary world in only one jar. **TH**

Taste: *Mustard seeds add sharp heat and fennel yields sweetness. Nutty and grassy flavors fill in between these extremes to completely engage the palate.*

Taste: *Sometimes hot from peppercorns and chiles, fresh batches usually feature mild citrus tastes on top of deep savory character, with considerable regional variations.*

Chinese Five Spice

Garam Masala

Ancient Chinese secrets are sometimes hard to uncover, but a recipe for classic five-spice powder is thankfully more forthcoming. Long ago, master chefs mixed fennel seeds, cassia, cloves, star anise, and Szechuan peppercorns into a blend big on both flavor and aroma. Walk into any Chinese community and you will smell these melded essences, one of the greatest culinary formulas of all time.

Five-spice has come to unify China's many distinct cuisines, and is ubiquitous in kitchens from Beijing to Xiamen. Although exact proportions vary, it is generally accepted in Chinese culture that five-spice is a balancing act on the tongue. Warm and cool, bitter and sweet, yin and yang—all seem to blend harmoniously.

After centuries of flavoring the full range of Chinese dishes, from roast meats to simmered rice, the authentic formula has made its way to star in fusion cuisines in urban centers around the globe, whether sprinkled over shrimp on a Brisbane beach or enlivening dessert cakes in New York. Multifarious different versions are available across Asia. **TH**

Like most creations of the Indian subcontinent, garam masala transports you to another world of flavor. The term means "hot mix," but most versions vary around a central theme of cinnamon, cardamom, cumin, and peppercorn to obtain a balance between sweet and savory tastes with relatively little by way of heat. Born of the spice bounty of India, a well-balanced masala will tickle the palate on many fronts, leaving an imprint of each component behind in delightful combination.

In India, packaged spice blends are virtually nonexistent, although local merchants will prepare blends to order; in expat communities and in the West, ready-made concoctions crop up regularly. Whichever formula is used, however, they are ideal for rubs on roast meats and vegetables where the high heat will bloom the spices into an aromatic frenzy. Similarly, a garam masala blend can be worked into dough for flatbread and naan where cooking will finish the melding of flavors. Some Western chefs use blends to add a spicy surprise to sweeter desserts like flan or chocolate torte. **TH**

Taste: *Best ground fresh for maximum aromatic impact. Licorice base notes meld with sweet top notes, accented with the slightly numbing effects of Szechuan pepper.*

Taste: *Sweet cinnamon and cardamom dominate the coriander base, but sharp peppery and grassy notes often intrude. Other pungent components are clove or mace.*

Berbere

Ethiopia might not be a world center of cuisine, but it does manage to make the most of what its surroundings offer. A long history of independence, especially compared to some of its less-stable neighbors, has ingrained a rich culinary history unique on the continent. Rich stews, called *wats*, are served with local *injera* flatbread and all is spiced by their own signature spice blend, berbere.

A base of fiery chiles is pounded with spices that can include ginger, fenugreek, cumin, cloves, rue, allspice, cardamom, and ajwain, most typically from regional sources and sometimes roasted to add flavor. Made at home, the mix usually forms a paste from the moisture of fresh chiles or added oil, onions, garlic, or shallots. Packaged versions appear as either a preserved paste or a dry powder that can be rehydrated with oil or water before use.

Despite its incredible heat, berbere is also found on the table as a condiment. In chicken and beef *wats*, the blend also becomes a rub for roasted meats and easily flavors the vegetarian dishes based on lentils and grains in Ethiopian cuisine. **TH**

Ras-el-Hanout

There is no greater mystery in the spice world than ras-el-hanout, the famed spice blend that populates the bazaars and markets of Algeria, Tunisia, and Morocco. Stall vendors lie in wait to expound the virtues of their own recipe, most probably handed down through generations and steeped in secrecy.

The name means "head of the shop" and spice merchants often strive to show their prowess by finding the most exotic ingredients. Grains of paradise, cinnamon, peppercorns, and rose petals are just the beginning: some blends contain over thirty ingredients. Some of the oddest additions include long pepper pods and edible beetles.

The blend's complexity and inherent balance make it ideal for seasoning and transforming simple ingredients such as beans or couscous into culinary delights. The huge variety of recipes ranges from pungent to mild. Like garam masala, the ingredients offer a wide variety of accent flavors, and, while most are suitable for roasting (especially lamb and eggplant) or simmering, experimentation with individual batches is essential. **TH**

Taste: *Searing heat is typical of most recipes, but the spice combinations can bring out aromatics, especially cardamom's camphor notes and ajwain's tarry pungency.*

Taste: *The best ras-el-hanout provides a balance on the tongue that marries savory with sweet, yet punctuates t his pairing with a peppery bite and a floral scent.*

Conical-shaped mounds of spices create an arresting sight at a Marrakesh bazaar. »

Shichimi Togarashi

Harissa

The Japanese art of balancing form and function is perhaps best seen in their cuisine. Every ingredient is carefully chosen to harmonize with others within a dish. This equilibrium is found everywhere from sushi to yakisoba and the spice blends they employ are no exception, not least of which is shichimi togarashi (also known just as togarashi).

Seven flavors combine in this mix: recipes vary but often include chile, orange peel, sesame seeds, seaweed, hemp seeds, Japanese pepper, and poppy seeds. Careful portions allow each taste to shine through in a progression that starts on one end of the tongue and works around to key each component of taste. What the Japanese strive for is the magical combination of all tastes that sums up as greater than its parts, and togarashi seems to deliver just that. The spices lend depth and intensity, and since balance exists within the blend, it can be added almost anywhere. Noodles, fish, and even grilled beef can all take a dose of togarashi well. Coarsely ground, even its appearance seems artistic with a rainbow of colors blended in perfect unison. **TH**

As if the sands of North Africa were not hot enough, the locals have developed a blistering hot spice paste that punctuates almost every food on local menus. Entrenched for centuries in the cuisines of Morocco, Tunisia, and beyond, a shrinking culinary world has made harissa a common staple in many Western groceries and delis.

Hot red chile, garlic, coriander, salt, and caraway serve as the base: variations additionally incorporate citrus, oil, cumin, and—increasingly in Western packaged versions—tomato, alongside a cornucopia of spices. Toasting of some ingredients is common and adds extra dimensions to the spectrum of tastes behind the dominant chile heat.

The kabobs and tagines that traditionally benefit from harissa's punch have inspired Anglo barbecues and stews with otherwise mundane roots to new heights. Adventurous chefs looking for convenient exotica have snapped up jars of the red paste and wrestle, sometimes in vain, to tame this fiery beast from Africa: it finds uses as diverse as an accent for roasted vegetables, or as a rub for meats and fish. **TH**

Taste: *Recipes range from mild to hot, but most have a base of sesame and other seeds, with a slightly numbing peppery impact from mild chiles and sansho in the finish.*

Taste: *The chiles are sharp and hot, but other robust flavors manage to emerge. Garlic adds another twist, while in caraway versions the woodsy taste shines through.*

Vendors in Morocco sell jars of harissa paste alongside fresh kebabs flavored with the spicy blend. ❯❯

Hazelnut Oil

Walnut Oil

Hazelnut oil is a relative newcomer to the range of culinary oils. It was developed in France in the 1970s and inventive chefs have been using it ever since. In the United States, hazelnuts are grown mainly in Oregon, where it is the official state nut. In Europe, the nuts used for oil come from France, Italy, or Turkey. The hazelnut is also known as a "filbert" or "cobnut." One theory of the origin of the former name is that it comes from St. Philibert, a seventh-century French abbot, whose feast day falls in August, in the middle of the nut-gathering season.

After the nuts are harvested they are sorted by hand and kept at a temperature of about 40°F (4–5°C) to prevent spoilage until they are crushed with millstones. The crushed pulp is roasted to enhance the flavor and then cold pressed to release the oil. This is mixed with any free run oil from the roasting process. Hazelnut oil is high in monounsaturated fatty acids, rather than the polyunsaturates found in walnut oil, so it has a longer shelf life. It is best served uncooked, however, as it can become slightly bitter when heated. **JR**

This wonderfully rich and well-flavored oil, made from roasted nuts, was first developed for culinary use in France in the nineteenth century. Before this, walnut oil was pressed from unroasted nuts and used mainly as a treatment for wood—most famously, perhaps, for Stradivarius violins.

The walnut tree is native to Asia, but now grows in Europe (particularly France), Turkey, and China, and California, which accounts for two-thirds of the world's nuts. The finest walnuts for oil come from the Dordogne region of France where the predominant variety is Le Grandjean.

Most walnut oils from France are unrefined virgin oils, cold pressed from dry nuts which have been lightly roasted. A similar process is used in California, but often the oil is extracted with solvents to give a refined oil with no odor or taste. This is mixed with virgin walnut oil to give a well-flavored walnut oil that is cheaper than virgin oil. Walnut oil does not have long-lasting qualities; once opened it should be kept in the refrigerator and used within three months. **JR**

Taste: *Nut oils generally taste of the nuts from which they are made and hazelnut oil is no exception. The aromas are strong but subtle, and the flavor is attractively toasty.*

Taste: *The rich, toasty aroma of walnut oil is very good when drizzled over warm vegetables or fish. It also goes well in salad dressings and added to stir-fry dishes.*

The walnut kernels are commonly ground into a paste, which is then poured into a press to extract the oil. »

Italian Extra Virgin Olive Oil

Italy offers the widest range of flavor in its extra virgin olive oils of all the olive-growing nations. Almost every province produces olive oil, and virtually every region has its own unique microclimate and cultivates its own varieties of tree. Italy also produces a higher ratio of extra virgin olive oil—the fresh fruit juice of the olive with the water removed—than anywhere else. Tuscany is one of the smallest of the Italian producing areas, but has gained a reputation as producing some of the best extra virgin oils. Many of these come from estates owned by a single family.

In the south of the region, set on the slopes of Monte Amiata, is the town of Seggiano. It is here that the film director Armando Manni organically farms the local Olivastra olive to produce the acclaimed extra virgin oils, *Per Me* (For Me) and *Per Mio Figlio* (For My Child), which are probably the most expensive in the world. Because they are pressed from Olivastra olives rather than the northern Tuscan varieties, Manni's indulgent oils are not, however, typical of Tuscany. **JR**

Taste: *Armando Manni extra virgin olive oils are light and sweet, but still have the immense depth of flavor typical of classic Tuscan olive oils*

Spanish Estate Olive Oil

Spain is the largest producer of olive oil in the world, and usually accounts for more than half the world's supplies. Most is produced by small farmers working together in large cooperatives. The very best Spanish extra virgin olive oils, however, usually come from large, family-owned estates. The single unit enables great care to be taken with every aspect of cultivation and production. The olives are harvested as single varietals and processed on the estate. The resulting oils are only ever blended with others from the same estate.

The major producing area is Andalusia, in the south. Here the olive groves stretch as far as the eye can see under an overbearing sun, producing the sweet and intense oils characteristic of Cordoba and Granada. One of the top estates in this area belongs to the Núñez de Prado family, which owns 160,000 trees in total. The other important area for export oils is Catalonia, in northern Spain. This region is widely planted with Arbequina olives, which produce more delicate oils: lightly nutty in character with a touch of apples and sweet herbs. **JR**

Taste: *Núñez de Prado extra virgin olive oil has intense flavors of lemons, melons, and tropical fruit. Despite light pepperiness, it is so sweet that it can be used in desserts.*

Olives being milled in Andalusia, the world's biggest olive oil–producing region. ❯❯

Greek Monastery Olive Oil

The ancient Greeks revered the olive and in later times Greek monasteries, which have always had their own olive groves, played a very important role in insuring the continuity of olive oil production throughout Greece. While some monasteries, like the ones at Mount Athos and Karpenisi, keep the oil for their own use in holy services and in their kitchens, others such as the monastery at Toplou, on the island of Crete, produce olive oil on a commercial scale.

Olive trees are to be found everywhere in Greece and fourteen regions benefit from a Protected Designation of Origin, but it is the mountainous regions of the island of Crete and of the Peloponnese that are best known for olive oil. The main variety pressed for olive oil is the Koroneiki; the more-famous Kalamata is used almost exclusively for table olives. Production is based on numerous small farms and large single estates are rare. Farmers sell their produce to privately owned mills or belong to local cooperatives, which sell to secondary cooperatives that blend and market the oil. **JR**

Taste: *Some oils are delicate with soft salad leaves and apple fruit in their flavor tones, whereas others are more robust with notes of dried grass and nutty almond skins.*

Olive oil from the Toplou monastery is entirely organic. »

Argan Oil

Hemp Oil

The argan tree, *Argania spinosa,* grows only in the southwestern part of Morocco and is in decline. Over the last century more than a third of the argan forest has disappeared, so UNESCO has added the argan tree to the World Heritage list of plants at risk.

Local Berber women have extracted oil from the fruit of the argan tree for centuries, but it remains largely unknown outside its home territory. The fruit looks somewhat like a large, round olive, but the oil comes only from the kernel, which is encased in a nut with an extremely hard shell.

Until recently everything was done by hand. After removal from the shell the kernels were toasted and ground to a flour, then mixed with water to make a dough from which the oil was extracted. This was a lengthy process and producing one gallon of oil could take twenty hours.

Today, mechanical presses similar to those used for olive oil are being installed to crush and grind the kernels to extract the oil. This considerably speeds up the process and improves the quality of the oil as it removes the need for water. **JR**

The hemp plant—*Cannabis sativa*—has been grown in Asia and the Middle East for more than five millennia, a period during which cultivation has spread east to China and west to Europe and North America. Although some varieties have provided a valued high for many cultures, the type pressed for oil is not among them, and probably its most dominant use has been in the production of rope. But hemp seeds have been a valued food in many countries. Before sunflower oil, hemp oil was the basic cooking oil of Russia and parts of Poland; toasted hemp seeds are eaten as snacks in China, and increasingly elsewhere. The cold-pressed hemp oils developed at the end of the twentieth century take the delicate flavor of hemp to a new level.

Rich in polyunsaturated fatty acids, particularly omega-6 and omega-3, hemp oil has real nutritional benefits. Unfortunately, essential fatty acids are very unstable, making hemp oil extremely susceptible to heat and to light. It should be packed in dark bottles and stored in the refrigerator; it should never be used in high-temperature cooking. **JR**

Taste: *Its light roasted flavor is reminiscent of toasted hazelnuts. Good for cooking and flavoring, it makes an interesting salad dressing mixed with lemon juice.*

Taste: *Cold-pressed hemp oil has a sweet and delicate flavor, reminiscent of pine nuts, with a slightly vegetal element. It is best used in salad dressings and cold food.*

Toasted hemp seeds are eaten as snacks in China, and are increasingly popular elsewhere. »

Mustard Oil

Almost any seed can be pressed to exude a flavorful oil and Indian cooks have long extracted mustard seed oil to use in cooking. Mustard seeds are still processed, mainly in Asia and on the Indian subcontinent, for use as a cooking oil (and a topical rub in Ayurvedic medicine). The raw oil preserves the compounds that give mustard its characteristic "hot" taste: it is very pungent with a distinct aroma.

Heating mustard oil brings out a nutty, subtly sweet character that is ideal for vegetarian cuisine, especially in the stir-frying of mustard's brassica cousins like cauliflower. Bengali cuisine uses the oil in dishes such as the classic fish curry, *maacher jhol*. Similar treatments of potato dishes are seen widely across Bangladesh and most of coastal Indochina.

Recently, in the West, the erucic acid content of some types of mustard oil has led to health concerns. Although found naturally in many brassicas, erucic acid is classified as dangerous both in North America and in Europe, and is banned for food uses in high concentrations. As a result, mustard oil can sometimes be difficult to source. **TH**

Taste: *The oil is sharp and bright with the bitterness and heat expected from mustard. A high cooking heat pleasantly mellows both the flavor and the aroma.*

Lord Shiva is said to have had his food cooked in mustard oil rather than the more common ghee.

Avocado Oil

The avocado takes its name from an Aztec word, and it was in Mexico that Westerners first encountered the large, pear-shaped fruit growing in abundance on the exuberant trees that still flourish there.

Today, avocados are cultivated in many parts of the world, including the United States, where they are a major crop on the coastal mountain ranges of southern California. But it is only in recent years that the flesh of the fruit has been pressed for oil. The first oils were made in California as part of an effort to use up less-than-perfect fruit. Avocados are now grown specifically to press for oil not only in California but countries such as Australia, New Zealand, Israel, and Chile.

Cold-pressed avocado oil is considered healthy because it is very rich in monounsaturated fatty acids. It is also immensely useful in culinary terms, thanks to a very high smoke point, which means cooks can work at extremely high temperatures without the oil burning. The thick, velvety texture, usually paired with a wonderful deep green color, makes it one of the more attractive oils to use. **JR**

Taste: *Cold pressed avocado oil is full and fruity with a definite taste of avocado. Some brands have flavor tones of globe artichokes, celery, spinach, or bay leaves.*

Single Estate Grapeseed Oil

A by-product of the naturally occurring grape marcs that are left over after the fruit is pressed for winemaking, grapeseed oil is a versatile vegetable oil. As the oil is cholesterol free and rich in vitamin E and essential fatty acids, it is especially valued for its health properties. Its mild flavor does not overpower delicate foods as some oils are prone to do and it has a high flashpoint, which means it is particularly good for frying at high temperatures.

To make the oil, grape seeds are separated from the marcs and dried gently in rotary driers to avoid any degeneration in the resulting oil due to heat. They are subsequently crushed to extract the oil, which is then filtered before bottling. The quality of the oil largely depends on the raw material; oil content can be anything from 6 to 20 percent according to the grape variety and a good yield is needed to produce a first-rate product.

In Italy, grapeseed oil is the third most commonly used fat after extra virgin olive oil and butter. It is good for dressing salads and vegetables, such as asparagus, as well as sautéing. **LF**

Taste: Grapeseed oil has an attractive pale green color and a light, fresh flavor with vaguely nutty nuances. Its "neutrality" makes it ideal for use with delicate flavors.

Pumpkin Seed Oil

Although pumpkins originated in Central America, it was the Austrians of Central Europe who developed pumpkin seed oil. A mutant variety of pumpkin, *Cucurbita pepo* var. *styriaca,* produces seeds without the stringy skins of other pumpkin seeds, and sometime during the early eighteenth century the Austrians started to extract oil from them.

Today, fields of these pumpkins slowly ripen in the warm summer sunshine. At harvest time they are cut open and the seeds picked out of the pulp. Traditionally, the whole family worked together, but today this is more often done by machines. The seeds are cleaned, dried, ground, and finally toasted, in a crucial process that is the subject of much secrecy. Variation of a degree or two in temperature or a small change in timing can result in a very different flavor.

The best Austrian pumpkin seed oil has PDO status and must be entirely Styrian in origin. It is high in polyunsaturates and must be kept in a cool, dark place. It is so susceptible to light that the oil in a salad dressing will coagulate in sunlight. **JR**

Taste: Pumpkin seed oil is dark green-brown in color, with a sweet, distinctive flavor of toasted nuts. It is good with cold preparations, but can also be heated briefly.

Cold-Pressed Canola Oil

Sesame Oil

Rape (*Brassica napus*) is a member of the cabbage family, which was not widely cultivated until the last few decades of the twentieth century. In the 1980s, Canadian breeders then developed a new variety called canola that was nutritionally more acceptable than earlier varieties and is now widely grown for its seeds. These are crushed and processed at high temperatures to produce a clear, bland oil that is now Canada's most widely used cooking oil, and gaining popularity in the United States and across Europe. In 2005, for example, British farmers began to experiment with cold pressing their rapeseed and developed a new product with much more flavor than the original oil. Whole-food stores now sell numerous brands of cold-pressed oil.

The increased popularity of canola oil is credited to its health benefits. Made up predominantly of monounsaturated fatty acids, it is also rich in omega-3 and omega-6 polyunsaturated essential fatty acids. It is often described as "extra virgin" or "virgin," but these words have no official meaning in relation to canola oil. **JR**

The origins of this oil, pressed from the seed of the sesame plant—*Sesamum indicum*—stretch back a very long way. Some sources claim the Chinese were using sesame oil in their lamps as long ago as 5000 BCE. Others believe sesame seeds first originated in India or Africa and they were taken to China at a later date. Early references can be found to the use of the oil in Babylonia and Arabia. A charming story suggests the "open sesame" of *Arabian Nights* reflects the fact that the sesame pod bursts open quite suddenly when the seeds are ready to be released.

In fact, there are two types of sesame oil: a dark, amber-colored oil that is very popular in Chinese cooking, and a lighter, pale beige oil used in Indian cuisines. The darker oil is pressed from roasted sesame seeds and is ideally added as a flavoring. It should not be used for cooking as it burns very easily. The lighter colored oil is cold pressed from uncooked sesame seeds. It has a light, delicate flavor and is not a suitable substitute for the stronger oil, but ideal for using in dressings. **JR**

Taste: *Cold-pressed canola oils are generally light and nutty, often with a vegetal tone reminiscent of cabbage, broccoli, or fresh peas. They are viable for all culinary uses.*

Taste: *Dark sesame oil tastes of toasted nuts and seeds with a hint of burnt chocolate. The light oil smells similar to fresh sesame seeds and has a delicately vegetal taste.*

Goose Fat

A mature goose of any breed popular today can lay down 2 pounds (900 g) soft fat around its internal organs, or even more. Rendered down, this fat is used for cooking in the same way as lard. While once closely identified with the Jewish cuisine of Central Europe, goose fat is now more commonly associated with southwest France. It is a key ingredient in *rillettes d'oie*, potted goose, all forms of confits, and, very often, *garbure béarnaise*, the cabbage-based soup-stew simmered in an earthenware pot.

In nutrition and diet, *graisse d'oie* has been linked to what is known as the French paradox: the question of why, despite a high-fat diet, cardiovascular disease in France has been historically low. Goose fat is rich in monounsaturated and polyunsaturated fatty acids. The British, too, once valued goose fat for its health-giving properties—they spread it on laborers' undershirts in winter as a protection against respiratory diseases. Roast goose has always been a popular festive dish and Anglo-Saxon cooks know goose fat makes absolutely the best roasted potatoes. **MR**

Red Palm Oil

This vibrantly colored oil is to African cooking what extra virgin olive oil is to Mediterranean cuisines. As with the finest olive oils, red palm oil adds its own unique color and flavor to a dish and contains just as many health-giving properties.

Extracted from the fibrous pulp of the grape-size fruit of the African oil palm tree, red palm oil—not to be confused with white palm oil, which is produced by crushing the fruit's inner kernel—is non-hydrogenated and trans fat free. The distinctive flame red color comes from the oil's high levels of beta-carotene and lycopene, the powerful antioxidants that make carrots and tomatoes immune-boosting superfoods.

Also known as *zomi*, red palm oil adds a strong and unique flavor to many traditional West African dishes such as *ndolé* (a bitterleaf soup that is the national dish of Cameroon), *egusi* (a Nigerian meat and fish soup), and *moi-moi* (a steamed cake made with black-eye peas). Today, most red palm oil can be bought ready-made, but traditionally African cooks prepare their own. **WS**

Taste: *Although goose fat absorbs other flavors, it is never bland. The rich farmyard taste lingers on the palate, adding to any ingredient with which the fat is combined.*

Taste: *Foods such as chicken, seafood, or potatoes will be tinged a rich, golden-red when fried or sautéed in red palm oil, absorbing its nutty, sweet, and slightly creamy flavor.*

Workers are housed on an oil palm plantation in the rain forest. »

Varietal Red Wine Vinegar

Corinthian Vinegar

The Greek doctor Hippocrates first extolled the virtues of vinegar in writing some time about 400 BCE, but its cleansing, healing, and preservative properties were well known in biblical times. Its origin was probably the result of a happy accident, as suggested by the name, which comes from the medieval French words *vin aigre* (sour wine).

Vinegar is formed when the naturally occurring bacterium *Acetobacter xylinum* gets to work on the alcohol in an alcoholic liquid and converts it to acetic acid. For the very best wine vinegars this process is long and slow. Grape juice is allowed to ferment into wine and then matures for some months before acetification with a carefully prepared bacterial culture. The vinegar itself then matures for an additional period of months or even years.

The better the base wine the better the mature vinegar will be. The finest examples come from single varietal wines produced in the famous red wine regions of the world: in Piedmont, Cesare Ciaconne produces outstanding varietal vinegars from Barolo and Barbera. **JR**

Corinthian vinegar is made from Zante currants— the small, intensely flavoured, dried fruit of Black Corinth grapes grown in the Peloponnese peninsula of southern Greece.

The word "currant" comes from the Old French term, *raisins de Corauntz* or "raisins of Corinth." For centuries, production of the fruit was centred around Corinth, however, trade shifted to the island of Zante in the sixteenth century. Production of the vinegar is based on an ancient method of making sweet wine from raisins. The grapes are harvested and left out in the sun to dry. The semi-dried fruit is then pressed, and the resulting juice along with the must (the skins, seeds, pulp, and stems of the grapes) is gently boiled for hours until greatly reduced. The mixture is then strained and the juice is transferred to wooden barrels and left to age.

Full-flavoured, dark, and fruity, Corinthian vinegar works well with roasted and grilled meats and vegetables, or stirred into savoury dressings and sauces. Like balsamicos, it is also good drizzled sparingly over fruit and ice cream. **LF**

Taste: *Varietal red wine vinegars give wonderfully fruity flavors reminiscent of black currants, raspberries, plums, and cherries. They are mellow and harmonious.*

Taste: *An intense vinegar with a complex sweetness that softens the vinegar's innate sharpness; it has a delicate fruity flavour and a clean aftertaste.*

Sherry Vinegar

Aceto Balsamico Tradizionale

Sherry wine has been produced in Jerez de la Frontera, deep in the southwestern corner of Spain, since the sixteenth century and maybe even before then. In those days vinegar was the inevitable result of poor winemaking practices and was given to family and friends for cooking. Today, formal regulations govern production.

There are two basic types of sherry. One grows a form of yeast on it called "flor" and one does not. The latter is known as "raya" and it is this wine that goes on to become oloroso sherry and which is fermented to make the most popular sherry vinegar. Raya is poured into oak casks and placed in the full heat of the sun while the wine turns to vinegar. The vinegar is then left to mature in a solera system for anything from two to twenty-five years. This means only one-third of the vinegar in the oldest barrels is taken each year for bottling. These barrels are then filled up with vinegar from the previous year and so on down the line until new vinegar goes into the youngest barrels. Fruitier than other wine vinegars, it gives a real lift to dressings, bastes, and sauces. **JR**

Written records of this famous condiment start in the mid-nineteenth century, although then its creators made it only for family and friends. Today, Modena is defined as the producing region by a DOC, although this elite artisanal product should not be confused with the much newer "balsamic vinegar of Modena," which is largely factory made and can include caramel and preservatives.

Traditional balsamic *aceto* (in many countries, it is not technically classed as a vinegar due to its low levels of acetic acid) is made from the juice or must of local grape varieties, reduced by cooking to a very sweet liquid that is placed in small wooden barrels with a starter of regular vinegar. After the first year, a small amount of liquid is taken out and placed in a second cask: the first barrel is topped up with new concentrated grape must. Over the years a series of barrels of different woods—oak, mulberry, chestnut, cherry, and juniper—are built up, each barrel holding a mixture of vinegars of varying ages. No vinegar can be released from the system until it is at least twelve years old. **JR**

Taste: *Sherry vinegar retains the taste of full oloroso sherry with its balsamic and dried fruit flavors. It has a light acidity, but is sweeter than other wine vinegars.*

Taste: *Penetrating aromas of mixed dried fruits like raisins, apricots, and prunes. The flavor tones are rich and mellow, the liquid smooth, sweet, and velvety thick.*

Tarragon Vinegar

Tarragon, *Artemisia dracunculus,* has been known as "the dragon" in different times and places. The thirteenth-century Arab botanist Ibn Baithar knew it as *turkhum,* perhaps for its strong, at times numbing flavor, but more likely because of its serpentine roots: its botanical name is Latin for "little dragon."

Tarragon, however, is associated most of all with France, and it was the French who were the first to produce tarragon vinegar on a commercial scale. The base vinegar for this product is often made in an acetator. Here white wine is placed in an 8,000-gallon (30,000-liter) vat, the vinegar-producing bacteria are added, and warm air is filtered through the vat to raise the temperature and aid the conversion of alcohol to vinegar. The process takes a couple of weeks: the resulting liquids are flavored with natural extracts or chemicals to simulate the taste of tarragon. The very best tarragon vinegars are made by a much slower method, similar to that used to make varietal vinegars. Once the white wine vinegar is ready, sprigs of French tarragon are infused either in the vat or in the bottle. **JR**

Taste: *It should have a strong aroma of tarragon with a spicy, gingery note, but not too sharp. Excellent with chicken, it also makes a good vinaigrette with walnut oil.*

Apple Cider Vinegar

In regions like England and northern France, where apples have been cultivated for at least two millennia, vinegar made from apples has a history as ancient and unwritten as that of wine vinegar. Like wine vinegar, apple cider vinegar is formed when naturally occurring bacteria get to work on the alcohol in a base liquid—here cider—and convert it to acetic acid.

Today, most commercial vinegar is made in large quantities under controlled, industrial conditions and then pasteurized to inactivate the enzymes and kill microorganisms. However, a number of smaller producers still use slower, more traditional methods, similar to those used for good red wine vinegar. Unpasteurized and preservative free, these vinegars can be fermented from sweet apples, cider apples, or a mixture of the two. They are excellent in salads, salsas, bastes, and pickles, when a sharp vinegar kick is not required. Apple cider vinegar has a reputation as a healthy food and even an effective medicine. However, there is no scientific evidence of any medicinal value. **JR**

Taste: *Apple is, not surprisingly, the predominant note in both the aroma and taste of apple cider vinegars, which are often mellowed by tones of light honey or maple.*

Somerset in England is well known for its age-old traditions of growing and pressing cider apples. »

Verjuice

Raspberry Vinegar

Verjuice comes from the French *vert jus* or "green juice," and was the name given to the sour juice pressed from unripe fruit. In other countries, there are similar products such as *agresto* in Italy, *argraz* in Spain, *hosrum* in Lebanon, and *abghooreh* in Iran.

In winemaking regions such as France, grapes were the fruit in question, but crabapples, plums, gooseberries, and bitter oranges have been used elsewhere. Some believe verjuice was known in Roman times, but the first written reference to it appears in 1375 in a recipe book belonging to Taillevent, the master cook of French king Charles V.

Verjuice gradually fell out of favor as lemons became more widely available, but has enjoyed something of a comeback during the latter part of the twentieth century. Maggie Beer, the Australian chef and food writer, led the way, and other producers in California, Australia, South Africa, and parts of Europe followed. Grapes are picked very early in the season, pressed, and the juice is then stabilized and bottled immediately. Occasionally the juice is left to ferment before bottling. **JR**

Raspberry vinegar probably began as a homemade product in those temperate areas where raspberries grew easily. (In northern England, it was served with the traditional Yorkshire pudding before roast meat.) There are few historical references to raspberry vinegar, however, before the twentieth century. Commercial production began in France and it was chefs there who popularized its use in the 1980s.

The best raspberry vinegars are made by infusing the fresh fruit in a good-quality wine vinegar for about a month. At the end of this period the vinegar is filtered and sometimes a few fresh berries are placed in the bottle with the vinegar. The list of ingredients of any decent raspberry vinegar should feature raspberries. The words "natural ingredients" usually mean the vinegar has been made by adding essences or extracts, rather than the fruit itself. Mix with a good, easy-going extra virgin olive oil to dress avocados or combine with blue cheese to make a dip for endive spears. Chefs also use it in cooking to counter the richness of ingredients, such as pan-fried chicken livers. **JR**

Taste: *Verjuice has the acidity of vinegar and the tartness of lemons, but it is softer on the palate. It can be used whenever a dash of lemon juice or vinegar is specified.*

Taste: *Good raspberry vinegar tastes of sweet, ripe raspberries with a lightly acidic kick. The flavors should linger in the mouth.*

Unripe grapes are removed from the vines to thin
⊗ out the crop at the beginning of the season.

Shanxi Extra Aged Vinegar

Mochi Gome Su

Chinese aged vinegars have a richness, concentration, and complexity that can rival some Italian aged balsamicos and, like their Italian equivalents, are used sparingly as the best are very expensive. They are also extremely difficult to find outside China: usually only mass-produced versions are available elsewhere, which, like supermarket balsamic vinegar, only hint at the complexity of the aged versions.

While vinegars can be made from many different ingredients—notably grapes, fruits, and grains—in China, they are made primarily from glutinous rice mixed with other grains. Shanxi aged vinegar (and a similar type made in Jiangsu province) starts off as all Chinese vinegars do: the grains are cooked to produce a liquid that is fermented, then bacteria convert the alcohol into acid. While regular vinegars are bottled immediately, both Shanxi and Jiangsu aged vinegars undergo a controlled exposure to the elements for months, even years, which concentrates the liquid and tempers its acidity. In fact, the acidity of the best kind is so low that in some markets they cannot be legally classed as vinegars. **KKC**

The key ingredient in *tamago-su*, a potent Japanese folk remedy, is the vinegar made from brown rice and credited with many health-giving properties. As revered as Modena's balsamic vinegar, the best mochi gome su comes from Japan's Kyushu island, where it is made in a thousand-year-old process.

The process begins when steamed brown rice is mixed with rice koji—a rice that has been treated with the same *Aspergillus* mold used to make miso and soy sauce. After several weeks the liquid is mixed with a mother vinegar and spring water, and transferred to clay crocks, which some producers bury in the ground. When it is a rich, dark vinegar it is diluted again and left to mature for up to ten months. This lengthy process creates amino acids that enhance both the flavor and the health benefits of the vinegar: it is said to stimulate the appetite, aid digestion, and prevent cholesterol build-up.

Brown rice vinegar balances saltiness in foods and its antiseptic qualities are used to marinate fish. Its delicate sweetness is perfect in dressings, mixed with oil or miso, and added directly to food. **SB**

Taste: *Colored a brown so dark it is almost black, Shanxi extra-aged vinegar is sticky, thick, sweet, and only mildly acidic, with intense, complex flavors.*

Taste: *Exceptionally mild, with a light flavor and underlying sweetness, mochi gome su is much less acidic than most vinegars (although not as sweet and viscous as balsamic).*

Commonly brown rice vinegar is used to season rice when making sushi. »

Moutarde de Dijon

Dijon, Burgundy's capital, has been famous for its *moutardes* since the early eighteenth century. Stores once sold them by the ladleful, and rival artisans vied with each other to devise the latest fashionable flavors: nasturtium, caper and anchovy, and lemon. Some mustards made eyes water, whereas others tasted sweet and aromatic. Today, the Maille store in Dijon still creates exotic mustards, such as raspberry and Champagne, but the yellow, pungent but not overpowering, moutarde de Dijon is the real focus of attention.

Dijon mustard is made from brown or black mustard seeds. When crushed, the seeds are odorless and almost tasteless, but a moistening triggers a chemical reaction that gives the kick. Dijon mustard was created in the 1850s in a recipe that substituted verjuice (unripe grape juice) for vinegar, leading to a less acidic, smoother-tasting mustard. Freshly ground, the paste is noticeably hot. Within a day it carries a real punch. Eaten fresh like this— the Maille store sells it from a pump—moutarde de Dijon has a unique zing. **MR**

Taste: *Dijon mustard is strong enough to seem sharp, its aroma powerful enough to tickle the back of the nose, and its texture smooth without seeming floury.*

Grey Poupon mustard has been produced since 1777 ⊘ *and is still sold in the Rue de la Liberté in Dijon.*

Moutarde de Meaux

Moutarde de Meaux is often described as a mustard that has been prepared *à l'ancienne* (in the old way). Sold in earthenware pots with cork stoppers and a red-wax seal, it looks very much a traditional product. Monks initially cultivated and prepared mustard in France, but J. B. Pommery, a company that made millstones, claims to have a recipe for the mustard dating to 1632. It developed the mustard into a brand and although it has been much imitated around the world, it has kept its unique identity.

Like its close cousin from Dijon, moutarde de Meaux uses brown mustard seeds, *Brassica juncea*, but the manufacturing process is different. Instead of discarding the husks, they form an integral part of the recipe. The seeds are soaked in verjuice, salt, and spices, then they are crushed and blended with the husks that have been sieved and returned to the mixture. Today, most mustard seeds are imported from Canada rather than grown in central France.

A gastronomic mustard favored by chefs around the world, moutarde de Meaux is best eaten simply, as a relish to accompany broiled or grilled meat. **MR**

Taste: *Milder than Dijon mustard, but still very spiky when fresh, it is also more vinegary. The texture is intentionally gritty because of the mustard bran.*

Bavarian Sweet Mustard

Mostarda di Frutta

Eating sausage without mustard is regarded as unthinkable in Germany. And Bavarian sweet mustard—brown in color, mild and sweet in flavor—is considered the only worthy accompaniment to Munich's celebrated white veal sausage, *weisswurst*. In fact, it is even known as white sausage mustard throughout Germany.

Bavarian sweet mustard was invented in the mid-nineteenth century by Johann Conrad Develey. He opened a mustard factory in Munich that adopted the best principles of artisan production. Constantly trying to create new flavors, Develey spotted a gap in the market for a sweet mustard. He experimented with the traditional mustard mix, adding spices and sugar that had been caramelized. The mixture went through various changes, until brown sugar and roughly ground mustard seeds proved to be the winning ingredients.

As well as being the quintessential partner to *weisswurst*, Bavarian sweet mustard is also eaten with another southern German specialty, *leberkäse* (a liver meatloaf), and knuckle of pork. **LF**

This wonderful concoction of fruits preserved in grape must and spiked with mustard originates from northern Italy, and is a particular delicacy of the city of Cremona in Lombardy. Its beginnings can be traced back as far as Roman times, when gourmets combined honey, mustard, vinegar, and oil in quest of the perfect balance of sweet, sour, and spice.

Mostarda di frutta, or fruit preserved in grape must and spices, was originally a country food, a pragmatic means of preserving whatever was left over after the harvest, but seems to have acquired some status during the Middle Ages, when sugar was an expensive luxury. A base of grape must or sweetened water was used to cook fruits such as apricots, cherries, pears, plums, and figs. The fruit was then removed and the sauce was seasoned with mustard and vinegar before being simmered until it thickened to an almost jamlike consistency. Today the fruit is usually candied first and then bottled in the spicy syrup. Traditionally, this unique relish is eaten with *bollito misto*, but it is also good with boiled or cured meats, game, and cheese. **LF**

Taste: *Sweet Bavarian mustard has a grainy texture and soft piquancy with predominantly sweet overtones. It is wonderful as a spread, particularly on dark rye breads.*

Taste: *Mostarda di frutta delivers bold, fruity flavors against a wine-rich backdrop. The spice is balanced by a pleasing sweetness: the definitive sweet and sour.*

Mostarda di frutta is a particular delicacy of the city of Cremona in Lombardy, Italy. »

Kimchi

For thousands of years, Koreans have taken pickling to the limit with kimchi (or kimchee). Countless variations play around the themes of spice, color, and composition, with piquant flavors that put Western pickles to shame. At least one kimchi appears alongside rice at every Korean meal, and there is a museum in Seoul devoted to the subject.

Asian cabbage is cleaned, salted, and stacked in large pots to age for a few days to yield the most basic versions of kimchi. More complex recipes add spices such as chiles, garlic, and paprika, other vegetables such as cucumber or radish, or shrimps and other seafood: whole stuffed cabbage heads are known as *tongbaechu*. Traditionally, earthen pots were used to promote aging and fermentation, either in buried chambers or outside the home in the back garden to benefit from the climate of each season: "summer" kimchis are typically fermented only for a short time. Today, specialized refrigeration is now available and, while many homes continue the ritual of kimchi preparation, modern demand has given rise to myriad prepackaged versions. **TH**

Taste: *Despite considerable salt, most kimchi has a well-balanced taste that preserves the essence of each component. Heat can range from nonexistent to severe.*

Earthenware kimchi pots absorb the climatic
ⓚ *conditions outside a temple in South Korea.*

Cwikla

Although the origin of this tangy pickled beetroot relish is buried in time, the first recorded recipe for cwikla was provided by the sixteenth-century writer Mikolaj Rej, sometimes known as the "father of Polish literature." Rej's recipe called for oven-baked beetroot, sliced thin and seasoned with horseradish, fennel, and vinegar. Nowadays, the beetroot is usually diced or grated and caraway is the more common flavoring. A splash of red wine can be added. Unfortunately, many commercially available brands of cwikla have the somewhat less appetizing texture of a nondescript mashed puree.

Naturally, the individualistic Poles usually have their own idea on how fine or coarse, how mild or potent, and how tart or sweet their "national" relish should be. The mellower (lower horseradish and vinegar content) version may be regarded as a salad, whereas the more potent variety is more of a piquant condiment. Either way, nothing brings out the flavor of the sausages, hams, roasts, pâtés, jellied pork knuckles, and other cold meats that reign supreme at the Polish table better than cwikla. **RS**

Taste: *With a deep ruby-red color and a grainy texture, the faint sweetness of the marinade mellows the earthy beetroot flavor.*

Piccalilli

Its name has an exotic, even Italian ring, but piccalilli is a venerable, English mixed-vegetable preserve. The first half of the word no doubt derives from "pickle" and food historians suggest the second might be a contraction of "chili." The added tag "Indian pickle," along with the inclusion of mango in some of the earliest recipes, such as Hannah Glasse's from 1759, suggests it might have been an Anglo-Indian invention.

During the Victorian era piccalilli appeared alongside large joints of cold beef, mutton, and ham served in gentlemen's clubs and is still, despite changes to modern eating habits, eaten as a part of cold meals. Today, it is a pickle consisting of some mix of cauliflower flowerets, green beans, gherkins, and other vegetables preserved in a thickened vinegary sauce and colored with turmeric to give it a bright mustard color. It can be spiced with ginger or chile and mustard. While modern proprietary brands tend to be acetic, domestic versions can be distinctive and more subtly flavored. Piccalilli is frequently featured on English pub menus. **MR**

Taste: *The vegetables keep their original shape and are crunchy, never soggy, but have absorbed the flavor of the vinegar. The spicy yellow sauce should not be harshly acid.*

Mango Chutney

Despite its culinary and etymological origins in India, chutney owes much of its fame to word-of-mouth advertising from travellers and colonists who passed through the subcontinent. There are countless chutney recipes containing ingredients ranging from aubergine to coconut, but few are better known than those featuring underripe mango.

Mango chutney has become a standard partner to Indian fare the world over. Domestic versions are made fresh daily using the produce that is seasonally available, whereas foreign sources come preserved in brand-name jars. Although the former tend to be spicier and balance the natural sweetness of the fruit with vinegar and savory vegetables such as onion, the latter are made sweeter for foreign tastes, by adding tamarind and palm sugar.

Mango chutney is often eaten with poppadoms as an appetizer, but it can also be used to cool hot curries or to pep up blander dishes such as rice or dal. It also goes well with some cheeses. Innovative chefs have taken the chutney into yet another realm, as a pastry filling and as a glaze for roast meats. **TH**

Taste: *The sweetness of the mango is balanced by the naturally tart notes of vinegar and citrus. Spice flavorings commonly include chile, peppercorns, turmeric, and clove.*

Mango and other chutneys are popularly sold from roadside stalls in Madagascar, Africa. ❯❯

Gari

Once a word known only to sushi aficionados, "gari"—thinly sliced ginger root pickled in sweet vinegar—is beginning to reach a wider audience. Ginger neutralizes strong fishy flavors and gari is commonly eaten alongside sashimi and sushi, to cleanse the palate between courses.

Gari is an indispensable part of the sushi store ritual, but sushi stores themselves are a relatively new phenomenon. Centuries ago, fish was packed with rice to preserve it: the rice fermented giving the fish a sour taste, and was thrown away, while the fish was eaten. Over time, this grew into sushi—rice was mixed with vinegar to replicate the sour taste, and was itself eaten. A type of pressed sushi developed first and then, in the nineteenth century in Edo (now Tokyo), finger-style sushi (*nigiri-zushi*) gained popularity, and this is probably when gari was introduced to the experience.

To make gari, thinly slice fresh ginger, sprinkle it with salt and leave it for an hour or so until it gives off water. Pat dry and pour a warm mixture of three parts vinegar and two parts sugar over. **SB**

Taste: *Sweet, hot, and refreshingly sour, crunchy gari is a perfect palate cleanser. Japanese pickled ginger ranges in color from pale pinkish to yellowish.*

Preserved Lemon

Moroccans are ingenious chefs. A prime example of their creativity can be seen in their technique of making preserved lemons with little more than salt, water, lemons, and time. The fruit matures into a completely unexpected taste and texture that helps define North African cuisine.

Preserved lemons are available to buy, but most chefs will have a jar maturing on the pantry shelf at any given time. The process involves little more than stuffing whole lemons liberally with salt, packing them into glass jars, and covering with water. After roughly a month of aging at room temperature, the texture of the peel softens and becomes chewy. The resulting lemons can be cut up and used as both condiment and ingredient. Most jars last only as long as it takes the next batch to be aged.

Lamb tagines and curries are often laced with preserved lemons to add a tart lift to otherwise heavy fare. They are served on their own in tiny bowls as a flavorful accent with the evening meal or as a sort of palate cleanser between the courses of more elaborate dinners. **TH**

Taste: *Tart, slightly sweet, and pleasantly bitter, the texture of preserved lemons is soft and pliable but should not be mushy. Rinse or dilute with fresh water as desired.*

Lemons can be easily preserved at home using a good quality, coarse sea salt. »

Katsuobushi

In the famous Nishiki food market in Kyoto, an old-fashioned red enamel rotating drum churns out freshly shaved katsuobushi for sale by the bagful. The cured fillet of the skipjack tuna, *Katsuwonus pelamis*, katsuobushi is at the heart of *dashi*, the flavorful stock that underpins all Japanese cooking.

The drying process is unique to Japan, and dates back more than three centuries. Skipjack fillets are simmered, and the bones removed, before being hot-smoked for up to two weeks, then trimmed and sun-dried. Next they are cured using the mold *Aspergillus glaucus*, until they are as hard as wood and rich in the *umami* flavor. The dried fillets can then be shaved into fine flakes, or *kezuribushi*, using a tool that looks like a carpenter's plane.

Besides *dashi* (best produced by a fast infusion of freshly shaved katsuobushi in boiling water), very fine shavings can be used as a garnish for vegetables and fish, or mixed with soy sauce and eaten with rice. The flavor disappears rapidly on exposure to air, and the fragrance of freshly shaved katsuobushi is far superior to packaged flakes. **SB**

Taste: *The finely shaved flakes seem to dance upon the food they garnish, but they take some chewing. The aroma is smoky, and the taste is of the ocean.*

The tuna fillets used for katsuobushi are shaved
❰ *using a tool that looks like a carpenter's plane.*

Shiokara

Originally produced as a way of preserving fish during the winter, shiokara is the salted and fermented guts of fish, most usually squid and cuttlefish, although regional variations are made with sardines, bonito, and mackerel. Pickling in Japan is almost always a salt-based procedure, rather than a vinegar one, and the process produces amino acids that are beneficial to health and full of flavor. Shiokara is used to flavor dishes, as well as eaten as an accompaniment to rice.

In Nagasaki, on the southern island of Kyushu, shiokara is made with the locally caught anchovies, *katakuchi iwashi*, or, in the local dialect, *etari*. After the catch, the whole anchovies are scaled, washed in sea water, packed under layers of salt, and covered in rice straw, which contains microbial flora and aids fermentation. Unfortunately, *etari* stocks in the area are declining, although efforts are being made to revive them.

Similar salted and fermented fish products are found throughout Asia, such as Thailand's *nam pla* and Vietnam's *nuoc mam*. **SB**

Taste: *Shiokara is strong, salty, and highly savory with a slight bitterness that lingers in the mouth. It has a pleasantly chewy and slippery texture.*

Doubanjiang

Coconut Milk

An essential flavoring in the cooking of China's Szechuan province, this thick, richly flavored paste with its reddish-brown hue is based on fresh red chiles, salt, and fermented lima beans: an unusual ingredient, since most other Chinese bean pastes are made only from soybeans. It is made in various areas of Szechuan, but the best is said to come from the town of Pixian, near the capital, Chengdu.

Although it is made from just a few ingredients, doubanjiang can have very different levels of heat and flavor. It all depends on the long and careful process of fermenting and aging: each step can take anywhere from a few months to two years, or even longer. In older pastes, the heat level decreases and the complexity increases as age mellows and softens the chiles.

Unlike other chile-bean pastes, doubanjiang is almost always used as a flavoring ingredient, in the same way as garlic, ginger, and rice wine. It is rarely used on its own as a dipping sauce. In English, doubanjiang is usually labeled "spicy [or hot] chile-bean paste" or "spicy [or hot] lima-bean paste." **KKC**

The coconut tree (*Cocos nucifera*) has a plethora of uses across the tropics where it grows. The fronds can roof a hut, the fibrous husks can mulch a garden, and hollowing out the trunk provides a ready-made canoe. In just one meal, the fruit can yield a drink, flavor a soup or curry, and make a sweet dessert.

Coconut milk is not the water found inside the coconut. It is produced by infusing the shredded white flesh of the fruit with boiling water; the liquid is then strained from the pulp through a cloth. Using less water in the infusion produces a thicker liquid known as coconut cream. This is not to be confused with the product sold commercially, which needs reconstituting with hot water. For the freshest taste, coconut milk can easily be extracted at home.

In the South Pacific, coconut milk is a staple used in everything from *thom kha gai*, a classic Thai chicken and coconut soup, to modern fusion treatments of Australian shrimp curry. In India, coconut milk is made into sweets like *burfi* and simmered into curries. New World chefs are also aware of its delights, using it to concoct exquisite rice puddings and cream pies. **TH**

Taste: *Good doubanjiang has a spicy yet mellow complexity that is delicious with meats and complements subtler ingredients, such as fish, without overwhelming them.*

Taste: *Good coconut milk is silky smooth with a deep aroma. Older or inferior versions will be chalky in texture. Shake canned versions before opening to redistribute fats.*

Coconut milk is freshly prepared on the shores of Tuamotu, French Polynesia. ❯❯

Cassareep

A trip to the local market of any Caribbean island is a true adventure of sight and sound. The cacophony of parrots and stall hawkers is matched with an equally heady mix of colors and smells, amid which the dull brown cassava root looks almost out of place.

Known locally as yuca or manioc, cassava is grown both in the Caribbean and in West Africa as a staple dietary starch and is, curiously, the parent of tapioca. To make cassareep, grated cassava is pressed or squeezed to release the juice, then mixed with raw sugar and spices such as cinnamon or clove. This is simmered and reduced to a moderately thick consistency with a pungency and sweetness that varies considerably between recipes.

The real value of cassareep is in the kitchens of the Caribbean and along the northeastern coasts of South America. There it is synonymous with the many versions of the classic pepperpot, a regional stew made from pork, chicken, onions, and chiles gently simmered with the syrup. Less commonly, cassareep is the basis for more elaborate chili or fruit sauces used with both meats and seafood. **TH**

Taste: *Cassareep tastes like the bitter elements of molasses. Rather unpleasant when consumed directly, its complexity adds a unique layer of flavor to pepperpot.*

Once the tough, brown skin of cassava is peeled, the crisp, white flesh grates easily to make cassareep.

Umeboshi

In Japan, the appearance of the first *ume* blossom signals the start of spring, a moment enshrined in poems, paintings, and festivals. When the fruits appear in June it is time to make umeboshi, the brine-cured, sun-dried fruit that has been an indispensable part of the Japanese diet for centuries.

Beloved of the seventeenth-century feudal lord and gourmand Mito Komon, these highly acidic delights are still a daily feature of the Japanese table. *Ume* fruits (*Prunus mume*), despite their alternative names of Japanese apricots or Japanese plums, are acid and bitter when raw, and toxic when unripe. Their characteristic color comes from red shiso leaves, which also add flavor and minerals.

The flavor of umeboshi marries well with green vegetables, and oily fish simmered in an umeboshi broth is particularly fine. One single plum on top of white rice resembles the Japanese flag, thereby gaining this food a symbolic as well as nutritional place in the hearts of the Japanese. A puree of the flesh of umeboshi, *bainiku*, adds piquancy to dressings and sauces. **SB**

Taste: *Small umeboshi can be crunchy and tart, but larger ones can be soft, juicy, and fruity. All are exceptionally salty and acidic, with a palate-cleansing zestiness.*

Mayonnaise

Aïoli

The origin of the word "mayonnaise" has long been controversial. Some food historians suppose it to be a corruption of *bayonnaise* (from Bayonne in southwest France) or linked to an Old French word for egg yolk, *moyeu*. It is generally accepted, however, that its earliest spelling—*mahonnaise*—ties it to the capital of the Balearic island of Minorca, Mahón.

A simple, seasoned, emulsified sauce made from egg yolk and olive oil, it may have evolved from mortar and pestle emulsions such as aïoli into the whisked sauce that was fashionable by the early nineteenth century. Over time, the sauce has added a wide palette of variations such as flavoring with vinegar, mustard, or lemon juice and the use of different oils. Science has demystified the process by putting mayonnaise under the microscope to show how the droplets of oil and yolk coalesce. Modern electric blenders allow its making in under a minute.

At its simplest and best, prepared with egg yolks from free-range chickens and a golden extra virgin olive oil that is soft and sweet, rather than harsh and overly green, it stands the test of time. **MR**

Jean-Baptiste Germain, an eighteenth-century Provençal poet, wrote a poem about a divine fish stew, *La Bourrido dei Dieoux*, in which he memorably described a perfect aïoli: "Venus made it so stiff for him, / That the pestle stood upright in the mortar." Erect pestles and love goddesses aside, however, the couplet gives an indication as to how the garlic-and-olive-oil sauce that is the "national" dish of Provence should be. Like many other sauces, it is made into an emulsion—the difference here is that this is done in a mortar. First the garlic is crushed, then it is mixed with egg yolk, and finally oil is added, drip by drip.

In nineteenth-century farmhouses, aïoli was made in large quantities—the pestle was attached to the ceiling by a cord so the cook's arms did not become too tired blending in the oil. In winter it was eaten with vegetables, but restaurants today present it with fish, salt cod, or the *bourride* to which it plays the same supporting role as *rouille* does bouillabaisse. Neighboring Catalans often omit the egg and call their sauce *allioli*. **MR**

Taste: *Creamy, smooth, and unctuous, fresh mayonnaise should be light and well-aerated, too. The taste should reflect a perfect balance between the oil and the egg.*

Taste: *Aïoli should be thick and unctuous, almost to the point where a spoon will stand up in it. The fresh flavor of garlic should be softened by a gentle Provençal olive oil.*

Aïoli is traditionally made using olive oil and garlic, although some recipes add egg as an emulsifier. ❯❯

Tartare Sauce

Banana Ketchup

In its modern incarnation, tartare sauce is a hybrid containing elements of a seventeenth-century sauce, remoulade, and a nineteenth-century derivative of mayonnaise. It has nothing to do with the Mongolian Tartars who overran China in the thirteenth century and its link to the raw, chopped steak tartare may be either incidental or accidental.

The earliest remoulades were a kind of broth mixed with anchovies, capers, onions, garlic, and parsley. The first English recipe for tartare sauce, using mayonnaise, capers, and herbs was published by Eliza Acton in 1845—forty-one years after the first printed reference to mayonnaise. Since then this piquant sauce has become an omnipresent partner to fried fish, initially in aspirational, French-inspired cooking, but more recently in pubs and fish and chip shops. Overly acidic manufactured versions skimp on the capers, cornichons, scallions, and fresh parsley that give the recipe interest.

In France, the sauce is traditionally prepared with a hard-boiled egg-yolk, sometimes with the chopped white added to it. **MR**

Since the eighteenth century, ketchups based on various ingredients have seen highs and lows of popularity. In the Philippines, and from the South Pacific into Indonesia and the Caribbean, it is mashed bananas that mutate the now-classic pairing of ripe tomatoes and exotic spices into an experience worthy of the most intrepid gourmand.

Although most likely invented in imitation of the tomato version, banana ketchup vastly expands both its sweet and heat dimensions. It uses little or no tomato paste, relying instead on locally available fruits, vegetables, vinegar, a litany of spices, and, of course, fresh bananas, but is generally colored red, either naturally or artificially.

Variations on the theme vary as widely as the culinary cultures that create them, and each region will add its own local twist to the recipe. Wherever they are, they gain favor as a principal ingredient in barbecues, as additions to soups and stocks, and as a condiment on a huge variety of dishes from noodles to *lumpia,* the spring rolls of the Philippines and Indonesia. **TH**

Taste: *The smoothness of the mayonnaise contrasts with the texture of the diced vegetables. It should taste herby and only a little sharp without eclipsing the olive oil flavor.*

Taste: *Curiously reminiscent of tomato ketchup in color and consistency, but sweeter and with more spice. The banana flavor, surprisingly, can even be hard to spot.*

The buds of the Mediterranean caper shrub are
❿ *picked before they open and are then pickled.*

Mole

Throughout the thirty-one states of Mexico, there are countless culinary opinions, which makes the task of defining authentic tastes challenging. No more so than in the case of the classic sauce, mole.

Many misconceptions about this elusive group of sauces exist. For example, while many do contain chocolate, it is not always a defining ingredient. (The bitter dark chocolate used enriches the mole sauce rather than sweetens it.) However, what seems to define mole is a complex formula, rich in chiles, that takes careful, often long preparation. The most famous mole sauces come from Oaxaca and Puebla, where current recipes are thought to first originate.

Recipes can call for twenty or more ingredients, including chocolate, seeds, nuts, raisins, allspice, cinnamon, and several different chiles. The ingredients, often roasted, are ground up, often with oil, and then simmered in a stock. In one popular dish, poultry is cooked in a dark brown *mole poblano* sauce until it almost falls off the bone. Another incarnation is *mole verde*, a green sauce made with tomatillos that is perfect with roast pork. **TH**

Taste: *Most versions are complex enough to redefine the flavors of the component ingredients. Rich and smoky, mole often has chocolate and chile undertones.*

A Mexican woman offers mole in tortilla at the family altar. »

Hummus

Tahini

A Middle Eastern meze table without a bowl of hummus is like an Arabian Night without a tale. This simple dish of mashed or pureed chickpeas, usually now flavored with tahini, garlic, lemon juice, salt, and often olive oil too, was originally an inexpensive, vegetarian protein source. Today, it is enjoyed by rich and poor on a daily basis throughout the Arab world, as well as in Israel, Turkey, Greece, and Cyprus. It is a national food for many countries, several of which claim credit for its creation, and most of which compete for the best recipe.

Available in supermarkets and delis around the globe, hummus is easy to make. Both texture and flavor profile vary from region to region, depending on the balance of ingredients and how they are blended: Syrian versions often include herbs and spices. Hummus is served with a variety of garnishes, often in combination with each other: olive oil, whole chickpeas, parsley, cilantro, paprika, cumin, and anardana (pomegranate seeds) are just a few of the adornments that find their way onto the plate. It can also be used as a sandwich filling. **BLeB**

Hummus, baba ghanoush, and tarator would all be much lesser culinary treats if they lacked the subtle, earthy flavor of this creamy paste. Although not usually eaten on its own in its natural state, tahini is an essential flavoring element in many traditional Middle Eastern dips and sauces. In Israel, it is thinned with water and drizzled over just-fried falafel and hot kabobs; in Lebanon, it is made into a simple lemony sauce that is served with fresh fish. It even finds its way into some of the numerous different recipes for halva, a sweet confection that appears in many guises in every country of the Middle East.

The versatile paste is laboriously extracted from sesame seeds in a process that involves crushing, grilling, milling, and two periods of soaking. The paste, which is sold in jars in Middle Eastern food shops, delis, and some supermarkets, is thick and varies in color from light to dark beige. Aficionados favor the lighter versions, which come from earliest pressings, but either quality adds a depth of flavor to other ingredients. Tahini is known in Arabic, and sometimes in English, as tahina. **BLeB**

Taste: *The best-made hummus has the key notes of tahini, garlic, and lemon juice blended so no one flavor dominates. Texture ranges from smooth to chunky.*

Taste: *Rich, thick, and smooth, tahini paste has a quite pronounced, earthy sesame flavor that combines very well with lemon juice and other sharp flavors.*

Hummus is traditionally served as one of the
◈ **small appetizer dishes that make up meze.**

Genoese Pesto

Pâté di Carciofi

Essentially a pounded blend of herbs and other flavorings, pesto must be one of the oldest sauces in the world. It is probably also one of the most copied—with, on occasion, some of the worst results. The real McCoy was a Genoese invention, a delicious concoction highlighting the magical flavor of the sweet, fragrant leaves of the local Ligurian basil. (Today, much of Italy's commercial pesto production is centered around the village of Pra in Liguria, an area noted for its basil farms.)

Genoese pesto has always been made using a mortar and pestle: the word comes from the Italian verb *pestare*, which means "to crush." Garlic, pine nuts, salt, olive oil, and cheese—customarily a mixture of Pecorino and Parmigiano-Reggiano—are the only components apart from basil.

Fresh, handmade Genoese pesto is one of the world's true delights, best stirred into hot pasta, soup, or slathered over warm focaccia as it is in its home region. While pairing it with hot or warm ingredients accentuates its flavor, cooking kills its essence: fresh crushed basil. **LF**

Artichokes are an utterly sublime vegetable that belongs to the thistle family, but, like so many superlative foods, they are seasonal. In Italy, where artichokes have long been especially valued, the age old art of conservation comes to the rescue in the form of pate di carciofi, a glorious pâté with a texture similar to tapenade, usually made simply from artichokes, extra virgin olive oil, white wine vinegar, salt, and garlic, and sometimes herbs. There are also versions available containing ground almonds, Parmigiano-Reggiano cheese, and even truffles.

Pate di carciofi—also referred to as crema di carciofi—is always available from good Italian food stores and delis. It is especially popular in Sicily and Apulia, two of Italy's major artichoke growing areas. A versatile spread, it creates a fabulous topping for bruschetta and crostini, makes a tasty sandwich filling and, stirred into hot pasta, makes a stunning, yet simple, sauce. It is easy enough to make at home too, either by using fresh artichokes in season, or by pureeing good-quality artichokes that have been preserved in extra virgin olive oil. **LF**

Taste: *Heady with sweet, perfumed basil, the subtle suggestions of garlic combine with a creaminess helped by slightly buttery pine nuts and balanced by salty cheese.*

Taste: *Depending on the recipe, pate di carciofi will display a balance of smooth, grassy, and buttery characteristics, along with a gently muted sweetness.*

The regular harvesting of basil
❷ **promotes generous new growth.**

Tapenade

Ajvar

Ancient Roman cooks had a recipe for crushed olives—*epityrum*—that they mixed with cumin, coriander, rue, mint, and oil. It predates tapenade by almost two millenia. What it lacks, however, are capers. The Provençal word for a caper tree—*tapeno* or *taperié*—gave its name to a caper sauce *tapenado* that has since evolved into what is known as tapenade today—the flavored blend of crushed olives, extra virgin olive oil, anchovies, and capers. (Somehow anchovies joined the mix along the way.) Not exactly a dip, a paste, or a sauce—it is really all three depending on how it is used. It may be spread on toast, offered as a dip with raw celery, or served as an accompaniment to grilled fish.

Both green Picholine and black olives can be made into tapenade, although black olives from Nyons in the Drôme are ideal. The capers themselves are the buds from the tree, picked before they flower, and pickled in salt or vinegar. Making tapenade with an electric blender takes only a few moments today, but its texture and taste seem to improve when it has been ground slowly by hand in a mortar. **MR**

In the Balkans, at the end of the autumn harvest, a delicacy arises from the surplus that rivals mustard and mayonnaise in versatility: ajvar. Most kitchens will hold a jar of this blend of sweet red peppers and eggplant, whether homemade or packaged, to use as a spread or condiment.

Recipes blossom from this simple base into more complex affairs featuring smaller amounts of squash, tomatoes, onions, and garlic. Traditionally the ingredients are hand-prepared, skins and seeds, are stripped off, then slowly simmered together to preserve their flavors. Wood fires are often used to impart mild smoke notes, but spicing and heat are never overpowering. The brilliance of ajvar is the ingenuity that sees individual ingredients married into a blend that is greater than the sum of its parts.

Texture varies from smooth to chunky and, while almost always a brilliant fresh red, some versions can be green or amber depending on the vegetables involved. Perfect on sandwiches and antipasti, ajvar can also be tossed with warm pasta or used as a dip with pita bread. **TH**

Taste: *Tapenade can be smooth, coarse, or granular. Its dominant flavor is of olives, but the anchovies and capers should also contribute their distinctive notes.*

Taste: *The sweetness of pepper flesh is accented by the mild bitterness of eggplant. There are "mild" and "hot" varieties, as well as some with a stronger smoked taste.*

Baba Ghanoush

Muhammara

It is not for nothing that this popular Middle Eastern dish is known as "poor man's caviar." The intriguing combination of smoky eggplant blended with tahini, garlic, lemon juice, and salt create a tasty dip or spread that belies its simple ingredients.

The origins of this essential meze dish are lost in the mists of time and culinary folklore, although medieval Arabic manuscripts indicate the passion for eggplants dates back to at least the thirteenth century. Baba ghanoush appears in many guises throughout the region, sometimes under its alternative name of moutabel, and in Ottoman times it was said that the women of the harem prepared it to win the Sultan's favor. A Lebanese version omits the tahini, making a less indulgent dish; in parts of Syria yogurt replaces the tahini.

The essential smoky flavor comes from grilling the eggplant over hot coals or baking it in a very hot oven until it simply collapses, making the flesh easy to blend with the other ingredients. The dip is served chilled or at room temperature with pita or other kinds of flatbread. **BLeB**

Smoky, slightly textured, and red, a glowing mound of muhammara awaits the invasion of a triangle of crisp flatbread to escort it to an eager mouth. Less well known than its meze cousins hummus and baba ghanoush, this roasted red bell pepper dip originated centuries ago in Aleppo, within the borders of modern-day Syria, where the spice routes of the Mediterranean, and Turkish and Armenian culinary traditions, influenced its zesty complexity.

Muhammara is made by grinding scorched and skinned red bell (capsicum) peppers with oil, walnuts, lemon, garlic, cumin, and pomegranate molasses. The local piquant Aleppo pepper adds a spicy, but subtle kick. This lush, highly flavored puree makes a stronger statement than other meze dips and is equally good as an accompaniment to grilled meats or fish. In western Turkey, it is sometimes called *acuka*, whereas in the Lebanon mint leaves might be added to the exotic mixture to spread on toast. The flavor of muhammara is best when it has been prepared a few hours in advance and served at room temperature. **RH**

Taste: *Grilled, rather than baked, eggplants give a more pronounced smoky flavor, which is complemented by the tang of lemon juice and garlic. The texture should be light.*

Taste: *Tantalizing complex, the slightly nut-textured mouthfeel of muhammara bursts with a smoky sweetness leveled out by the tartness of the pomegranate and lemon.*

Bumbu Kacang

Yeast Extract

In Indonesia the special peanut sauce, known locally as bumbu kacang, is used on everything from chicken satay to rice noodles.

While peanut sauces are common throughout Southeast Asia, this elaborate version gains fame by the inclusion of shrimp paste and chile, whether chopped fresh or via prepared *sambal oelek*, a paste made of chile and garlic. Soy sauce, citrus juices, ginger, kaffir lime leaves, and even fruit chutneys further round out the taste of bumbu kacang, offering a cascade of flavors, layer upon layer. The peanuts are usually roasted fresh in most recipes, with the newly expressed oil contributing to the end consistency. Palm sugar, garlic, and onions balance the heat of the chile and bring more complexity. Purists refrain from overcooking the sauce and rely on time to meld the flavors into their final form.

Satays of any kind are traditionally accompanied by bumbu kacang, as is *gado-gado*, the famous salad of Indonesia, but the sauce appears elsewhere for both table and kitchen use throughout the archipelagoes of Southeast Asia. **TH**

The dark brown, savory paste, known to millions as Marmite, is made from the yeast that is a by-product of the brewing industry. Marmite is a British brand owned by the food giant Unilever and has been spread on bread and toast for more than a century. The name refers to a French cooking pot, pictured on the label, which was perhaps chosen because the color, appearance, and aroma of Marmitea vaguely resemble the juices produced by pot-roasting beef. Marmite trades on its "love it or loathe it" image.

The process of converting waste yeast into a protein-rich paste was discovered by the German scientist Baron Liebig. Salt added to the yeast triggers a process known as autolysis whereby the biological cells self-destruct. To complete the recipe, the outer husks of yeast cells are removed and the remaining "sludge" is blended with a similar vegetable extract, natural flavorings, and added vitamins.

Marmite is made under license in New Zealand, but to a different recipe that includes sugar, giving it a less assertive flavor. The rival brand Vegemite is much loved in Australia. **MR**

Taste: *Freshly prepared bumbu kacang is simultaneously salty, sweet, and sour on top of an intense, roasted peanut flavor. Flavor accents vary according to the recipe.*

Taste: *A little goes a long way because it is sticky, sharp, and salty. The taste is heightened by the naturally occurring* umami *in it, caused by the protein's breakdown.*

Marmite has the reputation of a highly nutritional food, a fact alluded to in this 1929 advertisement. »

Yellow Bean Sauce

Hoisin Sauce

The ancient Chinese discovered that fermenting different types of beans was a way to both preserve them as well as enhance their flavor. Yellow bean sauce gets its name not from the color of the finished product—which is actually brown—but from the Chinese name for the main ingredient—*huang dou* or yellow soybeans.

Yellow bean sauce is made by first soaking the soybeans, then cooking them, and letting them ferment before adding rice wine and sugar. The fermented beans are then aged before being mashed and mixed with other ingredients. Depending on the producer and the region where it is made, the salty sauce can be chunky, smooth, sweet, or spicy. In Vietnam, where it is known as *nuoc tuong*, lemongrass, coconut, ground peanuts, chiles, and garlic are usually included in the sauce.

Yellow bean sauce is popular in Chinese and Thai cooking. It can be mixed with other ingredients to make a dipping sauce or condiment, or incorporated into cooked dishes. It works well with fish and seafood, as well as chicken and beef. **KKC**

In China, hoisin sauce is used in much the same way as ketchup is in the West—although, fortunately, a little more sparingly. It may be used as a dipping sauce straight from the jar or bottle, added judiciously during cooking to add depth and complexity, or mixed with other ingredients to make a coating for barbecued meats—hence its occasional name of "barbecue sauce."

One of the better-known Chinese condiments, hoisin sauce is made from fermented soybeans, vinegar, salt, sugar, garlic, chile, and five-spice powder, thickened with starch and colored with food colorings. It is often served with Peking duck—the laboriously prepared whole duck with golden, crisp skin and moist, succulent flesh—but in China the traditional accompaniment is thinner and less sweet, yet also based on fermented soybeans.

Although some of the less expensive Chinese restaurants have hoisin sauce on the table for diners to use at will, any talented Chinese chef will be every bit as horrified by this notion as an American or French counterpart. **KKC**

Taste: *Thick, glossy, and brown, yellow bean sauce varies in texture. The saltiness of the sauce should be balanced by the flavor of the other ingredients added to it.*

Taste: *Hoisin sauce should always be used sparingly— a little goes a long way. The best versions are beautifully balanced with salty, sweet, and spicy flavors.*

Oyster Sauce

Even in the bad old days of experimental fusion cooking, when chefs were haphazardly adding all sorts of Asian ingredients to their food, oyster sauce never really made the culinary leap from East to West. Commercial oyster sauce—the kind sold on supermarket shelves—is made by cooking oyster extract with other ingredients, such as soy sauce, sugar, cornstarch, caramel coloring, and preservatives. Yet a few artisans in Chinese seaside villages or Hong Kong's New Territories still make it the traditional way. They harvest oysters and cook them according to secret family recipes, without any of the industrial additives. You might have to go to the source to buy these small-batch sauces, but it should be worth every step of the journey.

While oyster sauce is at times used as a dipping sauce, it is more often used in small quantities to flavor dishes. It goes well with eggs, noodles, vegetables, and meats, such as beef and chicken, but should be used with care In seafood dishes so as not to overwhelm the delicate flavors. A vegetarian version is made from mushrooms. **KKC**

Taste: *Authentic, small-batch oyster sauce has a strong, pure, oyster flavor. Despite the unappealing color, this is a different creature from the factory-made ingredient.*

XO Sauce

Although it has its namesake in XO cognac, XO sauce contains no alcohol. The name is meant to evoke a luxurious, expensive, and very special product, something with a status and cost equivalent to the fine cognac that is a cult item in China. XO sauce was invented in Hong Kong during the 1980s and its popularity spread quickly. Many chefs claim credit for its creation, but what is certain is that it was originally made only at the top Cantonese restaurants, and these places still produce the best: most restaurants that make it sell their own recipe in jars on the premises.

The essential ingredients in XO sauce are dried scallops, oil, chiles, and garlic. It can also contain dried shrimp, dried Chinese ham, and salted fish. It is usually used in small quantities, often as a dipping sauce with dim sum. The sauce shines in simple preparations. It is delicious tossed with noodles; paired with minced scallions, it makes a delectable topping for fresh oysters. As it is relatively expensive, XO sauce is a popular gift in Christmas and Chinese New Year hampers. **KKC**

Taste: *The best brands contain larger quantities of dried scallops, which are more expensive than other ingredients. The intense, chunky sauce is salty, spicy, and oily.*

Terasi

Sheto

Foul-smelling and rotten, Indonesian terasi, a paste made from shrimp that have been left to ferment, can entirely overwhelm the uninitiated. Yet like garlic or asafoetida, this unappealing ingredient can utterly transform a dish, as the aroma of rotting shrimp thankfully dissipates, leaving behind a taste that puts common fish sauce to shame.

The shrimp turn a mahogany color during fermentation and are often sun-dried, pulverized, and pressed into blocks before packaging. It is also sold in jars as a thick paste, sometimes capped with wax or oil as a preservative, and more rarely as a powder. Salt is always added, but other ingredients vary from producer to producer. Connoisseurs seek out artisan producers who use the very smallest shrimp, and ferment them the longest.

In Indonesia, the chili paste sambal is mixed with shrimp paste and other ingredients like tamarind and vinegar to produce the hot sambal terasi. Elsewhere in Southeast Asia terasi, or its siblings such as Malaysian *belacan* or Thai *kapi*, are added to hot oil before starting meat or vegetable sautés. **TH**

Situated on the west coast of Africa and the beneficiary of great ocean bounty, Ghana has put its own unique twists upon the culinary influences spread by seafaring traders over the centuries. Sheto is one of the distinctive hot condiments found across Africa and locals will argue to the death about the origins and recipe permutations of their own beloved pepper sauce.

Pronounced shee–toe, it partners two foods found in abundance locally, dried chiles and dried shrimp. These are blended with other ingredients such as ginger, garlic, and tomato paste into a salted oil base much like the harissa found elsewhere in Africa. Made from only dried ingredients, it can keep for months; versions featuring fresh chiles, herbs, and vegetables require quicker consumption.

Sheto is used to flavor many dishes. *Waakye*, simply rice and beans cooked in the local fashion, is almost always heightened with a dose of sheto. Similarly, starchy *fufu* balls made from cassava or yam can be dipped in shito and groundnut stew can have a few spoonfuls stirred in to give extra kick. **TH**

Taste: *Terasi tastes like an extremely concentrated fish sauce, but leaves, surprisingly, far less aroma than the raw paste suggests. Use the fluid paste in tiny amounts.*

Taste: *Hot chile and rich salty shrimp flavors are prominent but accented by other additions. Improves with age as the flavors meld and slightly mellow.*

Small shrimps are laid out to dry in the sun. The color ❸ of the paste varies from village to village.

Tamari Shoyu

Shiro Shoyu

Traditionally made soy sauce, or shoyu, in the style of many centuries ago, when soy sauce first arrived in Japan from China, makes up only one or two percent of Japan's entire production. There are only a handful of families who continue to make it the traditional way.

One such is the Aoki family, in Aichi, who still handcraft tamari shoyu to their original, 500-year-old recipe, using multiple, complex fermentations over a period of two years. They soak soybeans in spring water, then steam and crush them. Aspergillus spores and roasted barley flour are added, before the whole is left to incubate for three days, transforming into a fluffy mass of mold-covered beans. This is dried and mixed with sea salt and water to make a mash called *moromi*, which ferments in century-old cedar kegs over two summers, as enzymes, yeasts, and bacteria break down the proteins and carbohydrates. It seems that the microorganisms and natural oils in the wood of the cedar casks are crucial to the sauce that is ultimately pressed from the mash. **SB**

A white soy sauce, shiro shoyu is the product of a process that reverses the usual ratio of wheat and soybeans, using only twenty percent soybeans and eighty percent wheat. (The Shichifuku company in Aichi make an organic shiro shoyu using an even higher ratio, of ninety percent wheat and only ten of soybeans.) Soy sauce has been used in the Orient for centuries, and was brought to Japan by Buddhist monks from China in the thirteenth century, but it was only around 400 years ago that wheat was used in its preparation—before then it was made only with soybeans. Using such a high proportion of wheat gives the sauce a much lighter amber color and a sweet mellow flavor.

In Japan, shiro shoyu is used mainly for cooking, not as a dipping sauce, and it is especially prized when the cook wants to preserve the natural color of an ingredient. It is popular in the cuisine of Kyoto when the natural color of vegetables, such as the *Kyo ninjin* red carrot and white daikon, must be displayed to their best advantage. It is also used in the delicate, steamed egg custard, *chawan mushi*. **SB**

Taste: *Tamari shoyu has the prized umami taste. With its thick, viscous texture and rich savory, but mildly salty, taste, it is ideal both for dipping sauces and for cooking.*

Taste: *Sweet, mellow, and lightly smoky, while still being salty, shiro shoyu has a background muskiness of wheat. The color darkens with age, but does not affect the flavor.*

Kecap

Nuoc Mam

Soy sauce, Asia's most famous culinary export, is believed to have its roots in the sixth century when Buddhists in China developed a salty, grainy paste as a meat substitute. Popular in all oriental cuisines, styles of soy sauce vary widely from country to country, and Indonesia's kecaps are quite unique.

Kecap manis is sweet, thick, dark, and syrupy from the addition of palm sugar. If unavailable, it can be made by simmering a Chinese or Japanese dark soy sauce with sugar, star anise, and garlic, or replaced in recipes with a blend of molasses, dark soy sauce, and vegetable or chicken stock. Kecap asin is lighter, thinner, and saltier than its manis cousin. Kecap manis needs the richness of beef and lamb to balance its strong flavor, whereas kecap asin is more versatile and complements dishes where retaining the fresh flavor and color of the food is necessary, such as chicken or seafood dishes.

One theory links kecap to ketchup, a generic word used to describe sauces and condiments long before it became synonymous with a well-known brand of tomato sauce. **WS**

In Southeast Asia, where fermented fish sauces play a similar role to the soy sauces of Japan and China, Vietnam's nuoc mam is probably the most sublime, and the most revered. A warm, rich brown in hue, its finely nuanced flavor is the foundation for many dipping sauces; when used in cooking, its natural glutamates and other proteins enhance the overall taste profile of a dish without domineering it.

Nuoc mam is made by layering fresh anchovies and sea salt in wooden or earthenware vats and letting them ferment for several months to a year. The first, most treasured tapping of the vats is sold as nuoc mam nhi, an "extra virgin" nuoc mam. Later "pressings" are based on what remains from the first tapping, and labels often—but not always—bear a rating expressed in degrees, which is a guide to quality. Higher grades have undergone less dilution and are suitable for table use; lower grades are reserved for cooking. Phu Quoc, a Vietnamese island whose surrounding waters teem with especially prized anchovies is famous for its nuoc mam, which now has protected appellation status. **CTa**

Taste: *Dark, thick, and almost treacly in consistency, kecap manis packs a powerful sweet-savory punch. Lighter, saltier, kecap asin can season all kinds of dishes.*

Taste: *Top-grade nuoc mam has an intensely marine savor that is never pungent or harsh. Its saltiness is balanced by caramel notes and a natural sweetness.*

Chimichurri

The Argentines, purveyors of some of the world's best beef, allow very little to come into contact with their sublime steaks. Chimichurri is the notable exception. Across South America there are countless recipes for this blend of herbs, spices, vinegar, salt, and olive oil, which vary not only by region but according to each chef's secret recipe. In Argentina, fresh parsley, garlic, oregano, and chiles form the basis of the blend; in other parts of Latin America, cilantro is a popular ingredient; tea, lemon, honey, mint, and other herbs might also feature.

Most think this herb-packed sauce originated with the gauchos who roamed the fertile grasslands that are now in Argentina, Uruguay, and Paraguay during the nineteenth century. Some folktales attribute its name to a corruption of the name of a European immigrant—maybe Jimmy McCurry, or Jimmy Curry—who concocted the sauce, using vinegar to tenderize the lean beef of the highlands. Whatever the truth of the matter, the taste clearly reflects the manifold flavors brought by the waves of arrivals from different European nations. **IA**

Taste: *Chimichurri has a vibrant flavor, the piquancy of which depends on the vinegar content. Its green herb freshness works nicely as a condiment to grilled steak.*

Gauchos traditionally ate chimichurri with their steak. »

Tabasco Sauce

Worcestershire Sauce

On Avery Island, Louisiana, the buzz of bayou insects amid trees draped in Spanish moss might lull the unsuspecting visitor into thinking the calendars were stuck a century or so earlier. Any illusions soon come crashing down, however, once the factory that makes Tabasco pepper sauce comes into view.

Edmund McIlhenny founded the company in 1868 based on the initial success of an aged pepper sauce that has since become a benchmark of piquancy, not only in the southern United States but all around the globe. The chile peppers are all started locally in the spring from hand-selected heirloom seed gathered from previous crops. Although some seedlings are matured in Latin America, like their local siblings they are picked by hand using a painted red baton as a color guide, then returned to Avery Island for processing. Ripe peppers are immediately ground into a mash, mixed with locally mined salt, sealed in oak barrels, capped by a sealing layer of salt, and aged in warehouses for three years. Ultimately the mash is blended with vinegar, stirred, and strained before bottling. **TH**

Early in the nineteenth century, there was a fashion in England for "store sauces"—or sauces that could be kept in the pantry—among them mushroom ketchup, Harvey's sauce, and Lord North's sauce.

About the time Queen Victoria was coming to the throne in 1837, a retired governor of Bengal asked two Worcester pharmacists, Messrs Lea and Perrin, to make a recipe he had acquired during his stay in the subcontinent for a sauce that included tamarind, soy, garlic, anchovy, and spices. The chemists' efforts failed to please their client, so they put the barrel away and forgot about it until 1838 when they tasted it again. Realizing the aging had improved the sauce, they put it on sale. The sauce's popularity was instantaneous and by 1843 it was being served in the first-class dining room of Brunel's steamship, the *Great Western*. A hidden ingredient in many dishes, notably Caesar salad, it is closely identified with the Bloody Mary cocktail and pairs wonderfully with melted cheese on toast. The Lea & Perrin's brand, the only authentic Worcestershire sauce, is now owned by H. J. Heinz. **MR**

Taste: *A distinctly clean chile flavor. Balanced heat, salt, and vinegar are persistent, and the attuned palate can detect an oaky ripeness from the aging process.*

Taste: *Worcestershire sauce's main attraction is the balance and complexity of its flavor. The overall impression is of a tangy, flavor-packed composite.*

A whisky barrel is recycled by Tabasco to age its famous pepper sauce.

Grain

Sunflower Seed

Sunflowers (*Helianthus annuus*) have a long history. Indigenous Americans were eating the energy-rich seeds of these bright flowers thousands of years ago. When sixteenth-century colonists brought the seeds back to England with them, the plants were at first grown only for decoration. However, when Peter the Great (1672–1725) brought the flowers to Russia, their arrival coincided with an edict banning the eating of oily plants on fast days: sunflowers, as a new introduction, were omitted from the list and thus their seeds gained popularity. Today, sunflower oil is still the most important cooking oil in Russia, while plants are greatly cultivated in North America.

Sunflower seeds are a popular snack, particularly around eastern Europe. They can be purchased with or without the stripy hull, salted or unsalted, roasted or plain, from street vendors or at farmers' markets. While for many the ritual of cracking the salty hull with their teeth, extracting the smooth seed, and spitting out the shell Is a blg part of the fun, the hulled seeds also make a fine addition to breads, cakes, cookies, muffins, muesli, or granola. **SH**

Taste: *Plain sunflower seeds are crunchy and slightly oily with a lively, nutty taste that can be overwhelmed by too much salt. The roasted seeds have a richer, toastier flavor.*

Sunflowers are known for their ability to grow to great heights; the heads can contain up to 2,000 seeds.

Pumpkin Seed

People have been eating pumpkin seeds since pumpkins were first cultivated probably more than 7,000 years ago. And for good reason. These flat green seeds with a yellow-white hull are extremely nutritious and tasty. Spanish conquerors probably learned of them from the Aztecs and then introduced them to Europe.

Today, since pumpkins are grown everywhere except Antarctica, the seeds are available and eaten around the world. Most are consumed either raw or toasted as a snack food, but they also play a role in cooking. Called *pepitas* in Spanish, they are an ingredient in Mexican moles, derived from an ancient Aztec recipe made with pumpkin seeds, tomatillos, cilantro, and other ingredients, and served with chicken or duck. Tossing the seeds in olive oil and soy sauce before toasting is another way to make a delicious snack. Pumpkin seeds can also be turned into a delicious pesto. They are frequently used by vegetarians, who add them to salads and baked goods and use them ground in soups, stews, and casseroles. **SH**

Taste: *Pumpkin seeds have a chewy texture and a nutty flavor with just a hint of pumpkin. If some pumpkin pulp is left on before toasting, the pumpkin taste is stronger.*

Wattleseed

For nearly a century Australians have celebrated Wattle Day by wearing a wattle-blossom as a show of patriotism. There are many hundreds of varieties of this Australian acacia, from scrambling woody shrubs to tall trees, but all are recognized by their clusters of golden (or sometimes pink) flowers.

For thousands of years, Australian Aborigines in different groups around the country collected, cleaned, parched, and milled the seeds from about 120 varieties, baking the coarse flour into nourishing seed cakes, high in protein and unsaturated fats. As wheat flour has become increasingly easy to come by, however, this practice is becoming rare.

The humble wattle's fortunes were changed forever when, in 1984, Australian Vic Cherikoff accidentally overroasted a unique species, creating the modern day product known as Wattleseed. The result of this happy accident is now available as a ground-seed product, a liquid extract, and a paste, and is used around the world in ice cream, cream, chocolates, spreads, butters, breads, pancakes, cookies, beverages, and other savories. **VC**

Taste: *The short chocolate palate offers ongoing coffee notes, but without the bitterness and with a nutty finish. Cream or milk unmasks these subtler flavors well.*

Lotus Seed

Somewhere or other in Asia, almost every part of the lotus plant is eaten. The rhizome is consumed in myriad ways: in Thailand, Vietnam, and parts of India, the stems and young leaves are valued vegetables; older leaves are used as wrappings; even the petals can be used as a garnish, or even eaten. The seeds, which grow in a curious, bowl-shaped pod, are also beloved. They are sometimes eaten fresh out of hand, but are more versatile when dried: in Vietnam, they are cooked in soups and stews.

In China, dried lotus seeds are used in sweet preparations. A thick sweet lotus paste is used to fill buns, particularly the mooncakes eaten during the mid-autumn festival and the buns, shaped like a peach to symbolize long life, that are traditionally served at birthday parties. Candied, they are a traditional part of *cheun hup*—the box of candy presented to visitors over Chinese New Year.

When buying dried lotus seeds, tiny holes indicate the presence of bugs. Seeds that are too yellow are too old; seeds that are too white have been bleached. **KKC**

Taste: *Lotus seeds have a starchy, subtly sweet flavor. They are delicious when roasted, which enhances the sweetness and gives them a flavor similar to corn.*

Lotus seeds can be seen growing in the top of curious, bowl-shaped pods. ❯❯

Pine Nut

Macadamia Nut

These small, creamy, ivory-colored seeds, also known as pine kernels, have been appreciated for their exquisite flavor since prehistoric times. The ancient Greeks and Romans knew and loved pine nuts: they are one of the foods archaeologists discovered in the ruins of Pompeii.

Although all of the numerous varieties of pine trees around the world produce seeds, only some are edible. Of these, the seeds of the Mediterranean (or Italian) stone pine, *Pinus pinea*, are particularly prized for their pronounced nutty flavor. It can take up to twenty-five years for a pine tree to crop, and seven years for the cones to mature sufficiently to release their seeds, so they are naturally expensive.

An essential ingredient in the exquisite Italian basil sauce pesto, pine nuts are paired with raisins and spinach in many Mediterranean cuisines. They are also fabulous added to salads and vegetables. They are high in monounsaturated fats (the good kind) and rich in protein, which does mean they tend to become rancid very quickly; they are best stored in the refrigerator. **LF**

Australian Aborigines have been eating macadamia nuts for millennia, gathering them from the tree they called *kindal kindal*. The Western culinary world, however, discovered them comparatively late. It was not until 1857 that two botanists came upon the trees in a Queensland rainforest and recorded the nuts' existence: Baron Ferdinand von Mueller described the tree botanically and Dr. Walter Hill named it after the pharmacist Dr. John Macadam.

Despite the difficulty in cracking their rock-hard shells, the nuts' qualities were soon recognized and small-scale commercial cultivation began. The Hawaiians made the first large-scale commercial planting in 1882, sparking an industry that now accounts for about ninety percent of world production. *Macadamia integrifolia* and *M. tetraphylla* are the main edible species found in the wild, and have been widely hybridized for agricultural use.

Most nuts are eaten plain or salted, but they can be made into cookies, confectionery, and ice cream. Small quantities of macadamia nut butter are also produced and available in whole-food stores. **SC-S**

Taste: *Raw pine nuts have a soft, milky texture and a sweet, buttery flavor. Light toasting without fat releases a more prominent nutty flavor, inviting aroma, and crisp texture.*

Taste: *Mellow-flavored and buttery, macadamias are best eaten unadorned with, at most, a little salt. Less brittle than harder nuts, they nonetheless have a satisfying crunch.*

The torpedo-shaped Italian nut is easily distinguished
❸ *from the Chinese nut, which is more triangular.*

Ginkgo Nut

Baobab Seed

The ginkgo tree is considered a living fossil, the last surviving species of a type that ruled the earth about 200 million years ago. Today the nuts—technically seeds—that appear during autumn are an important part of Chinese vegetarian cuisine.

Ginkgo biloba trees are either male or female, and pollination has to take place before the female bears seeds. Sadly for ginkgo-loving humans, who might relish the thought of harvesting the abundant seeds of the female tree there is, however, a big drawback to having a ginkgo tree in your backyard: the soft pulp around the seed has a highly pungent, unpleasant smell, and gives off a sticky substance. Fortunately, ginkgo is cleaned before being sent to market. The smelly exterior is removed, leaving a pristine, easy-to-crack, beige shell around the edible core, which is also sometimes removed for ease.

In China, ginkgo seeds are used in the well-known and appropriately named vegetarian dish, "Buddha's delight." In Japan, they frequently appear alongside other elements in the savory custards known as *chawan mushi*. **KKC**

The monumental baobab tree (*Adansonia digitata*) provides one of the most striking silhouettes on the landscapes of Africa and Australia: its vast trunk sprouts tangled, root-like branches that look as if the tree has been planted upside down. Indeed, legend has it the tree was uprooted by the gods and replanted after it complained about its appearance.

Taken from the elongated, velvet pods borne by the large, white pendulous flowers of the tree, baobab seeds are covered in a powdery white pulp that is rich in citric and tartaric acid, as well as having high levels of vitamin C, calcium, iron, and dietary fiber. The tart fruit pulp of the seeds is used to make a refreshing, astringent drink, which locals use to treat fever and diarrhea. The pulp can substitute for cream of tartar and is also used in powder form to thicken sauces. The seeds are ground to make a creamy butter and a soft porridge.

The baobab tree offers vital shelter, food, and water (its trunk stores large quantities), among many other things. With so many valuable uses, it is no wonder it is also known as "the tree of life." **HFi**

Taste: *Ginkgo nuts are waxy, tender, and slightly chewy; the flavor is like chestnuts, especially when roasted or broiled. Avoid canned, peeled, or vacuum-packed versions.*

Taste: *Encased in a hard brown kernel, the seeds are coated in a powdery pulp, which has a mildly sour, light lemony taste. The seeds can be eaten raw or roasted.*

The ginkgo tree is the official tree of Kumamoto; it can
Ⓚ *often be found planted in avenues around the city.*

Cashew Nut

Marcona Almond

Toasted and salted, the cashew nut's wonderful combination of delicate flavor, tangy salt, and smooth, but crunchy, texture have made them one of the world's favorite appetizers. Yet they have many other uses, too. Native to the coast of Brazil, the cashew tree, *Anacardium occidentale*, was exported by Portuguese colonizers first to Africa, then to Asia; it has since reached Australasia, too. Its curved nut is part of the cuisine of many countries, including India, Indonesia, China, and Vietnam.

In Brazil, the cashew nut finds a staggering range of uses. Fresh cashews star, with egg whites and other additions, such as shrimp and coconut, in the delicious *frigideira de maturi*; they can also be a part of the Bahian fish stew *moqueca*. The nuts are also used in baking and sweet-making; ground and crushed, they decorate the rim of ice-cream goblets; they are at the heart of cashew butter, a tasty spread used in a similar way to peanut butter. In South China, India, and Vietnam, cashews appear in many savory dishes; in Indonesia, they are part of the spicy fruit salad known as *rujak*. **AL**

Marcona almonds are cultivated throughout the Mediterranean provinces of Spain, from Catalunya down to Murcia. They were probably introduced to the region by the Moors in the thirteenth century, but it was only during the twentieth century they became widely cultivated when demand for dried fruits and pâtisserie products grew worldwide. The most highly prized marcona almonds are harvested in the mountainous regions of Alicante.

The marcona almond is a short, round almond appreciated for its sweet flavor and high levels of fat. Various traditional almond products in Spain can only be made with marcona almonds if they are to comply with quality standards of their respective PDOs. In Spain, marcona almonds are widely used for making traditional Christmas specialties such as *turrón de Jijona*. Similar to Middle Eastern *halva*, the main ingredients of turrón are almonds and honey.

Almond growers assess the quality of marcona almonds by eating them raw, straight out of the shell, because heating them allows some of the essential oils to escape. **RL**

Taste: *With a flavor between hazelnut and pistachio, the toasted cashew nut can win over most palates. It is also enticing when mixed with chocolate in sweets or truffles.*

Taste: *The sweet, buttery flavor of the marcona is evident when the nuts are drizzled in olive oil and lightly roasted. Fabulous with a little salt and enjoyed with a dry sherry.*

Almonds ripen on the tree; they can be harvested once the shell has split open to reveal the nut. »

Iranian Pistachio

Wild Green Hazelnut

The green, alluring nuts, brought to earth by Adam according to an Islamic legend, are indigenous to Iran and their name derives from the Persian *pesteh*. In their native soil, they grow to be larger than elsewhere. *Pesteh khâm* are the plain kind and *pesteh shoor*, the roasted salted ones.

The outer shell of a pistachio nut is hard. When the fruit reaches ripeness it starts to gape. Referred to as "laughing" in Iranian, it reveals a kernel covered in a reddish skin. This is an indication of the freshness of the nut, because it turns darker over time. Iranian pistachios have pale-green flesh, which is probably the reason behind the artificial green color of "pistachio" ice cream. The color of Iranian pistachios distinguishes them from Californian varieties, which are yellowish, but not those from Turkey, which are equally good to eat.

In classic Persian cooking, raw pistachios are ground, and combined with green cardamom, cinnamon, and saffron to flavor basmati rice dishes. Pistachios are an ingredient of the Persian toot—a nut paste bonbon served as a New Year treat. **MR**

In spring, the furry catkins of the wild hazelnut, less obtrusive than other hedgerow blooms, tell country dwellers all over North America and Europe where they will find nuts in August and September. Unlike blackberries , elderberries, crabapples, and rosehips, a reminder is needed: the nuts themselves will be very well hidden underneath the leaves.

Sometimes called filberts—probably because St. Philibert's Day, 22 August, traditionally marked the beginning of the season—fresh hazelnuts are a true wild delicacy. In Europe, larger, cultivated varieties, notably Kentish cobnuts, are sold fresh locally, but the pleasure of finding and eating out of hand lifts them to another level.

In nineteenth-century England, many regions of the country gave children a vacation on Holy Cross Day—14 September—so they could go nutting. While hazel twigs were traditionally used as dowsing rods, and the nuts used in love divinations, the main reason for collecting the nuts was always to eat them as fresh as possible. They lose their succulence in less than a week. **AMS**

Taste: *In texture, a fresh pistachio is less brittle and less moist than an almond, but very oily. Its taste is unique, and is at once recognized regardless of how it is served.*

Taste: *Fresh hazelnuts are crisp, milky, and sweet in the way a raw pea is, but with a savory twist. They are not that "nutty," but still as delicious as any ripe nut.*

Pistachio nuts command high prices; they cost three or four times as much as other nuts.

Grenoble Walnut

Chestnut

When it comes to walnuts, the milky, magical nuts of Grenoble, in southeastern France, are the crème de la crème. They were introduced to the region by the Romans and now carry an AOC certificate, which sets strict criteria for their production.

Walnuts are among the oldest tree-grown foods known to man—archaeologists uncovered petrified walnut shells dating back 8,000 years. The ancient Romans and Greeks thought walnuts so closely resembled the human brain that they must have special properties. They believed walnuts could cure headaches, but while there is little evidence to prove this theory, walnuts are now recognized as a so-called superfood because they are highly nutritious.

September heralds the new season for walnuts; the freshly picked walnuts are an unquestionable treat. As the season moves on, the nuts are kiln-dried and so the shells harden and the flesh develops vaguely bitter characteristics, although pronounced bitterness signals a rancid nut. It is possible to restore the newly picked flavor and texture by soaking the shelled kernels in milk overnight. **LF**

Throughout history, chestnuts have obligingly succumbed to canning, candying, drying, flour-making, and more, but one of the simplest and most splendid ways to enjoy them is freshly roasted. Hot roasted chestnuts are one of the truly great joys of late autumn and early winter, especially when bought fresh from the glowing braziers of street vendors on crisp days during the run up to Christmas; the glorious aroma wafting through the air is almost as enjoyable as eating the actual nut itself.

On the tree, chestnuts are encased inside a green-colored prickly burr. When the ripe burrs fall to the ground it can be opened to reveal the familiar brown-shelled nuts. A quick tip: if cooking chestnuts at home, cut slits in the shells beforehand to make them easier to open.

Chestnut flour is another seasonal specialty well worth trying. It's usually available for only a short period each year because of its limited keeping qualities, and is typically used in cakes, pasta, gnocchi, fritters, and batter. **LF**

Taste: *Grenoble walnuts have a delightful light crunch and an effortless chewiness. The tender, very succulent kernel has a sweet milky flavor and mild nutty taste.*

Taste: *Inside its robust brown armor, the chestnut yields soft, faintly floury and deliciously sweet flesh; roasting brings out rich, nutty, but slightly floral nuances.*

Traditionally, chestnuts were roasted on an open fire in a special perforated roasting pan. »

Pecan

Pecans take their name from the Algonquian word *paccan*, and were used by Native Americans for many thousands of years. Pecans were growing in Georgia, generally the largest pecan-producing state, long before the first European settler arrived. They were mainstays in the local diet—especially during the winter months—and eaten out of hand or ground into a thickener for stews.

Today, there are more than 1,000 varieties of pecans. Although they are also grown commercially in Mexico, Australia, South Africa, and parts of Latin America, they remain most associated with the United States: *Carya illinoinensis* is native to parts of the southern United States and northern Mexico.

Pecans can be eaten out of hand, used in batters for waffles and pancakes, turned into pecan butter, or included in stuffings for turkey, chicken, or duck. They are most often used, though, in various desserts, most famously the all-American pecan pie. Spiced pecans are often served as an appetizer, while sugared pecans appear on wedding buffet tables throughout the South. **SH**

Taste: *Pecans are crisp, but not hard. They are light to mild tasting nuts with a rich, buttery flavor similar to that of a walnut, yet without its bitterness.*

Brazil Nut

In the Brazilian Amazon, the enormous tree called *Bertholletia excelsa* is known as the "forest ceiling" for good reason. It can grow to as much as 200 feet (60 m) tall, with a trunk more than 10 feet (3 m) in diameter. The fruit it bears—known as the *ourico*— can weigh up to just under 4½ pounds (2 kg). Inside the fruit, like jewels in a casket, nestle up to twenty-four seeds surrounded by hard, almost triangular shells—Brazil nuts.

Indigenous tribes have used Brazil nuts as the basis of their diet for centuries, but it is only relatively recently the nuts have gained importance in the rest of Brazil and elsewhere. They are harvested wild in the virgin rain forest from fruit that have fallen the long drop to the forest floor; in fact, the tree requires virgin rain forest to grow, since it relies on specific orchids and bees to pollinate it, and on animals known as agoutis to extract the seeds from its fruit.

Brazil nuts make a tempting addition to candies, cakes, and ice creams, and are scrumptious coated in good-quality dark chocolate. They are also fantastic toasted, whole, or in slices. **AL**

Taste: *Nothing beats eating Brazil nuts whole and raw. They have a pleasant, smooth crunch combined with a measured sweetness and a gentle oiliness.*

Brazil nut trees provide welcome shade from the searing heat of the Amazon rain forest. **»**

King Coconut

Coco-de-Mer

The king coconut (*Cocos nucifera*) is native to Sri Lanka, where it is known as *thembili* or *weware*, although it has also been introduced to India, Fiji, Indonesia, Malaysia, and Philippines. The coconuts are frequently sold at the roadside, and the water of fresh, tender, young, green coconuts is prized as a refreshing drink called *kurumba* to combat the oppressive heat. Sellers cut off the top of the coconut and buyers drink the tender coconut water through a supplied straw.

The soft, spongy, and tangy kernel is eaten straight from the split nut by scooping it out with a spoon or using a piece of nut shaved from the shell. King coconut is widely used in cooking. Coconut milk—made from grated coconut meat and warm water—is added to curries, and coconut meat can be grated onto salads or ground and mixed with red chiles and lime, and then heated to make sambols. It is also used as an ingredient in sweet dishes such as *halapes,* made from coconut meat and jaggery (unrefined brown sugar from palm sap), and *kiri bath*, a thick rice pudding made with the creamy part of coconut milk. **CK**

Native to just two islands in the Seychelles' 115-island archipelago—Praslin and its near neighbor Curieuse—coco-de-mer is the giant, prehistoric nut of a variety of fan palm. The nut is the world's largest seed, and can weigh up to 50 lb (22 kg).

The mature nuts are, famously, an almost-perfect representation of the lower torso of a rather shapely lady, so it comes as no surprise they caused much comment among sailors and early explorers who found them floating in the sea. If that were not enough, both male and female trees are needed to produce the nut: one local legend tells how at certain times of the year the enormous trees uproot themselves from Praslin's dense Vallée de Mai forest and make their way down to the beach in order to mate.

Inevitably the distinctively shaped nuts are in high demand as souvenirs, which has forced the Seychelles Government to place strict controls on the 7,000 or so remaining trees. The government has registered each tree and issues every harvested nut with an individual ID number to deter the black-market trade. **WS**

Taste: *King coconut water has a very refreshing, sweet, mild flavor; the coconut meat has a tangy flavor and a soft, spongy texture.*

Taste: *The milky jelly inside can be scooped out and eaten as a soft pudding, similar to Turkish delight. The flesh has a hint of mint and some consider it a powerful aphrodisiac.*

The coco-de-mer tree not only produces giant nuts, but also grows extraordinarily large palm leaves. »

Puy Lentil

Urd

Lentilles Vertes du Puy were the first French legume to enjoy AOC status. These small green lentils are farmed in a unique area of the Massif Central, in south-central France, that surrounds the village of Puy-en-Velay and benefits from a unique microclimate, referred to as the "Foehn effect."

In summer, the mountains to the southwest trap the cloud formations brought by the prevailing winds. The result is a high level of sunshine and clear skies in the zone, which generates extra heat that serves to stress the plants, which duly sweat out moisture. The plants then develop seeds (lentils) that are small, with lower protein levels and thinner skins than similar varieties—an evolutionary defect that becomes a gastronomic advantage. In cooking, the lentils soften more readily and are sweeter and less starchy than most other varieties.

Although featured by star chefs as a garnish, Puy lentils are best eaten as a simple rustic food, cooked with onions, garlic, herbs, and the local dry-cured *ventrèche* bacon, or dressed with a mustard-flavored vinaigrette to make *salade de lentilles*. **MR**

This small, oval, richly nutritious bean is one of India's most highly valued legumes. Also known as urad, black gram, urid beans, and matpe beans, urd have been cultivated since ancient times and are believed to be a relative of the mung bean. The seed of a trailing, very hairy annual herb, the beans grow in slim, cylindrical pods. Although native to southern Asia, they have now been planted in other tropical areas, mostly introduced by Indian immigrants.

Urd are a staple in the Punjab, where they are known as *maanh*. There they are often cooked with red kidney beans for a contrast of color and texture. In northern India, Muslims cook them whole; in the south the beans are skinned and ground to a flour for making waferlike *dosas*, crisp *papads*, and steamed *idlis*, while across the subcontinent they are hulled, split, and eaten as urad dal. Naturally low in fat, high in fiber, and protein rich, urd have a dull, black skin covering the creamy yellow beans inside. With their skins on, they are often sold as "black lentils," whereas split and with their skins removed, they can be labeled as "white lentils." **WS**

Taste: *Properly cooked Puy lentils should not be hard and gritty, nor mushy or floury. The taste has a delicate hint of sweetness that blends with the ingredients around it.*

Taste: *More gelatinous than either mung beans or other varieties of lentil and split pea, whole urd have a comfortingly creamy texture and a rich, earthy flavor.*

Lentils grow in flat, delicate pods in Puy-en-Velay,
◎ *France; they were introduced there by the Gauls.*

Azuki Bean

Tolosa Bean

These tiny oval beans, also known as adzuki and adanka beans, are used in many cuisines, but they are particularly popular in Japan, China, and South Korea. Usually shiny, dark ruby-brown and with a distinctive white stripe running down one side, other colors of azuki bean exist, including green, black-orange, mottled, and straw-colored.

In the West, azuki beans tend to be eaten as a vegetable or in savory dishes such as salads, soups, and stews, but in Asia they are more common in sweet recipes, either cooked whole with rice or turned into a sweetened red bean paste. As the beans retain their color when cooked, they tint rice an attractive purple-pink. The Chinese add coconut milk to them, whereas in Japan red-cooked festival rice is served at weddings and birthdays. The Japanese also eat red bean paste dumplings to celebrate New Year and set it with agar-agar to make the popular confection *yokan*.

To cook, the beans need to be simmered in a pan of water for two hours but this can be reduced to forty-five minutes if they are presoaked. **WS**

Grown in fields along the banks of the Oria River in the Basque Country, *alubias de Tolosa* are small, roundish beans that are sold in the markets of the provincial town of the same name. The Tolosa bean is valued for its fine dark skin, which varies in color from deep blackberry to matte black, punctuated with a small white spot. The origins of the bean are disputed, but it seems likely that they were brought to Spain from the Americas in the sixteenth century. They are cultivated at the base of corn plants, a technique still in common use in Central America.

The microclimate around Tolosa provides the ideal growing conditions for the beans. Their cultivation is labor intensive: they are hand planted and the bean pods are individually harvested after ripening on the vine, which ensures a consistent high quality. In the classic Basque stew, *alubias a la Tolosana*, the beans are first cooked with water and possibly an onion in an earthenware pot. Chorizo, cabbage, and cooked morcilla are often then added to the pot. The flavorsome dish is served with *guindillas de Ibarra*, or pickled green peppers. **RL**

Taste: *Strong, nutty azuki beans are sweeter and less mealy than other beans. This sweetness accounts for their popularity in Asian desserts, cakes, and confectionery.*

Taste: *Plump Tolosa beans are appreciated for the satisfying creaminess of their flesh which have a rich, pure taste of bean. The beans require pre-soaking.*

Garbanzos Pedrosillano

Fasolia Gigandes

Garbanzos pedrosillano are the tiny tots of the chickpea dynasty: garbanzo is Spanish for chickpea and pedrosillano means "the little one." One of the most prized varieties of chickpea, they are grown in the Castilla-León region of northwest Spain.

Chickpeas have been cultivated for thousands of years, and were among the first crops farmed on the fertile plains of Mesopotamia. The Carthaginians took the chickpea from North Africa to Spain, where it became one of the most significant ingredients of the Spanish *cocidos* or stews, particularly in Castilian cuisine. Until not long ago, they featured in the average Castilian diet on an almost daily basis. They have a natural affinity with gutsy stews, but marry equally well with flavorsome fish dishes and good extra virgin olive oil.

Garbanzos pedrosillano tend not to be treated with pesticides or preservatives, and many Castilians swear the diminutive chickpeas can be stored in glass jars or even in paper bags, as long as they are within close proximity of an unpeeled garlic clove, apparently an effective method of bug control! **LF**

Fasolia gigandes, also known as fasolia gigantes, are the big boys on the bean scene, and utterly divine they are, too. Creamy white when dried and somewhat flat, gigandes feature prominently in the cuisines of both Greece and Spain. It is thought the beans originated from South America, before subsequently flourishing in the ideal clement environment of the Mediterranean.

The best gigandes are grown in the Prespa-Florina region of northern Greece. They are particularly popular in a traditional meze offering known as Gigandes Plaki, a must-do dish in which the beans are cooked in a rich tomato sauce. If Greece is a little far and a good local Greek restaurant isn't an option, they are usually readily available in to buy in their dried state. Simply soak them overnight (this is essential) and then cook for an hour or until soft. Once tender, douse them in good-quality extra virgin olive oil, along with lemon juice, a smattering of salt, maybe a little garlic, and a scattering of finely chopped parsley, and you have a little taste of heaven on a plate. **LF**

Taste: *The soft skin gives way to a smooth, delicate texture. The flavor is slightly sweet, vaguely milky, and nutty. Always soak them overnight before cooking.*

Taste: *Creamy and elegantly yielding in the middle, the beans have a delightfully sweet, buttery flavor, but marry well with punchy oils and gutsy sauces.*

Tiger Nut

Tiger nuts (*cyperus esculentus*) are not really nuts at all, but small tubers. They look a little like crumpled peanuts. In Spain, they are more commonly known as chufa nuts and are the principal ingredient in one of Spain's most famous drinks, horchata de chufa, a refreshing summery concoction made from ground chufa nuts mixed with sugar and water and often embellished with cinnamon and fresh lemon.

The plant is known to have been cultivated since ancient times, with evidence of their use having been found in early Egyptian tombs. It is thought the Moors introduced the plant to Spain, as Valencia was found to provide an ideal growing environment. They have, subsequently, flourished in the region.

Once the tubers are harvested, they are dried over the course of several months, after which they can be stored for a number of years. They can be reconstituted by a period of soaking and then boiling, which nudges out a subtle sweetness that isn't as pronounced in the dried nut. **LF**

Taste: *Chewy on the outside, soft and milky on the inside, tiger nuts have a delightful flavor that can be compared to a young hazelnut, with hints of almond and coconut.*

In Spain, cafes sell the popular drink horchata de chufa. »

Basmati Rice

A variety of *Oryza sativa*, this rice's name says it all—*bas-mati*, or "the fragrant one." It is said to be the grain of the gods, a native of the snow-fed terraces of the temple-studded Himalayan foothills and the alluvial Indo-Gangetic plains of northern India and Pakistan below. These two countries, in fact, insist only this unique terroir can give basmati the incomparable aroma and flavor that has been immortalized in subcontinental scriptures and chronicles down the millennia.

This delicate long-grain rice has fought off transgenic imposters and hybrids from the United States and Australia to remain de rigueur for special meals, especially since the September to December harvest coincides with the North Indian festive season. Celebratory dishes like pulao (with peas, almonds, raisins, and aromatic spices) and mutton biryani are always made with white basmati, as its fragrance enhances the appeal of vegetables, meats, and spices. But basmati rice, like many wines, is best consumed after aging for at least twelve to eighteen months. **RD**

Taste: *Grains are at least ¼ inch (5 mm) long and double in size when cooked, but do not become sticky. The scent is delicately floral and the flavor has a creamy nuttiness.*

Jasmine Rice

Exported as "jasmine rice" or "Thai fragrant rice," it is known in its native Thailand as *Thai Hom Mali* or *Khao Dawk Mali*. As a specific strain of long-grain rice, jasmine rice originated in the Central Plain close to Bangkok some sixty years ago, but is now mainly grown in the northeastern Isan province.

Depending on whether it is eaten soon after harvesting or at the end of the year, jasmine rice can have two very different characters. In the first instance, the long grains are soft, but not sticky, even though they cling together when steamed or cooked by the absorption method. Later the grains become more like basmati rice: drier, more chewy. Thais refer to jasmine rice as *khao suai*, beautiful rice, to distinguish it from other rices, which can be somewhat more tacky, especially the glutinous "snake fang" rice that is used for desserts.

Thai Hom Mali is organically produced by farmers and has its own national quality mark. The United States, however, grows and manufactures a "Thai" jasmati rice that is effectively a rival product, though it lacks the subtlety of the genuine item. **MR**

Taste: *The new-season rice has more aroma, reminiscent of jasmine flowers. The older rice is more flaky when cooked, ideally suited to* khao pad, *the popular Thai fried-rice dish.*

Carnaroli Rice

Calasparra Bomba Rice

Carnaroli rice is a white rice belonging to the short-grained japonica variant of the *Oryza sativa* family. It is grown mainly in the Lombardy region of northern Italy and typically used in risottos. There are three grades of rice grown in Italy for risotto: semifino, which is the smallest; fino; and superfino, which is the largest. Carnaroli is a superfino.

Risotto rice consists of two different starches. The outer is amylopectin, a soft starch that swells and dissolves to a degree during cooking. The middle is amylase, a firmer starch that does not break down during the cooking process and keeps the rice *al dente*. The balance of the two starches differs with each rice variety; carnaroli is high in amylopectin, so, therefore, produces a creamy risotto because it absorbs more liquid than Arborio and Vialone Nano, the other two varieties.

Originating in Asia before 4000 BCE, it is not known exactly when rice was introduced into Italy, but it is thought Italian Venetian or Genoese merchants brought it in on trade ships returning from the Far East. **LF**

Think of rice and Spain together and thoughts immediately turn to Valencia and paella. And it is true most of the country's rice paddies are located in the marshlands near that city or to the south in Alicante. The finest rice, however, is grown in a hilly inland region of Murcia, around the small town of Calasparra.

Rice was introduced to Spain by the Moors during the eighth century. It has been cultivated around Calasparra since the seventeenth century, and the local specialty, a dish of rice cooked with rabbit and snails in an open pan, might date from that time. Today, the region produces the ideal rice for Spanish cuisine, plump grains that absorb the flavors of stocks and seasonings beautifully.

Calasparra Bomba (DOP) is the smallest variety produced in Calasparra today (the others are Balillax and Sollana). Packed with starch, it keeps its shape and texture well when cooked. It is grown without the use of pesticides as part of a traditional system of crop rotation that acts as a natural protection against plant diseases. **MR**

Taste: *Cooked in risotto, carnaroli`s ratio of starches creates a wonderful degree of creaminess balanced with bite; perfect for ingredients such as shellfish and saffron.*

Taste: *Calasparra Bomba has the ideal texture for paellas in that the grains remain separate and are never sticky—unless simmered in milk for long periods.*

Purple Rice

Also known as black glutinous or red rice, this native of Thailand is the Rolls Royce of the rice world. It's inappropriately named, though, as the grains do not contain any gluten and are black or rust-red, rather than purple. When raw, the grains can best be described as looking like brown rice that has been burned. As they cook, however, color seeps out, staining the whole grain and giving the cooked dish a uniform indigo hue.

Although purple rice is gluten-free, it contains two kinds of starch, amylose and amylopectin, and the more amylopectin the grains contain, the stickier they are when cooked.

This rice is most commonly eaten as a feast day dessert in Southeast Asia, in the form of a sticky pudding. The grains are first soaked for several hours or overnight to shorten their cooking time and then steamed for about forty-five minutes, rather than being boiled. As the color leaches out, it dyes the inside of the bamboo steamer (and the hands of the cook) a vivid purplish-black and while this will not wash away, it does fade very quickly. **WS**

Taste: *Purple rice has a natural, subtly sweet flavor, but many cooks add extra sugar according to personal taste. Purple sticky rice pudding is served hot with coconut milk.*

Wild Rice

Not actually a rice, but an aquatic grass, wild rice (*Zizania aquatica*) is native to North America. It has been eaten since prehistoric times and was a staple in the diets of the early inhabitants of North America. Native Americans call it *manomin* or "good berry." It is also known as Canadian rice, squaw rice, water oats, and marsh oats. In French, it is *riz sauvage*.

In its natural state, wild rice grows along lake and river banks in the Great Lakes region, which includes the Canadian provinces of Ontario and Quebec and eight U.S. states. A slightly different species is also native to ecologically similar habitats in Asia. Cultivated wild rice is grown in flooded fields or paddies in Minnesota, California, and elsewhere.

Aromatic kernels of wild rice have a black-brown hue and open like a butterfly when cooked. The quality of the rice depends a great deal on how carefully it is harvested. Long, slender, unbroken grains are the best and the most costly. Lumberjacks once ate wild rice mixed with honey as a hot cereal similar to oatmeal. Today, it is used in pilafs, stuffings, salads, soups, and many other dishes. **SH**

Taste: *Wild rice blends well with other ingredients. It has a firm texture and a nutty, grassy taste. Some varieties have an earthy flavor somewhat like wild mushrooms.*

The wild rice plants grown in Texas have been declared an endangered species. »

Buckwheat Groat

Despite its name, buckwheat (*Fagopyrum esculentum*) is not a cereal like wheat or barley. Belonging to the same family as rhubarb and sorrel, it is native to Siberia and northern China. Crusaders brought it to Europe during the Middle Ages.

Buckwheat is commonly ground into a dark, gritty flour that can be used to make anything from pancakes to noodles. It has dark, roughly triangular seeds that when left whole are known as "groats." These can be hulled, cracked, or even sprouted and used as a green vegetable in salads. Raw groats can be used as a seasoning, but their bitter flavor means that they are usually hulled and toasted in oil for a few minutes before being used in cooking.

Buckwheat groats can be added to pilafs, soups, and stews. Russian and Polish immigrants introduced buckwheat groats to the United States, where they are known as kasha. They are used as a filling for the fried or baked snacks known as *knishes* or served with noodles and vegetables as *varnishkes*. In Eastern Europe, however, kasha refers to a number of cooked grains including buckwheat. **CK**

Taste: *Raw buckwheat groats are rather bitter. Toasted they have a sweet, nutty earthy flavor and are plump and tender in texture. They make an ideal stuffing.*

The buckwheat from meadows in Japan is used mainly in noodles. ❯

Pearl Barley

Freekeh

Barley was once a staple, the most important European food grain, but it has been supplanted by wheat and is now used primarily for making beer.

To turn the grains into pearl barley, the outer husks are discarded and the kernel is polished. This process, known as pearling, produces fine, medium, or baby "pearls" that can be left whole, flaked, cut (grits), or ground into flour. Containing about eighty percent starch, it looms large in vegetarian cooking. However, it also has its place in European regional cuisines. *Orzotto,* a barley equivalent of risotto, is popular throughout northern Italy. In Russia, it occurs in both savory and sweet *kasha,* grain dishes midway between oatmeal and puddings. In Scotch broth, a traditional soup-stew, partly pearled barley (pot barley) contributes body and texture.

The flour does contain some gluten, the protein that gives elasticity to bread, but a barley loaf requires the addition of some wheat flour to the dough for it to rise satisfactorily. Scalded pearl barley is also the basis of the cordial lemon barley water, drunk in England since the eighteenth century. **MR**

Since ancient times this highly nutritious wheat grain has played an important part in Middle Eastern cuisines, particularly those of Jordan, Lebanon, and Syria. The wheat is harvested while still young, soft, and green and the stalks are then roasted and smoked over open wood fires to preserve the nutritional value and "green" taste before being hulled. In the past, tiny stones would sometimes creep in among the wheat and threaten the teeth of unsuspecting diners, but modern harvesting and processing methods keep dentists' bills to a minimum.

High in fiber, low in carbohydrates, and with a low GI, freekeh (pronounced free-ka) can replace rice or couscous in salads, stuffings, vegetarian burgers, breads, or pilafs, but in Middle Eastern homes one of the most popular ways to serve it is in a stew. Wholegrain freekeh is very coarse and dark greeny-brown and needs to be simmered for about forty-five minutes in water or stock to tenderize it. Cracked-grain freekeh is browner and blander and requires a shorter cooking time. **WS**

Taste: *Grains of pearl barley have a chewy texture allied to an almost slippery surface. The taste is relatively bland, but it soaks up the flavors of accompanying ingredients.*

Taste: *The cooked grains have a slightly smoky, rich —almost meaty— flavor and add a pleasingly nutty texture to both hot and cold dishes.*

Ripened barley ready for cutting by
◑ *a loch in the lowlands of Scotland.*

Polenta

Couscous

Polenta is a cornmeal grain that has become very fashionable outside of Italy, even though it was traditionally a food favored by the poor. When meat and fresh foods were scarce during World War II, polenta became a key part of the Italian diet in many regions, but in fact, it had been an important staple in the north of Italy for hundreds of years. In the Fruili and Veneto regions, it was more popular than bread.

The name polenta is taken from the Latin *pulmentum*, which was the mainstay of the Roman legionnaires' diet. *Pulmentum* was made from an ancient variety of wheat, with the grain toasted on hot stones. When explorer Christopher Columbus introduced corn into Europe in the fifteenth century, the abundant rainfall in the north of Italy meant the new crop flourished. Polenta was traditionally cooked over the fireplace, with a stream of the golden grains poured into boiling water and stirred forty-five minutes until it formed a thick yellow mass. It was then served with cheese, or a small amount of meat if it was available. **LF**

It is a sign of the times that couscous granules, which have required slow and careful steaming to render them tender and edible since at least the thirteenth century, are now available in quick-cooking varieties that soften within minutes in boiling water. The tiny dried dough balls that were traditionally handmade from freshly ground whole grains are now a mass-produced global comfort food.

Durum wheat couscous is still a staple of its home territory, the Maghreb, where the steamed grains are served in many guises, just like rice. Couscous is best known in the dish that bears the same name: the grains are steamed over a spicy stew in the top of a two-tier, perforated vessel called a *kiskis* in Arabic, but better known in the West by its French name *couscoussier*. The stew is eventually served on top of the soft grains that have cooked in its steaming juices.

Generic, uniform grains are readily available in Western supermarkets, but in the Middle East and in Middle Eastern food stores overseas there is more variety, and dry grains can vary in size. **BLeB**

Taste: *Polenta has a granular texture and bland flavor in its basic form. With strong cheese or other ingredients, however, it is wonderful served with stews and sauces.*

Taste: *The slightly sweet but neutral flavor of couscous makes it an ideal backdrop for highly spiced meat and vegetable mixtures. Leftover grains make excellent salads.*

Handmade, ceramic tagines are used to cook the stews traditionally served with couscous. ❯

Fregola Pasta

Tajarin

Although it is often mistaken for a type of grain because of its coarse appearance, fregola is a golden wheat pasta specialty from Sardinia. It is similar in some ways to couscous, and is, in fact, sometimes referred to as "Sardinian couscous." Both products consist of fine pasta pellets created when durum wheat (semolina) and water are rubbed together; the name "fregola" comes from the Italian verb *fregare*, which means "to rub." Little known outside Sardinia until relatively recently, fregola is becoming increasingly more popular because, unlike couscous, it is lightly toasted after being dried and, therefore, takes on an exquisite nutty flavor. Fregola beads are larger than couscous, too.

Little is recorded about the arrival of pasta fregola on the culinary scene; some Sardinians are adamant fregola was their own creation, but it is more likely it was first introduced to Sardinia when Genovese navigators returned from the last crusade.

Fregola is incredibly versatile. Often served in soups and broths, most notably with clams, it can also be used as a substitute for couscous. **LF**

Tajarin (pronounced ta-ya-reen) is a wonderful specialty pasta that originated in The Langhe, a hilly area in Piemont, northern Italy. It is similar to fine tagliatelle, with long, flat strands that are usually no wider than ⅛ inch (2mm). It has a glorious flavor and beautiful golden color. In Italy, it is easy to buy special eggs, with strikingly yellow yolks, for pasta making, as they come from hens that have been fed with a particular dye. The color of tajarin, however, is pronounced because it contains a far higher proportion of egg yolks than more common varieties of egg pasta.

Traditionally tajarin was always homemade, and mixed and cut by hand. All but the wealthiest of women would once have been taught the art of creating it as a matter of course.

Alba is the principal town in The Langhe and is famous for its exquisite white truffles. Tajarin has a wonderful affinity with them; the combination is unforgettable. Fresh white truffles grated over butter-tossed tajarin, or tajarin with truffle butter, must surely be on the menu in heaven. **LF**

Taste: *Cooked until al dente and served unadorned, pasta fregola has a moist, pleasantly chewy bite and appealing nutty taste. It will also happily absorb other flavors.*

Taste: *Tajarin has an elegant, faintly eggy richness and exhibits superb buttery nuances. Cooked until al dente, its texture is velvety, but with a graceful robustness.*

Alba market is famous for the fresh white truffles that partner tajarin pasta so well. »

Durum Wheat Spaghetti

Tortelli di Zucca

There are two basic types of pasta that Italians eat and have made famous around the world; fresh egg pasta and dried pasta. Neither is seen as better in the eyes of the Italians; each kind simply serves a different purpose.

Dried pasta is made from durum wheat flour; *durus* being the Latin word for hard. A law passed in Italy in 1967 states that all dried pasta, including that which contains egg, must be made with durum wheat; it is the high-gluten content that gives the pasta its distinctive texture and bite when cooked. Pasta made outside Italy is often made with other types of flour and, hence, can never be cooked *al dente* as pasta should. As with most traditional Italian foods, the exact beginnings of pasta are disputed. Many give Marco Polo the credit for bringing it across from China; the Chinese were eating noodles as long ago as 2000 BCE. On the other hand, frescoes found in ancient tombs near Rome show people making flour and water pastes, although it is believed the dough might have been baked on flat stones, rather than boiled. **LF**

Not to be missed, tortelli di zucca are gorgeous little Italian pasta packages with a pumpkin-based filling. The ingredients combined with the pumpkin vary from region to region, but perhaps the most famous tortelli di zucca are those from Mantua (or Mantova as it is known in Italy). In Mantua, the pumpkin used to make the filling is usually a local variety, *Marina di Chioggia*. It is cooked and mixed with crushed amaretti biscuits, grated Parmesan cheese, and mostarda, a wonderful savory-sweet conserve typical of the area and made from fruit and mustard oil. The intriguing piquant, but syrupy, mostarda complements the sweet flesh of the pumpkin wonderfully. Tortelli di zucca are sensational tossed with melted butter and sage, but occasionally a tomato and bacon sauce is offered as an alternative.

Tortelli di zucca are eaten throughout the autumn and winter, but they are traditionally always served as part of the feast on Christmas Eve. As with all things Italian, each family will have its own secret recipe, handed down through generations from mother to daughter. **LF**

Taste: *Good dried pasta shouldn't simply be a vehicle for sauce, but should have a voice of its own, with a subtle, almost nutty flavor and pleasing toothsome texture.*

Taste: *Tortelli di zucca have a buttery, vaguely sweet, pleasantly salty filling with a delightful smack of mustard fruits, enhanced by a wrapping of egg-rich pasta.*

The art of making perfect fresh pasta for tortelli parcels requires great attention to detail. »

Kisoba Noodle

Japanese soba noodles are buckwheat noodles—but because pure buckwheat flour doesn't bind well, most soba noodles are, in fact, made with a combination of buckwheat flour and wheat flour. Aficionados, however, believe the best taste comes from noodles made with buckwheat alone. Such noodles are known as kisoba.

Soba noodles are something of a paradox in Japan. They are a sustaining everyday food, available on every train station platform, but also a sacrosanct food, associated with shrines and temples. It is at the shrines and temples that kisoba will most often be served, from the specialist noodle stores that are usually found there.

Purists eat them entirely on their own, cold and without any dipping sauce, in a style known as *mori soba* (mori means "to heap"). They are, however, usually served with a little dried nori on top and a small cup of soy sauce-based broth in which to dip them, and from which they are noisily slurped. Such slurping is thought polite, and it's said that taking in air while eating kisoba enhances the flavor. **SB**

Sanuki Udon Noodle

Sanuki udon are thick wheat-flour noodles that originate from the Sanuki (now known as Kagawa) prefecture in Japan. The area does not have enough rainfall for extensive rice cultivation, and so wheat, and wheat noodles, have become a specialty.

Sanuki noodles are famed for their strong body and chewy texture, as well as their smoothness, which gives an attractive *nodogushi*—the feeling as the noodles slips down the throat. The other crucial factor in their appeal is the ratio of salt and water used when they are made, which changes according to the season; 1:3 is considered optimum in summer, making them saltier than in winter, when a ratio of 1:6 is preferred.

Udon noodles have always been popular in western Japan, while in the East buckwheat noodles (see *kisoba,* left) have traditionally been preferred. The 2002 publication of an enormously successful Sanuki Udon travel guide (*Osorubeki Sanuki Udon—Magic of Sanuki Udon*), however, led to a boom in popularity. Specialist stores have now sprung up in Tokyo, nationwide, and even overseas. **SB**

Taste: *Rich and earthy, with a delicate, satisfying sweetness. When cooked al dente, the noodles have a firmness akin to whole-wheat pasta.*

Taste: *Silky smooth with a chewy texture. The slightly salty, breadlike taste complements the delicate dashi and soy-sauce flavor of the broth the noodles are cooked in.*

Fen Si Noodle

Laksa Noodle

Fen si is better known in English as glass noodles, cellophane noodles, or mung bean noodles. Their resemblance to glass or cellophane is more apparent after they have been rehydrated—the dry whiteish, pliable, slightly wrinkled noodles then become smooth and translucent.

The noodles do not have any particular taste of their own, but have a pleasantly tender "bite" and absorb the flavor of whatever they are cooked with. They are made from the famously versatile mung bean, which is ground into a smooth paste and then shaped and dried.

Usually sold in convenient packages perfect for home cooking, the tidiest way to separate a large bundle of noodles into smaller portions is to pull it apart while still in its bag: this stops the small pieces that break off from flying everywhere. They are then easily prepared for cooking by soaking them in hot water for about ten minutes. Although less common, dry (unhydrated) noodles can also be fried, which makes them puff up slightly and turn white and crunchy, to make a striking garnish. **KKC**

Modern-day laksa noodles are intimately linked to the "Nonya" cuisine, a hybridized form of regional Chinese and Malayan cookery styles.

Round, slippery, and made from rice, laksa noodles are the basis of spicy soups that are eaten as snack meals. They are classic street food, sold by hawkers at all hours, night or day. These soups may be thick and curry-like, containing bean curd and prawns and seasoned with *rempah*, a paste made from chiles, candlenuts, and fermented fish paste, or the broth can be paler, similar in texture to hot and sour Thai soups.

Laksa has also been adopted by fusion cooks working in Australia and New Zealand, who have added their personal imprint. Many local recipes exist, but the broth usually includes coconut milk and chile. The island of Penang, for instance, is famed for its *assam laksa*, which contains shredded mackerel and is flavored with tamarind, galangal, lemongrass, and mint. Instead of the traditional laksa noodle, some cooks prefer rice vermicelli or even wheat-based noodles. **MR**

Taste: *Although it has no real taste itself, Fen si's texture and consistency make it a popular base for a wide range of Asian dishes, from soups to spring rolls.*

Taste: *In a curry-style laksa, the noodles are almost coated by the sauce and the dish can be eaten without a spoon, but the more soupy laksas have the texture of a broth.*

Cornish Pasty

Samosa

The Cornish pasty, as its name suggests, does indeed originate from Cornwall, the most southwestern county of England. This substantial filled pastry was once a traditional, regional, working man's food but is now widely produced and consumed. Easily portable, pasties were historically eaten for lunch by Cornish tin and copper miners. Legend has it that the thick pastry crimp characterizing the Cornish pasty was used as a convenient handle by miners. The miners' wives were said to mark their husband's initials on their pasties when they made them.

Pasties range in shape from oval to semicircular and are generally made from shortcrust pastry. Meat pasties are the best known, filled with chopped (not minced) beef skirt or chuck steak, turnip, onion, and potato, and simply flavored with salt and plenty of pepper. There are several variations, however, including cheese and potato, cheese and leek, and egg and bacon. To make a pasty, the filling ingredients are added uncooked, sealed in the uncooked pastry, and baked. Ideally, Cornish pasties should be eaten warm from the oven. **JL**

Of all South Asia's myriad snacks, this filled, fried or baked pastry parcel is probably the best-known. A popular street food in India, Pakistan, Bangladesh, and Sri Lanka, it is also found around the world, reflecting the South Asian diaspora. It is one of a large "family" of filled pastries eaten in many regions, such as the Middle East's *sambusak*.

Traditionally, samosas are triangular in shape, varying, however, considerably in size, from dainty bite-size morsels, served at parties, to large, substantial creations. Key to its popularity is its versatility; this is a food with many forms. Fillings range enormously—potato with ginger and garlic, cauliflower, spiced lamb mince, minced fish, or chicken—and can be mild, fragrant with aromatic spices, or formidably hot, laced with green or red chile. A crisp, flaky pastry coating is characteristic, but the pastry can also vary in texture. In South Asia, samosas are often served with a fresh mint or coriander leaf chutney. Production varies from domestic or small-scale to large-scale industrial, making both frozen and ready-cooked samosas. **JL**

Taste: *A pasty at its best has a fine layer of crumbly, golden-brown pastry wrapped around a peppery and moist, meaty filling of steak, potato, onion, and turnip.*

Taste: *It is the contrast of textures that makes samosas so satisfying—the fine, crisp, golden pastry coating gives way to a deliciously spiced vegetable or meat filling.*

Deep-fried samosas, also known as patties or curry puffs, are popular across South Asia. »

Empanada

Believed to have been unassumingly created in Galicia, Spain, when ground meat or fish was wrapped in two layers of pastry, the empanada is one of Spain's most popular culinary contributions to Hispanic America. Taking the shape of a *media luna* (half moon) and traditionally sealed one at a time, empanadas can be bake or fried. Although their size and fillings vary, they are generally enjoyed as a snack, an appetizer, or a quick meal.

The pride of the national cuisines of Bolivia, Colombia, Peru, Uruguay, Venezuela, and Mexico, the empanada has, however, found its richest expression in Argentina. Popular both at home and in bars and restaurants, Argentina has its own particular pastry recipe using wheat flour and beef fat. Among the fillings, nothing beats beef minced with a knife and mixed with fresh seasoning, spices, chile, boiled egg, and olives, all fried in beef fat. Versions with chicken, white corn, ham, and cheese are equally delicious. The empanada even makes an appearance as a dessert, for example filled with the country's famed *dulce de leite* (sweet milk syrup). **AL**

Taste: *Although very tasty when fried, it is best to eat empanadas fresh from the oven, made with a juicy filling and crunchy pastry. Heavenly with chili sauce.*

Tamale

This Mexican, Central American, and South American delicacy dates back at least to the time Columbus discovered the New World, and quite possibly much earlier. Tamales might have been made when prehistoric peoples began processing corn with ashes or slaked lime. This process softens the corn, making it easier to both grind and digest. To make a tamale, the corn dough is then wrapped in corn husks or banana leaves and steamed or baked.

Plain tamales can be made very simply, but they often are mixed with other ingredients, including spices; vegetables such as squash and beans; meats such as beef, pork, and chicken; and fish. Tamales are commonly served plain, but they are delicious eaten with a savory and spicy sauce. They can even be served as desserts: *tamales de dulce,* or sweet tamales, are filled with sugar, jams, fruits, or nuts.

A basic tamale recipe includes textured cornmeal, salt, fat (most often lard), and a liquid such as chicken broth, milk, or water. Although tamales can be eaten on any occasion, they are traditionally served at Christmas celebrations. **JH**

Taste: *Plain tamales boast a sweet corn taste and a soft, spongy texture. Always best warm, flavored tamales should showcase the flavorings of the other ingredients.*

Kulebiaka

Melton Mowbray Pork Pie

The naming of this rich Russian pie is often disputed. Does it derive from *kulebyachit*, to knead with the hands (the pastry part is a kind of brioche), or does it come at one remove from the German *kohlebacken*, which means to bake with coals? Etymology apart, it gained prominence at the turn of the twentieth century as coulibiac, when it joined the repertoire of international haute cuisine.

The standard version is a large salmon *pâté en croûte* filled with hard-boiled eggs and rice flavored with dill. Auguste Escoffier's *Guide Culinaire* (1903) insisted that it should include vesiga, a sturgeon's spinal marrow. In Russian cookery, though, there are many different kinds. At its simplest, it can be filled with cabbage, but this can be substituted with meat, mushrooms, or other combinations of savory ingredients. In effect it is the big brother of the smaller Russian patties known as *pirozki*, that can be both simple street food or delicacies fit for a Tsar. Kulebiaka is normally shaped in a rectangular parcel, although some fanciful interpretations resemble a sucking pig. **MR**

The first printed recipe for the pork pie apparently appeared in an English court cookbook in the fourteenth century. It is a raised pie in which a hot-water crust encloses a ball of simply seasoned chopped or ground pork, and its easy portability perhaps explains its popularity among huntsmen.

Pork pies have long been associated with the Leicestershire market town of Melton Mowbray, and producers there—among them Dickinson & Morris, which bakes 4,000 pies a week, and the award-winning Nelsons of Stamford—take pride in the Melton Mowbray difference. After the pastry has been pressed into shape using a wooden implement called a dolly, it is filled with seasoned, chopped, fresh pork—which becomes gray after baking—then sealed. The pies are baked without hooped supports, producing the characteristic saggy sides. As the pie cools, the meat contracts, leaving a space between pastry and filling. This is filled with jelly made from pigs' feet, which is poured into one of two holes cut into the lid of the pie. This was originally done to prolong the life of the pie. **ES**

Taste: *The kulebiaka pastry should be crisp and buttery. The moist, thick strip of wild salmon fillet contrasts with a creamy layer of eggs and rice with dill notes.*

Taste: *Crisp, dark, lard-rich pastry makes a delicious casing for a firm pork filling with a slight spiciness from the seasoning of ground white pepper.*

Injera

Tortilla

Injera is so central to Ethiopia and Eritrea's way of life that the standard daily greeting is "Have you eaten injera today?" This spongy, pancakelike flatbread is the staple food that lays the foundation for every meal. It is prepared daily and can take up to three days to be ready to cook. Injera is usually made from ground tef, a grain native to Ethiopia and the country's most important cereal crop. However, it can also be made using ground barley, corn, sorghum, or wheat. A mix of flour, water, salt, and sometimes yeast are left to ferment for up to three days. The batter is then cooked on a clay plate known as a *mogogo,* which is placed over a fire or on top of a special electric plate.

Injera is served with most meals and traditionally accompanies another Ethiopian classic dish, *wat,* a spicy meat or vegetable stew. An injera is laid down, rather like a plate, and then *wat* is spooned on top. Additional injera is served and small pieces of this are torn off and used to scoop up the *wat.* Once the food is eaten, the "plate"—having soaked up all the tasty juices—is also eaten. **SBI**

When Spanish conquistadores landed on Mexican shores in the sixteenth century, they discovered corn, or maize, a crop that had been cultivated for several millennia by the Aztec and Maya peoples, possibly as far back as 10,000 BCE. Considered a gift of the gods, corn was a staple food of these ancient peoples, and legend has it tortillas, known as *tlaxcalli* in the indigenous Nahuatl language, were invented by a peasant for a hungry king.

Corn was often soaked in lime and then ground up into a paste or dough called *masa.* It would then be flattened and cooked on both sides over a hot griddle. The Spanish named them tortillas or "little cakes." While homemade corn tortillas are the most authentic and tasty kind, wheat or flour tortillas evolved when Mexicans moved north in the 1700s into what is now Texas, Arizona, and California, where corn was not as plentiful as wheat.

Tortillas are used to sop up food, but they can also be combined with meats, cheeses, chile sauces, and vegetables. They are also used to make burritos, quesadillas, and enchiladas. **JH**

Taste: *Light, airy, and spongy in texture, injera has a tangy, sour flavor. Its fundamentally bland taste is ideal for absorbing the spicy, strong flavors of other foods.*

Taste: *Proper tortillas only contain corn or wheat flour, water, and salt. Corn tortillas should have a chewy, slightly dense texture and a slightly sweet, but mild, taste.*

Tortilla dough is shaped by hand and then slapped straight onto a hot griddle to cook. »

Pane Carasau

This delightful Sardinian flatbread is so wafer thin it is also known as *carta di musica*, from the term for the paper on which music was written. An ancient bread, it was eaten in great quantities by shepherds, who had to live in the mountains with their grazing flocks for many months. They wrapped the flatbread in cloth and tucked it easily into their bags. It was light to carry on their long and solitary journey, and formed an invaluable staple in their limited diet. The bread's crisp, dry texture gives it fantastic keeping qualities; stored away from moisture, it will make excellent eating after many, many months.

Explorers and hermits aside, pane carasau's longevity is possibly less likely to be tested nowadays, but it remains remarkably delicious and versatile. It can be nibbled at just as it is, or drizzled with olive oil and baked for added crunch. It can be moistened with water and rolled around a filling, used as pasta would be in a makeshift lasagne, or star in the wonderful Sardinian recipe *pane frattau*, moistened with stock and topped with tomatoes, pecorino, and a poached egg. **LF**

Taste: *Usually found in feather-light disks, pane carasau is pale parchment in color. It has a pleasant, slightly grainy texture and a subtle salty crunch.*

The dough blows up into a bubble in the oven and is then split in two. »

Barbari

Nan

This traditional Persian bread can be found all over Iran, freshly baked and piled high in bakeries ready to be taken home for the next meal. Its full name is *nan-e-barbari*, meaning bread of the Barbars—a people who live near the eastern borders of Iran in Afghanistan—and it is said that it was the Barbars who introduced barbari to Iran.

There are many regional breads in Iran, but as well as barbari, there are three other national flatbreads: *sangak*, *lavash*, and *taftun*, and bakeries tend to specialize in making an individual bread. Barbari is the second most common type of flatbread. It can be made from white or whole-wheat flour, and is made into long, oblong shapes about 1 inch (2.5 cm) thick and lightly baked until they are a pale, golden color.

The baker marks grooves down the length of the dough before it is baked. Traditionally, the baking is done in a domed brick oven heated by coals, and the bread bakes quickly—in about five minutes. Barbari is most often eaten at breakfast and is popularly served with the fetalike cheese *tabriz*. **SBI**

The word "nan" is actually a Persian word, meaning bread, although it is now used in India, Pakistan, Afghanistan, and into central Asia. Most people in the West think of nan as the leavened bread commonly served in Indian restaurants. The bread's distinctive teardrop shape comes from the flattened dough that is cooked stuck to the side of a clay tandoor oven and stretched downward during baking. Yogurt and milk are often added to give volume to the dough. Nans can be plain, brushed with ghee, or sprinkled with seasonings, such as sesame seeds. Nans can also be stuffed; *keema* nan is stuffed with ground meat, whereas *Peshwari* and *Kashmiri* nan are stuffed with nuts and raisins.

There are, however, numerous other examples of nan breads. Uzbekistan makes *goshtli nan*, which is stuffed with ground meat, *shirmay nan*, which is made with chickpeas, and a bran bread, *jirish nan*. Iran makes a sweetened nan called *nan-e-shir*. In its various incarnations, nan is a staple food at meals throughout central and south Asia, and is usually torn into pieces and used to scoop up the food. **SBI**

Taste: *Crisp, golden, and often sprinkled with salt or sesame seeds on the outside, freshly baked barbari is soft and tender when broken into.*

Taste: *Tastes and textures vary, but a classic plain nan, such as that found in India, has a light smoky flavor, is crisp on the outside, and tender in the middle.*

Stretched nan dough is smacked against the clay walls of the oven, and a lid put in place to retain heat. »

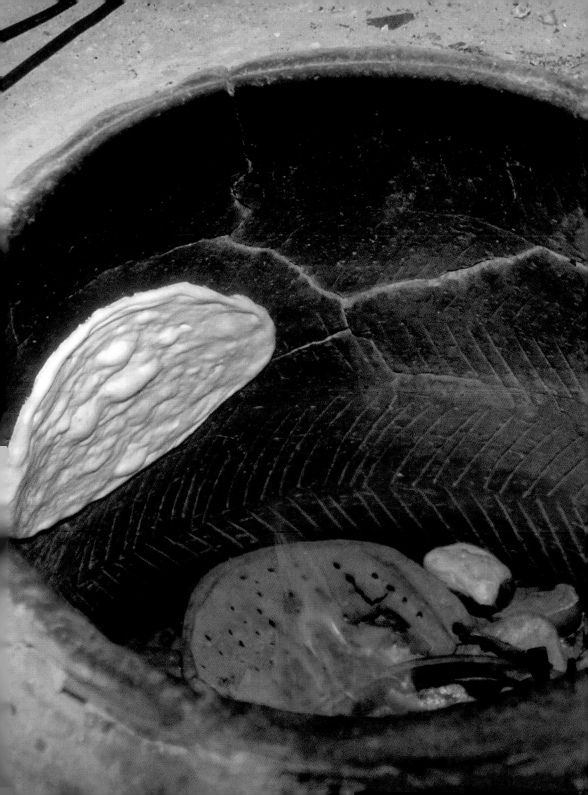

San Francisco Sourdough

Pain au Levain Naturel

Nearly as well known a symbol of San Francisco as the Golden Gate Bridge, sourdough bread began its rise to fame in 1849 when the influx of "gold rushers" brought a subsequent increase in bakeries. To bake leavened bread, in this era before the invention of bakers' yeast, "starters" were used. A fermented mixture of flour and water was saved from making one batch of bread and used to start off the next. Leavened bread was most likely discovered by accident by the Egyptians thousands of years ago.

Bakers who came to San Francisco found that when they baked their bread, it had a different and unidentifiable taste. Some say it was the San Francisco fog; others suspect it was wild yeast from the nearby grape-growing region that changed the flavor. They called it sourdough and the name stuck.

Although there are many bakeries making sourdough in San Francisco and elsewhere, the original San Francisco sourdough was made by the Boudin family from France. The legendary bakery still makes sourdough bread from a starter derived from the one made in 1849. **SH**

Pain au levain is delicious, gutsy sourdough bread made with a fermented starter rather than commercially made yeast. It is believed the Egyptians inadvertently gave us the first leavened bread as long ago as 2300 BCE when they discovered that dough left uncovered for several days began to rise (as a result of being infected with airborne yeast spores). They baked the batch of dough regardless, and it produced a wonderful light bread.

Although manufactured yeast allows bread to rise in one to two hours, naturally leavened breads take many hours. When the starter is mixed with whole grain flour and salt, carbon dioxide is made and fermentation continues. The slow rising of the dough creates a loaf with good old-fashioned flavor.

The name Poilâne is synonymous with pain au levain naturel. In 1932, Pierre Poilâne opened a bakery in Paris and made bread using stoneground flour, natural fermentation, and a wood-fired oven. Slowly but surely, he transformed what was essentially a rustic sourdough bread into an artisanal product, still sold all around the globe. **LF**

Taste: *Sourdough bread has a slightly sour, yet wheaty, taste, which makes it great for dipping into seafood stew. It has a chewy crust and a firm texture.*

Taste: *Dense, chewy, and flavorsome with a thick, golden crust, pain au levain naturel has a pleasant sour taste that goes well with both savory and sweet foods.*

The Poilâne bakery's trademark is a curly initial "P." It is carved into each loaf at the bakery in Paris. »

Pain de campagne
Pain Poilâne
3,87 le kg

Pane di Altamura

Soda Bread

Pane di Altamura (DOP) is a fabulous crisp and fragrant bread with a distinctive straw-colored crumb. It is made in the Alta Murgia region of Apulia, in Italy, from the milled grain of specified varieties of durum wheat according to strict criteria.

It is a leavened bread made with a fermented starter and methods that can reputedly be traced back at least as far as the first century BCE, when the Roman poet Horace praised the local bread in his "Satires." Traditionally, this bread was made, kneaded, and fashioned into large loaves at home and then taken to public ovens to be baked. Each individual loaf would be stamped with the initials of the head of the family, so it could be easily identified after it had been baked.

Like many breads customarily produced in the hills and mountains of Italy, Pane di Altamura has good keeping qualities: an essential requirement for the peasants and shepherds who lived and worked in remote farms across the hills of Alta Murgia. Just before eating, it was dipped briefly into boiling water and dressed with olive oil and salt. **LF**

A staple of the Irish table and an indicator of a good meal to come, soda bread's history is surprisingly short. Baking soda, which reacts with soured milk or buttermilk to lift the bread, became available in Ireland only in the early-to-mid nineteenth century. Early breads would have been baked over the fire in a lidded cast-iron pot, or bastible.

Soda bread is traditionally shaped in rounds and "blessed" by cutting a deep cross through the middle. Many cooks also prick each of the four resulting segments with the tip of their knife, to "let the fairies out" lest the bread be jinxed.

The finest soda bread is made with Irish flour— either white or a combination of whole wheat and white—which is famously soft, and the bread should be eaten on the day it is made. Although it is quick to make (no kneading is required), fresh soda bread is a sign of a generous host.

Variations on soda bread tend to include relatively expensive ingredients, such as dried fruit (to produce what is known as "spotty dog") or chocolate. Small soda scones are also made. **ES**

Taste: *Pane di Altamura has a delicious crisp crust and a well-balanced, uniform crumb. Good extra virgin olive oil and salt draw out the unique flavors of the wheat.*

Taste: *Soda bread is best eaten just warm, with salted Irish butter. It has a compact, but not heavy, crumb and a crisp crust. The sour milk or buttermilk lends a faint acidic tang.*

Pane di Altamura should be stone-baked and its crust ⊘ *should be a minimum of an eighth of an inch thick.*

Challah

Butterzopf

Challah is the traditional Jewish Shabbat (Sabbath) bread. The challah is made from a slightly sweetened dough made with many eggs and white flour, which is then braided, glazed, and sprinkled with sesame or poppy seeds before being baked.

Two loaves of challah are served at each of the three Shabbat meals, with prayers said over the bread. The loaves represent the double portion of *manna*, which is said to have fallen from heaven on the sixth day while the Israelites were in the wilderness, providing them with food both for that day and the Sabbath day that followed.

For certain festivals or celebrations, challah can be formed in different shapes. For Rosh Hashanah (Jewish New Year), the loaf might be shaped into a ball or crown. Small individual challah rolls, known as *boulkas*, are often served at weddings and are shaped into balls, braids, or spirals.

Classic Shabbat breads belonging to the Sephardi tradition include jam-filled *mouna* from the Algerian community, and the coiled, steamed breakfast bread, *kubaneh*, from Yemen. **SBI**

Similar in appearance to challah, butterzopf is a type of braided butter loaf from Switzerland. It originates in the dairy pastures of the Emmental valley in the canton of Bern in west central Switzerland. It is also known simply as *züpfe* or *zopf*. The latter name comes from the distinctive shape of the bread and means "braid." Butterzopf is usually eaten for breakfast or brunch on Sundays, with butter and fruit preserves or cheese. It is sold in bakeries, although it is also commonly made at home. The rich bread is made from *zopf* flour that is ninety percent white wheat flour and ten percent white spelt flour. Butter, milk, egg, salt, and yeast are the other ingredients. A dash of kirsch, golden raisins, nuts, sunflower seeds, or bittersweet chocolate chips are often added to the dough.

The dough, which is made with hot melted butter, is left to rise to double its size before being divided into two or four strands that are braided together. It is then left for thirty to sixty minutes under a cloth. Before baking, the dough is brushed with egg yolk to produce its shiny golden crust. **CK**

Taste: *Soft, sweet, and tender, challah is not dissimilar to French brioche in flavor and texture, although the sprinkling of seeds on top gives it a slightly different taste.*

Taste: *Butterzopf bread has a very rich, white bread flavor with a light inner texture and a crispy crust. It is ideal eaten warm from the oven with jam or honey.*

Kosher challah, as sold by this Jewish bakery
❸ *in France, is made without dairy ingredients.*

Ciabatta

Focaccia

Ciabatta is one of the most well known of all the Italian breads outside Italy. In translation it simply means "slipper," a name the bread earned because it looks just like a flat, elongated slipper. It has a crisp crust and a chewy, often holey texture.

As so often in Italy, recipes for ciabatta vary from region to region, but all are generally made with wheat flour and a fermented dough starter called a *biga*, a rising agent that has been used in Italian baking for thousands of years. Breads made with *biga* generally share a characteristically moist, permeable texture and a deliciously pronounced flavor. Ironically, what has now become a highly fashionable bread was once a food of the poor. After World War II, a shortage of grain meant white dough was reserved for the most prosperous people. But the odds and ends of dough that were left over from the bread-making were stretched into slipper shapes—and the ciabatta was born.

Ciabatta is best served warm alongside good Italian cheese or cured meats, but it can also be enjoyed alone with good extra virgin olive oil. **LF**

Like ciabatta, this traditional Italian bread is becoming known worldwide. Yet focaccia arrived on the scene even before the oven did. A precursor of pizza, it is one of Italy's most ancient breads, and is thought to have originated with the Etruscans. The earliest focaccia were unleavened flatbreads made from flour, water, and salt. This simple composition meant they could be cooked using any available heat source at the time—most often in the hearth of domestic fires. The dough was flattened over a stone slab and cooked under the hot ashes, hence its Latin name *panis focacius* (hearth bread).

Over the centuries recipes for focaccia have become more elaborate. Today, yeast is commonly added, the basic dough includes olive oil, and loaves are often baked with herbs, bacon, cheese, or other ingredients. In its homeland, focaccia is probably most closely linked to Genoa, on the Italian Riviera, where it is known as pizza Genovese and topped with thinly sliced sautéed onions. Around Bologna, it is known as *crescentina*; in Tuscany and parts of central Italy, it becomes *schiacciata*. **LF**

Taste: *Artisanal ciabatta has a crisp golden crust, a pleasantly chewy, but porous, middle, and a subtly yeasty aroma, almost reminiscent of Champagne.*

Taste: *The best-known focaccias have a golden, dimpled, slightly salty crust and a soft middle. Texture, however, varies according to region and flavors vary with ingredients.*

Before baking, slits are sometimes cut into the focaccia dough and stuffed with herbs or other ingredients. ❯❯

Hardough

Limpa Bread

This classic bread—most frequently associated with Jamaica—is the most popular bread within the Caribbean islands. Made from white flour, the plain white bread is baked in loaf pans or, sometimes, shaped into braids. It has a dense, chewy texture, a slightly sweet flavor, and is surrounded by a soft, pale-golden crust. Outside of the Caribbean, you will find hardough in countries such as the United States and the United Kingdom where there are large Caribbean populations.

The loaves are sold whole and are delicious cut into chunky slices. Hardough is popular for its firm texture, which does not crumble nor become soggy when spread with butter or served with wet foods, such as soups or stews. It should be noted wheat is not a staple crop of the Caribbean and most of the wheat there is imported to be ground and then used in bread and other products.

Caribbean bun also has a dense texture, but is slightly stickier and darker in color due to the addition of molasses, allspice, and moist dried fruit—all of which contribute to its distinctive flavor. **SBI**

Limpa bread is the dark, sweet, deliciously aromatic bread also known as Swedish rye bread. It is flavored with molasses, anise or fennel seed, and orange peel. There are two types: *vort limpa*, which is typically made with light rye flour, and *Stockholm limpa*, which is made from a blend of white and rye flours and is often brushed with butter after baking to give it an appealing soft, well-flavored crust.

Little has been written about the origins of limpa bread, but rye goes back thousands of years. On the whole, the ancient Greeks and Romans gave rye a wide berth and it became synonymous with poverty. The grain thrived in Scandinavia and eastern Europe, however, and has long been valued in culinary terms.

Swedish cuisine has been built largely on the need for preserving and storing. Brief summers and long, dark winters meant pickles and preserves were customarily made and rye bread was baked slowly into loaves that could be stored for long periods. The ironic thing is that limpa bread is so delicious there seems little chance its capacity for storage will be put to the test. **LF**

Taste: *Hardough is firm and moist, with a dense texture that makes it great for sandwiches, or served alongside traditional Caribbean dishes, such as fish or soup.*

Taste: *Fragrant, dark, treacly, and satisfyingly sweet, limpa bread has a dense chewiness and a wonderful composed spiciness. Try it with butter and lingonberry jam.*

A family prays before breaking bread in this 1909 stained-glass window in the Tiska Kyrka, Stockholm. »

Gestiftet u Fredrik Althaus u seiner

Pumpernickel

Pumpernickel is a type of whole-grain rye bread that originated in Westphalia, Germany. An unusual bread with a dark color and dense texture, when sliced it has a similar appearance to small, heavy-duty carpet tiles, yet is surprisingly delicious. It has a particular affinity with luxury fish products such as caviar and smoked salmon, and, as such, is often served as a base for these delicacies in hors d'oeuvres. Unlike some imitation breads colored with molasses or caramel, however, traditional pumpernickel gets its dark, almost black color from a chemical browning reaction. It happens as a result of the long, slow cooking of the bread, which can be baked or steamed for up to twenty-four hours.

Rye flourished in the sandy soils of Westphalia; it was ground into course meal and made into dough that was mixed in hollowed-out tree trunks and trampled by barefoot laborers until pliable. The hefty loaves weighed in excess of 110 pounds (50 kg) and were baked in huge ovens. Machinery has now taken over where the feet left off, but the bread's unique properties have remained the same. **LF**

Taste: *With faint hints of bitter chocolate and slightly sour overtones, German pumpernickel has a big, bold, gutsy flavor that marries well with salty ham, oily fish, and beer.*

Roggenvollkornbrot

Roggenvollkornbrot is a German whole grain rye bread made from a sourdough starter. It is a highly nutritious bread with a heavy, dense texture and pronounced sour flavor. It is regarded as a very acquired taste, but complements sweet foods, such as jam and honey, and makes a wonderful base for canapés with oily fish toppings such as smoked salmon and eel, and is also superb with caviar. Roggenvollkornbrot is considered good bread for anyone trying to lose weight because it is slow to digest, so it is particularly filling and satisfying.

There is somewhere in the region of 300 types of bread on offer in Germany, but rye breads have long been top of the popularity polls. Like pumpernickel, good artisan-baked Roggenvollkornbrot gets its dark coloring from a chemical reaction that occurs naturally in some foods when they are heated. It is the same process that causes the change in the color of bread when it is toasted. The inferior industrially made varieties are usually baked for a much shorter time, so the flavor and color must be enhanced by caramel syrup and beet sugar. **LF**

Taste: *Roggenvollkornbrot has an earthy aroma and sour flavor, balanced by a vaguely sweet aftertaste. Splendid with oily fish, creamy cheeses, and sweet preserves.*

Rye breads are common in northern European countries because rye grows well in cooler latitudes.

Rúgbraud

Rich in molasses and crumbly in texture, rúgbraud is an Icelandic dark rye bread. What makes "hot spring bread" unique is that it is traditionally cooked inside steam boxes in the burbling, spouting geysers that dot Iceland's bleak lunarlike landscape.

Icelandic cuisine has evolved out of the skills and resourcefulness of its people. With its shortage of natural light and a harsh environment, not much can be grown on the land and fresh food is hard to come by. Once fuel was also in short supply. Icelanders, therefore, developed methods of drying, pickling, and fermenting foods that would last them through the relentless winters. Ingeniously, they also harnessed the geothermal power generated by vents in the volcanic soils to cook their food.

Once a fundamental part of the Icelandic diet, rúgbraud (also known as thunder bread) continues to be enjoyed today. Icelanders typically serve rúgbraud with salted butter, fish, and potatoes, but it is also good with cheese, pickled herring, and cured meats. The steaming process also provides an unusual spectacle for visiting tourists. **LF**

Taste: *Rather like traditional pumpernickel in appearance and texture, rúgbraud has sweet, slightly burned taffy overtones that hint of bittersweet chocolate.*

The geothermal power of geysers is used to steam Icelandic rúgbraud. ⟩⟩

Pane Siciliano

Kavring

Pane Siciliano is a delicious Sicilian specialty bread made with a high percentage of semolina flour and scattered with sesame seeds.

Although little is documented about the origins of pane Siciliano, the scattering of sesame seeds over bread is nothing new. The decorated tomb of an Egyptian noble dating back about 4,000 years portrays a baker going about his trade, adding sesame seeds to his bread dough. The ancient Greeks were known to have used sesame seeds in bread, but some believe the tradition of sesame bread in Sicily came about through Arab influence.

Typically eaten at breakfast or lunch with anything from jam to hams or cheese, pane Siciliano is one of the most popular breads on Sicily and has been prepared for centuries to traditional recipes by the women of Sicilian households. The different forms have interesting names, such as *occhi di St. Lucia* (eyes of St. Lucia) and *corona* (crown), but perhaps the most popular is a serpentinelike configuration with a final straight piece of dough being laid along the entire length of the center. **LF**

Kavring is the collective name for many different kinds of Swedish soft breads that are good to store and can be kept fresh for a long time. Kavring breads even improve if left to mature for a few days.

In Sweden, where the climate limits harvesting to a relatively short period in the warmer season, finding ways to store food was an important issue. The longevity of kavring made this particular bread an important staple in the Swedish diet, and the difference between life and death for some.

In medieval times kavring was baked from rye, the dominant crop at the time, but the bread is now baked with any flour. Scalding part of the rye flour and adding sourdough gives the bread a moist feel and slightly acidic flavor. It is also characterized by its spices and other flavorings, such as cumin, aniseed, or bitter orange. Baking the bread twice creates a hard crust that stops the bread drying out; this baking method also gives the kavring a dense consistency.

Kavring is an indispensable part of the Christmas smorgasbord, but is eaten all year-round. **CC**

Taste: *Bite into pane Siciliano and the soft, golden crust gives way to a delightful crunch of sesame seeds that yield a creamy, almost peanutlike flavor.*

Taste: *Black syrup gives kavring a slight taffylike taste and the hard crust a pleasant toasted tone. Delicious with pâté or skagenröra, a dill, shrimp, and mayonnaise mix.*

Crown-shaped loaves of Sicilian bread are
Ⓚ distributed for the feast of San Paolo in Sicily.

Bammy

In the 1990s, the widespread availability and popularity of bread made from wheat flour threatened to relegate Jamaica's national flatbread to an "old-time" dish. Fortunately, bammy lovers revived the dish and agricultural authorities stepped in to support the cassava farmers and their industry.

Bammy is said to have originated with the Arawak Indians, who once inhabited the West Indies. They harvested the tuberous edible root from the cassava plants, which grow in hot climates, including the Caribbean, South America, and West Africa. It was found to be a natural ingredient for making flatbreads.

Cassava is the source of tapioca, which is used as a thickener and to make puddings. Because the different varieties of cassava contain varying levels of toxic substances, the tuber must be peeled, washed, and cooked before eating. To make bammy, the cassava is grated and the liquid is pressed from it. It is then seasoned with salt, formed into a flat cake, and deep-fried, pan-fried, or baked. Often, it is soaked in coconut milk before frying. Once cooked, bammy is served with fried fish or other fried foods. **SH**

Taste: *The texture and flavor are very bland. The taste is slightly sweet, a little bready, and resembles hash brown potatoes. It picks up a little of the flavor of the oil used.*

A mobile vendor sells bammy to a hungry stallholder in Jamaica. »

Bagel

A Jewish bread originating in central Europe, bagels have an uncertain history. Polish statutes from 1610 are said to contain records that bagels were presented to women who had given birth. There is no doubt, however, that two centuries later, Eastern European Jewish immigrants brought bagels to the United States and Canada. With their relatively large Jewish populations, New York City and Montreal soon became the bagel capitals of North America.

This round yeast bread with the hole in the middle is one of the few breads that is cooked twice. In New York City, where all bagels were once handmade, the dough is first dropped into rapidly boiling water and then baked in a moderately hot oven. In Montreal, bagels, or beugels, are smaller and have larger holes. There the dough is dropped into honey-flavored boiling water and then baked in a wood-fired oven. Often the bread is finished off with a sprinkling of sesame or poppy seeds.

Bagels are traditionally eaten with a "shmear" of cream cheese and some sliced lox (smoked salmon), red onion, tomato, and capers. **SH**

Taste: *Plain bagels are pleasantly sour and taste like dense, slightly moist bread. Montreal bagels are sweeter than New York bagels and usually have seeds.*

Bialy

Slathered with butter and washed down with hot lemon tea or coffee, these warm, flavorful onion rolls are a breakfast favorite of many New Yorkers. They look similar to a bagel with a diameter of up to 6 inches (15 cm), but, instead of a hole in the middle, they have a depression that is filled with a delicious diced onion mixture, often containing poppy seeds and a little crushed garlic.

In *The Bialy Eaters* (2000), food writer Mimi Sheraton tried to retrace the bialy's journey from the Polish city of Białystok to Manhattan. In the old country, the bialy (a Yiddish word) was a Jewish specialty, known as *Białystok kuchen*. When Ashkenazi Jewish immigrants brought it with them to the United States at the beginning of the twentieth century, however, the name was shortened to bialy. The Jewish bakers who remained in the Polish city perished in the Nazi camps of World War II. In today's Poland, the closest equivalent to the bialy is the *cebulak*, a type of onion cake. Bagel bakery owner Harry Cohen is said to have been the first to market bialys in the United States. **RS**

Taste: *The bialy is not boiled before baking, so is lighter and less chewy than a bagel, although still with a touch of chewiness. The flavor is subtly yeasty.*

Crumpet

English Muffin

A popular delicacy served for afternoon tea, recipes for these traditional English griddle cakes date to the eighteenth century, but their origins reach back beyond that. Predecessors of the crumpet are thought to have been the fourteenth-century crompid cake and the buckwheat griddle cake, known as a crumpit, which appeared from the seventeenth century. It has also been associated with the Welsh pancake, *crempog*, and the Breton buckwheat pancake, *krampoch*.

Crumpets are made from a yeasted batter. Once the batter has been left to ferment, invariably baking powder (or a mixture of baking soda and cream of tartar) is added to the batter just before cooking. Unlike the similar pancakes, pikelets, which are popular in the north of England and are also cooked on the griddle, crumpets are cooked inside a ring to give them their uniform round shape. The cooked crumpet is golden and flat on its underside with a deeply holed top, which gives it its distinctive texture. Crumpets are always toasted before eating, and are delicious eaten hot and oozing with butter. **SBI**

Distinct from the familiar muffins of the United States, English muffins are unsweetened round pats of yeast dough enriched with milk and butter and cooked on a griddle to produce a disk that is crisp and flat on its top and bottom, but spongy and yeasty in the middle. They feel more like a bread than their holey relatives, crumpets and pikelets.

Homemade muffins can be eaten fresh from the griddle, but store-bought examples are warmed by toasting on both sides. They are traditionally split in half around the circumference with the fingers, due to the belief that cutting with a knife will make them heavier. They are usually spread with butter, and also form the basis of the breakfast dish eggs Benedict, topped with bacon or ham, poached eggs, and hollandaise sauce.

Muffins enjoyed their heyday during the nineteenth century. Muffin men would walk English city streets with baskets of warm muffins, advertising their wares with the ringing of a bell. Their popularity is confirmed by the words of the nursery rhyme, which asks "Have you seen the muffin man?" **ES**

Taste: *Crumpets have a plain, slightly salty flavor. Their real appeal lies in their spongy texture. Served toasted, they are best slathered with butter and sometimes jam.*

Taste: *English muffins have a crisp top and bottom, and a soft, fairly damp crumb. Spread with salted butter, they are one of the simplest treats of the English tea table.*

Croissant

Although there are earlier culinary references to "croissants," the first recipe for the croissant we know today only emerged as recently as 1906 and the huge growth in popularity of this fabulous pastry appears to have been a twentieth-century sensation.

This classic, crescent-shaped French pastry is made from a yeast-based dough, which is rolled and layered to incorporate butter. Because of the cost of butter, many bakers use cheaper substitutes such as margarine, so you will find that most bakeries in France offer two types of croissants: croissant and croissant au beurre. The former tends to be breadier, whereas the latter is much richer and, as you would expect, more buttery. A popular habit among bakers is to bend the butterless croissant into a distinctive curve, while straightening out the croissant au beurre to distinguish between the two.

Croissants are also sold stuffed with sweet and savory fillings. The classic sweet-filled croissants are almond croissants, whereas savory croissants might be filled variously with fillings such as cheese, spinach, or ham. **SBI**

Taste: *Golden, buttery croissants should be crisp and flakey on the outside and wonderfully soft and tender on the inside, with a texture that can be almost pulled apart.*

The unusual crescent shape is part of the croissant's appeal. »

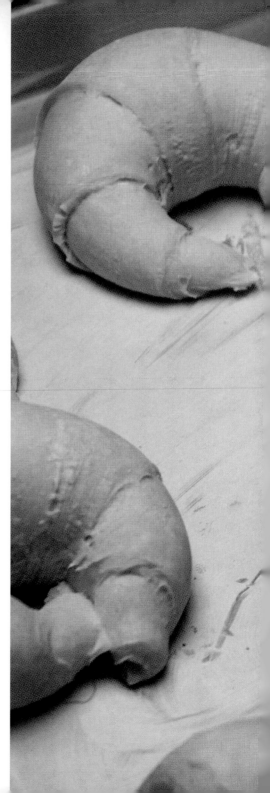

Brioche

This delectable treat from the French bakery had arrived in Paris by the seventeenth century, and the word "brioche" has been in use since at least the fifteenth century. The yeasted bread is enriched with butter, eggs, milk, and a little sugar to create a wonderfully soft, crumbly texture. The butter ratio is very high—often half to three-quarters butter to flour—and the bread is usually kneaded three times, as opposed to twice as in ordinary bread-making.

One of the best-known varieties is the brioche à tête, which is cooked in a fluted pan with sloping sides and has a little brioche ball nestled on top. Brioche Nanterre is made up of balls of dough arranged along the bottom of a loaf pan, whereas the similar brioche Parisienne has balls of dough arranged in a circle. A specialty brioche comes from the village of St. Pierre-d'Albigny: flavored with saffron or anise, it is known as the hand of St. Agathe, which refers to the severed hand of the patron saint of young mothers and wet nurses. As well as these more interesting loaves, you can also find plain loaves and simple brioche rolls. **SBI**

Taste: *Brioche has a deliciously tender, golden crumb and a slightly sweet flavor. In France, it is popularly served for breakfast or at teatime with coffee or hot chocolate.*

Pan de Coco

Every Caribbean island and Latin American country has its own unique style of coconut bread. According to some, pan de coco dates from the arrival of the Garifuna people, a cultural mix of Africans and West Indians who have lived along the coastline of Belize and Honduras since the eighteenth century. One hundred years before, their forebears escaped from slavery to settle and live on St. Vincent as free men and women, intermarrying with the island's indigenous people. They later resisted British efforts to establish a slave plantation on St. Vincent and eventually settled in Belize and Honduras.

A profusion of local coconuts suggests early pan de coco, cooked over glowing coals, became a survival food for the new settlers. Today's loaves are still served at nearly every meal, but are baked in conventional ovens and are commonly made using only flour, coconut milk, grated fresh coconut, and yeast or baking powder. In remote areas, however, basic recipes still exist for making flatbreads from just coconut milk and flour. These breads are baked on a hot iron skillet in a similar way to corn tortillas. **WS**

Taste: *Pan de coco is a simple bread with a crisp, brown crust and a moist, pale, very heavy crumb—perfumed and flavored with the sweet creaminess of fresh coconut.*

A perfectly formed brioche à tete, topped
❸ *with its characteristic small dough ball.*

Malt Loaf

This quintessentially British treat is a yeasted loaf usually made with wheat flour and barley malt. It is traditionally the size of a small brick, with a dark color and dense texture, and studded with juicy golden raisins. The bread is fairly soft, so it is best cut with a serrated knife, pulled gently across the grain, so as not to squash the loaf.

The dark color and dense texture come from the addition of malt extract and treacle, which also give the bread its delicious flavor. Malt extract is a dark brown, syrupy concentrate obtained from malt. Barley grains are germinated, dried, and ground; the ground malt is then "mashed" in hot water to make brewer's wort, and the malt extract is obtained from this by process of evaporation in a partial vacuum.

Although the history of malt loaf is uncertain, it is thought the habit of adding malt extract to bread began near the end of the nineteenth century. Malt was then incredibly popular as an ingredient because of its reputation as a tonic and restorative. It featured in malted cocoa, malted preserves, malted jellies, and, of course, malt loaf. **SBI**

Kugelhopf

Many variations of this enriched, yeasted cake-bread are baked all the way from the Alsace region of France through parts of Germany and Poland and into Austria. Its name varies, too, according to region; it tends to be known as kugelhopf in the western part of its range and gugelhupf in the east. It is held in great esteem and in the tiny village of Ribeauville, in Alsace, there is even a fete held every summer in its honor.

The defining feature of a kugelhopf is its shape, produced by the pan in which it is baked—a high, round, fluted pan with a central funnel. The resulting cake is tall and ring-shaped, not dissimilar to a Bundt cake. It is frequently dusted with confectioners' sugar to highlight the fluted pattern and sometimes decorated with slivered almonds.

Kugelhopf contains eggs, butter, and sugar as well as yeast and flour and in that respect is similar to the French brioche, but it is also often flavored with lemon peel and raisins. In the Alsace, there are also savory versions made with bacon, lard, and fromage frais or cream cheese. **SBI**

Taste: *Despite an uninspiring appearance, malt loaf has a chewy, almost fudgy texture. Fruity, but not too sweet, this teatime treat is usually eaten sliced and buttered.*

Taste: *Sweet kugelhopf has a taste and texture like well-flavored brioche. The less-common, savory version still has a tender, enriched crumb, but flecked with bacon bits.*

A copper mold signals that kugelhopf can be bought from this baker in Ribeauville, Alsace. »

Bara Brith

Paasiaisleipa

One of the best-known Welsh fruit breads, bara brith literally means "speckled bread." The dried fruit, usually currants, raisins, or golden raisins, and candied peel, with which the bread is packed, is frequently soaked in tea before adding to the batter, which gives it a very moist texture. Traditionally, bara brith was always yeasted, although modern versions are often leavened with rising agents such as baking powder or baking soda, which affects the finished flavor and texture.

In Wales, there are many different variations of this bread in stores, bakeries, and in the home, and most families will have their own closely guarded recipe. But bara brith is not just confined to Wales and the British Isles. As far away as Argentine Patagonia there are versions of this moist Welsh bread, where it was introduced by Welsh settlers who arrived in Chabut province from 1865. There it is known as *torta negra*, meaning black cake, but despite its change in name and the distance it has traveled, torta negra still bears a striking resemblance to the original bara brith. **SBI**

As with other Easter breads from around the world, rich, sugar-dusted paasiaisleipa, from Finland, is full of everything traditionally eschewed during the Christian fast of Lent. The dough is enriched with eggs, butter, and milk, and flavored with cardamom, orange and lemon peels, nuts, and dried fruit, which are kneaded into the dough. This is then traditionally baked in a milk pail to give the loaf a sloped, cylindrical shape. (Modern recipes suggest using a round cake pan instead of a milk pail.)

Paasiaisleipa's roots are thought to hark back to pre-Christian times. Cylindrical breads have a long history in pagan celebrations: some theories suggest their phallic shape made them important in spring festivals; others believe the shape resembles the long skirt of a woman, a symbol of fertility.

Paasiaisleipa takes pride of place at the center of an Easter buffet piled high with homebaked breads, alongside rich spring butter, creams, and cheeses, and one of the oldest Finnish Easter dishes known as *mämmi*—a mixture of molasses, water, and rye flour flavored with raisins and orange peel. **SBI**

Taste: *Bara brith is a moist, lightly spiced loaf with a fairly dense, fruit-packed texture. Although it is delicious buttered, some purists believe it should be served plain.*

Taste: *Lightly spiced, with a citrus tang, and studded with dried fruit and nuts, this bread is not unlike panettone. Slightly cakey, it has a briochelike taste and texture.*

Lussekatter

The Christmas season would not be Christmas for Swedes without lussekatter, the sweet, yellow saffron buns, whose name means "St. Lucy's cats." Still celebrated in homes, churches, schools, and concert halls across Scandinavia with processions led by a white-clad girl wearing a crown of candles, St. Lucy's Day was marked by the Swedish gentry as early as the eighteenth century. Lussekatter are believed to have originated during this period from a Germanic forerunner known as *dövelskatter*, or "devil's cats," named after an evil figure that used to follow St. Nicholas and spank naughty children.

Lussekatter are baked with yeast, flour, milk, egg, butter, sugar, raisins, and a generous amount of expensive saffron, used specifically because of its exclusivity. The dough is traditionally formed in patterns and shapes that date back centuries, notably crosses, sheaves, "priests' hair," "swaddled baby," and "golden cart." The pig is as associated with Christmas in Sweden as the turkey is in the Britain, and so the most popular kind today is the S-shaped "Christmas-pig." **CC**

Taste: *Best eaten warm, fresh out of the oven, lussekatter are slightly sweet with a wonderful scent and taste of saffron. They are usually served with tea or coffee.*

Birnbrot

This dense fruit-and-nut bread is popularly served throughout Switzerland for Christmas. Although it contains many different dried fruits, its name literally means "pear bread." The rustic loaf has peasant origins, but these simple beginnings belie its delicious flavor. Packed with dried pears, prunes, dates, figs, and golden raisins, and dark raisins, which give the bread a wickedly dark color when cut, the bread also contains candied orange and lemon, pine kernels, nuts, and kirsch, and the dough is flavoured with spices, vanilla, and a little sugar.

The fruits and nuts are bound together with dough, then encased in a thin layer of plain dough to make a densely packed loaf. The bread has great storage qualities and traditionally it is made in large quantities before Christmas so there are enough loaves to last until Candlemas (February 2nd).

Birnbrot has been likened to the Christmas spice cake *berawecka*, which originates from the Alsace region of France. The French cake is similar in flavor and texture, except it is baked without an outer covering of plain, enriched bread dough. **SBI**

Taste: *This heavy, chewy, spiced bread is naturally sweet from all the fruit it contains. It should be cut into thin slices and served either plain or thinly spread with butter.*

Stollen

Originating in Germany, this classic bread-cake has become almost ubiquitous in many parts of the world as traditional Christmas fare. The origins of stollen have been traced back to the city of Dresden in the Middle Ages, although it should be noted the early versions of stollen were not the luxurious treat that we know today. The stollen of the Middle Ages was made to a much more austere recipe, with a dough made only from flour, oats, and water—in line with church doctrines that did not allow the use of richer ingredients over the Christmas period.

Today's stollen, however, is a veritable treat. The yeasted dough is enriched with eggs, butter, milk, sugar, and spices into which dried currants, golden raisins, and candied peel are kneaded. Almonds are sometimes finely chopped and added to the dough, and sometimes ground to a marzipanlike paste and rolled into the bread to give it a moist, sweet middle. The loaf is then shaped into an oval or oblong with tapering ends to represent the form of the baby Jesus wrapped in swaddling clothes—hence stollen's sometime name of Christstollen. **SBI**

Taste: *Stollen offers a perfect not-too-sweet bread base, packed with dried fruit and dusted with confectioners' sugar. It is rich and dense, so serve in thin slices.*

Panettone

Gloriously scented and enriched with butter, eggs, sugar, raisins, and candied fruit, panettone is essentially *the* Italian Christmas cake, traditionally eaten over the festive period and New Year. It is made like a bread, using a fermented starter to raise the dough, and acquires its characteristic dome shape as it hangs upside down to cool.

The legends behind panettone are as rich as the cake, although all agree that panettone was first made in Milan, and most Italians like to believe its name was originally *pan di Toni* (Tony's bread). One story has it that a young Milanese nobleman fell in love with Toni, the daughter of a local baker. He bluffed his way into the kitchen masquerading as an apprentice and won her heart by creating a huge, dome-shaped confection. Another fable tells of Toni, a young kitchen boy working in the court of Ludovico il Moro, a duke of Milan during the Renaissance. When the chef ruined the Christmas dessert, Toni saved the day with a bread he had made from leftover dough and enriched with eggs, fruit, and butter, impressing the duke immensely. **LF**

Taste: *Panettone has an outwardly firm texture, which gives way to a soft, exquisitely buttery middle studded with fruit, and flaunting tempting vanilla overtones.*

The distinctive light texture of panettone comes from proving the dough for an unusually long time. »

Blini

Scots Pancake

To the Russian poet Alexander Kuprin (1870–1938) blinis were "yellow gold and hot like the sun, the symbol of sublime days, rich harvests, harmonious marriages, and healthy children." Today, these pancakes are so popular that in St. Petersburg a chain of fast-food blini restaurants has been dubbed "Blindonalds" by the local population.

Traditionally made with buckwheat flour and known as red or *krasnyj* blinis, other ground grains such as millet and barley can also be used. Modern recipes favor a mix of buckwheat and ordinary wheat flour to give a lighter, less brittle result.

Blinis can be served piled up with fillings layered between or stuffed and rolled. The range of fillings is as wide as the cook's imagination and could be caviar, sour cream, honey, jam, hard-boiled eggs, chopped herring, or fruit. As with all pancakes, blinis are best eaten as soon as they are made and guests in traditional Russian homes were allowed to sit in the kitchen with the hostess ready to enjoy her labors the moment the lightly puffed dough clouds were flipped off the hot cast-iron griddle. **WS**

The simplicity of making these little pancakes belies their versatility. Also known as "drop" or "dropped" scones in England and in some parts of Scotland, Scots pancakes are traditionally sweet and made with white flour, cream of tartar, baking soda, sugar, eggs, and milk. The resulting batter is then dropped onto a griddle, which is a hot metal plate set over an open fire. As the pancakes begin to bubble they are ready to be turned over; this usually takes about a minute on each side because Scots pancakes are thicker than other varieties.

They are a popular dish to make for unexpected guests because the batter can be made and cooked very quickly, and the pancakes served warm with butter and jam. A savory version can also be made with whole wheat or buckwheat flour and without sugar. It is similar to a blini and is often served with crème fraîche and smoked salmon.

Scots pancakes are easy to buy in Britain, but because of the simple recipe and the fact they are most delicious fresh from the griddle, they are best made at home. **CTr**

Taste: *With the robust, nutty taste of buckwheat, blinis should be eaten warm, before they become tough, and be slightly puffed like a thicker version of the French crêpe.*

Taste: *Scots, or Scotch, pancakes are more of a vehicle for other foods, not having great flavor in themselves, but the texture is light and spongy with a sweet aftertaste.*

Hopper

In the tropical splendor of Sri Lanka they are called hoppers; in Kerala, southern India, *appams*, but both are the same rice flour pancake, fried in a kind of wok and eaten for breakfast. They are made from a light dough that is fermented overnight with a little palm toddy. Once it has risen like a sponge, it is thinned with coconut cream. To make each one, a little batter is poured over a heated round cast-iron pan (*cheena chatti*) and baked so it is crisp and curling at the edges and still fluffy in the middle. It is eaten in many ways, with hot sambals, chile relishes, grated coconut, or curries. The favorite way in the subcontinent is with a fried egg sunny-side up. Like pancakes, hoppers can be consumed in quantity, and Sri Lankans will have little difficulty in polishing off half a dozen while watching a cricket match.

The name "hopper," an Anglo-Indian invention, derives from the Tamil *appam*, used to describe a fried snack. *Iddiappams,* or string hoppers, are a related snack-cum-breakfast food, also made from rice flour, but formed like a string by being forced through a mold and steamed. **MR**

Taste: *Brittle at the edges, almost lacelike, hoppers become progressively softer toward the middle where they are almost spongy. They have a mild taste of rice.*

Arepa de Choclo

Visitors to Venezuela will not have to travel far before they find a bar or small *arepera* restaurant serving these sweet corn cakes. Made from yellow arepa meal (*masarepa* or *masa harina*)—a gluten-free flour ground from starchy cooked corn, which should not be confused with cornmeal, cornstarch, polenta, or hominy grits—arepas de choclo were originally a food staple of the poor, but have now become a national dish. Before technology stepped in, preparing arepa meal was time-consuming. Dried corn kernels had to be soaked in water and lime to remove their skins, then cooked, drained, dried, and ground between stones. Traditionally sweetened with an unrefined, brown sugar cubes called *papelón*, modern recipes simply call for sugar.

Arepas de choclo are eaten at any time of day as a snack, appetizer, or accompaniment to a meal instead of bread. They can be fried, baked, or griddled, eaten plain, or with *queso fresco* and chopped chiles added to the mix. They can also be split and sandwiched with slices of chicken, meat, or strong cheese, or topped with guacamole. **WS**

Taste: *Best eaten warm, so the golden outside is crusty and the inside light and soft. The freshly cooked ground corn kernels give a creamy texture and extra sweetness.*

Bath Oliver

In the mid-eighteenth century, Dr. William Oliver was the most fashionable physician in ultra-fashionable Bath—the spa town to which England's rich and famous flocked as a retreat from the smell and squalor of London. Bath's sulfurous mineral waters had been famous since Roman times, but the eighteenth century brought a renewed focus on their health benefits, and Dr. Oliver apparently created these fairly plain, unsweetened biscuits to be "taken" with the waters. Today, of course—but for the chocolate-coated versions, which were allegedly John Lennon's favorite cracker—they are mostly eaten with cheese.

The plain Bath Olivers have been continuously in production since Dr. Oliver's death in 1764. The story goes that he bequeathed the recipe for the famous cracker to his coachman, a Mr. Atkins, together with a sack of flour and a large sum of money. Mr. Atkins promptly set up a baking business and became rich on the proceeds. The production rights have since been transferred several times, and Bath Olivers are no longer made in Bath. **AMS**

Oatcake

The unique crumbly texture of the Scottish oatcake has made it known across the world. Developed in the seventeenth century, when oats took over from barley as Scotland's staple food grain, it was quick and easy to make in front of the open fire: a simple mix of meal and water blended into a paste and baked on the hot hearthstones. Historical references are many. The fourteenth-century French chronicler Jean Froissart noted how Scottish soldiers mixed meal with water and seared it over the fire to produce a "biscuit." The English diarist Dorothy Wordsworth observed in 1803 that they were "kneaded with cream and were excellent." (Today warm lard is more traditional than cream.)

Commercial oatcakes are usually made with wheat flour to hold them together. They have retained their popularity as they make as good an accompaniment as bread to many dishes, and are seen as healthier because of their low-gluten content and the perception that they absorb cholesterol. They can be eaten with oily fish, cheese, jams, butter, and honey, as well as with soup. **CTr**

Taste: *These mild crackers are slightly soft, rather than crisp, with a fine grain. The texture and smooth, almost creamy flavor make them an ideal partner to cheese.*

Taste: *Commercial oatcakes tend to be smooth with a nutty crunch. Homemade versions can be very thin and brittle, with a fuller flavor and delightful toasty edge.*

People enjoy the healing waters of Bath—home of the
❸ *famous cracker—in this eighteenth-century illustration.*

Knäckebröd

Matzo

Thin, hard flatbreads have been baked in Sweden since the sixth century, when they were originally based on barley, then the dominant grain. For the last thousand years, rye has been the grain of choice, although versions are made using wheat, barley, and oats. Knäckebröd has remained remarkably popular, both in its homeland and abroad, where it is generally known as crispbread.

Recipes and styles vary from region to region, but when making knäckebröd a dough of flour, water, yeast, and salt is rolled out into thin, flat circles. A special rolling pin creates the distinctive cratered texture, and a large hole is made in the middle before the bread is baked at high temperature. After baking, numerous breads are then hung by the hole in the middle on a long wooden rod to dry. This method gives the bread its distinctive dry feel, as well as the long shelf life, which was a necessity in older days. Today, knäckebröd is rarely baked at home, but is a central feature of any Swedish smorgasbord. It also comes in smaller rectangular shapes. **CC**

Derived from the Hebrew word *matzah*, flat, brittle matzo is the traditional Jewish unleavened flatbread baked for Passover—or Pesach, as it is known in the Jewish calendar. Matzo is symbolic of the flight from slavery in Egypt, when there was not any time for leavened bread, and every year unleavened matzo is eaten for the eight days of Passover.

Matzo is the only flour product that can be eaten during Passover. Guidelines on preparation are strict and once the flour has been mixed with water, no longer than eighteen minutes can pass before the baked matzo is removed from the oven. To make sure the production of the matzo has adhered to these regulations for Passover, the packaging is always marked "kosher for Pesach."

Other matzo products include matzo meal, which can be used for making cakes and cookies, as well as the Jewish classic recipe *knaidlach* (matzo balls for serving in chicken soup), and binding ingredients in dishes such as *gefilte* fish (fish balls) and *latkes* (potato pancakes), and matzo farfel, which is lightly crushed matzo. **SBI**

Taste: *Knäckebröd should be crisp and hard. It is neutral in taste, sometimes with a faint smoky note. It is served as a sandwich with cheese, sausage, or pickled herring.*

Taste: *Crisp, dry matzos come in large oblong sheets, creamy colored and speckled with brown. They are very versatile and taste somewhat like water biscuits.*

The mother of a Jewish family breaks wrapped matzo in a fourteenth-century Hebrew manuscript. ❯❯

אחת משלש המצות אֵ
אשר כסל ומוצע אותה
לשתים ומניח חציה בין
שתי השלמות וחצה הם
המצה והנכסל שני

Nürnberger Elisenlebkuchen

The first traditional German Christmas cookies known as *Lebkuchen* are thought to have been baked by monks in Franconia, Germany, during the thirteenth century, but the most famous variety is from Nürnberg and dates from 1395. Since 1808, the very best *Lebkuchen* has been Elisenlebkuchen (PDO), and one of Nürnberg's most celebrated Elisenlebkuchen bakeries is the Lebkuchen Schmidt.

Unlike other gingerbreads, this elite cookie contains little or no flour, the most important ingredients being nuts (hazelnuts and/or almonds) and a special spice blend. Each bakery adds its own characteristic blend and the mix of spices used is a jealously guarded secret. Some ancient recipes use honey instead of sugar; the forerunner of today's *Lebkuchen* was known as honey cake and can be traced back to the Egyptians, Greeks, and Romans.

Elisenlebkuchen can be baked as circles decorated with whole nuts and dusted with confectioners' sugar, cut into decorative shapes and frosted, or set on wafers and covered with a glistening layer of smooth dark chocolate. **WS**

Basler Leckerli

Since the mid-fourteenth century, these spicy honey cookies have been baked to celebrate every festive occasion in Basel, Switzerland. The first recipes were devised by local spice merchants.

Lebkuchen (gingerbread) makers plied their trade in the markets of Strasbourg, Nürnberg, and Memmingen and it was to escape the fierce competition from them that a self-employed baker moved to Basel and opened a small store selling leckerli. The sugar-glazed cookies proved popular with the Basel elite and a new craft established itself, the first mention of leckerli appearing in the city's council records of 1720. Today, one of the leading producers is the Läckerli-Huus, established in 1903.

As well as baked cookies, the original shop also stocked candied lemon and orange peels, nuts, honey, spices, and kirsch, so customers could bake their own. Similar in texture and flavor to *panforte di Siena*, leckerli can be stamped out using a special cutter or simply cut into bars with a knife. *Lecker* means delicious in German and the cookies are a powerhouse of complementary flavors. **WS**

Taste: *A range of spices, including cinnamon, coriander, nutmeg, clove, allspice, cardamom, and ginger, adds a warm, spicy taste to the soft and crumbly Elisenlebkuchen.*

Taste: *The honey gives a mellow flavor, candied peels add the tang of citrus, almonds give a nutty crunch, and cinnamon provides the warmth of exotic spice.*

Heart-shaped lebkuchen bearing a huge
☾ *variety of messages are widely sold in Germany.*

Amaretto di Saronno

Brandy Snap

Amaretti—"little bitter ones"—are perhaps the most famous of all Italian cookies. As with most Italian recipes, there are regional specialties from all over the country, each reflecting the customs, traditions, and tastes of their district. Styles range from soft and sugary to hard and crunchy, and most contain both sweet almonds and bitter almonds.

Yet of all the multifarious amaretti, those from Saronno, in Lombardy, are best known. The Lazzaroni brand is found the world over and the cookies have a history almost as colorful as the papers they are wrapped in. According to legend, almost three centuries ago, the Cardinal of Milan visited the town. To honor him, two young lovers, Giuseppe and Osolina, created bittersweet cookies made from sugar, apricot kernels, and egg whites, and wrapped them in pairs as a symbol of their love. The cardinal blessed the couple, who went on to marry; their recipe has remained a secret ever since.

Amaretti are served with coffee, dessert wines, and liqueurs. Crumbled, they are used in Italian desserts. They enjoy a special affinity with peaches. **LF**

These crisp, lacy, wafer-thin cookies that literally "snap" as you bite them are traditional English treats. They are made from a mixture of butter, golden syrup, sugar, and flour, often flavored with ginger. The mix is melted in a pan, then dropped onto cookie sheets and baked. As the mixture bakes, it spreads to create the dimpled texture that is so distinctive. While still warm and soft, the cookies are lifted off the sheet and rolled around a spoon handle or horn molds to make hollow tubes. Once cool, they are eaten plain or filled with whipped cream.

Brandy snaps, or "fairings," were sold at English fairs, and were sometimes sold flat rather than rolled. Despite their name, brandy snaps are not always flavored with brandy. It is thought that earlier recipes used brandy, but that the ingredient was dropped because it was so expensive and had a minimal effect on the taste. Other early versions of the cookies were made with molasses.

Today, you will also find brandy snaps shaped into baskets rather than tubes, creating edible containers in which desserts can be served. **SBI**

Taste: *At first bite, Amaretti di Saronno are crunchy and sweet, but the texture soon becomes chewily soft. They have an almond flavor, reminiscent of fine marzipan.*

Taste: *The texture of sweet, buttery brandy snaps is between a cookie and a taffylike wafer that melts in the mouth and crackles around the teeth. Delicious with tea.*

The act of unwrapping amaretti to take with coffee ❨❩ is enjoyed as much as the cookies themselves.

Appenzeller Biber

Florentine

Known for its elaborate embroidery and delicious cheeses, the Appenzell canton of Switzerland is also home to an addictive pastry. Appenzeller Biber (or Appenzeller Baerli-Biber) is a special gingerbread filled with almond paste.

Made for centuries, the gingerbread is believed to have originated in the abbey of St. Gallen, but today it is made in bakeries throughout the region. Although the gingerbread shares similarities with the German *lebkuchen*, Appenzeller Biber is unique in that it starts with a layer of dough pressed into a decorative mold (often of a bear). This dough is then topped by a layer of marzipan or homemade almond paste, and finished with another layer of dough.

The gingerbread often has honey in it, sometimes has liquor, and always has spices, but the exact amount of spices and exactly which spices depend on the baker. Most often it has ginger, cinnamon, and nutmeg, and sometimes rose water is also added. It can come in the form of large cakes known as *Fladen*, but is also served as cookies known as *Biberli*, traditionally served as a Christmas treat. **JH**

The word "florentine" is commonly used in reference to the city of Florence, and frequently to describe dishes containing spinach. This is not the case, however, with regard to these delicate, sweet little cookies. Their exact history and provenance appears to have been lost in the mists of time, but what is certain is that they are not specific to the city of Florence, but are popular all over Europe and beyond.

The base of these rich, chewy nut cookies is made of slivered almonds and candied fruit and usually coated in chocolate marked with distinctive wavy lines. They make a popular petit four (a collective term for any number of pretty little cakes and cookies, such as macaroons and meringues).

There are countless variations of florentine when it comes to the combination of fruits and nuts and the coating of chocolate—whether it be bittersweet, semisweet, or white. The classic florentine uses almonds, but other ones are made with pistachios, walnuts, and others. And, the candied fruit used is as varied as the candied fruits available—be it citrus, apricot, pineapple, mango, fig, or cherry. **SBI**

Taste: *The gingerbread has a dry, cakelike texture and is not overly sweet, which goes nicely with the very sweet almond paste filling. Perfect with good hot chocolate.*

Taste: *Florentines are irresistibly sweet, chewy, and mouthwatering. Whether served after dinner with coffee or a cup of midday tea, one is never quite enough.*

For the hungry passer-by, few sights are more enticing than confections in an Italian pasticceria. ❯

Shortbread

Although similar styles of cookie are made elsewhere, shortbread has become synonymous with Scotland. It appeared in 1736 in the first Scottish cookbook, Mrs. McLintock's *Receipts for Cookery and Pastry-work*: she made her recipe with flour, butter, and "barm" (yeast). Ninety years later, when Meg Dods wrote *The Cook and Housewife's Manual*, it had become the sweet food it is today.

Shortbread has a distinctive crumbly texture and is made using three main ingredients—flour, butter, and sugar. The dough is rolled out, cut into shapes, and baked in a slow oven until golden. While today's commercial manufacturers sometimes add chocolate and ginger, and use ground almonds and different flours in their basic recipe, the round style that breaks into triangular pieces known as "petticoat tails" tend not to include additions, except, perhaps, caraway seeds, which purists consider the traditional method. Quality varies, and shortbread made with fats other than butter is best avoided. Walkers, of Aberlour, in Scotland, produce fantastic petticoat tails. **CTr**

Chocolate Chip Cookie

The North American cookie is generally richer and chewier than an English biscuit, and has been made under that name since at least the beginning of the eighteenth century, and probably much longer. But the chocolate chip cookie—the most famous cookie of all—was invented only during the 1930s.

Ruth Graves Wakefield and her husband bought the Toll House Inn in the town of Whitman, Massachusetts, in 1930. Ruth did the cooking, and she became locally known for her desserts. While experimenting with an old cookie recipe for Butter Drop Do, she chopped a bar of semisweet chocolate into tiny bits, and added it to her cookie dough. The pieces did not melt, but held their shape, softening slightly to a creamy texture.

A large baking-chocolate manufacturer astutely acquired the rights to her recipe, and printed it on their package. Then they created "chips" of chocolate specifically for her recipe. Today, Nestlé owns the Toll House Cookie trademark. Other chocolate chip cookies are marketed commercially in a range of shapes and sizes. **SH**

Taste: *The thin petticoat tail has a crisp, almost brittle, yet buttery texture with a sweet flavor. The thicker cookie is denser, but still with the distinctively rich flavor.*

Taste: *The texture of chocolate chip cookies can vary from crisp, even crunchy, to deliciously chewy. The taste is nutty and chocolaty with brown-sugar notes.*

Chocolate chip cookies were airlifted to U.S. front-line troops in the Gulf to boost morale. ❯❯

Liège Waffle

Madeleine de Commercy

Also known as *gauffres*, waffles are one of Belgium's best-known culinary inventions. The Liège waffle, created in the town of Liège, is best described in terms of how it differs from its better-known counterpart, the Brussels waffle. The Brussels waffle is the rectangular waffle, made from a yeasted batter cooked in a waffle iron, then served with toppings, such as confectioners' sugar, whipped cream, strawberries, or chocolate sauce and served on a plate with a knife and fork. (It was this waffle that was introduced to the United States and has become the ubiquitous breakfast treat, whereas in Belgium it remains a snack food enjoyed at any time.)

In contrast, the Liège waffle is smaller and has a more rounded shape. The batter is made without yeast and the resulting golden waffle has a denser texture and sweeter flavor, with a caramelized burned sugar coating that is produced as a result of adding small lumps of sugar to the batter. Liège waffles are sold by street vendors and from small stores all over Belgium and they are simply wrapped in paper and eaten in the hand as a snack. **SBI**

It was famously the recollection of eating a madeleine that sparked Proust's *À la Recherche du Temps Perdu*, and these scallop-shaped little sponge cakes are, indeed, delicious. But opinions differ as to their precise origin. Some say the recipe came from the convent of St. Mary Magdalene, in Commercy, during the eighteenth century, when nuns made cakes and sweets and sold them to support themselves. When the French Revolution led to the abolition of convents and monasteries, the nuns sold the recipe to village bakers for a handsome fee.

Another story centers on a different Madeleine, a young servant girl, who made them for the Duke of Lorraine in the eighteenth century. He was so impressed with them he gave some to his daughter Marie, the wife of Louis XV, who subsequently took them to Versailles where they were a huge hit. Others credit Jean Avice (1754–1838), a celebrated pastry chef, with their distinctive shape. Whatever their beginnings, their delicate flavor can be appreciated with tea and coffee, or alongside creamy desserts and sweet wines. **LF**

Taste: *Liège waffles are best eaten while still warm to fully enjoy their crunchy outside and fluffy inside. They are naturally sweet and do not need extra toppings.*

Taste: *The madeleine's crisp, lightly browned edges rise into a golden dome of springy, closely textured crumb that is light, moist, and buttery with hints of lemon and vanilla.*

Traditionally, madeleines are baked in scallop-shaped molds. »

Scone

Brownie

Although they can be large, savory, made with soda-bread dough, or cooked like pancakes, the popular notion of scones in their British home is now the small, slightly sweet, but very simple baked item served mainly with tea. The word is originally Scottish and there is a strong tradition of scone-making in that country: like other similar Scottish goods, they would originally have been cooked on a heavy metal plate known as a "girdle" or "griddle."

Most common recipes today include white flour, baking powder, and butter, with eggs and milk. The dough is cut into thick circles or, sometimes, triangles and baked in a hot oven. Sweet scones served with clotted cream and jam form part of the traditional cream tea, a delicious ritual observed happily by tourists in Devon and southwest England, where it originated, and increasingly in the quainter corners of other counties. Like other plain mixtures, scones take happily to additions, such as dried fruit, grated cheese, or a sugar topping, but restraint should be exercised. Scones stale quickly and should be eaten soon after baking. **ES**

This square bar of dark, rich, chocolate indulgence is not as dense as fudge, nor as light as a cake, yet strikes the perfect balance of texture between the two. Nuts, particularly walnuts, often add crisp notes to the blend, but, as so often with popular American recipes, embellishments are endless: anything from crumbled taffy to dried fruit to chocolate chips can be added to the batter.

The word "brownie" was used in reference to various confections before it became firmly attached to the baked dish it denominates today. The cooking teacher and writer Fannie Farmer is credited with printing the first modern brownie recipe in the 1906 edition of her *Boston Cooking School Cook Book*. It gained popularity in the United States as an easy alternative to homebaked cakes and pies for mothers who were becoming increasingly time-pressed as the twentieth century gained pace: they are still popular packed in a lunch bag or a picnic basket, or served at a casual dinner. Topping with ice cream and chocolate sauce or caramel sauce creates the ever-popular brownie sundae. **CN**

Taste: *A fresh scone should be light and not too crusty, with a soft texture more like soda bread than cake. Simply serve split and spread with butter. Its plainness is a virtue.*

Taste: *The brownie is all about its rich chocolate flavor. Texture is a matter of personal taste. Some like brownies chewy and dense, whereas others prefer them lighter.*

Scones with clotted cream and jam are
❸ *always served as part of an English cream tea.*

Berliner Doughnut

Dating back to at least the early 1800s, the Berliner doughnut goes by different names in different regions of Germany. Outside of Berlin it is known simply as Berliner, but in Berlin itself it is better known as *Berliner Pfannkuchen* or *Pfannkuchen*, which means Berlin pancake, or pancake.

Whatever its name, a Berliner doughnut is essentially a classic jelly doughnut made from a sweet yeast dough that has been deep-fried in oil, filled with jam or plum sauce, then usually dusted or rolled in sugar. Other recipes include custard-filled varieties, or a type of doughnut known as *fastnachts*, which are traditionally served on Shrove Tuesday. These differ from Berliners in that they are round or diamond-shaped and made from a yeast-raised potato dough; traditionally they are sprinkled with sugar and served with syrup.

Since 1961, the Berliner doughnut has been inextricably tied to the U.S. president John F. Kennedy, after he famously tried to say, "I am a citizen of Berlin." But instead he said, "*Ich bin ein Berliner,*" which translates as "I am a doughnut." **SBI**

Taste: *Soft, golden Berliner doughnuts are a treat, indeed, oozing with jam as you bite into them. They are best when fresh, so be sure to seek out a bakery with a good turnover.*

Mooncake

Mooncakes are as central to the Chinese Mid-Autumn Festival as lanterns, candles, and gazing at the full harvest moon. Traditionally these round or square pastries were simple: a thin, slightly sweet pastry molded around a rich filling generally made of lotus seed paste. A some time in history, a whole salted egg yolk was added to symbolize the moon.

Today, mooncakes are varied, as top hotels and restaurants from Beijing to Singapore vie to create exotic (and expensive) new versions. Some bakeries add four or more salted egg yolks in their recipes, while fillings can include red bean paste, nuts, seeds, salted ham, durian paste, mashed taro, and even bird's nest. "Snowy" mooncakes have a wrapper of sweetened rice flour paste; ice cream mooncakes come in various flavors with a core of mango sorbet to stand in for the egg yolk.

Mooncakes allegedly played a role in the overthrow of the Mongol Yuan Dynasty that ruled China in the fourteenth century. Messages outlining plans for the revolts were hidden in mooncakes, which were given as gifts to supporters. **KKC**

Taste: *Mooncakes are smallish, but they are rarely eaten whole because of their rich filling. Instead, they are cut into wedges, the better to appreciate the "moon" in the middle.*

In 2007 a mooncake weighing 13 tons was baked in China; it incorporated ten of these smaller cakes. »

Baba

Honey Cake

Italy, Ukraine, and Poland (where it is known as *babka*), all claim to be the originators of baba, the sweetened, cylindrical shaped cake. Baba means old woman or grandmother (*babka* is its diminutive—little old granny), and the cake's name is said to come from its tapered shape, which resembles the full skirts once worn by peasant women.

While the shape of baba is Slavic in origin, the recipe seems to have traveled around Europe, gaining various culinary influences along the way. Recipes vary from simple yeast-raised cakes and fruited breads to its alcohol-laden incarnation as the celebrated *baba au rhum*, a development that took place in France (perhaps thanks to an exiled Polish king who might have taken *babka* there in the eighteenth century).

Frosted or sugar-dusted babas are traditional Easter fare in Russia and Poland. Their luscious golden dough can be scented with saffron and studded with raisins, and the white frosting dripping down the sides is often sprinkled with slivered almonds, although the original baba was plain. **RS**

This traditional confection known as *mézeskalács* is more of a cookie than a cake. Today, you will see the highly decorated honey cakes sold not only all over Hungary, but also across central Europe, and they make a popular token of love or for friendship.

The earliest honey cakes date to before the fourteenth century. They were made from a soft dough of warmed honey, sugar, and flour pressed into intricate molds frequently carved with religious characters, indicating that the cakes were probably used as offerings to saints on special occasions. Later molds depicted images of outlaws, animals, and dancing couples. The shapes of the molds were so beautiful that no additional decoration was added to the baked cakes.

Today, the cakes are cut, not cast, into simple shapes and then decorated with frosting and decorations. Red is a popular color and, unusually, mirrors are often used within the decorations. To this day, the most-favored shape is the heart and honey cakes often bear the words *szívküldi szívnek*, which means "from a heart to a heart." **SBI**

Taste: *Light, porous, and buttery, with yeasty undertones, baba sometimes has a subtle hint of saffron, vanilla, almonds, or rum, depending on the flavorings used.*

Taste: *Honey cakes are very similar in taste to some gingerbread, although with a lighter, more honeyed flavor. They are often treated as an object of admiration.*

A cylindrical mold gives baba its distinctive shape, but the cake can also be baked in small individual rounds.

Maid of Honor

These golden-colored, almond-flavored, dainty English curd tartlets have a venerable history. As their name suggests, they are associated with royalty. Legend links them with the Tudor monarch Henry VIII, who is said to have first come across the tarts when he met Anne Boleyn and other maids of honor eating them. Such was Henry's fondness for the tarts that he insisted the recipe be kept secret within Richmond Palace. Another version of the story links them to the royal palace of Hampton Court.

Historically the tarts have a long association with the town of Richmond in Surrey, where a local shop was famous for its maids of honor during the eighteenth century. Today the tradition of making the tarts is maintained by a charming bakery and tea shop called Newens, situated by Kew Gardens. The connection between the Newens family and making maids of honor goes back to the mid-nineteenth century, when Robert Newens served an apprenticeship at the Richmond shop, before setting up his own business baking the tartlets and offering them on his own premises. **JL**

Tarte Tatin

This legendary French caramelized apple upside-down tart is the subject of much culinary folklore. In one story of its origins, Stephanie, one of the two Tatin sisters who ran the Hotel Terminus in Lamotte-Beuvron in the Loire Region, accidentally placed the apples in a tart dish before she had lined it with pastry. She then layered the pastry on top of the apple and proceeded to cook it, inverting it when serving. Another version simply credits the Tatin sisters with producing particularly fine examples of a tart traditionally made in the region.

Whatever the truth of the matter, tarte tatin is a culinary treat of such importance to the French that their restaurants are assessed on their ability to make it successfully. For a classic tarte tatin, sliced dessert apples are first fried with butter and sugar, then topped with pastry and baked in the oven; the result is turned upside-down to reveal caramelized apple on a fine, golden pastry base. The tart is served warm from the oven. Variations exist, using fruits such as pineapple, pear, or quince instead of apple, but made according to the same principles. **JL**

Taste: *This little, open tart has a crisp puff-pastry case containing a sweet, almond-flavored curd filling. The tart is at once moist and slightly crumbly.*

Taste: *The bitterness of the caramel contrasts deliciously with the sweetness of the apple, enhanced by the melting buttery richness of the pastry.*

The Newens family tea shop, famed for its maids of
◐ *honor, moved to its current location in Kew in 1887.*

MRS. RORER'S
NEW COOK BOOK.

Devil's Food Cake

A chocolate lover's delight, this cake became popular in the United States in the early 1900s. Although there are different versions of the recipe and the cake's first creator is unknown, a recipe for devil's food cake first appeared in *Mrs. Rorer's New Cookbook* in 1902. Other recipes soon followed. The cake acquired its reddish-brown color from the mix of baking soda and cocoa in the recipe, which has led it to sometimes be confused with Waldorf Astoria cake or red velvet cake. Purists still make it with cocoa, but only alkalized European cocoa will do as natural cocoa will not make the cake rise.

Whatever recipe is used, devil's food cake is made from chocolate layers topped with white or chocolate icing to produce a dark, "sinfully" delicious cake. The cake may have gained its name for its contrast to the light, airy, and white angel food cake, known in the United States by about 1870.

Devil's food cake is wonderful topped with a scoop of vanilla ice cream and a glass of ice cold milk or dark, rich coffee. Many believe it tastes better after being refrigerated for a day. **SH**

Taste: Devil's food cake has a rich, chocolate taste and a tender, moist crumb. Because cocoa is used, it is only moderately sweet, but with slightly bitter undertones.

Mrs. Rorer's book distills the experience she ◔ *gained in her Philadelphia cookery school.*

Dobos Torte

A contemporary of Auguste Escoffier, Josef Dobos became equally famous outside his native Hungary as his fellow master baker did outside France. Born into a family of chefs in 1847, Dobos became particularly renowned for the extravagant layered cake he created in 1887.

Gourmets gasped at the five or more extra-thin layers of sponge—each individually baked—sandwiched with rich buttercream and sometimes topped with a layer of crisp sugar caramel. The Dobos torte was an instant sensation and, thanks to its appearance at the 1896 Millennium Exposition, it became a Hungarian institution.

Dobos shrewdly designed packaging sufficiently robust to send his masterpiece abroad. But, when the market was flooded with inferior imitations, he decided to release his secret recipe; when he retired in 1906, he donated it to the Budapest Pastry and Honey-Bread Makers' Guild. In 1962, Hungary's pastry chefs celebrated the anniversary of the creation of his classic cake by parading a giant-size Dobos torte through the streets of Budapest. **WS**

Taste: The thin vanilla cake layers of Dobos torte have a characteristic dryness, providing the perfect foil for the melt-in-the-mouth chocolate buttercream frosting.

Sacher-Torte

Sacher-torte, a chocolate cake to die for, hails from Vienna. It has two glorious tiers of rich, intensely flavored chocolate sponge, sandwiched together with apricot jam, and swathed in a glossy chocolate coating. The cake was invented in 1832 by Franz Sacher, a sixteen-year-old apprentice working in the kitchens of Prince Metternich, the legendary Austrian diplomat. When Metternich ordered a grand dessert for distinguished guests and the head chef was taken ill, Sacher stepped in to create a splendid chocolate cake. To this day, Sachertorte continues to be baked to the original, well-guarded recipe.

In 1876, Sacher's son, Eduard, opened the Hotel Sacher in Vienna, and an authentic Sacher-torte must carry the official hotel seal on the face of the cake, made in chocolate. Cakes to carry away should be packed in a gold-cornered wooden box, bearing the registered trademark "Hotel Sacher Wien" on the lid, and have a wood engraving of the Hotel Sacher Wien inside the cover. The box should then be gift-wrapped in Bordeaux-colored paper and decorated with a Biedermeier design. **LF**

Taste: *Dense, but deliciously yielding, the sublime cocoa-rich crumb and silky glaze are complemented by a tangy apricot fruitiness. Serve with clouds of whipped cream.*

Sacher-torte is still made at the Hotel Sacher today. »

Café~Garten

Baumkuchen

Black Forest Cake

A specialty of German bakers for more than 200 years, the German word *baumkuchen* literally means tree cake. The name refers to the layers of golden rings that are revealed when the cake is cut into, which are not dissimilar to the rings of a tree trunk.

This unusual effect is produced by a labor-intensive cooking method. A thin layer of batter is brushed over a spit and baked until golden. (Originally this would have been over a wood fire, but nowadays it is usually under a broiler.) Another layer of batter is then brushed on top and cooked, and so the process is repeated, with ten to twenty layers, until a full cake has been created. For special occasions, chefs can bake very large cakes weighing 100 pounds (45 kg) or so. The finished baumkuchen is usually covered with a sugar or chocolate glaze.

In Luxembourg, where it is known as *baamkuch*, baumkuchen has become a traditional dish for special celebrations, in particular weddings. Other national variations include the Polish *sekacz* with its distinctive fingerlike protrusions that make the cake look somewhat like an ice formation. **SBI**

Known as *Schwarzwälder Kirschtorte* in its homeland of Germany, which literally translates as Black Forest cherry cake, this wonderfully indulgent dessert is popular the world over, and became something of an iconic dessert in the 1970s.

The cake is constructed from several thin layers of chocolate cake, which are frequently sprinkled with the cherry liqueur kirsch, and sandwiched together with pitted, cooked, sweetened sour cherries, and whipped cream. The whole cake is then decorated with more whipped cream and chocolate shavings, and perhaps more cherries. The sharpness of the cherries set against the richness of the cream and the dark bitterness of the chocolate, plus that indefinable punchy kick provided by the kirsch, should all come together to make a slice of Black Forest cake an utterly luxurious taste sensation.

The history of this dessert is elusive, but it is generally dated to 1930s Berlin. In Germany, there are very few variations on the classic recipe, but in Austria it is sometimes made with rum. **SBI**

Taste: *The long, slow cooking of baumkuchen, along with the ground nuts used in the batter, gives it a very distinctive taste and texture. Serve it in slices with coffee.*

Taste: *A slice of genuine Black Forest cake should be a truly sublime experience, with a perfect balance of flavors. It is worth searching high and low for one.*

A boy carrying a pretzel and a baumkuchen
☮ *traditionally signals a bakery in southern Germany.*

British Fruitcake

There are many types of fruitcake in Britain, and most of them are good. Made with dried fruits, nuts, and candied citrus peel, these sturdy creations have been linked with celebrations for at least three centuries. Perhaps because of the ingredients—which were once huge luxuries and remain relatively expensive even today—they are usually baked for weddings and Christmas. They keep unspoiled for months, or even years, during which time the flavor is believed to improve—hence the old practice of reserving the smallest tier of a wedding cake to eat at the christening of the couple's first child.

Although a fruitcake is never light, they have always been leavened. They probably began as fruit breads, leavened with yeast, during the Middle Ages, with eggs replacing yeast as a rising agent in the eighteenth century and baking powder added later. Its solidity makes it ideal for decoration; a layer of marzipan is applied to protect the cake and stop the traditional white frosting from being stained by the fruit. Or, sometimes glacé fruits and nuts make a simple topping. A moist texture is prized. **ES**

Madeira Cake

Known in the United States as the pound cake, this confection is actually a traditional English cake from the nineteenth century. Moist and closely textured, but buttery rich, it is most often flavored with lemon peel, and usually baked in the shape of a loaf. The link with Madeira is that it was originally served with a glass of this celebrated fortified wine, with which it pairs fantastically well.

Combining wine with cake was a practice enjoyed by upper-class English ladies, arising from their habit of waking late and subsequently eating breakfast late. Dinner was usually an early evening meal, and so a light, stopgap affair was needed to keep hunger pangs at bay: a sort of precursor to the meal that later became recognized as lunch. (The working class already had an established bread-and-ale habit, but the leisurely lifestyle of the rich meant it took a while to catch on.) When eventually lunch became an accepted meal of the day, the custom developed of offering a slice of cake and a drink (be it wine or tea) to visitors who called in the middle of the morning or of the afternoon. **LF**

Taste: *Recipes vary greatly, but the British fruitcake eaten at Christmas, for example, is dark and dense. Brandy, nuts, candied peel, or dried fruits can all emerge in the flavor.*

Taste: *A golden soft outer layer gives way to a dense, moist interior. Although the cake typically contains lemon peel, the prevailing flavors are those of vanilla and butter.*

Potato Apple Cake

Cheesecake

This is an ancient dish with ancient roots, but no less charming for it. Mashed potatoes mixed with butter, ginger, and flour are kneaded to a soft dough, then rolled into farls (a circle, which is scored into triangles) and layered with apples, sugar, and more butter. They are then cooked on the griddle until golden, with the apples tender and the butter and sugar melting into a sweet, succulent sauce.

Potato apple cake is a classic dish to serve on Halloween in England—the eve of the Christian celebration of All Saints' Day. Halloween can be seen as an amalgamation of Christian, Celtic, and Roman traditions. Samhain is an ancient Celtic festival celebrated annually at the end of October. By 43 CE, the Roman Empire had conquered most of the Celtic regions and the Roman festival of Pomona, whose symbol was an apple, became incorporated into the festivities of Samhain. The eve of All Saints' Day used to be a day of strict abstinence and traditional fare tended to consist of meatless dishes favoring potatoes; this unusual potato apple cake soon became a favorite at that time. **SBI**

Of all the variations on this American classic, the New York–style cheesecake reigns supreme. That is not to say cheesecake is a New York invention—not in the least. Similar custardy, cheese-based sweet cakes had been introduced to the city by European immigrants, and it is possible a similar dish was enjoyed in ancient Rome. But it was in the hands of New York City bakers that cheesecake became the denser, creamier product it is today.

The classic cheesecake recipe sees a blend of cream cheese, eggs, and sugar on top of a crust, commonly made from crushed graham crackers. But this simple formula offers almost a blank slate for the creative cook. Although cream cheese is classic for the New York version, cheesecake can be made with ricotta cheese, sour cream, or cottage cheese replacing some or all of the cream cheese; the crust can be pastry, cookie dough, or chocolate cookie crumbs; the cheese topping can be flavored or decorated in endless ways. Savory variants include a blue cheese cheesecake served either as a first course or in place of a cheese course. **CN**

Taste: *Potato apple cake is a sweet-savory griddle cake. It is best served hot in wedges drizzled with thick cream, if you like, and accompanied by steaming cups of strong tea.*

Taste: *New York–style cheesecake has a rich tangy dairy character from the cream cheese, with moderate sweetness, and a subtle flavor from vanilla or lemon zest.*

Pashka

This creamy molded confection of curd cheese, lemon zest, nuts (usually almonds), and dried fruits was created by Russian Orthodox Christians to eat as a dessert at the end of Lent. The name comes from *Pascha*, the Hebrew word for Passover.

Pashka is similar to an unbaked cheesecake, but without the crust. Curd cheese is used to celebrate the first rich milk of spring. The curd cheese is sweetened, softened with cream, and sharpened with lemon, before the nuts and fruits are added and the finished batter spooned into a perforated mold. (Traditionally, the mold is pyramid shaped and leaves an imprint of the orthodox cross on the surface of the pashka.) It is then pressed and left for twelve to twenty-four hours to give the whey time to drain from the curds.

When ready to serve, the pashka is unmolded onto a plate and nuts or fruit are used to form the initials "XB"—meaning "Christ is risen"—on the side. At Easter, pashka is traditionally served with *kulich*, a tall, iced fruit bread similar to an Italian panettone, and colored hard-boiled eggs. **WS**

Taste: *The tangy curd cheese and lemon zest give a slight sourness and perfectly temper the creaminess of this wonderfully rich dessert. Serve in small portions.*

Pavlova

A large, thick disk of swirled meringue that is soft and marshmallowlike in the middle, the pavlova is like life itself to both Australians and New Zealanders, who compete for ownership of what is in both countries an iconic national delicacy. Perhaps the most misused of all culinary terms, a pav is not a pav unless it has that ethereal soft layer in the middle, produced by the addition of vinegar, cornstarch, or both to the egg whites and sugar that would otherwise create a crisp meringue.

The name commemorates the fluffy tutus of the Russian prima ballerina Anna Pavlova, who toured Australasia in 1926 and 1929. The question of which nation first celebrated her in pâtisserie is vexed, but Professor Helen Leach delivered a paper at Tasting Australia 2007 showing that a recipe for pavlova appeared in New Zealand as early as 1929.

Today, specialist stores sell several sizes of pavlova, and imaginative chefs come up with elaborate contemporary versions of the classic dessert, featuring roasted peaches, orange-flower water, loganberries—even chocolate. **GC**

Taste: *The mouth experience of pavlova is a rich, changing swirl of mousselike meringue and whipped cream accented by the crisp crust and sharp fruit topping.*

A signed portrait of prima ballerina Anna Pavlova on stage at the Imperial Palace in 1912. ❯❯

Torta di Castagne

Chestnuts have long flourished along the Apennines. The ancient Greeks ate them boiled or roasted; the Romans made them into flour and turned them into a type of bread; today, more than 300 different types of chestnut grow all over Italy.

Torta di castagne is a traditional northern Italian chestnut cake that seems to have originated in the town of Pontestura, in Piedmont. The first written reference dates back to 1800, when the town's bakers were making and selling the cakes at Easter. (They would also bake cakes prepared at home by families with no suitable oven of their own.)

The basic ingredients are pureed chestnuts, butter, eggs, sugar, and, nowadays, vanilla, but any number of ingredients can be added, depending on the preferences of the cook. Typical additions might include citrus peel, amaretti, cocoa, nutmeg, and usually some form of alcohol such as marsala or rum. The egg whites are whipped separately before adding to the cake, which helps give the cake its light texture. It is best served in thin slices alongside coffee, the perfect foil for its gratifying richness. **LF**

Taste: *Torta di castagne has a dense, but moist, texture that is never cloying or heavy; the chestnuts add a nutty, candy-sweet creaminess to the other ingredients.*

Torta Caprese di Mandorle

Dark, dense, and utterly divine, Torta Caprese di Mandorle could well make you fall head over heels in love at first slice. Although the Italians produce some fantastic chocolate, by tradition they are not particularly big on chocolate cakes. However, this glorious exception confirms quality comes first and foremost over quantity. It really is a stunner.

Torta Caprese takes its name from Capri, the beautiful island in the Bay of Naples where it is a specialty. The cake is made with the best-quality bittersweet chocolate, butter, eggs, ground almonds, and in some recipes the vaguest hint of flour. Sometimes a splash of strega liqueur is added and it is decorated with a stencil image of the island and a palm tree. It is best sampled in the wonderful pastry stores of Capri or in Naples alongside the dock from where ferries sail to the island.

Little is recorded about the true origins of the cake. Locals say it was the result of a happy accident when a forgetful baker omitted baking powder and flour from his mixture. Whatever its provenance, the cake makes essential eating. **LF**

Taste: *Ground almonds and little or no flour give a dense moistness to the cake. The deep flavor is rich with the essence of cocoa, but without any obvious nuttiness.*

Torta Caprese is the obvious choice at coffee time for visitors relaxing in Capri. »

Linzer Torte

This classic fruit tart originated in Linz, in Austria, and recipes for Linzer torte can be found dating back to the seventeenth century. In the earliest recipes, butter, almonds, sugar, flour, and spices were used and little has changed in the intervening years. It was clearly a favorite tart in Baroque times and has lasted in popularity through to modern times.

The Linzer torte is distinctive in appearance with a golden lattice top and red fruit filling shining through. The golden, crumbly pastry crust dough is usually made with ground almonds, butter, sugar, flour, and egg yolks; it is rolled out, spread with a sweet red-currant preserve, then topped with a pretty lattice made with more rolled dough. When baked, it is crumbly, without being dry, with a moistness added by the fruit preserve in the middle.

Although red-currant preserve is the traditional filling for Linzer torte, there are others as well: raspberry is a particularly popular alternative. Likewise, almonds are the classic nut of choice in the pastry, but there are many variations made with other nuts such as hazelnuts. **SBI**

Taste: *Linzer torte is stunning in its very simplicity: a rich, nutty, pastry with fruit preserve. It is best midmorning or midafternoon, perhaps with cream on the side.*

The Old City of Linz is lined with bakeries and other specialist stores. »

Treacle Tart

A traditional English dessert, comforting in its simplicity, treacle tart dates back to Victorian times. Popular nursery fare, it also features on the menus at gentlemen's clubs and old-fashioned British restaurants. These days the name is the source of some confusion, as "treacle" in England refers to black treacle or molasses, the dark, sticky, strongly-flavored sweet by-product of sugar processing. Treacle tart, however, is usually sweetened with golden syrup or pale treacle, another by-product of the sugar industry. The market for golden syrup or "goldie" in England was recognized by businessman Abram Lyle, who began canning and selling the sweet, sticky syrup in 1885.

Treacle tart draws on a thrifty tradition of using basic ingredients to make a treat. The classic recipe mixes fresh breadcrumbs with a generous amount of golden syrup and a touch of lemon juice and grated lemon peel. This sticky filling is then spread into a shortcrust pastry case and baked until set. Some versions add cream or eggs to the filling, and often the tart is decorated with a pastry lattice. **JL**

Taste: *One of the pleasures of treacle tart is its distinctive texture, as the stickiness of the filling melts away into a yielding, buttery sweetness with a hint of lemon.*

The distinctive packaging of Lyle's Golden Syrup,
◈ used in treacle tart, has changed little since 1885.

Tarte aux Fraises

With its bright, scarlet berries, the classic French strawberry tart is a delectable sight, one that is seen in the windows of pâtisseries in villages and cities throughout France. This pretty creation is one manifestation of France's rich and varied tradition of fruit tarts. A simple concept, the secret of a truly great tarte aux fraises rests with the quality of the ingredients used and the care taken in its making.

There are numerous variations on the theme. The pastry, for example, may be a simple shortcrust or a richer *pâte sucrée*, enriched with egg yolks and sweetened with sugar. Either way, the pastry should be rolled out very finely and used to make a pre-baked pastry case. In some versions, whole strawberries are simply arranged in the pastry case, then glazed with red-currant Jelly. A more indulgent tarte aux fraises, however, sees the addition of a layer of *crème pâtissière* spread over the base of the tart. This pastry cream is a thick, creamy-textured custard, made from eggs, sugar, butter, flour, and milk, the latter infused with a vanilla bean. The cream contrasts beautifully with the fresh strawberries. **JL**

Taste: *The flavor of ripe, sweet strawberries should dominate, combined with the rich, vanilla-scented* crème pâtissière *and the crisp, fine texture of the pastry.*

Apple Strudel

Most closely associated with German and Austrian cuisine, but enjoyed all over central Europe, the delight that is apple strudel is made from layer upon layer of wafer-thin sheets of pastry, wrapped around a tender filling of apples and golden raisins. In traditional recipes, the pastry is wrapped around the filling to make a long sausage shape, then twisted into a horseshoe before baking. The word "strudel" comes from the German for "whirlpool," reflecting the swirling layers that characterize this dessert.

The pastry with which strudels are made is all-important, and the making of it is judged an art form. Similar to phyllo, strudel pastry dough is made from flour, eggs, butter, and water. It must be kneaded until smooth and elastic and left to rest. The dough is then rolled and stretched by hand over a large table until so thin as to be almost transparent. Then, and only then, is it ready to be made into a strudel.

Apple strudel is the best loved of all strudels, but other fillings are extremely popular, too. Cherry strudel is an absolute classic, and there are also savory versions filled with, for example, spinach. **SBI**

Taste: *Apple strudel is sweet, but not too sweet, with a sharp filling and a delicate pastry jacket. It can be eaten hot or cold, and is a popular choice for serving with coffee.*

Apple strudel comes with a liberal serving of
ⓒ *whipped cream in this restaurant in Mosel, Germany.*

Belgian Frangipane Pastry

Variations of frangipane have been enjoyed for centuries—with recipes dating back to seventeenth-century France. Today, although frangipane pastries can be found all over Europe, the Belgian version is not to be missed. Usually baked as individual tartlets, the crisp golden pastry shell is filled with sweet frangipane—a mixture of ground almonds, butter, and sugar combined to make a sweet, tender filling. The pastry might then be finished off with a striped pattern on top, or a swirl of frosting.

Other popular frangipane tarts include the French *amandine*, which is enjoyed sprinkled with slivered almonds and brushed with a translucent glaze: the *galette des rois* (cake of kings) is a larger French frangipane tart. Similar to a pithivier, it is traditionally baked for the festival of Epiphany, when Christians celebrate the visit of the three wise men to the newborn baby Jesus. Often made of puff pastry, the case is usually filled with frangipane, then topped with another disk of pastry and a bean or charm is hidden inside. The lucky person who finds the bean is crowned "king" for the day. **SBI**

Taste: *These sweet, crisp, delicious pastries are utterly enticing. The combination of nuts, sugar, and butter in the frangipane is rich, but not too sweet or overpowering.*

Éclair

Danish Pastry

The origins of these choux pastry confections filled with cream and topped with frosting or chocolate are vague, suggesting that they have evolved over time into the delicacy that we know today. Certainly—according to the *Oxford English Dictionary*—the word can be traced back to 1861.

The classic éclair is made of choux pastry piped into a finger shape and baked until hollow in the middle. In France, you will find two types: *éclairs au chocolat*, filled with a chocolate-flavored *crème pâtissière* and topped with chocolate frosting, and a coffee version with a coffee-flavored filling and coffee frosting. The English version, in contrast, is usually filled with whipped cream and topped with melted chocolate. A similar choux-based pastry is the profiterole: round choux buns filled with cream and topped with chocolate sauce, usually served as a dessert. Another confection found in France is the *religieuse* (nun). Flavored with coffee or chocolate, a *religieuse* consists of two filled choux buns topped with frosting, a smaller one sitting on top of the other to resemble a little fat nun. **SBl**

Although associated with Denmark, the "Danish" pastry is not one hundred percent Scandinavian. In its homeland, it is called *wienerbrød*, which means "Viennese bread," whereas in Austria it is known as *Kopenhagener*. According to one story, when Danish bakers went on strike during the mid-nineteenth century, Austrian bakers migrated to the country to work, bringing with them recipes for a pastry known as *plundergebäck*. When the Danes returned, they refined the Austrian recipes, creating pastries with ever more and ever finer layers of dough and butter.

Today, Danish pastries come in many shapes and sizes. (A large pastry shaped like a pretzel is known as a *kringle*, and is the official sign for bakeries in Denmark.) Fillings include custard, jam, and, most typically, *remonce*—butter creamed with sugar, and nuts or cinnamon. They are often topped with frosting. For Danish families it is a Sunday tradition to have pastries at breakfast. It is almost a rite of passage for young people to knock on the back door of the local bakery for freshly baked pastries on their way home in the early hours from a night out. **CTj**

Taste: *This truly indulgent pastry is light in texture, yet rich, sweet, and creamy in the mouth. Éclairs are wonderful fresh from a pâtisserie and eaten out of hand.*

Taste: *Biting into a piece of freshly baked Danish pastry is a very sweet experience. The texture is fluffy and crispy, with the buttery softness of the remonce in the middle.*

Superb éclairs are available from French pâtisseries
⊗ *such as this impeccable example in Montmartre, Paris.*

Mince Pie

Pastéis de Nata

In Britain, these small, sweet pies are synonymous with Christmas—although they are not usually served as part of the Christmas Day meal, but kept in a tin as an offering for visitors during the festive season. The most famous of these visitors, of course, is Father Christmas, for whom children often leave a mince pie and a glass of sherry on Christmas Eve.

Mince pies owe their existence to a medieval pastry called a chewette, which was first made with meat and spices, then later with the addition of dried fruit. Today, they are made with a crust and top of shortcrust or puff pastry, and filled with mincemeat—a mixture of dried fruit, spices, grated apples, citrus, nuts, and perhaps a little brandy. The mincemeat is traditionally based on beef suet: the last remnant of the old, meat-based recipes. Although meat had fallen from popular use by the nineteenth century, *petits pâtés de Pézenas*, the sweet meat pastries from Herault in the Languedoc, are similar to earlier mince pies. Local lore has it the recipe derives from a visit to Pézenas by the British colonial general Robert Clive in 1768. **ES**

These creamy, buttery little pastry tarts, dusted with cinnamon and confectioners' sugar, are emblematic of Portugal and the wonderful Portuguese way with pastry. They can be found in pastry stores and cafés across the country, and wherever the Portuguese gather around the globe.

As with a number of other traditional pastries and sweetmeats, it is thought it was nuns who originally created pastéis de nata: in this instance, the sisters at the Mosteiro dos Jerónimos (the Hieronymite monastery) in Belém, near Lisbon, some time around the turn of the eighteenth century. In the capital they were, and still are, most likely to be known as pastéis de Belém, after their original home, and in 1837, a little shop called Casa Pastéis de Belém opened its doors. This was the first place outside the convent to sell the much-loved cakes, and to this day locals and tourists alike travel to the store to enjoy them fresh and warm from the oven: velvety rich custard encased in layers of buttery, crisp puff pastry, topped with a delicate powder of cinnamon and sugar. **LF**

Taste: *Much depends on the mincemeat, which should be dark and fruity with notes of cinnamon and ground ginger, and the pastry, which should be crumbly.*

Taste: *Best eaten warm, pastéis de nata yield melt-in-the-mouth layers of crisp yet buttery puff pastry, which give way to a glorious silky, sunshine-yellow custard.*

Gerbet Macaroon

Millefeuille

These colorful, flavored sweetmeats—almond and egg white cookies stuck together in pairs with a near-infinite variety of fillings—are a Parisian pâtisserie that originated during the Belle Époque. Their name links them to the Ladurée family that owned a celebrated salon de thé in the capital's Rue Royale—a business still flourishing today.

Although popular since their creation, these macaroons owe their current form to the celebrated pastry chef Pierre Hermé, who worked for Ladurée as a young chef, but started experimenting with the recipe after he went to work at Fauchon, the most famous food store in Paris. Until Hermé began developing his own recipes, gerbets were smooth and dry on the outside and a little chewy: a thin butter cream or ganache held the pairs together. He transformed the range of fillings, adding fruit, nuts, and a galaxy of textures and tastes. His signature gerbet—"Ispahan"—is scented with rose water and filled with fresh raspberries, but each year he brings out a new range of gerbets in much the same way as a fashion house brings out a new collection. **MR**

The French name of this classic, indulgent pastry literally means "a thousand leaves," reflecting the numerous wafer-thin layers of puff pastry contained in just one heavenly slice. This name is not far off the mark when one considers that a typical sheet of puff pastry has 729 layers and a millefeuille can consist of two, three, or more layers of pastry.

This confection is usually rectangular in shape and made up of three sheets of crisp, golden puff pastry with a layer of rich, creamy filling spread between each one. The top is dusted with confectioners' sugar before the pastry is sliced into individual millefeuille. The filling is made of whipped cream, or sometimes *crème pâtissière*, with fruit.

In France, there is an oval-shaped millefeuille known as a "Napoleon," which is made of two layers of pastry sandwiching a creamy, almond filling. (In the United States, however, this name applies to all kinds of millefeuille.) A caramel-coated version is known as *Szegedinertorte*, after the Hungarian town of Szeged, which some attribute to the birth of the original millefeuille. **SBI**

Taste: *The surface of each macaroon should be crisp; the inside should be moist and chewy, having been left, ideally for twenty-four hours, to absorb moisture from the filling.*

Taste: *Crisp, buttery pastry contrasts delightfully with the soft, luscious cream, which oozes out from between the layers. Fruit cuts across the rich creaminess of the filling.*

Güllaç

Found in every local bakery during the month-long Muslim festival of Ramadan, this Turkish confection dates back to the Ottoman Empire. Records suggest güllaç was served at the circumcision ceremony of the sons of Suleiman the Magnificent, who ruled the empire from 1520 to 1566. Some say güllaç is an early version of baklava, the classic sweetmeat made of layers of phyllo pastry, nuts, and sugar syrup.

Sweet and milk-based, it consists of layers of güllaç leaves (thin wafers made of cornstarch, wheat flour, and water) that have been soaked in milk, sugar, and ground nuts. Although walnuts are the traditional choice, they tend to color the milk so almonds are often favored to produce a snowy-white hue. Güllaç can be flavored with rose water or vanilla and is often decorated with vibrant red pomegranate seeds and pale green pistachio nuts. This distinctive confection is traditionally brought out after the *iftar*—the evening meal served to break the day's fast. Although güllaç can be bought, homemade is best, and güllaç leaves can be purchased at most Turkish food stores. **SBI**

Gaziantep Baklava

Gaziantep, the largest city in southeast Turkey, can claim to be the country's gastronomic capital. It is also the spiritual home of the syrupy, nutty, flaky pastry: baklava. Across the Middle East and the Balkans, baklava changes its character: sometimes larger, sometimes drier, sometimes sweeter, sometimes more sticky. In Gaziantep, each piece is small, moist, and packed with the finest pistachios grown in the surrounding countryside. Above all, its pastry, rolled out with a long, tapering pear-wood pin, is unequaled in its fineness. The pastry, referred to as *yufka*, is transparent and thinner than the thinnest strudel pastry; when baked it becomes a pile of brittle layers. After they are taken from the oven, boiling syrup is poured over them and they separate into leaves.

The origin of the pastry is not clear but it might have evolved from the flatbreads layered with nuts eaten by nomads living in the region that was once Kurdistan, where Gaziantep lies. Indeed, what are considered the best pastry stores in Istanbul today are owned and run by Kurds. **MR**

Taste: *Intensely sweet with a milky richness, güllaç is distinctly lighter than other similar classics, such as baklava, and is ideal for completing the Ramadan meal.*

Taste: *Baklava is a complex mixture of textures and tastes. The crisp, buttery upper layers give way to the moister lower ones, blending with a filling of pistachios and syrup.*

After baking, baklava pastries are cut into individual portions for display to customers. »

Sbrisolona

Sbrisolona, which is also known as sbriciolona, is a delightfully crisp, buttery cake from Mantua, in Lombardy, northern Italy. The name means "crumbly," and that is exactly what this cake-cum-cookie is. Too brittle to be cut with a knife, sbrisolona is generally broken into pieces and often served with coffee or sweet dessert wines, such as Malvasia or vin santo. Although it is enjoyed throughout the year, it is a particular favorite at Christmastime.

Sbrisolona was traditionally a frugal affair: a treat for the poor, based on inexpensive, easily available ingredients. Typically a sweetened mixture of cornmeal and hazelnuts, shortened with lard, it was a far cry from the rich cakes the wealthy enjoyed. Yet the hazelnuts were replaced by almonds and butter took the place of lard, giving the cake an entrée to Mantua's upper class.

A recipe for the indulgent version of sbrisolona appeared in Pellegrino Artusi's landmark recipe book, *La Scienza in Cucina e l'Arte di Mangiar Bene*, which was first published more than 150 years ago and is still highly regarded today. **LF**

Vatrushka

Vatrushki are sweet cheese pastries that are a classic of the Slavic cuisine, and are particularly associated with Russia and Ukraine. Their name comes from the word *vatra,* which means "fire" or "fireplace" in various Slavic languages, including Czech, Polish, Ukrainian, Serbian, and Croatian.

Typically, vatrushki are made from a yeasted wheat-flour dough enriched with butter, eggs, and sugar, rather like brioche, shaped into a flattened round that is pinched up and then filled with *tvorog* —a version of farmer's curd cheese similar to German quark or Italian ricotta. The *tvorog* filling is usually sweetened, often simply with sugar or honey, or flavored with vanilla or lemon zest. The filling can have raisins added and you will also find jam vatrushki, although less common. Every family tends to have their own recipe and tradition.

Savory vatrushki are also delicious, the dough of which is usually made of wheat and rye flours and the filling flavored with onion. A similar pastry is the Siberian *shangi*, made with sourdough and a simple potato and sour cream filling. **SBI**

Taste: *Wonderful served next to creamy zabaglione, sbrisolona has a fabulous crisp texture and rich buttery flavor. Beyond the almond edge are hints of lemon zest.*

Taste: *Sweet, tender vatrushki resemble rustic cheese Danish pastries and are typically served with strong black Russian tea. Savory vatrushki are served with soup.*

Vatrushki are popular as a quick snack bought from vendors such as this one in Warsaw, Poland. »

Struffoli di Napoli

Mochi

Fans of the sweet, sticky, and sublime should stop right here. Struffoli di Napoli are little golden balls of fried dough drenched in honey. Especially popular at Christmastime when they are found piled high in mounds on restaurant tables, struffoli is a specialty of southern Italy, particularly Naples.

The Greeks probably introduced the antecedent of struffoli to the Italians; the name comes from the Greek *strongulos*, which means "rounded." Central Italy has its own version of struffoli, known as *cicerchiata*, which also feature chopped almonds and candied fruit. Fried sweets such as these are descended from *frictilia*, which were popular at Carnival time in ancient Rome.

For years, struffoli were prepared by nuns in convents and were given as gifts to the aristocracy in thanks for charitable deeds. Today, they are sold in pastry stores, although many people still make their own, following old family recipes. Each home has its own special touches, but apparently the secret is to make the balls as small as possible so that each one gets an ample coating of honey. **LF**

In *A Diplomat in Japan* (1853–64), Sir Ernest Satow described these glutinous rice cakes as "prepared and decorated in proper fashion with a Seville orange and fern." And o-mochi (the honorific is commonly used for this sacred food) remain an indispensable part of the New Year celebrations even today, displayed alongside a satsuma orange in the family seasonal alcove.

Making mochi is a winter ritual, traditionally performed by husband and wife, and an exercise in trust as she deftly turns and wets the steamed glutinous rice in a large wooden tub before her husband brings the large wooden mallet crashing down to pound it. Mochi is an essential item at the New Year breakfast, eaten in a hot soup called *zoni*. Its glutinous texture, however, calls for careful chewing—many old people end their lives choking on the New Year mochi, and numbers are duly reported in the newspapers next day. Dried mochi keeps a long time, and is sold in individually wrapped pieces—simply broil or simmer in soup to soften. It is always satisfyingly filling. **SB**

Taste: *Each mouthful of struffoli combines the sticky, sweetness of honey with soft, light dough. Recipes vary, but can include chewy peel and crunchy nuts.*

Taste: *The taste and texture of freshly pounded mochi, with a little soy sauce and wasabi, is unforgettable. Sweet and sticky, it forms an appealing golden crust when toasted.*

One after the other, Japanese men pound glutinous rice with mallets to make mochi. ❯

Crystallized Ginger

Candied Citrus Peel

Amid the barren expanses of inland Queensland, Australia, fields of green fronds flourish in the shade of long, black tarpaulins. The crop enticing farmers to sustain a living in this harsh climate is gingerroot.

The hardy rhizome that flourishes under these extreme conditions produces particularly pristine "hands"—or clumps of roots—that reach their best when sweetened and transformed into crystallized versions. The rhizomes are peeled and chopped or sliced into a variety of shapes, then cooked briefly in sugar syrup. This mellows the hot nature of ginger, creates a candylike texture, and partially preserves the flesh. Once dried, the pieces are typically rolled in sugar; occasionally, they are packed in the cooking syrup and sold as "preserved ginger." The potency and sweetness depends on factors ranging from the age of the roots at harvest to the recipe.

Crystallized ginger is worked into countless desserts from ice cream to chocolates, but can also be eaten out of hand like candy. This expression of ginger works especially well in classic treats, such as gingerbread and ginger cookies. **TH**

Once associated primarily with domestic baking and cake decorating, candied citrus peel is now commonly considered a luxurious, sweet treat. Eating deliciously chewy and succulent orange peel that has been carefully candied and dipped in dark chocolate, for example, is a truly heavenly experience.

Candied fruit peel is perhaps one of the oldest confections in the world; the ancient Egyptians, Chinese, and Arabs all candied fruits using honey, which was later substituted with sugar. By the sixteenth century, candied citrus peel was being sold as candy. Some were preserved in syrup and known as "wet sucket," whereas simply dried and coated with sugar they were called "dry sucket." Up until the twentieth century, this is largely how most people encountered citrus fruits. Candied citrus peel remains popular across the world from Europe to Asia.

Oranges, lemons, grapefruits, and citron all make excellent candied peel. In Italy, the fruit is candied whole to make a stunning window display. Candied citrus peel also features in Italian confections, such as cassata, panettone, and panforte. **LF**

Taste: *Peppery flavors echo the fresh ginger origins, but the process sweetens the rhizome considerably. A mild heat remains, an almost fruity variant on the ginger theme.*

Taste: *Tender, with a delightful crunchy sugar coating, the best candied peel will retain the essence of the fruit and have a juicy tang without any bitterness.*

Marron Glacé

Ameixas d'Elvas

These famed specialties from the Ardèche area of France are essentially sweet chestnuts preserved in a particularly strong sugar syrup, which also adds the typical fine, flaky glaze of all glacé, or candied, fruit. But these are not the chestnuts you might roast on an open fire. They are a particular variety: the marron has only one chestnut per shell, whereas better known varieties have two, hence the satisfying, compact presentation of marrons glacés.

The heightened sweetness dictates both what you can and cannot do with them; preservation rather overpowers the nutty flavor of the basic marrons so using small pieces in, say, an ice cream or in a creamy cake filling only works if they dominate the mixture. Generally marrons glacés should be enjoyed just as they are, absorbed and savored slowly after a meal with coffee, a liqueur, or brandy. If left to sit in brandy or rum for some time, much of the sugar dissolves out and you then have a chestnut-flavored liqueur and an alcoholic chestnut with bigger flavors. Broken pieces in syrup are sometimes sold very cheaply. **GC**

Ameixas d'Elvas (DOP)—sugar-coated, dried plums from the town of Elvas, in eastern Portugal—are an unbelievably luscious specialty. The green-amber colored fruit used, similar to a greengage, is thought to be among the elite of all dessert plums.

The Portuguese have been candying plums since the fifteenth century. They were originally produced by nuns from convents in the Elvas area, as a luxury food confined to the wealthy. Production moved on to dedicated producers, and since the nineteenth century their delights have been enjoyed by a growing international audience. Today, Ameixas d'Elvas carry a DOP certificate, protecting the production methods. Harvested between June and August, the plums are boiled gently, first in water, and then again in a sugar-and-water mixture. They are then left to soak in the syrup before being dried in the sun or special chambers.

Ameixas d'Elvas are wonderful served after dinner with liqueurs. In Portugal, they are often eaten with an egg custard-style dessert known as *sericaia*, a magical combination. **LF**

Taste: *Their firm texture is made smooth and unctuous by the sugar syrup content. Best enjoyed slowly, so the sweetness dissipates, leaving vestiges of chestnut flavor.*

Taste: *Succulent, juicy, and very sweet, Ameixas d'Elvas hold on to the fruit's fresh plummy tang. This is superbly contrasted by the slight crunch of the sugar coating.*

Titaura

Made with the pulp of Lapsi fruit, titaura originates from Nepal. Lapsi trees need a cold climate to grow and hence most titaura is made during the winter months. Lapsi is boiled and the pulp extracted is then sun-dried; it is seasoned with sugar, salt, and spices. Most households in Kathmandu make it at home, and it is also sold at almost all food and beverage shops in Nepal. Young, old, rich, and poor, titaura does not have any social or economic boundaries, but it is most popular with children, teenagers, and women.

The sweetmeat is unique to Nepal; however, countries such as Bhutan, India, and Tibet tend to import it on demand. Titaura is made and sold in all shapes, sizes, and flavors. It comes in dried or gravylike varieties in salty, sweet, sour, and chile flavors. Shapes vary from round or square, to rectangular or long thin strips. In Kathmandu, Ratna Park is famous for housing a number of stores dedicated to selling titaura. Most Nepalese living abroad tend to stock up before leaving the country, and titaura makes a popular gift when traveling. **TB**

Taste: *To an untrained taste bud, the sweet variety is still very spicy. Titaura contains Nepalese spices and is mostly tangy due to the Lapsi fruit, somewhat like gooseberry.*

Women trade all kinds of candies in Maktinath, Nepal. »

Licorice Drop

Whereas some countries, such as the United States, prefer licorice to be sweet, in Scandinavia and the Netherlands it is usually eaten salty. "Drop" is the Dutch word used for hundreds of licorice candies in all shapes and sizes, the consumption of which can almost be classed as a national addiction. The licorice plant is a legume that looks like a purple flowered bean. Its straggling woody roots contain a sweet compound called glycyrrhizin. Once mixed with water they are pulped, boiled, and processed into a syrupy extract that is poured into molds. The result is block-drop. This can then be reprocessed to make licorice candies that range from hard and toffeelike to soft and sweet or extra salty.

Alongside Boerderijdrops (farmyard animals) and Katjes (cat-shaped drops), highly salty Haring drops are perennial favorites. The name describes their fishy shape and the salt dusting gives them an immediate salty hit. Doctors have been known to prescribe them for patients with low blood pressure, and drops are sold in drug stores in the Netherlands, as well as in candy stores and supermarkets. **MR**

Taste: *Licorice drops have a chewy texture similar to gum drops. The salty coating helps salivation and enhances the natural licorice taste.*

Maple Candy

Before the United States and Canada were first settled by Europeans, the First Nations (Canada) and Native Americans knew what it meant when the "sap was running." It is when maple trees are ready to be tapped to provide a source of sweetener for the year ahead. The sap is boiled down into syrup, but some of it is cooked even longer so it crystallizes and forms a "sugar" that can be stored in blocks. As it is late winter or early spring, snow might still be on the ground. When droplets of hot syrup hit the cold snow, jack wax or "maple in the snow"—a toffeelike confection—forms.

Maple-in-the-snow is still made where sugar maples are tapped, but commercial maple candy is more sophisticated. The maple sap is heated to the crystalline stage; then it is whipped and poured into molds, often shaped like maple leaves. Since the candy can also be made from maple syrup, it is available year-round: this is a soft candy and the most popular. Maple sap or syrup, however, is also turned into a hard candy and into a fudgelike candy, sometimes called Ohio maple cream. **SH**

Taste: *Maple candy is made from different grades of syrup: the darker the syrup the richer the taste. The best candy is not overly sweet and tastes like brown sugar.*

Children sample maple syrup cooled in snow at the Elmira Maple Syrup Festival in Ontario. »

Doncaster Butterscotch

Buttermint

Butterscotch is a smooth, caramel-like candy made by boiling butter and sugar syrup together with cream. It is similar to a toffee, but boiled longer so it becomes hard and crunchy, rather than chewy like traditional pulled toffee.

The first written records appear in 1817, when an enterprising confectioner and grocer named Samuel Parkinson in the town of Doncaster, in the north of England, began making a brittle toffee; before long, his invention became one of the town's most famed exports, and the town was synonymous with butterscotch. In 1851, when Queen Victoria opened the famous St. Leger horse race, she was presented with a tin of Parkinson's butterscotch and the company gained royal approval. In 1893, the business was sold and by 1977 production had halted. Twenty-six years later, however, a Doncaster businessman came upon an old box in a cellar that contained one of the old St. Leger tins. His wife took a fancy to the tin and Parkinson's Butterscotch was resurrected, apparently using the original recipe she had found, neatly folded, in the tin. **LF**

A traditional wedding reception confection in the United States, buttermints have long been made at home by candy makers. They were perfected for commercial production, though, in 1932 by American Katherine Beecher. Her candy company was acquired by another candy manufacturer in 1974, but the Beecher buttermints are still among the many brands sold throughout the world today.

Made from butter, cream, peppermint flavoring, and confectioners' sugar, buttermints are sometimes also known as party mints, after-dinner mints, pastel mints, and wedding mints. They come individually wrapped, often with custom logos, and in a variety of colors, including pale green, yellow, and pink. Some are filled with liquorice or various flavors of jelly.

Sometimes confused with flat mints or a hard candy also called buttermints, true buttermints are small and pillow shaped, although slightly larger ones can be found. Also consumed as a breath freshener, buttermints are sugary and quickly melt in the mouth, leaving a lingering mint flavor. **SH**

Taste: *Smooth and creamy, Doncaster Butterscotch has a gloriously addictive buttery-sweet caramel flavor and a pleasantly crunchy texture that delights toffee fans.*

Taste: *Buttermints taste like peppermint with a hint of butter. They are sweet and creamy and leave a refreshing coolness in the mouth.*

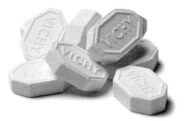

Vichy Mint

These distinctive, octagonal white pastilles with an invigorating mint flavor were invented in 1828. A local pharmacist in the famous spa town of Vichy, in central France, discovered a method of extracting minerals from the town's thermal waters, created by volcanic activity in the nearby Massif Central. He then mixed the minerals with sugar and natural peppermint to produce a mint pastille that was used as a cure for heartburn.

Vichy mints were doubtless also enjoyed for their singular, fresh minty taste. They were particularly popular throughout the nineteenth century and were a favorite of the Empress Eugenie, wife of the Emperor Napoleon III. Emblazoned with the name of their place of origin, Vichy mints remain much in demand today, and it is said eating eight of the pastilles daily is as beneficial to your health as a course of spa treatments. The mineral rich water is also used to prepare *carrots à la Vichy*, a dish of thinly sliced carrots that have been cooked in the spa water, along with butter and sugar, and garnished with minced parsley. **FP**

Chicle Gum

Chewing gum might be the bane of the modern sidewalk, but the confection's roots go back centuries to the Mayans and Aztecs. Chicle is the resin that comes from the sapodilla trees native to Central America. In the Mayan language the chewing gum made from chicle, lake-asphalt, and oily yellow grease obtained by crushing the axin insect was known as *tzictli*, and in Spanish the word for chewing gum remains *chicle*.

Mexican general Antonio López de Santa Anna was the one who came up with the idea of commercial chewing gum. It was taken up in 1869 by American businessman Thomas Adams, who added sugar and flavorings to make chewing gum.

However, chicle as the base for chewing gum soon disappeared as companies opted for cheaper synthetic alternatives that could feed the growing demand in the 1950s and 1960s. But gum based on chicle is still available from Mexico. The resin is filtered and stirred to remove impurities, resulting in an elastic white substance that is molded into a compact block to be used as the gum base. **CK**

Taste: *Vichy mints have a clean, fresh flavor with a slight peppermint heat and are smooth and pleasingly chalky as they dissolve in the mouth. A mint of distinction.*

Taste: *Chewy, sticky, and elastic, with a subtle taste, although the flavor depends on what might have been added to the base gum, such as clove or peppermint.*

Lowzina

Ur, the ancient name for modern Iraq, is the oldest country on earth and it was here, in this crescent-shaped land spanning the mighty Euphrates and Tigris rivers, that the almond tree become one of the first food crops to be cultivated. The almond tree is now grown all over the world for its creamy, oval-shaped nut, which plays a part in practically every cuisine. Back in its homeland of Iraq, the almond has retained its popularity and is used in many everyday dishes as well as celebratory foods such as lowzina.

Lowzina b'Shakar, to give the sweetmeat its full Iraqi name—*shakar* means grateful in Arabic, and is also an Arabic name—is a diamond- or triangular-shaped white sugar confection made with almonds and flavored with rose water, lemon juice, and the warm-scented spice, cardamom. The rose water and lemon juice are first boiled with water and sugar to make a concentrated syrup. When it has reached the correct consistency and has been allowed to cool, freshly ground almonds and cardamom—either seeds from cardamom pods or the powdered spice—are stirred in. The mixture is then spread out in a shallow tray and left until it is firm enough to cut into pieces, while remaining quite soft.

This special sweetmeat is reserved for special occasions such as weddings, when the lowzina is covered with delicate sheets of the finest gold leaf and sent by the family of the bride as a gift to their relatives and friends. Edible gold is a popular enhancement of celebratory dishes all over Asia, from Turkey to Japan. Although the gold used to make it is genuine, the sheets are so fine that their cost is not prohibitive. Asian celebratory dishes may also be sprinkled with edible gold dust. **WS**

Taste: *Soft and creamy, lowzina has a delicate nuttiness. Its sweetness is balanced by the warm spice of cardamom, the exotic perfume of rose water, and a hint of citrus.*

Peppermint Rock

Alongside bawdy postcards and mini golf, this garish confection embodies the traditional British seaside holiday. Sold in coastal resorts and known as candy sticks in the United States, it displays in cross-section the name of the town where it was bought. Traditionally, people vacationing by the seaside would bring home sticks of peppermint rock as gifts for those not fortunate enough to join them.

As a reminder of home, rock-making traveled to the Antipodes, where the unique confection can be found in Sydney and in Tasmania. Peppermint rock has also been made since 1859 in Gränna, Sweden, where it is called *polkagris* after the polka dance. In Gränna, rock-making began as a one-woman operation, but now tourists flock to see it being made in a number of bakeries.

The child's query—"How do the words get inside the rock?"—can best be answered by watching the hot, heavy, sometimes dangerous work that goes on at a traditional rock shop. Sugar, glucose, and an anti-foaming agent are boiled together, with some of the mixture set aside and colored for use as the outside layer. The rest is flavored, cooled, and worked to form the core. The lettering is added by interleaving long bars of colored sugar (each cross-section is a letter) with white to create a long strip with letters running through it that can be wrapped around the core of the rock. The outer layer is added, resulting in a large cylinder that is then stretched to form sticks.

Made in Scotland, Edinburgh rock is a slightly different confection. Soft and crumbly, it melts in the mouth and comes in many flavors. It is the original rock but does not enjoy the same popularity. **ES**

Taste: *Hard, minty, and very sweet, if crunched too keenly peppermint rock can break into shards that hurt the soft tissues of the mouth. This is, of course, all part of the fun.*

Classic peppermint rock has a bright pink coating, but now many other colors and flavors are available. ❯❯

Pear Drop

Pear-shaped, like a droplet, pear drops are among the old-fashioned hard candies that were sold loose, by the quarter-pound (115 g), from rows of large jars behind a candy-store counter. Nostalgia has seen a resurgence in their popularity during the early twenty-first century, but as local corner stores give way to supermarkets, fans are more likely to find their fix online.

Pear drops are made with sugar, glucose syrup, water, and citric acid. The sugar mixture is boiled, flavored, and colored, then cut, shaped, and rolled in superfine sugar to give a slightly rough coating. The finished candies are usually pinkish red, yellow, or a mixture of the two, and vary in shape from flat and elongated to stubby and squat. They are flavored either with jargonelle pear essence or the less-appealing pentyl acetate.

Like the sour sweets known as lemon drops, pear drops evolved from boiled sugar recipes that date to the seventeenth century, and which used acid fruit juices to guarantee the boiled sugar syrup stayed hard and clear on cooling. **ES**

Taste: *For fans, sucking the sugar off these hard candies is a true pleasure. The taste is sweet, sour, and synthetic—of pear flavoring, rather than actual pear.*

Jelly Bean

Jelly bean lovers around the world might have the Turks and the French to thank for this many-flavored, all-American confection. The chewy candy middle possibly derives from Turkish Delight, while the hard outer shell might just have been inspired by French sugared almonds. The term "jelly bean" first appeared in 1861, when an advertisement recommended sending them to soldiers fighting the Civil War.

Traditional jelly beans, egg-shaped and about the size of a red kidney bean, were sold first as Christmas candy and then, from the 1930s, as Easter candy. They came in just a few flavors, mostly fruit, although licorice has always been popular.

It was, of course, an American company that produced the first "gourmet" jelly bean in 1976. Smaller than traditional jelly beans, Jelly Belly® beans are richer in flavor and have taste and color inside and out. Today there are more than fifty varieties of Jelly Belly® beans, including strawberry cheesecake, margarita, and a watermelon version with a green shell and a chewy red middle. **SH**

Taste: *Gourmet jelly beans are chewy, very sweet, and more intensely flavored than traditional beans. They create a tangy mouthful of shamelessly artificial pleasure.*

Ronald Reagan sent Jelly Belly® beans into space in 1983. This portrait was made in tribute. ❯❯

Fondant

Rasgulla

Genoa has a long-standing reputation for producing cool candy creations. In the eighteenth century, Antonio Maria Romanengo began producing elegant candied fruits and sugar-coated dragées. When Parisian confectioners opened stores later in the century, Romanengo was suitably inspired to expand his repertoire. Fans included such eminent members of society as Giuseppe Verdi and Prince Umberto, whose wedding feast in 1868 featured an impressive array of Romanengo's sugary goodies.

The fondants are considered with particularly high regard and the process of making them is complex. A syrupy solution is made by dissolving sugar and glucose syrup in water, and then boiling. The liquid is worked with a spatula into a crumbly solid, then kneaded until smooth and left to stand overnight. The consistency of the fondant makes it an ideal coating for small fresh fruits, and the acidity of the fruit combined with the extreme sweetness of the fondant makes the confection even more special. For sightseers in Genoa, a visit to the ornate premises of Pietro Romanengo is a must. **LF**

For centuries Indians have been cooking down milk to keep it from souring, and along the way they invented their own distinctive range of candies. A fresh, crumbly curd cheese, known as *chhenna*, is used many Indian confections, including rasgulla. These are soft, porous curd cheese and semolina balls that have been boiled and soaked in a sugar syrup, often infused with rose water. Rasgulla can also be dry and stuffed with nuts and fruit.

Believed to originally hail from Puri, in the east-coast state of Orissa, where they are used as temple offerings, rasgulla are also considered a typical Bengali dessert. They are popular throughout the subcontinent on occasions such as weddings, birthdays, and Hindu festivals like Diwali. A variation on rasgulla, *rasmalai* are made with a sweetened, screwpine-infused milk, rather than a sugar syrup.

Rasgulla are highly perishable and need to be eaten quickly. They are also available canned. Any place in the world with an Indian community is sure to have its own Indian candy store where aficionados can stock up on these dumpling delights. **TB**

Taste: *Sweet, soft, sugary, smooth, melting fondants launch the taste buds on a path toward paradise— only a hard-edged dentist could possible resist.*

Taste: *Rasgullas are light and spongy with a slightly squeaky texture. Generally sweet and milky, with a refreshing hint of rose, flavors depend on the recipe.*

Rolls of fondant await cutting into bite-sized
❸ *pieces at a confectionery shop in Istanbul, Turkey.*

Marshmallow

Cotton Candy

Food mythology attributes the invention of marshmallows to the ancient Egyptians, but the word was first used to describe a sweetmeat in the nineteenth century. Then they were prepared using an extract from wild marshmallow plants. Today, their spongy texture most often comes from gelatin. The basic ingredients of a marshmallow are sugar, syrup, and flavorings, which can include chocolate, strawberry, or vanilla, or, in the case of the celebrated chef Pierre Gagnaire, additions such as rose or rosemary. These are whipped with gelatin and starch, then baked, cut up, and rolled in a fine dusting of confectioners' sugar and cornstarch.

Marshmallows feature in the game "Chubby Bunny" where children fill their mouths with them then try and pronounce a difficult sentence. This pastime is not as harmless as it sounds, however, and at least two victims are known to have choked to death. Americans have found more culinary uses for marshmallows than the rest of the world; they occur in many cake and cookie recipes, as well as in the celebrated Rocky Road ice cream. **MR**

No more, no less than spun sugar, prototype cotton candy was probably an Italian invention of about 1400. It did not become the fairground attraction it is today, however, until 1897 when two candy makers, William J. Morrison and John C. Wharton, patented a machine that cooked the sugar with added flavor and color and then, using centrifugal force, push the melted mixture through a screen to create a dense sugar cocoon.

This fluffy, sugary mass was introduced to the world at the Paris Exhibition of 1900 as fairy floss. An instant hit, it soon made its way to the United States where it was sold to thousands of visitors at the St. Louis World's Fair of 1904. It became an archetypal fairground treat and stallholders quickly learned to spin the cotton candy onto beech sticks or into cardboard cones. The attraction in terms of profit was not lost on these traders. Although inextricably tied to popular food culture, the cotton-candy machine has been adopted by the Spanish über-chef Ferran Adrià, who uses cotton candy in his gastronomic recipes at his el Bulli restaurant. **MR**

Taste: *The marshmallow's appeal lies in its texture. Heated over the embers at a barbecue, the crisp skin sits on a layer of hot syrup atop a center that is both fluffy and chewy.*

Taste: *The first mouthful is the best, because the fine strands crackle as the mouth gets to grips with them, while the sugar sticks to the lips. The taste is sweet and synthetic.*

 *Modern marshmallows are pink and white like the wild marshmallow flower once used in their manufacture.*

Turkish Delight

This soft, jewel-like sugar bomb became popular among the people of Turkey—who know it as lokum—about the turn of the nineteenth century. The Turkish confectioner Hadji Bekir, who arrived in Istanbul from Anatolia in 1776, is often credited with its invention. Some claim the sultan was so enamored of the sweetmeat he deemed Hadji Bekir the palace's chief confectioner.

Until refined sugar reached Turkey at the end of the nineteenth century, their sweetmeats had been a sticky mix of honey or dried fruit and wheat flour. Lokum transformed the culinary scene. It earned world fame from the 1830s when an English traveler brought a sample of "Turkish Delight" back home. The author C. S. Lewis played up the sweet's alluring properties by giving it an important role in *The Lion, the Witch, and the Wardrobe* (1950). The child Edmund becomes so intoxicated by Turkish Delight he betrays his siblings in an effort to get more.

Today, the fifth generation of Bekir's family runs Ali Muhiddin Hadji Bekir confectioners in Istanbul. It exports Turkish Delight around the world. **DV**

Taste: *The sugar-dusted jelly collapses into a sticky paste in the mouth. Rose water provides a heady fragrance and floral taste. Lemon, mint, and nuts are common additions.*

Turkish delight and other mouthwatering
❻ *confections are piled high at a bazaar in Istanbul.*

Qum Sohan

The holy city of Qum, situated 96 miles (155 km) south of the Iranian capital Tehran, is famous for three things: as the center of Shi'ite Islam, it has more sacred shrines than anywhere else in Iran; its local carpet makers weave beautiful, handmade silk rugs prized by collectors around the world; and its bakers sell sohan, an irresistible honey-and-nut confection. Similar to peanut brittle, aficionados agree the very best sohan comes from Qum.

Iranian people adore their cakes and pastries and their collective sweet tooth is legendary. As Qum boosts a patisserie on virtually every street corner and side of the bazaar, cooks seldom take the trouble to make sohan at home. Flat and rectangular in shape, sohan is made from an aromatic dough of honey, sugar, butter, saffron, cardamom, and nuts, usually a mixture of toasted almonds and local pistachios. Less sickly than most Iranian sweets, Qum sohan is eaten with morning coffee or afternoon tea or with other sweetmeats after a meal. With great "crunch appeal," sohan is addictively delicious once you have first tasted it. **WS**

Taste: *Qum sohan is buttery and crunchy with the tantalizing scent of cardamom and saffron, the mellow sweetness of honey, and the warmth of toasted nuts.*

Turrón de Jijona

Montelimar Nougat

Turrón di Jijona (IGP) is a soft nougat made in a small town close to Alicante, in the Valencia region of central Spain. Made from ground Marcona almonds, egg whites, sugar, and honey, it has a similar texture to peanut butter. There is also a hard version—turrón de Alicante—that is similar to peanut brittle.

To make turrón de Jijona, whole almonds are shelled and peeled before being roasted. The honey is heated with the almonds, the mixture is bound by eggs whites and then cooled. The mixture is then milled before being transferred to cauldrons; there it is cooked even more while at the same time being kneaded, until it takes on its characteristic smooth consistency and golden hue. The best turrón, labeled "suprema," must contain sixty percent almonds.

Turrón is an old confection, believed to have been introduced to Spain more than 500 years ago by the Arabs. It is a popular sweet, traditionally eaten at Christmas. There is a museum dedicated to its history at the factory where the El Lobo and 1880 brands are made, which are considered the finest examples of this distinctive nougat. **LF**

An aristocrat of confectionery, the nut-studded nougat of Montelimar, France, has roots in ancient recipes from Greece and the eastern Mediterranean, where honey and nuts were traditionally cooked together. Such ideas then came to the Mediterranean coast of Provence, perhaps with the Romans. When almond trees were grown inland in the seventeenth century, Montelimar created nougat.

There are several methods of manufacture: long-cooked syrup of honey with almonds and pistachios is whisked into whipped egg whites, or honey and egg whites are slowly cooked and nuts are added at the end. It is the proportion of one ingredient to the other that is the touchstone, said to be twenty-eight percent almonds and sixteen percent honey. The final temperature reached by the mixture gives either soft or hard nougat. Such variations as using a lavender honey, and Sicilian or Greek pistachios, add to the claims of superiority by one manufacturer over another, but all agree, only the very finest local almonds can make a true nougat de Montelimar. **GC**

Taste: *Sugary, soft, and with a pleasantly sandy texture, turrón de Jijona has superb honeyed qualities that sweep over the taste buds, with a light caramel aftertaste.*

Taste: *Honey adds unique richness to the bland background, so slowly chewing or sucking nougat gives a greater flavor spectrum than perhaps expected.*

Good confectioners ensure that nougat is fresh for the customer by slicing it only a little at a time. »

Kaju Katli

Habshi Halwa

Sparkling silver foil often anoints the dense, fudgy richness of these ground-cashew candies. One of the vast constellation of sticky Indian treats (*mithai*), kaju katli, and its various derivations, is made in the south of India in Kerala and Tamil Nadu, and in the west in the Goan and Gujarati regions. In the north, almonds are often used as a substitute for cashews.

Crushed, softened raw cashews are ground with palm-sugar syrup flavored with cardamom and rose essence until a thick spreadable paste is formed. The oil-rich, emollient mass is spread out, cut into diamond shapes, and adorned with edible silver foil. During festivals, such as Hindu Diwali, gold foil might replace the silver.

Used more as a gesture of hospitality than an end-of-meal palate refresher, such India candies are symbolic of welcome. An essential part of all celebrations, they serve an important function in a country with a large vegetarian population. Nuts, cow's milk, and sugar formed into rich sweets will not offend any of the major religions practiced in India, so they make the perfect gift. **RH**

Connoisseurs of Indian cuisine consider habshi halwa to be one of the country's great dessert delicacies. Halwas are a specific type of Indian sweet. They are a type of thick pudding, made with caramelized milk, sugar, ghee, and wheat flour, and of the different varieties, habshi halwa is considered the *shezhada,* or crown prince, of halwas. Although habshi halwa shares its name with a Middle Eastern dessert made of sesame paste, the Turkish candy is nothing like this Indian treat.

Nuts, especially almonds, cashews, or pistachios, are always mixed into the smooth, almost polenta-like consistency of the pudding, and sometimes raisins are also added. Cardamom, mace, nutmeg, and even saffron can also be used to enhance the flavor. Some versions are very sweet, whereas others offer only a small taste of sugar.

Halwa is traditionally served more often during the winter months, from September to March, than summer months in India, but in the United States and the United Kingdom, it is made year-round in Indian candy stores. **RD**

Taste: *Kaju katli has a soft, but slightly grainy, unroasted nut taste and is not as sugary as some Indian candies. The pale nuts absorb the flavors of rose and cardamom.*

Taste: *Silky textured habshi halwa is almost unctuous on the tongue, with layers of sweetness and just a little bit of spice. The boiled nuts in the halwa add a gentle crunch.*

Kaju katli is just one of several types of candies
⊙ *sold at this beautifully presented stall in India.*

Pista Burfi

Burfis (or barfis) are popular Indian candies that are synonymous with most special occasions in the country. Although it originated in India, today the candy is also part of tradition and culture in Pakistan, Nepal, and Bangladesh. In India, it is a common tradition to give candies to family, friends, and neighbors for special festivities, and no *mithai* (sweet) box is complete without burfi. At weddings, burfi is exchanged between the families of the bride and groom as a gesture of good will.

Made from real silver, the silver coating on burfis is shaped into edible leaf, which is used in many other Indian sweets, too. Indeed, its excessive use in India sees tons of silver churned every year to make it.

Burfis are expensive delicacies made from condensed milk, which is cooked with sugar, water, clarified butter, ground pistachio, and powdered milk until it makes a thick paste. The mix is then spread out and, once cool, cut into diamond shapes or squares and decorated with silver leaf, or *varak*, to give it shine. The sweetmeat also comes in different flavors, such as coconut or cashew. **TB**

Taste: *Pista burfi has a sweet and creamy taste. The pistachio gives it a slightly nutty and heavy texture. The silver leaf lends the sweet a cool and metallic taste.*

Confectioners are among the busiest traders in Delhi. »

Cornish Fudge

Honeycomb Toffee

For a substance that tastes so timelessly sweet, fudge is a surprisingly recent arrival. The creamy, chewable blend was first made by female college students in the United States during the 1880s. Other possible ancestors include Scottish tablet—a hard blend first recorded in the early eighteenth century—or the Mexican nut fudge *penuche*. Some Indian candies also have a fudgelike character.

Confectioners in many countries boil fudge from sugar, milk, and butter. Fudges where the mixture is cooled before being beaten are softer and creamier than those manipulated while the mixture is still hot, which tend to be harder and grainier. Fudge is often flavored with chocolate, vanilla, coffee, fruit, and nuts, and then coated with chocolate.

British fudge is most commonly associated with Cornwall, where a hard, grainy fudge (or tablet) along the old Scottish lines, was traditionally popular. Soft styles, often based around clotted cream, now dominate the tourist market. This cream, a Cornish specialty, gives a benign creaminess and pale color to the finished fudge. **ES**

Honeycomb toffee, also known as cinder toffee in England, puff candy in Scotland, and sponge candy in parts of the United States, is one of those confections that has to be tasted to be appreciated. Nostalgically part of the childhood years of many people in the United Kingdom, it is still one of the most popular confections there.

Toffee first became popular in the 1800s when sugar and treacle, a molasseslike syrup, became inexpensive enough to be made into a treat. Honeycomb toffee is simply a regular toffee to which a little bit of vinegar and baking soda have been added. These ingredients, which do not affect the taste, give the toffee a light, airy texture, like a honeycomb.

In New Zealand, honeycomb toffee is an integral part of hokey pokey ice cream, whereas in Britain it is enjoyed coated in chocolate in the form of the popular Cadbury's Crunchie bar. Confectioners in the United States, especially in Buffalo, New York, make a similar treat called sponge bar: caramelized crisp candy dipped in creamy milk chocolate. **SH**

Taste: *Cornish butter tablet is firm, granular, and crumbly at the edges. Fudge is much softer, with a more obvious creaminess. Both are terrifyingly, magnificently sweet.*

Taste: *Sugary with a foamlike texture, honeycomb toffee is extremely crunchy at first bite before melting in the mouth. The flavor is of molasses and light butterscotch.*

Soft Caramel

Soft caramels occupy a delicious place between hard taffy and really soft butterscotch or buttercrunch, an American specialty. Their origins seem to be in western Europe and Britain, with different countries adding twists according to national preferences. The essential ingredients are those of taffy: butter and sugar, to which milk or cream are added. By varying the type of butter, by using white or brown sugars, and by varying the proportions of milk and cream or using just one of these, a different texture and flavor is easily made. Like taffy, you first make a light butter/sugar caramel, and once the milk or cream is added the mixture is cooked only to the firm-ball stage.

Caramels are particularly good with high cocoa-fat dark chocolates, as these add both acidity and a touch of bitterness, thus presenting a fuller and more gratifying mouth experience. The rich sweetness of soft caramels is the perfect complement to practically every fruit and citrus flavoring, and exploring the choice can become a life-long pleasure. **GC**

Salt Caramel

These confections are also known as salted caramels or sea-salt caramels, if such salts are used. Like all caramels, their basis is a hard taffy of butter and sugar, but this mixture is softened and extended by the addition of milk or cream. They are also cooked only to the firm-ball stage, at a much lower temperature than taffy.

Their origin is thought to be a French custom of sometimes making caramels with salted rather than unsalted butter (*caramels au beurre salé*). In these the salt taste is subtle and sweetness still dominates. The sudden worldwide popularity of salted caramels is perhaps generated by the better availability of single-origin salts and of super-special *fleur de sel*, salt naturally crystallized by the wind on wave tops and collected by hand. As the world celebrates the increasing choice of salt caramels, so chefs have explored deeper. They now offer salt caramels with chocolate and such flavors as lemon, orange, coffee, or lavender, and with every type of salt, from the flat white crystals of English Maldon to the pink salts of Hawaii and Australia's Murray River. **GC**

Taste: *Buttery sweetness and a satin-smooth texture give way to a hint of bitterness provided by the caramelization of the sugar; there should not be any graininess.*

Taste: *A sweet and satiny taste dissolves into one of salt. The salt increases our ability to taste flavors, heightening the characteristics of the caramel and other ingredients.*

Single-Estate Chocolate

The first taste of single-estate chocolate can be a shock to the unaccustomed palate. Unlike mass-market chocolate, usually made from a mix of traded cocoa beans, serious chocolatiers purchase or partner with plantations to make chocolate sold as single-estate chocolate. At this elevated level, chocolate becomes somewhat like wine: the variety of bean, the *terroir* in which it grows, and the treatment of the pods from the cacao tree—from which cocoa and chocolate are derived—all hugely affect the finished product.

The artisan French chocolatier Bonnat was probably the first to produce a single-estate chocolate, in 1996, but the idea really took off when another French company, Valrhona, began making their Gran Couva in 1998. Today, there are many good examples, perhaps most famously Amedei's Chuao, from a legendary Venezuelan plantation accessible only by boat. Michel Cluizel makes Los Anconès, from the Dominican Republic, and Maralumi from Papua New Guinea, which is—unusually—also available as a milk chocolate. **MC**

Taste: *Flavors such as tobacco, berries, grass, and citrus are common. The chocolate should have a good melt and mouthfeel; the "length" can last as long as forty minutes.*

Untouched, bricks of chocolate pass from molds along a conveyor belt in the Valrhona factory.

Milk Chocolate

A delight for young and old alike, milk chocolate is the approachable face of chocolate. Milk softens the bitterness and strong flavors found in many cacao beans. Sir Hans Sloane, a scientist and founder of the British Museum, first came up with the idea of adding hot milk to chocolate drinks while traveling in Jamaica at the end of the seventeenth century. Solid milk chocolate arrived in 1879, when Daniel Peter added Henri Nestlé's newly invented milk powder to cocoa butter and ground cacao beans and began a famous Swiss tradition. Swiss milk chocolate, like U.S. and British milk chocolate, tends to be very sweet: too much so for purists.

Recently there has been a trend for high-strength milk chocolate. The French chocolatier Valrhona has produced what is recognized as one of the best milk chocolates: their Jivara contains forty percent cocoa solids, more than some mass-market bittersweet bars. The French artisan chocolate maker Bonnat and the Italian company Slitti have both experimented with milk chocolate containing at least sixty-five percent cocoa solids. **MC**

Taste: *Good milk chocolate melts well and is never greasy: it strikes a delicate balance between creamy dairy and the tart notes often found in cacao beans.*

Cocoa Bean

The essence of chocolate, cocoa beans grow in pods on the tropical tree, *Theobroma cacao*, the name of which so appropriately means "food of the gods." For the Aztecs, the beans were so precious they were used as currency. The drinks made from them were reserved—as one would expect of liquid gold—for the emperor and aristocracy. After early reticence, the conquering Spanish began to experiment with cocoa: *mole poblano*, the rich chile-cocoa sauce, is probably an early example of this. When cocoa reached Europe, it was the Italians who led the way, using the new spice in savory dishes, and creating some of the earliest chocolate candies.

More recently, chefs have utilized the textures and flavors afforded by cocoa beans, which are often crushed or chopped into "nibs." These can be added to balsamic vinegar to make a salad dressing or sprinkled on ice cream; they can add thickness to a sauce or texture to a cake. Nibs are available from companies such as Scharffen Berger, in the United States, while the Italian company Domori produces Kashaya, beans roasted especially for eating. **MC**

Taste: *Eating a whole cocoa bean can be like eating a bitter chocolate almond. The flavors tend to be strong, pungent, and untamed, while quality is very obvious.*

Cocoa beans dry in the sun at a farm near the town of Assin Adadientem, Ghana.

Dried Fruit in Chocolate

The simplest of chocolate centers, dried or candied fruit coated with chocolate makes a luscious, mouth-watering delight. Candied orange peel is a favorite among chocolatiers; the bite and texture of the peel and the slow melt of the chocolate create a multi-level taste sensation. Some products, however, use low-grade chocolate or, even worse, a substitute made with vegetable fat. Because preserved, candied and dried fruits lose flavor as they age, it is best to eat these chocolates freshly made.

Most fruits have been combined with chocolate at one time or another, but some of the most interesting are prunes soaked in vodka, cherries in kirsch, and chinotto—whole baby citrus fruits from Italy. Candied orange or lemon are classic choices and usually come in thin strips.

Bucking the Belgian trend for sweetness in chocolates, Brussels chocolatier Laurent Gerbaud imports dried kumquats from China and coats them in Domori chocolate from Italy. His square bars sprinkled with sun-dried Persian cranberries are to die for, if not strictly speaking chocolate-coated fruit. **MC**

Taste: *A high-percentage dark chocolate like Valrhona works best with the tartness of candied orange, bringing out the citrus notes and adding depth of flavor.*

Truffle

Lübecker Marzipan

The chocolate lover's favorite, this classic mix of chocolate cream filling, crisp chocolate coating, and a dusting of cocoa powder creates a wave of delight when popped in the mouth.

Created as imitations of the highly prized fungi, chocolate truffles probably originated in France around the start of the twentieth century, following the invention of modern, solid chocolate. Fillings vary from hand-rolled, fresh chocolate, and cream ganaches with a shelf life of only a few weeks to industrial mixtures dominated by vegetable fat, sugar, and preservatives. Some of the best examples are found in Paris from chocolatiers such as Jean-Paul Hévin or Pierre Hermé. New World artisans such as Fran's of Seattle also make excellent truffles.

Although "champagne" truffles are endlessly popular and perceived as luxurious, they are rarely made with real Champagne. Instead *marc de Champagne*, a young brandy from the same region, is substituted, or worse still, artificial flavorings. Working with real Champagne is a difficult art. Rare exponents include London's Paul A. Young. **MC**

Intensely almondy and utterly divine, Lübecker marzipan (IGP) is considered to be the finest in the world. Produced in the pretty Hanseatic town of Lübeck, in northern Germany, the town also claims to be the inventor of the almond confection, but it is more likely to have first originated in the Orient.

The delicacy arrived in Europe by way of Venice during the time of the Crusades and was introduced to Spain, Portugal, and Germany. Marzipan, at its simplest a ground paste of almonds and sugar, was initially regarded as a medical remedy and made by pharmacists. By the fourteenth century, it had found its way onto the table of aristocratic diners as a luxurious dessert. After the discovery of the New World and the introduction of sugar into Europe, marzipan began to be produced by confectioners, who transformed basic marzipan into an elegant art form, sculpting the paste all manner of shapes.

Marzipan makers in Lübeck, such as the companies Niederegger and Carstens, make a dark-chocolate-coated marzipan that is wonderful eaten with a dark roasted coffee after dinner. **LF**

Taste: *As you bite into the chocolate shell, cocoa powder falls on the tongue and the soft, creamy filling inside melts. The chocolate flavor floods out as the textures combine.*

Taste: *Lübecker marzipan has a pleasant, lightly grainy texture, and a delicious almond aroma. The flavor is not overly sugary, but delivers a balanced sweetness.*

The cocoa powder coating of chocolate truffles
contrasts with their smooth texture and sweetness.

Creole Praline

Praline

A popular sweet souvenir of New Orleans, pralines (pronounced prah-leens in that city) actually originated in France, reputedly during the seventeenth century. There the confection was made by sugar-coating almonds. New World tastes and ingredients, however, subverted that tradition, and New Orleans made Creole pralines one of its many culinary claims to fame. They are made throughout the city, often in storefront windows. Tourists line up to watch the women stirring the big vats of light corn syrup, sugar, milk, butter, vanilla extract, and pecans, then dropping the mixture by the spoonful onto wax paper to harden and cool. The result is a sugary, fudgelike confection that looks very like a cookie.

Although true Creole pralines are made in the New Orleans way, other pralines come in different varieties and can be made with brown sugar, maple syrup, or other sweeteners. Commercial producers have even added flavorings like chocolate and banana. The best and the most authentic, however, are still made the old-fashioned way. **SH**

Legend has it that in 1671, an angry chef spilled boiling sugar over almonds a clumsy kitchen boy had dropped on the floor. Short of a dessert for his master—the Maréchal du Plessis-Praslin—the chef served the sugared almonds, which were a great success. The latter part of his master's name is said to be the origin of the word "praline."

The name initially referred to single almonds covered in caramelized sugar, but over time it also came to refer to a ground mixture that could be used in cakes and pastries. After solid chocolate was invented, this was often added to the nut mix, which duly became a popular filling for chocolate bonbons. So much so, confusingly, that in countries such as Belgium, all filled chocolates are known as pralines.

The best praline is prepared by hand using freshly roasted nuts. In Europe, almonds or hazelnuts are almost always used; pecans and pistachios are popular in the United States. The use of peanuts by newcomers such as New York's Chocolat Moderne makes a scrumptious treat, but would be frowned upon back in Europe. **MC**

Taste: *Creole pralines have a flavor and texture not unlike a light cookie: a slight crunch gives way to a creamy fudge. The nutty flavor of the pecans offsets the sugary taste.*

Taste: *The strong, nutty, toasted flavor, combined with slightly burnt sugar, makes praline an addictive delight. It is even better when coated with dark chocolate.*

Ganache Chocolate

For the connoisseur, chocolates filled with ganache are the ultimate expression of the chocolatier's art. In the freshest, most skillfully made examples, the combination of chocolate, cream, and sometimes a little butter create a semiliquid filling that allows the chocolate's natural flavor to flow over the tongue in a sensual wave of pleasure. Ganache can be the perfect base for combining traditional and exotic flavors with chocolate: the best are infused by hand from natural ingredients. Examples worth trying include cinnamon and chile, as well as even more unusual flavors, such as yuzu or the Swedish licorice-flavored ganaches.

The recipe for ganache was invented in the mid-nineteenth century, but fell out of fashion in the twentieth century until Robert Linxe founded La Maison du Chocolat in Paris during the 1970s. The French are still the true masters of ganache, with Paris, Bayonne, and Lyon—where the legendary Bernachon house is based—among the most prolific areas. The art of ganache has recently spread to North America, Scandinavia, and London. **MC**

Taste: *Textures vary from soft and buttery to firm as fudge. A good ganache will really open up the flavor notes of the chocolate and deliver a clean aftertaste.*

Gianduja

Perhaps the perfect combination of chocolate and nuts, gianduja pairs chocolate with the famous *Tonda gentile* hazelnuts from the Langhe, in Piedmont. The British, however, can take some credit for this Italian invention. Naval blockades during the Napoleonic wars helped create cocoa shortages across Europe that lasted for much of the first half of the nineteenth century. Inventive chocolate-makers in northern Italy began adding ground paste made from toasted local hazelnuts to their chocolate, extending what little cocoa they had and creating a new tradition in the process. They named their creation after the comic carnival character and mask that represents Piedmont.

One of the first commercial producers was Pierre Paul Caffarel, who perfected his recipe in 1865 and began selling it in the famous "upturned boat" shape, wrapped in gold foil paper. Others followed, including Ferrero, whose gianduja-filled Rocher is now ubiquitous, but a pale imitation of the original recipe. Venchi's gianduja sticks, elegantly disguised as cigars, are popular with connoisseurs. **MC**

Taste: *The best gianduja has a crisp, toasted-nut flavor, a silky smooth texture, and pleasant chocolate overtones without the cloying sweetness of mass-produced versions.*

Chocolate Spread

Dulce de Leche

Whether loading a knife with mountains of rich, thick chocolate to spread on hot buttered toast or getting caught red-handed with the spoon in the jar, chocolate spread has a childlike appeal many adults never manage to shake off.

Although chocolate has been spreadable for a long time—more than two centuries—chocolate spread itself is a relatively recent invention. Cocoa shortages caused by rationing during World War II led the Ferrero company in northern Italy to begin producing a version of gianduja—a blend of ground local hazelnuts and chocolate—by adding vegetable fat. About twenty years later they marketed an improved version, and the Nutella brand was born.

Most chocolate spreads on the market imitate the Nutella recipe, but are often overly sweet and use hydrogenated vegetable fat: even organic brands rely on a high proportion of vegetable fat. However, many good quality chocolatiers—among them Venchi and Paul A. Young—produce higher-quality chocolate spreads, which are often freshly made with a short shelf life. **MC**

This ambrosial "milk jam" is nothing short of an obsession in South America, particularly in Argentina and Uruguay, around the Rio de la Plata. It is a source of great national pride for both countries, although neither has a DOC classification. (In 2001, Argentina unsuccessfully tried to get UNESCO to recognize dulce de leche as part of its national patrimony.)

Essentially a slow-boiled mix of cow's milk and sugar, generally enhanced with a little vanilla and baking soda, the origins of dulce de leche are nebulous. Popular Argentine legends suggest it was discovered by accident in the early nineteenth century when a maid left sweetened milk on the stove, only to come back and find it transformed into a thick and creamy mixture. It is also closely related to a number of caramelized milk goodies— such as the dessert known as *manjar blanco*, which is popular in Peru, Chile, and Colombia, and the French *confiture de lait*. South Americans apply it to all kinds of desserts—from pancakes to cakes and ice cream. It is the traditional filling for the South American cookie sandwich known as *alfajor*. **IA**

Taste: *The best chocolate spreads should balance a good chocolate flavor with toasty notes from the nuts. The texture should be thick without being waxy in the mouth.*

Taste: *This thick, milky, brown sauce is wonderfully sweet, silky smooth, and glossy, with a milky flavor. It lacks the intensity and burned notes found in sugar caramels.*

Green Walnut Gliko

There are many types of gliko, the delicious Greek specialty known as "spoon sweets": wonderful preserves made from fruits or nuts that are often harvested while slightly underripe, and conserved in thick, sweet syrup. Green walnut gliko is just one variety, but it is considered very special because it is made from the famous walnuts of Arcadia, on the Peloponnesian Peninsula in Greece. The walnuts are harvested while they are young and still sheathed in a downy green jacket, before the inner shell has formed. The sugar syrup in which they are preserved is often spiced with cinnamon and cloves.

There is a long tradition of preserving nuts and fruits in syrups; the ancient Greeks were particularly fond of combining nuts with honey. The name "spoon sweets" evolved because the preserves were offered on small spoons, usually as a sign of welcome and hospitality, although legend attests that the habit of taking a spoonful from one dish insured the sweetmeats were safe to eat and not poisoned. Small-scale artisanal production means it is still possible to enjoy these wonderful treats. **LF**

Taste: *Glossy and smooth with a uniquely alluring bite, the syrup-soaked walnuts display exotic notes enhanced by the gentlest intimation of warm spices.*

Black Butter

The English "black butter" should not be confused with the French "beurre noir," burned butter served with skate. The English version is a form of syrup made by boiling apples that was popular during the Regency period and still made today on the Channel Island of Jersey. It was made at the novelist Jane Austen's home and, in a letter to her sister Cassandra in 1808, she described eating a pot of it: "Though not what it ought to be; part of it was very good."

Before its agriculture was dominated by the cultivation of new potatoes, Jersey was covered in orchards. Cider is still pressed at La Mare Vineyards and Distillery in the middle of the island. Black butter is made by boiling and crushing apples (traditionally with sweet hard cider and spices, especially licorice) until they are reduced to a sticky, dark brown mass. Left to mature, the syrup's color deepens to that of molasses. Young Jersiaise farmers hold an annual black butter-making party—*La séthée d'nièr beurre*—when the apples are boiled slowly for most of the night over an open cauldron. The recipe itself most likely evolved from a medieval applesauce. **MR**

Taste: *Black butter can have a faintly smoky aroma mixed with the sweetness of apples. Its taste is a tempting combination of toffee and fruit that lingers on the palate.*

Amardine

Across the Middle East dried fruits are a staple part of the local cuisine, but sweet and succulent as many of them are, none can match the glistening orange opulence of Syria's apricot leather, or amardine.

Each July the new season's crop of ripe apricots is harvested, the best fruit coming from the orchards around the town of Malatya, on Syria's northern border, where both the soil and climate suit the unpredictable apricot tree perfectly. The fruit is carefully transported to the leathermaker's workplace, where it is gently crushed and then tipped into large vats to be simmered with a little water until pulpy. The pulp is then pushed through a sieve to remove the skins and pits and the thick puree sweetened before being cooked down to a paste. The apricot paste is poured into shallow, oblong trays greased with olive oil and the trays are left on a sunny rooftop for forty-eight hours until the paste dries out. The amardine is then removed and cut into sheets, for sweet-toothed customers to snack on, use to make drinks and desserts, or add to wonderful Middle Eastern lamb and vegetable stews. **WS**

Membrillo

Membrillo is a delightful, amber-pink-colored Spanish preserve in the form of a firm paste, the type often referred to as "fruit cheese." It is made from the pulp of the fruit the Spanish call membrillo (quince). The quince (*Cydonia oblonga*) is too hard and acerbic to be eaten raw, but when sweetened and cooked for several hours, the pulp softens and takes on a glorious fire-red color and a flavor of apples and pears.

Quinces are high in pectin, a compound that helps to set fruit pulp, and this makes them well suited to preserving. Membrillo paste was, in fact, the original "marmalade" (rather than the orange conserve we usually associate with the word today).

Membrillo is characteristically served with slices of Manchego, Spain's deliciously spirited sheep cheese; the combination of sweet quince with piquant Manchego is heavenly. As its reputation spreads internationally, membrillo is increasingly being eaten alongside other hard cheeses, too. The preserve also has a particular knack for cutting rich and fatty foods, such as lamb and duck, and will melt happily into divine glazes and simple sauces. **LF**

Taste: *The chewy amardine sheets have a concentrated fruity flavor and are sweet enough to satisfy even the most intense sugar craving.*

Taste: *Sweet and delicately flowery, with a superb, compact jellylike consistency, membrillo makes the most wonderful partner for salty and savory foods.*

In a market sheltered from the heat of Aleppo, Syria,
Ⓚ *vendors sell many preserved rather than fresh foods.*

Lekvar

European plums have been cultivated since ancient times. The first trees probably grew in central and southeastern Europe, where each year much of the harvest is turned into a thick fruit butter called lekvar. The first written reference to this jamlike conserve can be traced back to 1350, but today some East European villages still hold a feast where plums are pureed and slowly simmered in big copper pots until thick enough to spread on bread.

Lekvar is traditionally packed into small wooden barrels lined with waxed paper, from which the fruit butter is then scooped out with a wooden paddle. As plums contain a natural preservative, lekvar has a long shelf life, so the barrels were shipped around the world. Today, however, it is more common to see lekvar packed in jars sitting on delicatessen or supermarket shelves alongside the jams.

Lekvar is a popular filling for pastries, such as *pierogies* and the croissant-shaped Austrian *kipfels*. The prune butter is also used as one of the fillings for *hamantashen*, the traditional triangular pastries eaten at the Jewish festival of Purim. **WS**

Taste: *The long, slow process of boiling down the plum puree gives lekvar butter an intense prunelike flavor, so a little goes a long way if you are spreading it on bread.*

Lemon Curd

The most luxurious of custard-style tart or pie fillings (although it is also now used as a spread), lemon curd is a direct descendant of the lemon creams and orange butters of Hannah Glasse's eighteenth-century *Art of Cookery*. It is made from only lemons, eggs, butter, and sugar, so it does not keep for more than a few weeks even if pasteurized—it must be kept refrigerated. Much commercially available "lemon curd" is a travesty of the real thing, being thickened with cornstarch and a little dried egg, but of course these do keep well without refrigeration. Unfortunately, they are not worth eating.

Limes and Seville oranges are also used to make citrus curds, and some gourmets would rate orange curd above lemon curd. In all cases, however, it is necessary to cook the mixture over a very low heat to stop it from curdling. Hannah Glasse's lemon cheesecakes were filled with the mixture and then baked—a far cry from a modern cheesecake. Her most extravagant recipe called for two lemons, half a pound *each* of sugar and butter, twelve egg yolks and eight egg whites! **AMS**

Taste: *Lemon curd can be spread on biscuits and toast, as well as including it in puddings. It is a superior filling for lemon meringue pie than one thickened with cornstarch.*

Homemade lemon curd is best made in small amounts because it does not keep well. »

Seville Orange Marmalade

The qualities that make the Seville orange ideal for marmalade are almost exactly those that mar its viability as an eating orange: its thick, rough skin encases a pulp that is extremely sour, even bitter, and chock full of seeds.

Bitter oranges (*Citrus aurantium*) probably first originated in China and India, but by the twelfth century the Moors had brought both oranges and irrigation technology to southern Spain. There, despite Andalusia's arid climate, the fruit began to flourish: bitter oranges took their generic name, Seville, from the region's capital.

Although the name derives from a Portuguese quince paste called *marmelada* and the oranges come from Spain, modern marmalade is very much a British affair, and appears on the national culinary list along with roast beef, Yorkshire pudding, and fish-and-chips. Most stories concur marmalade took its current form—a transparent spreadable jelly enriched with pieces of peel—during the eighteenth century in Scotland: some attribute its creation to James Keiller of Dundee. **LF**

Taste: *Fruity and jellylike with an intense bittersweet orange tang and chewy slivers of peel, Seville orange marmalade is a perfect topping for hot buttered toast.*

A Victorian marmalade factory in Seville, Spain. »

Rowan Jelly

Fig Jam

An English West Country name for the bright vermilion-orange berries that cluster on a rowan tree is "poison berries." And the rowan tree or mountain ash (*Sorbus aucuparia*), that grows wild in Europe and northern Asia, does, indeed, bear a toxic fruit. When raw, it contains parasorbic acid, but cooking converts this into the harmless, easily digested sorbic acid.

Berries ripen in autumn, but are not ready to be harvested before the first frosts. In their raw state they are bitter and astringent, which does not bother the birds that seem to crave them. Made into a sweetened jelly, they develop an unusual, almost citric flavor that retains more than a hint of their initial bitterness. The fruit is very low in the setting agent pectin and recipes for rowan jelly suggest combining it with an equal quantity of crabapples to achieve a proper set. Whole clusters of berries are stewed until soft and the juice they render is boiled with sugar. In Britain, where there is a tradition of eating jellies with meat, rowan jelly is served alongside mutton or, especially, venison. **MR**

The Mediterranean produces some of the world's best figs. Fig trees there bear two crops: the first flush comes in June or July, the second from the end of August. The latter produces the juiciest, sweetest fruit, perfect for the best jams. The many varieties of fig that grow divide into "white," which (confusingly) have green or yellowish outer skins, and "black" ones, which are dark purple. Both are suitable for jamming, and recipes abound, featuring extra ingredients such as vanilla, walnuts, and lemon juice. A Spanisha *mermelada de higo* is no different, in essence, from an Italian *confettura de fichi*. (Note, however, that the delicious Sicilian preserve *fichi d'India* is made from prickly pears.)

As experienced jam-makers know, setting depends on the amount of pectin in fruit. Figs can be tricky in this regard, as they can set without it, but not always. The Tuscan town of Carmignano, near Florence, famous for its dried figs, makes jams, too, using the local varieties: Dottato, Verdino, Brogiotto Nero, and San Pietro. Italians eat fig jam with white meats and cheese, such as Gorgonzola. **MR**

Taste: *The set jelly, similar to red-currant jelly, is clear, bright, and orange in color. Both color and flavor make it comparable to a unique form of marmalade.*

Taste: *Dense, brightly colored, and grainy in texture from the seeds, fig jam should smell sweet, fruity, and fragrant. The flavor should be rich, intense, and persistent.*

Sour Cherry Jam

Damson Jam

Sour cherry jams are made with an infinite number of variations throughout the Balkans, in Turkey and Iran, and as far east as Russia. Each culinary culture has seized on the contrast between the sweetness of the sugar, or honey, used for preserving and the tartness of the fruit. Greek *víssino glikó* is essentially the same recipe as Turkish *vişne reçeli*, in which juice from the pitted cherries (morello or similar) is mixed with sugar and boiled. The fruit is cooked in the light syrup, left overnight to stand, and boiled again until the syrup thickens. It can then be stored like a jam. The result though is different from some jams, in that cherries are low in pectin, but will keep their shape. Elena Molokhovets, doyenne of nineteenth-century Russian cooking, recommended *vishni i chereshni*, in which the *vishni* (sour cherries) were cooked together with *chereshni* (sweet ones).

These preserves are not intended for eating with bread, but are enjoyed in small quantities as a spoon sweet. In Persia, the syrup is poured over a glass of crushed ice and sipped as a sherbet (*sharbat-e albaloo*), a prototype of the modern sorbet. **MR**

Damsons produce a quintessentially English jam. In the Middle Ages, these small blue-purple plums were also called "Damascenes," which reveals their link to Damascus. However, they belong to a native European species (*Prunus instititia*), which includes the rounder bullace plum and the wild, astringent sloe. Even when perfectly ripe, damsons are sour and their popularity as a country garden fruit rests entirely on their suitability for jamming.

In Cumbria, England, Damson Saturday was celebrated each year up to the outbreak of World War II. Carts and trailers brought loads of semiwild and cultivated fruit to be sent to the jamming factories in the neighboring county of Lancashire. A traditionally poor, rural area, the income often helped to pay the tenant farmers' rents.

Nowadays, damson jam is mainly the preserve of hobby cooks. It is naturally rich in pectin, sets well, and has more body than other kinds of plum jam. The fruit is not usually pitted before cooking, but the pits rise to the surface of the pan during boiling and can easily be removed with a slotted spoon. **MR**

Taste: *The syrup's color will reflect the variety of cherry used: dark or bright red. The taste of fruit is not dominated by the sugar and retains a memory of its original sourness.*

Taste: *Damsons make a dark purple, almost black, jam. The high proportion of skins gives a sense of texture and body. The taste is of wild plums, powerful and dense.*

Plum Slatko

Wild Beach Plum Preserve

Plum slatko is a fruit preserve from Bosnia-Herzegovina. In neighboring countries, it is also made from other fruits such as strawberries, raspberries, blueberries, and cherries. Typically made at home, a spoonful of slatko is traditionally served in a special cup to guests on special occasions. Commercial production of the preserve, based on the traditional recipe and using the local blue Pozegaca plums has, however, begun in the country's Upper Drina valley, spearheaded by local women keen to reinvigorate the economy, replant old plum orchards, and create new ones.

The second crop of plums, harvested in mid-September, is used to make slatko. The plums are peeled and pitted, and placed in a solution of water and lime to firm up their flesh. They are then boiled in a clear sugar syrup flavored with lemon slices. Cloves, walnuts, and almonds are sometimes added.

Plum slatko is usually eaten with young cheeses, *kaymak*, Turkish coffee, or goat-milk tea, although it also makes an excellent topping for ice cream, pancakes, and waffles. **CK**

Prunus maritima, or beach plum, grows wild in sand dunes and by the roadside on the east coast of North America. Explorer Henry Hudson found them when he landed in 1609 on what is now Long Island, but Native Americans had been eating them long before Hudson and other Europeans arrived.

A member of the rose family, beach plums have fragrant white blossom and produce crimson to blue-black fruit, although a variety native to New England produces yellow fruit. Early settlers to New England and other areas where beach plums grow turned the fruit into jams, jellies, and preserves. No large-scale commercial enterprise lasted long though, because beach plums continually defy attempts to cultivate them successfully. Thus, the production of commercial beach plum preserves remains for the most part a cottage industry.

Wild beach plum preserves and jellies are difficult to find outside the plant's native habitat. Some producers do, however, provide a mail-order service and the product can be bought through gourmet and specialty food stores online. **SH**

Taste: *Slatko has a light, creamy consistency with a delicate, sweet flavor reminiscent of the best Turkish rose-petal preserves.*

Taste: *Raw wild beach plums have an astringent flavor and can be sweet or very tart. The preserves, however, strike a balance and have some regular plum flavors.*

Beach plum's showy flowers resemble cherry blossom. The shrub produces cherry-sized fruit. »

Maple Syrup

In late winter and early spring, across New England, the northern American states, and Canada's eastern provinces, warmer daytime temperatures spur the sugar maple (*Acer saccharum*) into life and stimulate its sap flow. A single tree can produce several gallons a year. A thin, clear liquid in its natural state, with only a faint sweetness, when the sap is boiled down it becomes the thick, sweet syrup beloved for topping pancakes and waffles, making maple-walnut ice cream, or glazing carrots. A special treat is "maple in the snow" made by longer reducing the syrup before drizzling it on fresh snow: the syrup sets into a chewy candy.

Syrup grading is a complicated subject, and each region has different standards. All, however, rely on the color, which can range from light to dark amber, as a primary yardstick. The flavor intensity echoes the color: lighter syrups have a more delicate maple flavor, while darker syrups are more pronounced. Vermont's maple syrups are especially prized for their higher viscosity, but generally "best" is a matter of personal taste. **CN**

Taste: *Sweetness is the distinguishing characteristic of maple syrup, but beyond that intense first impression, a maple, almost smoky flavor lingers on the palate.*

Tapping maples for their sap is an expensive process.
Inferior imitations are made with cheaper ingredients.

Beech Honeydew

The ancient black and red beech trees growing in New Zealand's pristine southern wilderness host two aphids that part-process their aromatic sap. The sweet liquid they produce is known as honeydew, and bees that feed on this, rather than on the more common flower nectar, produce a unique honey. Marketed as "beech honeydew," it is the nation's largest honey export, and is very popular in Germany.

The makeup of honeydew honeys is very different from flower honeys. Their mineral content is higher; they have fewer simple fructose and glucose sugars and more complex sugars, meaning they are much less likely to crystallize. These complex sugars—oligosaccharides—are thought to help the human gut promote beneficial bacteria, and studies suggest honeydew honeys offer greater antioxidant and antiseptic properties than manuka honey.

Beech honeydew has a distinctive dark color, partly because it is stored in darker combs closer to the brood nest in the hive and partly because it contains a residue of sooty molds from the forest, a typical marker of genuine honeydew honeys. **GC**

Taste: *There is a definite earthy tang of the forest in this malty, intense, amber to golden honey. It is used in European folk medicine, in cooking, and as a spread.*

Heather Honey

As summer fades to autumn, the heather that covers the moors of northern Europe erupts into a carpet of variegated purple on Scottish glens and jagged Scandinavian hillsides. The bees that feed on these late-blooming flowers produce a honey that is far more intense in flavor than summer-blossom honey.

Heather is an iconic plant for both Scots and Norwegians, although it was Norwegian heather honey that Ian Fleming's James Bond favored for his breakfast. In Scandinavia and Scotland, people have harvested heather honey from the wilds for centuries and used it as a sweetener in favor of the more-expensive sugar. The aromatics of heather honey pair particularly nicely with Scottish staples, notably oatmeal and whisky.

Bees feed on three main varieties of heather to produce their honey. Ling heather (*Calluna vulgaris*) makes a thick honey with a strong aroma and flavor. Bell heather (*Erica cinerea*) is thinner and has a bitter edge, whereas cross-leaved heather (*Erica tetralix*) produces a thin honey with a distinctively lighter tasting flavor. **CTr**

Taste: *Resiny on the nose, with a waxy, firm texture that melts slowly in the mouth. The flavor is intense and sweet, not cloying, but rich, mouthfilling, and lingering.*

Hymettus Honey

Honey from Mount Hymettus, southeast of the city of Athens, has enjoyed a reputation for about 3,000 years. The honey was sold in the Via Sacra of ancient Rome and has fueled numerous legends and poetry. The Roman orator, Cicero, claimed that as a baby the philosopher Plato was left on its slopes, and bees filled his mouth with honeycomb, leading Homer to record: "Speech sweeter than honey flowed from his tongue."

Hymettus honey is classified as *uniflora* or monofloral, which means the bees have usually had access to only one type of flower. In this case, a variety of wild thyme (*Thymus capitatus*), from which the foraging Cecropian bees—named after a legendary Athenian king—gather their nectar. This produces a potent honey, still runny, but denser than most varieties.

The proximity to the Greek capital insures it features on the menus of gastronomic restaurants and ice cream parlors alike. It is an ingredient of the best baklava and other syrupy desserts, as well as being served with thick yogurt for breakfast. **MR**

Taste: *Hymettus is a liquid or runny honey with brownish tints. In its natural state it has a light aroma of wild herbs, but this disappears when the honey is used in cooking.*

Sidr Honey

Manuka Honey

The most expensive honey in the world, sidr honey is harvested only twice a year in the remote Hadramaut Mountains of Yemen and Saudi Arabia. Prized for its rich flavor and reputed medicinal properties, this organic honey is often given as a gift.

The honey, which has been gathered by nomadic beekeepers for about 7,000 years, comes from bees that feast on the pollen of the sidr tree (*Ziziphus spina-christi*). Also known as the Lote tree and Christ's Thorn, the tree is regarded as holy and is mentioned in the Koran. In Yemen, the beekeepers brave harsh conditions to harvest the honey over a forty-day period. The beekeepers smoke the bees, which have been captured from wild swarms, out of the wooden hives with burning dried camel skin, and gather the honeycombs using knives. The harvesting method accounts for the honey's high price, as well as the fact the bees are allowed to die rather than feed them nectar. It is said that bees fed only on the nectar of the potent sidr flower die after making about three trips—bees typically make 37,000 trips to make 1 pound (450 g) of honey. **CK**

Fast becoming one of New Zealand's best-known food exports, manuka honey is named after the extraordinary native plant on whose nectar the producing bees feed. The manuka plant or New Zealand tea tree (*Leptospermum scoparium*) is a scrubby bush with tiny leaves and flowers that vary from white to pink. Its characteristic, comforting scent with eucalyptus overtones makes manuka wood a favorite for cold-smoking food.

Like most of the unrelated plants that are known as "tea" trees in other countries, including the Australian tea tree (*Melaleuca*), oil from the manuka is used widely as an insect repellent and bactericide. Some honey made from manuka nectar carries very strong bactericidal powers and can heal wounds. This is marketed as "active manuka honey" and its potency is measured by its UMF (Unique Manuka Factor)—a rating of ten or more is considered desirable. Waikato University leads research into the therapeutic qualities of the honey, which appears to be helpful in treating fungal skin diseases and ulcers, as well as some internal or digestive complaints. **GC**

Taste: *Sidr honey is particularly viscous and has a rich, distinctive, sweet, floral flavor. Honey harvested during the winter is considered to be the very best.*

Taste: *Manuka honey is loved for its rich, dark color and big, aromatic flavor that only rarely exhibits eucalyptus overtones. It is delicious as a spread, sweetener, or a drink.*

Dibis

Blackstrap Molasses

For thousands of years, humans have cultivated dates, and for almost as long, they have used them to create a sweet syrup. This is believed to be the "honey" of the "land of milk and honey" that Moses led the Israelites to after their enslavement in Egypt.

That syrup, known as dibis, is today perhaps the most popular date product produced in the Middle East. Also known as date syrup and date honey, this thick-as-molasses sweetener is used to flavor pastries, spooned onto bread instead of jam, and mixed with tahini as a spread (*dibis w'rashi*). It can also be drizzled onto ice cream or yogurt, used in place of maple syrup on pancakes, and added to warm or cold milk for a sweet drink. Sometimes, date syrup is used to soften and preserve dates, too.

While most dibis is factory made, traditionally it was produced at home by extracting and then boiling down the juice. In villages, production of date syrup has been used to celebrate special occasions, such as the birth of a child or the birthday of the Prophet Muhammad. On such occasions, it is poured on a cooked dough known as *asseeda*. **JH**

Sugar is a complex beast. Modern industrial refining processes work hard to deconstruct it into individual components to meet contemporary tastes, but some of the most interesting parts of raw sugar are what is left at the end: blackstrap molasses.

In a curious sort of reverse engineering of cane-sugar juice, refined white sugar crystals are removed with each of several boiling stages. After the third such boiling, the results are thick and viscous. Sulfur is occasionally added to aid processing, but typically in amounts small enough to leave the flavor unaltered. Light, dark, and blackstrap molasses have similar qualities and uses to light, dark, and black treacle found in the United Kingdom.

Blackstrap found its way into the peasant foods of the southern United States where refined sugars were too expensive. Recipes commonly call for molasses in lieu of other sweeteners. Perhaps most famously, slow-cooked baked bean recipes of Boston rely on molasses for depth of flavor. Modern cane sugar producers now recognize blackstrap's value and capture it as a premium product. **TH**

Taste: *Thick and viscous, dibis is darker in color than most honeys, and its sweetness is tempered by acidity and what some describe as a slightly bitter flavor.*

Taste: *Blackstrap molasses is certainly sweet, but with decidedly bitter components not found in other sugars. Mineral tastes are noticeable when sampled directly.*

Before being turned into molasses, raw sugarcane is shredded and the juice extracted at the sugar mill. ❯❯

Muscovado Sugar

Jaggery

Atop its signature sweetness there are many flavors in sugarcane, most of which emerged in the rough-hewn cane sugars of the past. The problem with modern efficiency is that these tastes are lost during processing to a contemporary standard. Most of the richness the cane acquires from growing in mineral-laden soils is stripped out, leaving something behind with little to interest the taste buds.

Thankfully, the antiquities of sugar processing are not completely forgotten when it comes to muscovado sugar. Unlike brown sugar lookalikes, muscovado's dark molasses character is found in the sugarcane juice and stays with the sugarcane juice, rather than being extracted then returned to the mix at a later stage. This preserves all the subtle character imparted by the local conditions and results in a more varied taste.

Sticky muscovado grains are often rougher than processed brown sugars, but can be used in the same way. Darker fruitcakes and cookies flavored strongly with ginger or cinnamon seem best suited to the heady character muscovado offers. **TH**

Sugar evaporators ply their trade in India hunched over giant shallow pans perched atop intense fires. They start the process billowing with steam and heat and end with a thick pliable syrup coating the bottom, which will ultimately be formed into solid shapes. From these cottage industries come the dense, rich sugars packed with robust natural flavor that have become a pillar of Indian cooking.

Both date palm and sugarcane juice can be distilled down to make the raw sugar blocks known as "gur" or "jaggery." Both terms are applied to such reductions and, while similar in process, the flavor is noticeably different depending on the source ingredients. Jaggery has consistencies ranging from coarse crumbling to rock hard and is sold in square or cone-shaped blocks, graded by colors.

Jaggery makes its way into Indian cuisine in many ways, from the expected sweets to the less-obvious chutneys and sauces for grilled meats. Even simple rice can be elevated to special status, with jaggery and spices balancing the heat and intensity of curry without losing the sugar's signature character. **TH**

Taste: *Eye-opening to anyone used to bland, white sugar, a deep, dark molasses and wild honey character predominates with noticeable earthy flavor in the finish.*

Taste: *The flavor of jaggery is only faintly reminiscent of common brown sugars and is almost chocolaty in the darker grades. Rich mineral character lingers in the finish.*

Rapadura

Granita Siciliana

Simultaneously a sweetener and a dessert, rapadura is one of the most primitive derivatives of sugarcane. High in energy, it is popular with people in the rural regions of Brazil, such as Bahia, Pernambuco, and Ceará in the northeast, and Minas Gerais in the southeast. Its production dates back to the early decades following Brazil's discovery in 1500, when it was made by slaves in mills on large colonial estates. Since then, apart from mechanization, very little has changed in the production process. Sugarcane is pressed to remove its juice, called *garapa*. This green, cloudy, very sweet liquid is collected and put in copper pots to boil on the stove. The thick molasses produced is then placed in large wooden molds to solidify and form rapadura.

The locals intuitively improved on this basic sweet treat by adding cinnamon, cloves, and fennel seeds. It is also customary, before the rapadura hardens, to add fruit pieces such as orange, pineapple, papaya, guava, banana, and coconut. Today, in addition to the traditional large slabs, rapadura comes in tempting mini-bar sizes. **AL**

Granita is an Italian iced dessert made from sugar and water; it belongs to the celebrated family of ices that also includes gelato and sorbet. Granita Siciliana is the best in the world; the characteristically crystalline granita from Palermo is legendary. The way granita is made varies across the island; in some areas it is made by machine and, therefore, has a smooth, almost sorbetlike, consistency, whereas in other areas it is literally shaved ice. Sicilian lemon juice, coffee, chocolate, and almonds are among the traditional flavorings, as are local fruits as they come into season. In the wonderful ice-cream parlors of Palermo, granita is customarily served with brioche and is a traditional breakfast food.

Granita Siciliana is believed to be based on an iced dessert that was popular with the ancient Romans. Special foot runners would bring snow down from the peak of Mount Etna, and it was then flavored with honey and local berries or nuts and served to the rich diners. Thankfully, now anyone visiting Sicily can (and most definitely should) enjoy the superb granitas, regardless of social standing. **LF**

Taste: *Rapadura melts in the mouth, leaving behind a trace of caramel. It reaches even greater heights when embedded with pieces of succulent tropical fruit.*

Taste: *Granita Siciliana has a glorious crystalline, snowy texture that melts on the tongue, releasing a burst of cool, refreshing, thirst-quenching flavor over the taste buds.*

Lemon Sorbet

For some, a light and luscious lemon sorbet is considered a tangy and mouthwatering dessert; to others, including nineteenth-century gourmet August Escoffier, it serves as a palate cleanser for serving between savory courses.

There is no hard evidence detailing the precise history of sorbet, but it is widely believed to have been around for a thousand years or so longer than its equally cool cousin, the ice cream. The late great Roman Emperor Nero is credited by many with inventing sorbet during the first century CE, when he is said to have had servant runners carry snow down from the mountains that was subsequently mixed with honey and wine and served as a dessert. Others profess that the sorbet arrived in Italy via China and the Far East.

The name sorbet was taken from the Turkish word *sherbet*, meaning fresh drink. From Turkey, sorbet was introduced to Sicily; this time it was Mount Etna that provided the ice. Juice from the magnificent sweet Sicilian lemons was added to the ice and lemon sorbet was born. **LF**

Agraz

For lovers of unusual ices, agraz should certainly be high on the list of flavors to try. It is a tangy and deliciously different sorbet that is very popular in North Africa. It is also eaten in southern Spain, in areas where there has been an Arab influence.

Agraz is the name given in these particular regions to the cooking condiment that is made from the juice of immature grapes; it is essentially the same thing that is known as verjuice in other parts of the world. It can be used in both savory and sweet dishes, and adds a wonderful depth of flavor and a pleasant tartness. Agraz sorbet is simply a mixture of verjuice and almonds, which is then sweetened with sugar and frozen.

Little is known as to how agraz first came to flavor an iced dessert, but like verjuice, agraz was created when wine makers pruned the grape vines to strengthen them and concentrate the flavor of the fruit left behind. Rather than discard the unripe grapes, they were pressed to make agraz. Although a firm favorite in sorbets, agraz is used primarily to add tartness to rich soups and stews. **LF**

Taste: *Lemon sorbet is a zingy, lip-smacking, full-flavored ice with a light, smooth texture and an invigorating freshness that energizes and cleanses the taste buds.*

Taste: *Agraz sorbet has an unusual but enticing flavor and aroma that is all at once tart and sweet. It leaves a distinct, but delightful, hint of perfume on the palate.*

Gelato

Green Tea Ice Cream

Sweets and drinks have been cooled using ice or snow since ancient times and every region of the world has its own history of iced desserts—from the cone-shaped *kulfi* of India to Turkey's delicacy, *salep dondurma*. But it was probably in sixteenth-century Italy that the first gelato was made. An account of a Florentine banquet in 1595 recalls the amazing, carved shapes of *sorbetti* (water-based ices) and *gelati* being consumed at the court of the Medici dukes. As Italy's gelato-makers migrated, their recipes spread rapidly across Europe and beyond.

Gelato (Italian for "frozen") is handmade from whole milk, sugar, and other flavorings, typically fruit, chocolate, and nuts. It uses high-quality, fresh ingredients, slowly incorporating air as they are frozen, resulting in a thick, firm, yet soft, cream that is slow to melt, with a well-defined taste and color. Gelato contains less air than ice cream produced in the United States (which also has more butterfat) and is denser and more intensely flavored. Industrial ice cream, often made with powdered milk, tastes very different to real gelato. **HFa**

The ritual drinking of powdered green tea, matcha, was introduced to Japan by the Japanese priest Eisai in the twelfth century. It was adopted by Buddhist monks because the caffeine-rich brew helped to keep them awake during long hours of meditation. By the sixteenth century, the tea master Sen no Rikyu had refined the ritual into the tea ceremony— a celebration of the seasons, art, and nature, and path to enlightenment—built around the drinking of strongly flavored, powdered green tea.

The leaves for matcha are especially protected from the sun during their growth. After drying, stems and veins are removed and the leaves ground to a fine powder—matcha. It is this tea that is used to make ice cream. The Japanese have long used matcha in cakes, jellies, and noodles, but green tea ice cream is a recent invention of the post-war years. Ice cream is not a traditional Japanese food, but it is sweet; green tea is always drunk with something sweet to counteract its bitterness. Matcha ice cream is now on the menu of restaurants all over the world, and has become a standard flavor alongside vanilla. **SB**

Taste: *The best artisanal gelato does not contain any ice crystals and should have a well-balanced intensity of flavor and creaminess, without being too sweet.*

Taste: *Sweet and bitter on the palate all at once. The smoky and grassy flavor of green tea ice cream is offset by a creamy smooth texture.*

Kashta

Salep Ice Cream

As a former part of the Ottoman Empire, the Lebanon shares some of its culinary heritage with Turkey. Known as *kaymak* in Turkey, kashta, or kishta, is a thick white cream that often tops rich pastries. The finest quality is prepared with buffalo milk, but the Lebanese dairies that make it for the pastry stores use cow's milk. They dissolve milk powder in untreated milk and simmer it very gently for several hours (the process is similar to that used to make Cornish clotted cream) until a white, elastic membrane forms on the surface. This is drawn to the back of the tray and the simmering continues until several more layers of skin form. These are then raked off and the kashta is ready to eat.

Although kashta contains over fifty percent fat, it is sometimes eaten simply sweetened with honey, but it is more often an ingredient in desserts and pastries. At Abdul Rahman Hallab, a famous Tripoli patisserie founded in 1881, it is used as a filling for a rice-flour sweet called *halawet el riz*. Flavored with rose water or orange-flower water, it decorates a range of pastries also known as kashta. **MR**

Imagine the rhythmic thud of wood against metal, deadened by chilled elastic ice cream. Elastic? In Turkey the 300-year-old method of creating thick ice cream by mixing milk and sugar with salep—a flour made from the dried ground tuber of wild orchids—was developed as a way of retarding the melting process and creating a magnificent texture. The polysaccharide (bassorin) in the tuber acts as a thickening agent to produce a dense ice cream. This is then hung on hooks, stretched, shaped, dipped into shards of pistachios and eaten, all without dissolving into a puddle.

The name salep comes from an Arabic term meaning "fox testicles," a graphic description of the appearance of the ovoid root tubers of the orchid, and a hint at salep's alleged reputation as an aphrodisiac. Called *salepi dondurma* (*dondurma* is the Turkish word for ice cream), it was first made in the town of Kahramanmara in southeastern Turkey. It continues to be made throughout Turkey, Syria, and the Lebanon (where it is known as *bouza bi haleeb*) in traditional ice cream parlors. **RH**

Taste: *Kashta has the texture of a smooth, thick white pomade that holds its shape on a spoon. Its rich, milky taste is neutral and absorbs other flavors very well.*

Taste: *Salep ice cream has a chewy, nougatlike texture and sometimes needs eating with a knife and fork. It has a sweet, nutty taste and an earthy fragrance.*

A vendor in Bursa, Turkey, uses long paddles to stretch salep ice cream and keep it workable. »

Glossary

Aemono
A Japanese term for chilled foods that have been cooked and mixed with a dressing that complements the flavors of the ingredients. It particularly applies to vegetables such as broccoli, green beans, carrots, and white radish.

Affinage
The ripening of cheese until it reaches its optimum maturity and taste. Apart from cellaring, this can also include brushing, beating, washing, and rotating, the process and timescale depending on the requirement of individual cheeses.

Agar-agar
A vegetarian alternative to gelatine produced from sea vegetables. Neutral in flavor, it can be used in both sweet and savory dishes.

Annatto
A red food coloring that is produced from the pulp surrounding the seeds of the anchiote tree. Often linked to food related allergies, it is used to color foods including smoked fish, rice, butter, and some cheeses.

Antipasti
A selection of hors d'oeuvres served in Italy as appetizers before the pasta course. Usually cold, they might consist of olives, marinated anchovies or sardines, cured meats, roasted or raw vegetables, cheeses, seafood, and salads.

AOC (Appellation d'Origine Contrôlée)
A French system devised in 1935 to protect and maintain the quality of the country's wines. AOC status has now been extended to cover other products such as meat, poultry, and cheese.
See **PDO**

Artisan
Foods made by small local producers following traditional methods without the intervention of factory production lines, the widespread use of pesticides, and growth promoters or intensive farming. Typical foods produced in this way include cheeses, preserves, honey, poultry, eggs, rare breed cattle, bread, olive oil, vinegar, wine, cider, and liqueurs.

Bagna cauda
A dish from the Piedmont region in northwest Italy, similar to a Swiss fondue. A sauce of garlic, extra virgin olive oil, anchovies, butter, and sometimes lemon juice is slowly simmered in a pot and then served with raw vegetable crudités and crusty bread.

Bain-marie
A deep roasting tin containing warm water in which custards and similar dishes are oven-baked. The water prevents the delicate custard mix from getting too hot in the oven, which could cause it to curdle or overcook. The water should be warm, not boiling—the temperature of "Mary's bath."

Bearnaise sauce
A rich, creamy sauce from the Bearn region of southwest France made from an emulsion of egg yolks and butter flavored with shallots and fresh tarragon or chervil. Traditionally served with grilled steak or fish.

Beurre blanc
Another rich French sauce based on an emulsion of dry white wine and butter, flavored with shallots and sharpened with lemon juice. Served with asparagus, fish, and white meats.

Bouillabaisse
Marseille's legendary fish soup traditionally made by fishermen as a way of using up the very small or spiny specimens from their catch. The soup, which contains chunks of fish that are eaten before the saffron and tomato flavored broth, is traditionally served with toasted

croûtes of French bread, grated Gruyère cheese, and *rouille*, a fiery mayonnaise spiked with chile, paprika, or red pepper and saffron.

By-catch
This unwanted part of a catch trapped in a fisherman's net has two devasting effects on wildlife. Seafood waste that is thrown back and picked up by sea birds is low quality "junk food," acceptable for adult birds but potentially disastrous for chicks. Also, large creatures such as dolphins can become accidentally caught in nets with fatal results.

Ceviche
Latin American dish in which slices or chunks of raw fish are marinated in lime or lemon juice, the acid in the juice having the effect of "cooking" the fish.

Cochineal
A natural, bright red food coloring obtained from the crushed shells of the female species of a cactus-dwelling insect indigenous to Central America.

Cordon bleu
The French for "blue ribbon" and originally the highest order of chivalry in the gift of the

Bourbon kings. The term later came to mean the recognition of excellence in a particular field but was especially associated with chefs. *Le Cordon Bleu ou Nouvelle Cuisiniere Bourgeoise* cookbook was published in 1827, followed by cookery classes that started at Paris' Palais Royale in 1896.

Coulis
A smooth sauce made by pureeing and/or sieving fruit or vegetables. Popular fruit coulis are made with strawberries, apricots, peaches, or raspberries. Vegetables such as peppers, carrots, and tomatoes make good savory coulis.

Court bouillon
Meaning "short boil" in French, this is a light, aromatic liquid for poaching fish and shellfish, made from water or light stock, white wine, lemon juice, and aromatics such as onion, carrot, lemongrass, and whole peppercorns.

DO (Denominación de Origen)
The Spanish equivalent of the French AOC has all quality Spanish wines (except cava) bearing the official black *contraetiqueta* label denoting DO status on the back of the bottle. As in France, other foods such as rice, olive oil, cured hams, and cheese can be given DO status.

DOP (Denominazione di Origine Protetta)
See **PDO**

Epicure
A person concerned with the sensual pleasures of sourcing, preparing, serving, and eating good food.

IGP (Indicazione Geografica Protetta)
See **PGI**

Marine Stewardship Council (MSC)
A global, independent, non-profit making organization that promotes responsible fishing practices via a certification program, allowing well-managed fisheries to display the council's seal of approval.

O-hitashi
A Japanese dish of boiled vegetables dressed with dashi, mirin, and soy sauce.

Omega-3, Omega-6 oils
Essential fats that help the body conserve carbohydrate while at the same time shedding fat. Alpha-linolenic acid (omega-3) and linoleic acid (omega-6) are found in nuts, seeds, oily fish, and unrefined whole grains.

Organoleptic

The process of evaluating the quality of a food by using the senses of sight, taste, and smell.

Pot au feu

Meaning "cooking pot on fire" in French, meat and vegetables are very slowly simmered in a covered casserole with stock or water. The broth is served as an appetizer and the meat and vegetables as a main course.

Potage

A thick French soup where vegetables are simmered in stock or water until tender and then pureed with the cooking liquid.

PDO (Protected Designation of Origin)

European Union (E.U.) trademarks legally protecting the names and reputations of those regional foods whose particular qualities depend primarily or exclusively on the territory in which they were produced. This includes natural factors such as climate and human factors such as craftsmanship, which combined create a unique product. These trademarks, enforced in the E.U., are gradually being extended internationally. The PDO is similar to the French AOC, Italian DOP, and Spanish DO.

PGI (Protected Geographical Indication)

See **PDO**

Sashimi

Meaning "raw" in Japanese, sashimi is bite-sized pieces or slices of the highest quality and freshest fish. Eaten raw on its own, dipped into soy sauce, and accompanied with wasabi and pickled ginger, sashimi can also be a topping for sushi.

Single-Estate (varietals)

Used to describe produce such as coffee, wine, chocolate, and olive oil made on a single, named farm, plantation, or winery (rather than a cooperative) from one variety of coffee bean, grape, cocoa bean, or olive.

Shojin ryori

Zen Buddhist vegetarian dishes served in Japan. The teachings of Buddha prohibited those seeking enlightenment from drinking alcohol, eating meat and fish, and the five strongest members of the lily family—garlic, scallions, onions, shallots, and leeks.

Soffrito

Meaning "sub-fried" in Italian, this mix of sautéed onion, celery, and carrot provides the base of many soups, stews, and pasta sauces.

Superfood

Although there is no legal definition of "superfood," the term is generally applied to any foods—examples are blueberries, tomatoes, oats, broccoli, papaya, goji berries, and strawberries, that contain particularly high levels of nutrients.

Sushi

Bite-sized Japanese snacks made with cooked short-grain rice, seasoned with vinegar and topped or filled with raw, cooked, or marinated seafood, meat, or vegetables. The rice can also be wrapped in nori seaweed and cut into small rolls.

Umami

The "fifth" basic taste after sweet, sour, salty, and bitter. First identified in the sea vegetable *konbu* by Japanese scientist, Dr. Kinunae, this amino acid imparts a savory taste, expanding and rounding out other flavors, to foods such as ripe tomatoes, Parmesan cheese, cured hams, and mushrooms.

Velouté

A classic French sauce, similar to a bechamel but stock-based and then enriched with cream. Served with poultry, veal, or fish.

Contributors

Ismay Atkins (IA) is an editor, journalist, and restaurant critic based in Buenos Aires, Argentina. She has worked on dozens of the the *Time Out City Guides*.

Tara Basnet (TB) is a culinary arts graduate of Westminster Kingsway College. After a stint at the Savoy Hotel in London, she edited the trade magazines *Dubai Means Business* and *Tandoori*. She works in food and drink PR in London.

Stephen Beaumont (SBe) is a leading writer on beer, known for his work involving the partnership of beer and food—a passion that led to his ownership of Beerbistro. He writes for *Flavor & the Menu*, *The Malt Advocate*, and *City Bites*.

Jose Luis Alvarez Bernal (JAB) has a passion for Spanish food. Drawing on his father's knowledge as a chef, along with his own travels around Spain, he created the online delicatessen Delicioso.

William Black (WB) is the author of *Al Dente* and the coauthor with Sophie Grigson of several books including *Fish, Organic*. He won a Glenfiddich award for his TV program *A Question of Taste* and has sourced ingredients for many top British restaurants.

Susannah Blake (SBl) is a food writer and editor. She has written more than ten books and her work has appeared in publications such as the *Daily Express*, *New York Daily News*, and *Food and Travel*.

Shirley Booth (SB) is an award-winning writer and documentary director, and a leading authority on Japanese food. She is the author of *Food of Japan* (Winner, Japan Festival Prize, 2001) and a contributing editor to Harumi Kurihara's *Japanese Cooking* (2006).

Frances Case (FC) writes about food for publications including the *Guardian*. She has contributed to radio and television, written copy for major brands, and researched the food scenes of twenty-odd cities across five continents.

Charlotte Celsing (CC) is a journalist and writer based in Stockholm. She has lived in Indonesia, Fiji, and Australia and has a passion for travel and food.

Victor Cherikoff (VC) was nominated for the Australian of the Year award (2007) in recognition of his pioneering work in the commercialization of indigenous plants, building a new segment of the food industry, creating opportunities for Aborigines, and Australian cuisine development.

Glynn Christian (GC) has been cooking on British TV since 1982. His most recent book—*Real Flavors: The Handbook of Gourmet and Deli Ingredients*—won Food Guide of the Year at Le Cordon Bleu World Food Media awards and a Special Jury award at the Gourmand World Cookbook awards (2007).

Martin Christy (MC) is editor of the chocolate connoisseur's website Seventypercent.com and a Founder Member of the Academy of Chocolate. He has sampled and reviewed hundreds of fine chocolate bars and written many articles online and for magazines.

K. K. Chu (KKC) is a food writer whose work has been published online and in newspapers, books, and magazines in Hong Kong, the United States, and Europe.

Stephanie Clifford-Smith (SCS) is a journalist and author specializing in food writing and restaurant reviewing. She coedits Sydney's longest-running independent restaurant guide *Sydney Eats* and wrote the biography of Australia's first celebrity chef, Bernard King.

Reshmi Dasgupta (RD) is an editor and food and drink columnist for *The Economic Times*, India's largest business daily.

Anna Maria Espsäter (AME) is a Swedish food and travel journalist. She has traveled in Latin America and Mexico, where she learnt how to make a mean *mole poblano*.

Helmut Failoni (HFa) teaches food sciences and food and wine criticism at the University of Bologna. He is enogastronomical critic for *L'Espresso* magazine.

Hennie Fisher (HFi) is a food and wine writer in Pretoria, South Africa. He writes about restaurants for the annual guide *DINE* and also teaches professional cookery.

Liz Franklin (LF) is the award-winning author of eleven cookery books. She lives in Italy, where she also runs a cookery school.

Barb Freda (BF) began her food writing after nearly ten years of work in the kitchens of restaurants such as New York City's Union Square Cafe. She is food editor for the magazine *Florida Table*.

Heidi Fuller-Love (HFL) is a food and travel writer/photographer based between France, Spain, and Greece. She is the author of *Crossing the Loire*.

Mark Gilchrist (MG) is a game chef whose company Game for Everything has won numerous business awards.

Suzanne Hall (SH) is a U.S.-based food, wine, nutrition, health, and travel writer who contributes to publications and online.

Rebecca Harris (RH)

A. B. Heyns (ABH) is a food writer and erstwhile restaurateur who lives in Pretoria, South Africa. He loves to spend time with like-minded individuals over good food.

Tony Hill (TH) is a writer and the founder of Seattle's World Spice Merchants. His book *The Spice Lover's Guide to Herbs and Spices* (2005) was an IACP award finalist.

Jeanette Hurt (JH) writes about food, wine, and travel. Her books include *The Complete Idiot's Guide to the Cheeses of the World*.

Carol King (CK) is a freelance journalist based in London and Sicily, who has tried many foods during the course of her travels.

Beverly LeBlanc (BLeB) has written on French, Indian, and Spanish cuisines, and is the author of nine cookery books, including *The Student Cookbook*.

Clare Leschin-Hoar (CLH) is a freelance journalist who writes food and agricultural stories for a variety of magazines and newspapers in the United States.

Jenny Linford (JL) is a food writer based in London. She is the author of a number of books including *Food Lovers' London*, a guide to the capital's food shops and eateries.

Rupert Linton (RL) is a translator in Spanish food production. He has visited artisan food manufacturers on behalf of Brindisa Ltd.

Arnaldo Lorençato (AL) is one of Brazil's foremost food writers and the gastronomic editor of *Veja São Paulo* magazine.

Giles MacDonogh (GM) has written books on wine and French gastronomy, and is an expert in central European food.

Kate Magic Wood (KMW) is the author of *Eat Smart Eat Raw* and *Raw Living*. She runs her own company, Raw Living.

Julian Matteucci (JM) is a lawyer and freelance writer who lives between Umbria, Italy, and London. He has published on food, cinema, art, law, and business.

Dora Miller (DM) is a Portuguese journalist who is passionate about food. She has traveled widely and also writes about hotels and spas.

Jade Ng (JN) was born in Malaysia and now lives in Sydney, Australia. She has maintained a healthy obsession with the food of her childhood and enjoys new cuisines.

Cynthia Nims (CN) is a food and travel writer living in Seattle, Washington. She has written ten cookbooks and contributes to magazines in the United States.

Michael Raffael (MR) is a writer whose *West Country Cheesemakers* won the British Cheese Awards prize in 2006. *Truffles* won a World Gourmand Cookbook award in 2002.

Genevieve Rajewski (GR) writes about snacking and sipping for publications including the *Washington Post Magazine*, *The Boston Globe*, and *Edible Boston*.

Judy Ridgway (JR) is an olive oil expert and an acknowledged authority on wine, cheese, vinegar, mustard, condiments, and charcuterie. She has written more than fifty-five books including *Judy Ridgway's Best Olive Oil Buys Round the World: The New Edition* (2005).

Seafood Training School (STS) is a charity based at London's Billingsgate fish market. It provides training and courses for fishmongers and the general public. Its director, C. J. Jackson, is a well-known food writer.

Emma Sturgess (EM) is a food writer and restaurant critic who trained with Darina Allen at the Ballymaloe Cookery School in County Cork, Ireland.

Rob Strybel (RS)

Anne-Marie Sutcliffe (AMS) lives in Norfolk and the Mani. She especially enjoys seasonal foods—whether samphire in England or horta in Greece—and the challenge this presents in deciding when to be where.

Wendy Sweetser (WS) is a food, wine, and travel writer. She has written fourteen cookbooks and travels widely, eating and drinking, all in the name of research.

Christopher Tan Yu Wei (CTa) is a writer, food consultant, and cookbook author who was raised partly in Singapore, partly in London, and mostly in the kitchen. His cookbooks include *Inside the South East Asian Kitchen*.

Camilla Tjellesen (CTj) is a Danish journalist and writer based in London, where she writes for various lifestyle magazines.

Christopher Trotter (CTr) is a chef, consultant, and food writer. He is the author of *Scottish Cookery*, *The Scottish Kitchen*, and *Scottish Heritage Food and Cooking*.

Dani Valent (DV) is a journalist and screenwriter based in Melbourne, Australia, where she reviews restaurants for the *Sunday Age*. She has written many books for Lonely Planet including *World Food: Turkey*.

Lindy Wildsmith (LW) is a food writer and the author of several books, including *Preserves*.

Carol Wilson (CW) is a freelance food writer, inspector of restaurants, and member of the Guild of Food Writers. She has written several cookbooks and is a jury member for the Slow Food Biodiversity Awards.

General Index

marionberry, 31
marjoram
  sweet, 624
marlin
  blue, 395
marmalade
  Seville orange, 924
marmalade plum (sapodilla), 79
Marmite, 734
marron, 430
marron glacé, 885
marrow
  bone, 525
marshmallow, 899
marula, 41
marzipan, Lübecker, 915
Matteuccia struthiopteris, 178
matzo, 834
mayonnaise, 722
mazhanje, 41
medlar, 81
  Japanese (loquat), 72
meggyleves, 44
Melicoccus bijugatus, 43
melokhia, 172
melon
  Charentais, 96
  Shizuoka, 96
  watermelon, 98
membrillo, 921
mesclun, 164, 166
Mespilus germanicus, 81
methi, 606
Mexican potato
  (jicama), 201
"Mexican truffle"
  (huitlacoche), 221
Mexican turnip, 201
microgreen (microleaf), 159
midshipman's butter
  (Hass avocado), 150
milk cap, saffron, 226
millefeuille, 875
"millionaire's salad," 131
mint
  Cambodian (rau ram), 616
  Moroccan, 602
  Vichy, 891
mirabelle, 54
miracle berry
  (miracle fruit), 36
miraculin, 36
miso
  Hatcho, 256
  Saikyo, 256
mitsuba, 610
mocetta, 590
mochi, 880
mochi gome su, 704

mocororó, 48
mojama, 416
mojarra, 353
molasses
  blackstrap, 934
mole, 726
moleche, 439
mombin
  red, 50
Momordica carantia, 153
monkey peach (golden kiwi fruit), 69
monkfish, 389
  liver, 418
mooli, 206
mooncake, 848
moose, 494
morel, 231
Moreton Bay bug, 434
Moringa oleifera, 141
morogo, 159
Morus nigra, 28
Moscatel raisin, 117
mosciame del tonno, 416
mostarda di frutta, 708
"mountain eel" (Japanese yam), 214
moutarde de Dijon, 707
moutarde de Meaux, 707
muffin
  English, 819
muhammara, 733
mui choy, 246
mulberry
  black, 28
mullet
  red, 381
muscadine, 93
Muscari comosum, 236
mushroom
  cep (*porcino*), 229
  chanterelle, 229
  "dancing" (maitake), 224
  horn of plenty, 229
  matsutake, 222
  morel, 231
  oronge (Caesar's), 226
  oyster, 224
  saffron milk cap, 226
  shiitake, 231
  winter (enokitake), 222
mussel
  date-mussel, 448
  green-shelled, 449
  Mont St. Michel, 449
mustard
  Bavarian sweet, 708
  moutarde de Dijon, 707
  moutarde de Meaux, 707
  oil, 693
mutton

Villsau, 506
muuch'ae kimchi, 206
myoga, 634
myrtle, lemon, 627

N
nan, 798
naranjilla, 82
naseberry (sapodilla), 79
nasturtium, 128
natto, 252
nduja, 534
nectarines, 55
nedr, 208
nèfle du Japon, 72
Nelumbo nucifera, 208
Nephelium lappaceum, 63
Nephelium mutabile, 63
nepitella, 606
nespola giapponese, 72
nettle, 177
níspero (sapodilla), 79
noodle
  fen si, 787
  kisoba, 786
  laksa, 787
  Sanuki udon, 786
nori, 251
nougat, Montelimar, 902
nuoc mam, 741
Nürnberger Elisenlebkuchen, 837
nutmeg, 118
nut
  Brazil, 762
  cashew, 756
  chestnut, 760
  coco-de-mer, 764
  gingko, 755
  Grenoble walnut, 760
  Iranian pistachio, 759
  macadamia, 753
  marcona almond, 756
  pecan, 762
  tiger, 770
  wild green hazelnut, 759

O
oatcake, 833
obatza, 272
octopus, 458
  Akashi tako, 458
oil
  argan, 690
  avocado, 693
  canola, 695
  grapeseed, 694
  hazelnut, 684
  hemp, 690
  mustard, 693

Picture Credits

Every effort has been made to credit the copyright holders of the images used in this book. We apologise for any unintentional omissions or errors and will insert the appropriate acknowledgement to any companies or individuals in any subsequent edition of the work.

Acknowledgments

Appetit/Alamy **650** Steve Atkins Photography/Alamy **652** Rob Walls/Alamy **654** Pat O'Hara/CORBIS **655** Jignesh Jhaveri/StockFood UK **657** blickwinkel/Alamy **658** Vibrant Pictures/Alamy **661** Photolibrary **663** Simon Grosset/Alamy **664-5** Owen Franken/CORBIS **666** Bill Bachmann/Alamy **671** Bob Sacha/Corbis **673** Lindsay Hebberd/CORBIS **674** Hemis/Alamy **677** CHRIS LEWINGTON/Alamy **681** Jeremy Horner/Corbis **683** Sergio Pitamitz/CORBIS **685** JUPITERIMAGES/Agence Images/Alamy **687** Felix Stensson/Alamy **688-9** Paul Cowan/Alamy **691** WoodyStock/Alamy **692** World Religions Photo Library/Alamy **697** Edward Parker/Alamy **701** Mark Bolton Photography/Alamy **702** ZenShui/Laurence Mouton/Getty Images **705** Andrea Matone/Alamy **706** Russell Kord/Alamy **709** AA World Travel Library/Alamy **710** Radius Images/Alamy **713** Danita Delimont/Alamy **715** Bon Appetit/Alamy **717** Fabian Gonzales Editorial/Alamy **719** Iconotec/Alamy **720** Wolfgang Kaehler/Alamy **723** Owen Franken/CORBIS **724** cesare dagliana/Alamy **726-7** Danita Delimont/Alamy **728** foodfolio/Alamy **730** Richard Bickel/CORBIS **735** Burt Hardy/Getty Images **738** dbimages/Alamy **742-3** Javier Etcheverry/Alamy **744** Goss Images/Alamy **746-7** Photolibrary **748** Photolibrary **751** Photolibrary **752** Vincenzo Lombardo/Getty Images **754** Frederick Fearn/Alamy **757** Nature Picture Library/Alamy **758** Photolibrary **761** foodfolio/Alamy **763** Jacques Jangoux/Alamy **764** Alison Wright/Corbis **765** Photolibrary **766** Holt Studios International Ltd/Alamy **770-1** DAVID NOBLE PHOTOGRAPHY/Alamy **775** Joel Sartore/National Geographic/Getty Images **776-7** JTB Photo Communications, Inc./Alamy **778** David Cairns/Alamy **781** Vova Pomortzeff/Alamy **783** Photolibrary **785** Walter Cimbal/StockFood UK **788-9** Photolibrary **791** Neil McAllister/Alamy **792** Cynthia Brown/StockFood UK **795** Woman Making Tortillas **796-7** Nick Haslam/Alamy **799** Photolibrary **801** Owen Franken/CORBIS **802** CuboImages srl/Alamy **804** Robert Holmes/CORBIS **807** CuboImages srl/Alamy **809** The Art Archive/Corbis **810** Photolibrary **812-3** Bob Krist/CORBIS **814** CuboImages srl/Alamy **816-7** Cris Haigh/Alamy **820-1** Istock **822** Alan Richardson/Getty Images **825** imagebroker/Alamy **829** Cristofani/ANSA/Corbis **832** Victoria Art Gallery, Bath and North East Somerset Council/Bridgeman Art Library **835** The Art Archive/British Library **836** Amazing Images/Alamy **838** Jo Kirchherr/StockFood UK **841** Anne-Marie Palmer/Alamy **843** Tsgt. H. H. Deffner/Department Of Defense (DOD)/Time Life Pictures/Getty Images **845** Iconotec/Alamy **846** Adam Woolfitt/CORBIS **849** Zhang Wenkui/ChinaFotoPress/Getty Images **850** Alberto Moretto/StockFood UK **852** Travelshots.com/Alamy **856-7** Photolibrary **858** imagebroker/Alamy **859** Gaby Bohle/StockFood UK **863** Mansell/Time Life Pictures/Getty Images **865** Travel-Ink/Chris Stock **866-7** Photolibrary **868** Redfx/Alamy **870** Frances M. Roberts/Alamy **872** Barry Lewis/Corbis **877** IML Image Group Ltd/Alamy **879** john norman/Alamy **881** john lander/Alamy **882-3** Photolibrary **886-7** Michael S. Lewis/CORBIS **889** Bill Brooks/Alamy **893** Manor Photography/Alamy **895** David Paul Morris/Getty Images **896** Rebecca Erol/Alamy **898** keith burdett/Alamy **900** OJPHOTOS/Alamy **903** J-Charles Gérard/Photononstop **904** Photolibrary **906-7** John Birdsall/Alamy **910** Jean Pierre Amet/BelOmbra/Corbis **912** Olivier Asselin/Alamy **914** Photolibrary **920** Bill Lyons/Alamy **923** Jonathan Little/Alamy **924-5** Mary Evans Picture Library/Alamy **929** Photolibrary **930** Rogan Coles/Alamy **935** Arco Images GmbH/Alamy **941** JTB Photo Communications, Inc./Alamy

Additional commissioned photography by:
Masami Bornoff **254**
Craig Fraser **377, 414**
Kenzaburo Fukuhara **198, 345, 370, 438, 718**
John Hollingshead **39, 46, 108, 121, 750**
Ricardo Lagos **45, 132, 353**
Simon Pask **180, 208, 246, 253, 254, 254, 264, 311, 328, 330, 357, 359, 360, 363, 367, 369, 372, 381, 386, 396, 400, 410, 414, 422, 443, 445, 455, 458, 474, 514, 529, 533, 553, 592, 790, 820, 823, 853, 866, 869, 873, 875, 876, 878, 886, 890, 897, 905, 909, 940**
Gerson Sobreira **39, 45, 67, 92, 98, 354, 437, 465, 641, 937**
Jeremy Sutton-Hibbert **92, 96, 105, 214, 221, 224, 400, 404, 453, 458, 470, 510, 610, 632, 634, 717, 740**

We would like to express our gratitude to the following:

The Ice Box, New Covent Garden Market, London

Editors:
Phil Hall
David Hutter
Felicity Jackson

Indexer:
Kay Ollerenshaw

Food Sourcing:
Masami Bornoff
Wendy Sweetser

Artworking:
Don Ward
Chris Taylor

Image Libraries

Alamy — Maria Kuzim
Corbis — John Moelwyn-Hughes
Getty — Hayley Newman
Photolibrary — Tim Kantoch
StockFood — Kathy Sinclaire